LIFE EVENTS AND ILLNESS

LIFE EVENTS AND ILLNESS

Edited by

GEORGE W. BROWN
TIRRIL O. HARRIS
Royal Holloway and Bedford New College
University of London

FOREWORD BY DAVID MECHANIC

London
UNWIN HYMAN
Boston   Sydney   Wellington

© 1989 The Guilford Press

Published by the Academic Division of
Unwin Hyman Ltd
15/17 Broadwick Street, London W1V 1FP, UK

Unwin Hyman Inc.,
8 Winchester Place, Winchester, Mass. 01890, USA

Allen & Unwin (Australia) Ltd,
8 Napier Street, North Sydney, NSW 2060, Australia

Allen & Unwin (New Zealand) Ltd in association with the
Port Nicholson Press Ltd,
Compusales Building, 75 Ghuznee Street, Wellington 1, New Zealand

First published in 1989

British Library Cataloguing in Publication data
Life events and illness.
 1. Man.   Stress.   Medical aspects
 I. Brown, George W. (George William), 1930–
 II. Harris, Tirril
 616.8
ISBN   0-04-445426-0

Contributors

HARRY ANDREWS, MA, DM, MRCPsych, Department of Clinical Neurophysiology, The Maudsley Hospital, Denmark Hill, London SE5 8AZ, England.

GEORGE W. BROWN, PhD, FBA, Department of Social Policy and Social Science, Royal Holloway and Bedford New College, University of London, 11 Bedford Square, London WC1B 3RA, England.

PAUL CALLOWAY, MD, MRCPsych, MRCP, Fulbourn Hospital, Cambridge CB1 5EF, England.

TOM K. J. CRAIG, MB, BS, MRCPsych, Division of Psychiatry, United Medical and Dental Schools, Guy's Hospital, London SE1 9RT, England; National Unit for Psychiatric Research and Development, Lewisham Hospital, Lewisham High Street, London SE13 6LH, England.

FRANCIS CREED, MD, MRCP, MRCPsych, University Department of Psychiatry, Rawnsley Building, Manchester Royal Infirmary, Oxford Road, Manchester M13 9WL, England.

RICHARD DAY, PhD, Department of Biostatistics, Graduate School of Public Health, University of Pittsburgh, Pittsburgh, PA 15213 USA.

RAYMOND DOLAN, MD, MRCPsych, National Hospitals for Nervous Diseases, Queen Square, London WC1 N3BG, England.

ROBERT FINLAY-JONES, MBBS, PhD, DPM, MRCPsych, FRANZCP, Research and Evaluation Unit, Psychiatric Services Branch, Health Department of Western Australia, Selby Centre, Corner Selby Street and Stubbs Terrace, Shenton Park, Western Australia 6008, Australia.

IGOR GRANT, MD, FRCP(C), Department of Psychiatry, University of California at San Diego School of Medicine, La Jolla, CA 92093 USA; Veterans Administration Medical Center, San Diego, CA 92161 USA.

TIRRIL O. HARRIS, MA, Department of Social Policy and Social Science, Royal Holloway and Bedford New College, University of London, 11 Bedford Square, London WC1B 3RA, England.

ALLAN HOUSE, BSc, MRCP, MRCPsych, DM, Medical Research
    Council Project, Department of Neurology, Radcliffe Infirmary,
    Woodstock Road, Oxford OX2 6HE, England.
MICHAEL MARMOT, BSc, MBBS, MPhil, PhD, Department of Com-
    munity Medicine, University College Hospital, Gower Street,
    London WC1E 6BT, England.
W. IAN MCDONALD, PhD, FRCP, National Hospitals for Nervous
    Diseases, Queen Square, London WC1N 3BG, England, and
    Maida Vale, London W91TL, England.
EILEEN NEILSON, MSc, Department of Social Policy and Social Sci-
    ence, Royal Holloway and Bedford New College, University of
    London, 11 Bedford Square, London WC1B 3RA, England.
THOMAS PATTERSON, PhD, Department of Psychiatry, University
    of California at San Diego School of Medicine, La Jolla, CA
    92093 USA; Veterans Administration Medical Center, San
    Diego, CA 92161 USA.
PAUL G. SURTEES, PhD, Medical Research Council Unit for Epide-
    miological Studies in Psychiatry, University Department of Psy-
    chiatry, Royal Edinburgh Hospital, Morningside Park, Edinburgh
    EH10 5HF, Scotland.
MICHAEL R. TRIMBLE, MRCP, FRCPsych, National Hospitals for
    Nervous Diseases, Queen Square, London WC1N 3BG, England,
    and Maida Vale, London W91TL, England.

Foreword

The insight that illness may involve in some important measure factors not encompassed by the physical and biological sciences has been a source of speculation for more than a century, but it was not until recently that systematic efforts were made to investigate the effects of such mental states as fear, rage, depression, and anxiety on physical illness. While early efforts in psychosomatic medicine focused on mental states and illness, the concern with personal status and social circumstances is only now attaining the centrality it merits.

George Brown, Tirril Harris, and their collaborators bring together in this volume an impressive range of theoretical thought and empirical study organized around the Life Events and Difficulties Schedule (LEDS). In presenting an ingenious approach to examine the relationship between "attitudes" and illness using the richness of data elicited by the LEDS, and in comprehensively and critically examining the literature and prevalent research models, they reveal a deep and complex array of issues that will occupy the attention of researchers well into the next century. In its scope, boldness, and erudition, this book is a *tour de force*. It is not a volume to be read quickly, but rather one to be savored and re-read because it deals with fundamental issues and controversies and delves deeply.

The research issues examined here have long intrigued scientists and physicians. The attentive clinician has always noted variations among patients in resilience and a "will to live." Every patient when questioned carefully has a story to explain his or her illness, and these stories, and the emotional states associated with them, seem to cluster by illness. Such observations were the basis of vigorous interest in developing psychosomatic medicine and continue to be a source of inquiry in the growing field of behavior and health. If fields of inquiry are to prosper, however, they require theories that suggest searching questions and methods that allow them to be attacked systematically and rigorously. The issues of specificity, addressed so creatively in this volume, have been of longstanding interest. There has been no shortage of hypotheses about attitude, personality, and organ specificity, but the field of "psychosomatics" bogged down because there were no good research models essential to studying these hypotheses. By the late 1950s, psychosomatic medicine was in the doldrums.

Research on stress and disease was reactivated with the introduction of life events scales in the 1960s that allowed investigators to examine links between such occurrences and a variety of disease outcomes. The early rating scales were simplistic; the items were often vague and ambiguous; and the use of these instruments raised many new methodological issues. Their contribution was neither in their content, nor in the new findings they elicited, but mostly in showing a way that the link between life events and disease could be studied in populations. These approaches gave a new optimism to such investigation and attracted many new and talented research workers to life events research.

The editors of this volume have an impressive record of innovative research in mental illness. George Brown, whose pathbreaking work extends back to the 1950s, has for three decades moved back and forth between intensive clinical assessment and the conscious effort to design measures and instruments that capture the real complexity of social situations, assigned meanings, and personal response to crisis. And this approach has been extraordinarily successful, as evidenced by Brown's discovery of the importance of "expressed emotion," the differential role of life events in schizophrenia and depression, and, more recently, his seminal work on the social etiology of depression with Tirril Harris. These efforts have had three defining characteristics: sensitivity to clinical material and capitalizing on serendipity; self-consciousness about methods and methodological advances; and focus on theory with careful efforts to specify intervening processes and the links between macro events and personal meanings. I address each briefly.

Excellence in research on health requires not only good ideas and rigorous methods but also intimate understanding of the phenomena being addressed. Too many researchers study diseases they know only casually and patients they have never personally seen. They are often too distant from disease processes to appreciate the subtleties in experiences and meanings that define the illness situation. From the start, the work of Brown and Harris has been characterized by an intimate knowledge of their respondents that has been an inspiration to their creativity. Appreciation of the experience of these research participants has contributed importantly to Brown and Harris's theoretical formulations and research questions and has assisted them in focusing their interviewing in a highly productive way. Maintaining a close connection between clinical and research materials gives their work unusual richness that makes it special.

The clinical richness relates to the development of the LEDS and the issue of contextual judgments and timing of life events that also characterize their work. This instrument has been developed meticulously over many years in a productive interplay between research interviewing and theoretical elaboration. The impressive research findings and innovative ideas justify the labor intensiveness of the methodology, but research styles in the study of life events remain divergent and yield somewhat different results. Readers can make their own judgment of the LEDS, since this entire book is in some sense its product. It remains to be seen to what degree the LEDS can be simplified and adapted to new research contexts, but it is evident that this methodology – and even more, the careful thought that underlies it – has brought the study of life events and disease to a new stage.

The comprehensiveness of the data the LEDS provides fits nicely the sophistication and complexity of the theoretical ideas it serves. Brown and Harris have successfully woven their theoretical thinking about depression and other conditions into the context of the life course and the contingencies that may push a life on one or another trajectory. The examination of the origins of life events and difficulties and the notion of "conveyor belts" to continuing adversity capture the real uncertainties of life and usefully link concerns with life events and disease to larger issues of human development.

In sum, let me invite readers to "drink from these streams." For whatever your theoretical and methodological persuasions and commitments, you cannot come away from this volume without enrichment – without a greater appreciation of the diversity of adversities and how people define and deal with them and the inventions of method that allow us to glimpse these processes in a multidimensional way. Having achieved this is no small contribution.

David Mechanic, PhD
University Professor and
René Dubos Professor of Behavioral Sciences
Rutgers University

Preface

This volume is best introduced by giving a little history. In 1978 we published *Social Origins of Depression*, which became a focus for a certain amount of debate within sociology, psychology, and psychiatry. Paradoxically, however, this did not center around the issue we had seen as the most controversial – namely, the approach to the measurement of life events. In setting the scene for the investigation of depression by outlining this approach, we continued the critique of existing work (mainly using checklists) that had been started earlier in the decade when one of us spoke at a conference on Stressful Life Events convened by Barbara and Bruce Dohrenwend in New York in June 1973, arguing for the use of a flexible interview and the use of the investigator rather than the respondent to carry out the job of measurement. At about the same time, Eugene Paykel, an advocate of the verbal interview who was moving toward this same position, returned from Yale University to work in England. In the curious fashion that afflicts such intellectual debates, the two sides of the Atlantic seemed to become identified with the two sides of the controversy, with the result that most research in the United States remained in the checklist tradition, although there can be no doubt that disenchantment with the existing checklist instruments is now widespread. We had therefore anticipated that the interest aroused by *Social Origins of Depression* would have stimulated an equal interest in rethinking the American method of research into life events. We saw our approach to life stress as an attempt at a new integration between the quantitative analyses of epidemiology and the depth understanding of the case history approach, with room left both for examination of statistically significant associations between classic epidemiological variables and life events, and for exploration of the phenomenology and meaning of individual experience. Instead, a different controversy developed, over the nature of vulnerability factors and the statistical approach required to demonstrate such a theoretical model. (The most recent exchange concerning the vulnerability issue, which has drawn in North American commentators, can be found in the November 1986 issue of *Sociology*; the original findings concerning depression were published in this journal in 1975.)

The two traditions of life events research appear today, if anything, as an even more entrenched division between the United States and Europe. The predominant role played by the checklist tradition has been probably more a reflection of the increasing demand by funding bodies for projects that are cheap and speedy than of the philosophy of researchers themselves. Nevertheless, despite our running a regular training course in the Life Events and Difficulties Schedule (LEDS) since the mid-1970s, publications using it in North America have been very few. Charles Costello carried out a general-population inquiry in Calgary (which was in fact published in a European journal), and more recently Ron Kessler has used a version of the LEDS in Detroit, which was considerably amended in order to meet the economic requirements of large-scale survey work. We have therefore chosen an American publisher for the current volume in the hope it will reach a genuinely transatlantic audience. With this in mind, we have been persuaded to make every attempt to come out to meet our American readers by abandoning our English spellings and idioms. We hope readers from this side of the Atlantic will forgive us surprises such as "one-time" rather than "one-off" which result from this. But, in compensation, there was a certain piquancy in substituting the greater "forest" for the smaller "wood" in "not seeing the wood for the trees."

The volume assembles examples of findings where the LEDS is used to examine the onset of a range of disorders, in the hope of illustrating the importance of contextual meaning in rating life stress. It moves from a largely methodological to a more substantive message about specificity in the etiology of illness. In short, does the specific nature of life events and vulnerability factors differ in different disorders; and do the vulnerability factors relevant for a particular disorder have a similar specificity to those life events? This classic issue could fill several volumes, and inevitably our coverage has failed to do justice to the complexity of the field. The focus of the volume has been upon life events (and difficulties); by contrast, vulnerability factors and their possible specificities have received scant attention, despite the critical importance we have allotted them in our model of depression elsewhere. This has been purely a function of space. We are increasingly aware that such a line between types of factors is somewhat arbitrary, and that their separation as different building blocks in a model may represent a phase in the progress toward a total perspective. This is particularly clear in studies of depression where the intimate link over the total life span between provoking agents and vulnerability factors has become clearer as work has progressed and is reflected in some results discussed in Chapter 14 of this volume. However, there is no reason, in principle, to expect vulnerability factors and their links with provoking stress factors to be any less important in the etiology of the other disorders discussed here, although their nature is almost certainly often different from the nature of factors involved in depressive onset. We look forward later to the elaboration elsewhere of such issues.

It remains for us to thank the many people who have made this book possible: our many colleagues who have patiently collected data and rated contextual meaning with us in consensus rating meetings; Laurie Letchford and Warren Hilder, whose unpossessive style of work with the computer allowed us to continue to work at ground level with the data alongside their elegant programming; Eve Branston, Anne Wigger, and Helen Durrant for their stoical secretarial support; our families for equally stoical support of another kind; the Medical Research Council for its continuing support, especially in providing resources that have allowed us to train so many others in the use of the LEDS; and our medical colleagues for their collaboration and advice on diagnostic issues. As we made clear in *Social Origins of Depression*, we have never seen any reason not to take seriously existing diagnostic categories, although we accept that refinements might be made and believe that psychosocial categorization might help to further such refinements. Special thanks must go to our psychiatric colleagues in this regard: to John Wing, John Cooper, and John Copeland, whose Present State Examination (PSE) we used under their instruction initially, and who have seen us in later years superimpose upon it a refinement of diagnostic categorization (Bedford College Caseness); and particularly to Ray Prudo, Robert Finlay-Jones, Elaine Murphy, and Tom K. J. Craig who, as members of our team, calmly piloted our lay suggestions concerning nonhierarchical regrouping of syndromes and their thresholds, when others might have recoiled at the invasion of the province of psychiatric diagnosis by outsiders. We must also particularly thank Andrew Steptoe, Raymond Dolan, and Tom Craig for helpful comments on a draft of this volume.

Finally, our warmest thanks must go to the thousands of men and women who have been the subjects of the research described here, often revealing their most private thoughts and sorrows only because they believed that in this way they might further medical understanding and thus alleviate future suffering. This is our task.

George W. Brown
Tirril O. Harris

Contents

PART ONE

INTRODUCTION

1

Life Events and Measurement

GEORGE W. BROWN

"If you estimate it correctly, there is a shipwreck everywhere."
– From the title page of the first edition of Milton's *Lycidas*
(original in Latin), quoted by Christopher Hill (1977, p. 11)

On the morning of March 7, 1957, an oil tanker collided with a freighter
in the Delaware River. Intense explosions in the tanker killed eight men
instantly, including all the officers, but the rest of the crew survived in
spite of being surrounded by fire on the ship and in the water. In the
short term, psychological symptoms such as nervousness, tension, or
anxiety were common among the survivors, as were somatic reactions
such as gastrointestinal complaints. Of the 35 men, 4 showed severe psychiatric disorder. When the men were seen a few years later, the amount
of psychological deterioration that had taken place was impressive. At
least 26 of the 35 men had received some form of medical help for complaints of a psychiatric nature, and 12 of these had received hospital
treatment. Ten had suffered from severe gastrointestinal illnesses. In
general, there was a marked increase in restlessness, phobic reactions,
and depression. Sleep disturbance was reported by 22, and over half
complained of continuous and sometimes disabling headaches (Leopold
& Dillon, 1963). The account is generally persuasive and rather puzzling: The men were for the most part experienced sailors, and yet a
surprisingly large proportion appeared to be some kind of casualty.

By contrast, a psychologist, Stanley Rachman, in his book *Fear and
Courage* (1978), takes as a major theme that individuals are far more
resistant to stress than is commonly recognized; he cites, among many
other instances, the very low rates of psychiatric casualties during air
raids in World War II.

George W. Brown. Department of Social Policy and Social Science, Royal Holloway
and Bedford New College, University of London, 11 Bedford Square, London WC1B
3RA, England.

These two examples demonstrate the kind of difficulty faced in coming to terms with the issue of health and illness after the experience of stress. First, although everyday experience tells us that some immediate emotional disturbance, perhaps with accompanying minor physical symptoms, is common following such occurrences, there is a good deal of evidence that even after apparently major crises only a minority develop serious physical or psychiatric disturbance. The Leopold and Dillon (1963) study showing long-term adverse effects in the majority of the tanker crew is probably exceptional. Indeed, it is clear that stress-like experiences may at times prove beneficial and may even be actively sought, as in dangerous sports. The pleasure in the sense of competence that can emerge may far outweigh any untoward effects.

It is useful to isolate three issues at this point. The first is the principle of "event specification." It is the most basic of the three issues and is designed to maximize the correlation between a particular class of event and a physical or psychiatric disorder or range of disorders, or even disorder in general. Perhaps if we were better able to classify events and to reject more as not being truly "stressful," we might find their impact as high as that among the tanker crew following the explosion. It is possible to approach such specification in terms of either a general notion of severity of threat or a more specific notion of the emotional significance of the event. Perhaps some of the tanker crew, if the matter could be examined in more detail, had a less threatening or unpleasant experience in terms of severity – say, they were well away from the main explosion – and this would explain why some suffered no ill effects. Measures of severity of threat or unpleasantness have, in fact, proved to be extremely effective in exploring the etiological role of events for a wide range of psychiatric and physical disorders. But events also differ in the quality of cognitive-emotional response they typically call forth. Events may produce much the same degree of distress in response to their threat or unpleasantness, but may do so through quite different emotions. In this sense, severity of threat and emotional significance can differ independently. A number of such basic emotions have evolved as mankind has developed, and it is possible to outline in broad terms the kind of situation that will call them forth – emotions such as anxiety, anger, joy, and shame (Tomkins, 1962, 1963; Ekman, 1982; Oatley & Johnson-Laird, 1987). (They rarely occur without accompanying cognitive activity, and no tidy distinction between emotion and cognition is attempted here.) Emotional significance of events has so far proved to be particularly important in differentiating between different disorders; that is, certain emotional categories of events tend to relate to certain disorders, acting as provoking agents. The exploration of such links is one of the main concerns of the present volume. New measures have been developed for this. It has been necessary because, although the measurement of severity of threat involves consideration of emotional reactions, it fails to distinguish different kinds of emotional response.

But even if event specification in terms of severity of threat and emotional significance allows us to identify more accurately the type of event leading to a particular disorder, it is still necessary to explain why the disorder does not always follow. On the assumption that severity and emotional significance have been dealt with, it is possible to move on to deal with the role of factors more removed from the event itself. This is the issue of "vulnerability": to explain why only some break down following an event of a certain type. It is possible, for instance, that those who suffered long-term effects in terms of depression among the tanker crew had less support after the event from relatives and friends. Although the role of psychosocial variables is emphasized in this volume, a wide range of other factors, including constitution and personality, may be involved in vulnerability.

The third issue is "diagnostic specificity." This has already been touched on in discussing event specification, when it is noted how events with particular kinds of emotional significance tend to lead to specific kinds of disorders. Like event specification, diagnostic specification can follow varying principles, but most students of stress aim to illuminate the etiology of illness in a way that may ultimately serve some pragmatic function, and they therefore usually follow the specific diagnostic categories used in current medical practice. These continue to evolve as progress is made in charting the physiological mechanisms underlying the disorders, so that hierarchies of subtypes have developed, and among these regroupings often occur: For example, the status of "postpill amenorrhea" (i.e. amenorrhea following the use of birth control pills) as a separate diagnostic subtype of amenorrhea is currently subject to some debate (see Chapter 10). In the absence of a proven theory regarding the differing etiologies of these subtypes, resolution of such debates usually relies on the degree of statistical overlap between them *vis-à-vis* the clustering of clinical symptoms. A classic example of this kind of debate concerns the distinction between neurotic and endogenous depression. Although this anticipates a further exposition later, an elaboration of this example may serve to illuminate these several points about specificity in stress-disorder models. Elsewhere (Brown & Harris, 1978b), we have discussed evidence that specification of provoking events and vulnerability issues for depressive disorders as a whole (in contrast, say, to schizophrenia) does not help to predict the neurotic-endogenous subtypes of depression. This suggests a need for a separate third set of "symptom formation" factors to explain the development of one of these subtypes rather than the other. Specifying a patient's experience of major loss *in the past* in terms of whether it

TABLE 1.1. Specification of etiological factors

	Stressor		Diathesis	Outcome
Broad class	Provoking agent	Vulnerability	Symptom formation	Psychiatric
Specific type	Recent loss	Lack of support	Past loss	Depression (not schizophrenia)
Subtype			Past loss by separation versus death	"Neurotic" versus "psychotic" depression

occurred through death or separation did predict the subtype of depression (Brown & Harris, 1978b, Chap. 14; note that major losses in the year before onset would have counted as provoking events). But the presence of a separate group of symptom formation factors for diagnostic subtypes is not inconsistent with a model where specification of events provoking disorder (provoking agents) and vulnerability factors can also determine the *broader* diagnostic grouping. For example, while recent events do not appear to relate to subtype of depression, recent experience of a specific type of life event, involving loss and disappointment, raises the risk of depression in some form rather than some other type of disorder (see Table 1.1). Once again, as with vulnerability, several symptom formation factors may operate simultaneously. Furthermore, some may be genetic and others may be psychosocial.

So far in this consideration of diagnostic specification, one type of psychosocial factor (say, loss) has been related to one type of disorder (say, depression). But it is also possible to explore why one event can relate to more than one type of disorder. For instance, gastrointestinal disorder was particularly common among the survivors of the tanker disaster, but a number of other disorders were also present. It is possible in this instance that the event was not experienced in the same way by all the members of the crew; perhaps it was those who were placed under greatest conflict by the event (because, say, they had the greatest need to return to sea to earn a living) who tended to develop gastrointestinal disorder. But equally, as with the issue of vulnerability, the explanation may lie in processes more removed from the event itself. For example, the way a person copes with an event may change its meaning and thereby its impact. And, equally, genetic or constitutional factors may again be involved. Thus with diagnostic specification we face what Roessler and Engel (1974) have called "individual response specificity," and ask whether there is some further factor that determines the fragility of one organ system so that the subject succumbs with, say, arthritis rather than bronchitis.

To sum up:

1. "Event specification" considers whether taking account of severity of threat or emotional significance increases the correlation of events with a disorder, a group of disorders or disorder in general.
2. "Specification of vulnerability" considers how, once an event has occurred, other factors may help to predict who will respond to a particular type of event with a disorder.
3. "Diagnostic specification" involves the categorization of these disorders in different groupings and subgroupings.
4. The term "symptom formation" is used to refer to factors that differentiate subtypes of disorder once other etiological agents (provoking and vulnerability factors) have brought about some form of the broader condition.

The wide range of factors potentially involved in diagnostic specificity and vulnerability presents a daunting research task, which, even if restricted to psychosocial factors, is far too big for this volume. However, it would be quite unrealistic to keep rigidly to our main task, the issue of event specification. For one thing, the processes implied by particular vulnerability and diagnostic specificities appear at times to involve the same cognitive-emotional quality as the event itself; when this occurs, there is bound to be an arbitrary element in any decision about where the event "ends" and other processes begin. It is also important to give the reader some idea of how event specification can help in tackling the fundamental etiological issues involving vulnerability and diagnostic specificity. However, it should be realized that what is done in this volume, particularly concerning vulnerability, can be only cursory, and is intended to be largely introductory to and illustrative of issues to be addressed in a companion volume.

Life Events and Stress

Defining Life Events and Stress

Complaints about the misuse of the term "stress" are common: It is used by some to refer to the external environment and by others to refer to an internal state that in turn can be psychological or physiological. But agreement to use the term in only one way will not in itself banish confusion, as either approach on its own leads to untenable positions. To take a preliminary example, if stress is something a person experiences, it cannot reside in an event. But if it can only be characterized as stressful in terms of someone's response to that same event, how do we avoid the self-defeating tautological error of defining life events only by what is found stressful? How do we, for example, study coping if we rule out events not experienced as stressful (however this is defined) because of successful coping?

Selye warned some time ago that the external approach of listing of stressors is "arbitrary" and that "the stressor effects depend not so much upon what we do or what happens to us but on the way we take it" (1956, p. 370). The trouble with pursuing the implications of this view is that, if we are concerned with etiological issues, it may be difficult to distinguish with confidence an internal response from the disorder itself or some early sign of it. Given that we wish to examine the triad of event-response-disorder, we will be fortunate indeed in epidemiological research if we are in a position to establish that the measurements of the final pair, response-disorder, have not been conflated. Moreover, it is by no means clear that the respondent will always have the ability to report accurately on his or her response to an event. In such a situation, there is much to be said for the alternative – for putting weight on the measurement of the event in an external sense; at least there is something there that can be grasped. This has undoubtedly contributed to the increasing interest in recent years in life events research. Although an event certainly cannot get "inside" a person until it has in some way been translated, it does exist independently of any such translation.

By and large, events are important because of the way they match or mismatch with concerns of the individual (Fridja, 1986). And to this it is important to add what has come to be termed a "transactional" perspective: There is likely to be such an interplay between organism and environment that neither will necessarily remain stable (Temoshok, 1983, p. 217). But this very duality and reciprocity are what can cause confusion, and the study of life events has suffered from a failure to face up to the full complexity of what follows from the acceptance of such views. Let us follow some of the implications.

It is unnecessary to argue for the need for competent description of the event itself. But since the decline of behaviorism, it has become clearer that we cannot rest content with only this – with remaining outside the person. If we leave aside the issue of physiological measures, the most usual way of tackling the question of translation has been to go on to assess meaning (i.e., the event's relevance for a person's concerns). In the end, we deal here with the event's internal representation and a person's cognitive and emotional responses to it. This has been discussed earlier in terms of event specification and the term "meaning" is used here to cover both severity of threat and emotional significance.

Once this step has been accepted, there have been two ways of proceeding. Judges from much the same social world can be asked to say how the individual experiencing the event is likely to think and feel in response to it. This will require us to deal with the twin problems of how the event should be described to the judges and how to deal with lack of agreement among them. Alternatively, we may proceed by asking the person experiencing the event about how he or she felt. This will require us to deal with the possibility that the report and the disorder we wish to understand have in some way been confounded, and also the possibility that the person's response may not always be able to reflect adequately the sum total of the event's meaning for him or her because the basic postulates on which his or her emotional response was based are not fully open to awareness. In an insightful discussion of this issue, Epstein (1983) makes clear that important preconscious postulates about self and about the world often have to be inferred from repetitive patterns of behavior and from emotions. In what follows, I emphasize the advantages of this approach – that is, the use of investigator-based judgments of a person's likely response in terms of an assessment of his or her plans and concerns. I emphasize that they can be assessed individually by concentrating on the person's behavior. This has methodological advantages and helps to overcome the problem of lack of awareness. But this second approach does not rule out asking a person how he or she felt, in order to make a *further* rating of self-report.

However, there is still one other way forward, and this has the advantage of avoiding the daunting complexities presented by the issue of meaning. This can be done if events are defined in terms of disruption or promise of disruption of an individual's activities (Dohrenwend & Dohrenwend, 1969; Holmes & Rahe, 1967; Thoits, 1983). If we make this assumption, events can then be dealt with in straightforward descriptions of what happens in terms of behavior. It is not unreasonable to hope to establish the amount of disruption of behavior following an event, and this would avoid the question of personal meaning in terms of severity of threat or emotional significance. But while this approach has been common and is probably good enough to get research under way, its avoidance of any consideration of internal representation suggests that it can be highly misleading if taken literally. Ingmar Bergman, in his film *The Lie*, describes the struggle of a man to come to terms with the knowledge that his wife has had an affair throughout their 14 years together. This is obviously a life event, and, as we will see later, one capable of provoking an affective disorder, even if (to amend Bergman's script slightly) *the man's life in outward display were not to change at all* – say, if he chose not to tell anyone of his discovery and continued the routines of his daily life without disruption in behavioral terms. To pursue the implications of this example, life events can be seen as essentially about readjustments in *thoughts*, albeit provoked by something in the world and usually paralleled by some change in behavior. Such a view has the advantage that it leaves open to be settled empirically how far actual changes in routine and behavior are involved in the stress process, as contrasted with mental and emotional changes. Changes in activity can be seen as part of the description of the event itself, and meaning as how the event is translated internally. One can, of course, further add to this approach the many bodily changes (of which a person may or may not be aware) that have been seen as signs of stress – neuroendocrine changes, blood glucose levels, increased heart rate, and so on. In much of this book their existence is taken for granted, as is the need to move toward their study in conjunction with the event-response-disorder triad.

This change in emphasis, from life events as involving altered behavior to life events as involving cognitive and emotional changes, is consistent with the emerging agreement that if life events are involved in the etiology of affective disorders, it is because of their meaning. But here research into psychiatric disorders and research into physical disorders took somewhat different courses, which have only begun to converge again in recent years. One of the purposes of this volume is to document just this coming together.

The foundation of life events research can be traced to the laboratory work of W. B. Cannon, which, insofar as it was concerned with illness, dealt largely with physical disorder (Dohrenwend & Dohrenwend, 1974; Mason, 1975; Thoits, 1983). Cannon demonstrated that emotion-provoking stimuli can produce the physiological alterations necessary for fight or flight (e.g., rapid clotting, circulatory changes, and increased blood sugar). He also proposed that physical illness would result from "the persistent derangement of bodily functions . . . due to persistence of the stimuli which evoke the reactions" (Cannon, 1929, p. 261). And much life events research has continued to be concerned with the etiology of physical illness. However, in the growth of systematic inquiries over the last 15 years, the study of psychiatric disorder has held an increasingly important place. Perhaps because of the obvious similarity between affective disorder and ordinary emotions, it is here that the role of meaning has probably been most clearly documented and the most definite break has been made with the tradition of seeing events in terms of disruption of behavior. This was first done by establishing the degree of undesirability or unpleasantness of events – the degree to which they threaten the physical survival or emotional well-being of the individual (e.g., Paykel, Prusoff, & Uhlenhuth, 1971; Brown, Sklair, Harris, & Birley, 1973). But this went with or was soon followed by more discriminating concepts (Lazarus & Launier, 1978) and measures such as "exits" (Paykel *et al.*, 1969) and "loss" and "danger" (Finlay-Jones & Brown, 1981). The importance of undesirable events in the onset of psychiatric disorder has now been documented in many studies. By contrast, Thoits (1983) notes in a recent review that "I know of only three studies that compare the relative predictiveness of total changes and undesirable changes for physical health outcomes. . . . These studies indicate that the total amount of change best predicts physical health outcomes whereas undesirable change best predicts psychological outcomes" (p. 59). In later chapters of this book, a different conclusion emerges: namely, that current research leaves little doubt about the importance of emotional response to events for physical health as well.

A Choice of Methods

Acceptance that meaning is likely to be critical brings would-be investigators face to face with measurement issues that have afflicted sociology since its inception and have been the source of countless discussions and disputes. Indeed, this ambience of complexity is probably an important reason why so many have hoped that it would be enough to record simply the "external" event – a birth, a move to a new house, a broken love affair. Much life events research has done just this, and in doing so has employed a simple checklist approach. In a recent review, Cohen and Wills (1985) conclude that roughly 90% of existing studies were using such life events measures; it can be added that practically every study from the United States to date has used them. A checklist is used to obtain information about events that have occurred, with a person simply checking off whether, say, "someone in the family has been ill." In a parallel but quite distinct exercise, "weights" are obtained to characterize each class of event. The weights are derived from averaging the scores of a number of judges asked to assess the disruption caused by such events, in relation to a standard maximum score provided by an event such as "death of a spouse." This procedure has the advantage that it is possible to subject the ratings of the judges to various refinements and controls. However, in practice this latter possibility has been largely thrown away by dealing only with average ratings made in response to extremely brief event descriptions. In the commonly used Schedule of Recent Experiences (SRE), where 100 is the standard provided for death of a spouse, any birth of a child is simply given a score of 39 in terms of the readjustment required by the event; any dismissal from work is given a somewhat higher score of 47; and any divorce receives a still higher one of 73 (Holmes & Rahe, 1967). "Birth," for instance, is therefore seen in terms of a lexical decoding of the kind that is involved in the definition given in a dictionary, "the production of offspring," with no further attempt at differentiation. At a third stage, scores of events that have occurred in a set period of time are summed and individuals are allocated an overall score.

There are many reasons why such a checklist-dictionary approach has proved to be ineffective. The resulting measures have had low reliability, both when the subjects have been reinterviewed about the same events and when different judges have rated the "stress" involved in particular events. They have also shown poor accuracy in terms of across-respondent agreement about the same event. Probably as a direct result, research findings have been disappointingly inconsistent. At heart, the problem appears to be one of variability within particular event categories such as "move to a new house." A brief description of this kind (given to judges in order for them to assess weights and to respondents in order to gather the basic research material) can mean many things. Is the move planned or enforced, or to a more or less desirable house? Does it mean losing friends? Does it involve financial problems? Is it associated with difficulties in a marriage? The problem of variability within each event category illustrated by these examples is nicely documented in an exercise carried out by Bruce Dohrenwend and his colleagues in New York (Dohrenwend, Link, Kern, Shrout, & Markowitz, 1987). They took the unusual step of asking respondents for an account of what had actually happened in each event established by a checklist. The investigators then rated each of these replies in terms of the amount and desirability of changes involved. To their apparent surprise, there was a wide range of responses. For example, in terms of amount of change, "laid off" was considered to involve "no change" in 10% of the applicable cases, "little change" in 13%, and at least "moderate change" in 77%. Puzzled, the investigators noted, "If what one has in mind here is the effect of a plant shutdown on its workers, it is difficult to see how being laid off can lead to little or no change for almost a quarter of those experiencing such an event" (Dohrenwend *et al.*, 1987, p. 109). But when they went back again to look at the specially elicited replies, they found that they should have been thinking about more than plant shutdowns: "Some of those laid off, for example, were people employed as musicians, dancers or actors, who had come to the end of a contracted engagement. For them, this was a non-event since it was part of their occupational pattern to be laid off several times a year" (p. 109). Dohrenwend *et al.* conclude, "Our results suggest that differences in amounts of change may be as large within event categories as between them. With this amount of error, it is hardly surprising that the associations found between life events and adverse health changes are frequently small" (p. 109).

This insight has come after more than a decade of work with such instruments, involving hundreds of research studies. One of the reasons for the delay in recognizing and dealing with such shortcomings has probably been the fact that most checklist studies have not been concerned with the impact of particular events, but with an overall score based on the weights of all events occurring in a given period of time. In this sense, they have been one step removed from the problem of such event variability. Moreover, it has for the most part been assumed that events summate in their impact. There are, as yet, few or no empirical data to support this assumption. As far as the etiology of depression is concerned, evidence reviewed in the next chapter suggests that, if anything, just the reverse may occur. But, leaving this aside, one unfortunate consequence of this assumption of additivity has been to divert interest from the issue of meaning and from the need to date events as accurately as possible *vis-à-vis* any onset of disorder. The rest of this chapter concentrates on studies that have taken a quite different route: They have set out to consider the etiological role of particular events, and have left it to be settled empirically how far the impact of such events is additive. But before completing this review of the alternative approach to the one we have taken, it should be noted that there have been some moves to introduce the idea of meaning into the kind of questionnaire-based instrument developed by Holmes and Rahe (1967), and at the same time to tackle the issue of event variability. The most important innovation has been to ask individual respondents to rate the importance of particular events for them (e.g., Hurst, Jenkins & Rose, 1979; Uhlenhuth, Balter, Haberman, & Lipman, 1977; Sarason, Johnson, & Siegel, 1978). This is a major departure, and it is clearly reasonable to expect that something of the true complexity of meaning will be reflected in such an approach. In practice, however, improvement in prediction has been minimal. Probably part of the reason for this is that summed scores for events occurring in a given time period have continued to be used.

But such a subjective approach, however used, runs in any case into formidable methodological difficulties. For instance, there is no control over what the respondent will have in mind when rating the event. Will the reply relate to the time of the first occurrence of a child's illness, when there seemed some risk of his or her dying, or to the perspective a few days later, when it was clear that there had been no risk in fact? There are even more fundamental problems. A critical one concerns the possibility that reports about the "severity" of the event may be influenced by the fact that the respondent has probably already developed the illness which is the focus of investigation. One way in which bias may occur is through "effort after meaning" (Bartlett, 1932). A man whose wife has developed a severe depressive illness may exaggerate the importance to her of her pet dog, who died 2 months before her illness, as a means of coming to terms with her recent symptoms. His wife might exaggerate for a similar reason or because she is depressed. We know that this kind of distortion can occur (Brown, 1974). However, the critical point is not whether or not it has, but that an approach based on the respondent's assessment is unable to rule out the possibility.

The problems of life events measurement are therefore not just related to error. Even if this were ignored and research were based on the assumption that measures are sufficiently accurate to give some idea about the presence of an etiological effect, there is still the problem of bias. It is difficult to conceive of any scientific measurement without error or inaccuracy (although time invested in developmental work can often keep this within manageable limits). The major concern is therefore not inaccuracy but bias. It may still be possible to arrive at valid conclusions about causal processes with inaccurate measures; the inaccuracy merely reduces the size of the link. Bias is more serious because it can produce a link where none in fact exists. As far as life events are concerned, a viable alternative is to continue to listen to what respondents have to tell us, but to use ourselves to filter this. In so doing, however, we have to go beyond the mere documenting of the world in an empirical sense to create a picture in terms of the meaning both of what has happened and of what might have been. A restatement of the *facts* about a birth (e.g., weight, age of mother, parity, and physical complications) is not enough. Their likely meaning to those involved must be considered, and this must be done by taking into account the wider social context. For example, in the case of a birth, factors that must be considered include the likely relevance of the mother's housing (is there overcrowding?), financial security (is it uncertain?), career plans (will it mean giving up going to college?) and even apparently minor matters (e.g., is a grandmother willing to babysit?). Concern with meaning ultimately reflects a commitment on the part of an investigator to explore the likely significance of an event for those involved in terms of their role identities or lives as a whole. Fortunately, since we all spend much of our time doing just this for ourselves, the human mind is a suitable instrument for the task.

Measurement and Meaning

To recapitulate: We are faced with the problem of the translation of an event into an internal representation. And in doing this, we need to bear in mind that for methodological reasons it is highly advantageous to place as much weight as possible on characteristics of the event itself. Given this daunting task, it is useful to begin by considering how an individual in everyday life becomes aware of meaning. (The assumption to be pursued is that there is some comparability between this and how an investigator might gain insight into the meaning of events.)

There can be little dispute about the critical role of emotion in such translation. Indeed, Lazarus has argued that the study of stress is in essence the study of a variety of emotional responses (Lazarus & Folkman, 1984). In an accomplished review, integrating current theories of emotion, Howard Leventhal (1980) emphasizes the frequent passive quality of emotion, as something that comes over us. He first marshals evidence that emotional experience precedes the social labeling of it (emhasized by Schachter's cognition-arousal theory; see Schachter and Singer, 1962). For example, the cognitions of a child are linked to innate emotional states, and it is these states that in adulthood supply the basis for the universality of affective communication found across different cultures. Leventhal argues that these emotional experiences are critical if the individual is to retain contact with his or her "true feelings," and that they can in fact provide a sense of what is going on even when social learning has from the individual's point of view distorted the interpretation to be given to a situation. Indeed, the most effective way an individual may have of dealing with "false consciousness" is to pay heed to his or her own emotional reactions. A "modern" woman in today's Nairobi may experience shame and despair when her husband takes a second wife, although the cultural standards still prevailing in Kenya make it clear that this is an acceptable and even desirable thing to happen. But Leventhal also places considerable weight on social learning. For example, although blind children show easily recognizable patterns of emotion in their faces, as they grow older these gradually decrease in clarity; this suggests that social experience is important in maintaining innate facial expressions of emotion, and that it is also capable of amending them.

Leventhal emphasizes the way in which perceptions are automatically referred to memories of past emotions and the circumstances that evoked them. Fear or anger, for example, may occur in response to the perceived status of someone in authority, without any obvious awareness on the part of the person of the full basis for his or her reaction. A person may only be aware of the emotion and the immediate eliciting conditions. Another influential commentator states that emotions "are aroused easily by factors over which the individual has little control, they are controllable with difficulty by factors that she or he can control, and [they] endure for periods of time that she or he controls only with great difficulty. They are in all these respects somewhat alien to the individual" (Tomkins, 1981, p. 323). However, Epstein (1983) is surely correct here in emphasizing the importance for emotion of implicit beliefs and values. He particularly emphasizes preconscious material that can be brought to conscious awareness by an act of attention, but in practice is often left implicit; it is the emotion or mood that we are often first aware of, and the need to interpret its significance. Perhaps this is one reason why emotion has been a surprisingly neglected topic in modern social science, although its critical importance is increasingly becoming recognized in sociology (Collins, 1973, p. 198).

Zygmunt Bauman (1978), in an insightful discussion of the literature on hermeneutics, relates the somewhat alien character of emotion to the issue of meaning. Emotion tends to come first; meaning is something that in ordinary circumstances has to be constructed in retrospect when memories of experience and emotional response are dwelled upon. A significant disappointment may be enough to set such introspection in train, with emotions an integral part of it. Crises, including obvious discrepancies between experience and expectation, may lead us to dwell on what our lives have been about, what we have done with them, and what will become of us (Brown & Harris, 1978b, Chap. 5). This is often accompanied by painful emotions, and perhaps weeks or months of obsessive rumination about the crisis (Horowitz, 1976). Take, for example, the case of a working-class woman who, with her husband's help, put considerable effort over a number of years into running a highly successful youth club in south London. Quite unexpectedly one evening, a quarrel developed at the club, and her son was seriously attacked without obvious motive by two youths who were not at the beginning involved in the quarrel. Before the police arrived, the youths had left, but a brick had been thrown through one of the windows. Later, the woman related to a research interviewer how this incident led to a gamut of thoughts and emotions, the most central of which focused on the safety of her son – particularly whether he would be recognized locally and set upon again. She insisted that he avoid the club, although he had been attending it for several years. She reported a sense of being let down, and of having recurrent thoughts about how the whole incident might have been prevented if her husband had been present. It also raised for her the question of whether or not she should give up the work and, if so, whether her husband should carry on at the club alone. She made clear, however, that though painful, her struggle to make up her mind had led to some good thoughts about their success as a family in running the club and how much they had achieved. But these same thoughts also highlighted how any withdrawal on her part would jeopardize the achievement. She related how she had found herself in the weeks following the incident thinking a good deal about the increase in violence among young people, and she gave a number of impressively sophisticated reasons, based on her own experience, for this social change.

This woman's observations therefore spanned the immediate consequences of the event, her own life, and the fate of young people today in our cities. The most salient thoughts concerned danger to those close to her – that is, she felt that the incident heralded even worse things to come. Apparently less significant was her sense of disappointment (i.e., her feeling that they had been misused); good thoughts about herself and her family came a poor third. It is easy to see that such themes were likely to be linked to characteristic emotions: for example, danger to anxiety, loss and disappointment to sadness, and past achievements to pride. The incident in this way was placed in a broader context, and this resulted in a gamut of emotions and reflections – in short, in its meaning for the woman.

The question therefore arises how far this kind of process can be reflected in our measurement procedures. How far can an investigator, by taking account of context, make a judgment about likely meaning? This was an issue dealt with by Weber in terms of "explanatory understanding" (*erklarendes verstehen* – Weber, 1964, p. 75; see also Marsh, 1982). Weber makes clear that systematic measurement needs to consider a person's values, plans, and goals in order to relate two things, which can be provisionally labeled "situation" and "meaning." Therefore an assessment of meaning or understanding on the part of an investigator can take into account not only the immediate situation (say, a woman losing a job), but the wider context (say, she is unmarried, in debt, and living with her school-aged child) – that is, in Weber's words, a "more inclusive context of meaning."

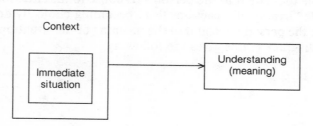

Diagram 1. Explanatory understanding – basic assessment.

A critical feature of explanatory understanding is the self-evident character of its assessment of meaning. Karl Jaspers has emphasized in his classic *Allgemeine Psychopathologie* the way in which such understanding "depends primarily *on the tangible facts* (that is the verbal contents, cultural factors, people's acts, ways of life and expressive gestures) in terms of which the connection is understood, and which provide the objective data" (Jaspers, 1923/1962, p. 303; emphasis his). In any particular instance, the force of this self-evident quality will differ, as this depends on the extent of the tangible facts known to us. "The fewer these are, the less forcefully do they compel our understanding; we interpret more, and understand less" (Jaspers, 1923/1962, p. 303). He also makes clear that this self-evident quality does not depend on the actual frequency of the connection in real life: "A poet, for instance, might present convincing connections that we understand immediately though they have never yet occurred" (p. 304).

Alfred Schutz (1971) has added further insights: Such understanding has nothing to do with introspection, but results from being brought up in a particular world. It is, if you like, self-evident that the woman described earlier would feel anxiety for her son and attempt to protect him as a result of the incident. Schutz emphasizes the public quality of the understanding; it is something we all participate in by the fact of being human and part of our society. Any knowledge of the circumstances surrounding the situation, however, acquired, is potentially relevant. Most important are people's goals, choices, and plans "originating in *their* biographically determined circumstances" (Schutz, 1971, p. 496; emphasis his). Schutz's emphasis on typicality stems from the fact that it would be foolish to be overconfident about the accuracy of any particular assessment, even though it has a self-evident quality. Accuracy of an interpretation will in practice depend on the range of tangible facts we possess, but even with a full account we merely have an assessment of what it is reasonable to expect a particular set of circumstances to mean to a person.

Once such a judgment about understanding (or meaning) is made, it is possible to relate it to the person's response to the situation, including possible "irrational" reactions (e.g., becoming clinically depressed), and also to the person's account of the meaning of the situation. To elaborate on Diagram 1, this gives the following:

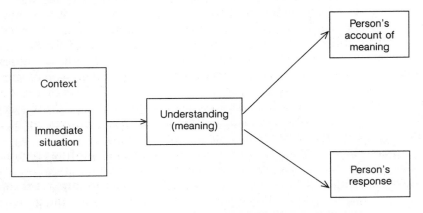

Diagram 2. Explanatory understanding – further links.

Now that the various possibilities have been outlined schematically, it is still necessary to settle how far it is legitimate to consider a person's *account* of meaning when dealing with understanding, or to use understanding to explain consequences, such as the onset of an anxiety disorder. Both questions require a closer consideration of the notion of cause.

In a good deal of social research, the phenomena examined are fairly closely associated in time, and it is usually possible to obtain detailed descriptions of what has occurred – say, the different behavior of nurses toward those with something "legitimate," such as a broken leg, and those admitted after a suicide attempt. Moreover, it is often possible to be reasonably convinced about the part such circumstances have played in the nurses' response. Like all causal imputations, this judgment is still an inference, but one that many would feel to be reasonable, and there is on the whole little criticism of the way such judgments about "situational causality" are continually employed in field research in the social sciences. Much social research, however, deals with "distal causality," involving considerable discontinuity in time, space, or the level of the systems studied, which cannot (if only for practical reasons) be reduced to such simple linkages (Brown, 1973). The outcome of activity may well be unintentional and in no way foreseen by those involved. For instance, war may lead to lowered rates of suicide, or schizophrenic patients who return to live with parents may relapse more often as a function of their greater participation in the daily round of family activities. Much of the doubt about the use of understanding has been consequent upon its use to unravel such possible distal causes. It does not matter whether or not a respondent cites such a link. One woman, for example, insisted that her extremely disturbed depressive reaction to the birth of her first child was due to the fact that the baby reminded her of a foster child whom she had wanted to adopt some years before and who was taken from her. It was, however, possible that it was being depressed that led the woman to believe this. Distal links therefore may concern time (e.g., loss of foster child → birth several years later → reawakening memory of child → depression), or distinction of the systems involved (e.g., birth → biological changes → depression → ideas about foster child). It follows that just at the point in someone's life when commentators such as Schutz agree that a person is most likely to be aware of meaning, the investigator is likely to have trouble ruling out the presence of bias.

Given these problems, I can conceive of no way of settling potential distal links by mere talk with respondents about the memory of events. Nonetheless, understanding or meaning can still play an important role in causal inquiry. But for this it is essential to move beyond the individual to study a number of persons – that is, to undertake a comparative inquiry and to look for associations in a statistical sense. Since many individuals are studied, the occasional error will not be of much moment, as long as it does not reflect serious bias in the measuring instruments. As already noted, inaccuracy is by no means fatal for scientific research as long as bias is avoided. Fortunately, unbiased judgments (if not always accurate ones) in terms of understanding are possible if the investigator is content to utilize *only* material about situation and context. Under these circumstances, since persons are studied in aggregate, it is still possible for powerful effects to emerge.

The argument can be summed up by adding to the earlier diagrams a distinction between the immediate response and the distal response, giving five phenomena that can be linked:

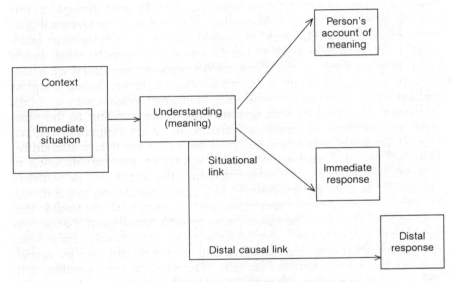

Diagram 3. Full scheme for explanatory understanding.

As already made clear in Diagram 3, the distal link should not (and often cannot) be tackled by understanding, and we should not ask whether the occurrence of a particular distal response makes sense in the light of understanding. But understanding or meaning can still be used to explain distal response in a comparative inquiry, as long as account and immediate response are ignored in its assessment. To return to the woman who witnessed the attack on her son (immediate situation), one could assess the likely meaning of the event in terms of her history of involvement in the club and her close ties with her own children (context), while ignoring her account of the meaning of the event, the fact that she insisted that her son not go back to the club (immediate response), and her development of an anxiety state (distal response) 2 weeks later. The latter set of factors involves distal causality, and it would only be possible to feel confident about the role of the understanding of the event in this if it were supported by the results of a comparative and statistics-based inquiry. In short, can we show that other events with this kind of meaning also tend to be associated with the onset of anxiety?

The Bedford College Life Events and Difficulties Schedule

The Establishment of "Equivalence" Classes for Events

The Life Events and Difficulties Schedule (LEDS), used throughout this volume, at its core utilizes this notion of *verstehen* or understanding to deal with meaning. However, the initial step in its development was a good deal less fundamental. It was first necessary to settle what should count as a life event. If the attack on the woman's son described above were to be included as an event, what other incidents should count as equivalent in the sense of deserving inclusion? What about a child's admission to a hospital with appendicitis, or an accident to the same child and subsequent emergency treatment in an outpatient department? This initial step in the design of the LEDS involved a straightforward but rather tiresome exercise of setting up comparable units of analysis. For example, it was decided that the attack on the woman's son should be seen as "equivalent" to a child's admission to a hospital, but not to attendance at a general-practice surgery with ear trouble that was likely to clear up. The task of creating such "equivalent classes" was carried out in two stages: first, by drawing up a set of rules about what should and what should not be included as events; and then by supplementing this with extensive examples. The need for prior detailed definitions is obvious when one considers the temptation for an investigator interested in the etiology of, say, anxiety states to include a son's routine outpatient visit if it happened to be followed by serious disturbance in a mother, and to exclude it if it did not.

Therefore, to return to the development of the LEDS, it was necessary to settle in advance of the main study what would count as a life event. The approach at this stage was based on earlier work with schizophrenic patients (Brown & Birley, 1968). Because we believed that a florid episode could be brought about in a susceptible individual by marked emotion of any kind, events were conceived in terms of the emotional response they might arouse, irrespective of whether this emotion was "positive" or "negative." In order to do this, the critical decision was made to define events in terms of their likelihood of producing strong emotion of any kind. The interviewer is provided with a comprehensive list of incidents that would be likely for most people to be followed by negative or positive emotion. Events are largely restricted to those involving the subject and "close ties" (i.e., spouse, fiancé[e], or cohabitee; parent; sibling; child; or confidant – a close friend in whom the subject can confide problems and worries with complete trust), but at times particularly dramatic incidents involving more distant relatives or even strangers are included as long as the subject was present (e.g., witnessing a serious road accident).

The list contains 40 types of events falling into the following eight groups, in every instance involving change in an activity, role, person, or idea:

1. Changes in a role for the subject, such as changing a job and losing or gaining an opposite-sex friend for the unmarried.
2. Major changes in a role for close ties or household members, such as a husband's staying off work because of a strike.
3. Major changes in subject's health, including hospital admissions and development of an illness expected to be serious.
4. Major changes in health for close ties or household members.
5. Residence changes or any marked change in amount of contact with close ties or household members.
6. Forecasts of change, such as being told about being rehoused.
7. Fulfillments or disappointments of a valued goal, such as being offered a house to rent at a reasonable price.
8. Other dramatic events involving either the subject (e.g., witnessing a serious accident or being stopped by the police while driving) or a close tie (e.g., learning of a brother's arrest).

We found it necessary to define in some detail for each of the 40 types of events just what should be included, illustrating each definition with a range of examples. For "changes in health," all hospital admissions for the subject are included, but only those that were urgent or lasting 1 week for other persons, and these only for close ties or household members. Illnesses not followed by admission are counted in a similar way, but only if in the rater's judgment they involved a possible threat to life or were alarming enough for serious implications to be suspected. Accidents are covered by similar criteria. Any new contact with a psychiatric service by a close tie is included. The death of anyone living at home or of a close tie is also included; all other deaths are excluded unless the subject was present or involved in its immediate aftermath (such events are rare). Therefore, incidents reported by respondents are often excluded, and in practice the threshold for inclusion is sufficiently high for only fairly rarely occurring events to be covered. Women interviewed in 1969-1970 at random in Camberwell, an inner-city London district, experienced on average only about three "events" in the year before they were seen (although this number ranged from none to over 20).

Therefore, there are detailed instructions to guide the interviewer about what to include. We were concerned that in the study of schizophrenia itself, if anything were left open, the decision as to whether to include an incident as an event could be influenced by knowledge that it antedated the attack or any other type of disorder. The use of a comprehensive and detailed set of definitions allows this possibility to be largely ruled out. The interviewer is tightly controlled in terms of what can be counted as an event; of course, a case can often be made for including or excluding a particular incident. As we saw it, the important point was to settle the matter before the main research began, and then to apply a common set of standards to everyone.

At this stage of the development of the instrument, we were concerned to establish not only that an event had occurred, but *when* it had occurred in the period before onset (or interview, in the case of those without schizophrenia). We attempted to place an event within a week of its occurrence, although on occasion it was necessary to record a range of weeks; when this was used, it was most often of the order of 2-3 weeks. Respondents often found it easier to pinpoint its occurrence when there was some anchor point to which they could relate; and we quite often attempted to provide one, such as a bank holiday (i.e., British legal holiday) or an important public event. The respondent was in any case always encouraged to relate "events" to each other and also to any onset of the florid schizophrenic episode with which we were concerned, but we did not ask about the possibility of a cause-and-effect relationship with the latter.

Contextual Ratings and the Question of Meaning

When the LEDS was extended to the study of depression, it was essential to go beyond this simple listing of events, since there was every reason to believe that depression would only relate to events with a particular kind of meaning. It was necessary to find some way to bring meaning into the research, but at the same time to avoid the kind of circularity that can come from taking a respondent's account of his or her response to an event. The second procedure therefore involved the more complex measurement task outlined above in the discussion of understanding. As already noted, most life events research (and sociological research on many other issues, for that matter) has ignored uniqueness of context by taking a dictionary approach to measurement. Therefore, once it is settled in the interview itself that an incident is to count as an event, it is necessary to go on to cover in as informal a way as possible a lengthy list of questions about what led up to and what followed it, and the full set of circumstances surrounding it. Respondents are asked in detail not only about what may be relevant circumstances, but also what they can tell about their reaction. But, as already made clear, the use of the latter runs the risk that any attempt to deal with meaning will lead to circular arguments about causality. To deal with this possibility, we decided upon *contextual* ratings of threat, based on the notion of the likely response of an average person to an event occurring in the context of a particular set of biographical circumstances. These ratings are closely related to the notion of situational causality discussed earlier, but a different term is used in order to emphasize that the contextual ratings should exclude any self-report about immediate response to the current situation. The ratings should reflect what most people would be expected to feel about an event in a particular set of circumstances and biography, taking no account either of *what the respondent says about his or her reaction or about any psychiatric or physical symptoms that followed it.*

The questioning is standardized only in the sense that there is a fairly lengthy list of topics to be discussed and a number of suggested probes. It is, however, the interviewer's job to question until he or she is confident that enough information has been obtained to rate the various "qualities" of each event. For this, there are 28 rating scales. They deal with (1) basic characteristics; (2) prior experience, plans, and preparation; (3) immediate reactions; and (4) consequences and implications. Most emphasis is placed on obtaining a full account of the situation at the time of the event.

The task of interviewing is not usually as exacting as might have been suggested so far. Interviewers are encouraged to follow two broad principles: to show curiosity about everything they are told, and to respond as much as possible to what is said as a story. This involves, for example, looking out for possible links between answers, although they may be far apart in the interview. Or, to give another example, a certain hesitation in a reply should be followed by another question along much the same lines if there is any hint that the respondent has something extra to impart. But curiosity will often need a focus, and so the interviewer, as already noted, is encouraged to react to what is said as if it were a story. The decision to stop asking questions is then not so much settled by coming to the end of a list of standard questions, but by the feeling that the material makes sense or hangs together. (Many questions are supplied, but it is left to the interviewer to decide whether to use them and in what order.) This means that it is often necessary to work backward and forward in time from a particular incident and to follow unexpected leads as they are brought up. But since respondents often talk in these terms, and since they usually react favorably to anyone showing genuine interest and curiosity about their lives, the approach can give every appearance of being natural and straightforward. It is also difficult not to be repeatedly surprised by the eloquence, detail, and clarity of accounts of quite ordinary individuals. Of course, there are exceptions. At times it is necessary to work patiently through a long list of questions, but even here the respondent can become unexpectedly involved and caught up in relating a particular incident. Training in the use of the instrument is essential.[1] Courses are held regularly and last about 2 weeks. They include an opportunity to listen to tape-recorded interviews, to rate them, and to discuss discrepancies with original ratings. Interview methods are discussed, and the trainee then carries out interviews, which are subsequently subject to criticism.

A good deal of the material required tends to come up spontaneously or in response to a minimal amount of encouragement to say more. But vague evidence is not enough, and the interviewer has to be thoroughly conversant with a manual of several hundred pages covering events to be able to decide during the interview whether enough has been established to complete the various scales once it is over (Brown & Harris, 1978a). Interviewers develop a facility for quickly rehearsing ratings (at least the key ones) during the course of the interview. However, interviews are tape-recorded, and final ratings on the various scales concerning each event are only made after listening to these later and making notes about all relevant statements. As will emerge later, the thoroughness of this interviewing style probably also contributes to the accuracy and reliability of the LEDS.

Short-Term and Long-Term Contextual Threat

The two most important scales in terms of etiological studies have proved to concern contextual threat and unpleasantness at two points of time. The consequences of some events, such as a child's unexpectedly developing a high temperature and being admitted to a hospital in an emergency with suspected meningitis, may well be resolved in a day or so – in this case, when the child's temperature returns to normal and extensive tests rule out a recurrence. However, other events, such as learning unexpectedly of a husband's infidelity, inevitably have longer-term implications. "Short-term threat" is defined as that implied on the day of the event or soon afterward, and "long-term threat" as that implied about 1 week after its occurrence. Each employs a 4-point scale of degree of threat: "marked," "moderate," "some," or "little or none."

1. Appendix 5 of *Social Origins of Depression* gives the full interview schedule, and also some suggested probes for the 28 scales covering each event (Brown & Harris, 1978b). But it should now be clear that this schedule cannot be used without the set of rating scales; the accompanying manual giving definitions, instructions, and examples; and participation in a training program.

In the standard procedure, the interviewer reads to the rest of the research team an account of the event and its surrounding circumstances, leaving out any mention of reactions and whether or not the subject was psychiatrically disturbed. The threat ratings are then made independently by each member of the team without discussion. Ratings are then compared, and if there is any disagreement, a consensus rating is reached. Raters are helped in three ways. First, there is a series of anchoring examples to illustrate the four points on each scale. Second, a rating is followed by a discussion about any discrepancy in the group of raters, and a final rating is agreed upon; in the longer term, this undoubtedly contributes to reliability of the ratings. Third, fairly "standard" ratings are applied to events such as routine childbirths. These standard ratings are not subtle and on the whole are adhered to fairly strictly. There is a convention, for instance, that childbirth is only rated high on long-term threat when it occurs in obviously difficult circumstances (e.g., poor housing, acute financial shortage, or very poor health of child or mother). These are considered to be integrally part of the context of the birth, and therefore relevant to its degree of threat. For example, caring for a new child is likely to be much more difficult where there is overcrowding, interpersonal tension, and financial hardship, and the suffering caused by all three of these problems will be likely to be considerably increased with another mouth to feed. In practice, what should be taken into account as relevant for contextual threat rarely causes difficulty. However, it must be added that the examples are intended to provide a grid in terms of which to view an event. Often events have unusual features, and it is always possible to depart from a rating given in the manual in the light of the differing context of another highly similar event. Events not covered by the manual occur from time to time and have to be judged in relation to the existing examples.

Therefore, contextual interpretations are not pushed too far. The woman mentioned earlier who reported being upset by her baby's likeness to one she had once wished to adopt was rated as having a non-threatening birth; we ignored what she said about her reaction, and there was nothing about her marriage, living arrangements, or other circumstances to make it particularly threatening. Although the interviewer was aware of the child she wished to adopt, no attempt was made to speculate on the kind of symbolic importance the birth might have had for her under the circumstances. It should perhaps be added that this was a borderline example; in a somewhat similar case – that of an otherwise childless widow who was reunited at the age of 70 with a daughter she had given up for adoption at birth – the rating of the event's probable meaning did take the adoption into consideration. Such a decision is a matter of judgment. For the woman who had previously lost the baby she had wanted to adopt, it was felt that it was impossible to sense whether a woman's *likely* response to the birth would be positive or negative, given this history. For the woman whose own child had been adopted and who had never had any subsequent children, it was considered that the reunion might well awaken ideas about what she had missed by having her child adopted, and therefore for most women would be a highly threatening event.

For the most part, events are easier to assess than these examples, and with an experienced team of raters the ratings can usually be completed fairly quickly. However, raters are encouraged to ask the interviewer for more information (i.e., "context") if they are in any doubt, and this process can be time-consuming. This is particularly so when interviewers are being trained, as such questioning is an important and convenient way of conveying the kind of material it is necessary to collect. One of the main requirements is to assess the amount of material required. The death, for example, of a woman's father closely antedating the birth of her child would not be relevant to the context of the birth, even though the new mother might herself repeatedly refer to the close juxtaposition of the death and the birth as having caused her to be particularly upset. According to our rating, the earlier event would not be part of the context of the second one unless the father had previously been substantially involved in the woman's plans concerning the birth (e.g., if it had been planned that he would help take care of the baby while she continued her career). The rating is based on a judgment about a woman's usual plans and expectations surrounding the birth and her life after it; in our geographically mobile society, the presence and support of a husband at the time of a birth is taken for granted in a way in which that of a parent usually is not. However, it is always possible to visualize exceptions. A woman whose husband, although in no way estranged, is often away for weeks at a time on his job may plan, in the absence of a substantial income, to continue her job soon after the birth, leaving the new baby with her mother-in-law, who is to receive no payment for this. The mother-in-law's unexpected death 6 weeks before the birth now becomes part of the context of the birth, in the sense that it crucially affects the young woman's plans and lifestyle: She may not be able to afford live-in help or find a suitable babysitter, and so now she may be unable to continue working, with all the attendant financial problems.

This standard rating procedure has on occasions been amended to adapt to different circumstances. For example, as a team accumulates experience, only the more threatening events and difficulties may be brought to the group for rating. Or, alternatively, ratings may be checked by just one rater, and these may only be brought to a full consensus meeting when there is a difference between interviewer and rater. But whatever alterations are made to the standard rating procedure, it is essential to have at least *one* other rater in addition to the interviewer. Whatever procedure is followed, there is a convention that when there is disagreement, the rating of the interviewer is not followed without very good reasons. It would be permissible, for example, if in discussing the reasons for the disagreement it emerges that the other rater has been inadvertently kept ignorant of a vital piece of biographical material. While it is essential for methodological reasons to have at least two people, it has also proved far easier to make the contextual ratings when a rater knows that it will be possible for obvious errors in his or her ratings to be corrected. Without this, it is easy to slip into a mood of uncertainty and to enter a spiral of doubt either that some critical part of the context has not been considered, or that knowledge of personal response or psychiatric condition has influenced ratings. The rating team at Bedford College, University of London, has often rated events for other researchers (and, indeed, for a number of the studies reported in this volume). Sometimes these ratings have been made from written accounts, but most often they are made during a personal visit. However, as the method becomes more widely used this will become more difficult, and other teams, particularly abroad, have already begun to support each other in this way.

At times, evidence for the validity of the rating procedure can be particularly impressive. For example, in Chapter 8 of this volume, Francis Creed documents how only one form of appendectomy ("functional" or "morphological") was preceded by an elevated rate of severely threatening life events. In the study itself, he collected material about events without any knowledge about diagnosis, while the Bedford College team supervising his ratings had no knowledge of whether the material to be rated concerned a patient or someone from the general population. The ratings were thus doubly "blind" – and to this it can be added that the patients were also in the dark about whether or not their condition was "functional."

While the role of the investigator in making contextual ratings has been emphasized, the LEDS does not rule out the additional use of the respondent's account of what occurred, although this material is ignored in the contextual ratings. The use of reported threat once the ratings of contextual threat are made may well lead to significant insights. The final five-factor diagram (see Diagram 3, above) illustrates the possibilities for such "triangulation." It is also useful to bear in mind that in the long-term such material may quite legitimately influence contextual ratings. There is no reason why raters should not be informed of the person's account of his or her own feelings *after* the contextual ratings have been made, and evidence of these in time should change the standards for contextual ratings, which are supposed to reflect average responses. In our own research (carried out over a period of 15 years) this has happened, particularly in the area of sexual behavior. For example, in 1977 we explicitly changed our "rules" in order to lower the minimum threat rating of the experience of termination of pregnancy, on the basis of the self-reports we had collected of numerous termination experiences in the early 1970s. (Of course, contextual factors can still always raise a threat rating in any particular instance of termination – say, if a woman is childless and in her late 30s, so that it may be her last chance to become a mother.) In addition, at this writing, we have begun to consider the implication of the growing public concern about acquired immune deficiency syndrome (AIDS).

Before this discussion of contextual threat is concluded, it is worth commenting on its relationship to the notion of the undesirability of life events (see Sarason *et al.*, 1978). Leaving aside the complications introduced by the contrast between contextual and reported threat, it is important to spell out from the start that the category of undesirable events is much broader than our group of severe events. The former would include all events that are threatening in the short term but that have no threat after 1 week. It would also include those with minor long-term threat. From this, it will be obvious that the degree of overlap between the two categories may not be very large.

Long-Term Difficulties

Life events occurring at one point in time do not constitute the only form of adversity relevant to stress research. A person may live in a dismal, overcrowded, and damp flat without necessarily having an "event" in our terms during the year of inquiry. Life events research has been muddled and unsystematic about this, often including a handful of ongoing difficulties with questions about events. We have collected such material systematically and have extended the principle of contextual ratings to such difficulties that last at least 4 weeks (Brown & Harris, 1978b, Chap. 8). Since we date the time the difficulty has lasted, and in particular its course during the year before interview, it is also possible to use these measures to document the outcome of events occurring in the year. A similar manual to that for events covers several thousand examples (Brown & Harris, 1979).

Criticism of the Contextual Approach

Some of the serious problems of the checklist approach have been discussed. Nonetheless, Dohrenwend and his colleagues in New York working in this tradition have been particularly skeptical about the contextual approach and have continued to seek an alternative. They note that although the contextual approach is more precise than the checklist method, "it is also more gross in that it involves collapsing in non-explicit ways the event, the social situation in which it occurs and the personal history of the individual involved, into a single measure. The resulting ambiguity is an obstacle to our understanding of statistical associations, since there is no way to tell which of the components that go into rating account for a particular association" (Dohrenwend *et al.,* 1987, p. 113). Given, as will be seen in the following chapters, that the contextual approach has provided the clearest results, and given that no satisfactory alternative has yet been developed, it is important to consider these criticisms and the possibility of a credible alternative. In their most recent statement about such an alternative, Dohrenwend and his colleagues finish by noting "that variability within categories is very large," but remain optimistic: "[D]ifferences between the events within each category do not seem to be infinite[,] neither are the major distinctions between the major sub-types inaccessible. Ultimately, it should be possible to revise life event lists to include in each event category examples of almost all the important variants of the events" (Dohrenwend *et al.,* 1987, p. 113).

First, how realistic is the kind of alternative they envisage? Here it should be borne in mind that, as it stands, the checklist approach gives judges and research subjects the *same* list. Such an extended approach is conceivable: The LEDS manual of examples follows along much the same lines and gives approximately 5,000 vignettes of events in terms of some 800 categories. However, it is almost certainly unrealistic to see this kind of extension as a means of rescuing the checklist approach. Certainly, in order to find out whether events have occurred to particular respondents, various short cuts are possible, and the whole list need not be presented. (But for this it would be essential to move to an investigator-based style of interviewing.) However, in order to obtain weights from the judges it is clearly necessary to present each a brief description of each event variant, and it is the formulation of this description to be presented to the judges that is the central focus of the divergence between the two approaches.

So far, the New York group has tackled the problem in terms of an instrument called the Psychiatric Epidemiology Research Interview (PERI), a list of 102 event labels under the headings of School, Work, Love and Marriage, Having Children, Family, Residence, and Crime and Legal Matters, with weights for each event obtained from averaging the responses of a series of judges (Dohrenwend, Krasnoff, Askenasy, & Dohrenwend, 1978). In terms of its usefulness, the first major problem is that the central figure involved in the event is not specified; this is left open for the judge (or respondent) to provide. This staggering shortcoming must obviously be rectified. The authors point out themselves that the considerable variability in their own judgment of the severity of events reported in response to two questions selected for special study, "family member other than spouse or child died" and "close friend died," was due to the fact that "Most of the deaths were of biologically distant relatives who were living far away at the time, and of acquaintances or long absent friends with whom the respondent was no longer close". (Dohrenwend *et al.*, 1987, p. 109). A solution would probably mean in most instances asking judges to rate events at least five times in terms of self, spouse, child, close relative, or friend, though there would be difficulty in conveying to judges who should be seen as "close."

But this would be only a preliminary step. In practice, many events are not dealt with by the current list even if the 102 categories are interpreted broadly. Some examples of events that can be collected by the LEDS but are not covered by the PERI are "serious trouble of child at school," "a mother's discovery that her child has been stealing from her" (only childhood *illnesses* are covered by the PERI), "a broken love affair" (only "broken engagements" and "broke with a friend" are covered), "the family pet dog biting two local children," "mother with schizophrenia discharging herself while still disturbed," "learning of a future layoff" (there is no allowance in the PERI for learning that an event is likely to occur or for decisions about future actions such as "a child deciding to emigrate"), "learning that a child is gay," "a threatened miscarriage," "learning that a twin sister has been separated from her husband for two years," "a sterilization." (Thoits [1983, pp. 50-53] discusses how event checklists typically omit many kinds of events and also deals with a number of related problems, such as the inclusion of events likely to be contaminated by any psychiatric disorder.)

But even if such gaps are filled, most of the descriptions in the PERI are patently too brief as they stand, whatever view is held about taking context into account. If we consider as an example a woman's break with a boyfriend, her actual response to the event is likely to be influenced by the following:

- Whether there was a commitment to get married or live together.
- Duration of relationship (e.g., weeks or years).
- Whether the relationship was a sexual one.
- Who took the initiative in bringing it to an end.
- Degree to which the woman was insulted and rejected in any final crisis (e.g., boyfriend went off with her best friend).
- Degree to which it was expected (e.g., the woman always knew that the boyfriend would return to live abroad).
- Social circumstances of subject (e.g., she lives alone, she is a single mother).

- Whether there is an obvious alternative (e.g., whether the woman already has another boyfriend in mind).

Some of the same considerations would be involved in a break with a friend. It would probably be relevant to know the following, for example:

- Whether they were living together, and, if not, how often they met.
- The distance of any move and the extent of any continued contact (e.g., by telephone).
- Irreversibility of the break.

The practical problems of presenting to a panel of judges an adequate list of event variants is clearly immense. Any such list would almost certainly run to thousands of examples. Now it may be argued that it is possible to rescue the situation by a retreat to cruder event descriptions – to take a defiant position that whether or not there were plans for marriage is not an integral part of the event "break with a boyfriend." But this flies in the face of reality. A person does not respond to some disembodied category, but to an event with links with past and present and with implications for the future. Moreover, leaving aside how an event is reacted to in real life, judges who are asked to rate degree of threat will almost certainly provide for themselves such a context, imagining aspects of past, present, and future. This can be done more or less consciously or, to use computer language, by default. That is, unless judges are told otherwise, they will automatically make assumptions – say, that a woman had been engaged or that there would be no hope of restoring a tie with a close friend. At this point, the matter is further muddled by the practice of ignoring any variability on the part of judges and using only an *average* score based on the ratings of a number of judges. In all these ways, the checklist approach is far more ambiguous than contextual ratings. The LEDS at least brings the issue of the dependence of meaning on context (indexicality) into the open, and the fundamental ambiguity of the alternative approach is bound to increase as event descriptions are truncated and decontextualized.

An alternative to that proposed by the Dohrenwends would be to keep an extended list of event variants but to obtain ratings from a panel of judges in the course of the investigation as particular events occur. But this would come close to the procedure employed in contextual ratings. Indeed, as this is written, the very latest discussions of the PERI by Dohrenwend and his colleagues (September 1987) appear to be moving in the direction of verbal interviews and consensus meetings to rate dimensions such as fateful loss (see also Dohrenwend, Shrout, Link,

Martin, & Skodol, 1986). But it is too early yet to tell what effect this will have upon the instrument. The approach would in any case continue to be plagued by the problem of event variability if the descriptions of events were insufficiently detailed.

Another response to the problem would be to keep a shortened list, but to collect material about various "dimensions," such as "degree to which event was expected" and "rate of contact with a person before the crisis." This is, in fact, an integral part of the present LEDS; however, there would remain the formidable and perhaps insuperable problem of developing effective event categories from these dimensions, since values on varying scales would often be incommensurable in the sense that their significance would depend on both the type of event and its general level of threat. The impact of an event's being "unexpected," for example, is almost certainly different for a broken love affair and for learning that one's married daughter is to have her first child.

It is perhaps insufficiently recognized that the problem of intraevent variability stems from the great range of events that need to be studied in any population survey. The problem is reduced in research dealing with people who have been victimized by a particular crisis, such as widowhood or rape, but even here the issue of variation requires some consideration. Parkes and Weiss (1983), for example, have convincingly argued in a study of widows and widowers for the importance of three factors: amount of forewarning of the death, ambivalence in the marital relationship, and amount of dependence. It would perhaps be easier for critics to accept the contextual approach if they could see it as approximating to the takeoff point of such studies of a single type of catastrophic event. In the present LEDS, any death of a husband would be classified as "severe"; to proceed further with analysis (given that sufficient numbers were present), it would still be necessary to take into account, in addition to the contextual rating, the kind of dimensions discussed by Parkes and Weiss. Indeed, this is just how the analysis proceeded in a study in the Outer Hebrides, where the women were more likely than in urban centers to develop an affective disorder after the death of a close relative (Brown & Prudo, 1981; Prudo, Brown, Harris, & Dowland, 1981). Paradoxically, therefore, one answer to critics is to emphasize the highly approximate nature of the present contextual threat ratings. Although they are good enough to give an impressively high etiological effect for onset of depression, the next chapter illustrates how much can still be done once the contextual ratings have been made to increase the association of severe events with the onset of this disorder, and to specify what is involved in terms of etiological processes. To put it in more technical terms, the achievement of the contextual ratings has probably been to greatly reduce "false negatives" (i.e., the number of onsets without severe events), but to create a large number of "false positives" (i.e., the number of severe events without onsets). That is, the ratings create a broad category of "equivalent" events that, in the development of etiological models and theory, parallel events such as death of spouse or rape in studies of particular crises.

The importance of this initial sorting of threat by severity, however, should not be underestimated. For example, as an exercise, PERI weights were given to 314 events collected by the LEDS in a recent study (to be reported in the next chapter) in the north London district of Islington. Of these events, 23% could not be allocated weights, and others had to be "forced" into a PERI category – for example, "ending a relationship with a boyfriend" was classified under "broken engagement" and "electricity cut off because of nonpayment" under "suffered a financial loss or loss of property not related to work." However, although this exercise was crude, it is of interest that there were no differences in average scores in terms of the four categories of long-term threat in the LEDS: "severe," "moderate," "some," and "little or none." (It will be seen in the next chapter that this differentiation is highly related to whether an event leads to depression.) Indeed, if anything, "severe" events had a lower average score than the rest – 435.9 ($n = 123$) versus 464.3 ($n = 120$). Since it becomes abundantly clear in the following chapters that this fourfold distinction has been central in getting research under way, then in this sense, at least, the PERI scores appear to be flawed.

Comparisons of the Checklist and LEDS Approaches

At this juncture, it is appropriate to mention other studies that have attempted to make comparisons between the LEDS and various checklist approaches along lines not dissimilar to the exercise just outlined. Despite the frequency with which critiques of the diverse methods have suggested they were tapping quite different sources of stress, there has been remarkably little empirical confirmation of this, possibly because a little thought about the instruments is enough to show that logically this must be so. Katschnig (1980) interviewed 42 suicide attempters in Edinburgh, first with the SRE (Holmes & Rahe, 1967) and then with the LEDS, and demonstrated that the congruence between these two methods was very low. This study also showed poor reliability between two administrations of the SRE just 2 weeks apart; only about half the events listed on either of the two occasions were identical in both trials. A further study on 147 depressed patients in Vienna gave a similar picture. Although pictures obtained from group means suggested a satisfactory degree of concordance, cross-tabulations at the level of the individual patient gave very low kappa values – .04 for the presence of at least one life change/event, and .19 for the presence of a "marked" LEDS event and a life change unit (LCU) score above the mean on the SRE (Katschnig, 1986). Another study (Bebbington, Tennant, Sturt, & Hurry, 1984) involved an attempt to fit events derived from a LEDS interview on 70 psychiatric outpatients and 310 subjects in a general population sample into the rubric of the inventory designed by Tennant and Andrews (1976). The authors report that the inventory failed to cover 26% of the events rated as "severe" according to the LEDS despite the fact that the exercise only utilized events obtained by the LEDS in the first place. With discrepancies of such size, it is clear that the problem of choice of instrument must be taken very seriously.

Reliability, Validity, and Falloff in the Reporting of Life Events

A certain level of accuracy and interrater reliability is, of course, essential for any research instrument, and a key issue concerns the mere occurrence of an event, rather than its qualities or dimensions of meaning. This is usually tested by the comparison of the independent reports of two informants (typically the respondent and a household member), although test-retest studies (e.g., Jenkins, Hurst, & Rose, 1979) and record checks based on written records (e.g., Belloc, 1954) can also be used. Low agreement using checklists has generally been due to a failure to report actual incidents rather than to invention of fantasy experiences. Kessler and Wethington (1986) have reviewed procedures to combat such inaccuracies, and the LEDS appears to embody a large number of these procedures. These authors list three broad sources of inaccuracy. First, there is simple failure to understand how much information the interviewer requires (Cannell, Oksenberg, & Converse, 1979). The conversational style of the LEDS interview provides several antidotes: On the one hand, interviewers are given explicit instructions that emphasize the importance of accurate recording of all that has happened in the given period (see Cannell, Miller, & Oksenberg, 1981); on the other hand, they question in a way that encourages the respondent to describe in a narrative style as many of his or her experiences as possible – a style of reporting that is usually enjoyed. Trained to show interest in even the most mundane incident, interviewers pause before moving on as a sign that they would be happy to hear more. They ask, for example, "Any other hospital admission in this time? Are you sure?" and reward any sign of serious memory search. Second, respondents may be too embarrassed to disclose certain experiences. Here again, the accepting style of listening of LEDS interviewers helps to desensitize respondents with such anxieties (Cox, Rutter, & Holbrook, 1988). This desensitization is further promoted by the length of the LEDS interview.

Not infrequently, it is just as the tape recorder is about to be switched off that interviewers are told, "Well, there is one other thing – I didn't want to tell you earlier, but . . . "; in this way, interviewers can leave with information that has not been imparted to anyone previously.

Third, respondents may genuinely forget incidents. Here not only the interpersonal stimulation and flexible probes of the LEDS, but also its basic structure and the reliving of emotions that the narrative style encourages, can jog a flagging memory. Once an incident has been obtained, it is pursued in terms of things occurring before and after, using this narrative approach. Moreover, asking about a large number of concrete possible incidents elicits more experience than does a small number of more general questions (Biderman, 1983, cited in Kessler & Wethington, 1986). Ordering these questions so that they occur in blocks covering a particular domain of life where each has some common relevance (e.g., housing, relationship with children) may facilitate recall, perhaps because the same memory schema can be used to structure information search (Higgins, Rholes, & Jones, 1977). But a set of rather more general questions must still be asked at the end of the interview, since some experiences do not readily fit into the structure of such domains. For example, hearing from an acquaintance that one's best friend has never repaid a £500 loan, but continuing to see the friend just as frequently (albeit seeing him or her in a new light), fits neither into the domain of the subject's own finances nor into that of changing contacts. There are six or seven of these general questions probing for revelations, disappointments, and decisions of which the respondents may not have been reminded by questioning in the earlier sections.

While the procedures help to combat inaccuracies stemming from lack of information about genuine events or the low validity of the measure, as implied earlier, detailed training and the use of directories of precedents increase the interrater reliability of ratings in regard to what is included as an event; this increases accuracy in the sense of precision and standardization (see Katschnig, 1986, for elaboration of this theme).

Some studies comparing reports of events by two close informants record a low rate of agreement about the occurrence of events. For example, Neugebauer (1983), using the PERI on 18 schizophrenic outpatients and their relatives, reported a 22% agreement (Wilcoxon signed-rank test), and Hudgens, Robins and Delong (1970) reported 57% agreement between 80 psychiatric patient-relative pairs (of whom half were diagnosed as depressives and the other half had a variety of conditions, including organic brain syndrome). But results with the LEDS have so far shown satisfactory levels of agreement, both for occurrence and for ratings of the contextual dimensions of events. To take occurrence of any event first, there was 81% agreement between schizophrenic patients and relatives, and 79% between depressed patients and relatives (Brown & Harris, 1978b, p. 71).

In order to review the evidence concerning dimensions of events, it is necessary to anticipate certain results concerning the role of what have been called "severe" events in the onset of depression (see Chapter 2). These, based on ratings of contextual long-term threat, form only about 15% of all events measured by the LEDS as occurring in the general population. This type of event has been clearly implicated in the onset not only of affective disorder, but also of "functional" physical disorders (Chapters 8, 9, 10, and 13) and of multiple sclerosis (Chapter 11).

In the original Camberwell study, interrater reliability of the basic ratings of short- and long-term contextual threat of events was high, and several reports by independent investigators have confirmed these results (e.g., Tennant, Smith, Bebbington, & Hurry, 1979; Parry, Shapiro, & Davies, 1981). Even more significant was the fact that there was a high level of agreement between ratings of contextual threat based on the accounts of depressed patients and on those of close relatives when seen by different interviewers. When ratings for the *same* events were compared, there was a 91% agreement about particular severe events occurring in the year before interview (Brown, Sklair, *et al.*, 1973).

There is, however, a complementary way of dealing with the difficult issue of accuracy (or validity) in terms of falloff in reporting of events. When a period of a year is considered, there is little or no evidence for a falloff in the reporting of severe events, supporting the evidence of accuracy based on across-informant agreement (Brown & Harris, 1978b, 1982). Given the critical etiological role of severe events, such results are of considerable importance. There is, however, often a falloff in the reporting of events of lesser severity (see Figure 1.1). It appears that significant error may occur when the gap between interview and event is 5 months or more. (For an exception and a fuller treatment, see Chapter 12.) It is the salience of the event that appears to be critical for recall, and Surtees *et al.* (1986) have recently published a paper in broad agreement with these conclusions.

A group in Zurich using the same list of events asked about in the LEDS interview obtained quite different results (Schmid, Scharfetter, & Binder, 1981). Whereas in Camberwell a decline of only 8% was found in the reporting of all events for the 21 weeks before interview, this figure was 62% in Zurich. This went with a total rate of events that was five times greater. This extraordinary difference must have been due to the way the two centers conducted and rated the interviews (Brown & Harris, 1982, p. 25), and the differing results provide dramatic confirmation that the basic procedures developed in the LEDS do control the range of incidents that can be included as events. However, training in the use of the instrument is essential, and the Zurich group did not

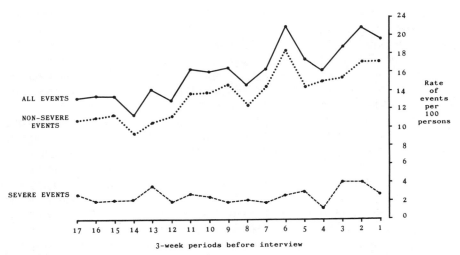

FIGURE 1.1. Rate of events over 12 months for seventeen 3-week periods before interview for Camberwell (south London) and Lewis (Outer Hebrides) by severity of threat of events. The final period covers 4 weeks, but the rate is readjusted as for a 3-week period.

receive this or have access to the manuals providing criteria for inclusion or exclusion of incidents.

    The much greater overall rate of events in the Zurich sample must have been due to the fact that the investigators included almost every incident mentioned in response to one of the standard questions. Thus, for example, they probably accepted *any* illness, rather than one reaching defined standards of severity. It is also possible that they included far more people among those covered. When the LEDS is used, respondents frequently mention events occurring to cousins, aunts, and the like whom they rarely see, even though the persons the interviewer wishes to to cover have been specified in detail at the beginning of the interview. (Such events are, of course, excluded.) This interpretation is supported by the low reliability reported for checklist instruments such as the SRE of Holmes and Rahe (1967) (e.g.,) Yager, Grant, Sweetwood, & Gerst, 1981). Paykel (1983) has recently carried out a comprehensive review and arrived at similar conclusions.

Time Order and Interviewing Methods

Perhaps the most puzzling aspect of life events research has been the widespread failure to deal seriously with time order. This is puzzling, since the idea of time is built into the very notion of a stressor-disorder link. But the question of dating onset is often ignored altogether, and events are only dated in the sense that respondents are asked to report whether particular incidents have occurred in a circumscribed period (typically 6-12 months in length). The reason for this startling indifference must be the almost universal use of respondent-based checklists and overall scores. If we wish to concern ourselves with the extraordinary variety of events that occur in the general population, there are two possible ways of insuring that events will be accurately dated.

First, as with the LEDS, the investigator can question respondents in detail, helping them to reconstruct the sequence of their experiences. Certain interviewing techniques that are a routine part of the LEDS, such as using the respondents' own salient experiences or personal marker dates (e.g., birthdays) or anniversaries of previous salient experiences (e.g., mothers' deaths) to narrow down the ranges of uncertainty over timing, have recently been reported as improving the accuracy of dating information (Loftus & Marburger, 1983; Baddeley, Lewis, & Nimmo-Smith, 1978; see also Kessler & Wethington, 1986). Respondents at times will be able to consult documents or give the investigator permission to consult records held by others. Others living at home may also be consulted. In general, discussing events in terms of a narrative with a beginning and an end is essential. However, such questioning, relying heavily on the judgment of the interviewer, runs counter to the tradition of questionnaire-based research with its emphasis on the advantages of "standard questions"; it has thus rarely been used to supplement a checklist approach.

A second strategy has been to use a longitudinal design, in which the respondent fills in the checklist before the development of any disorder. This was done in a number of influential early studies; particularly important were those of Rahe with naval personnel (Rahe, 1969). Large-scale population studies are far more costly, but several with longitudinal designs have recently been published. True time order is certainly established, but, given the cost of such inquiries, what has emerged has been disappointing. It has become clear that such longitudinal designs on their own are unlikely to provide an effective answer. (However, they can be invaluable in sorting out temporal order where ongoing processes such as self-esteem or marital adjustment are concerned.) The first necessity is to exclude persons already suffering from psychiatric disorder at the time of first interview and therefore not at risk in the follow-up period. The basic problem, however, is that the time between a possible stressor and any onset is often only a matter of weeks, and many events will therefore inevitably be missed. If such events are to be recorded, what happens in the follow-up period will also need to be covered, and this can only be done by retrospective questioning after the depression has occurred. This brings us once again back to the fact that the necessary fine-grained dating cannot be done with a checklist approach. Such longitudinal research therefore does not obviate the need to reconstruct time order by questioning of a "nonstandardized" type.

Recent longitudinal studies have reinterviewed subjects after periods ranging from as little as 2 months (Grant, Yager, Sweetwood, & Olshen, 1982) or 4 months (Henderson, Byrne, & Duncan-Jones, 1981) to 1 year (Theorell, Lind, & Floderus, 1975). All have used checklists to obtain life events and psychiatric state, and none has attempted to date onset in the follow-up period. The studies could not hope to be effective in the sense of Meyer and Haggerty's (1962) classic study of streptococcal infections of the throat, where children were seen every 2 weeks. (Frequent interviewing was here a practical possibility, because such infections are common and the study of a relatively small number of children was all that was necessary to obtain a sufficient number developing the disorder.) The study coming nearest to this design was that of Grant and his colleagues, employing a 2-month period (Grant *et al.,* 1982); however, because of events missed in the follow-up period, the studies as a whole are bound to have underestimated the etiological role of events.

The issue of the accuracy of dating in studies using the LEDS remains to be considered. Interviewers are instructed that if they are in doubt about time order, they should ask directly about the juxtaposition in time of event and onset. Although onset and events are covered at different points in the interview, respondents quite often mention a life event when asked about the development of the disorder. (See Brown & Harris, 1978b, Chap. 2, for details about dating onset.) It is also our experience that respondents usually have little difficulty in sorting out time order, and that they appear most at ease in reporting events in a narrative way in which time order is at least implicit. If events are not reported in this way, or if there is ambiguity, respondents usually readily respond to such questions as "Was it before or after your mother's death that you became depressed?" That there is likely to be a need for this kind of questioning is apparent from the fact that over half the women with an onset of depression in the recent Islington study reported it to occur within as little as 2 weeks after an important life event.

These issues concerning the dating of onset are raised in an optimistic frame of mind. They are offered to counter the pessimism that occasionally afflicts life events research, although there is insufficient space here to take readers through all the stages of designing an onset-changepoint schedule. Detailed outlines of how this has been done for depression can be found in *Social Origins of Depression* (Brown & Harris, 1978b, p. 347). The interested reader may also benefit from the debate between Cooke and Gorman, in which Gorman describes his onset schedule for alcoholism (Cooke & Allan, 1985; Gorman, 1986). This sets a pattern by which onset can be charted for any reasonably well-defined diagnosis, either physical or psychiatric. While claims for the accuracy of such dating are as yet only indirect, there are a number of reasons for confidence. First, in the Islington study just mentioned, onsets of psychiatric conditions were exactly equally distributed over the three 4-month periods of the follow-up year (Brown, Craig, & Harris,1985). Second, given the seriousness of the events of etiological importance, the dramatic nature of most of them (discussed in the next chapter), and the amount of detail collected about them, it is difficult to imagine respondents' inventing them. It follows that bias would have to arise either from rating an event as having more threat than it actually possessed or from pushing an event back in time that in fact occurred after rather than before onset. The contextual approach to rating events, using the consensus of a team of raters blind to the dependent variable, is geared to dealing with the first possibility, and no evidence has so far emerged to cast doubt on its effectiveness. The example already given of the "double-blind" rating of events in the appendectomy study is an example of the kind of evidence that can be formulated. This leaves the possibility that severe events have been in some way "pushed back" in time to occur before rather than after onset. It is certainly not possible to claim that this never occurs, but as a general explanation it appears unlikely. It would mean as an alternative that the true picture involves an accumulation of events *after* onset, and this would be even more difficult to explain. The only reasonable explanation for an accumulation after onset would seem to be that the events are in some way the *result* of the disorder. But in this case there would be no explanation for the findings showing that associations of events and onset hold equally for "independent" and "possibly independent" events (see Chapter 15, this volume, pp. 392-396).

Although we do not wish to encourage complacency or to underplay the problems of establishing time order, it does appear possible to reject the possibility that the dating of event and onset is so open to bias that bias provides an explanation for the associations reported. However, some investigators have responded to the possibility of *some* bias by changing some of the features of the approach that has been so far outlined, and it has become clear that this can cause problems. For example, if two different interviewers are involved in collecting the information about events on the one hand and date of onset on the other, it may not be possible to obtain final clarification on the time order between the two. Thus an interviewer may know that a subject's father died some time in mid-February and the other that onset occurred about mid-February, but will not be able to use both items in a further probe of the kind, "Was it before or after your father died that you started to feel so depressed?" One or the other item may then be incorrectly dated at the rating stage, with consequent invalidity of data and conclusions. The degree to which investigators feel it necessary to change the original approach must be a matter of individual judgment. But it is worth bearing in mind that there are Type II as well as Type I errors – that is, that research may produce too low as well as too high an association between etiological agent and onset. In the context of establishing whether or not stressors play a significant etiological role, the decision by the Edinburgh group (Surtees and colleagues) not to question subjects directly about relative dating of events and symptoms is probably of little moment. However, as investigators move on to consider more complex etiological issues, such as vulnerability and diagnostic specification, the possibilities of confusion become greater. For example, a vulnerability effect cannot by definition occur without the presence of a stressor, so a sizeable reduction in the association between stressor and onset may well lead to the conclusion that lack of social support makes an independent etiological contribution. This may occur because subjects are quite often recorded as having a vulnerability factor *and* an onset without the occurrence of a preonset stressor, because the latter has been dated as occurring later.

This chapter has set out to provide an introduction to the measurement of life events and difficulties. Further points are made in the context of reviewing the results of etiological research. The following chapter on depression develops a number of the points raised so far and begins to deal more directly with criticisms of the contextual approach.

References

Baddeley, A. D., Lewis, V., & Nimmo-Smith, M. I. (1978). "When did you last . . .?" In M. M. Gruneberg, P. E. Morris, & R. N. Sykes (Eds.), *Practical aspects of memory* (pp. 77-83). London: Academic Press.

Bartlett, F. (1932). *Remembering: A study of experimental and social psychology.* Cambridge, England: Cambridge University Press.

Bauman, Z. (1978). *Hermeneutics and social science.* London: Hutchinson.

Bebbington, P. E., Tennant, C., Sturt, E., & Hurry, J. (1984). The domain of life events: A comparison of two techniques of description. *Psychological Medicine, 14,* 219-222.

Belloc, N. B. (1954). Validation of morbidity survey data by comparison with hospital records. *Journal of the American Statistical Association, 49,* 832-846.

Brown, G. W. (1973). Some thoughts on grounded theory. *Sociology, 7,* 1-16.

Brown, G. W. (1974). Meaning, measurement, and stress of life events. In B. S. Dohrenwend & B. P. Dohrenwend (Eds.), *Stressful life events: Their nature and effects* (pp. 217-243). New York: Wiley.

Brown, G. W., & Birley, J. L. T. (1968). Crises and life changes and the onset of schizophrenia. *Journal of Health and Social Behavior, 9,* 203-214.

Brown, G. W., Craig, T. K. J., & Harris, T. O. (1985). Depression: Disease or distress? Some epidemiological considerations. *British Journal of Psychiatry, 147,* 612-622.

Brown, G. W., & Harris, T. O. (1978a). *The Bedford College Life-Events and Difficulty Schedule: Directory of contextual threat ratings of events.* London: Bedford College, University of London.

Brown, G. W., & Harris, T. O. (1978b). *Social origins of depression: A study of psychiatric disorder in women.* London: Tavistock.

Brown, G. W., & Harris, T. O. (1979). *The Bedford College Life-Events and Difficulty Schedule: Directory of severity for long-term difficulties*. London: Bedford College, University of London.

Brown, G. W., & Harris, T. O. (1982). Fall-off in the reporting of life events. *Social Psychiatry, 17*, 23-28.

Brown, G. W., & Prudo, R. (1981). Psychiatric disorder in a rural and an urban population: 1. Aetiology of depression. *Psychological Medicine, 11*, 581-599.

Brown, G. W., Sklair, F., Harris, T. O., & Birley, J. L. T. (1973). Life events and psychiatric disorders: 1. Some methodological issues. *Psychological Medicine, 3*, 74-78.

Cannell, C. F., Miller, P. V., & Oksenberg, L. (1981). Research on interviewing techniques. In S. Leinhardt (Ed.), *Sociological methodology* (pp. 389-437). San Francisco: Jossey-Bass.

Cannell, C. F., Oksenberg, L., & Converse, J. M. (1979). *Experiments in interviewing techniques*. Ann Arbor: Survey Research Center, University of Michigan.

Cannon, W. B. (1929). *Bodily changes in pain, hunger, fear, and rage*. Boston: C. T. Branford Co.

Cohen, S., & Wills, T. A. (1985). Stress, social support and the buffering hypothesis. *Psychological Bulletin, 98*, 310-357.

Collins, R. (1973). *Conflict sociology*. New York: Academic Press.

Cooke, D. J., & Allan, C. A. (1985). Stressful life events and alcohol misuse in women: A critical review. *Journal of Studies on Alcohol, 46*, 147-152.

Cox, A., Rutter, M., & Holbrook, D. (1988). Psychiatric interviewing techniques. A second experimental study: Eliciting feelings. *British Journal of Psychiatry, 152*, 64-72.

Dohrenwend, B. P., & Dohrenwend, B. S. (1969). *Social status and psychological disorder: A causal inquiry*. New York: Wiley.

Dohrenwend, B. P., Link, B. G., Kern, R., Shrout, P. E., & Markowitz, J. (1987). Measuring life events: The problem of variability within event categories. In B. Cooper (Ed.), *Psychiatric epidemiology: Progress and prospects* (pp. 103-119). London: Croom Helm.

Dohrenwend, B. P., Shrout, P. E., Link, B. G., Martin, J. L., & Skodol, A. E. (1986). Overview and initial results from a risk-factor study of depression and schizophrenia. In J. E. Barrett & R. M. Rose (Eds.), *Mental disorders in the community* (pp. 184-215). New York: Guilford Press.

Dohrenwend, B. S., & Dohrenwend, B. P. (Eds.). (1974). *Stressful life events: Their nature and effects*. New York: Wiley.

Dohrenwend, B. S., Krasnoff, L., Askenasy, A. R., & Dohrenwend, B. P. (1978). Exemplification of a method for scaling life events: The PERI life events scale. *Journal of Health and Social Behavior, 19*, 205-229.

Ekman, P. (1982). *Emotion in the human face*. London: Cambridge University Press.

Epstein, S. (1983). The unconscious, the preconscious, and the self-concept. In J. Suls & A. G. Greenwald (Eds.), *Psychological perspectives on the self* (Vol. 2, pp. 219-247). Hillsdale, NJ: Erlbaum.

Finlay-Jones, R., & Brown, G. W. (1981). Types of stressful life events and the onset of anxiety and depressive disorders. *Psychological Medicine, 11*, 803-815.

Frijda, N. G. (1986). *The emotions*. Cambridge, England: Cambridge University Press.

Gorman, D. M. (1986). Comments on D. J. Cooke and C. A. Allan's "Stressful life events and alcohol abuse in women." *British Journal of Addiction, 91*, 651-654.

Grant, I., Yager, J., Sweetwood, H. L., & Olshen, R. (1982). Life events and symptoms: Fourier analysis of time series from a three-year prospective inquiry. *Archives of General Psychiatry, 39*, 598-609.

Henderson, S., Byrne, D. G., & Duncan-Jones, P. (1981). *Neurosis and the social environment*. London: Academic Press.

Higgins, E. T., Rholes, W. S., & Jones, C. R. (1977). Category accessibility and impression formation. *Journal of Experimental Social Psychology, 13*, 141-154.

Hill, C. (1977). *Milton and the English Revolution.* New York. Viking Press.

Holmes, T. H., & Rahe, R. H. (1967). The Social Readjustment Rating Scale. *Journal of Psychosomatic Research, 11,* 213-218.

Horowitz, M. J. (1976). *Stress response syndromes.* New York: Jason Aronson.

Hudgens, R. W., Robins, E., & Delong, W. B. (1970). The reporting of recent stress in the lives of psychiatric patients. *British Journal of Psychiatry, 117,* 635-643.

Hurst, M. W., Jenkins, C. D., & Rose, R. M. (1979). Life changes and psychiatric symptom development: Issues of content, scoring, and clustering. In J. E. Barrett (Ed.), *Stress and mental disorder* (pp. 17-36). New York: Raven Press.

Jaspers, K. (1962). *General psychopathology* (J. Hoenig & M. W. Hamilton, Trans.). Manchester, England: Manchester University Press. (Original work published 1923)

Jenkins, C. D., Hurst, M. W., & Rose, R. M. (1979). Life changes: Do people really remember? *Archives of General Psychiatry, 36,* 379-384.

Katschnig, H. (1980). Measuring life stress: A comparison of two methods. In R. Farmer & S. Hirsch (Eds.), *The suicide syndrome* (pp. 116-123). London: Croom Helm.

Katschnig, H. (1986). Measuring life stress: A comparison of the checklist and the panel technique. In H. Katschnig (Ed.), *Life events and psychiatric disorders: Controversial issues* (pp. 74-106). Cambridge, England: Cambridge University Press.

Kessler, R. C., & Wethington, E. (1986). *Some strategies of improving recall of life events in a general population survey.* Ann Arbor: Survey Research Center, University of Michigan.

Lazarus, R. S., & Folkman, S. (1984). *Stress, appraisal, and coping.* New York: Springer.

Lazarus, R. S., & Launier, R. (1978). Stress-related transactions between person and environment. In L. A. Pervin & M. Lewis (Eds.), *Perspectives in interactional psychology* (pp. 287-327). New York: Plenum Press.

Leopold, R. L., & Dillon, H. (1963). Psycho-anatomy of a disaster: A long term study of post-traumatic neuroses in survivors of a marine explosion. *American Journal of Psychiatry, 119,* 913-921.

Leventhal, H. (1980). Towards a comprehensive theory of emotion. In L. Berkowitz (Ed.), *Advances in experimental social psychology* (Vol. 13, pp. 139-206). New York: Academic Press.

Loftus, E. F., & Marburger, W. (1983). Since the eruption of Mt. St. Helens, did anyone beat you up? Improving the accuracy of retrospective reports with landmark events. *Memory and Cognition, 11,* 114-120.

Marsh, C. (1982). *The survey method: The contribution of surveys to sociological explanation.* London: Allen & Unwin.

Mason, J. W. (1975). A historical view of the stress field. *Journal of Human Stress, 1,* 6-12.

Meyer, R. J., & Haggerty, R. J. (1962). Streptococcal infections in families. *Pediatrics, 29,* 539-549.

Neugebauer, R. (1983). Reliability of life-event interviews with outpatient schizophrenics. *Archives of General Psychiatry, 40,* 378-383.

Oatley, K., & Johnson-Laird, P. (1987). Towards a cognitive theory of emotions. *Cognition and Emotion, 1,* 29-50.

Parkes, C. M., & Weiss, R. S. (1983). *Recovery from bereavement.* New York: Basic Books.

Parry, G., Shapiro, D. A., & Davies, L. (1981). Reliability of life-event ratings: An independent replication. *British Journal of Clinical Psychology, 20,* 133-134.

Paykel, E. S. (1983). Methodological aspects of life events research. *Journal of Psychosomatic Research, 27,* 341-352.

Paykel, E. S., Myers, J. K., Dienelt, M. N., Klerman, G. L., Lindenthal, J. J., &

Pepper, M. P. (1969). Life events and depression: A controlled study. *Archives of General Psychiatry, 21,* 753-760.

Paykel, E. S., Prusoff, B. A., & Uhlenhuth, E. H. (1971). Scaling of life events. *Archives of General Psychiatry, 25,* 340-347.

Prudo, R., Brown, G. W., Harris, T. O., & Dowland, J. (1981). Psychiatric disorder in a rural and an urban population: 2. Sensitivity to loss. *Psychological Medicine, 11,* 601-6161.

Rachman, S. J. (1978). *Fear and courage.* San Francisco: W. H. Freeman.

Rahe, R. H. (1969). Life crisis and health change. In P. R. A. May & J. R. Winterborn (Eds.), *Psychotropic drug response: Advances in prediction* (pp. 92-125). Springfield, IL: Charles C Thomas.

Roessler, R., & Engel, B. T. (1974). The current status of the concepts of physiological response specificity and activation. *International Journal of Psychiatry in Medicine, 5,* 359-365.

Sarason, I., Johnson, J. H., & Siegel, J. M. (1978). Assessing the impact of life changes: Development of the Life Experiences Survey. *Journal of Consulting and Clinical Psychology, 46,* 932-946.

Schachter, S., & Singer, J. E. (1962). Cognitive, social and physiological determinants of emotional state. *Psychological Review, 69,* 379-399.

Schmid, I., Scharfetter, C., & Binder, J. (1981). Lebensereignisse in Abhangigkeit von soziodemographischen variablen. *Social Psychiatry, 16,* 63-68.

Schutz, A. (1971). Concept and theory formation in the social sciences. In A. Schutz, *Collected papers* (Vol. 1, pp. 48-98). The Hague: Nijhoff.

Selye, H. (1956). *The stress of life.* New York: McGraw-Hill.

Surtees, P. G., Miller, P. M., Ingham, J. G., Kreitman, N. B., Rennie, D., & Sashidharan, S. P. (1986). Life events and the onset of affective disorder: A longitudinal general population study. *Journal of Affective Disorders, 10,* 37-50.

Temoshok, L. (1983). Emotion, adaptation, and disease: A multidimensional theory. In L. Temoshok, C. Van Dyke, & L. S. Zegans (Eds.), *Emotions in health and illness: Theoretical and research foundations* (pp. 207-233). New York: Grune & Stratton.

Tennant, C., & Andrews, G. (1976). A scale to measure the stress of life events. *Australian and New Zealand Journal of Psychiatry, 10,* 27-32.

Tennant, C., Smith, A., Bebbington, P., & Hurry, J. (1979). The contextual threat of life events: The concept and its reliability. *Psychological Medicine, 9,* 525-528.

Theorell, T., Lind, E., & Floderus, B. (1975). The relationship of disturbing life-changes and emotions to the early development of myocardial infarction and other serious illnesses. *International Journal of Epidemiology, 4,* 281-293.

Thoits, P. A. (1983). Dimensions of life events that influence psychological distress: An evaluation and synthesis of the literature. In H. B. Kaplan (Ed.), *Psychosocial stress: Trends in theory and research* (pp. 33-103). New York: Academic Press.

Tomkins, S. S. (1962). *Affect, imagery, consciousness: Vol. 1. The positive affects.* London: Tavistock.

Tomkins, S. S. (1963). *Affect, imagery, consciousness: Vol. 2. The negative affects.* London: Tavistock.

Tomkins, S. S. (1981). The quest for primary motives: Biography and autobiography of an idea. *Journal of Personality and Social Psychology, 41,* 306-329.

Uhlenhuth, E. H., Balter, M. D., Haberman, M. D., & Lipman, R. S. (1977). Remembering life events. In J. S. Strauss, H. M. Babigian, & M. Roff (Eds.), *The origins and course of psychopathology* (pp. 117-134). New York: Plenum Press.

Weber, M. (1964). *The theory of social and economic organization* (T. Parsons, Ed. and Trans.). London: Collier-Macmillan.

Yager, J., Grant, I., Sweetwood, H. L., & Gerst, M. (1981). Life-event reports by psychiatric patients, non-patients, and their partners. *Archives of General Psychiatry, 38,* 343-347.

PART TWO

LIFE EVENTS AND PSYCHIATRIC ILLNESS

2

Depression

GEORGE W. BROWN AND TIRRIL O. HARRIS

It has long been recognized that clinical depression can be provoked by happenings in the environment, as indicated by the widespread use in psychiatry of the terms "reactive" and "endogenous" depression. In this chapter, we are primarily concerned with the success of research in characterizing these events. Recent work has confirmed that the experiences of loss, disappointment, and failure are most often involved. But these, the shipwrecks of everyday lives, are common. Among so many such experiences, is it possible to isolate those that are most likely to provoke a depressive disorder? To take the example of loss, are modest losses among the vulnerable capable of ushering in such a catastrophic response? Or, on the whole, are losses that are the stuff of tragedy more likely to do so?

Research in the general population must be an important part of any such effort, as it avoids the possibility that answers will be biased by the type of depressive disorders that happen to be channeled into psychiatric care. So far, such research has largely been carried out with women. The rarity of studies of men is probably explained by the fact that depression is less commonly found among them, at least in urban settings. However, there have been some population-based studies of men, and these suggest that the etiological ideas developed from the study of women are also applicable to them (Bebbington, Hurry, Tennant, Sturt, & Wing, 1981; Bolton & Oatley, 1987; Eales, 1985).

In what follows, the term "caseness" of depression is defined in terms of the characteristic bodily and psychological symptoms met in outpatient psychiatric practice. It was this principle that underlay the Bedford College caseness threshold, which was first developed upon the basis of the Present State Examination (PSE; Wing, Cooper, & Sartor-

George W. Brown and Tirril O. Harris. Department of Social Policy and Social Science, Royal Holloway and Bedford New College, University of London, 11 Bedford Square, London WC1B 3RA, England.

ius, 1974) in 1969, before the development of the category of major depression in the Research Diagnostic Criteria (RDC; Spitzer, Endicott, & Robins, 1978) and in the third edition of the *Diagnostic and Statistical Manual of Mental Disorders* (DSM-III; American Psychiatric Association, 1980). Subsequently, a discriminant function elaborated an algorithm embodying its criteria, and this was summarized in the following simpler checklist discriminating cases from borderline cases (the latter have symptoms that are less severe than the average outpatient, but are still the source of considerable distress): (1) depressed mood; (2) these 10 key symptoms, of which a case should have at least 4 and a borderline case between 1 and 3: hopelessness, suicidal ideas or actions, weight loss, early waking, delayed sleep, poor concentration, neglect due to brooding, loss of interest, self-depreciation, and anergia (see Finlay-Jones *et al.*, 1980). The criteria are thus in many ways similar to those of RDC and DSM-III. One epidemiological study using three different caseness criteria suggested that the Bedford College system was at least as strict as the RDC requirements for major depression and stricter than threshold level 5 of the ID-CATEGO system of other PSE users (Dean, Surtees, & Sashidharan, 1983).

When defined in this way, depressive disorder is common among women, but the rate differs according to the social characteristics of the population. Surveys have shown that most psychiatric disorders in the general population have an important depressive component, and probably at least 15% of women in inner-city areas can be expected to suffer from a depressive disorder at caseness level within the compass of any 1 year (Brown & Harris, 1978; Bebbington, Hurry, Tennant, & Sturt, 1984; Surtees *et al.*, 1983). A number of these conditions may be fairly short-lived, but about half at any one point of time will have lasted for at least 1 year. In a survey in 1986 of working-class women with at least one child at home living in Islington (a north London district), 18% suffered from caseness of depression and 22% from a caseness condition involving depression, anxiety, alcoholism, or drug addiction. On average, those with depression had 6.7 of 11 possible core symptoms of depression and a total of 19.1 symptoms on a shortened version of the PSE (Brown, Craig, & Harris, 1985). If those with borderline-case conditions are also included, these figures are doubled (Brown & Harris, 1978). In the Islington survey, the overall rate of case and borderline-case conditions in a 12-month period was 49%. Undoubtedly some urban populations have much lower rates, but these are melancholy statistics, and longitudinal research in Sweden has suggested that the problem may have grown in the last two decades (Hagnell, Lanke, Rorsman, & Ojesjo, 1982).

But, while there can be little doubt that psychosocial factors can play a critical role in bringing about such depressive disorders, not even the most severe of losses are necessarily followed by depression at a caseness level. Some women appear much more likely to develop depression in a crisis. This has been taken into account in etiological models of depression by the introduction of the idea of "vulnerability factors." Although it is not an issue tackled systematically in this chapter, any fully effective interpretation of the role of events has to take the role of such factors into account. Insofar as they are psychosocial, they can be measured either in terms of personal attributes such as low self-esteem or in terms of characteristics involving roles and relationships. Vulnerability factors on their own are not related to a higher risk, but are associated with an increased chance of breakdown in the presence of a provoking event. Lack of social support appears to play a particularly key role in depression. The importance of such vulnerability was illustrated in the first study of depression using the Life Events and Difficulties Schedule (LEDS), where only some of the social class difference among women in the general population in Camberwell in south London was shown to be due to the greater number of adverse life events and difficulties occurring among working-class women. Most of the greater risk of depression among working-class women was explained (at least in statistical terms) not by the fact that their lives were tougher in this sense, but by the more frequent presence of vulnerability factors, such as lack of intimate ties with their husbands. As noted in Chapter 1, there is also a third set of factors in the model, called "symptom formation"; these factors influence the *form* of the depressive condition rather than whether it will occur (see Brown & Harris, 1978, Chaps. 13 and 14).

In theoretical terms, we have gone on to speculate that for depression low self-esteem is often the common feature behind the vulnerability factors that have so far been isolated. It is not so much the situation brought about by a crisis that is important, as the capacity of a woman to hope for better things once the crisis has occurred. In response to a loss, relatively specific feelings of hopelessness are likely to occur; the person has usually lost an important source of value or reinforcement, which may have been derived from a person, a role, or an idea. If this develops into a general feeling of hopelessness, it may form the central feature of the depressive disorder itself; in Aaron Beck's (1967) terms, a feeling that the world is meaningless, the future hopeless, and the self worthless may quickly usher in the well-known affective and somatic symptoms of clinical depression. What may be critical in any such generalization of hopelessness is a woman's self-esteem, her sense of her ability to control her world, and her confidence that alternative sources of value will be available. If self-esteem is low before the onset of any depression, it may be that much more difficult for the woman to see herself emerging again. And, of course, once depression has occurred, feelings of confidence and self-worth can sink even lower.

But how convincing is the research behind such theoretical speculation? Are we really in a position to estimate accurately the relative importance of life events and vulnerability factors? The answer is probably "no." We will only be able to do this when research has given us a reasonably full explanation, and it has yet to achieve this sophistication. For a start, it is only in recent years that methods of measurement have been developed that begin to match the sensitivity of clinical accounts and manage to retain the methodological standards necessary for sophisticated causal inquiry. And if and when such knowledge has been achieved in one population, it will certainly be necessary to take account of differences across populations. In one study, for example, women in small rural populations of the Outer Hebrides were found to be particularly susceptible to loss by death of a close relative, and, as was not the case in an urban population, much of the chronic affective (depressive and anxiety) disorder appeared to have been originally provoked by such an experience (Prudo, Brown, Harris, & Dowland, 1981). Because of this, they might well have had a higher rate of affective disorder than would be expected from the relatively low rate of stressors and vulnerability factors in the community, if it were the case that they were no more subject to bereavement than London women. In general, however, the model developed in London appeared applicable in the Outer Hebrides, though the research is a useful reminder that etiological models may have to be adapted to take account of special cultural features. But whatever factors are included, all models of depression so far have depended critically on the study of the situation immediately before onset and particularly of life events, since these allow the role of other components – vulnerability and symptom formation factors – to be tested.

It is therefore to the work on etiological agents and particularly on life events that we now turn. Research, in fact, is only now beginning to emerge from a period of uncertainty, even as to whether events play any etiological role at all. Most of the research that has fueled this controversy has derived from the checklist approach discussed in the preceding chapter. Some of the most skeptical statements came from the St. Louis group of researchers (Hudgens, Morrison, & Barchaa, 1967; Hudgens, Robins, & Delong, 1970), but a recent review concludes that even in the instance of this early checklist research "the hypothesis that severely unpleasant life events, particularly events involving loss, are a cause of depression has not been refuted" (Finlay-Jones, 1981, p. 229). We return to the status of the research in this tradition in Chapter 15 of this book, where we also discuss the skepticism and frequent misunderstanding with which the alternative, contextual approach has been received. This chapter confines itself to reviewing the findings on depression using contextual measures. In the course of the review, we also present new data from some of our recent studies that bear on the issues discussed.

Contextual Measures of Life Events: Three Population Studies

We have already referred to some of the results of three large-scale population surveys of psychiatric disorder carried out by our group at Bedford College, University of London. The first population inquiry to use the LEDS was based in south London in the early 1970s (Brown & Harris, 1978). Two separate random samples of a total of 458 women aged between 18 and 65, living in Camberwell, were seen; details of their lives and psychiatric histories were collected using a shortened version of the ninth edition of the PSE. Although it was predominantly a working-class, inner-city district, the population included a middle-class area to the south of the borough. The study as a whole also included a special survey of 114 women treated by local psychiatric services for a recent onset of depression. In 1975 and 1976, the population survey was repeated among women living in two rural populations in the Outer Hebrides (Brown & Prudo, 1981; Prudo et al., 1981; Prudo, Harris, & Brown, 1984). Most of the women had been born and brought up on the islands. They were predominantly Gaelic-speaking; many lived on small farms or crofts; and the vitality of religion on the islands was still very evident.

A third study was carried out in the early 1980s in Islington, an inner-city area in north London. Unlike the first two, this study was longitudinal and designed to contact women at one point in time and investigate onset of an affective disorder at a caseness level during a follow-up period of 1 year. It was designed to test some of the theoretical ideas emerging from the earlier cross-sectional studies, including those concerning the role of self-esteem and support, and a good deal of weight is therefore placed here on the results of this third inquiry. Working-class women with at least one child at home were studied, since prior research had suggested that they would be particularly likely to develop a depressive disorder. In addition, all single mothers found in the initial screening survey were included regardless of occupational or class criteria, as there was evidence that they would have a high rate of depressive disorders. The main investigation was conducted in two phases approximately 1 year apart. In the first, measures of the quality of personal ties, amount of support received, and self-esteem were collected, together with an account of psychiatric disorders both at the time of interview and in the preceding 12 months. The second phase covered any psychiatric disorders, life events, and difficulties during the follow-

up year, together with actual social support received during any significant crises and the women's responses to the events or difficulties
(Brown, *et al.*, 1985; Brown, Andrews, Harris, Adler, & Bridges,
1986).

Event Dimensions

There are many ways of describing a life event – that is, many dimensions. The version of the LEDS used in Camberwell contains 28 dimensions, and new ones continue to be developed. However, for most disorders long-term contextual threat has proved to be critical and has
provided the basis for most further exploration of etiological processes.
(Henceforth, because of our focus upon the predictive causal role of
events, with the consequent need to reduce reporting biases, we are
dealing mainly with the contextual rather than the reported measure of
threat, and may on most occasions omit the term "contextual.") In
terms of the two measures of threat, only events with marked or moderate long-term threat, focused on the woman herself or jointly with someone else – referred to hereafter as "severe events" – appeared to be capable of playing a critical etiological role in depression. Such threat (in
contrast to short-term threat) was still present some 7-10 days after the
event's occurrence. The short-term threat of events was unrelated to
onset once the rating of long-term threat was taken into account. The
results of the first Camberwell population survey have been replicated
on at least 10 occasions (see Table 2.1, "Severe events" column). An
11th study in Edinburgh has so far only published results for *all* psychiatric disorder as defined by the RDC (Surtees *et al.*, 1986), but there
are indications that the data are of much the same order as those in
Table 2.1 when major depression is examined on its own (P. G. Surtees,
personal communication, 1987).

The Camberwell patient inquiry, in contrast to the population survey, was based on women specially selected on the basis of having a
recent onset of a depressive episode and being seen by a psychiatrist.
The proportion experiencing a severe event before onset was much the
same as among those with a new depressive episode in the population
series (61% vs. 65%), and this has now also been found on a number of
occasions. But psychiatric patients have proved more difficult to study,
and there must be somewhat more uncertainty about the role of events
among them. For example, such patients are more likely to have had a
continuing history of severe depression, which complicates the process
of determining the date of the most recent onset. Katschnig and his colleagues found that only half of their sample of depressive patients had
had as long as 6 months symptom-free before the index episode

TABLE 2.1. Summary of population studies using LEDS of women in the 18-65 age range, giving relationship of severe events and major difficulties to onset of caseness of depression

Studies (random sample unless stated)	Length period studied	Onset cases			Noncases
		Severe event[a]	Major difficulty[a]	Severe event or major difficulty[a]	Severe event or major difficulty[a]
Brown & Harris (1978): Camberwell	38/52 (weeks)	25/37 (68)	18/37 (49)	33/37 (89)	115/382 (30)
Brown & Prudo (1981): Lewis, Outer Hebrides, Scotland	1 year	11/16 (69)	6/16 (38)	13/16 (81)	42/171 (25)
Costello (1982): Calgary, Alberta, Canada	1 year	18/38 (47)	20/38 (53)	–	–
Campbell, Cope, & Teasdale (1983): Oxford (working-class with at least one child)	1 year[b]	6/11 (55)	6/11 (55)	10/11 (91)	21/60 (35)
		5/12 (42)	5/12 (42)	9/12 (75)	17/52 (33)
Cooper & Sylph (1973): London (general practice)	3/12 (months)	16/34 (47)	–	–	–
Finlay-Jones & Brown (1981): London (general practice)	1 year	27/32 (84)	6/32 (19)	27/32 (84)	32/119 (27)
Martin (1982): Manchester (pregnant women)	1 year	13/14 (93)	4/14 (29)	13/14 (93)	25/64 (39)
Brown, Andrews, Harris, Adler, & Bridge (1986): Islington (working-class with at least one child)	6/12[b] (months)	29/32 (91)	15/32 (47)	30/32 (94)	92/271 (34)
		25/33 (76)	14/33 (42)	28/33 (85)	107/323 (33)
Parry & Shapiro (1986): Sheffield (working-class with at least one child)	1 year	12/20 (60)	3/20 (15)	14/20 (70)	62/172 (36)
Bebbington, Hurry, Tennant, & Sturt (1984): Camberwell	10/12 (months)	–	–	13/21 (62)	45/131 (34)
Totals		212/312 (68)	107/279 (38)	218/261 (84)	558/1745 (32)

Note. All study locations were in England unless otherwise specified. Chronic cases of depression were excluded. Average population attributable risk = 73.1%.

[a] Percentages of those with at least one event/difficulty are in parentheses.

[b] Sample seen on two occasions 12 months apart; first line refers to follow-up period, and second, to anterior period.

(Katschnig *et al.*, 1981; Katschnig, Pakesch, & Egger-Zeidner, 1986); this suggests that unless considerable care is taken, patient samples may contain substantial numbers of chronic disorders, and this may well distort conclusions concerning the role of life events in etiology. A related problem is the greater likelihood that onset will be associated with some change in antidepressant medication. It can be added that there are almost certainly some subgroups of psychiatric patients who develop depression without any obvious involvement of psychosocial factors. However, these depressive subgroups may well not be characterized by differences in symptom pictures. For example, in a series of patients all apparently suffering from a *similar* clinical picture of major depression associated with pregnancy or childbirth, the development of the depressive condition within 2-3 weeks

TABLE 2.2. Summary of recent studies of life events and onset of depression among psychiatric patients

Source	Number of subjects		Percentage with at least one event			
	Patients	Comparison group	Patients	Comparison group	Period covered	Type of event
Paykel *et al.*(1969): New Haven, CT, USA	185	185	44	17	6 months	"Undesirable"
Brown & Harris (1978): London	114	382	61	19	8 months	"Severe threat"[a]
Barrett (1979): Boston	130	–	58	–	6 months	"Undesirable"
Glassner, Haldipur, & Dessauersmith (1979): New York	25[b]	25	56	16	12 months	"Major role loss"
Fava, Munari, Pavan, & Kellner (1981): Padua, Italy	40	40	73	30	6 months	"Uncontrollable"
Benjaminsen (1981): Odense, Denmark	89	–	63	–	6 months	"Severe loss"
Vadher & Ndetei (1981) Nairobi, Kenya	30	40	67	8	12 months	"Severe threat"[a]
Murphy (1982): London	100[c]	168	48	23	12 months	"Severe threat"[a]
Katschnig *et al.*(1981): Vienna	176[d]	–	42[d]	–	12 months	"Severe threat"[a]
Bebbington, Tennant, & Hurry (1981): London	45[e]	257	18	10	3 months	"Marked and moderate threat – independent"
Perris (1984): Sweden	38	–	62	–	12 months	"Exit event"

[a] Either independent or possibly independent events.

[b] Manic-depressive, bipolar sample.

[c] Elderly sample aged 65-87 years.

[d] Special analysis for this chapter.

[e] Includes some anxiety states.

of childbirth was less likely to be associated with psychosocial factors than the development of depression in the prepartum period (Martin, Brown, Brockington, & Goldberg, in press).

Each of these points may well contribute something to the somewhat greater variability in findings in patient series. Nonetheless, research has so far confirmed that psychosocial factors play an important etiological role; relevant studies concerning events and using the LEDS or a fairly comparable approach are summarized in Table 2.2. There also appears to be growing agreement that there is little association between *type* of depression, defined along the traditional lines of "neurotic" and "psychotic" depression, and the presence of a recent life event of etiological significance (see Brown & Harris, 1978; Katschnig *et al.*, 1986; Perris, 1984; Calloway & Dolan, Chapter 5, this volume). The only exception so far of which we are aware is a study of 45 patients by Bebbington and his colleagues (reviewed in Table 2.2), and there appear to be fairly obvious methodological reasons for this (Brown & Harris, 1982). There is, therefore, as yet no justification for the commonly held belief that something sets depressive *patients* aside and requires a quite different etiological model from that for cases in the general population (see Calloway & Dolan, Chapter 5). Nonetheless, we have already noted that there are probably subgroups of depressions that may prove to have lower rates of stressors, although it remains an open question how far it will be possible to define these subgroups in clinical terms.

In this context, it is interesting that there is some evidence that type of early loss experience can have an influence on the *form* of depression – that is, can act as a symptom formation factor in terms of a full three-factor etiological model. In two separate studies of depressed patients, early experience of death was found to be associated with a "psychotic" picture of depression and early experience of separation with a "neurotic" picture (Brown, Harris, & Copeland, 1977). This research was carried out by interviewing patients directly and requires replication. However, there are other results in the general population suggesting that such symptom formation effects of early experiences may be of importance. Two studies in the general population have shown that early loss of the mother by separation (but not by death) relates to "acting-out" behavior during a depressive episode, especially in terms of displays of violence and suicidal gestures, as contrasted with suicide attempts in which there is a serious intent to die (Brown, Craig, & Harris, 1985; Harris, Brown, & Bifulco, 1988). It is possible that early separation from the mother acts in this way because of the experience of rejection, which often leads to enduring dispositions to display hostile and attention-seeking behavior, especially in the crisis circumstances that accompany an onset of depressive disorder.

Findings concerning difficulties have been somewhat less consistent than those for events in both population and patient series. In Camberwell, *major* difficulties were associated with onset – that is, those (1) on the top 3 points of a 6-point scale of severity, (2) lasting at least 2 years, and (3) *not* involving purely health problems. In a number of other studies, *major* difficulties have made an additional contribution to risk of depression (see Table 2.1), and the term "provoking agent" is used hereafter to refer to the presence of either a severe event or a major difficulty. The process by which major difficulties contribute to depression is less intuitively apparent than the role of severe events, because it is not easy to see why onset should occur at that particular point in time rather than earlier.

On the other hand, these major difficulties embody many of the same features found in severe events – that is, they are the same in terms of meaning, containing elements of disappointment and loss of self-esteem. Elsewhere, we outline the possibility that in these circumstances quite everyday events may serve to bring home the full implications of a situation that has been going on for some time. Thus, for example, a short hospital stay for an operation with only minor threat may cause a woman to reassess the distressing nature of her marriage or the housing conditions to which she must return (Brown & Harris, 1978, p. 145). But, clearly, such reassessments can occur even without an event. One Camberwell subject became depressed soon after a stranger asked her whether her child was a "spastic" – an occasion that did not meet the threshold for inclusion as an event. Although she had known the full details of her child's handicap for at least 2 years, it seemed possible that it was not until this incident in the park that the meaning of the difficulty was brought home to her.

It is also possible that the investigation of difficulties acts as a "safety net" for severe events missed by the interviewer. (An example would be a failure to report a particularly threatening letter during the course of continuing litigation. The litigation itself would very easily be picked up by the LEDS, but the letter might be missed – for example, if the respondent had already reported two other events in response to our standard question about the experience of "shocking news.") A further reason for collecting information about difficulties is to chart their linkage with severe events. Later, we discuss evidence that severe events that "match" ongoing difficulties are particularly likely to be followed by depression. But before we consider such evidence, it is necessary to consider the etiological implications of these results concerning provoking agents from the point of view of their statistical interpretation.

The Statistical Assessment of the Importance of
Provoking Agents

In a review of life events research published in 1982, Judith Rabkin
asserts that "the large majority of studies of stress and psychiatric disorder have failed to demonstrate a clinically significant association,
although small statistically significant relationships repeatedly have
been found" (p. 566). Tausig (1982), in the same year, had reached this
conclusion on the basis of research with the Holmes and Rahe (1967)
Schedule of Recent Experiences (SRE). Although part of the pessimism
of such reviews is undoubtedly due to the indifferent results obtained
by such checklist measures, it is not just due to this. The conclusions
echo the spirit of an earlier review in *Psychological Medicine* by
Andrews and Tennant (1978) that included studies using the LEDS.
Another recent review notes that "the weak explanatory power of events
is an embarrassment" and seeks the reason in methodological and conceptual shortcomings (Thoits, 1983, p. 42). Such comments – and they
are by no means the only ones to be found – fail to consider, to use
Rabkin's own words, what is meant by a "clinically significant association." Instead, they have in an apparently unthinking way based their
conclusion on a *particular* measure of statistical association – that is,
"variance explained." David Cooke (1987), in a cogent review of the
issue, concludes that variance explained is not a good measure of causal
impact.

The issue can be most easily illustrated by taking an etiological
agent of undisputed importance: cigarette smoking. Although most
instances of lung cancer are associated with heavy smoking, much less
than 1% of the variance is explained by this link. This failure to reflect
the obvious etiological importance of smoking is due to the fact that
variance explained takes into account not only that most people with
lung cancer are heavy smokers, but also that *most heavy smokers do not
have lung cancer.* Since those without lung cancer greatly outnumber
those with it, the fact that most people with lung cancer are heavy smokers gets swamped in the "two-way" measure of association. This has
close parallels with the findings for depression: Although for the majority of people developing depression a provoking agent occurs before
onset, most people experiencing a provoking agent do not develop
depression. It would therefore be useful to have an index reflecting the
fact that those developing a disorder such as lung cancer and depression
tend only to do so after the experience of an etiological agent. However,
given the fact that heavy smoking and severe events are common in the
general population, such an index would need to take into account that
agent and disorder will at times be juxtaposed by chance.

A frequently used index in epidemiological research, Levin's "attributable risk percent" – or to use another name, "population attributable risk" (PAR) – is a particularly satisfactory index of the importance of an etiological effect, as it does just this (see Markush, 1977). It gives the proportion of the instances of the disorder associated with the putative causal risk factor, allowing for the fact that the two will in some instances be associated by chance. Because the index has been independently developed on a number of occasions, it has a variety of names, but its underlying rationale is straightforward (Brown & Harris, 1986; Waltner-Toews, 1982).[1] In the Outer Hebrides, 84% of onset cases of depression had a provoking agent; PAR was 73%, whereas variance explained was only 12%. This is a typical result. The 10 studies reviewed in Table 2.1, using the LEDS in the general population, had an average PAR of 73%. That is, nearly three-quarters of onset cases had a provoking agent of etiological importance.

However, it is also important to recognize that only about 1 out of 5 women experiencing a provoking agent according to the LEDS have so far been found to go on to develop depression at a caseness level, and it is this that is reflected by the low level of variance explained. As already noted, most of the effort to understand the reason for this has been through the study of vulnerability factors. However, it is possible that better conceptualization and measurement of provoking agents would contribute by showing that only *certain* types of severe events and major difficulties are of importance – thereby, say, increasing the proportion developing depression following the relevant type of severe event from 1 in 5 to 1 in 4 or even 1 in 3. We therefore need to turn to additional ways of characterizing provoking agents.

1. The index x produced by Julian Peto and used in our earlier studies is in essence the same index (see Brown & Harris, 1986). The formula for PAR is

$$\frac{ad - bc}{(a + c)\,(c + d)} \times 0.100$$

where

Provoking agent	Case	Noncase
Yes	a	b
No	c	d

For case-controlled studies (see Cooke, 1987), the formula is

$$\frac{ad - bc}{(a + c)\,d} \times 0.100$$

New Ways of Looking at Provoking Agents

The full LEDS as used in Camberwell dealt with 28 dimensions of life events; however, once long-term threat and the focus of the event were taken into account, no other dimension (e.g., "amount of change in routine") was associated with an increased risk of depression (Brown & Harris, 1978; pp. 115-116). This has been confirmed by subsequent studies. However, dimensions have continued to be developed and added to the original 28 (Finlay-Jones & Brown, 1981; Miller & Ingham, 1983), and these have had a certain amount of success – but, so far, only by specifying among those with a severe event the individuals most likely to develop depression.

In the longitudinal Islington study, we used essentially the same measure of loss as did an earlier study in the Regent's Park area of London, which explored the different characteristics of severe events leading to depressive and anxiety disorders (Finlay-Jones & Brown, 1981; see also Finlay-Jones, Chapter 3, this volume). The criteria used to define loss were straightforward, although it should be noted that they included loss associated with the subject's physical health and loss of a cherished idea. The latter type of loss proved to be crucial. It included either (1) disruption of an expectation of someone's commitment, faithfulness, or trustworthiness; (2) an event that might lead the subject to question such qualities in herself (e.g., learning that her daughter had been taking heroin); or (3) incidents that might be an even more fundamental challenge to identity (discovering that a spouse was bisexual). Also included as losses were certain "disappointments," defined as the re-establishment of a problem that had been dormant or much improved, and where it would have been reasonable to assume there had been a more or less permanent change for the better.

The Islington research also divided severe events into those with "upper" and "lower" severity. The severe event rating was the result of combining the two dimensions of threat and focus where it appeared that those focused on the subject were often more threatening than those focused only upon other people. We argued that if this division could be made more straightforward in terms of "higher" and "lower" (i.e., more moderate) threat, the effectiveness of the ratings would be improved. A "lower" severity rating would be given to a woman working as a secretary whose husband, employed in a specialized occupation where jobs are difficult to get, had been warned of a possible layoff. An "upper" severity rating would be given where the layoff had actually occurred and was already giving rise to considerable financial problems affecting the family. In practice, three-quarters of severe events were placed in the "upper" division.

In the following presentation of results concerning the etiological role of events, women suffering from depression at a caseness level at first interview have been excluded. Of the remaining 303, half (150) experienced a provoking agent in the 1-year follow-up period; the majority of these (130) experienced at least one severe event in this time. As already noted in Table 2.1, most of those with an onset of caseness of depression in the follow-up year had had a severe event in the 6 months before (29 out of 32), and the PAR was therefore again large (81%). Taking account of whether or not a severe event was a loss, and dividing the severity ratings into "upper" and "lower," somewhat improved the original association (Table 2.3). Thus 32%, or 1 in 3.2 (23/73), of the women with an "upper" severe event that involved a loss of developed depression, compared with 11%, or 1 in 9.5 (6/57), of the rest with a severe event. (These figures compare with 22%, or 1 in 4.5 (29/130), of all women with a severe event.)

In order to give this account more life, events occurring immediately before onset and involving some element of loss are described in terms of what it would have been reasonable for the women to feel, given the circumstances surrounding the event (i.e., in contextual terms). (In order to increase numbers, onsets in the year *before* first interview have been included with those for the follow-up period.) Only the severe event occurring closest in time to onset was considered. Forty-five women had such a loss event, and these events were classified in terms of either a loss of a person, a loss of a cherished idea, or a loss of something material. The notion of "cherished idea," already discussed to some extent, assumes that ideas that have emerged in the course of ordinary everyday life about oneself and one's close ties are likely to be critical for a sense of self-worth, although they may also provide a sense of security and meaning. Such ideas usually have a strong prescriptive element concerning what should or should not be done or

TABLE 2.3. Onset among 303 women in Islington by characteristics of any provoking agent

	Percentage with onset
No provoking agent	1 (2/153)
Provoking agent[a]	
Major difficulty only	5 (1/20)
"Lower" severe event	6 (2/32)
"Upper" severe event, other than loss	16 (4/25)
"Upper" severe event, loss	32 (23/73)
Total	11 (32/303) *

Note. n's for the percentages are in parentheses.
[a] Percentage with onset among women with a provoking agent = 20 (30/150).
* $df = 4$, $p < .001$.

felt, and any failure on the part of the woman or those close to her is likely to reflect on her sense of worth and competence (e.g., a husband's turning out to be homosexual or a son's being arrested for violent behavior).

The initial threefold classification of losses was then elaborated to include further categories. The first took account of the fact that it is possible to lose a person *and* a cherished idea (e.g., a husband's leaving shortly after revealing his infidelity). The second and third were introduced to take account of the complexity of the notion of loss of a cherished idea. Where it reconfirmed a loss already suffered in an earlier crisis, "reconfirmation of loss of a cherished idea" was rated (e.g., learning of a lover's infidelity after getting involved in the relationship as a sequel to discovering that one's spouse was having an affair). Where the loss of a cherished idea appeared to relate more to security or meaning than to self-worth, "loss of cherished aspirations" was rated (e.g., learning that a husband would never recover from the severely handicapping consequences of a head injury sustained some time before). Such aspirations had often grown out of some prior frustration or disappointment and contained an element of wishing to restore what once had obtained.

Only the most salient aspects of an event were taken into account in the ratings. For example, a husband's leaving home to live with someone else would be rated as "loss of a person" and "loss of a cherished idea" but not as "material loss," except under circumstances where he was refusing to make support payments.

The six classes of events contained roughly similar numbers of women (see Table 2.4). Loss of a person with no implications for a cher-

TABLE 2.4. Type of loss events occurring immediately before onset of depression in follow-up and anterior years in Islington survey

Type of loss	n	(%)	Typical events
A. Person	7	(16)	Death of husband
B. Person *and* cherished idea	9	(20)	Husband leaves; son leaves after argument – no contact
C. Cherished idea	9	(20)	Husband's infidelity; son's delinquency; ex-husband remarried
D. Reconfirmation of loss of cherished idea	7	(16)	Son arrested again
E. Aspiration concerning cherished idea	6	(13)	Miscarriage; rehousing falling through
F. Material/financial	7	(16)	Husband's loss of job; evicted at time of baby's birth
Total	45	(100)	

ished idea (category A) accounted for 16% of the loss events. All of these involved the death of someone close. Since the ratings were contextual, how the women actually reacted to the loss in each case was ignored, but in no instance were the circumstances surrounding the event or the women's prior relationship with the dead person such that she could be said to have grounds for guilt in the sense that she had shown neglect or too little concern during the final crisis. A further 20% of the events fell into category B. Here, the woman in each case not only lost contact with a person (only in one instance by death), but also could be said to have lost a cherished idea (e.g., a woman's ending an affair after learning of her lover's infidelity, or a child's dying in an accident that could possibly be seen to relate to the mother's negligence). For each event in category C, there was also reason to see the woman as losing a cherished idea, but, unlike the situation in B, contact with the person continued at much the same rate (e.g., learning of a husband's love affair and continuing to live with him). Category D covered the confirmation of an existing situation of failure or inadequacy (e.g., finding that a son whose behavior had been difficult for some years had returned to taking heroin). The final category dealing with the loss of an idea, E, concerned loss of an aspiration. All involved a highly valued goal (e.g., miscarriage in a woman who very much wanted a child). In contextual terms such events did not involve a threat to the woman's sense of self-worth, but in practice some of the women might well have interpreted such events in terms of personal failure. A final category, F, involved material and financial loss. Again, while the events did not obviously threaten a woman's sense of self-worth, they might in practice have done.

Leaving aside the possibility of loss of self-worth in categories E and F, 56% of the 45 loss events involved loss of a cherished idea of a kind that would usually be expected to bring a direct threat to the woman's sense of self-worth. But only a third of the events involved actual loss of a person in the sense that contact was broken for a period of time. However, two-thirds of the events brought about important changes in the quality of a close interpersonal relationship, and some of the remaining events might have done so (e.g., a husband's being home much of the time after being laid off [category F – material loss] in the context of a difficult marital relationship). It should finally be recalled that a small proportion of the severe events occurring immediately before onset (17%) did not involve a loss, although it is likely that some events were interpreted in terms of failure (e.g., a sister's attempted suicide and the woman's subsequent difficulty in looking after her).

This account so far contains one ambiguity: Priority has been given to nonmaterial aspects of the events. However, even with a fairly liberal interpretation, only a further 5 events concerned financial difficulties – that is, at most only about a quarter of the events (12/45) involved an important "material" aspect – although other events certainly occurred in the context of an important financial or material problem.

In the opening paragraph of this chapter, we have asked whether the events ushering in clinical depression are the stuff of tragedy. While some of events assessed in the Islington study could be fairly described in this way, we no longer find the question a strategic one. We would rather emphasize that the events almost always threatened some core aspect of identity and self-worth, and perhaps, leaving aside the drama of tragic events this is what in essence defined them. Elsewhere (Brown, in press), we have divided the 29 women developing depression after a severe event in the follow-up year into roughly three equal categories, and this simpler account gives a useful additional perspective. In the first category, the event in each case presented a threat to the woman's identity as a wife or mother about which she could do very little, at least in the immediate future. In almost every case, it was part of a history of failure in that area of life. The second set of women had more diverse experiences, but in all instances they were imprisoned in nonrewarding and deprived settings, and the events underlined how little they could do about extracting themselves; any way forward appeared to be blocked. A number of these events concerned housing and debt, but others concerned physical handicap, and the ramifications were often wide. (Although in the first group we have emphasized the threat to identity and in the second we have stressed the experience of being trapped, in practice both could hold to differing degrees; allocating these cases to one category or the other was somewhat arbitrary.) The final set of experiences involved the loss of someone a woman had known for a long time – in most instances, a close relative. Probably in almost every instance the woman felt some degree of rejection; in fact, in two-thirds of the cases, there was the same theme of failure as in the first two categories. However, there were three deaths (a mother, a husband, and a friend) in which there was no obvious reason for the women to feel in any way responsible or, for that matter, rejected. Perhaps only a few of the 29 events reached truly tragic proportions; but when context and history are taken into account, most of the women had ample reason to experience marked distress and despair.

To sum up this section on loss and refinement of severity, the improvements in prediction of depression were much as we expected, and future users of the LEDS will therefore have a choice. The proportion experiencing onset of caseness of depression after a provoking agent can be increased by the exclusion of all severe events other than those with both an "upper" severity rating *and* a loss rating. However, this may have certain unwanted consequences. In the Islington study, it would have resulted in losing nearly a quarter of the onsets associated with a provoking agent, and this would undoubtedly have affected the results of some analyses, particularly of vulnerability effects. The results are therefore probably best seen as an indication that the current classification of "provoking agents" can be improved. It is only with the next step – the more complex issue of "matching" – that we arrive at more fundamental insights into the etiological role of provoking agents, and we now deal with the three kinds of matching events we have so far identified (for a full account, see Brown, Bifulco, & Harris, 1987).

Matching Events

Commitment

Chapter 1 has explained how contextual ratings of threat take into account a person's plans, purposes, and commitments that are likely to have been frustrated by the event, insofar as these can be *indirectly* assessed from situational and biographical material. However, the use of a longitudinal design in the Islington inquiry allowed us to make a *direct* assessment of commitment at the time of first contact, before the occurrence of any severe event, and to compare this with an indirect assessment already incorporated within the contextual ratings.

At the first interview with each woman, five domains of her life were discussed at considerable length: children, marriage, housework, employment, and other activities outside the home. In rating commitment to these, we were primarily concerned with feelings and ideas, a good many of which were usually conveyed in the course of a woman's description of her day-to-day activities. For a married woman, for example, information about her commitment to the idea of marriage usually emerged from talking about her relationship with her husband. But in making the rating, we kept in mind that it was possible to be highly dissatisfied with a particular situation and yet to be highly committed to the *idea* of marriage. In addition to these five domains, we took into account any relationship (other than with husband or child) that the woman named as "very close" (O'Connor & Brown, 1984; Brown *et al.,* 1986). We did not rate commitment as such with regard to these relationships; as an alternative, a woman was considered committed in such a relationship if she was rated high in terms of dependency, on the assumption that this provided a reasonable approximation of what we had in mind for this exercise.

All but 17% of the 303 women followed up had at least one marked commitment, with an average of 1.5 for the six domains. Matching was judged by whether a severe event was logically part of an area of high commitment (e.g., a husband's infidelity would match high commitment to "marriage"). Of the women with a severe event in the follow-up year, 24% (31/130) had one that matched a domain in which they had shown marked commitment; that is, they experienced what we refer to hereafter as a "C-event."

The significance of such commitment was confirmed: Women with a C-event were three times more likely to develop depression than those with a severe event not matching a commitment (see Table 2.5, middle section). The result also adds credibility to the assumption made about the relevance of plans and commitments for the rating of contextual threat, although it suggests that such ratings are only partially successful in reflecting such commitments. However, these contextual ratings were clearly good enough to get research under way, and their importance is underlined by a further point. The matching analysis itself was based on severe events. When we considered events with *any* degree of long-term threat (i.e., 237 women with at least one event with a rating of 1-3 on the 4-point scale), no difference in risk of depression emerged: 14% (15/109) of those with a matching event and 12% (15/128) of those without a matching event developed depression. The contextual threat ratings were therefore highly effective in selecting events capable of pro-

TABLE 2.5. Onset among the 130 women in Islington with a severe event in terms of matching

Severe event	Percentage with onset
Severe event matching prior difficulty (D-event)	
Yes	46 (16/35)
No	14 (13/95)
Total	22 (29/130) *
Severe event matching prior commitment (C-event)	
Yes	40 (16/40)
No	14 (13/90)
Total	22 (29/130) **
Either C-event or D-event	
Yes	37 (24/65)
No	8 (5/65)
Total	22 (29/130) *

Note. *n*'s are in parentheses.
* $p < .001$.
** $p < .01$.

voking a depressive episode, and without this initial screening the matching exercise would have been to no avail.

Difficulties

An equally important form of matching concerned marked difficulties (rated 1-3 on severity). For each severe event, a judgment was made as to whether there was a match with an ongoing marked difficulty present at the time of the first interview. Difficulties were often the source of severe events occurring in the follow-up period, and they undoubtedly tended to generate events throughout their course. In the great majority of instances of matching, difficulties and events were related in this straightforward sense (e.g., a husband's leaving home in the context of a history of marital disputes over his heavy drinking and violence, or a difficulty with a child involving an event with the same child). However, a *causal* link between difficulty and event, though usual, was not essential for matching. It could occur if the event was rated as severe because of the presence of the background difficulty (e.g., a pregnancy rated as severely threatening because of poor housing was considered to match this difficulty). Of the 130 women with a severe event, 35 had one matching an ongoing marked difficulty that had lasted at least *6 months* at the point of first interview.

There was a threefold increase in risk for those with an event matching a difficulty (a "D-event"), and the greater risk of depression that we had anticipated was therefore confirmed (see Table 2.5, top section). Eales (in press), in a study of unemployment among men, established a very similar effect: An event bringing unemployment was much more likely to lead to depression among men who had had a history of financial or employment difficulties.

As it turned out, matching in terms of commitment and difficulty were unrelated to each other, and they contributed independently to risk of depression (see Table 2.5, bottom section, and Table 2.6). Of the

TABLE 2.6. Onset among 303 women in Islington by characteristics of provoking agent

	Percentage with onset		
	C-event	No C-event	Total
D-event	73 (8/11)	33 (8/24)	46 (16/35)
Both "upper" and loss event (and not D-event)	44 (7/16)	14 (5/35)	24 (12/51)
Remaining provoking agents	8 (1/13)	2 (1/51)	3 (2/64)
No provoking agent	–	–	1 (2/153)

Note. n's are in parentheses.

women with depressive onsets in the follow-up year, 72% had either a C-event or a D-event. If severe events were considered, a ratio of 1 onset to every 4.5 women with a severe event was obtained; however, if only C-events or D-events were considered, the ratio rose to 1 onset in 2.7 among women with such matching events – a considerable improvement in specification of events of importance.

The reason for the high rate of onset associated with D-events is not immediately apparent. One possibility is that they were more threatening than other severe events, and, since the rating of long-term threat was based on a simple dichotomy, the contextual measure used did not reflect this. However, three sets of interrelated results suggest instead that something associated with having lived with the marked difficulty for so long was the critical element. (Most of the difficulties involved had lasted over 2 years, and, by definition, none had lasted less than 6 months.)

The first result confirmed what was already implicit – that a marked difficulty on its own was insufficient to produce depression. Both event and difficulty were needed. There was no instance of depression among the 15 women with a marked difficulty and a matcning *nonsevere* long-term threatening event, compared with one-fourth of the 75 with a nonmatching severe event ($p < .05$).

But, given that both event and difficulty were required, it might still be the greater threat of D-events that was involved. Because the 2 points of the scale of severe long-term threat were not enough to test this possibility, all severe events were rerated on a new 7-point scale. This indicated that D-events were indeed more severe: 45% (17/38) fell in the top 2 points of the new scale, compared with 14% (4/28) of

TABLE 2.7. Occurrence of severe events in terms of type of match, a 7-point measure of long-term threat, and onset of depression

Type of severe event	Rating of long-term threat			
	1-2	3	4	5-7
D-event (n's)	6/17	7/11	1/6	2/4
Percentage with onset		46		30
C-event (and not D-event) (n's)	2/4	3/8	1/6	1/10
Percentage with onset		42		13
Other severe events (n's)	2/18	2/30	2/30	0/23
Percentage with onset		8		4

Note. Based on 167 severe events among 130 women in Islington with a severe event.

C-events and 18% (18/101) of the remaining severe events ($df = 2$, $p < .01$). Nevertheless, they were still associated with a greater risk of depression at all levels of severity of the new 7-point scale (see Table 2.7). (The findings for C-events were broadly similar in this last respect.)

Therefore, something over and above severity appears to be required to explain the greater risk associated with D-events. One possibility is that the difficulty lowered self-esteem, and that this was what increased risk once the event occurred. (Low self-esteem at first interview is related to a higher risk of depression once a severe event occurs; see Brown & Bifulco, 1985; Brown et al., 1986.) However, this still does not appear to provide an answer. While there was some tendency for those with a D-event to have low self-esteem more often (half, compared with a third of those with other provoking agents), the greater risk of depression remained, irrespective of level of self-esteem (Brown, Bifulco, & Harris, 1987).

The issue is at present unsettled, but elsewhere evidence has been presented suggesting that these women were particularly likely to respond to a D-event with profound feelings of hopelessness – a reaction that our theory assumes is often an integral part of the development of a depressive disorder. Among the Islington women, 38% reported complete lack of hope in response to a D-event, compared with only 9% responding in this way to other forms of severe events. Since the rating was based on material collected after any onset of depression, it was open to bias, but the interpretation is made more plausible by the fact that this difference in hopelessness also held for those *not* developing caseness of depression (see Table 9 in Brown, Bifulco, & Harris, 1987).

Role Conflict

Before we leave the issue of matching, a third type needs to be mentioned. The presence of role conflict in a woman's life was rated at first interview, particularly any arising from diverging obligations, such as that between domestic and external spheres. In order to be rated, conflict had to be directly reflected in the woman's actual social circumstances (e.g., full-time work vs. time spent with children), although its severity was based on the expression of feelings (Brown & Bifulco, 1985). But at the same time, conflict was rated only where a woman reported definite feelings of strain or tension between two domains in her life, both of which made demands on her. Role conflict was also rated where strain was reported by the woman in the way she related to others – for instance, if she experienced conflict over having high hostility as well as high dependency needs in a key relationship, or if her desire to get close to people conflicted with her mistrust of others.

There was an increased risk of depression among those with role conflict, and this was entirely explained by the "match" between such conflict and any severe event preceding onset (an "R-event"): 43% (9/21) of women with an R-event and 18% (20/109) of those without one developed depression ($p < .02$). For instance, a single mother, whose conflict arose from the clash between the obligation to work and her sense of being a good mother, developed depression when she found out that her school-age daughter was pregnant, thus underlining her failure in one of her central obligations. Like D-events, R-events were unrelated to C-events. However, they were highly related to D-events – 62% (13/21) of R-events were also D-events – and only two instances of a new onset of depression occurred in the follow-up period for women with an R-event without a D-event. Despite this considerable overlap, R-events are relevant to the issue of additivity, to which we now turn.

Additivity of Events and Difficulties

So far, we have not addressed the possibility that the effects of events and difficulties can summate to increase risk of depression. In fact, as discussed in Chapter 1, most checklist approaches to measurement, such as the SRE of Holmes and Rahe (1967), have simply *assumed* that such additivity takes place by using a total event score. But an effective evaluation of this issue not only has to deal with individual events; it has to face the complication that some events are clearly linked – for example, a woman's learning that her husband has cancer, his operation within 8 days, and his death 4 weeks later. (An example of a series of unrelated severe events would be the death of a woman's father, her husband's loss of his job, and her only close confidant's emigrating to Australia.) But the question of additivity presents us with a fundamental choice: whether to start from "inside" an event complex, and first consider the effect of more than one form of related event, ignoring any unrelated events; or to start from unrelated events, ignoring the fact that an event may have additional related events, and first ask whether the number of such events is associated with increased risk. In the original Camberwell survey, we took the second approach, thereby underplaying the possible contribution of related events. We concluded that, for the most part, it was the impact of just one event of sufficient severity that was critical, and that this held when difficulties were also considered. A more recent review of the evidence supports this view (Brown & Harris, 1986).

Scott Monroe (personal communication, 1986) has, however, raised one objection to this approach to the issue. He points out that we concentrated on the fact that multiple unrelated events were uncommon in the period before onset, and that we underplayed the magnitude of the effect of two or more such events when they *did* occur (which was considerable). And in so doing, we may have missed an important theoretical insight into the graduated effect of stress. Thus, to spell out the argument, it was true that only 19% (28/151) of the combined patients and onset cases in the community had two or more unrelated severe events before onset, and in practical terms the importance of any additive effect must therefore have been small. However, if the total Camberwell study population was considered (i.e., 114 patients with onset, 37 onset cases in the community, and 382 "normals"), then 80% (28/35) of those with two or more severe events before onset were depressed, compared with 50% (67/135) of those with only one event ($p < .01$). Monroe's contention appears reasonable. Although our main point concerning the importance of just one severe event remains, the occurrence of two or more unrelated severe events can apparently appreciably raise risk. With the possibility in mind that we strove too hard with the Camberwell material for a simple all-or-none solution to the problem of additivity, we now turn to consider our findings with the Islington material.

We took as a starting point the success of matching events in predicting subsequent onset of depression, as these effects (leaving aside Scott Monroe's point) demanded some reconsideration of the notion of additivity. Given that an event could be at the same time a C-event, a D-event, and an R-event, was it possible that the occurrence of an event with more than one form of matching would be associated with a greater risk of depression? Whether any such effect of multiple matches should be seen in terms of additivity is doubtful, but it is difficult to avoid the cogency of the argument that any increase in risk should be taken into account before the role of various forms of additivity is considered.

Given the importance of multiple matching dimensions, in contrast to the earlier Camberwell analysis, we chose to place emphasis on starting from "inside" an event or event complex. The approach appeared to make greater theoretical sense: If the human mind is going to "add" things, it is likely to begin with phenomena that are in some way related. Therefore, we proceeded by first considering the effect of characteristics *within* the event itself, then moved to external but related phenomena, and only then moved to clearly "unrelated" events and difficulties. We proposed to follow a stepwise procedure and to consider risk of depression in terms of the following stages:

- Presence of more than one "matching" dimension of a particular severe event.
- Presence of a related severe event.
- Presence of an unrelated severe event.
- Presence of an unrelated marked difficulty.

At each stage, we asked whether taking account of the new information increased risk of depression over that of the previous stage.

Three forms of matching have been discussed here: two involving characteristics of the woman herself (commitment and role conflict), and the other the presence of a linked marked difficulty. When we took into account that the *same* severe event could involve more than one type of match, there was a doubling of risk of depression with each additional matching dimension: 27% (14/52) for one, 50% (7/14) for two, and 100% (4/4) for all three ($p < .001$). Whether the effect of the presence of different matching dimensions should be seen as truly additive is doubtful, but it is clear that the effect was taking place *within* the context provided by a particular severe event.

The next stage of the analysis dealt with related severe events. Here we did not wish to prejudge the issue of the relevant length of period to be covered, so we took account of the fact that material on events had been collected not only in the follow-up period, but also for the 12 months before the first interview. For those with an onset in the follow-up period, we had data for an *average* of 83 weeks before this (range 61-108 weeks), and the same period for the remaining women was taken in all calculations concerning related events. Such events were common. Of the 130 women with a severe event, 57 had at least one other related severe event; in all, there were 66 clusters of such events. The majority (40/66) of these were straightforward developments of the same crisis (e.g., a husband's revelation of his infidelity, a marital separation, and a court appearance for a legal separation). Most of the rest (22/66) involved a common theme, although there was not the same clear development of a single crisis: One woman, for example, found that her 15-year-old daughter was on the "pill" and 6 months later received a letter threatening her daughter's expulsion from school because of her general misbehavior. Finally, there were 4 instances where the events were considered related only because of a linking marked difficulty: For example, one husband's general undependability was reflected in a rating of a marked marital difficulty, and because of this his losing his job due to heavy drinking was considered to be "linked" to his wife's finding out about a love affair he was having. The difficulty itself took into account a wide spectrum of behavior, including his giving her hardly any money after he lost his job and his generally truculent behavior when drinking.[2]

2. Miller and Ingham (1985) have developed a different classificatory system for much the same kind of undertaking. Type S involves an obvious and strong relationship between events; Type M (medium) reflects a lesser degree of relationship, where the first event

(continued)

With this scheme, it was possible to consider whether related or linked severe events would add to the impressive result concerning the summing of matching dimensions.[3] Two measures of linkage were developed: (1) the number of linked severe events in a cluster (if there was more than one cluster, the one with most events was taken), and (2) the length of time between the first and last severe events in the cluster. Both turned out to be associated with an increased risk of depression, but in practice we counted a woman positive in terms of a "link index" if she had either (1) a cluster with three or more severe events, or (2) a gap of at least 6 months between the first and last events in the cluster. The rationale underlying the index was that an increased experience of strain would relate to the number of linked events that had occurred and to the amount of time over which such linked events were experienced. These assumptions appeared to be supported, since the index was associated with an increased risk even when the number of matching dimensions was taken into account (see Table 2.8, middle section). (This is confirmed by logistic regression.) One further point is of interest: The effect of the index was entirely confined to clusters involving a D-event. Of those with a D-event, 71% (10/14) positive on the link index and 29% (6/21) negative on it developed depression, compared with 14% (11/82) and 15% (2/13), respectively, for the remaining women with a severe event but no D-event.

Therefore, if the results so far are seen in terms of some notion of additivity, it was a highly restricted effect; in every instance, the raised risk was due either to the number of matching dimensions of one severe event, or to the clustering of linked severe D-events.

The next stage provided the clearest test of an additivity effect as this is usually understood. However, there was no suggestion that unrelated severe events served to increase risk over and above the two prior indices (see Table 2.8, bottom section). There was also no suggestion that nonsevere events increased risk in any way; finally, when difficulties were considered, various analyses gave essentially the same (entirely negative) results.

---

seems to be necessary for the second but not sufficient (e.g., separation from one girlfriend and getting another); and Type W (weak) reflects the rater's belief that there might *possibly* be a link (e.g., a severe marital argument, the husband's walking out, and 2 days later his admission to a hospital after a car crash). This approach therefore emphasizes throughout the presence of a causal link, whereas the second category of our scheme avoids such a judgment and may therefore be somewhat more comprehensive. However, our impression is that the two schemes arrive at much the same conclusions about linkages between events.

3. Where there had been a matching event in the first stage of the analysis, we used this as the focus and considered only events linked to it.

TABLE 2.8. Three indices of additivity concerning severe events for 130 women in Islington with a severe event in the follow-up year

	Matching index
Number of matches	Percentage with onset
2-3	61 (11/18)
1	27 (14/52)
None	7 (4/60)

	Linked index	
	Percentage with onset	
Number of matches	Positive link index	Negative link index
2-3	88 (7/8)	40 (4/10)
1	36 (4/11)	24 (10/41)
None	20 (2/10)	4 (2/50)

	Further nonlinked severe event			
	Percentage with onset			
	Positive link index		Negative link index	
Number of matches	Further nonlinked severe event	No such event	Further nonlinked severe event	No such event
2-3	100 (4/4)	75 (3/4)	33 (2/6)	50 (2/4)
1	40 (2/5)	33 (2/6)	27 (4/15)	23 (6/26)
None	0 (0/3)	25 (2/7)	7 (1/14)	3 (1/36)
Total	50 (6/12)	41 (7/17)	20 (7/35)	14 (9/66)

Note. n's are in parentheses.

Therefore we arrived at the surprising conclusion that there was no evidence for an additive effect once characteristics of a single severe event and any related severe events were taken into account. In the earlier analysis based on the Camberwell material, we took the alternative approach of excluding from consideration related provoking agents. This did reveal, as already noted, some suggestion of an additive effect. Women developing depression in the general population had more often experienced two or more unrelated severe events or major difficulties, but the overall impact was modest. If a 38-week period was used as in Camberwell, the same tabulation for Islington women was less striking and no longer reached statistical significance: 28% (8/29) of onset cases and 16% (16/101) of other women had two or more unrelated severe events, compared with 36% (9/25) and 9% (7/75) in Camberwell. At best, therefore, this alternative approach indicated a modest additive effect. Therefore, nothing emerged from the Islington material to detract from our original conclusion that just one severe event is likely to be of critical importance in bringing about depression. However, within a severe event or cluster of severe events, it is certainly possible to argue for some kind of cumulative effect.

Another approach to the question of additivity has been developed by Surtees, who considers all events, not just severe ones. He argues that with the passage of time the chance of an event producing depression is reduced, and that the chances of prior events producing depression can be calculated at any point in time. This can be done by assuming that the effects of events decay and calculating an overall score of residual adversity stemming from a range of events. The approach *assumes* that the effects of events are in some way cumulative (see Surtees, Chapter 6, this volume). When applied to the original Camberwell material, the approach did not show any superiority when compared with using the occurrence of just one severe event; the PARs were 61.0% and 59.7%, respectively (Surtees & Rennie, 1983). For the Islington data, exactly comparable results were obtained by the two approaches, and there therefore appears to be no reason to incorporate the additional assumption that the effects of events are additive. But this analysis employed a simple dichotomous index of decay, and Surtees would argue that this does not do full justice to the flexibility of his approach and its ability to deal with continuous scores (see Chapter 6). However, the results in terms of a fourfold adversity score were in no way superior to the matching exercise reported in Table 2.8. Results in terms of decay were 69% with onset of depression (9/13 for scores of 1,000 or more), 32% (8/25 for scores of 500-999), 14% (12/80 for scores of 150-499), and 2% (3/182 for scores of 0-149), compared with 61%, 27%, and 7% for the matching index (see Table 2.8, top section); of course, even greater discrimination was achieved when the link index was also considered (see Table 2.8, middle section). Finally, when the residual adversity score itself for nonsevere events was incorporated into the results for the link index (see Table 2.8, bottom section), it added nothing to predicting onset.

We discuss Surtees's approach more fully in Chapter 15. However, we still conclude there that, as at present conceived, it does not seriously threaten the conclusions we have reached about the limited role of additivity. But we must confess that the conclusion is in a number of ways surprising: The presence of a powerful effect across unrelated events would have made sense, in that yet another event might well have increased the chance that hopelessness would generalize or might have led to some critical change in the neurochemistry of the brain (e.g., Anisman & Zacharko, 1982; Willner, 1985). At the same time, it is possible to see some sense in the results. There is clear evidence for a limited form of additivity with an event or cluster of related events, and it is easy to see how this may serve to enhance any generalization of hopelessness: If, for example, a husband's first stroke was followed by another, a woman's sense of optimism about life in general might be more than doubly disturbed by the cumulative blows to his prospects of recovery.

Additivity: Some Theoretical Speculations

Given this evidence for the etiological importance of just one event, or cluster of events, it may be useful to begin a more theoretical discussion by describing the experience of one of the Islington women. She was a widow whose husband had been killed in an accident when her daughter was 3. Since then, she had remained unmarried and had devoted much of her time to her daughter and to her job, which had become increasingly demanding.

There were several severe events concerning her daughter, the main and final one involving a letter from her school saying that she had been playing truant and seriously misbehaving. In discussing the crisis, the woman said, "I was very disappointed. I felt absolutely wretched because I felt helpless. I felt ashamed – it was all my fault. What will people think? I had a daughter who was not a nice daughter any more. People had always said, 'Oh, you're wonderful, making a home and bringing her up so well.' I must admit I liked that flattery, and here I was in a situation where she wasn't a well-brought-up daughter. It wasn't a wonderful situation. I had absolutely nothing to be proud of any more. It had all been shattered."

She developed fears that the girl would get involved in the drug scene and become pregnant; she blamed herself and felt responsible "because I'm her mother." She also felt guilty because of working late – "I blame myself because maybe I didn't react. . . . I didn't notice what was coming. It hit me a little bit hard." She tried many ways of getting closer to her daughter. Nothing worked, and she described how she developed a feeling of helplessness, believing that everything she did was wrong and nothing was working: "It came gradually, but once there it stuck." She developed a depressive disorder within 7 weeks of the first incident (discovering her daughter stealing) and within a day or so of receiving the letter from the school.

The nature of this woman's response is not unusual, particularly as a "matching" event was involved. Strong emotions are often experienced in this way – despair, anger, shame, anxiety, and the like. There is often an element of compulsive rumination of a kind described by Horowitz (1976) as following "traumatic" events. For this woman, thoughts "just kept coming back." This often goes, as Horowitz describes so well, with a need to talk about the incident and its implications. Thoughts about the self are common, and the kind of impact on self-esteem that is possible can be seen in comments made by women in Islington: "I somehow despised myself for becoming dependent on one person"; "I found it difficult to tolerate the thought that I could not sustain a relationship"; "I'm beginning to think it must be me – things are always happening to me and I wonder what the next thing will be."

Such feelings and thoughts can usually be directly related to the provoking event itself. But there can at times be marked inconsistency in mood: There may be both clear, if fleeting, feelings of mastery at getting out of a violent relationship, and also a sense of helplessness at not being able to find company. Added to such feelings, there are often changes in perceptions of relationships in general ("I asked how far it was possible to trust again") and of the future ("It was going to be back to the same round of work and child," or, by contrast, "I really felt I'm going to survive no matter what happens – I'm not going to depend on someone else for my happiness").

In considering these responses, Tomkins's (1979) formulation of script theory is illuminating. He places weight on the importance of both "scenes" and "scripts." It is from scenes that we construct our personal world. A scene is a "happening" that is likely to include the memory of persons, place, time, actions, and feelings. There are various types. "Transient" scenes remain relatively isolated in the experience of the individual and are often provoked by a minor incident, such as enjoying a film. Lives may nonetheless be made up in good part of transient scenes. There are also "recurrent" scenes, which typically represent habitual skills that can be drawn upon with minimal consciousness, thought, and affect. Tomkins notes the paradox that "it is just those achievements which are most solid, which work best, and which continue to work, that can excite and reward us least. The price of skill is the loss of the experience of value – and the zest of living. . . . [A] husband and wife who become too skilled in knowing each other can enter the same valley of perceptual skill and become hardly aware of each other" (1979, p. 212). Of course, life events often interfere with such skills, but paradoxically this can bring new zest to life as a person struggles to acquire new skills.

The most important scenes (certainly in terms of the origins of affective disorder) are a limited number of "nuclear" scenes, which "capture the individual's most urgent and unsolved problems and that continue to grow by recruiting even more thought, feeling and action" (Tomkins, 1979, p. 228). By such psychological magnification, one affect-laden scene is connected with another affect-laden scene: "Through memory, thought, and imagination, scenes experienced before can be coassembled with scenes presently experienced, together with scenes which are anticipated in the future. The present moment is embedded in the intersect between the past and the future in a central assembly via a constructive process we have called coassembly" (p. 217).

In these terms, the emotions provoked by a severe life event can set off an obsessive-like review of past, current, and future scenes. We have already noted in Chapter 1 Leventhal's (1980) emphasis on the critical role of emotion for memory: Incidents recall past emotions, and these in turn recall both further incidents and emotions. But Tomkins emphasizes that such recall will tend to have structure. The surfeit of ideas of the mother with the delinquent daughter ran very much along the paths defined by her role as mother and her past and future relationship with her daughter, although without the event many of these might, as discussed by Epstein (1983), have remained at the preconscious level. Nonetheless, the first interview with the mother before the crisis had occurred made clear that her life was dominated by the twin concerns of her daughter and her work. (There was high commitment in both domains and also role conflict, but no ongoing difficulty.) Her relationship with her boyfriend was of far less importance to her.

The importance of Tomkins's analysis is that it conveys how one event may be able to play such an important part in provoking depression; at the same time, it can be seen as another way of conceiving of plans and purposes. However, the mere review of a family of scenes, in our view, is not enough to bring about depression. The person must also experience hopelessness as a consequence. And here other factors are likely to come into play. Tomkins emphasizes "scripts" that parallel such scenes – an individual's rules for predicting, interpreting, responding to, and controlling a magnified set of scenes. This point is close to the widespread agreement about the importance of cognitive sets such as low self-esteem and feelings of helplessness in the development of depression. Indeed, so much importance has recently been given to such cognitive sets by psychologists and psychiatrists that there has been a tendency to downplay the importance of the environment in the development of depression. There has been a much greater emphasis on the fact that those who become depressed have in some way *distorted* experience by having maladaptive thoughts – that is, by overreacting in terms of how most people would have responded. Beck has documented, in fascinating detail, some of the ways in which this may be done (Beck, 1967; Beck, Rush, Shaw, & Emery, 1980).

However, an alternative perspective underlines the *naturalness* of depression, emphasizing that it is understandable, given an evolution-based propensity to react in a specific way to loss and disappointment, and given the degree of adversity inherent in a person's life (Brown & Andrews, 1986; Gilbert, 1984). It is, in fact, usually fairly easy to present the same data in terms of either perspective – that is, as a cognitive distortion, or as a natural response. What is described as one woman's "clinging, maladaptive personality" can be reformulated by an emphasis on the way women are encouraged to serve and live for others, and how, to a much greater degree than men, they are caught up in axiomatic relationships that cannot be broken except at the greatest cost. Similarly, a so-called "catastrophizing response" can be reinterpreted as a recognition of the real-life implications of the loss.

Undoubtedly, both distorting and natural processes play a role in depression, and Tomkins has illustrated how "maladaptive" cognitive sets may be built up in relation to particular nuclear scenes. It is therefore inappropriate to argue for either perspective alone. Depression can certainly follow from a realistic assessment of one's prospects, perhaps as part of the re-experience of negative emotions from the rehearsal of past scenes. It also seems possible that in some cases a major depression can be brought about by some apparently trivial event, with a depressogenic cognitive set or schema playing the dominant etiological role. Perhaps in most instances it is some combination of these extreme positions, with further factors such as current social support also playing a key role. For example, a fairly upsetting experience cannot be said to be "distorted" if a woman reacts with depression, nor yet is it entirely natural for the reaction to be as extreme as clinical caseness.

A good example here is the death of a parent for a woman well on in life with her own husband and grown-up children flourishing around her. Such an event very rarely leads to the onset of major depression in London. Horowitz et al. (1981) have discussed such experiences with considerable insight. As a result of an intensive study of psychiatric patients with depression following such a loss, they argue that the death may change the balance of a person's self-image in an unfavorable direction. One patient in the series, for example, was interpreted as having an idealized model of her relationship with her father as an important source of strength, and his death resulted in special problems with self-images of weakness, helplessness, and lack of internal resources – aspects that had not been predominant while her father was alive. There can be little doubt that such effects do occur and that we know too little about them. One of the problems is that such cognitions are unlikely to be readily available beforehand and are likely to require a good deal of skilled interviewing to reveal. There may also, of course, be some problem over the validity of the interpretations. In Islington we had only 1 instance of such a possible "overreaction" among the 32 onsets in the follow-up year, and this, as it happened, was in response to the death of a mother. The woman had an excellent marriage and a wide circle of friends, and there was an element of inexplicability in the seriousness of her reaction, recalling the clinical impression of some of the undue reliance on others among those developing depression (e.g., Arieti & Bemporad, 1980).

It is possible that in an inner-city area such responses are more difficult to isolate because of the plethora of "real" social problems. It is also possible that such responses are common even among those with such problems and help to explain why one woman rather than another develops major depression after events that are apparently equally severely threatening in contextual terms. Most probably, in most instances, it is some combination of the extreme "external" and "internal" positions. But any position along such a continuum is compatible with one event's playing a critical role. At this point it may be objected that one implication of our theory (i.e., that generalization of hopelessness is involved in leading to depression) is that those with more than one severe event, being further from the very specific loss of hope pertaining to only one severe event, will be at greater risk of onset. However, the theory posits that the tendency to generalize springs primarily from sources *other* than provoking agents – vulnerability factors, and particularly some sense that the self or supportive others will be unable to restore something of the loss. It is therefore quite possible that one loss is no less effective than two or three in setting in train this cognitive process by which other plans and roles are negatively evaluated and the conclusion is drawn that "my life as a whole is no good."

Although not as concerned as ourselves with the issue of additivity, Freden (1982) outlines a perspective on depression that has definite similarities with this account. He builds upon the theories of Ernest Becker (1964, 1971), who saw three main components in "the fundamental human motive" – strivings toward action, strivings to minimize anxiety, and strivings to maximize self-esteem. The five stages that Freden sees in the depressive process allow him, like ourselves, to take a halfway position in the debate about how natural or how distorted it is, placing equal weight on restrictive extrinsic circumstances and the subject's rigid action patterns. He sees the discriminating features as involving situations that do most to impair action opportunities – an emphasis reminiscent of Oatley and Johnson-Laird's (1987) focus upon plans, and one that would therefore embrace the possibility of there being no additivity of losses as such.

So far, our conclusions echo Thomas Hardy's comment in *The Woodlanders:* "Two simultaneous troubles do not always make a double trouble; and thus it came to pass that Giles's practical anxiety about his houses, which would have been enough to keep him awake half the night at any other time, was displaced and not reinforced by his sentimental trouble with Grace Melbury" (Hardy, 1887/1920, p. 112). But there is an important qualification. Our conclusion about additivity refers only to the onset of a discrete episode of clinical depression. If we extend our perspective to the worsening, improvement, or recovery of an established depressive condition, a somewhat different picture emerges that is perhaps not altogether incompatible with an "additive" perspective.

Change Points and Onset of Depression

In the original Camberwell study of 114 depressed psychiatric *patients,* somewhat over a third had at least one definite and discrete worsening of their condition – a "change point" – after the original onset of their depression in the year before their admission. These changes were a good deal less common among onset cases in the general population, and we therefore restricted our analysis of the phenomenon to the patient series. As expected, inpatients tended to have a more severe form of depression, but this was explained by the fact that they had more change points and tended to deteriorate more at such points; the two groups of patients did not differ in severity of disorder at the time of onset of caseness (Brown & Harris, 1978, pp. 207-210). For our present argument, the important characteristic of these change points – that is, worsenings of an established disorder – is that they were often preceded by a severe event.

In evaluating the etiological role of these events, we could not follow exactly the same procedure as at first onset; we needed to control for the possibility that the events were brought about by the depression itself, or that severe events occurring before onset (or prior change point) had led to others after onset. We therefore excluded altogether any events that could possibly be "illness-related," such as giving up a job (although they still might have brought about a worsening). To deal with linked events, we took for a comparison series the period after onset and before admission for women *without* a subsequent change point (Brown & Harris, 1978, p. 209). Once this was done, not only did change points more often have a prior severe event (47% vs. 16%), but the majority of the events involved were unrelated to any associated with the original onset. Therefore, once an episode of depression is under way, it appears possible for an unrelated severe event to bring about a definite worsening. There is no hint that nonsevere events can play this role. Whether or not this effect should be included under the rubric of additivity, it is clearly a related phenomenon, and one that would certainly have been confused with additivity if we had taken psychiatric state at the time of admission to represent "onset."

Recovery, Events, and Difficulties

It is also possible to consider recovery or improvement from depression, and here, of course, as with the worsening of the condition, it is important to examine the role of events irrespective of the issue of additivity. The original Camberwell survey underlined the important role played by ongoing difficulties in serving to perpetuate a depressive disorder (Brown & Harris, 1978, pp. 195-201), and Surtees and Ingham (1980) have used the LEDS and their decay model to show that the occurrence of threatening events of marked and moderate severity was related to lack of recovery in a follow-up of 71 patients treated for depression. Giel, Ten Horn, Ormer, Schudel, and Wiersma (1978) used the LEDS in a 5-year follow-up study of 35 cases in the general population and found some suggestion that events could play a role in prolonging illness.

Other studies have suggested that social factors play a role in course and outcome (e.g., Huxley, Goldberg, Maguire, & Kincey, 1979; Mann, Jenkins, & Belsey, 1981). However, of particular interest have been two studies using the LEDS that have suggested that "neutralizing" events may play a role in recovery, though neither study paid systematic attention to difficulties. Tennant, Bebbington, and Hurry (1981) showed in a study of affective disorders in the general population that half the cases identified at first interview had remitted 1 month later. The occurrence of an event that neutralized the impact of an earlier threatening event or difficulty was related to remission. However, the effect was quite modest: 21% of remitted cases had a neutralizing event in the 3 months before, compared with an expected rate of 5% based on nonremitted cases. The study also utilized a category of "positive" events, but there was a substantial correlation between the two types of events, and positive events did not make an independent contribution to remission.

A second study, again using the LEDS, reinterviewed 42 patients after 6 weeks and contacted them again after 20 weeks by a postal questionnaire (Parker, Tennant, & Blignault, 1985). The study showed only modest effects for neutralizing and positive events occurring in the 6 weeks after first contact, and then largely only in terms of outcome after 20 weeks. However, the study used a regression analysis in which the effect of factors recorded at time of first contact were controlled before the effect of events occurring later was considered. One factor at time of first contact that was of predictive importance was the breaking of an intimate relationship in the previous 12 months. But such an incident was particularly related to the occurrence of a later "positive" event, and it is probably illegitimate to control for the prior event as a matter of course in this way. Nonetheless, these two studies strongly suggest that "neutralizing" events play some role in recovery from depression, although at the same time they suggest that the effect may be a modest one. It must also be borne in mind that episodes of depression of any length were considered, and that no systematic attention was given to the role of ongoing difficulties. A further study considered recovery in a series of patients with chronic depression, but the life events measure was a questionnaire covering events in the 5 months before *admission*, which almost certainly explains the lack of an association with outcome (Hirschfeld, Klerman, Andreasen, Clayton, & Keller, 1986).

For a stringent test of the role of such events among women in Islington, we selected the 48 with caseness of depression of at least 1 year's duration and followed them up for at least 2 years. To do this, we carried out a second follow-up interview somewhat over 2 years after the first contact. Of the 48 women, 26 made a significant improvement at some time in the whole study period: 19 recovered from depression altogether, and 7 improved but retained symptoms at a borderline-case level. In addition, 11 of the 19 full recoveries remained cases or borderline cases of a *non*depressive nature (in nearly every instance, anxiety). For convenience, we use the term "recovery" to refer to all 26 women.

We used three approaches to the role of "neutralizing" factors (Brown, Adler, & Bifulco, 1988). The first was a score for reduction of a difficulty by at least one-quarter in a 3-month period. For this, we started with the score at the beginning of the period. The score was calculated by adding the individual difficulty ratings of the top 4 scale points from 1 ("high unpleasantness") to 4 ("low moderate unpleasantness",) using 5, 4, 3, and 1, respectively, as weights. We considered the 3 months before any recovery, and, for the nonrecovered, *any* point in the total follow-up period at which such a reduction occurred and in which they also had caseness of depression. Fortunately, such changes were rare, and there was no problem over the multiple occurrence of such reductions. (Only 1 of the 48 women had two during the period.) Second, we took account of difficulty-reducing events; these were defined by the fact that they had been associated with a fall in the contextual severity rating of a particular difficulty – either from a score of 1, 2, or 3 to 4, or from a score of 4 to 5 or 6. Therefore the first approach dealt with the total difficulty score, and the second with an event reducing a particular difficulty. There was a marked overlap between the two indices, and we finally considered women as positive in terms of difficulty reduction if both had occurred, excluding the relatively rare occasions where one occurred without the other. (There was no indication that these were related to recovery, although the numbers involved were small.) The measure, though more complex, is obviously related to the one used by Tennant and his colleagues.

Third, we developed a new concept: "fresh-start" events. These were not, as in the earlier research, just "positive" events. They had to involve a new beginning in a significant aspect of a person's life (e.g., one woman was rehoused on a new housing estate; another took a new lover; a third woman's husband, who had frequently been violent, was sent to prison for a long sentence; and a fourth woman was "forced" to accept a divorce settlement by her husband and his lawyer). Usually they occurred in the context of a significant related privation or hardship that was reported as such by the woman (e.g., the woman who was rehoused had been in poor housing; the one who acquired a new lover had not been out with a man for 5 years). We did not include as fresh starts incidents occurring during an apparently unexceptional course of events, such as having a wanted third child or getting married as planned before our earlier interview. Such events did not have the necessary sense of discontinuity and beginning again. Indeed, as already hinted by these examples, it will be seen that fresh-start events were not necessarily "positive."

Both difficulty reductions and fresh starts occurred much more commonly in the 3 months before any recovery. One or the other occurred in this space of time in 69% (18/26) of the recoveries and in only 36% (8/22) of the nonrecoveries *at any point in the 2-year follow-up period* ($p < .02$). Difficulty reductions and fresh starts often occurred together, but both types of experiences appeared to be capable of making an independent contribution to recovery. The importance of fresh starts was most clearly seen among the women with low difficulty scores for whom, by definition, difficulty reduction was rare.

Table 2.9 summarizes these results in terms of the initial difficulty score at the beginning of the 3-month period before recovery (or, if no recovery, the level before any difficulty-reducing event, or, if no such event, the most usual score). When women with either difficulty reductions or fresh starts were taken into account, initial difficulty score made an independent contribution to outcome. (This was confirmed by logistic regression; see Brown, Adler, & Bifulco, 1988.) Life events and difficulties therefore appear to play an important role in recovery among those with chronic depression; and they often do so in terms of a kind of mirror image of the original onset. However, the recovery process cannot be reduced to the straightforward clearing up of long-term difficulties. In the first place, recovery among these women could occur despite the presence of difficulties: 8 of the 26 recoveries still had

TABLE 2.9. Recovery from or improvement in chronic depression by occurrence of a fresh start or difficulty reduction

Initial level of difficulty	Percentage with recovery	
	Fresh start or difficulty reduction	No such experience
0-2 (low)	100 (6/6)	63 (5/8)
3-6	71 (5/7)	50 (2/4)
7+ (high)	54 (7/13)	10 (1/10)
Totals	69 (18/26)	36 (8/22)

Note. n's are in parentheses. Average percentages of recovery or improvement for those with a difficulty score over 3 were 60 for those with a fresh start or difficulty reduction and 21 for those without such an experience.

a score of 6 (equivalent to two marked difficulties) at the point of recovery. Second, as already noted, difficulty reductions and fresh starts were not always without threat. Indeed, one-fifth of those taking place before recovery were associated with an event rated as severe on long-term threat (e.g., one woman was "forced" to accept a divorce settlement, and another decided to try to have her markedly handicapped son home to live with her once again). If there should be a common feature to difficulty reductions and fresh starts, it perhaps relates to a sense of hope inherent in the situation that life has taken some new turning or that there is a chance to restore something lost. This was clearest for the six women with a fresh start event who recovered *without* significant ongoing difficulties: Three got jobs after being unemployed, one gained a new confidant, one acquired a new lover, and one returned to her family after being widowed.

Finally, there is the question of the 8 of the 26 women who recovered who did not have a fresh start or difficulty reduction. These women provided a number of interesting insights. They contained, for instance, three of the six whose original depression had been provoked by a death of a child or husband. It is possible to see here that there is a natural tendency for the effects of bereavement to dissipate with time and that this dissipation can be relevant even when the loss has brought about a frank depression. The eight also included the only instance of a postpartum depression.

Another interesting issue concerns the unpleasantness of some of the incidents preceding recovery. Several women were quite clear that recovery had not only followed a threatening event (without a difficulty reduction or fresh start), but that some aspect of the threat itself had played a direct role in recovery. One of these same eight women had begun to recover from a depression that had lasted 4 years when, after an emergency operation, a surgeon had told her that she was "the luckiest girl in the world to be alive today." She said that this had had a great impact on her and that she had from that point started being more positive. She felt more easy and stopped worrying; she started cutting down on her Valium, took driving lessons, and planned a vacation in Scotland. Perhaps the knowledge that the situation could have been worse (with her death) somehow injected new hope.

Another of the eight women without a difficulty reduction or fresh start emphasized the importance of an incident that we had not included as an event – the death of a sister-in-law (not defined as a close tie) from cancer in Scotland. She had been very concerned about the illness and the fact that the sister-in-law had a young child. The family was a close one, and the woman felt she had to be supportive. After the death, she said that her brother and mother had expected her to break down, but she felt she coped very well and was able to be strong for the sake of the rest of the family, overcoming her fear of traveling and funerals to be there. "I realized I had to pull myself together. And whatever help I was going to be, I certainly wasn't going to if I went to pieces. I realized I had to." She said she began to see her problems as less in comparison with theirs (she had left her violent husband some time before): "It took something like that to really shake me up." Two weeks after the funeral, she decided to change her job; 11 weeks later she did so, but the main improvement in her depression had apparently taken place before she actually took up the new job. We may speculate that coping with the initial incident seemed to give this woman sufficient sense of competence to lead her to plan to change her life in a significant way. However, it would not affect the implication of our argument if her clinical improvement had actually occurred after the taking of the job; the implication still would be that after the funeral she had enough initiative to create a fresh-start event, which in turn led to recovery.

In his autobiography, John Stuart Mill (1873/1928) described a depressive disorder in which he could no longer find any interest or enjoyment in his way of life. He described his recovery as following closely on *reading* about the kind of experience described in this last example:

> I was reading accidentally, Marmontel's *Memories,* and came to the passage which relates his father's death, the distressed position of the family and the sudden inspiration by which he, then a mere boy, felt and made them feel that he would be everything to them – would supply the place of all that they had lost. A vivid conception of that scene and its feelings came over me, and I was moved to tears. From this moment my burthen grew lighter. The oppression of the thought that all feeling was dead within me, was gone. I was no longer helpless: I was not a stock or a stone. I had still, it seemed, some of the material out of which all worth of character, and all capacity for happiness, are made. (p. 145)

It seems, therefore, that it may at times be possible to get into the habit of depression, and that some "jolt" may be required to give a more positive perspective on life and a sense that one is needed. It is of interest that neither woman in the examples given above had, in terms of the LEDS, difficulties that dominated their lives, but both were very unhappy with aspects of it (one with loneliness and a low-key marriage, and the other with her single-parent status). However, as yet we are unable to provide systematic evidence to support this argument concerning "negative" events, and such examples (and a few others could be given) should not be allowed to detract from the more general conclusion regarding the apparently critical role of difficulty reductions and fresh starts.

A separate series of women who recovered without becoming chronic cases was also considered. Here there was no evidence for a role for difficulty reductions or fresh starts in those cases lasting less than 3 months, but the figures for chronic cases and for women with depression lasting between 3 and 12 months were almost exactly comparable (Brown, Adler, & Bifulco, 1988). It is therefore possible that future research should concentrate on psychosocial factors in the recovery of individuals whose depression has lasted at least 3 months. Finally, it is necessary to return to the point already made for the chronic conditions – namely, that there may well be a small group of depressions following the death of particularly close ties (e.g., child or spouse) that only dissipate given a set span of time, although this will certainly differ between individuals. Even more speculatively, this may also hold for a small group of "biological" depressions, such as that of the woman whose original onset occurred in very close proximity to a birth (see Martin *et al.*, in press).

Therefore, in terms of the issue of additivity, these results concerning recovery are mixed. The correlation of difficulty score with outcome suggests that different sources of adversity may summate to perpetuate depression, and this is consistent with the earlier research of Surtees and Ingham (1980). The frequent presence of fresh-start events before recovery indicates that change is not necessarily tied to the resolution of difficulties (related or unrelated to original onset), and that there is a role for a more general positive assessment of one's life. In short, the results as a whole are compatible with the critical importance of the role of hope. They illustrate that this may stem from a surprising number of sources, and that it need not necessarily be focused on the consequences of the crisis that originally provoked the depression or on difficulties that may have helped to perpetuate it. It seems possible that hope arising out of events entirely unrelated to the depression itself may alleviate it; in this sense, it may after all be necessary to include an important "additive" effect in our understanding of the phenomenon of clinical depression.

Concluding Remarks

This chapter has reviewed early work on depressive onset using the LEDS and has devoted a good deal of space to the presentation of new data from a recent prospective study of women in Islington. It is difficult to escape the conclusion that the Islington data confirm and elaborate the perspective of depression provided by the etiological model developed on the basis of the early studies – that is, that severe losses often lead to negative thoughts about oneself and one's world, which can then generalize, thus ushering in the familiar symptoms of major depression. One severe loss may be enough to do this, and several minor losses do not seem capable of adding up to an equivalent effect. Recovery from depression is often the mirror image of this process, as difficulty reduction or a fresh start breaks into this cycle of generalization, and the subject starts to hope once again.

There has not been enough space to embark on a discussion of the essential parallel issues of how vulnerability factors can potentiate the effects of provoking agents. But here improvement in the measurement of life events does suggest that the original estimate that only one-fifth of women will succumb to a severe event (resulting in the need to explain in terms of vulnerability why four-fifths will not) is too conse vative. Current work on matching suggests that the risk that the majority of women will develop clinical depression in response to the relevant type of stressor may be nearer to one-half (see Table 2.6). Thus the role of vulnerability, as opposed to provocation, may have been overestimated.

However, this result will need eventually to be interpreted theoretically in the light of the links of such matching events with vulnerability factors (e.g., low self-esteem) and protective factors (e.g., receiving emotional support in a crisis) (see Brown & Bifulco, 1985, and Brown et al., 1986, for a preliminary account). The task is sufficiently complex for us to delay its full consideration to a later publication, although in Chapter 14 we provide some material concerning it. Our present analysis sets the scene for this final step. But, to anticipate, it seems likely that the vulnerability process can be interpreted along the same lines as the process involving severe events – that is, in terms of generalization of negative cognitions. Moreover, part of the effect of matching events is related to the role of factors (e.g., low self-esteem) present at first interview and the fact that they are combined with failing to receive support from core ties once severe events occur. In other words, it will be necessary to deal with the way the various factors in our etiological model interrelate. (See Brown, in press, for a preliminary statement.)

Nonetheless, despite this complexity, the role of events is emerging with comforting clarity. There are, of course, still many questions left unanswered: For example, are there biological markers for this propensity to generalize negative cognitions? And what is the significance of the variations between persons in length of the "causal interval" between severe event and onset? How do life events relate to other factors in the model? And how far is the reaction to events caught up in unconscious or preconscious schemas from the past, which the LEDS does not attempt to establish in any systematic manner? Although this chapter may have portrayed our current state of knowledge about life events and depression as having reached a comfortable plateau, there are further heights that must still be scaled.

References

American Psychiatric Association. (1980). *Diagnostic and statistical manual of mental disorders* (3rd ed.). Washington, DC: Author.

Andrews, G., & Tennant, C. (1978). Editorial: Life event stress and psychiatric illness. *Psychological Medicine, 8*, 545-549.

Anisman, H., & Zacharko, R. M. (1982). Depression: The predisposing influences of stress. *The Behavioural and Brain Sciences. 5*, 89-137.

Arieti, S., & Bemporad, J. (1980). *Severe and mild depression: The psychotherapeutic approach.* London: Tavistock.

Barrett, J. E. (1979). The relationship of life events to the onset of neurotic disorders. In J. E. Barrett (Ed.), *Stress and mental disorders* (pp. 87-109). New York: Raven Press.

Bebbington, P., Hurry, J., Tennant, C., & Sturt, E. (1984). Misfortune and resilience: A community study of women. *Psychological Medicine, 14*, 347-363.

Bebbington, P., Hurry, J., Tennant, C., Sturt, E., & Wing, J. K. (1981). Epidemiology of mental disorders in Camberwell. *Psychological Medicine, 11*, 561-579.

Bebbington, P. W., Tennant, C., & Hurry, J. (1981). Adversity and the nature of psychiatric disorder in the community. *Journal of Affective Disorders, 3*, 345-366.

Beck, A. T. (1967). *Depression: Clinical, experimental and theoretical aspects.* London: Staples Press.

Beck, A. T., Rush, A. J., Shaw, B. F., & Emery, G. (1980). *Cognitive therapy of depression.* Chichester, England: Wiley.

Becker, E. (1964). *The revolution in psychiatry: The new understanding of man.* Glencoe, IL: Free Press.

Becker, E. (1971). *The birth and death of meaning: An interdisciplinary perspective of the problem of man.* New York: Free Press.

Benjaminsen, S. (1981). Stressful life events preceding the onset of neurotic depression. *Psychological Medicine, 11*, 369-378.

Bolton, W., & Oatley, K. (1987). A longitudinal study of social support and depression in unemployed men. *Psychological Medicine, 17*, 453-460.

Brown, G. W. (in press). Etiology of depressive disorder. In D. Bennett & H. Freeman (Eds.), *The practice of social psychiatry.* London: Churchill Livingstone.

Brown, G. W., Adler, Z., & Bifulco, A. (1988). Life events, difficulties and recovery from chronic depression. *British Journal of Psychiatry, 152*, 115-128.

Brown, G. W., & Andrews, B. (1986). Social support and depression. In M. H. Appley & R. Trumbull (Eds.), *Dynamics of stress* (pp. 257-282). New York; Plenum.

Brown, G. W., Andrews, B., Harris, T. O., Adler, Z., & Bridge, L. (1986). Social support, self esteem and depression. *Psychological Medicine, 16*, 813-831.

Brown, G. W., & Bifulco, A. (1985). Social support, life events and depression. In I. Sarason (Ed.), *Social support: Theory, research and applications.* (pp. 349-370). Dordrecht, The Netherlands: Martinus Nijhoff.

Brown, G. W., Bifulco, A., & Harris, T. O. (1987) Life events, vulnerability and onset of depression: Some refinements. *British Journal of Psychiatry, 150*, 30-42.

Brown, G. W., Craig, T. K. J., & Harris, T. O. (1985). Depression: Disease or distress? Some epidemiological considerations. *British Journal of Psychiatry, 147*, 612-622.

Brown, G. W., & Harris, T. O. (1978). *Social origins of depression: A study of psychiatric disorder in women.* London: Tavistock.

Brown, G. W., & Harris, T. O. (1982). Disease, distress and depression: A comment. *Journal of Affective Disorders, 4*, 1-8.

Brown, G. W., & Harris, T. O. (1986). Establishing causal links: The Bedford College studies of depression. In H. Katschnig (Ed.), *Life events and psychiatric disorders: Controversial issues* (pp. 107-187). Cambridge, England: Cambridge University Press.

Brown, G. W., Harris, T. O. & Copeland, J. R. (1977). Depression and Loss. *British Journal of Psychiatry, 130,* 1-18.

Brown, G. W., & Prudo, R. (1981). Psychiatric disorder in a rural and an urban population: 1. Aetiology of depression. *Psychological Medicine, 11,* 581-599.

Campbell, E., Cope, S., & Teasdale, J. (1983). Social factors and affective disorder: An investigation of Brown and Harris's model. *British Journal of Psychiatry, 143,* 548-553.

Cooke, D. J. (1987). The significance of life events as a cause of psychological and physical disorder. In B. Cooper (Ed.), *Psychiatric epidemiology: Progress and prospects.* (pp. 67-80). London: Croom Helm.

Cooper, B., & Sylph, J. (1973). Life events and the onset of neurotic illness: an investigation in general practice. *Psychological Medicine, 3,* 421-435.

Costello, C. G. (1982). Social factors associated with depression: A retrospective community study. *Psychological Medicine, 12,* 329-339.

Dean, C., Surtees, P. G., & Sashidharan, S. D. (1983). Comparison of research diagnostic systems in an Edinburgh community sample. *British Journal of Psychiatry, 142,* 247-256.

Eales, M. J. (in press). Affective disorders in unemployed men. *Psychological Medicine.*

Epstein, S. (1983). The unconscious, the preconscious, and the self-concept. In J. Suls & A. G. Greenwald (Eds.), *Psychological perspectives on the self* (Vol. 2, pp. 219-247). Hillsdale, NJ: Erlbaum.

Fava, G. A., Munari, F., Pavan, L., & Kellner, R. (1981). Life events and depression. *Journal of Affective Disorders, 3,* 159-165.

Finlay-Jones, R. (1981). Showing that life events are a cause of depression: A review. *Australian and New Zealand Journal of Psychiatry, 15,* 229-238.

Finlay-Jones, R., & Brown, G. W. (1981). Types of stressful life event and the onset of anxiety and depressive disorders. *Psychological Medicine, 11,* 803-815.

Finlay-Jones, R., Brown, G. W., Duncan-Jones, P., Harris, T., Murphy, E., & Prudo, R. (1980). Depression and anxiety in the community. *Psychological Medicine, 10,* 445-454.

Freden, L. (1982). *Psychosocial aspects of depression: No way out?* Chichester, England: Wiley.

Giel, R., Ten Horn, G. H. M. M., Ormer, J., Schudel, W. J., & Wiersma, D. (1978). Mental illness, neuroticism and life events in a Dutch village sample: A follow-up. *Psychological Medicine, 8,* 235-243.

Gilbert, P. (1984). *Depression: From psychology to brain state.* Hillsdale, NJ: Erlbaum.

Glassner, B., Haldipur, C. V. & Dessauersmith, J. (1979). Role loss and working-class manic depression. *Journal of Nervous and Mental Disease, 167,* 530-541.

Hagnell, O., Lanke, J., Rorsman, B., & Ojesjo, L. (1982). Are we entering an age of melancholy? Depressive illness in a prospective epidemiological study over 25 years: The Lundby Study, Sweden. *Psychological Medicine, 12,* 279-289.

Hardy, T. (1920). *The Woodlanders.* London: Macmillan. (Original work published 1887)

Harris, T. O., Brown, G. W. & Bifulco, A. (1988). *Loss of mother in childhood and depression in adulthood: The differential impact of death and separation.* Unpublished manuscript.

Hirschfeld, R. M. A., Klerman, G. L., Andreasen, M. C., Clayton, P. J., & Keller, M. B. (1986). Psycho-social predictors of chronicity in depressed patients. *British Journal of Psychiatry, 148,* 648-654.

Holmes, T. H., & Rahe, R. H. (1967). The Social Readjustment Rating Scale. *Journal of Psychosomatic Research, 11,* 213-218.

Horowitz, M. J. (1976). *Stress response syndromes.* New York: Jason Aronson.

Horowitz, M. J., Krupnick, J., Kaltreider, N., Wilner, N., Leong, A., & Marmar, C. (1981). Initial psychological response to parental death. *Archives of General Psychiatry, 38,* 316-323.

Hudgens, R. W., Morrison, H. R., & Barchaa, R. G. (1967). Life events and onset of primary affective disorders. *Archives of General Psychiatry, 16,* 134-145.

Hudgens, R. W., Robins, E., & Delong, W. B. (1970). The reporting of recent stress in the lives of psychiatric patients. *British Journal of Psychiatry, 117,* 635-643.

Huxley, P. J., Goldberg, D. P., Maguire, G. P., & Kincey, V. A. (1979). The prediction of the course of minor psychiatric disorders. *British Journal of Psychiatry, 135,* 535-543.

Katschnig, H., Brandl-Nebehay, A., Fuchs-Robetin, G., Seelig, P., Eichberger, G., Strobl, R., & Sint, P. P. (1981). *Lebensverandernde Ereignisse, psychosoziale Dispositionen und depressive Verstimmungszustande.* Vienna: Psychiatrische Universitatsklinik Wien, Abteilung für Sozialpsychiatrie und Dokumentation.

Katschnig, H., Pakesch, G., & Egger-Zeidner, E. (1986). Life stress and depressive subtypes: a review of present diagnostic criteria and recent research results. In H. Katschnig (Ed.), *Life events and psychiatric disorders: Controversial issues* (pp. 201-245). Cambridge, England: Cambridge University Press.

Leventhal, H. (1980). Towards a comprehensive theory of emotion. In L. Berkowitz (Ed.), *Advances in experimental social psychology* (Vol. 13, pp. 139-206). New York: Academic Press.

Mann, A. H., Jenkins, R. & Belsey, E. (1981). The twelve-month outcome of patients with neurotic illness in general practice. *Psychological Medicine, 11,* 535-550.

Markush, R. E. (1977). Levin's attributable risk statistic for analytic studies and vital statistics. *American Journal of Epidemiology, 105,* 401-407.

Martin, C. J. (1982). *Psychosocial stress and puerperal psychiatric disorder.* Paper presented at the meeting of the Marcé Society, London.

Martin, C. J., Brown, G. W., Brockington, I. F., & Goldberg, D. (in press). Psychosocial stress and puerperal depression. *Journal of Affective Disorders.*

Mill, J. S. (1928). *Autobiography.* In J. M. Robson & J. Stillinger (Eds.), *Collected works of John Stuart Mill* (Vol. 1). Toronto: University of Toronto Press. (Original work published 1873)

Miller, P. M., & Ingham, J. G. (1983). Dimensions of experience. *Psychological Medicine, 13,* 417-429.

Miller, P. M. & Ingham, J. G. (1985). Are life events which cause each other additive in their effects? *Social Psychiatry, 20,* 31-41.

Murphy, E. (1982). Social origins of depression in old age. *British Journal of Psychiatry, 141,* 135-142.

Oatley, K., & Johnson-Laird, P. (1987). Towards a cognitive theory of emotions. *Cognition and Emotion, 1,* 29-50.

O'Connor, P., & Brown, G. W. (1984). Supportive relationships: Fact or fancy? *Journal of Social and Personal Relationships, 1,* 159-175.

Parker, G., Tennant, C., & Blignault, I. (1985). Predicting improvement in patients with non-endogenous depression. *British Journal of Psychiatry, 146,* 132-139.

Parry, G., & Shapiro, D. A. (1986). Social support and life events in working class women. *Archives of General Psychiatry, 43,* 315-323.

Paykel, E. S., Myers, J. K., Dienelt, M. N., Klerman, G. L., Lindenthal, J. J., & Pepper, M. P. (1969). Life events and depression: A controlled study. *Archives of General Psychiatry, 21,* 753-760.

Perris, H. (1984). Life events and depression: Part 2. Results in diagnostic subgroups, and in relation to the recurrence of depression. *Journal of Affective Disorders, 7,* 25-36.

Prudo, R., Brown, G. W., Harris, T., & Dowland, J. (1981). Psychiatric disorder in a rural and an urban population: 2. Sensitivity to loss. *Psychological Medicine, 11,* 601-616.

Prudo, R., Harris, T., & Brown, G. W. (1984). Psychiatric disorder in a rural and an urban population: 3. Life events, social integration and the morphology of affective disorders. *Psychological Medicine, 14,* 327-343.

Rabkin, J. G. (1982). Stress and psychiatric disorders. In L. Goldberger & S. Breznitz (Eds.), *Handbook of stress: Theoretical and clinical aspects* (pp. 567-584). London: Collier-Macmillan.

Spitzer, R. L., Endicott, J., & Robins, E. (1978). Research Diagnostic Criteria: Rationale and reliability. *Archives of General Psychiatry, 35,* 773-782.

Surtees, P. G., Dean, C., Ingham, J. G., Kreitman, N. B., Miller, P. M., & Sashidharan, S. P. (1983). Psychiatric disorder in women in an Edinburgh community: Associations with demographic factors. *British Journal of Psychiatry, 142,* 238-246.

Surtees, P. G., & Ingham, J. G. (1980). Life stress and depressive outcome: Application of a dissipation model to life events. *Social Psychiatry, 15,* 21-31.

Surtees, P. G., Miller, P. M., Ingham, J. G., Kreitman, N. B., Rennie, D., & Sashidharan, S. P. (1986). Life events and the onset of affective disorder: A longitudinal general population study. *Journal of Affective Disorders, 10,* 37-50.

Surtees, P. G., & Rennie, D. (1983). Adversity and the onset of psychiatric disorder in women. *Social Psychiatry, 18,* 37-44.

Tausig, M. (1982). Measuring life events. *Journal of Health and Social Behavior, 23,* 52-64.

Tennant, C., Bebbington, P., & Hurry, J. (1981). The short-term outcome of neurotic disorders in the community: The relation of remission to clinical factors and to 'neutralizing' life events. *British Journal of Psychiatry, 139,* 213-220.

Thoits, P. A. (1983). Dimensions of life events that influence psychological distress: An evaluation and synthesis of the literature. In B. Kaplan (Ed.), *Psychosocial stress: Trends in theory and research* (pp. 33-103). New York: Academic Press.

Tomkins, S. S. (1979). Script theory: Differential magnification of affects. In H. E. Howe, Jr., & R. A. Dienstbier (Eds.), *Nebraska Symposium on Motivation* (Vol. 26, pp. 201-236). Lincoln: University of Nebraska Press.

Vadher, A., & Ndetei, D. M. (1981). Life events and depression in a Kenyan setting. *British Journal of Psychiatry, 139,* 134-137.

Waltner-Toews, D. (1982). Nomenclature of risk assessment in 2 × 2 tables. *International Journal of Epidemiology, 11,* 411-413.

Willner, P. (1985). *Depression: A psychobiological synthesis.* New York: Wiley.

Wing, J. K., Cooper, J. E., & Sartorius, N. (1974). *The measurement and classification of psychiatric symptoms: An instruction manual for the Present State Examination and CATEGO programme.* London: Cambridge University Press.

3

Anxiety

ROBERT FINLAY-JONES

"An attitude of playfulness towards the phrases and words with
which various issues are defined often loosens up the imagination."
– Mills (1970, p. 175)

Introduction

The idea for the study described here began in 1976 with some playful
thinking of the "what if . . .?" variety. Brown and his colleagues (Brown,
Harris, & Peto, 1973; Brown, Ní Bhrolcháin, & Harris, 1975) had just
published their work showing that there was an association between the
report of a recent severely unpleasant life event and the subsequent
onset of psychiatric disorder in a sample of women drawn from the general population. It seemed that loss was the salient aspect of most of
these unpleasant events, and that the psychiatric disorder was nearly
always depression. But what if some women with anxiety states had
been interviewed? Would they report severely unpleasant life events just
as frequently? It seemed likely that they would. For example, Uhlenhuth
and Paykel (1973) had recently published a paper concluding that there
was no difference in the amount of "life stress" experienced by anxious
and depressed patients.

I began to play with the life event descriptions that Uhlenhuth and
Paykel reported in Table 3 of their paper. First, they were sorted into
serious events and less serious events, and then the serious events were
divided into losses and events that were not losses yet, but that raised
the possibility of loss in the future. Examples of events that seemed to
be serious threats of future loss were major illnesses to the subject or to
a close family member, an unwanted pregnancy, a lawsuit, a court
appearance, and the drafting of a son into the army. The parsimonious

Robert Finlay-Jones. Research and Evaluation Unit, Psychiatric Services Branch, Health
Department of Western Australia, Selby Centre, Corner Selby Street and Stubbs Terrace,
Shenton Park, Western Australia 6008, Australia.

descriptions of events that are provided in checklists of life events do not warrant the reading of such deep meanings into them, but this was only play. It seemed that the frequency of such serious threats among the 22 anxious patients described by Uhlenhuth and Paykel was about twice that among their 15 depressed patients.

The same calculation was tried with serious losses. However, it seemed that serious losses were just as frequently reported by the anxious patients as by the depressed patients. Then a pattern emerged when losses were divided into those where the patients might have cause to blame themselves (e.g., failed an examination, were laid off, were fired, were demoted, broke an engagement, had a miscarriage, discovered a spouse to be unfaithful) and those where they could not really blame themselves (e.g., death of spouse, child, or close family member). Losses for which the patients might blame themselves were three times more frequent among the depressed patients than among the anxious patients. Deaths, on the other hand, were just as common in the lives of anxious patients. Thus, despite the conclusion of Uhlenhuth and Paykel of "no difference," a wobbly kind of inductive thinking was leading from their results to the notion that specific types of life events were associated with anxiety and depression.

Of course, this research idea might have occurred much more quickly to the hypothesizer/deductivist who had read Freud. In the addendum to "Inhibitions, Symptoms and Anxiety" (1926/1959), Freud concluded that both realistic anxiety and neurotic anxiety were responses to a danger situation. A danger situation was one in which the person was threatened with the occurrence of a traumatic situation, or one in which the memory of a previous traumatic situation was revived. And a traumatic situation was one in which the person lost a loved object or lost the love of that object, and was helpless to do anything about it. Freud concluded that anxiety was the reaction to the threat of the loss of a loved object, whereas mourning was the response to the actual loss of the object. There was also the suggestion that people who had suffered a traumatic situation in childhood were more likely to respond with anxiety to a danger situation in adulthood.

Bowlby (1975) discussed at length Freud's views on anxiety. He pointed out that "Freud was probably mistaken in claiming that missing someone who is loved and longed for is the key to an understanding of anxiety. As likely as not there is no single key: fear and anxiety are aroused in situations of many kinds" (1975, p. 51). Bowlby expanded on what these situations might be in a later section of his book: "Plainly, any situation that might lead to our own injury or death is classifiable as dangerous. The same would be agreed for anything that threatens injury or death to members of our family and to close friends" (p. 185).

My "what if . . . ?" thinking and the ideas of these authors constituted the background for the hypotheses examined in this study, which
were as follows: (1) Severely unpleasant life events may provoke anxiety
states as well as depressive disorders; (2) the severely unpleasant life
events that provoke anxiety states will be characterized by the quality
of danger, whereas the severely unpleasant life events that provoke
depression will be characterized by loss.

The Sample

The hypotheses were tested among a sample of young women who consulted on certain days any one of three doctors working in a general
practice in Regent's Park, London, in 1977 and 1978. The area was chosen because I was living in it. The practice was chosen because I was a
registered patient there too, and I thought I could use that link to persuade the doctors to give me permission for the research. The women
who took part in the study happened to consult on the days on which
I could find an empty interviewing room in the office. Some reasons
can be put forward as to why this was scientifically respectable.
     The most important criterion in selecting people to test the hypoth-
esis was that anxiety states of recent onset should be reasonably common among them. A study of psychiatric patients was ruled out immediately. Most studies of treated anxiety neurosis suggested that the
patients had endured the symptoms for years before seeking psychiatric
treatment. Trying to date accurately the onset of an anxiety state, and
the timing of any life events that occurred before that onset, seemed to
place an unwarranted faith in the memory of the patient and in the
interviewing skills of the researcher. It also seemed possible that psychiatric patients might be a biased sample of all anxious people – that is,
it might contain an excess of people with no precipitating event for their
symptoms, who therefore were referred not only because they were anxious, but also because it was not clear why they were anxious. For this
reason, a sample was sought of people who had recently become anxious
but had not yet been referred.
     A random sample of the general population would have been ideal
for ruling out the possible contaminating factors associated with referral. But in the real world, as opposed to the ideal world of research
design, anxiety states of the severity found among psychiatric patients
are not very common, and the project had to be finished in the 2 years
for which research funds were available. The anxiety states and depressive disorders that are detected by the General Health Questionnaire
(GHQ; Goldberg, 1972) are about twice as common among general-
practice patients as among community residents (Finlay-Jones &

Burvill, 1978). The greatly improved chance of finding a sufficient number of people with anxiety states in a short time outweighed the risk that general-practice patients with anxiety states would be a biased sample of all people with anxiety states.

The study was restricted to women because women consult general practitioners more frequently than men; they were more likely than men to have the time to be interviewed at home; they were more likely than men to have a psychiatric disorder; and the previous studies by Brown and his colleagues (e.g., Brown *et al.*, 1975) had been carried out on women. Young women between the ages of 16 and 40 were chosen because they were more likely than older women to have anxiety of recent onset. Regent's Park was a fortunate choice because it stood in marked contrast to Camberwell (where Brown and colleagues' research had been carried out) in socioeconomic status. Regent's Park is predominantly middle-class, and Camberwell is predominantly working-class. A replication of the Camberwell results in a different setting would reinforce the generality of the results.

The Psychiatric Diagnosis

Any woman aged 16-40 years who came into the general practitioners' office was asked to complete the 30-item GHQ while she was waiting to see the doctor. When she had completed it, she was asked by the receptionist to hand it to me. On the pretext of checking to see that all the questions had been answered, I added up her score. A GHQ score of 5 or more suggests that the person is a probable case of "minor psychiatric morbidity," which largely means anxiety states and depressive disorders. The aim was to ask every woman with a score of 5 or more for permission to interview her, but to ask only one in four of the women with a score of less than 5. The assumption behind this reasoning was that of every five women attending a general practice, one would have a high score, and four would have a low score. Thus the interviewed sample should contain a ratio of probable cases to probable noncases of 1:1.

Things did not work out so neatly, however. For reasons apparently peculiar to the young women of Regent's Park, one in two general-practice attenders had a high score on the GHQ. It was enough to ask every attender for an interview without looking at her questionnaire. However, asking each woman to complete it was not a waste of time, since after completing it, a quarter of the women declined to take any further part in the research. The proportion of the refusers with a high score on the GHQ was 50%, and the proportion of the accepters with a high score was 45%. Thus the interviewed sample was probably reasonably representative of the young female general-practice attenders in that area as far as the frequency of psychiatric disorder was concerned.

Each woman who agreed was interviewed at home by a psychiatrist (myself) trained to use the Present State Examination (PSE; Wing, Cooper, & Sartorius, 1974). The version used consisted of the first 48 questions in the ninth edition, which are the questions about "nonpsychotic" symptoms.

The symptoms of each woman were presented at rating meetings held at Bedford College, University of London, and attended by at least two psychiatrists and two sociologists who had been trained in the use of the PSE in community surveys. Raters other than myself were kept unaware of the woman's social circumstances, to remove the possibility that the knowledge of the life events reported by the woman would influence the rating of her as a case of psychiatric disorder.

First, each rater made a judgment about the severity of the symptoms as a whole by comparing the woman with a series of anchoring examples. If there was any disagreement, a consensus judgment was made. Women were rated as cases, as borderline cases, or as not having a psychiatric disorder, following rules described elsewhere in this book. Second, a rating was made of the predominant syndrome. The choice was confined to anxiety, depression, a mixture of the two, and "other" (i.e., symptoms of worry or tension without evidence of an anxious or depressed mood). Finally, the women were classified as having either a disorder whose onset could be clearly dated as beginning some time in the last year ("onset disorders") or as having a disorder whose onset was more than 12 months before the interview ("chronic disorders").

All of the women diagnosed as "cases of anxiety" met the following criteria. First, their disorder had lasted at least 1 month. Second, they showed one of the following sets of symptoms:

• Free-floating anxiety experienced intensely for more than half of the month. The person had to report both the feeling of anxiety and the autonomic accompaniments, such as palpitations, sweating, choking, stomach churning, breathing difficulty, trembling, and dry mouth. (Not all of these had to be present.)

• At least five panic attacks in the month. A panic attack was defined as intolerable anxiety with autonomic symptoms, leading to some action to end it (e.g., getting off a bus, seeking help from a neighbor, taking a tablet, etc.).

• A combination of free-floating anxiety and panic attacks, where the free-floating anxiety was present at least some of the time, and one to four panic attacks had been experienced in the month.

• Situational anxiety (including anxiety on meeting people), in which the person showed evidence of (1) avoiding the situation, and (2) marked generalization from the feared situation, so that the person had not left the house or had gone out only if accompanied.

These criteria meant that women diagnosed as "cases of anxiety" in 1977-1978 would meet *Diagnostic and Statistical Manual of Mental Disorders*, third edition (DSM-III) criteria for either generalized anxiety disorder, panic disorder, agoraphobia, or social phobia. The DSM-III criteria had not been published at the time of the study.

For the diagnosis of "case of depression," a person had to meet the criteria of depressed mood, lasting at least 1 month, with 4 or more of the following 10 symptoms: hopelessness, suicidal ideas or actions, weight loss, early-morning waking, delayed sleep, poor concentration, neglect due to brooding, loss of interest, self-depreciation, or lack of energy. The women who were diagnosed as both "cases of anxiety" *and* "cases of depression" fulfilled both sets of criteria. The diagnoses produced by using these criteria match commonly held conceptions of who is a case in terms of severity and type of syndrome (Finlay-Jones *et al.*, 1980).

The Rating of Life Events

During each interview, the presence of a psychiatric disorder and the date of its onset was first established. The time period of interest for inquiring about life events was then set as the 12 months before the onset for women whose symptoms had a clear onset in the last year. For women with chronic symptoms or no symptoms at all, the period of interest was defined as the 12 months before the interview. This meant that when cases and noncases were compared for their experience of life events, data for the same length of time were available for both groups.

Life events were recorded using the Bedford College Life Events and Difficulties Schedule (LEDS). Accurate dating of each event was emphasized. Care was taken to keep events that occurred before and after the onset of psychiatric symptoms separate. A team of raters was asked to make independent judgments about three aspects of each event, without any knowledge of whether the woman had any psychiatric symptoms. The three judgments were the focus of the event, the degree of short-term threat, and the degree of long-term threat (see Chapter 1). These ratings allowed the events to be classed as "severe" or not.

The next step was to ask a team of raters to study each event already rated as "severe" and to rate (1) the degree of severity of loss, and (2) the degree of severity or future danger associated with each event.

Loss

In rating the degree of loss, raters were asked to look for evidence of four general categories of loss:

1. The loss by death or by separation of a valued person.
2. The loss of the person's own physical health.
3. The loss of a job, career opportunities, or material possessions.
4. The loss of a cherished idea (e.g., the discovery of a husband's infidelity could be rated under the appropriate circumstances as the loss of the notion of a happy marriage.

We recognized the difficulty of saying that one type of loss was greater than another. However, it was expected that the loss of a valued person would in general be rated higher than the loss of a material possession. It was also agreed that a loss of physical health would be rated entirely on the objective evidence of disability; a permanent disability (e.g., an amputated leg) would be rated higher than a reversible disability (e.g., a broken leg).

Raters were encouraged to take into account all of the salient circumstances that surrounded each event before making a rating. For example, there was no fixed rating of the degree of loss when a woman's relationship with a man was broken. On the contrary, the rating depended upon the salient objective circumstances surrounding the event. It was agreed to rate this event higher if the two had been engaged or living together, or if she had been financially dependent upon him, or if it was his idea to part and not hers. On the other hand, the event might be rated lower on the degree-of-loss scale if they had not been going out together for very long, if they had been only seeing each other infrequently, if the breakup was anticipated well in advance, if the woman already had another boyfriend, or if the decision to break up was mutual. The only detail that was not taken into account was the woman's emotional reaction to the event, for reasons already discussed in Chapter 1 in connection with the minimization of possible bias.

"Severe losses" were severe events that had been given a rating of 1 or 2 on a 4-point scale of loss. Examples of severely unpleasant events that were rated as severe losses included the following:

• A divorced woman in her 30s worked as a professional dancer. After an operation to remove cartilage in her knee, the surgeon told her that the damage was more extensive than he expected, and that she would be unable to dance again.

• The father of a married woman in her 30s died in a hospital 2 weeks after being admitted and diagnosed as having advanced cancer. She had seen him weekly before his admission and visited him frequently in the hospital.

- A 30-year-old single architect was dismissed from her job. The reason given was the prevailing slump in the building industry. However, she was the only architect in the office who was dismissed, and there had been previous friction between her and her employer.
- A married woman in her 20s was pregnant for the first time. After an uneventful pregnancy, the baby was born dead.
- A single woman in her 20s had a boyfriend for 18 months. They had a sexual relationship, she confided in him, and she saw him at least three times a week. He was then transferred in his employment to a distant city, so that seeing each other regularly became impossible.

Danger

In the rating of danger, the raters were asked to approach each event by asking themselves the following questions:

1. Does the present event raise the possibility of specific unpleasant crises happening to the woman in the future?
2. Is there some probability of at least one of them happening? (The closer this probability was to 50%, the more likely was the event to be rated as dangerous. That is, the future crisis should be neither improbable nor inevitable.)
3. How unpleasant will be the effect of this future crisis?

Thus, the severity of danger was defined as the degree of unpleasantness of a specific future crisis which might occur as a result of the event.

The raters were given the example of a woman who heard that her father had been diagnosed as having cancer. The most salient future crisis stemming from the news would be that of her father's possible death. The severity of danger would depend upon the rater's judgment of how upsetting the death of her father would be for the woman. It was the specific crisis of his death that was to be considered, not the associated difficulties that might stem from the news of his cancer (e.g., the need for the woman to nurse her father during his illness). We ruled out rating such consequences because nearly every type of unpleasant event probably involves some kind of associated difficulty stretching into the future.

Although the future crisis stemming from the severe event had to have some probability of occurring for the rating of danger to be made, this crisis did not have to be inevitable. For instance, if the woman in the example given to the raters had been informed that her father was in a coma, that he had terminal cancer, and that he was unlikely to live through the night, then danger would not be rated, since it would be misleading to see his death as only a possible rather than an inevitable outcome of such circumstances.

"Severe dangers" were defined as severe events that were rated as 1 or 2 on a 4-point scale of danger. Examples of severely unpleasant events that were rated as severe dangers included the following:

• A 40-year-old woman discovered a breast lump, which was confirmed by her general practitioner and a surgeon. The surgeon told her she must have a biopsy, and that this might lead to a mastectomy if she was found to have breast cancer.

• A young woman who lived at home with her parents was told after the admission of her father to a hospital for tests that he had cancer. The physician was optimistic that he would respond to the treatment, but his general practitioner told him that it would be wise for him to get his affairs in order.

• A young woman became pregnant despite using contraception. The boyfriend's family had opposed their earlier attempt to become engaged. His elderly parents were relying on him to support them financially, and opposed any suggestion of marriage.

• A woman in her 20s began an affair with a married man who taught at the college where she was a student.

• A 30-year-old woman and her *de facto* husband had been renting a cheap apartment for 3 years. They were both unemployed and could not afford to move to a better apartment. Their landlady, who was noted for her odd behavior, had their electricity cut off for no reason. She also threatened to cut off the telephone, served an eviction order on them, and wrote unpleasant letters to them.

Loss and Danger Together

Ratings of severe loss and severe danger were not mutually exclusive. Some events, such as these examples, were rated highly on both loss and danger:

• A woman in her 20s, married to a laborer, with no children, was told by the police that her husband, who had left the house the previous night because he wanted "to clear his mind," had committed suicide. The loss was obvious. The danger was that of a future financial crisis for her, since she had been financially dependent upon her husband.

• A single woman in her 30s resigned her job as a nurse after another attack of multiple sclerosis. The other members of the nursing staff had been commenting upon how impaired she was. The loss of her job acted as a reminder of her deterioration and hence that her life was endangered.

• A married woman in her 30s, with no children, suffered her second miscarriage. Thus she had lost another baby, and there was also now an increased risk that she might never have a successful pregnancy.

• A divorced woman in her 30s was living with a man to whom she was engaged. After some weeks of unexplained disappearances, he came home, told her the engagement was off, and gave her an ultimatum to get out of the house. He employed her as a secretary at the office that he managed. She had lost him and was likely to lose her job in the future.

Some life events that had been initially rated as "severe" in the global sense were not rated as involving either severe loss or severe danger. For example, a 29-year-old woman underwent a laparoscopy operation to search for the cause of her abdominal pain. The event was rated as severe because of the subsequent development of a peritoneal abscess, which had to be drained. Although she was very sick at the end of the first week (the point in any event at which a rating of long-term threat was made), the doctors told her she could expect to be completely recovered in 6 weeks or so and would have no reason to expect any further complications, so the situation did not deserve more than minor ratings on loss and danger.

Reliability of Loss and Danger Ratings

Five raters working independently and using the two 4-point scales described above rated 138 severely unpleasant life events for the degree of severe loss and severe danger involved. The coefficient of agreement known as "weighted kappa" varied from .83 to .92 for different pairs of raters when rating loss; it ranged from .70 to .87 for pairs of raters when rating danger. The correlation between the loss and the danger ratings was calculated. The value of Spearman's rank-order correlation coefficient was -.60, and the value of Kendall's tau was -.52. Both of these were significant negative correlations ($p <$ .001), which was taken as evidence that the two scales were measuring different qualities.

Results

Subject Characteristics

The number of female general-practice attenders who were approached for an interview was 220, and 164 (75%) agreed to be interviewed. The average age of the women was 28 years. Half were single, one-third were married, and the rest were separated, divorced, or widowed. The fathers of two-thirds of the women had jobs placed in the top two classes of a seven-class occupational scale (Goldthorpe & Hope, 1974; Goldthorpe & Llewellyn, 1977). In short, these women were relatively young, unattached, and affluent.

Diagnoses

Of the 164 women, 13 (8%) were diagnosed as cases of anxiety of recent onset; 15 (9%) met the criteria for caseness of both anxiety and depression and were called "mixed cases"; and 17 (10%) were diagnosed as cases of depression of recent onset. This left 73% who were either chronic cases, borderline cases of recent onset, or normal.

The 45 cases of recent onset met other criteria for both severity and type of syndrome. For example, the PSE protocols were analyzed using the CATEGO and Index of Definition computer programs (Wing, 1976). According to the Index of Definition, 37 of the cases had "definite" disorders and 8 had "threshold" disorders. CATEGO placed 15 of the 17 cases of depression in a "depression" class. The other 2 cases of depression, one of whom had a clinical rating of borderline anxiety, were placed in a CATEGO "anxiety" class. Of the 13 cases of anxiety, 12 were classed as anxiety by CATEGO, and the 13th, who also had a clinical rating of chronic borderline depression, was classed as depression. CATEGO as presently used does not produce a classification of a mixed disorder, and depression symptoms generally take precedence over anxiety symptoms. Thus 14 of the 15 cases of mixed anxiety and depression were placed in a depression class, and the 15th was placed in an anxiety class.

The DSM-III criteria, which also treat anxiety and depression disorders as mutually exclusive and also give precedence to depression symptoms when the two occur together, produced results similar to those obtained with CATEGO. If the 13 cases of anxiety and the 15 mixed cases were combined and the depression symptoms of the mixed cases were ignored, then the DSM-III diagnoses were as follows: 1 case of agoraphobia, 7 cases of panic disorder, and 20 cases of generalized anxiety disorder. (The seven cases of panic disorder also met DSM-III criteria for generalized anxiety disorder, but DSM-III treats them as mutually exclusive, with panic disorder taking precedence.) However, if the symptoms of depression of the 15 mixed cases were not ignored, then these cases would have met the DSM-III criteria for major depressive disorder, the category into which the 17 cases of pure depression would have also fallen.

Life Events and Diagnoses

In a preliminary analysis, it was shown that although significant differences in the reporting of life events between cases and noncases were evident for events occurring in the year before onset/interview, most of the excess of events among cases occurred in the 3 months before onset/interview. For this reason, 3 months was taken as the period of interest.

Severely unpleasant life events were associated with the onset of anxiety, depressive, and mixed disorders (Table 3.1). On the other hand, severe dangers were associated only with the onset of anxiety disorders

TABLE 3.1. Percentage of women reporting at least one life event in the 3 months before onset, by diagnosis and type of event

Diagnosis	Percentage with severe event	Percentage with severe danger	Percentage with severe loss
Case of anxiety			
Yes	69 (9/13) *	62 (8/13) **	8 (1/13) ***
No	28 (43/151)	13 (20/151)	14 (21/151)
Mixed case			
Yes	60 (9/15) †	47 (7/15) ††	47 (7/15) †††
No	29 (43/149)	14 (21/149)	10 (15/149)
Case of depression			
Yes	76 (13/17) ∫	24 (4/17) ∬	65 (11/17) ∭
No	26 (39/147)	16 (24/147)	7 (11/147)
All cases			
Yes	69 (31/45) §	42 (19/45) §§	42 (19/45) §§§
No	18 (21/119)	8 (9/119)	3 (3/119)

Note. n's for the percentages are in parentheses.

* $\chi^2 = 9.2$, $p = .002$; ** $\chi^2 = 19.7$, $p = .0001$; *** $\chi^2 = 0.39$, n.s.

† $\chi^2 = 6.1$, $p = .014$; †† $\chi^2 = 10.2$, $p = .001$; ††† $\chi^2 = 15.7$, $p = .0001$.

∫ $\chi^2 = 17.6$, $p < .0001$; ∬ $\chi^2 = 0.56$, n.s.; ∭ $\chi^2 = 43.0$, $p < .0001$.

§ $\chi^2 = 39.6$, $p < .0001$; §§ $\chi^2 = 27.7$, $p < .0001$; §§§ $\chi^2 = 44.3$, $p < .0001$.

(pure or mixed), and severe losses were associated only with the onset of depressive disorders (pure or mixed) (Table 3.1).

Vulnerability Factors

Each woman had been asked for a number of details about her childhood (including a history of separation from her parents for various reasons) and other demographic, social, and personal characteristics.

The size of the sample was not large enough to confirm Brown and Harris's (1978) finding about the vulnerability to severe events of women who had lost their mothers in childhood. For example, there were only three women who were younger than 11 years of age when their mothers died.

There was one important negative finding. The degree of intimacy of the relationship that a woman enjoyed with her husband was not associated with the onset of anxiety, but was associated with the onset of depression (Table 3.2). An intimate, confiding relationship was found to protect women against depression after a loss, but not to be associated with depression in the absence of a loss; thereby lack of an intimate confidant acted as a typical vulnerability factor in the sense defined by the Bedford College team. This finding is not presented in more detail here, since the main concern in this chapter is with anxiety.

Some types of childhood trauma, such as the death of a parent or the temporary separation from a parent because of illness, were found to be unrelated to the onset of anxiety in adulthood. However, there was a significant association between the onset of pure anxiety (not mixed

TABLE 3.2. Percentage of women with no intimate confidant, by diagnosis

Diagnosis	Percentage with no intimate confidant
Case of anxiety	
Yes	69 (9/13) *
No	59 (89/151)
Mixed case	
Yes	80 (12/15) **
No	58 (86/149)
Case of depression	
Yes	88 (15/17) ***
No	56 (83/147)

Note. n's for the percentages are in parentheses.

* $\chi^2 = 0.53$, n.s.; ** $\chi^2 = 2.8$, n.s.; *** $\chi^2 = 6.4$, $p = .01$.

cases, and not pure depression) and a history of parental divorce during a woman's childhood – that is, before she reached the age of 11 years (Table 3.3). The association between anxiety and parental divorce in childhood was examined further. The 19 women who were children when their parents were divorced were divided into the 8 women who never saw their fathers again after the divorce, and the 11 women who continued to see something of their fathers. Of the 8 women in the former group, 3 were cases of anxiety, compared to 2 of the 11 women in the latter group. These numbers are too small to justify drawing firm conclusions, but the suggestion that the risk of anxiety in adulthood may be further increased when the parental divorce is complicated by the loss of the father in childhood is an interesting one.

The relationship among parental divorce in childhood, a recent severely dangerous life event, and the onset of anxiety was analyzed. Parental divorce was significantly associated with the onset of anxiety among women who had experienced a recent severe danger, but not among women who had not experienced such a life event (Table 3.4). Thus parental divorce acted as a vulnerability factor in the sense used by the Bedford College team. It increased the risk of the onset of an anxiety disorder after exposure to a severely dangerous life event, but was not significantly associated with anxiety in the absence of such a life event.

Discussion

This study was carried out on a relatively small sample of young and middle-class female general-practice attenders living in Regent's Park,

TABLE 3.3. Percentage of women who reported the divorce of their parents in early childhood, by diagnosis

Diagnosis	Percentage with early parental divorce
Case of anxiety	
Yes	38 (5/13) *
No	9 (14/151)
Mixed case	
Yes	13 (2/15) **
No	11 (17/149)
Case of depression	
Yes	6 (1/17) ***
No	12 (18/147)

Note. n's for the percentages are in parentheses.

* $\chi^2 = 9.96$, $p = .0016$; ** $\chi^2 = 0.05$, n.s.; *** $\chi^2 = 0.60$, n.s.

TABLE 3.4. Percentage of women diagnosed as cases of recent-onset anxiety, by exposure to a recent severely dangerous life event and by history of parental divorce in childhood

	Percentage with recent-onset anxiety		
	Childhood parental divorce	No childhood parental divorce	Total
Recent severely dangerous event	80 (4/5) *	17 (4/23)	29 (8/28)
No dangerous event	7 (1/14) **	3 (4/122)	4 (5/136)

Note. n's for the percentages are in parentheses.
* 80% vs. 17%: $\chi^2 = 7.9$, $df = 1$, $p = .005$; ** 7% vs. 3%: not significant.

London, in the late 1970s. In this sample, there was a significant association between events rated blindly as severe losses and the onset of depression, and between events rated blindly as severe dangers and the onset of anxiety. Furthermore, women diagnosed as both cases of anxiety and cases of depression were more likely to report both types of events. It has been argued elsewhere that these results constitute evidence for a causal link between a specific type of unpleasant life event and a specific type of psychiatric disorder (Finlay-Jones, 1981; Finlay-Jones & Brown, 1981). The findings support the theoretical ideas about the origin of depression and anxiety that have been put forward by Freud and Bowlby.

The status of mixed anxiety and depression has not been clarified by this study. On the one hand, when the life event findings alone were considered, it seemed plausible to regard women with mixed anxiety and depression as women with two symptomatically distinct disorders that coexisted because a severe danger and a severe loss occurred close together (or, in some instances, because one event was both a severe danger and a severe loss). On the other hand, there was no evidence that a history of parental divorce was related to the onset of mixed cases, although it was related to the onset of anxiety alone. Here it seemed that the mixed cases resembled cases of pure depression, supporting the argument that anxiety-depression cases can be classified as a subgroup of all depressed patients (Paykel, 1971). The mixed cases stood midway between the cases of anxiety and the cases of depression as far as their association with the absence of an intimate, confiding relationship was concerned. It seems that a further investigation of the recent and past life events experienced by a larger sample of mixed cases might help to answer some interesting questions about the classification of depression.

An association between a history in childhood of parental divorce and the onset in adulthood of an anxiety disorder does not seem to have been reported previously. Tennant, Hurry, and Bebbington (1982) found no association between a history of "marital discord" between the parents when the woman was a child and the later onset of an "anxiety syndrome" when the woman was an adult. However, the authors emphasized that many of those with an anxiety syndrome would have insufficient symptoms to be considered "cases" of the severity typical of those in the present study. They might have found an association if they had used a slightly higher threshold to define their anxiety syndrome, such as the definition of a "case of anxiety" that was used here.

Parker (1981) found that anxiety neurotics, when compared to a group of controls, rated their parents as significantly less caring and more overprotective. Three other studies of anxiety in nonclinical groups supported these findings (Parker, 1983). These results may not throw any light on the present ones, since there was no suggestion that the parents of Parker's subjects had been divorced. However, it is possible that parental divorce, particularly when the father has little to do with the children subsequently, may provoke or intensify a style of rearing children characterized by overprotection, perhaps by a mother who lacks the time or energy as a result of her single-parent status to show those behaviors that the children will later report as "caring." According to Parker, a possible explanation of the link between overprotection and lack of care in childhood and subsequent anxiety in adulthood is that this style of parenting interferes with the balance between attachment and exploratory behaviors, promoting what Bowlby (1975) called "anxious attachment."

One study of a group of social phobics, agoraphobics, and height phobics investigated the patients' perceptions of how their parents reared them (Arrindell, Emmelkamp, Monsma, & Brilman, 1983). It found that, compared with the controls, social phobics and height phobics reported both parents not only as lacking in emotional warmth, but also as having been rejecting and overprotective. Agoraphobics reported both parents as having lacked emotional warmth, but only their mothers as being rejecting, and neither fathers nor mothers as being particularly overprotective. It might be useful to pursue the connection between such perceptions and more readily confirmed facts, such as parental death, illness, or divorce during a person's childhood. If parents who divorce (particularly the parent who subsequently has little to do with the child) are perceived as lacking in warmth and as rejecting and overprotective, then, according to the present results, the findings of Arrindell et al. would seem to apply not only to phobics, but also to women with generalized anxiety disorder and panic disorder (such as those described here).

In summary, this study has shown that in a small sample of London women, anxiety disorders could be distinguished from depressive disorders not only by the quality of the life events that provoked them, but also by the factors that made the women vulnerable to the effects of these provoking agents. Women without an intimate confidant were more likely to become depressed after a loss, whereas the lack of an intimate relationship was not associated with the onset of anxiety disorders. Women who as children experienced the breakup of their parents' marriage were more prone to anxiety disorders after a danger event, but parental divorce was unrelated to the risk of becoming depressed.

References

Arindell, W. A., Emmelkamp, P. M. G., Monsma, A., & Brilman, E. (1983). The role of perceived parental rearing practices in the aetiology of phobic disorders: A controlled study. *British Journal of Psychiatry, 143,* 183-187.

Bowlby, J. (1975). *Attachment and loss: Vol. 2. Separation: Anxiety and anger.* Harmondsworth, England: Penguin Books.

Brown, G. W., & Harris, T. O., (1978). *Social origins of depression: A study of psychiatric disorder in women.* London: Tavistock.

Brown, G. W., Harris, T. O., & Peto, J. (1973). Life events and psychiatric disorders: Part 2. Nature of the causal link. *Psychological Medicine, 3,* 159-176.

Brown, G. W., Ní Bhrolcháin, M., & Harris, T. O. (1975). Social class and psychiatric disturbance among women in an urban population. *Sociology, 9,* 225-254.

Finlay-Jones, R. A. (1981). Showing that life events are a cause of depression: A review. *Australian and New Zealand Journal of Psychiatry, 15,* 229-238.

Finlay-Jones, R. A., & Brown, G. W. (1981). Types of stressful life event and the onset of anxiety and depressive disorders. *Psychological Medicine, 11,* 803-815.

Finlay-Jones, R. A., Brown, G. W., Duncan-Jones, P., Harris, T. O., Murphy, E., & Prudo, R. (1980). Depression and anxiety in the community: Replicating the diagnosis of a case *Psychological Medicine, 10,* 445-454.

Finlay-Jones, R. A., & Burvill, P. W. (1978). Contrasting demographic patterns of minor psychiatric morbidity in general practice and the community. *Psychological Medicine,8,* 455-466.

Freud, S. (1959). Inhibitions, symptoms and anxiety. In J. Strachey (Ed. and Trans.), *The standard edition of the complete psychological works of Sigmund Freud* (Vol. 20, pp. 75-175). London: Hogarth Press. (Original work published 1926)

Goldberg, D. P. (1972). *The detection of psychiatric illness by questionnaire* (Maudsley Monograph No. 21). London: Oxford University Press.

Goldthorpe, J. H., & Hope, K. (1974). *The social grading of occupations: A new approach and scale.* Oxford: Clarendon Press.

Goldthorpe, J. H., & Llewellyn, C. (1977). Class mobility in modern Britain: Three theses examined. *Sociology, 11,* 257-287.

Mills, C. W. (1970). *The sociological imagination.* Harmondsworth, England: Penguin Books.

Parker, G. (1981). Parental representations of patients with an anxiety neurosis. *Acta Psychiatrica Scandinavica, 63,* 33-36.

Parker, G. (1983). *Parental overprotection: A risk factor in psychosocial development.* New York: Grune & Stratton.

Paykel, E. S. (1971). Classification of depressed patients. A cluster analysis derived groupings. *British Journal of Psychiatry, 118,* 275-288.

Tennant, C., Hurry, J., & Bebbington, P. (1982). The relation of childhood separation experiences to adult depressive and anxiety states. *British Journal of Psychiatry, 141,* 475-482.

Uhlenhuth, E. H., & Paykel, E. S. (1973). Symptom configuration and life events. *Archives of General Psychiatry, 28,* 744-748.

Wing, J. K. (1976). A technique for studying psychiatric morbidity in in-patient and out-patient series and in general population samples. *Psychological Medicine, 6,* 665-671.

Wing, J. K., Cooper, J. E., & Sartorius, N. (1974). *The measurement and classification of psychiatric symptoms.* Cambridge, England: Cambridge University Press.

4

Schizophrenia

RICHARD DAY

Introduction

Over the past 25 years, investigators with a psychosocial bent have given considerable attention to the subject of recent stressful life events and the role they play in a number of psychiatric conditions. The findings that have emerged from this domain of inquiry have been most informative and helpful in certain areas, such as depression; in other areas, they have remained largely uncertain and speculative at best. This chapter focuses on what is generally taken to be one of the more speculative areas of life events research – that is, the extent to which research has documented the existence of a *causal* relationship between the occurrence of recent stressful life events and the onset of the active phase of schizophrenic disorders (see American Psychiatric Association, 1980, p. 185, for a definition of "active phase"). Since the answer to this question is neither obvious nor straightforward, it has been necessary to devote a substantial portion of this chapter to the problem of establishing practical criteria for assessing putative causal associations, in the absence of definitive research findings.

Recent Studies

This chapter selectively reviews the literature on life events and schizophrenia. Readers seeking further in-depth discussion of the studies cited here should take a look at three general review articles (Rabkin, 1980; Day, 1981; Dohrenwend & Egri, 1981; see also Day, 1986). These articles are comprehensive in scope and, except for the small number of studies published over the past 5 years, generally reflect the current state

Richard Day. Department of Biostatistics, Graduate School of Public Health, University of Pittsburgh, Pittsburgh, PA 15213 USA.

of the field. Two studies completed subsequent to these publications are briefly reviewed here. Both are cross-cultural studies – one from the World Health Organization (WHO) (Day *et al.*, 1987) and the other from Saudi Arabia (Al Khani, Bebbington, Watson, & House, 1986) – and both use the same modified version of the life events instrument originally developed by Brown and Birley (1968).

The WHO report (Day *et al.*, 1987) summarizes the findings from a series of 386 acutely ill patients examined as part of a cross-national study of life events and schizophrenia. The data for this study were collected from nine separate catchment areas that varied widely with regard to patterns of socioeconomic and cultural organization. Five of these catchment areas (Aarhus, Denmark; Honolulu, Hawaii, USA; Nagasaki, Japan; Prague, Czechoslovakia; and Rochester, New York, USA) were located in developed countries, and four (Agra, India; Cali, Colombia; Chandigarh, India; and Ibadan, Nigeria) were located in developing countries.

The patients for the WHO research were drawn from a larger first contact incidence series. In order to be eligible for inclusion in the life events study, the patients had to have (1) a diagnosis according to *International Classification of Diseases*, ninth edition (ICD-9) criteria of schizophrenia, paranoid state, or schizophreniform reactive psychosis; (2) an onset of florid symptoms occurring within 6 months of first contact with a psychiatric helping agency; and (3) an acute illness onset datable to within 1 week.

The WHO life events interview covered the 3-month period immediately preceding the onset of florid psychotic symptomatology. In addition to the identification of relevant life events, the field interviewers were required to calculate the number of weeks by which an event preceded the onset of florid symptomatology, and to classify each occurrence in terms of its common-sense impact and its relationship to the patient's illness. It should be noted that the WHO schedule was modeled after an early unpublished version of what has become the Life Events and Difficulties Schedule (LEDS), and the WHO instrument should be viewed as an offshoot of the early Bedford College instrument designed with problems of cross-cultural research in mind.

One of the primary objectives of the WHO study was to test the findings reported by Brown and Birley (1968) concerning an association between stressful life events and the onset of acute attacks of schizophrenia. Brown and Birley studied a series of 50 schizophrenic patients, comparing their life events reports with the information from a sample of 325 subjects from the general population. It was found that the proportion of individuals reporting life events was similar among the patients and the general-population subjects until the final 3-week period before onset. During the final 3-week period, there was a statistically significant and threefold increase in the number of patients reporting life events. Brown and Birley concluded that "environmental factors can precipitate schizophrenic attacks and such events tend to cluster in the three weeks before onset" (1968, p. 211).

Unfortunately, the collection of a series of matched comparison subjects from the general population was beyond the capacities of the WHO investigators. Although this narrowed the range of questions that could be addressed using the WHO data, it was possible to determine whether the *general pattern* of events observed by Brown and Birley was replicated.

Given the cultural diversity and the range of socioeconomic conditions characteristic of the centers taking part in the study, the overall rates of events reported showed a remarkable similarity across six of the nine patient series – Aarhus, Cali, Honolulu, Nagasaki, Prague, and Rochester. Besides standing in agreement with one another, the overall rates for these six centers were similar to the rates from Brown and Birley's patient series and to the rates reported in other life events studies of schizophrenic patients (see Day, 1981, p. 113).

In the case of the two Indian centers (Agra and Chandigarh), it could not be determined on the basis of the available evidence whether the observed differences in overall event rates were artifactual in nature or included true cross-cultural variations. In the Nigerian center (Ibadan), the situation was more clear-cut. Difficulties resulting primarily from cultural expectancies made the consistency and validity of the data highly problematic.

Despite these problems, the data collected from eight of the nine WHO centers were considered adequate, and a significant increase was found in the number of patients experiencing life events during the 2- to 3-week period preceding the appearance of positive psychotic symptoms in all six of the WHO centers analyzed statistically (see Tables 4.1 and 4.2). In five of these centers, this conclusion held true for the category of events determined to be "independent" of the patient's illness, as well as for the broader category of "all events." In a single case (Nagasaki), the increase in the number of patients reporting independent life events in the 2 to 3 weeks prior to onset was less marked than in the other centers. This was despite the fact that the overall pattern of the Japanese data was strongly in the predicted direction. Due to the small number of patients reporting an acute illness onset, statistical analyses were not carried out for the Honolulu and Rochester centers. However, the data from both of these centers showed strong trends in the predicted direction. Therefore, eight of the nine centers participating in the WHO study reported data that either confirmed the main hypothesis

TABLE 4.1. Percentage of patients in different study populations with at least one life event in the four 3-week periods preceding onset: All field research centers (FRCs)

FRC/event category	Percentage patients with life event in period:				Significance level	Remarks
	Weeks 1-2	Weeks 4-6	Weeks 7-9	Weeks 10-12		
1. Aarhus (n =31)						
Independent events	39	23	13	23	p =.03	
All events	55	29	26	29	p =.008	
2. Honolulu (n =13)						
Independent events	23	15	0	8		Due to small size of patient series, log-
All events	69	15	0	8		linear analysis was not carried out
3. Nagasaki (n =29)						
Independent events	24	14	10	10	p =.10	
All events	41	31	14	14	p =.02	
4. Prague (n =48)						
Independent events	38	15	21	17	p =.004	
All events	48	21	25	25	p =.002	
5. Rochester (n =15)						
Independent events	40	27	13	20		Due to small size of patient series, log-
All events	73	47	27	27		linear analysis was not carried out
6. Camberwell (n =50)						
Independent events	46	14	8	14	p =.0001	"Bunching" in weeks 10-12 significant
All events	60	20	18	30	p =.0001	at 5% level
7. Agra (n =48)						
Independent events	29	6	9	4	p =.0002	
All events	35	15	10	6	p =.0001	
8. Chandigarh (n =67)						
Independent events	42	21	10	9	p =.0001	Rate for weeks 4-6 significantly higher
All events	48	27	12	10	p =.0001	than for weeks 7-12
9. Cali (n =51)						
Independent events	53	14	14	16	p =.0001	
All events	65	22	18	22	p =.0001	
10. Ibadan (n =48)						
Independent events	13	5	4	6		
All events	13	11	6	7		

Note. From "Stressful Life Events Preceding the Acute Onset of Schizophrenia: A Cross-National Study from the World Health Organization" by R. Day, J. Nielsen, A. Korten, G. Ernberg, K.C. Dube, J. Gebhart, A. Jablensky, C. Leon, A. Marsella, M. Olatawura, N. Sartorius, E. Strömgren, R. Takahashi, N. Wig, and L.C. Wynne, 1987, *Culture, Medicine and Psychiatry, 11*, 1-123. Copyright 1987 by D. Reidel Publishing Company. Reprinted by permission of Kluwer Academic Publishers.

TABLE 4.2. Percentage of patients in different study populations with at least one life event in the four 2-week periods preceding onset: All FRCs

FRC/event category	Percentage patients with life event in period:						Significance level	Remarks
	Weeks 1-2	Weeks 3-4	Weeks 5-6	Weeks 7-8	Weeks 9-10	Weeks 11-12		
1. Aarhus ($n=31$)								
Independent events	35	23	16	10	16	13	$p=.01$	
All events	55	29	23	13	29	16	$p=.0001$	
2. Honolulu ($n=13$)								
Independent events	23	0	15	0	0	8		Due to small size of patient series, log-linear analysis was not carried out
All events	62	8	15	0	0	8		
3. Nagasaki ($n=29$)								
Independent events	17	10	10	7	7	7	$p=.14$	
All events	31	24	21	10	7	10	$p=.016$	
4. Prague ($n=48$)								
Independent events	38	10	8	15	12	13	$p=.0001$	
All events	46	13	15	21	15	21	$p=.0001$	
5. Rochester ($n=15$)								
Independent events	40	20	7	0	20	13		Due to small size of patient series, log-linear analysis was not carried out
All events	73	27	27	20	27	13		
6. Camberwell ($n=50$)								
Independent events	38	14	8	6	10	12	$p=.0001$	
All events	54	18	14	12	14	28	$p=.0001$	
7. Agra ($n=48$)								
Independent events	23	8	2	8	2	4	$p=.0001$	
All events	27	17	6	8	2	6	$p=.0001$	
8. Chandigarh ($n=67$)								
Independent events	36	16	15	10	6	3	$p=.0001$	
All events	40	19	19	12	7	3	$p=.0001$	
9. Cali ($n=51$)								
Independent events	45	18	10	6	14	10	$p=.0001$	
All events	59	21	14	10	16	14	$p=.0001$	
10. Ibadan ($n=48$)								
Independent events	11	5	4	3	3	6		
All events	12	7	8	4	6	7		

Note. From "Stressful Life Events Preceding the Acute Onset of Schizophrenia: A Cross-National Study from the World Health Organization" by R. Day *et al*, 1987, *Culture, Medicine and Psychiatry, 11*, 1-123. Copyright 1987 by D. Reidel Publishing Company. Reprinted by permission of Kluwer Academic Publishers.

or showed a strong trend in the direction predicted on the basis of the early research in London.

The study by Al Khani *et al.* (1986) examined the life events reported by a series of 48 schizophrenic patients and 62 general-population subjects, all of whom resided in the Njad region of Saudi Arabia. This study also had as its objective to test the findings reported by Brown and Birley. In contrast to the WHO research, where patients were used as their own controls, this study implemented a true case-control design. The clinical subjects included those with previous episodes of illness, as well as first-episode patients. However, the two studies were otherwise quite similar in design, instruments, and measures.

The authors examined subgroups of patients in detailed fashion, but only the data from first-episode acute schizophrenic patients are dealt with here. Data analysis was carried out in two steps. First, the investigators examined the homogeneity of the data across the four 3-week periods preceding the onset of positive psychotic symptoms. A statistic termed "specific inhomogeneity" was used to test the hypothesis that a significant difference would exist in the number of patients reporting life events in the final 3-week period before the appearance of positive psychotic symptoms, as compared to similar periods further removed from illness onset. A similar statistical procedure was applied in the WHO study, the results from which are reported in Tables 4.1 and 4.2. The second step in the analysis went beyond what could be accomplished in the WHO study. This step, involved the comparison of the life events data collected from the patients and the general-population subjects.

Even though the results from the initial phase of data analysis were weaker than the findings in the WHO research, a similar patterning of life events was observed. The first-episode patients ($n = 21$) showed a marked increase ($\chi^2 = 3.76$, $p = .053$) in the number of patients reporting life events in the final 3-week period preceding the onset of florid symptomatology. Moreover, the increase in reported events in the final 3-week period was clearly absent among the general-population subjects. Despite these promising initial findings, the data examined in the second phase of the analysis failed to permit the investigators to reject the global null hypothesis that the pattern of reported life events was similar among the first-episode patients and the general population. A trend in the expected direction was noted, but the null hypothesis could be rejected for only the small subgroup of married females.

Al Khani *et al.* (1986) consider three explanations that may account for the negative findings emerging from this second phase of analysis: (1) Life events do not provoke the onset of positive psychotic symptoms; (2) an association does exist, but it is comparatively weak (a hypothesis suggesting that the current study lacked the power required to reject the null hypothesis); and (3) the onset of illness among the clinical subjects was provoked by types of psychosocial stressors falling outside the definition of "life events." Al Khani and his coauthors clearly reject the first explanation and would appear to favor the third over the second. Alternative psychosocial stressors mentioned by the authors include family factors such as criticism and overintrusiveness on the part of close relatives (see Leff & Vaughn, 1985). Suffice it to say that the second and third explanations are not mutually exclusive, and both may be relevant to the findings in this study.

The Saudi Arabian data tend to confirm the pattern of findings reported for the WHO clinical subjects, while at the same time highlighting certain limits on the WHO data resulting from the use of patients as their own controls. Meta-analytic procedures (Hedges & Olkin, 1985; Rosenthal, 1984) could be applied to these data in order to demonstrate that the pattern of findings in both studies (i.e., the increase in the number of first-episode patients reporting life events just prior to the acute onset of illness) is highly unlikely to have occurred by chance. The obvious results of such an analysis would lend support to the suggested possibility that the Saudi Arabian study lacked sufficient power to detect a relevant difference between the clinical and general-population comparison subjects in the reporting of stressful life events.

The problems of interpretation involved in comparing the results from these two cross cultural studies have a certain exemplary character that is also worthy of comment. Clearly, neither study is definitive, and the limits of the data from both repeatedly interfere with our ability to address the issues that concern us most. This continuing equivocality in the results of the research is frustrating, particularly to the extent that investigators (and, by the same token, reviewers) are unable to resolve the sense of uncertainty that originally motivated their work. Two approaches to such a situation are possible. The first and more critical of these is to reject the conclusions of apparently flawed research, declaring that the questions under study remain moot, pending the achievement of more definitive findings. The second approach does not demand definitive results. It looks instead for important trends or directions in admittedly imperfect studies, which would serve to reinforce or further qualify our confidence in certain key hypotheses. My own writing (see Day, 1981; Day et al., 1987) has in the past emphasized the first, more critical perspective. In this chapter, however, I draw upon the thought of contemporary epidemiologists and meta-analytic methodologists in order to explore the possibilities of the second approach to the literature on life events and schizophrenia.

Causal Thinking in Epidemiology

The customary starting points for epidemiological notions of disease causation are the Henle-Koch postulates (Evans, 1978). Formulated in the mid-19th century, they require that before a microorganism can be declared the "cause" of a disease, the following conditions must be met: (1) The suspected microorganism must always be found to be present in cases of the disease; (2) one must be able to recover the microorganism from an affected patient and grow it in the laboratory; and (3) when reintroduced from the laboratory, the microorganism must always cause the disease. Within a medical context, these postulates reflect a positivist approach to causality (Cook & Campbell, 1979).

Even though the Henle-Koch postulates, when taken at face value, imply a rather narrow approach to the definition of "cause," a number of authors (Evans, 1978; Lilienfeld & Lilienfeld, 1980) have noted that they were never intended to be applied in a rigid fashion. More important, they soon required substantial modifications in order to accommodate rapidly expanding knowledge about other kinds of infectious agents (e.g., viruses, fungi, parasites).

Despite the various modifications to these postulates, the watershed for epidemiological reasoning about the causation of disease occurred in the mid-1950s, with a growing interest in the medical and public health implications of non-infectious and chronic diseases. The key feature of this change was the shift from a focus on single agents to an emphasis on multifactorial etiologies of disease (see Yerhushalmy & Palmer, 1959; Lilienfeld, 1959). Early investigators suggested that this was probably a temporary situation and one that was characteristic of the early phases of research into any disease (e.g., Yerushalmy & Palmer, 1959, p. 29). However, with time and the weight of the evidence from additional studies, this initial point of view waned, and the concept of a multifactorial etiology increasingly became a fundamental component of research into both the infectious and the noninfectious chronic diseases (see Susser, 1973; Lilienfeld & Lilienfeld, 1980; Breslow & Day, 1980; Schlesselman, 1982; Kleinbaum, Kupper, & Morganstern, 1982). It is from this point of view that probabilistic approaches to disease causation have emerged. Consider, for example, the following definition by Lilienfeld and Lilienfeld (1980): "A causal relationship would be recognized to exist whenever evidence indicates that the factors form part of the complex of circumstances that increases the probability of the occurrence of disease and that a diminution of one or more of these factors decreases the frequency of disease" (p. 295; cf. Breslow & Day, 1980, p. 85, and Schlesselman, 1982, p. 20).

Kleinbaum and his colleagues (1982, p. 29) refer to a "modified determinism"; drawing upon the theoretical work of Rothman (1976), they emphasize a model in which clusters of risk factors rather than single agents are treated as the causes of disease. Specific risk factors may interact with one another in a single cluster, and multiple independent clusters may exist that affect a single disease condition. Any risk factor that occurs in at least one but not all clusters is called a "contributory cause" (see Figure 4.1).

Multifactorial and probabilistic models of this kind raise the possibility of extremely complex causal chains, as well as subtle instances of confounding and interaction. Despite the use of increasingly sophisticated statistical techniques, this kind of conceptual approach tends to belie the very possibility that a single study can produce definitive evidence for a causal relationship. Observational studies with even the most complex designs cannot account for all possible variables or eliminate all possible biases. Even in nearly ideal circumstances, evidence must be accumulated in a piecemeal fashion from a series of limited but increasingly informative studies; over time, this process promotes the basic consensus among investigators that is required for them to finally accept or reject the causal significance of a specific risk factor for the etiology of a disease condition.

In reality, the process of adjudicating cause is usually a far more unruly affair. Even when confronted with reasonably convincing evidence from observational studies, methodological issues frequently intervene to insure that there is always continuing controversy about the "true" causal significance of specific risk factors. Indeed, it is normally the case that judgments about the causal nature of observed associations must be made on the basis of many incomplete and more or less flawed pieces of research.

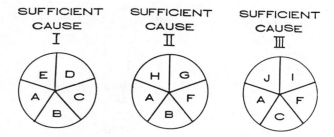

FIGURE 4.1. Conceptual scheme for disease causation. Contributory causes: B, C, D, E, F, G, H. Necessary cause: A. From "Causes" by K. Rothman, 1976, *American Journal of Epidemiology, 104,* 587-592. Copyright 1976 by the *American Journal of Epidemiology.* Reprinted by permission.

Over the past 25 years, a series of inferential criteria have developed to aid the working epidemiologist in deciding upon causal significance of specific risk factors. Historically, these criteria have their roots in the debate over the impact of smoking (U.S. Public Health Service, 1964) and were formalized in the textbook on medical statistics by A. B. Hill (1971, p. 304 ff.; see also Yerushalmy & Palmer, 1959; Lilienfeld, 1959). The following six criteria have been culled from Hill (1971) and a number of other epidemiological sources (Susser, 1973, p. 142 ff.; Breslow & Day, 1980, p. 86 ff.; Lilienfeld & Lilienfeld, 1980, p. 298 ff.; Schlesselman, 1982, p. 28 ff.; Kleinbaum et al., 1982, p. 33 ff.):

1. *Temporal sequence.* It is necessary to establish that the exposure to a risk factor preceded in time the appearance of a disease condition.

2. *Strength of the association.* The closer the association of a putative causal factor and the disease condition (e.g., the greater the relative risk among exposed individuals), the less likely it is that the association is due to bias or a noncausal association.

3. *Biological gradient.* The observation that the frequency of a disease increases in proportion to (a) the level and/or (b) the length of an exposure to a risk factor lends support to a causal interpretation.

4. *Specificity of the risks.* If a putative risk factor is found to be specific to certain (a) disease subgroups and/or (b) subcategories of exposure, this is strong evidence for inferring a causal relationship. At the same time, the absence of specificity cannot be taken as evidence against the existence of a causal relationship.

5. *Consistency of the findings.* The repeated observation of an association under different conditions (e.g., studies involving several populations, utilizing different methods, and/or using different observation periods) usually supports a causal interpretation.

6. *Coherence of the explanation.* A causal interpretation of an association is strengthened when the following conditions apply. First, the explanation is biologically plausible and does not conflict with current understanding of the disorder. Second, there are no alternative explanations of equal plausibility to explain the findings.

The professional consensus regarding the causal association between smoking and lung cancer is, perhaps, the foremost example of the process of scientific adjudication discussed in this section. Even though we remain ignorant of the precise biological mechanism involved in the etiology of this condition, few qualified individuals would question a causal link. All of this is simply to suggest that within the context of contemporary epidemiology, the very idea of a "definitive study" is something of a modern chimera. Given the complexity of our conceptual models and limits on our research tools, judgments regarding the causal significance of statistical associations must perforce be made upon the basis of partial, incomplete, and sometimes contradictory data. In other words, there comes a point at which most reasonable people simply cease to have doubts about the evidence.

Life Events and the Onset of Positive Symptoms in Schizophrenia

Its worth noting that most schizophrenia investigators conceptualize the factors leading to psychotic relapse in a multicausal framework similar to the etiological models described by epidemiologists. Moreover, the same limits on design affect both life-events research and the study of chronic noninfectious diseases. For example, it is impossible to apply a true experimental design to life events research; that is, we cannot randomly assign patients matched on key clinical characteristics to groups that will and will not have life events of a uniform kind or impact. Like most epidemiologists, we must be content with observational studies and the less definitive kinds of knowledge that usually emerge from them.

Temporal Sequence

Temporal sequence, the first of the six inferential criteria listed above, has received substantial attention from life events investigators. Of fundamental importance here is the possibility that life events may have been brought about by the unnoticed onset of the illness episode, rather than vice versa. The single most important methodological advance in this area came with the Brown and Birley's (1968, pp. 204-205) idea of classifying life events in terms of their degree of independence from the patient's illness. Since the publication of their pioneering work, some kind of equivalent measure of the degree to which events are outside the control of the patient has become a *sine qua non* for serious life events research.

A second consideration that bears on the matter of temporal sequence concerns the type of patients studied. It has been my experience that determining the independence of events is difficult with the chronically ill, for whom residual symptoms and disturbed behavior may be more or less continuously present between florid episodes. For many, the illness process is likely to have become an important feature of the way in which these individuals are viewed by their family and friends, and changes in the patients' lives (e.g., getting laid off work) may be uncritically viewed as part of the patients' psychopathology. Under such conditions, it may be difficult to obtain the information necessary to assign temporal precedence to the event or to the illness. A number of investigators (Brown & Birley, 1968; Jacobs & Myers, 1976; Day *et al.*, 1987) have avoided this problem by carrying out their research, in whole or in part, with first-episode patients who have not yet reached this kind of ambiguous situation.

Finally, the selection of only subjects reporting an *acute* illness onset also has important implications for the criterion of temporal sequence (Brown & Birley, 1968; Jacobs & Myers, 1976; Day *et al.*, 1987; Al Khani *et al.*, 1986). Among these patients, the onset of positive symptoms is relatively swift, usually marking a distinct boundary between states of illness and health. This clearly distinguishable boundary permits an accurate determination of temporal relationships between life events and symptomatology.

Strength of the Association

Developing effective methods for assessing the type and strength of the association between life events and the onset of positive symptoms is a particularly difficult issue. Perhaps, the most successful strategy to date is the concept of "brought-forward time." In developing this measure, Brown, Harris, and Peto (1973) argued that this permits investigators to estimate both the proportion of patients for whom life events are causally involved in the onset of positive symptoms and the amount of time by which this onset has been "brought forward" over a spontaneous occurrence. The assumption here is that the effect of events is to "insert independent (provoked) onsets into the ongoing (spontaneous) illness process" (Brown, Harris, & Peto, 1973, p. 164). The authors argued that the length of this brought-forward time permits a decision, on common-sense grounds, between two competing causal hypotheses. If the brought-forward time is short (say, a matter of weeks), it emphasizes the importance of predispositional factors at the expense of the influence of events. The role of events in such a case can be referred to as a "triggering effect." Should the onset of illness be substantially advanced by the event (say, a year or more), it is possible to speak in terms of a "formative effect," which generally suggests that the event has some fundamental etiological significance (Brown & Harris, 1978).

When applied to the data from the early London research, this technique suggested that life events had a causal role in the onset of positive symptoms in approximately 50% of the patients studied and that onset was brought forward by an average of 10 weeks. On the basis of these results, Brown, Harris, and Peto (1973) concluded that they could not rule out the possibility that life events "in a majority of cases triggered an onset which might well have occurred quite soon anyway" (p. 122). They also noted the possibility that a triggering effect may, in fact, be formative if the kind of event occurring before onset is actually rarer than it appears to be in light of the measurement system. This may be the case in schizophrenia if, for example, patients are breaking down after events that have some further dimensions that have not yet been codified. One real possibility here, the dimension of intrusiveness, is considered shortly.

Paykel (1978) has suggested that established measures such as "relative risk" can be used to quantify the strength of the association between life events and schizophrenic onset. The estimates of relative risk provided by Paykel (1978, p. 249) on the basis of the New Haven, Connecticut, data (see Jacobs, Prusoff, & Paykel, 1974; Jacobs & Myers, 1976) were in the range of 3.0-4.5 for a 6-month period. When Paykel reanalyzed Brown and Birley's London data, he reported relative risks of 2.4 for a 6-month period and 6.4 for the 3-week period immediately preceding onset.

My colleagues and I in Pittsburgh have also attempted to apply the concept of relative risk within an ongoing cohort study. A total of 33 chronic schizophrenic patients residing in the community and receiving outpatient treatment were rated on a weekly basis for psychopathology (using the Schedule for Affective Disorders and Schizophrenia, Change Version [SADS-C]) and life events (using the WHO instrument) over a 6-month period. Each life event was assumed to put the patient at risk for the onset of positive symptoms within the succeeding 3-week period (see Brown & Birley, 1968; Day *et al.*, 1987). A 2×2 table (see Figure 4.2) was constructed in order to estimate the relative risk of a negative change in the patients' mental status following reported life events. Using the information from the SADS-C, we rated three levels of change in mental state: (1) asymptomatic or nonspecific symptoms to suspected psychotic symptoms; (2) asymptomatic, nonspecific, or suspected psychotic symptoms to definite psychotic symptoms; (3) asymptomatic, nonspecific, suspected, or definite psychotic symptoms to acute psychosis. The results in terms of relative risks are presented in Table 4.3. For this cohort of chronically ill patients, the occurrence of life events was indeed associated with negative changes in the patients' mental state, and this association tended to become stronger as the degree of change became more negative.

A second way of looking at these results was suggested by the observation that even though very few cigarette smokers develop lung cancer, smoking is still an important risk factor, because almost all lung cancer victims are smokers. This involved looking at our data from two points

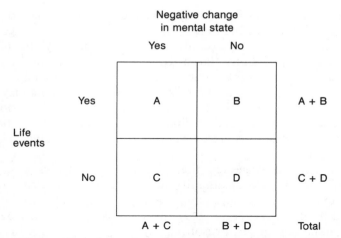

A = Life event reported *and* negative change in mental state within 3 weeks.
B = Life event reported *but* no negative change in mental state within 3 weeks.
C = Negative change in mental state *but* no life event in preceding 3 weeks.
D = No negative change in mental state *and* no life event in preceding 3 weeks.

FIGURE 4.2. Table for estimating relative risk of negative change in mental status following reported life events.

of view – a task that could be accomplished by comparing the answers to two specific questions. First, there was the prospective issue: What proportion of the reported life events in the study were followed within 3 weeks by an observed negative change in the patients' level of psychopathology? On Figure 4.2, this would be the equivalent of dividing cell A by cells A + B; in probabilistic terms, it would be the equivalent of conditioning on the occurrence of life events – that is, Pr(relapse l life event). Next, there was the retrospective issue: What proportion of observed negative changes in psychopathology were preceded within 3 weeks by a life event? On Figure 4.2, this would be the equivalent of dividing cell A by cells A + C; in probabalistic terms, it would be the equivalent of conditioning on relapse – that is, Pr(life event l relapse). The results of this analysis are presented in Table 4.3. For the most

TABLE 4.3. Preliminary results of Pittsburgh cohort life event study

Mental state changed to:	Relative risk	Pr (life event l relapse)	Pr (relapse l life event)	Relative risk	Pr (life event l relapse)	Pr (relapse l life event
	All events			Moderate- to high-impact events		
Suspected psychosis	4.33	.50	.18	2.26	.27	.10
Definite psychosis	7.35	.60	.18	7.78	.57	.18
Acute psychosis	11.31	.63	.12	4.16	.29	.07

inclusive category (i.e., all events), these data suggest that even though fewer than one in five reported life events were followed within 3 weeks by negative changes in psychopathology, over half of the new episodes of psychosis observed among our patients were preceded by some kind of stressful life event.

Biological Gradient

The key question concerning a biological gradient in life events research is whether we can identify a dose-response relationship in the data. Investigators studying the relationship between life events and positive schizophrenic symptoms have used a number of different measures of impact – for example, "hazardousness" (Beck & Worthen, 1972), "contextual threat" (see Chapter 2, this volume), "degree of upset and required readjustment" (Jacobs & Myers, 1976), and "objective impact" (Day et al., 1987). Despite this variation in the measures of impact used, very little evidence has emerged to date that would support the notion of a dose-response relationship between the impact of life events and the occurrence of negative changes in psychopathology. Jacobs and Myers (1976), for example, found that even though a significant proportion of their respondents reported at least one undesirable event preceding relapse, the majority of these events caused minor to moderate upset and required little or no readjustment on the part of the subjects. In a similar fashion, Beck and Worthen (1972) came to the conclusion that "schizophrenic patients . . . decompensate in the context of life situations which are independently judged as not particularly hazardous" (p. 128). The data from the Pittsburgh study, cited above, show similar findings. If a dose-response relationship existed between life events and negative changes in psychopathology, we would expect a significant increase in the proportion of moderate- and high-impact events followed by a negative change in mental status, compared to the proportion of all events followed by a similar change. In fact, the proportion of moderate and severe events followed by a negative change in the patients' mental status was smaller than the totals for all events (see Table 4.3).

Specificity of the Risk

To turn to the criterion of specificity, there has been a long-standing debate over whether or not there exist subgroups of schizophrenic and/or schizophrenic-like conditions that show a particular vulnerability to stressful life events (Garmezy, 1971; Vaillant, 1963; Chung, Langeluddecke, & Tennant, 1986). Scandinavian psychiatrists (Stromgren, 1965;

Noreik, 1970) identify a category of "reactive psychoses," which they feel represents an etiologically separate category of disorders standing between schizophrenic and manic-depressive conditions. They suggest that individuals with reactive disorders often respond in a negative fashion to specific kinds of environmental stressors that affect constitutionally vulnerable aspects of their personalities. The evidence available from certain studies (e.g., McCabe, 1975) suggests that these patients may be quite rare, perhaps representing less than 5% of psychotic patients. Birley and Brown (1970) argue against the identification of a separate group of psychogenic psychoses, suggesting instead a multifactorial approach to the course of the disorder. They conclude that "we have found no evidence that our findings apply only to patients of a certain age, sex or symptomatology" (p. 331).

A more controversial position has been taken by Dohrenwend and Egri (1981). Drawing upon the evidence from studies of extreme situations and battlefield psychoses, they argue that recent stressful life events combining the three elements of (1) the death of comrades, (2) the threat of severe physical harm to the subject, and (3) the disruption of social supports may play a primary etiological role (i.e., a necessary and sufficient cause) in the development of schizophrenic disorders. In other words, these authors appear to take the position that such extreme situations may provoke schizophrenic psychoses in healthy individuals who would not otherwise have become ill. Clinicians have replied that such schizophrenia-like psychoses are usually transient and largely self-limiting in nature, and should not be confused with "true" schizophrenic disorders. The latter position is reflected in the *Diagnostic and Statistical Manual of Mental Disorders*, third edition (DSM-III), which separates schizophrenic disorders from symptomatologically similar conditions, such as schizophreniform and brief reactive psychoses (American Psychiatric Association, 1980, pp. 199-202).

The question of whether certain subgroups of patients are particularly vulnerable to the effects of stressful life events remains largely a matter of speculation. The paucity of findings in this area is due at least in part to the fact that life events investigators have not studied random samples of patients. For methodological reasons, many researchers (Brown & Birley, 1968; Jacobs & Myers, 1976; Al Khani *et al.*, 1986; Day *et al.*, in press) have selected subgroups of patients with relatively acute illness onsets for inclusion in their studies. Inclusion criteria of this kind usually mean that significant numbers of schizophrenic patients are automatically excluded from life events studies.

With regard to specific subcategories of exposure, a number of proposals have been made. First, Beck (n.d.) and Gift and Wynne (1986) have suggested that events with a sexual content may be particularly troublesome for schizophrenic patients. So far, only fragmentary evidence has been provided for this hypothesis. Second, Harris (1987) has recently suggested that intrusive events creating paranoid feelings may be of central importance for schizophrenics. A reanalysis of Brown and Birley's (1968) data indicated that events involving intrusions by outsiders were 20 times as common in the 1 week before schizophrenic onset as they were in the 1 week before interview in a comparison group. These intrusive events included burglaries, attacks, visits by police, and communications by the bureaucracy or workplace management, all of which were intuitively identifiable as possessing a paranoia-stimulating quality. Many of these events had, at most, a mild long-term threat (e.g., a visit by the police turned out to be a mistake). A preliminary analysis of the data from the WHO study suggested a similar high proportion of intrusive events during the 1 week before onset in the developing-country centers. Third, Leff and Vaughn (1985), on the basis of earlier research (Leff, Kuipers, Berkowitz, Eberlin-Vries, & Sturgeon, 1982), have argued that "the threatening nature of life events is a crucial aspect of their role in precipitating episodes of schizophrenia" (p. 191). Chung et al. (1986) report similar findings for schizophreniform patients diagnosed according to DSM-III criteria. After a reanalysis of the data from the initial schizophrenia study, Brown, Sklair, Harris, and Birley (1973) reported results suggesting that about half of the patients experiencing events in the 3 weeks before onset were facing situations with at least moderate long-term threat. Further analysis suggests that only one-eighth of them had no short- or long-term contextual threat at all – that is, did not even have a rating of "some" threat (G. W. Brown, personal communication, 1986). Finally, to the extent that such concepts as "intrusiveness" and "threat" overlap with such variables as "undesirability," other studies have produced similar evidence. For example, Jacobs and Myers (1976) found that 82% of their schizophrenic patients reported at least one undesirable life event. In summary, these findings suggest that schizophrenic patients may indeed show a certain sensitivity to the impact of intrusive and/or threatening events, as opposed to the more general run of life events.

Consistency of the Findings

If all the studies dealing with a given relationship produce consistent positive findings, a causal interpretation is enhanced. In practice, however, most observational studies are flawed, and the exact meaning of the findings remains open to debate. My own reviews of the literature have argued, for example, that we still lack a study that definitively tests the findings reported by Brown and Birley in their pioneering papers (Day, 1981; Day et al., 1987). For the most part, this has been due to weaknesses in research design – for instance, confounded variables (Leff, Hirsch, Gaind, Rohde, & Stevens, 1973); missed events (Jacobs & Myers, 1976); a failure to determine the point of symptomatic onset (Harder, Strauss, Kokes, Ritzler, & Gift, 1980); insufficient precision in the dating of events (Malzacher, Merz, & Ebonther, 1981); and lack of adequate comparison subjects (Day *et al.*, 1987). To what extent should these weaknesses in design eliminate such studies from consideration? Here it is useful to recall the remarks by Glass (1976) regarding the consequences of a tendency in literature reviews (my own included) to integrate a difficult topic area by

> carping on the design or analysis deficiencies of all but a few studies – those remaining frequently being one's own work or that of one's students or friends – and then advancing the one or two acceptable studies as the truth of the matter. This approach takes design and analysis too seriously, in my opinion. I don't condone a poor job of either; but I also recognize that a study with half a dozen design and analysis flaws still may be valid. (p. 4)

Cook and Leviton (1980) have made a similar point in arguing that one important task in reviewing a body of literature is to get at the "facts": "These are the stubborn, dependable relationships that regularly occur despite any biases that may be present in particular studies or because of implicit theories behind the investigator's choice of measures, observation schedules, and the like" (p. 449).

If we evaluate the consistency of the evidence on the basis of the "facts," as described by Cook and Leviton (1980), and keep a rein on our impulse to "carp" about design, as suggested by Glass (1976), we find that a substantial majority of all the relevant studies in this area have produced findings that, although less than definitive, still support the existence of a causal association between stressful life events and the acute onset of positive symptoms in schizophrenic patients (e.g., Brown & Birley, 1968; Steinberg & Durell, 1968; Leff *et al.*, 1973, 1982; Jacobs & Myers, 1976; Harder *et al.*, 1980; Day *et al.*, 1987; Al Khani *et al.*, 1986). Indeed, it is difficult to point to more than a handful of studies that report uniformly negative findings (e.g., Malzacher *et al.*, 1981), and they too have their flaws (see Day *et al.*, 1987). Admittedly, there may be a "file drawer" problem here – negative findings do not get published – but I doubt that it is serious enough to reverse the balance of the evidence in this case.

Coherence of the Explanation

The final criterion to be assessed is the extent to which a coherent, biologically plausible explanation exists for the effect of the risk factor under study. Needless to say, the plausibility of life stress as a nonspecific cause of illness is still a controversial notion for many medical researchers. In the case of schizophrenia, however, there is an established and convincing body of evidence to suggest that schizophrenic patients suffer from a biologically founded "core deficit" that makes them particularly vulnerable to the effects of environmental circumstances. Perhaps the most closely reasoned formulation of this model has been put forward by Wing and Brown (1970; see also Wing, 1978a, 1978b, 1978c; Brown & Harris, 1978). Wing and Brown note that in schizophrenia,

> there seem to be at least two fundamental processes at work. On the one hand, an under-stimulating social environment tends to increase symptoms such as social withdrawal, passivity, inertia and lack of initiative. . . . On the other hand there is a tendency to break down, with an effusion of florid symptoms (delusions, hallucinations, incoherence of thought and speech, over-activity and various forms of odd behavior), under conditions of over-stimulation. . . . The sketch of a theory is discernible and depends upon the assumption that negative symptoms are a protective reaction against cognitive impairment. When a patient is allowed to withdraw, he does so and the process can easily go too far. When he is not allowed to withdraw, but faced with what seems to be impossible demands, the underlying thinking disorder becomes clinically manifest in florid symptoms. (1970, pp. 21-22)

Within this theoretical framework, stressful life events, of course, represent one of the most important potential overstimulating factors that may provoke the appearance of positive psychotic symptoms. Although, from a reductionist point of view, the actual biological mechanism underlying this "core defect" has yet to be identified, the evidence for this kind of general model has continued to accumulate from fields as varied as genetics (Rosenthal, 1970; Gottesman & Shields, 1976, 1982), psychophysiology (Neuchterlein & Dawson, 1984; Leff & Vaughn, 1985, pp. 195-209; Mirsky & Duncan, 1986), and psychopharmacology (Leff et al., 1973, 1982; Doan, West, Goldstein, Rodnick, & Jones, 1985; Hogarty et al., 1979). Only a few investigators (e.g., Crow, Cross, Johnstone, & Own, 1982) have proposed alternative explanations that explicitly reject a role for environmental stressors (including life events) in the onset of positive psychotic symptoms. Alternative perspectives are more likely simply to de-emphasize the significance of external stressors in favor of a number of other factors (e.g., discontinuation of maintenance neuroleptic medication or alterations in specific biological parameters).

Summary and Conclusion

It seems clear that research has demonstrated a statistical association between recent stressful life events and acute attacks of schizophrenia. The critical problem has been to determine whether this association is properly described as causal or noncausal in nature. Epidemiologists have customarily spoken about two kinds of noncausal associations: (1) artifactual associations, resulting from defects in research methodology, and (2) indirect associations that come about when the independent and the dependent variables are both related to a third prior factor but not to each other. The careful attention given by life events investigators to the issue of temporal sequence has had the effect of excluding from the literature the kinds of situations most likely to result in artifactual findings due to shortcomings of method – that is, situations in which there is a strong possibility that life events may have been brought about by the prior insidious onset of psychotic symptoms. An indirect noncausal association would seem to be an even more unlikely possibility, since it is difficult even to conceive of a third prior variable capable of systematically influencing both the occurrence of independent life events within such a limited 3-week period and the onset of positive psychotic symptoms. It therefore seems reasonable, on the basis of evidence in the literature, to conclude that the association between stressful life events and episodes of schizophrenia is probably causal in nature.

The conclusion that we are apparently dealing with a causal association raises additional questions concerning the directness of this relationship. Here it is worthwhile to recall certain negative findings: (1) Among acute-onset schizophrenic patients, a substantial proportion of their illness episodes may be expected to occur without the involvement of life events; (2) stressful life events that do not result in the onset of illness episodes: are frequently reported by schizophrenic patients; and (3) there is no clear dose-response relationship between the impact or number of reported life events and the onset of acute attacks of schizophrenia. All of these findings tend to suggest that the presence of other risk factors may have important implications for the probability of an illness episode following a stressful life event. The existence of additional risk factors also raises the possibility that, given proper circumstances, life events may play either a direct or an indirect causal role in the onset of psychotic episodes. Consider, for example, the case of a patient who is laid off work for reasons that are beyond his or her own control (i.e., an independent life event). Now, if the patient becomes discouraged and quits taking maintenance medication, and this in turn eventually results in a symptomatic relapse, the life event has played an indirect causal role (e.g., life event → quitting medication → relapse).

However, if the same patient relapses while continuing to take his or her medication, then the life event has played a direct causal role in the onset of symptoms. At the same time, it also may be necessary in most cases for other risk factors to be present before the life event can play this direct causal role. Potential risk factors may range from psychosocial conditions, such as the quality of the patient's family environment, to the current state of specific biological parameters. In other words, life events, even of the threatening or intrusive variety, may be relatively benign except when they occur in the presence of other important risk factors.

The model proposed by Rothman (1976) (see Figure 4.1) is particularly helpful in sorting out the complex relationships that may exist between different risk factors. It is multicausal and probabilistic, and it exemplifies the modified determinism proposed by Kleinbaum et al. (1982), which, as indicated earlier, is broadly representative of contemporary epidemiological approaches to the causation of disease. As shown in Figure 4.1, Rothman's model is composed of clusters of risk factors that *together* act as "sufficient causes" of illness. If a factor appears in every cluster, then it represents a "necessary clause" of illness – that is, it must be present for an illness onset to occur. If a risk factor appears in at least one but not all clusters, then it is termed a "contributory cause." It is the concept of contributory causes that seems most compatible with the evidence reviewed from life events studies. Rothman's concept of contributory causes is flexible enough to permit life events to play a direct or an indirect causal role in the onset of illness episodes, while also providing a framework for the interpretation of the troublesome negative findings outlined above. Illness onsets, for example, may occur without the involvement of life events, due to the existence of alternative risk factor clusters (i.e., sufficient causes). By the same token, life events may occur without provoking illness onsets in situations where one or more of the vital components of the risk factor cluster are missing. Finally, the complex relationships that may be expected to obtain among the various elements of a risk factor cluster serve to explain the lack of a clear dose-response relationship in the life events literature.

The adoption of such a multicausal and probabilistic model suggests that future research should focus less on life events per se than on the clusters of risk factors that make up Rothman's sufficient causes. We already have a number of important clues concerning the risk factors that compose such clusters. By far the most sophisticated and informative approach to this problem to date has come from the work carried out by Leff and Vaughn and their associates, building on the work of Brown, Birley, and Wing (1972) on expressed emotion (EE). Leff and Vaughn (1985, pp. 186-194) have recently proposed a model of schizophrenic relapse that attempts to account for the interaction among life events, relatives' EE, and prophylactic medications. They suggest that in the absence of prophylactic medications, patients may relapse as a consequence of either living in a high-EE household or experiencing a threatening life event. The general effect of prophylactic medications in this model is to protect patients against one or the other of these risk factors, but not both. Hence, patients living in high-EE households and taking prophylactic medications are not expected to relapse without the occurrence of a threatening life event. And, finally, maintenance medications in low-EE households prevent relapses by protecting patients against the impact of events that inevitably occur with the passage of time. Additional psychosocial risk factors that appear worthy of investigation in a similar fashion include long-term difficulties involving cognitively confusing, overdemanding, demoralizing, and physically threatening environments (Day, 1986).

It is an unfortunate fact that – contrary to the multicausal, probabilistic approach preferred by contemporary epidemiological investigators – putative risk factors for schizophrenic relapse have, for the most part, been studied intensively and in isolation from one another. As a result, there now exist a number of very complex and frequently esoteric assessment technologies that, despite their positive findings, are both time-consuming and limited in terms of the overall amount of variance they explain. This type of situation is probably the inevitable consequence of any developmental phase of research, and is therefore quite understandable; yet a time also comes when complicated technologies of this sort need to be simplified, combined, and tested under practical day-to-day clinical conditions. The design and implementation of such multifactorial clinical studies would appear to be the next major step in the development of this field.

References

Al Khani, M., Bebbington, P., Watson, J., & House, F. (1986). Life events and schizophrenia: A Saudi Arabian study. *British Journal of Psychiatry, 148*, 12-22.

American Psychiatric Association. (1980). *Diagnostic and statistical manual of mental disorders* (3rd ed.). Washington, DC: Author.

Beck, J. (n.d.). *Life events and sex*. Unpublished manuscript.

Beck, J., & Worthen, K. (1972). Precipitating stress, crisis theory and hospitalization in schizophrenia. *Archives of General Psychiatry, 26*, 123-129.

Birley, J., & Brown, G. W. (1970). Crises and life changes preceding the onset of acute schizophrenia: Clinical aspects. *British Journal of Psychiatry, 116*, 327-333.

Breslow, N., & Day, N. (1980). *Statistical methods in cancer research. Vol. 1. Analysis of case-control studies*. Lyon, France: International Agency for Research on Cancer.

Brown, G. W. & Birley, J. (1968). Crises and life changes in the onset of schizophrenia. *Journal of Health and Social Behavior, 9*. 217-244.

Brown, G. W., Birley, J., & Wing, J. K. (1972). Influences of family life on the course of schizophrenic disorders: A replication. *British Journal of Psychiatry, 121*, 241-258.

Brown, G. W., & Harris, T. O. (1978). *Social origins of depression. A study of psychiatric disorder in women*. London: Tavistock.

Brown, G. W., Harris, T. O. & Peto, J. (1973). Life events and psychiatric disorders: 2. The nature of the causal link. *Psychological Medicine,3*, 159-176.

Brown, G. W., Sklair, F., Harris, T. O., & Birley, J. (1973). Life events and psychiatric disorders: 1. Some methodological issues. *Psychological Medicine, 3*, 74-87.

Chung, R. K., Langeluddecke, P., & Tennant, C. L. (1986). Threatening life events in the onset of schizophrenia, schizophreniform psychosis and hypomania. *British Journal of Psychiatry, 148*, 680-685.

Cook, T., & Campbell, D. (1979). *Quasi-experimentation: Design and analysis for field settings*. Boston: Houghton Mifflin.

Cook, T., & Leviton, L. (1980). Reviewing the literature: A comparison of traditional methods with meta-analysis. *Journal of Personality, 48*, 449-472.

Crow, T., Cross, A., Johnstone, E., & Owen, F. (1982). Two syndromes in schizophrenia and their pathogenesis. In F. Henn & H. Nasrallah Eds.), *Schizophrenia as a brain disease* (pp. 196-234). New York: Oxford University Press.

Day, R. (1981). Life events and schizophrenia: The triggering hypothesis. *Acta Psychiatrica Scandinavica, 64*, 97-122.

Day, R. (1986). Social stress and schizophrenia: From the concept of recent life events to the notion of toxic environments. In G. Burrows *et al.* (Eds.), *Studies on schizophrenia, Part 1* (pp. 71-82). Amsterdam: Elsevier.

Day, R., Nielsen, J., Korten, A., Ernberg, G., Dube, K. C., Gebhart, J., Jablensky, A., Leon, C., Marsella, A., Olatawura, M., Sartorius, N., Strömgren, E., Takahashi, R., Wig, N., & Wynne, L. C. (1987). Stressful life events preceding the acute onset of schizophrenia: A cross-national study from the World Health Organization. *Culture, Medicine and Psychiatry, 11*, 1-123.

Doan, J., West, K., Goldstein, M., Rodnick, E., & Jones, J. (1985). Parental communication deviance and affective style. *Archives of General Psychiatry, 38*, 679-685.

Dohrenwend, B. P., & Egri, G. (1981). Recent stressful life events and episodes of schizophrenia. *Schizophrenia Bulletin, 7*, 12-23.

Evans, A. (1978). Causation and disease: A chronological journey. *American Journal of Epidemiology, 108*, 249-258.

Garmezy, N. (1971). Process and reactive psychoses. In M. Katz *et al.* (Eds.), *Classification in psychiatry and psychology* (pp. 419-465). Bethesda, MD: National Institute of Mental Health.

Gift, T., & Wynne, L. (1986). *Life events in the sexual sphere*. Unpublished manuscript.

Glass, G. (1976). Primary, secondary and meta-analysis of research. *Educational Researcher, 5*, 3-8.

Gottesman, I., & Shields, J. (1976). A critical review of recent adoption, twin and family studies of schizophrenia. *Schizophrenia Bulletin, 2*, 360-400.

Gottesman, I., & Shields, J. (1982). *Schizophrenia: The epigenetic puzzle*. London: Oxford University Press.

Harder, D., Strauss, J., Kokes, R., Ritzler, B., & Gift, T. (1980). Life events and psychopathology severity among first psychiatric admissions. *Journal of Abnormal Psychology, 89*, 165-180.

Harris, T. O. (1987). Recent developments in the study of life events in relation to psychiatric and physical disorders. In B. Cooper (Ed.), *Psychiatric epidemiology: Progress and prospects* (pp. 81-102). London: Croom Helm.

Hedges, L., & Olkin, I. (1985). *Statistical methods for meta-analysis*. New York: Academic Press.

Hill, A. B. (1971). *Principles of medical statistics*. New York: Oxford University Press.

Hogarty, G., Schooler, N., Ulric, R., Mussare, F., Ferro, P., & Herron, E. (1979). Fluphenazine and social therapy in the after care of schizophrenic patients. *Archives of General Psychiatry, 36,* 1283-1294.

Jacobs, S., & Myers, J. (1976). Recent life events and acute psychoses: A controlled study. *Journal of Nervous and Mental Disease, 162,* 75-87.

Jacobs, S., Prusoff, B., & Paykel, G. (1974). Recent life events in schizophrenia and depression. *Psychological Medicine, 4,* 444-453.

Kleinbaum, D., Kupper, L., & Morgenstern, H. (1982). *Epidemiological research*. London: Lifetime Learning Press.

Leff, J., Hirsch, S., Gaind, R., Rohde, P., & Stevens, B. (1973). Life events and maintenance therapy in schizophrenic relapse. *British Journal of Psychiatry, 123,* 659-660.

Leff, J., Kuipers, L., Berkowitz, R., Eberlin-Vries, R., & Sturgeon, D. (1982). A controlled trial of social intervention in the families of schizophrenic patients. *British Journal of Psychiatry, 141,* 121-134.

Leff, J., & Vaughn, C. (1985). *Expressed emotion in families*. New York: Guilford Press.

Lilienfeld, A., (1959). Comments on the paper by J. Yerushalmy and C. Palmer. *Journal of Chronic Diseases, 10,* 41-47.

Lilienfeld, A., & Lilienfeld, D. (1980). *Foundations of epidemiology*. New York: Oxford University Press.

McCabe, M. (1975). *Reactive psychoses (Acta Psychiatrica Scandinavica*, Suppl. No. 259). Copenhagen: Munksgaard.

Malzacher, M., Merz, J., & Ebonther, D. (1981). Einscheidende Lebensegeignine im Vorfeld Akuter Schizophrener Episoden. *Archives für Psychiatrie und Nervenkrankheiten, 230,* 227-242.

Mirsky, A., & Duncan, C. (1986). Etiology and expression of schizophrenia: Neurobiological and psychosocial factors. *Annual Review of Psychology, 37,* 291-319.

Noreik, K. (1970). *Follow-up and classification of functional psychoses with special reference to reactive psychoses*. Oslo: Universitersforlaget.

Neuchterlein, K., & Dawson, M. (Eds.). (1984). Vulnerability and stress factors in the developmental course of schizophrenic disorders [Special issue]. *Schizophrenia Bulletin, 10,* 158-312.

Paykel, G. (1978). Contribution of life events to the causation of psychiatric illness. *Psychological Medicine, 8,* 245-253.

Rabkin, J. (1980). Stressful life events and schizophrenia: A review of the research literature. *Psychological Bulletin, 87,* 408-425.

Rosenthal, D. (1970). *Genetic theory and abnormal behavior*. New York: McGraw-Hill.

Rosenthal, R. (1984). *Meta-analytic procedures for social research*. Beverly Hills, CA: Sage.

Rothman, K. (1976). Causes. *American Journal of Epidemiology, 104,* 587-592.

Schlesselman, J. (1982). *Case-control studies*. New York: Oxford University Press.

Steinberg, H., & Durell, J. (1968). A stressful social situation as a precipitant of schizophrenic symptoms: An epidemiological study. *British Journal of Psychiatry, 114,* 1097-1105.

Stromgren, E. (1965). Schizophreniform psychoses. *Acta Psychiatrica Scandinavica, 42,* 483-488.

Susser, M. (1973). *Causal thinking in the health sciences*. New York: Oxford University Press.

U.S. Public Health Service. (1964). *Smoking and health*. Washington, DC: U.S. Government Printing Office.

Vaillant, G. (1963). Natural history of the remitting schizophrenias. *American Journal of Psychiatry, 120*, 367-375.

Wing, J. (1978a). *Reasoning about madness.* London: Oxford University Press.

Wing, J. (Ed.). (1978b). *Schizophrenia: Towards a new synthesis.* London: Academic Press.

Wing, J. (1978c). The social context of schizophrenia. *American Journal of Psychiatry, 135*, 1333-1339.

Wing, J., & Brown, G. W. (1970). *Schizophrenia and institutionalism.* London: Cambridge University Press.

Yerushalmy, J., & Palmer, C. (1959). On the methodology of investigations of etiologic factors in chronic diseases. *Journal of Chronic Diseases, 10*, 27-40.

5

Endocrine Changes and Clinical Profiles in Depression

PAUL CALLOWAY AND RAYMOND DOLAN

Introduction

There is a substantial body of research to indicate that depressed men and women have abnormalities of endocrine function. Most of the work in this field has concentrated on the hypothalamic-pituitary-adrenal (HPA) and hypothalamic-pituitary-thyroid (HPT) axes.

Early studies revealed that plasma and urinary cortisol levels, and the cortisol production rate, were high in depressed patients and tended to return to normal on clinical recovery (Board, Wadeson, & Persky, 1957; Gibbons & McHugh, 1962; Sachar et al. 1973; Carroll, 1976). More recently, dynamic tests of HPA function have been used. Dexamethasone, a synthetic corticosteroid, suppresses cortisol production by way of the negative feedback loop. Failure to do this normally implies overactivity of the HPA axis. This is the basis of the dexamethasone suppression test (DST; see Figure 5.1). It has been found that about 50% of depressed patients fail to suppress cortisol levels fully after administration of dexamethasone, although the proportion of patients showing this varies from study to study (Holsboer, Bender, Benkert, Klein, & Schmauss, 1980; Nuller & Ostroumova, 1980; Carroll, 1982).

Studies of thyroid hormone levels in depressed patients have been less consistent (Ferrari, 1973; Yamaguchi, Hatotani, Nomura, & Ushijima, 1977; Rinieris, Christodoulou, Souvatzoglou, Koutras, & Stefanis, 1978). However, longitudinal studies suggest that thyroid hormone levels are raised during episodes of depression and fall on recovery (Board et al., 1957; Kierkegaard & Faber, 1981). The response of depressed patients to the thyrotropin-releasing hormone (TRH) test has

Paul Calloway. Fulbourn Hospital, Cambridge CB1 5EF, England.

Raymond Dolan. National Hospitals for Nervous Diseases, Queen Square, London WC1 N3BG, England.

also been measured. TRH, a hypothalamic tripeptide, stimulates the release of thyrotropin (TSH) from the pituitary gland, which in turn stimulates the release of thyroid hormones from the thyroid gland (see Figure 5.2). An impaired, or blunted, TSH response to TRH may be due to a number of different factors, but in general implies either dysfunction of the pituitary gland or overactivity of the HPT axis (when the blunting is due to thyroid hormones acting homeostatically by way of a negative feedback loop). Blunting of TSH responses is thus most commonly seen in hyperthyroidism, but may also occur in hypothyroidism due to pituitary failure. It has been reported that 30-50% of depressed patients have a relatively blunted TSH response to TRH, although the significance of the phenomenon is as yet unclear (Loosen & Prange, 1982).

The early work on HPA-axis and HPT-axis function in depression suggested that endocrine abnormalities were related to the presence of anxiety or turmoil. Increased output of cortisols was shown to be associated with anxiety (Gibbons, Gibbons, Maxwell, & Willcox, 1960; Sachar, Hellman, Fukushima, & Gallagher, 1970; Stokes, Stoll, Mattson, & Sollod, 1976) and was found to rise on "crisis" days (Bunney, Mason, Roatch, & Hamburg, 1965) and on days when patients in psychotherapy were confronted with loss (Sachar, Mackenzie, Binstock, & Mack,

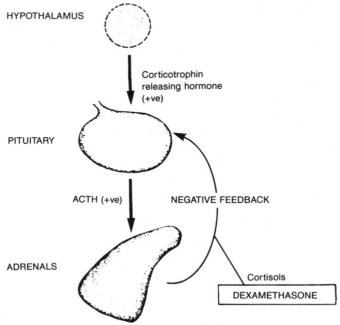

FIGURE 5.1. Schematic representation of the hypothalamic-pituitary-adrenal (HPA) axis.

1967). Raised levels of thyroid hormones were found in depressed patients who were most anxious or agitated (Ferrari, 1973; Kolakowska & Swigar, 1977). Results such as these may indicate that the endocrine abnormalities are due to distress in depressed patients rather than to the depression itself. It would thus be possible to hypothesize that the abnormalities represent an adaptive response to stress. Indeed, there is already much evidence showing that stress affects the HPA and HPT axes. The HPA axis in animals is affected by many different stimuli and situations, including increases in population density, isolation, and lowering of social rank. Marked rises of cortisols are provoked by situations involving novelty, uncertainty, and the anticipation of unpleasant stimuli, especially in situations where established rules are suddenly changed (Mason, 1968a). Increased output of cortisols in humans has been shown to occur as a result of flying, taking examinations, watching emotionally arousing films, and many other stress-provoking situations (Mason, 1975; Kennon, 1979). Blumenfield, Rose, Richmond, and Beering (1970) showed that air force personnel in training who became anxious or depressed had abnormal DST results, which returned to normal after completion of training. In depressed patients, it has been shown that hospitalization itself is a significant cause of increased cortisol output and of DST abnormalities (Sacher, 1967a, 1967b; Berger, Pirke, Doerr, Krieg, & von Zerssen,, 1984; Coccaro, Prudic, Rothpear, & Nurnberg, 1984). Similarly, studies have shown that thyroid activity increases after such stressful activities as watching certain films, taking examinations, or undergoing difficult interviews (Mason, 1968b; Levi, 1972).

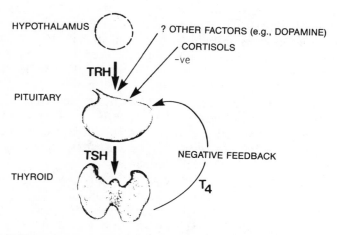

FIGURE 5.2. Schematic representation of the hypothalamic-pituitary-thyroid (HPT) axis.

However, it has also been argued that the endocrine abnormalities in depressed patients are unrelated to stress. Sachar (1975) showed that cortisol levels were high in sleeping depressed patients and also in patients who were taking tranquilizers. Moreover, he found that "apathetic" and retarded depressives had increased output. From these facts he argued that the phenomenon could not be considered a stress response in all patients. This case was further advanced by studies of the DST in depression, which suggested that patients with "endogenous" depression (i.e., patients for whom environmental etiological factors were considered to be unimportant) were more likely to have abnormal DST results than other depressed patients (Carroll, 1982; Holden, 1983). Both the DST and the TRH test have been suggested as possible markers for endogenous depression. The implications are that the endocrine abnormalities reflect underlying neurotransmitter changes that constitute the biological basis for depression. However, many studies have failed to find differences in the rates of endocrine abnormalities between patients with endogenous depression and other types of depression (Verghese et al., 1973; Holsboer et al., 1980; Davis et al., 1981; Rabkin, Quitkin, Stewart, McGrath, & Puig-Antich, 1983; Lesser, Rubin, Finder, Forster, & Poland, 1983; Berger et al., 1984). Thus, the case for using tests such as the DST or the TRH test to distinguish subgroups of depressed patients is far from being made. Moreover, the concentration of effort on trying to find "markers" for dubious diagnostic categories such as endogenous depression has perhaps obscured attempts to understand the significance of the endocrine changes themselves. Although it is clear that not all these changes are explicable in terms of an adaptive response to stress, it is impossible to investigate the field without taking this into account. In accounting for the endocrine abnormalities in depressed patients, it is necessary to take account of both environmental and biological factors, and in particular to allow for the effect of individual variation. It has been shown, for instance, that there are marked individual differences in the endocrine response to stress in both animals and humans. The same stressful experimental situations produced widely differing degrees of HPA and HPT activation in different animals of the same species (Mason, Brady, & Tulliver, 1968; Mason, Mousey, Brady, & Tulliver, 1968). Most of the studies of endocrine function in depressed or nondepressed human subjects also reveal wide individual variations, indicating the many different influences on the HPA and HPT axes.

Factors that could mediate between environmental stress and morbidity or endocrine response include the type of environmental change, the individuals biological and psychological attributes, and the characteristics of the social support system (Rabkin & Struening, 1976). The influence of hereditary factors is suggested by studies showing that patients with a family history of depression are more likely to have abnormal DST responses than those without such a history (Schlesser, Winokur, & Sherman, 1980), although this has not been found in all studies (Mendlewicz, Charles, & Franckson, 1982). Moreover, different genetic strains of the same species of animal show different biochemical responses to stress (Goodwin & Bunney, 1973). In human beings, early environmental factors such as parental loss in childhood have been shown to influence HPA-axis activity in adulthood (Mason, 1975). The importance of social support systems is suggested by a study showing that loneliness influences cortisol levels (Kiecolt-Glaser *et al.*, 1984). Attempts to relate personality to endocrine function are confounded by problems of measurement and of the extent to which personality measures can be considered enduring. There is, however, some evidence that personality attributes and endocrine status may be associated (Bridges & Jones, 1968; Persky, Zuckerman, & Curtis, 1968; Curtis, Fogel, McEvoy, & Zarate, 1970). Mattsson (1971) showed that the way in which children with hemophilia coped with their condition predicted cortisol output. Wolff, Friedman, Hofer, and Mason (1964) showed that the output of cortisols in the parents of terminally ill children was increased on "distress" days, but that these increases were greatest in those parents who had the highest baseline levels. These baseline levels were related to the coping strategies used by the parents. Those who were obviously distressed had the highest output, whereas the lowest levels were found in parents who showed little distress (e.g., those who believed that it was all in the hands of God). Similarly, in a study of schizophrenic patients, high cortisol output was associated with distress and turmoil, whereas output was normal in those with organized delusional systems (Sachar, 1970).

It is clear, therefore, that in any population – depressed or otherwise – many different factors influence endocrine function. Many of the studies in this field have considered only a limited number of the possible variables. Moreover, the instruments used to assess the variables have often been inadequate. The commonest tendency has been to employ sophisticated techniques for assaying the endocrine parameters, and increasingly effective means of quantifying symptomatology, but crude and subjective methods for assessing the role of environmental or social factors.

The purpose of the study reported in this chapter was to investigate endocrine function in depressed patients, with particular emphasis on the possible role of social factors. The Life Events and Difficulties Schedule (LEDS; Brown & Harris, 1978) was used to obtain accurate and quantifiable information about environmental influences. By including these measures in the clinical assessment of the patient population, we hoped to delineate more fully the significance of the endocrine abnormalities – in particular, those demonstrated by the DST and the TRH test – in depressed patients.

The Royal Free Hospital Study

Method

SUBJECTS

The study reported here has been described in more detail elsewhere (Calloway, Dolan, Fonagy, De Souza, & Wakeling, 1984; Dolan, Calloway, Fonagy, De Souza, & Wakeling, 1985). The patients were selected for the study from various sources, including a district teaching hospital, a psychiatric hospital, a psychiatric day hospital, and a general practice. Their ages ranged from 20 to 70, and all met Research Diagnostic Criteria (RDC) for primary depression (Spitzer, Endicott, & Robins, 1978). Out of 130 subjects interviewed over a 2-year period, 72 were considered eligible according to the RDC and our other criteria. No patients had serious physical illnesses, and all were drug-free for a minimum period of 1 week prior to endocrine investigations, except for a group of 13 who were prescribed 10-20 mg of temazepam at night.

CLINICAL ASSESSMENT

In the clinical assessment of the patients, the Hamilton Rating Scale for Depression (Hamilton, 1960) and the Present State Examination (PSE; Wing, Cooper, & Sartorius, 1974) were used as global measures of severity of depression. The Newcastle Diagnostic Index (Carney, Roth & Garside, 1965) was used to assign patients to diagnostic classes (i.e., "endogenous" vs. "neurotic".) We also used the CATEGO program of the PSE for classification; patients classified as R (retarded depression) and D (depressive psychosis) on this instrument were considered to be "endogenous," and patients allocated to class N (neurotic depression) were considered to be "neurotic." Demographic data were collected, and the LEDS was administered by two trained raters (ourselves). Events and difficulties were rated as present only if they met predefined inclusion criteria (i.e., the criteria for "severe events" and "major difficulties"; see Chapter 2, this volume). We restricted severe events to those occurring in the 6 months before onset. At the preanalytic stage of examining the relationship of difficulties to neuroendocrine change, a decision was made to include difficulties if they fulfilled the Bedford College criteria for "marked difficulties" and were present for 1 year or more before onset. This decision was made in order to obtain a reasonable sample size of patients with difficulties.

NEUROENDOCRINE ASSESSMENT

The neuroendocrine assessment was carried out in the following manner. After a 3-day acclimatization period, a 24-hour urine collection was taken from 11 P.M. on Day 1 to 11 P.M. on Day 2. A second 24-hour urine collection was started on Day 2 after the administration of 1 mg of dexamethasone at 11 P.M.. Blood was taken at 4 P.M. for plasma cortisol on Day 3. The first 24-hour urine sample was used to give a measure of baseline urinary free cortisol (UFC) production. The second 24-hour urine sample provided information on postdexamethasone UFC output. After an overnight fast, an intravenous butterfly needle was inserted at 8:15 A.M. on Day 5, and the line was kept open with heparin. Half an hour later, a baseline blood sample was taken, and 400 μg of TRH (Roche) was given over a 1-minute period. Further blood samples were taken at 20 minutes and 60 minutes after baseline. Cortisols in plasma and urine were measured in duplicate using a double-antibody radioimmunoassay (RIA) method (Amerlex Cortisol RIA kit). The coefficient of variation for repeated assays was 4.4%. Serum thyroxine (T_4) and T_3 update were measured in the baseline sample by RIAs using the RIA-UK kit. The intra-assay coefficients of variation were 6% and 7%, respectively. The free thyroxine index (FTI) was calculated by multiplying the two values and dividing by 100. TSH was measured in duplicate by double-antibody RIA techniques using the Amerlex TSH RIA kit. The interassay coefficient of variation was 3.2%. The variations found in the assay results were in line with findings from other studies in the field and did not affect the results significantly.

Results

CLINICAL PROFILE AND LIFE EVENTS/DIFFICULTIES

Table 5.1 summarizes demographic, clinical, and life events/difficulties data on the patients. The mean age of the population was 41.6 years; 43 (59.7%) of the subjects were female, and 20 (27.8%) were experiencing their first episode of depression. The RDC diagnoses of the patients were as follows: major depressive disorder, 54; probable major depressive disorder, 9; and minor depressive disorder, 9. Of the 72 patients, 70 met the criterion of caseness, utilizing the Index of Definition (ID) of the PSE – that is, an ID of 5 (Wing et al., 1974). The other 2 patients had an ID of 4. The PSE classifications of the patients were as follows: depressive psychosis (D), 6; retarded depression (R), 33; neurotic depression (N), 29; anxiety neurosis (A), 2; paranoia, 1; and obsessional neurosis, 1. The mean Hamilton score of the sample was 20.4 (± 7.1). On the Newcastle Diagnostic Index, half the patients were classified as endogenous and half as neurotic.

Twenty-eight (39%) of the patients had an independent or possibly independent severe life event before onset of their illness, and 15 (21%) had an independent or possibly independent major difficulty; 19 (26%) had a marked difficulty (i.e., present for over a year). Thirty-nine (54%) of the patients had either a severe life event or a major difficulty before onset. Most of the life events were either loss or danger events (see Chapter 3, this volume) and tended to reflect problems concerning work or significant relationships. Difficulties were predominantly danger difficulties, and about half of these were in the area of relationships. Fourteen patients (19.4%) had experienced the loss (by death or permanent separation) of one or both parents before the age of 11, and 24 (33.3%) had experienced either a loss or a separation of greater than 1 year before the age of 11. Forty-eight (66.6%) of the patients had either a

TABLE 5.1. Characteristics of the study population ($n = 72$)

Demographic variables	
Mean age (years)	41.6 (SD = 13.8, range 20-70)
Sex: Number (%) female	43 (59.7%)
Number (%) with family history of depression	30 (41.7%)
Previous history	
Mean age of onset of first episode (years)	32.9 (SD = 15.4, range 16-64)
Mean number of previous episodes	3.7 (SD = 2.9, range 0-8)
Mean number of previous admissions	0.8 (SD = 1.4, range 0-7)
Current episode	
Number (%) presenting with first episode	20 (27.8%)
Number (%) inpatients	28 (38.9%)
Mean duration of symptoms (months)	4.9 (SD = 3.2, range 1-12)
PSE diagnosis (CATEGO class)	
Depressive psychosis	6 (8.3%)
Retarded depression	33 (45.8%)
Neurotic depression	29 (40.3%)
Anxiety neurosis	2 (2.8%)
Paranoia	1 (1.4%)
Obsessional neurosis	1 (1.4%)
Life events/difficulties (from LEDS)	
Number (%) with severe life events before onset	28 (38.9%)
Number (%) with major difficulties before onset	15 (20.8%)
Number (%) with independent "provoking agents" before onset	39 (54.2%)
Number (%) with satisfactory relationship with spouse/partner	27 (37.5%)
Number (%) with loss of parent before age 11	14 (19.4%)
Endocrine variables	
Number (%) with raised 24-hour UFC secretion	38 (58.5%)
Number (%) nonsuppressors on DST	32 (44.4%)
Number (%) with raised FTI levels	16 (23.5%)
Number (%) with blunting of TRH test	31 (45.6%)

childhood loss/separation or a provoking agent before the onset. Forty-five (62.5%) of the patients did not have an "intimacy rating" of 1 (i.e., a warm, close, satisfactory relationship with spouse or partner – in other words, spouse/partner as "confidant"). Only 6 patients (8.3%) had no childhood loss/separation, no provoking agent, and an intimacy rating of 1.

Patients with severe life events had a greater mean Hamilton score (22.7 ± 7.0 vs. 18.9 ± 6.8), $F(1, 72) = 5.2$, $p < .05$, and a greater total PSE score (30.4 ± 11.3 vs. 24.1 ± 8.7), $F(1, 72) = 6.9$, $p < .01$, than those without such events. There were no differences between patients with and without major difficulties on these scales. Patients classified as endogenous according to the CATEGO program of the PSE (i.e., R and D) were as likely to have an antecedent severe life event or major difficulties as patients classified as neurotic (i.e., N). Furthermore, when the Newcastle Diagnostic Index was used to allocate patients to the diagnostic grouping of endogenous or neurotic, there were no significant differences between the groups in the incidence of severe antecedent life events or difficulties.

Those patients who were experiencing their first episodes of depression had a greater likelihood of a severe antecedent life event than those who had had one or more previous episodes (62% vs. 29%), $\chi^2 = 5.3$, $p < .05$. There were no differences in the incidence of major difficulties, in age, or in overall severity of illness between patients with a first onset of depression and those with a previous history.

NEUROENDOCRINE RESULTS

All 72 patients had a DST performed, and 68 a TRH test; 70 had predexamethasone and 65 postdexamethasone UFC estimations. The mean predexamethasone UFC was 158.6 µg/24 hours ($SD = 77.8$, range 33-378). As Table 5.1 indicates, 38 (58.5%) of the patients had predexamethasone UFC above the normal range (25-130 µg/24 hours). The postdexamethasone plasma cortisol level of 5 µg/dl was used as a cutoff point for nonsuppression (Carroll, 1982); by this criterion, 28 patients were classified as nonsuppressors. There were significant correlations between postdexamethasone plasma cortisol and postdexamethasone UFC levels, $r(67) = .79$, $p < .001$. With a linear regression function, the postdexamethasone UFC value corresponding to a plasma level of 5 µg/dl was found to be 58.01 µg/24 hours. The value 58 µg/24 hours was taken as a UFC cutoff point for nonsuppression. This produced 27 patients (37.5%) as nonsuppressors. When results from both methods were taken together, 32 patients (44.4%) were classified as nonsuppressors, and this group was used in the subsequent analysis.

The mean T_4 level of the patients was 11.9 nmol/liter ($SD = 3.7$, range 5.3-25.5), and the mean FTI was 38.9 nmol/liter ($SD = 10.9$, range

16.0-76.6). Sixteen (23.5%) patients had FTI levels above the upper limit of 45 nmol/liter. The mean maximum response of TSH to TRH was 10.0 μU/ml (SD = 10.5, range 0.5-71.0). When a cutoff point of 7 μU/ml was used, 31 patients (45.6%) had blunted responses. Patients with blunted responses had higher FTI values than those with normal responses, F (1, 58) = 4.32, $p < .05$.

DST STATUS AND CLINICAL PROFILES

It emerged that nonsuppressors appeared with above chance frequency among patients classified according to the RDC as having a definite or probable endogenous subtype of major depressive disorder than among those classified as nonendogenous (53% vs. 26%), χ^2 = 7.9, $p <$ .01. Those who were grouped as endogenous on the PSE were more likely to be nonsuppressors than those grouped as neurotic (64% vs. 24%), χ^2 = 10.6, $p < .001$. The proportion of nonsuppressors was similar in patients classified as endogenous and those classified as neurotic by the Newcastle Diagnostic Index (47% vs. 42%), n.s. According to the PSE syndrome scores, nonsuppressors were found to have more symptoms of depression anxiety. Discriminant-function analysis indicated that the PSE syndromes of general anxiety and slowness best discriminated between nonsuppressors and suppressors and were independently associated with nonsuppression.

HPA-AXIS FUNCTION AND LIFE EVENTS/DIFFICULTIES

Suppressor-nonsuppressor status on the DST was not associated with a greater or lesser likelihood of antecedent life events or difficulties. Thirteen (40.6%) of the nonsuppressors and 15 (37.5%) of the suppressors had a severe antecedent life event; 7 (21.9%) of the nonsuppressors and 8 (20%) of the suppressors had a major difficulty before onset.

Tables 5.2 and 5.3 present the UFC data for patients with and without severe life events and marked difficulties. Patients with severe life events in the 6 months before onset had significantly higher 24-hour UFC levels than those without severe life events (172.0 ± 62.3 vs. 147.9 ± 86.9 μg/24 hours), F (1, 62) = 4.25, $p < .05$. Similarly, patients with severe life events in the 6 months before incorporation into the study had significantly higher 24-hour UFC levels than those without such events (183.0 ± 68.3 vs. 146.1 ± 80.1 μg/24 hours), F (1, 63) = 4.6, p < .05. Patients with marked difficulties also had significantly higher 24-hour UFC levels than those without such difficulties (190.4 ± 57.8 vs. 146.4 ± 81.4 μg/24 hours), F (1, 55) = 10.53, $p < .005$). There were no differences in 24-hour postdexamethasone UFC levels between patients with life events or difficulties and those without life events or difficulties. Whether life events occurred between 1 and 3 months or

TABLE 5.2. Endocrine variables in patients with and without life events

Variable	Life events (n = 28)	No life events (n =44)
Mean UFC level (µg/24 hours)	172.0 ± 62.3	147.9 ± 86.9*
Number (%) of nonsuppressors	13 (46%)	19 (43%)**
Mean FTI level (nmol/liter)	41 ± 10	38 ± 11 ***
Number (%) with blunting	12 (43%)	19 (43%)**

*$F(1, 62) = 4.25$, $p < .05$ on analysis of variance.

**n.s. on chi-square test.

***$F(1, 68) = 7.68$, $p < .01$ on analysis of variance.

between 3 and 6 months before onset did not influence the results. Moreover, results were similar for independent and nonindependent life events and for the types of life events (e.g., loss or danger). The differences found were not explained by age, as there were no differences in age between those with and without life events or difficulties.

In addition to the analyses above, the relationship among UFC excretion, provoking agents (i.e., life events and difficulties), and vulnerability factors (e.g., early loss/separation) was examined for possible interactional effects, utilizing a multivariate analysis of variance (MANOVA). No significant findings emerged. Patients who had experienced loss of parents in childhood had similar UFC levels to those who had experienced a separation and those who had no loss/separation (161 ± 77.4 vs. 159.4 ± 82.4 vs. 158 ± 78.5). There was a nonsignificant trend for patients with a low intimacy rating to have higher cortisols than those with a high intimacy rating of 1 and those with an intermediate rating (182.3 ± 10.3 vs. 155.9 ± 80.4 vs. 152.7 ± 65.5).

BLUNTED TSH RESPONSE AND CLINICAL PROFILES

Patients with blunted TSH responses appeared with greater-than-chance frequency among those classified according to the RDC as having definite endogenous depressive disorder, as opposed to those with

TABLE 5.3. Endocrine variables in patients with and without marked difficulties

Variable	Difficulties (n = 19)	No difficulties (n = 53)
Mean UFC level (µg/24 hours)	190.4 ± 57.8	146.4 ± 81.4 *
Number (%) of nonsuppressors	9 (47%)	23 (43%)**
Mean FTI level (nmol/liter)	44 ± 12	38 ± 10 **
Number (%) with blunting	13 (68%)	18 (34%) ***

*$F(1, 55) = 10.53$, $p < .005$ on Brown-Forsythe test.

**n.s. on chi-square test.

***$\chi^2 = 4.34$, $p < .05$.

nonendogenous depressive disorder (62% vs. 30%), $\chi^2 = 5.5$, $p < .05$. The proportion of patients with blunted responses was similar in patients classified as endogenous and those classified as neurotic by the Newcastle Diagnostic Index. Similarly, the proportion of patients with blunted responses was similar in those classified as endogenous or neurotic (R and D vs. N) on the PSE. Discriminant-function analysis revealed that the PSE syndromes of depersonalization and agitation were associated with blunting. However, only half of the patients with blunting had one or both of these syndromes.

HPT-AXIS FUNCTION AND LIFE EVENTS/DIFFICULTIES

There was no difference in the proportion of patients experiencing a severe life event before onset or before the test and a blunted versus nonblunted response on the TRH test. However, patients with blunted responses were more likely to have experienced marked difficulties (42%) than patients with normal responses (16.2%), $\chi^2 = 4.34$, $p < .05$. When the patients with blunted responses were divided into two groups – those with abnormally high FTI levels (above 45 nmol/liter) and those with normal FTI levels – it was found that patients with blunted responses and high FTI levels were significantly more likely to have marked difficulties (73%) than those with blunted responses and normal FTI levels (25%), $\chi^2 = 6.64$, $p < .01$. The same calculation was made using an arbitrary cutoff point for FTI of 40 nmol/liter, which is at the upper end of normal. Of the 16 patients with high FTI values, 68.7% reported difficulties. Only 2 (13%) of the patients with FTI values below 40 nmol/liter reported difficulties, $\chi^2 = 8.88$, $p < .005$. Patients with blunting and high FTI levels (> 40 nmol/liter) were more likely to report a history of loss or separation from their parents before the age of 11 (69%) than patients with blunting and normal FTI levels (27%), $\chi^2 = 4.82$, $p < .05$. There was a definite pattern for women who had experienced childhood loss/separation from parents and who now had threats to their relationships (danger difficulties) to have high FTI levels and blunting.

Patients with severe events had higher FTI levels than those without such events (42.5 vs. 37.4 nmol/liter), $F(1, 68) = 7.68$, $p < .01$.

Patients who had lost a parent in childhood showed a nonsignificant trend to have higher FTI levels than those with separation or those with no loss/separation (41.1 ± 11.5 vs. 40.6 ± 10.9 vs. 38.3 ± 10.7). Interactions between these effects and other effects such as early loss/separation were examined using a MANOVA, but this did not reveal any significant findings. There was a nonsignificant trend for patients with life events between 1 and 3 months before onset to have higher FTI levels than those with events between 3 and 6 months before onset (45.9 ± 10.5 vs. 38.7 ± 10.4), $F(2, 63) = 2.64$, n.s. Moreover, patients with danger life events had higher FTI levels than those with loss events, who in turn had higher levels than those with no events (the few nonloss, nondanger events being excluded) (46.0 ± 8.3 vs. 39.3 ± 8.6 vs. 37.4 ± 11.3), $F(2, 63) = 3.5$, $p < .05$.

The Endogenous-Reactive Debate

Patients who were classified in the current study as having endogenous depression were just as likely to have an independent "provoking agent" or precipitant before onset as those classified as nonendogenous. This was found both with the CATEGO classification and the Newcastle Diagnostic Index, despite the fact that the presence of a precipitant on the latter is given a negative weighting for endogenous depression. This finding is in keeping with many earlier studies, which have thrown doubt upon the distinction between endogenous and nonendogenous (or situational and nonsituational) depression in terms of the presence or absence of precipitants (Leff, Roach, & Bunney, 1970; Thompson & Hendrie, 1972; Goodwin & Bunney, 1973; Paykel, 1974; Brown & Harris, 1978; Hirschfeld, 1981). A conflicting report is that of Bebbington, Tennant, and Hurry (1981). In a mixed sample of hospital outpatients and community cases, they found that those patients classified as R or D on the CATEGO were less likely to have a precipitant than those classified as N or A. This discrepant result could reflect the fact that the authors included only events occurring in the 3 months before onset. There was a low overall rate of events reported, particularly in the hospital outpatient population.

Our results, and those from the studies cited above, suggest that it is not valid to divide patients into categories on the basis of the presence or absence of precipitants. The dichotomous categorization of depressed patients has been called into question (Kendell, 1968). Indeed, these categories may simply reflect varying degrees of severity of depression rather than different conditions (Ní Bhrolcháin, Brown, & Harris, 1979). In this respect, it is of interest that in the present study patients with life events had greater total PSE scores and Hamilton scores than those without events. This could be seen as evidence that patients with precipitants were more severely ill, although it should be borne in mind that summed scores on rating scales can only partially reflect illness severity.

The DST, which has been suggested as an external validator or marker for endogenous depression, did not differentiate between patients with precipitants and those without. A blunted TSH response to TRH, which has also been suggested as a possible marker for endogenous depression, was associated with an increased likelihood of long-term environmental difficulties. These findings are in line with many other studies, which have also failed to find an association between endogenous depression and endocrine abnormalities.

Holsboer *et al.* (1980) found that the DST did not differentiate between patients diagnosed as having endogenous depression and those with neurotic or reactive depression. Lesser *et al.* (1983) reported on 37 patients with endogenous subtype of major depressive disorder, according to the RDC. Of 17 patients with "situational" depression, 8 were nonsuppressors, as compared to 5 of 20 with "nonsituational" depression. Berger *et al.* (1984), in a large study of the DST in depressed patients, found that it did not differentiate patients with endogenous depression from those with nonendogenous depression. Other factors, such as hospital admission, drug withdrawal, and weight loss, significantly influenced DST results. It is necessary to account for the discrepancies between such results and those of authors who find associations between nonsuppression on the DST or blunting on the TRH test and endogenous depression. One possible explanation is the confounding effect of psychotropic medication, in that many studies have been carried out on patients taking some form of medication. Severely depressed patients with anxiety or agitation who are treated with psychotropic drugs may experience relief from anxiety before other symptoms of depression are alleviated. These patients, who are likely to have endocrine abnormalities, thus may have a greater chance of being classified as endogenous depression (the Newcastle Diagnostic Index, for instance, loads negatively for anxiety) than if they had remained drug-free. This may cause a bias toward an association between endogenous depression and the endocrine abnormalities. It is important to be aware that *all* psychotropic drugs alter mental state. Results from studies that report associations between mental state (and therefore diagnosis) and other variables for patients on any medication should therefore be interpreted with caution.

A further source of error arises from the methodology used to determine the presence or absence of precipitants. In many studies, patients on admission have simply been asked in an unsystematic way about possible precipitating factors. Such assessments may not yield reliable data, and when used in the acute phase of depression may result in retarded or guilty patients' underreporting precipitants; such patients are less likely to seek external causes for their plight because of the retardation or self-blame. This may well result in a spurious association between these "endogenous" features (i.e., retardation and guilt) and the absence of precipitants. Instruments such as the LEDS, which can be applied retrospectively (and thus after recovery from depression) and which provide an objective measure of the importance of a precipitant, are less likely to result in such errors.

There is little evidence to support the central tenets of the concept of endogenous versus reactive depression: that patients with endogenous depression do not have important precipitating events, and that patients with precipitants are less severely depressed and are less likely to have biological changes. However, the habit of differentiating endogenous from nonendogenous depression in clinical practice is deeply entrenched, and probably has its basis, consciously or otherwise, in philosophical issues of mind and body. The view persists that "mental" disorders such as neurotic depression, grief, or distress are due to problems of living or "psychological" factors. If they are seen as clinical problems at all, it is thought that they should respond to "mental" treatment approaches such as psychotherapy or guided mourning. From this perspective, endogenous depression is then seen as a brain disease secondary to such physical abnormalities as neurotransmitter or receptor dysfunction; it is usually thought that these are inherited, that they need to be corrected by physical means, and that they are not influenced by psychological or environmental factors. However, there is no empirical basis for this dualist position, and, as summarized above, there is overwhelming evidence that environmental and psychological factors have profound physiological effects on the body. Despite this, attempts to find biological markers for "endogenous" depression persist, perhaps because of the wide spectrum of severity and clinical heterogeneity in depression. In severely depressed patients requiring urgent treatment, the relevance of environmental factors is often seen as merely theoretical, whereas it is easier to admit the role of precipitants when prescribing psychological or social interventions. This understandable but inaccurate perception helps to further the endogenous-reactive dichotomy. The reality would appear to be that environmental factors – early or late – are important in all the different syndromes of depression. It is obvious that some patients, generally those with more severe symptoms, have more physiological changes than others. These must reflect physiological processes as well as adaptive mechanisms. Future research should be directed at evaluating the contribution of these factors, as well as "biological" or hereditary factors, to the different syndromes of depression (as defined initially in terms of clinical profiles, and, eventually, in terms of structural or functional abnormalities).

The Endocrine Response to Stress

Patients with life events and difficulties in our study were found to have a greater 24-hour excretion of UFC than those without events or difficulties, although they were no more likely to be nonsuppressors. It has been shown that depressed patients who reported life events on the

Holmes and Rahe (1967) scale had higher cerebrospinal fluid cortisol levels than those without (Traskman et al., 1980). Baseline cortisol levels may reflect stress-related HPA-axis activity better than post-dexamethasone levels. Although both measures probably represent different degrees of HPA-axis activity, the DST abnormalities may be a result of more prolonged disinhibition of the axis (allowing time for impairment of the negative feedback mechanism), and so may be less likely to be related to immediate environmental influences. However, environmental factors can affect the DST in depressed and nondepressed subjects (Blumenfield et al., 1970; Berger et al., 1984; Coccaro et al., 1984). Moreover, the one previous study that has used the LEDS in an endocrine study of depressed patients reported a positive association between nonsuppression and the presence of life events, although the number of subjects was too small to be of statistical significance (Sashidharan et al., 1984).

Patients with life events and difficulties in our study were found to have higher FTI levels, indicating increased thyroid activity, and patients with difficulties were more likely than those without to have blunted TSH responses to TRH. This suggests that prolonged stress with frequent increases in thyroid output affects the negative feedback system, presumably by down-regulating pituitary TRH receptors, so that subsequent challenge with TRH results in a relatively impaired response (blunting). These results suggest that in some patients the endocrine changes represent an adaptive response to stress. The literature on the effects of stress on the HPA and HPT axes supports this, and suggests, moreover, that the nature of the response depends upon the duration of stress. Prolonged stress appears to be associated with abnormalities of thyroid function. In conditioned avoidance experiments with monkeys, there were early elevations of cortisols, whereas the measures of thyroid activity rose toward the end of the 3-day sessions, remaining elevated for longer (Mason, Brady, & Tulliver, 1968; Mason, Mousey, et al., 1968).

Not all of our patients with life events or difficulties showed endocrine abnormalities, because, as discussed earlier, there is wide individual variation in response to stress. Individual vulnerability depends on a number of different mediating factors. One effect that emerged from the present study was that of parental loss or separation in childhood. Patients with blunted TSH responses due to high thyroid hormone output (who were also those with an increased number of difficulties, and in whom the blunting probably reflected stress-related HPT activity) reported significantly more separations from parents before the age of 11. Such individuals may become "sensitized" to insecurity or danger in later life. Indeed, most of the difficulties reported by this group of patients represented threats to security in relationships or at work.

Women with losses or separations from parents in childhood appear to be particularly susceptible to threats to relationships in adult life. Such threats are perhaps more likely to produce physiological disturbances in subjects who are already vulnerable because of their childhood experiences. The present study was not able to demonstrate the influence of other mediating variables (personality, social isolation, adequacy of personal relationships, etc.), although patients with no confidants at all tended to have raised UFC levels – a finding in line with that of Kiecolt-Glaser *et al.*, (1984). A similar study carried out on a larger heterogeneous population would be more likely to reveal interactional effects of the various factors in producing the endocrine abnormalities. Longitudinal studies would have the additional benefit of being able to assess the specificity of endocrine response to duration of stress.

Implications for Psychosomatic Disorders

There is some evidence that psychological and environmental factors play a part in the etiology and onset of thyrotoxicosis, and that prolonged stress is particularly significant (Weiner, 1977). Weiner (1977) states that "central to most psychological formulations about patients with Graves Disease is that they have been predisposed to respond to danger or separation by previous environment." He reports a high incidence of loss of parents in childhood among patients, and reminds us that before current treatment methods the condition had a spontaneous remission rate of about 50%. In this context, the present findings (i.e., that patients with increased thyroid hormone output and blunting on the TRH test had a greater number of long-term difficulties and reported more childhood separations) are of considerable interest. These patients were not clinically hyperthyroid (although many had symptoms of anxiety, sweating, and tachycardia), and it would be of interest to know whether there are similar psychosocial factors in thyrotoxic patients. If this is the case, it will then be important to determine what features distinguish thyrotoxic patients from psychiatric patients with high thyroid output. It may be that biological factors (cf. the association of HLA-B8 tissue type with Graves disease) determine which subjects develop the full clinical syndrome of thyrotoxicosis. Another possible hypothesis is that psychiatric patients are capable of going on to develop thyrotoxicosis, but onset is prevented by the fact that they present as *psychiatric* patients, and thus alter their environment (as well as receiving treatments that affect the thyroid gland).

Severe depression is very common in patients with hypothalamic Cushing disease, but less common in Cushing syndrome (i.e., when there is some other cause, such as adrenal tumor, for increased cortisol output) (Starkman & Schteingart, 1981). Moreover, in Cushing disease, rather than Cushing syndrome, up to 50% of patients report either childhood losses or significant life events prior to onset (Cohen, 1980). Most of the tests of endocrine function are unable to distinguish between patients with severe depression and those with Cushing disease. However, depressed patients do not have the clinical signs of Cushing disease, and it would be premature to suggest that there is any overlap between the two conditions. It may, however, be reasonable to speculate that presenting as a psychiatric patient, with the changes in circumstances that ensue (e.g., admission, treatment), may modify the course of the illness and prevent Cushing disease from developing.

The HPA and HPT axes are of considerable interest in psychosomatic research because of their physiological effects and the fact that they provide a linking mechanism between the environment and somatic change. One area of obvious importance is the immune system. Cortisols have profound effects on the immune system (Stein, Keller, & Schleifer, 1979), and HPA activation could be a link between psychosocial stress and a range of conditions (e.g., infection and neoplasia) that are influenced by immunity.

Conclusion

Environmental factors influence HPA-axis and HPT-axis function in depressed and nondepressed men and women. This contradicts the assumption that if biological changes are present in psychiatric patients, then social factors such as life events are not relevant; it thus suggests that the classification of depression in terms of the presence or absence of precipitants (the endogenous-reactive dichotomy) is neither valid nor useful. Many factors, both biological and environmental, are important in the etiology and onset of the different syndromes of depression and in causing the endocrine changes associated with them. Future studies, using adequate measures of psychosocial variables, should be directed at trying to elucidate these. Only then will it be possible to establish what the marked abnormalities of HPA-axis and HPT-axis function mean in patients with depression and other disorders.

The HPA and HPT axes are of considerable interest in terms of their implications for psychosomatic disorder. In view of their responsiveness to the environment and their profound physiological effects, they provide a clear linking mechanism between psychosocial factors and physical change in the body.

References

Bebbington, P. E., Tennant, C., & Hurry, J. (1981). Adversity and the nature of psychiatric disorder in the community. *Journal of Affective Disorders, 3*, 345-366.

Berger, M., Pierke, K. M., Doerr, P., Krieg, J. C., & von Zerssen D. (1984). The limited utility of the dexamethasone suppression test for the diagnostic process in psychiatry. *British Journal of Psychiatry, 145*, 372-382.

Blumenfield, M., Rose, L. I., Richmond, L. M., & Beering, S. C. (1970). Dexamethasone suppression in basic trainees under stress. *Archives of General Psychiatry, 23*, 299-304.

Board, F., Wadeson, R., & Persky, H. (1957). Depressive affect and endocrine functions: Blood levels of adrenal cortex and thyroid hormones in patients suffering from depressive reactions. *Archives of Neurology and Psychiatry, 78*, 612-620.

Bridges, P. K., & Jones, M. T. (1968). Relationship of personality and physique to plasma cortisol levels in response to anxiety. *Neurosurgery and Psychiatry, 31*, 57-60.

Brown, G. W., & Harris, T. O. (1978). *Social origins of depression. A study of psychiatric disorder in women.* London: Tavistock.

Bunney, W. E., Mason, J. W., Roatch, J. F. & Hamburg, D. A. (1965). A psychoendocrine study of severe psychotic depressive crises. *American Journal of Psychiatry, 122*, 72-80.

Calloway, S. P., Dolan, R. J., Fonagy, P., De Souza, V. F. A., & Wakeling, A. (1984). Endocrine changes and clinical profiles in depression. *Psychological Medicine, 14*, 749-765.

Carney, M. W. P., Roth, M. & Garside, R. F. (1965). The diagnosis of depressive syndromes and the prediction of ECT response. *British Journal of Psychiatry, 111*, 659-674.

Carroll, B. J. (1976). Limbic system-adrenal cortex regulation in depression and schizophrenia. *Psychosomatic Medicine, 38*, 106-121.

Carroll, B. J. (1982). The dexamethasone suppression test for melancholia. *British Journal of Psychiatry, 140*, 292-304.

Cohen, S. I. (1980). Cushing's syndrome: A psychiatric study of 29 patients. *British Journal of Psychiatry, 136*, 120-124.

Coccaro, E. F., Prudic, J., Rothpear, A., & Nurnberg, H. G. (1984) Effect of hospital admission on DST results. *American Journal of Psychiatry, 141*, 982-985.

Curtis, G., Fogel, M., McEvoy, D., & Zarate, C. (1970). Urine and plasma corticorteroids, psychological tests, and effectiveness of psychological defences. *Journal of Psychiatric Research, 7*, 237-247.

Davis, K. L., Hollister, L. E., Math'e, A. A., Davis, B. M., Rothpearl, A. B., Faull, K. F., Hsieh, J. Y., Barchas, J. D., & Berger, P. A. (1981). Neuroendocrine and Neurochemical measurements in depression. *American Journal of Psychiatry, 138*, 1555-1562.

Dolan, R. J., Calloway, S. P., Fonagy, P., De Souza, F. V. A., & Wakeling, A. (1985). Life events, depression and hypothalamic-pituitary-adrenal axis function. *British Journal of Psychiatry, 147*, 429-433.

Ferrari, G. (1973). On some biochemical aspects of affective disorders. *Rivista Sperimentale di Freniztria e Medicina Legale delle Alienazioni Mentali, 93*, 1167-1175.

Gibbons, J. L., & McHugh, P. A. (1962). Plasma cortisol in depressive illness. *Journal of Psychiatric Research, 1*, 162-171.

Gibbons, J. L., Gibson, J. G., Maxwell, A. E., & Willcox, R. D. C. (1960). An endocrine study of depressive illness. *Journal of Psychosomatic Research, 5*, 32-41.

Goodwin, F. K., & Bunney, W. E. (1973). A psychological approach to affective illness. *Psychiatric Annals, 3,* 19-53.

Hamilton, M. (1960). A rating scale for depression. *Journal of Neurology, Neurosurgery and Psychiatry, 23,* 56-62.

Hirschfeld, R. M. A. (1981). Situational depression: Validity of the concept. *British Journal of Psychiatry, 139,* 297-305.

Holden, N. L. (1983). Depression and the Newcastle Scale: Their relationship to the dexamethasone suppression test. *British Journal of Psychiatry, 142,* 505-507.

Holmes, T. H., & Rahe, R. H. (1967). The Social Readjustment Rating Scale. *Journal of Psychosomatic Research, 11,* 213-218.

Holsboer, F., Bender, W., Benkert, O., Klein, H. E., & Schmauss, M. (1980). Diagnostic value of dexamethasone suppression test in depression. *Lancet, ii,* 706.

Kendell, R. E. (1968). *The classification of depressive illnesses* (Maudsley Monograph No. 18). London: Oxford University Press.

Kennon, F. T. (1979). Psychological correlates of serum indicators of stress in man: A longitudinal study. *Psychosomatic Medicine, 41,* 617-628.

Kiecolt-Glaser, J. K., Ricker, D., George, J., Messick, G., Spiechel, C. E., Garner, W., & Glaser, R. (1984). Urinary cortisol levels, cellular immunocompetency, and loneliness in psychiatric inpatients. *Psychosomatic Medicine, 46,* 15-23.

Kierkegaard, C., & Faber, J. (1981). Altered serum levels of thyroxine, triiodothyronines and diiodothyronines in endogenous depression. *Acta Endocrinologica, 96,* 199-207.

Kolakowska, T., & Swigar, M. E. (1977). Thyroid function in depression and alcohol abuse: A retrospective study. *Archives of General Psychiatry, 34,* 984-988.

Leff, M. J., Roatch, J. F., & Bunney, W. E. (1970). Environmental factors preceding the onset of severe depression. *Psychiatry, 33,* 293-311.

Lesser, I. M., Rubin, R. T., Finder, E., Forster, B., & Poland, R. E. (1983). Situational depression and the dexamethasone suppression test. *Psychosomatic Medicine, 8,* 441-445.

Levi, L. (1972). Stress and distress in response to psychosocial stimuli. *Acta Medica Scandinavica* (Suppl. 528).

Loosen, P. T., & Prange, A. J. (1982). Serum thyrotrophin response to thyrotropin-releasing hormone in psychiatric patients: A review. *American Journal of Psychiatry, 139,* 405-416.

Mason, J. W. (1968a). A review of psychoendorcrine research on the pituitary-adrenal cortical system. *Psychosomatic Medicine, 30,* 576-607.

Mason, J. W. (1968b). A review of psychoendocrine research on the pituitary-thyroid system. *Psychosomatic Medicine, 30,* 666-681.

Mason, J. W. (1975). Emotion as reflected in patterns of endocrine integration. In L. Levi (Ed.), *Emotions, their parameters and measurements* (pp. 143-207). New York: Raven Press.

Mason, J. W., Brady, J. U. & Tulliver, G. A. (1968). Plasma and urinary 17-hydroxycorticosteroid: Response to 72-hour avoidance sessions in the monkey. *Psychosomatic Medicine, 30,* 608-630.

Mason, J. W., Mousey, E. M., Brady, J. U., & Tulliver, G. A. (1968). Thyroid (plasma butanol-extractable iodine) response to 72-hr avoidance sessions in the monkey. *Psychosomatic Medicine, 30,* 682-695.

Mattsson, A. (1971). Psychoendocrine study of adaptation in young haemophiliacs. *Psychosomatic Medicine, 33,* 215-225.

Mendlewicz, J., Charles, G., & Franckson, J. M. (1982). The dexamethasone suppression test in affective disorder: Relationship to clinical and genetic subgroups. *British Journal of Psychiatry, 141,* 464-470.

Ní Bhrolcháin, M., Brown, G. W., & Harris, T. O. (1979). Psychotic and neurotic depression: II. The clinical characteristics. *British Journal of Psychiatry, 134,* 94-107.

Nuller, J. L., & Ostroumova, M. N. (1980). Resistance to inhibiting effect of dexamethasone in patients with endogenous depression. *Acta Psychiatrica Scandinavica, 61,* 169-177.

Paykel, E. S. (1974). Life stress and psychiatric disorder: Applications of clinical approach. In B. S. Dohrenwend & B. P. Dohrenwend (Eds.) *Stressful life events: Their nature and effects* (pp. 139-149). New York: Wiley.

Persky, H., Zuckerman, M., & Curtis, G. C. (1968). Endocrine functions in emotionally disturbed and normal men. *Journal of Nervous and Mental Disease, 146,* 488-497.

Rabkin, J. G., Quitkin, F. H., Stewart, J. W., McGrath, P. J., & Puig-Antich, J. (1983). The dexamethasone suppression test with mildly to moderately depressed outpatients. *American Journal of Psychiatry, 140,* 926-927.

Rabkin, J. G., & Struening, E. L. (1976). Life events, stress and illness. *Science, 194,* 1013-1020.

Rinieris, P., M., Christodoulou, G. N., Souvatzoglou, A. M., Koutras, D. A., & Stefanis, C. N. (1978). Free-thyroxine index in psychotic and neurotic depression. *Acta Psychiatrica Scandinavica, 58,* 56-60.

Sachar, E. J. (1967a). Corticosteroids in depressive illness: I. A re-evaluation of control issues and the literature. *Archives of General Psychiatry, 17,* 544-553.

Sachar, E. J. (1967b). Corticosteroids in depressive illness: II. A longitudinal psychoendocrine study. *Archives of General Psychiatry 17,* 554-67.

Sachar, E. J. (1970). Psychological factors relating to activation and inhibition of the adrenocortical stress response in man: A review. *Progress in Brain Research, 32,* 316-324.

Sachar, E. J. (1975). Twenty-four-hour cortisol secretory patterns in depressed and manic patients. *Progress in Brain Research, 42,* 81-91.

Sachar, E. J., Hellman, L., Fukushima, D. K., & Gallagher, T. F. (1970). Cortisol production in depressive illness. A clinical and biochemical clarification. *Archives of General Psychiatry, 23,* 289-298.

Sachar, E. J., Hellman, L., Roffwarg, H. P., Halpern, F. S., Fukushima, D. K., & Gallagher, T. F. (1973). Disrupted 24-hour patterns of cortisol secretion in psychotic depression. *Archives of General Psychiatry, 28,* 19-24.

Sachar, E. J., Mackenzie, J. M., Binstock, W. A., Mack, J. E. (1967). Corticosteroid responses to psychotherapy of depressions: I. Evaluations during confrontation of loss. *Archives of General Psychiatry, 16,* 461-470.

Sashidharan, S. P., Freeman, C. P., Lojomon, J. B., Novosel, S., Beckett, G. J., & Gray, S. (1984). Dexamethasone suppression test in depression: Association with duration of illness. *Acta Psychiatrica Scandinavica, 70,* 354-360.

Schlesser, M. A., Winokur, G., & Sherman, B. M. (1980). Hypothalamic-pituitary-adrenal axis activity in depressive illness: Its relationship to classification. *Archives of General Psychiatry, 37,* 737-743.

Spitzer, R. L., Endicott, J., & Robins, E. (1978). Research Diagnostic Criteria: Rationale and reliability, *Archives of General Psychiatry, 35,* 773-782.

Starkman, M. N., & Schteingart, D. E. (1981). Neuropsychiatric manifestations of Patients with Cushing's syndrome: Relationship of cortisol and adrenocorticotropic hormone levels. *Archives of Internal Medicine, 141,* 215-219.

Stein, M., Keller, S., & Schleifer, S. (1979). Role of the hypothalamus in mediating stress effects on the immune system. In B. A. Stoll (Ed.), *Mind and cancer progress* (pp. 85-101). New York: Wiley.

Stokes, P. E., Stoll, P. M., Mattson, M. R., & Sollod, R. N. (1976). Diagnosis and psychopathology in psychiatric patients resistant to dexamethasone. In E. J. Sachar (Ed.), *Hormones, behavior and psychopathology* (pp. 225-229). New York: Raven Press.

Thompson, K. C., & Hendrie, H. C. (1972). Environmental stress in primary depressive illness. *Archives of General Psychiatry, 26*, 130-132.

Traskman, L., Tybring, G., Asberg, M., Bertilsson, L., Lantto, O., & Schalling, D. (1980). Cortisols in the CSF of depressed and suicidal patients. *Archives of General Psychiatry, 37*, 761-767.

Verghese, A., Mathew, J., Mathai, G., Kothoor, A., Saxena, B. N., & Koshy, T. S. (1973). Plasma cortisol in depressive illness. *Indian Journal of Psychiatry, 15*, 72-79.

Weiner, H. (1977). *Psychobiology and human disease*. New York. Elsevier.

Whybrow, P. C., & Prange, A. J. (1981). A hypothesis of thyroid-catecholamine-receptor interaction. *Archives of General Psychiatry, 38*, 106-113.

Wing, J. K., Cooper, J. E., & Sartorius, N. (1974). *The measurement and classification of psychiatric symptoms*. London: Cambridge University Press.

Wolff, C. T., Friedman, S. B., Hofer, M. A., & Mason, J. W. (1964). Relationship between defences and mean urinary 17-hydroxycorticosteroid rates. *Psychosomatic Medicine, 26*, 576-591.

Yamaguchi, T., Hatotani, N., Nomura, J., & Ushijima, Y. (1977). Function of hypothalamo-pituitary axis in depressed patients. *Folia Psychiatrica Neurologica, Japonica, 31*, 173-181.

6

Adversity and Psychiatric Disorder: A Decay Model

PAUL G. SURTEES

During the early 1970s, the use of life events questionnaires rapidly increased, as the method appeared to provide a quick and inexpensive means of obtaining a composite measure of the event stress experienced by an individual during a given study period. Despite fervent criticism on methodological and theoretical grounds (Brown, 1974), and the development of the semistructured interview technique called the Life Events and Difficulties Schedule (LEDS), list or respondent-based methods have remained the technique of choice for most researchers. Although economic reasons are without doubt a primary factor in explaining this, it is also possible that researchers regard certain attributes of the LEDS approach with some skepticism.

The theoretical underpinning of the LEDS is that stressors are envisaged in binary rather than continuous terms. With few exceptions, published work in which the LEDS has been used reports results in a way that sets boundaries for presence versus absence of stressors. What is usually determined is either the presence or absence of an event, or the presence or absence of an event of a particular type (usually severe vs. nonsevere, as defined by a combination of long-term threat and focus ratings). The boundaries are also imposed on the basis of threat scales that have only a very limited range (originally only 4 points), and yet that are designed to accommodate the universe of stressful events. The particular cutoff point employed therefore takes on a crucial significance in terms of its meaning, reliability, and validity. The LEDS concentrates on characteristics of particular events and difficulties and does not attempt to provide an overall measure of life stress experienced (this not being a dominant objective in its development). The method enables a history of events and of long-term difficulties to be obtained

Paul G. Surtees. Medical Research Council Unit for Epidemiological Studies in Psychiatry, University Department of Psychiatry, Royal Edinburgh Hospital, Morningside Park, Edinburgh EH10 5HF, Scotland.

for an individual covering a chosen study period. This allows, for example, differences in event rates between groups to be examined, though this has not been the preferred method of analysis. Greater value has been placed on the results from analyses examining the presence or absence of a severe event within a study period, or, more usually, the joint index of a severe event and/or a long-term difficulty. This approach has enabled considerable advances to be made in understanding relationships between stressors and health state, as this volume testifies.

However, it is conceivable that such a procedure, by its dependence on a particular cutoff point for a stressor, may direct or even prejudice theoretical developments in adversity research and thus limit the potential for new substantive findings. In addition, the now-accepted procedure of combining two different forms of stress, events and long-term difficulties, each with their own separate etiological significance, may confound analysis (though, of course, events frequently lead to difficulties and difficulties to events). It is also possible that the relative causal importance of events and difficulties may be a function of the particular study period covered. This is evident if two hypothetical studies are considered, one assessing the 3 months before interview, and the other the year before interview. In both studies, all long-term difficulties that are current at interview and that satisfy duration criteria (e.g., continuing for at least 2 years) are determined; however, the two studies are bound to differ considerably in terms of the assessed significance of events.

A fundamental issue, however, and one that is often overlooked, is the relative neglect of timing in assessing the impact of stressors. Although the LEDS approach recognizes the ameliorative effects of elapsed time following the occurrence of events in assigning long-term threat ratings (some consensus is reached on the likely circumstances 1 week to 10 days after the event), the threat of events at times after their occurrence, especially those times of particular interest to the researcher (e.g., illness onset, change in health, admission to a hospital, etc.), cannot be determined. The approach of Brown and Harris and their colleagues has been to consider that certain categories of events have what they term an "etiological effect" within particular times (their "causal" periods) following their occurrence. However, the justification for attributing such qualities to events is based only on crude period analyses. It is clear, therefore, that if a method existed that would provide an estimate of the *residual stress* due to preceding events at *any* time within a study period, then the opportunity for testing hypotheses concerning vulnerability, stress tolerance, and issues of specificity would be enhanced.

It is with these aims in mind that a model of event stress has been developed and designed to provide a composite index of the residual adversity that is due to the combined effects of different life events occurring at different times. As long as events are rated on a common scale and are carefully dated, then the model can be applied. In practice, therefore, although it is feasible to apply the methodology to event data collected from respondent-based techniques, this has so far *not* been done.

All the results to be discussed in this chapter are derived from studies where the LEDS has been used. As a consequence, this permits a contrast between a binary and a continuous method of conceptualizing event stress. However, it is important to note that the decay model links *two* basic assumptions not made by Brown and Harris – namely, decay *and* additivity. The results also reflect the consequences of adopting certain refinements to the model.

The Decay Model

Two postulates concerning life events were incorporated in the simplest form of the model. (1) The stressful effect of a life event decays with time at a *constant rate*, with this rate being the same for all events; and (2) life events summate in their stressful effect.

The consequence of applying these postulates can be seen in the following simple example. Consider a study period of 18 months in which two life events (A and B) have occurred, as shown in Figure 6.1.

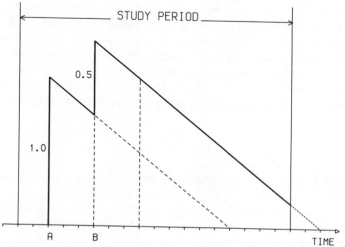

FIGURE 6.1. Schematic representation of the linear decay in stressful effect of two life events, A and B.

If it is assumed that the first event to occur (event A) is a severe event (e.g., it is of initial threat magnitude 1, and is assumed to decay completely in a year), and the second event (event B) is a nonsevere event (e.g., it is of initial threat magnitude 0.5 and is assumed to have no residual threat remaining after 6 months), then the level of residual threat remaining due to these two events can be determined for any time of interest. Note that the rate of decay is *constant*. Furthermore, the individual events are *not* assumed to decay *in vacuo*; summation in residual threat is postulated. Given the assumptions imposed on the two events, it is possible therefore to determine the residual stress remaining and attributable to them at any time in the study period following their occurrence. For instance, at the time event B occurs, 0.75 units of event A remain; 3 months later, the *combined* threat has decayed to 1.0 units; and by the end of the study period, 0.167 units remain.

Plan of the Chapter

This model has now been applied to data from several studies designed to investigate the relationship between life stress and psychological state. These analyses reflect stages in the development of the modeling procedure. One stage was concerned with contrasting findings based upon this model of linear decay with those based upon an approach that conceptualizes stress in binary terms. A series of empirical analyses also examined the extent to which variation in decay periods assigned to events altered the magnitude of association between residual adversity and symptom state among different clinical groups. More recent analyses have attempted to develop these ideas further – first, by modifying the assumption of linear decay underlying the modeling procedure, and, second, by attempting to allow for *individual* rather than *group* differences in stress-adaptive capacity. The greater part of this chapter presents results obtained during these developmental stages and based upon studies undertaken in London (Camberwell) and in Edinburgh.

The Camberwell Studies

Two community surveys of women undertaken by Brown and his colleagues during 1969-1971 and 1974-1975 in the London borough of Camberwell, and two patient samples obtained during 1968-1970 from women resident in Camberwell, provided the first opportunity to examine the use of the decay model in relation to the *onset* of depressive disorder. After women with chronic conditions were excluded, the community surveys provided information on 419 women, 37 of whom experienced an onset of depressive illness (with or without anxiety) at some time during the year covered by the interview. The patients included an inpatient sample of 73 women and an outpatient sample of 41 women selected from admissions to and attendance at the Maudsley Hospital (for details of the design, see Brown, Sklair, Harris, & Birley, 1973; Brown & Harris, 1978b). The LEDS was given to all the women for the year prior to interview. In addition, a modified form of the Present State Examination (PSE; Wing, Cooper. & Sartorius, 1974), covering the entire study period, was administered; this in conjunction with an onset schedule, enabled points of change in clinical state to be dated.

Details of how the event ratings derived from the LEDS have been incorporated within the decay model for these and other studies have been described in detail elsewhere (Surtees & Ingham, 1980; Surtees & Rennie, 1983). Although several methods have been used, the one found to have greatest salience was the direct linkage of long-term threat and event focus ratings to the postulates of the decay model. This strategy insured that the decay *periods* assigned to events could extend over a broader range than would otherwise have been possible if threat ratings alone had been used. The initial weighting assigned to each event is shown in Table 6.1. The weighting provided for a ratio of the most to the least stressful events of 16:1.

The initial analyses determined the levels of residual adversity at onset of illness or interview for those women interviewed in the community studies. Only those events considered logically independent of the illness episodes were included. The basis for determining the stress value was varied according to whether (1) all events were considered or just severe events, and (2) the decay period associated with the most severely rated event was 6 months or 1 year. This gave four sets of results. Two additional sets were obtained by assuming no decay, using

TABLE 6.1. Event weights assigned to LEDS event rating combinations (Camberwell analysis)

LEDS event ratings		Event weightings in relation to that of the most severe event
Long-term threat	Focus[a]	
1	S	1.0
1	O	0.75
2	S	0.5
2	O	0.375
3	S	0.25
3	O	0.1875
4	S	0.125
4	O	0.0625

[a] S, subject-focused; O, other-focused.

(1) severe events and (2) all events. The recorded adversity values determined by each of the six analyses were then ranked (high values to low), and the relative rate of selection of the onset cases to selection of normal women was determined. The results are shown in Figure 6.2.

The figure reveals that the relative rate of selection of women with illness onset to selection of those without was improved, regardless of event class, as soon as event decay was included. In addition, it is clear that the modeling procedure permitted considerable choice concerning the proportion of cases or normals selected. But how would these results

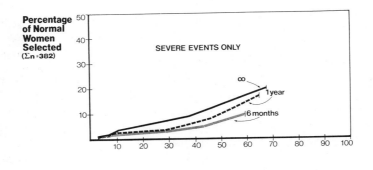

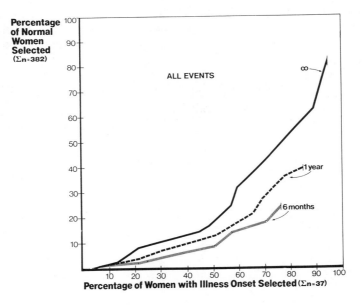

FIGURE 6.2. The relative rate of selection of women with illness onset to selection of normal women, determined according to their ranked level of residual adversity at onset or interview. Event classes and maximal decay periods were varied as shown.

compare to those obtained using a simple binary scale of experience or
not of a severe event? To undertake this comparison, *two* approaches
were adopted. The first was a comparison of the classical measures of
association obtained using the binary measure with those obtained
using the measure of residual event stress; the second was a logistic
modeling approach.

Classical Measures

The results of the first method of analysis are shown in Table 6.2. Three
measures are displayed: relative risk, variance explained, and population (percentage) attributable risk (PAR). This last measure was devised
by Levin (1953) and was designed to represent either the maximum proportion of a disease that could be attributed to a given agent or the
proportional decrease in disease incidence if the agent were removed
from the total population. Miettinen (1974) has more recently referred
to this measure as the "etiologic fraction" (see also Lilienfeld &
Lilienfeld, 1980). Results based on the decay approach revealed that for
the optimal selection of women with depressive disorder to a minimum
selection of normal women, a 6-month rather than a 1-year decay period
(assigned to the most severely rated event) was most appropriate, and
this has been used in what follows.

Of those women with an onset of illness, 67.6% ($n = 25$) experienced
at least one severe event, in contrast to 19.6% ($n = 75$) of the normal

TABLE 6.2. Measures of the association between event stress and onset of depression
(Camberwell data)

Basis for analysis	Population (%) attributable risk (PAR)	Relative risk	Variance explained (%)
Binary (severe event) measure (number of cases selected = 25)	57.4	6.65	10.18
Adversity index[a]			
A. Severe events only (cutoff point at maximum number of cases selected; $n = 22$)	53.0	9.12	16.90
B. All events (cutoff point chosen in order to select a number of cases equivalent to that selected with the binary measure[b]	61.7	8.17	12.74
C. All events (cutoff point at maximum number of cases selected; $n = 28$)	66.0	7.84	10.65

[a] With assumptions of linear decay and of the most severe event's having no residual effect 6 months
after occurring.

[b] Cases ranked 25th and 26th had identical residual adversity scores.

group. This gave a relative risk of illness associated with a severe event (based on the original approach of Brown and Harris) of 6.65. In addition, the PAR of onset of depression associated with event exposure (see Table 6.2) was found to be 57.4%. These measures were compared to those based upon the decay approach, though this was somewhat problematic, given the sensitivity of the decay-based measures to both the placement of any (arbitrary) cutoff point and the classes of events included in the modeling procedure. If the model was based only upon severe events *and* the cutoff point was placed in order to select the maximum number of cases, then the PAR value based on the decay approach (53.0%) was much the same as that obtained by the binary method. However, the values for both relative risk and variance explained were much improved beyond those obtained using the Brown and Harris criterion. It was quite clear, however, that although the relative rate of selection of cases to normals exceeded that produced by the no-decay analysis (22 onset cases could be selected to 36 normals), it remained impossible to select as many onset cases as when the severe event criterion alone was used (22 in the decay and 25 in the binary).

Table 6.2 also shows the results of two further analyses when the class of events in the analysis was broadened to include *all* events. In the first (B in Table 6.2), a cutoff was adopted in order to select a proportion of onset cases (67.6%) equivalent to that achieved using a binary (severe event) criterion. This produced a relative risk of 8.17 with a PAR of 61.7%. The second analysis (C in Table 6.2) showed that if the (arbitrary) cutoff imposed on the residual adversity measure was fixed at the point that selected the maximum number of cases, then all three measures of association *exceeded* those based upon the Brown and Harris severe event criterion.

Logistic Modeling Approach

The results above provided one basis for examining the relative magnitude of the association between the stress measures and case status, but required the imposition of cutoff points on the (continuous) adversity index – a procedure likely to synthetically limit the associative strength of the measure (see Breslow & Day, 1980). An alternative procedure that would avoid the problem was logistic regression. However, it was equally important that if a logistic procedure were chosen, then the modeling of the variables should be carefully explored in order to avoid overinterpretation of findings.

The relationship between the adversity indices and case status was therefore examined using logistic regression. Examination of the distributions of the raw index scores showed that few individuals had very high values, and suggested that in modeling the relationship between stress and illness, the consequence of setting an upper threshold limit should be investigated. The importance of this is shown in Table 6.3 for one adversity index – that based upon all events with linear decay assumed, and with any severe event considered to have no residual threat remaining after the lapse of 6 months.

The results shown in Table 6.3 clearly indicate that the measure of residual adversity was highly significant, producing a change in scaled deviance of 24.4 on 1 df (model 2 in Table 6.3). The analysis could, of course, have easily ended here. However, to take into account the distributional characteristics of the stress index, as mentioned above, a quadratic term in the index (the index squared) was additionally modeled. The consequence is shown as model 3. This analysis produced an *additional* change in scaled deviance of 15.8 on 1 df ($p << .001$). The final analysis (model 4 in Table 6.3) showed the consequence of imposing an upper "ceiling" threshold on the level of residual adversity at onset of illness or interview. The threshold was set at 500 units, which represented the scaled value of a moderately threatening severe event (long-term threat rating of 2, *and* subject-focused. The result of this analysis indicated that imposing this threshold would replace the need for the quadratic term by producing an equivalent change in scaled deviance, but on only *one* degree of freedom. Although the result in reality probably reflected the relative rarity of women with high (>500) levels of residual adversity at onset of illness or interview, it is nevertheless tempting to speculate that the result may also be evidence for a "ceiling" or upper threshold effect. Such a conclusion, if correct, would suggest that the LEDS severe-nonsevere threshold is "pitched" appropriately for discrimination purposes. This issue is raised again below in the context of another data set.

The procedure just described for the residual stress measure, based upon all events and incorporating a maximal event decay period of 6 months, was now repeated for those other indices contributing to Figure 6.2. The results of the logistic analyses based upon these measures

TABLE 6.3. Logistic modeling results of fitting one adversity index to case status (Camberwell data)

Model	Parameters	df	Residual deviance	Change in deviance
1	0	418	250.2	–
2	Adversity	417	225.8	24.4
3	Adversity + adversity[2]	416	210.0	+15.8
4	Adversity (C)[a]	417	209.3	40.9

Note. The index in this case was based on all events, with assumptions of linear decay and of the most severe event's having no residual effect 6 months after occurring.

[a] Upper "ceiling" threshold (C) imposed (see text).

are set forth in Table 6.4. They showed that regardless of whether or not the class of events was restricted (e.g., to severe events alone), allowance for decay in threat brought about an improvement in the fit of the stress measure to the case status data. Model 5 showed the degree to which the original binary severe event measure fitted the data, a highly significant result. However, models 6 and 7 indicated that this fit could be improved upon when allowance was made for threat decay. Finally, and perhaps most significantly, model 4 provided a better fit to the data than that achieved with the binary measure. The importance of this result was given further emphasis when the effects of models 4 and 5 were considered *together* in the same analysis (see model 8). The results revealed that although model 5 (i.e., the binary measure) made no significant additional contribution beyond model 4 (scaled deviance 3.5, $df = 1$, n.s.), the residual stress measure produced a significant *additional* reduction in scaled deviance of 8.9 ($df = 1$, $p < .005$) beyond model 5.

What, therefore, do the results based upon the classical measures of association and those from the logistic analysis reveal concerning the two approaches to dealing with event stress? Both sets of results confirm the predictive value and importance of the binary measure and illustrate its attractiveness. Much of its appeal lies in its simplicity; it embodies no complex assumptions concerning additivity or decay period. However, it is also clear that through the adoption of such assumptions as are

TABLE 6.4. Logistic modeling results of fitting other adversity indices to case status (Camberwell data)

Model	Basis for stress index	df	Residual deviance	Change in deviance	Standardized coefficient
1	0	418	250.2	–	–
	All events				
2	No decay	417	233.7	16.5	3.58
3	1 year decay	417	218.2	32.0	5.36
4	6 months decay	417	209.3	40.9	6.35
	Severe events only				
5	No decay[a]	417	214.7	35.5	5.79
6	1 year decay	417	210.6	39.6	6.32
7	6 months decay	417	203.2	47.0	7.02
	Joint effects				
8	Model 5				1.91
	+				
	Model 4	416	205.8	+8.9	2.91

Note. All indices had an upper threshold imposed.

[a] Equivalent to the binary measure.

included within the modeling procedure, PAR values, estimates of relative risk, and variance explained, together with changes in scaled deviance, can all be shown to be enhanced (to varying degrees) beyond those attainable through use of the binary measure. The results do suggest, therefore, that the decay model does provide an alternative approach and one that might give an opportunity for more flexibility in analysis.

The availability of the Camberwell data also permitted an examination of the relationship among residual adversity values, the timing of illness onset, and *subsequent* patient status. Such relationships could be investigated using event rates; however, if events have a "stressful lifetime," then rate analyses would tend to mask relationships, because they make no provision for duration of event effect. Analyses were therefore performed upon the 73 hospital inpatients and the 41 outpatients mentioned previously. The mean level of residual adversity that was due to *all* illness-independent events was determined for each of the weeks *preceding* and *following* illness onset. To provide a comparison group, similar analyses were performed upon the community sample up to the time of interview (all onset cases were excluded). The modeling procedure that was adopted assigned a 6-month decay period to the most severely rated events.

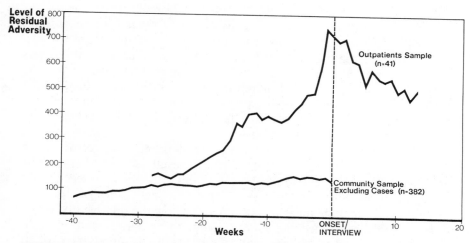

FIGURE 6.3. Mean level of residual adversity for weeks preceding and following time of illness onset (hospital outpatients) and preceding time of interview (normal women).

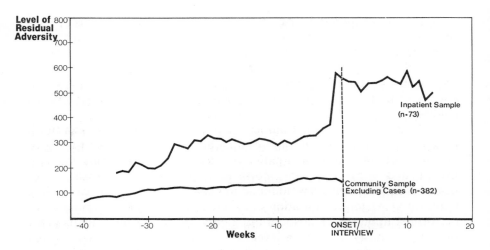

FIGURE 6.4. Mean level of residual adversity for weeks preceding and following time of illness onset (hospital inpatients) and preceding time of interview (normal women).

The results are shown in Figures 6.3 and 6.4. Figure 6.3 reveals that although mean adversity levels peaked close in time to illness onset, they *dropped* following onset for this group of patients who were given treatment on an outpatient basis. These results were in contrast to those for the inpatients (Figure 6.4). For this group, although illness onset again shortly followed the mean peak adversity level reached, this level was *maintained* for almost 15 weeks, equaling the average time to hospital admission following illness onset for this patient group. Figure 6.4 also shows that the maintained level of adversity for the onset group was about four times that of the community sample at interview. The results shown in Figures 6.3 and 6.4 therefore resembled those obtained on the basis of event rate analyses preceding illness onset (see Brown & Harris, 1978b), but revealed new relationships between levels of adversity and patient status *following* illness onset.

The Camberwell studies were single-interview retrospective designs; it was important, therefore, to establish whether results obtained in that context would be congruent with those based upon a multi-interview, longitudinal research design. Such a design however, would need to include measures that would allow the relative juxtaposition of event occurrence and illness change to be determined; in addition, it would need to utilize diagnostic procedures embodying explicit operational definitions. A community study undertaken in Edinburgh was designed to incorporate these objectives.

The Edinburgh Community Study

Methods

The study was undertaken in a discrete area of Edinburgh on a random sample of 576 women aged 18-65 years, selected from a total eligible population of approximately 44,000 (1981 census). A subsample of those women initially interviewed were approached for reinterview 6 months and 1 year later. Details of the design and methods of the survey are provided in two other publications (Surtees *et al.*, 1983; Surtees, Sashidharan, & Dean, 1986), and the present account is thus kept to the barest minimum. The principal aims of this longitudinal study were to compare and contrast different diagnostic schemes (e.g., see Dean, Surtees, & Sashidharan, 1983; Surtees & Sashidharan, 1986); to describe the course, prevalence, and incidence of psychiatric disorders in the general population (see Surtees, Sashidharan, & Dean, 1986); and to examine the relationship between psychosocial factors and disorder (e.g., see Surtees, 1984; Miller, Surtees, Kreitman, Ingham, & Sashidharan, 1985; Ingham, Kreitman, Miller, Sashidharan, & Surtees, 1986; Surtees, Miller, *et al.*, 1986).

At each of the interviews, the subject's psychiatric status was evaluated using a semistructured clinical interview schedule, the Psychiatric Assessment Schedule (PAS). This was based on the first 40 items of the PSE and selected items from the Schedule for Affective Disorders and Schizophrenia (SADS; Endicott & Spitzer, 1978). The PAS first provided a detailed assessment of each respondent's psychiatric status for the month preceding each interview. If significant symptoms of dysphoric mood were present (anxiety, loss of interest, or depression), then the interviewer followed a semistructured schedule to probe for illness change points and to establish accurately when the onset and remission of the illness episode had occurred. Following the 1-month assessment, whether this had revealed the presence of symptoms or not, the interviewer inquired about the occurrence of specified symptoms in the remaining interinterview period. For most women, this was about 5 months (Dean *et al.*, 1983).

If, after checking interview material, the staff found evidence of psychiatric illness, the audiotape of the interview was rerated. Consensus symptom ratings were then established by joint discussion between the interviewer and a staff rater. Finally, all clinical changes were re-evaluated by staff members, using the total available information, in order to date them in relation to each respondent's final interview and to apply the Research Diagnostic Criteria (RDC; Spitzer, Endicott, & Robins, 1978) scheme to all available symptom data (see Surtees, Sashidharan, & Dean, 1986).

The assessment of life stress resembled that developed at Bedford College, except that the initial procedure for eliciting potential life events and difficulties was a list (on which the subject checked off items) rather than a set of questions asked orally. The interviewer *then* obtained all necessary contextual information concerning each putative incident, in order to classify and assign ratings. Typically, the 6-month period preceding each interview was covered. Events were dated to the nearest week prior to final interview, and long-term difficulties were rated in terms of their duration and whether they were still continuing at the time of final interview. All events were assigned Bedford College threat and focus ratings (Brown & Harris, 1978b). Before completion of the interview, subjects were asked some additional questions about their experiences, in order to see whether any events had been missed by the initial use of a list rather than a full oral LEDS. Any events thus discovered were included and then rated contextually in the same way.

Results

Findings already reported (Surtees, Miller, *et al.*, 1986) have shown that deliberately biasing the selection of the follow-up sample in terms of presence of putative vulnerability factors was *not* in fact associated with *either* new onsets of RDC psychiatric disorder *or* event rates. In view of these results, the analyses performed on the follow-up sample were undertaken without weighting. The results that follow were based on longitudinal data available for 307 women, of whom 35 experienced onsets of RDC affective disorder (17 women with definite or probable major depressive disorder and 18 women with definite/probable minor depressive disorder, panic disorder, or generalized anxiety disorder) at some time during their followup. In addition, only those life events considered to be independent of psychiatric disorder were included.

Initial analyses contrasted the event experiences of the onset group ($n = 35$ women) with those of the normals ($n = 272$ women). For the onset group, it was found that the average period for which data were available before onset was 43 weeks. This interval was then used as the preinterview period for contrasting event exposure among the normals. Table 6.5 gives the event rates preceding onset or interview for the 307 women followed up, and shows that minor as well as severe events distinguished the two groups.

When event rates (based on all events) were determined for each 3-week preonset or preinterview period per 100 women (Figure 6.5), a marked rise was found in the 3 weeks just preceding onset of illness, suggesting recency of event challenge as a significant factor (see Surtees, Miller, *et al.*, 1986). Unfortunately, the rarity of severe events precluded similar rate analyses for them alone. However, based upon the binary

TABLE 6.5. Life event rates per 6 months per 100 women preceding onset of illness or interview (follow-up assessment, Edinburgh data)

Event class	Women with onsets (n = 35)	Normals (n = 272)
All minor events	181.4	129.1 *
All severe events	27.6	10.4 **
All events	209.0	139.6 **

* Mann-Whitney U <.05, two-tailed.
** Mann-Whitney U <.01, two-tailed.

measure of the presence or absence of a severe event (according to Bedford College criteria), analysis revealed that 31.4% ($n = 11$) of the onset group, in contrast to 12.9% ($n = 35$) of the normals, had experienced one or more severe events during equivalent (43-week) event risk periods ($\chi^2_c = 6.99$, $df = 1$, $p < .01$; relative risk among those exposed = 2.60).

Application of the Decay Model

The applications of the decay model to event data that have been reported thus far (e.g., to the Camberwell data) have incorporated the assumptions stated earlier. The justification for assuming a linear decay

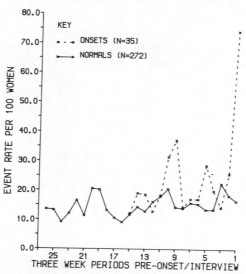

FIGURE 6.5. Life event rates per 3 weeks per 100 women preceding onset of affective disorder or final interview.

in threat rests almost entirely upon the ease with which this facilitates analysis. However, it represents only one proxy for what in general is being assumed to occur. An alternative, and perhaps more justifiable, representation of threat change over time would be one based on logarithmic laws (see Gaddum, 1945). Such an assumption would then coincide, for example, with the observed change in certain biological and naturally occurring phenomena (e.g., change with time in intensity of radiation from naturally occurring radioactive nuclides). This still speculative modification was used to investigate individual differences in stress response. The decay model incorporating an exponential change in adversity is described in the appendix to this chapter.

The modified model was now applied to the event data available from the 307 women followed up in the Edinburgh community study. For the purposes of the following analyses, *all events* were included. The initial weighting assigned to each event was the same as that used in the earlier (Camberwell) analysis, except that the value assigned to the least severely rated event (long-term threat rating of 4, other-focused) was modified to reduce the overall scale range slightly (modified weighting = 0.09375). The effect of this change was to extend the half-life of this most minor event from 5.75 days to 8.5 days (based upon the most severely rated event's having a 6-month decay period), but to reduce the ratio of the most to the least stressful events from 16:1 (Camberwell analysis) to 10.67:1 for the following analyses.

To illustrate something of the flexibility of the procedure, residual adversity levels at onset of illness or interview were determined, but under the assumption that the threat level of the most severely rated event (long-term threat rating of 1, subject-focused) had declined to *half* its initial stress level in 3.25 weeks (first analysis), 13.0 weeks (second analysis), or 52.0 weeks (third analysis). The resulting residual stress levels for each of the three separate analyses were then ranked (high to low), and the proportions of women with and without affective disorder were determined in relation to level of residual adversity. The complete results, in graphic form, are shown in Figure 6.6. The results reveal the considerable effect for case and noncase selection of allowing different maximal half-lives to be applied to events of *equal* initial magnitude. The figure provides all the necessary information to calculate the relative risk associated with the presence of minimum *particular* levels of adversity remaining at onset or interview, according to the three very different assumptions concerning decay periods.

MEASURES OF ASSOCIATION

As with the Camberwell data, the relationship among these measures of adversity, the binary (severe event) measure, the *inception of*

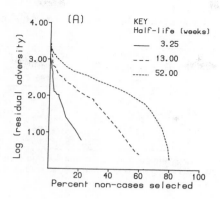

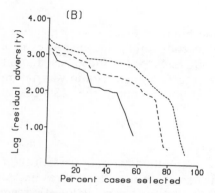

FIGURE 6.6. The percentages of women with and without affective disorder (lower and upper figures, respectively) in relation to their ranked level of residual adversity (log scores) at onset of illness or interview. The maximal event half-lives were varied as shown.

RDC disorder was investigated. The initial analyses derived estimates of the association between event stress (with and without imposing the modeling assumption) and disorder. The use of a binary measure selected 31.4% of the cases (all RDC conditions) and produced a relative risk of 2.60. This is shown in Table 6.6, together with the associated PAR and variance estimates.

The table also reveals the results obtained when the decay model was applied to all events, and when the half-lives assigned to those severe events with the maximum threat ratings were varied (as in Figure 6.6). However, the most important caveat regarding the interpretation of these findings is that they were based on measures of adversity that were constrained, both in a categorical sense and further by the particular placing of the cutoff point to select a number of cases equivalent to

TABLE 6.6. Measures of the association between event stress and onset of RDC disorder (Edinburgh data)

Basis for analysis	Population (%) attributable risk (PAR)	Relative risk	Variance explained (%)
Binary (severe event) measure	19.3	2.60	2.73
Adversity index[a]			
Half-life = 3.25 weeks	26.9	6.95	16.34
Half-life = 13.00 weeks	25.1	4.95	8.75
Half-life = 52.00 weeks	22.6	3.56	5.10

[a] Based on all events and with the assumption of exponential decay in event threat. The cutoff point was imposed to select a number of cases equivalent to that selected with the binary (severe event) measure.

that selected with the binary (severe event) measure. As can be seen, despite these artificial constraints, the measures of association based upon the adversity indices exceeded those based upon the binary measure. If, however, the cutoff point constraint was not imposed, then PAR values, based, for example, upon the 13-week half-life analysis, exceeded 55%.

LOGISTIC ANALYSES

As a parallel to the methods employed with the Camberwell data, the relationship between these stress measures and the onset of RDC conditions was investigated further using logistic regression. As before, the need to impose an upper stress threshold, and the influence this had on the strength of the relationship between adversity and case status, were also studied. The results of these analyses – although based on adversity measures assuming an exponential change in threat with time, rather than linear decay (as in the Camberwell analyses) – were broadly confirmatory of the earlier findings from Camberwell, in that imposing an upper stress threshold improved the explanatory significance of the adversity measure. In consequence, subsequent analyses incorporated such a threshold.

Of particular interest, however, is the relative predictive power of the binary measure (presence or absence of a severe event preceding onset of disorder) as opposed to the decay-based measure. Table 6.7 examines this issue in relation to two different measures of case status: first, all RDC cases (major and minor depressive disorders and anxiety disorders); and, second, a case criterion *restricted* to include only those with disorders meeting the RDC for major depressive conditions. As the table indicates, model 2 showed that the result of fitting the measure of

TABLE 6.7. Logistic modeling results of fitting combinations of binary and continuous stress scaling to different measures of case status (Edinburgh data)

Model	Parameters	df	All RDC cases		Major depression only	
			Residual deviance	Change in deviance	Residual deviance	Change in deviance
1	0	306	217.9	–	131.4	–
2	Adversity (all events)[a]	305	192.3	25.6	109.2	22.2
3	Severe events (yes-no)	305	210.9	7.0	120.8	10.6
4	Models 2 + 3	304	190.5	+1.8	109.1	+0.1

[a]With the assumption of exponential decay in event threat and with the severe event half-life set at 13 weeks

adversity to case status was highly significant; the change in scaled deviance was comparable to a chi-square statistic with one degree of freedom. Model 3 showed the strength of association for the binary (severe event) measure, with the result indicating an improved fit for the major depression criterion. However, model 4 indicated that although the binary measure added nothing to the predictive power of the adversity measure, that measure added substantially to the binary criterion (all RDC cases, deviance change = 20.4, $df = 1$, $p << .001$; major depression only, deviance change = 11.7, $df = 1$, $p < .001$).

To illustrate further the relationship between the binary scaling and the score provided by the decay model, the two measures were contrasted as shown in Table 6.8, and the proportion of women fulfilling the RDC for anxiety or depressive disorders was determined. The residual adversity measure (as used in Table 6.7) was divided into three lev-

TABLE 6.8. Proportions of women with onset of RDC disorder by severe event experience and level of residual adversity (Edinburgh data)[a]

Preonset/ preinterview severe event	Residual adversity at onset or interview			
	≥ 250	< 250 but ≥ 100	< 100	Totals
Yes	10/29 (34.5)	1/8 (12.5)	0/9 (0.0)	11/46 (23.9)
No	6/17 (35.3)	4/34 (11.8)	14/210 (6.7)	24/261 (9.2)
Totals	16/46 (34.8)	5/42 (11.9)	14/219 (6.4)	35/307 (11.4)

Note. Percentages are in parentheses.

els; the upper level (≥ 250 units) was chosen to select the *same* total number of women who had experienced a severe event. Logistic analysis of the cell proportions, shown in the table, clearly indicated that the measure of adversity *alone* provided an excellent fit to the data (change in scaled deviance = 23.7, df = 2, $p \ll .001$). The same analysis also estimated the odds ratio for the high-stress group to be 7.81, in contrast to 3.11 for those experiencing at least one severe event.

RELATIVE OPERATING CHARACTERISTIC ANALYSES

An alternative way of illustrating the relative abilities of the adversity and binary measures to discriminate between those women with and without RDC disorder was to examine the sensitivities (proportion of women correctly identified by each measure as being ill) and false-positive rates (those identified by each measure as ill, but found on examination to be disorder-free) associated with each scale. These indices could then be used to produce a relative (or receiver) operating characteristic (ROC) curve for each measure. Although the ROC method

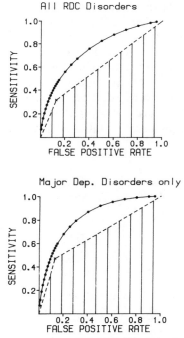

FIGURE 6.7. ROC curves based upon residual adversity scores (full lines) and presence-absence of a severe event (dashed lines) by RDC case status.

was initially developed for assessing radar technology, in recent years it has proved useful for investigating the differing abilities of radiological imaging systems (e.g., see Swets *et al.*, 1979). Its use in general epidemiology (e.g., see Erdreich & Lee, 1981), and in epidemiological psychiatry in particular, is much more recent. For instance, it has been used in psychiatry to investigate the relative advantages of different screening instruments to detect psychiatric disorder (e.g., see Mari & Williams, 1985; Bridges & Goldberg, 1986; Surtees, 1987). To produce an ROC curve, successively broader and broader categories of "abnormal" on a given scale are used.

The result of applying the method to the adversity measure and to the binary scale (only a single point) is illustrated in Figure 6.7. Analyses were based on the "ROCFIT" program developed by Metz, Wang, and Kronman (1984) and undertaken in relation to the two case status criteria used previously. An understanding of what the figure conveys may be enhanced when one realizes that a linear ascending diagonal perfectly dividing the figure would represent no discrimination whatsoever (the area beneath such a line would be 0.5). However, with any tendency for the curve to move toward the upper and left boundaries of the graph, discrimination would increase (and so the area below the curve would approach 1.0). Figure 6.7 shows the point representing the binary (severe event) measure to be *below* that of the smoothed ROC curve representing the adversity measure. The figure therefore indicates, just as the logistic analysis did in a more formal way, that the adversity measure exceeded the binary criterion in its (statistical) ability to discriminate cases from noncases. The figure also additionally indicates that *both* stress measures discriminated women with major RDC depressive disorders from those without (lower part of figure) better than they discriminated women with all RDC disorders from those without (upper part of figure).[1]

Theoretical Issues

To date, investigator-based binary stress scaling has provided the basis for Brown and colleagues' specification of a psychosocial framework for attempting to understand the etiology of affective conditions. Essential elements in that framework, discussed in detail elsewhere in this vol-

---

1. This can be confirmed by determining the areas beneath the curves, the trapezoidal rule being used for the binary (presence-absence) curve. The results are as follows: upper part of figure, adversity ROC (0.704), severe event ROC (0.593); lower part of figure, adversity ROC (0.827), severe event ROC (0.670).

ume, include emphasizing the primary meanings of the stressors; the role of hopelessness; the relevance of "matching" between areas of role conflict in an individual's life and areas targeted by severe events; the role of self-esteem and support; and the integration of all these elements under the rubric of vulnerability (e.g., see Brown & Harris, 1978b; Brown, 1981; Brown & Andrews, 1986; Brown, Andrews, Bifulco, Adler, & Bridge, 1986; Brown, Bifulco, & Harris, 1987). This theoretical framework, and the analytic procedures used to test hypotheses concerning the interrelationship of elements within it, remain controversial (e.g., see Tennant & Bebbington, 1978; Brown & Harris, 1978a; Everitt & Smith, 1979; Shapiro, 1979; Bebbington, Sturt, Tennant, & Hurry, 1984; Tennant, 1985).

Brown and Harris's theory development continues to depend on the stress measures determined from the LEDS. The very basis, therefore, of the theory rests on making due and considered allowance for the contextual circumstances surrounding the occurrence of each and every stressful incident. In recent years, debate on this core issue of whether such allowance should or should not be made has become increasingly heated. In essence, Brown and Harris suggest that a human being responds emotionally according to the "cortical relevance" of *all* the important elements, as they are perceived, that are associated with a stressful incident. In consequence, they believe that the measurement of a stressful life event or of a major long-term difficulty can never be completely divorced either from its context or from the individual to whom it occurs. The Dohrenwends have expressed an alternate view (e.g., Dohrenwend & Dohrenwend, 1984; Dohrenwend, Link, Kern, Shrout, & Markowitz, 1985), conceiving of life stress processes as involving three main structural components: events fairly closely preceding the time of interest; ongoing social situations (intended to include some long-term difficulties as measured by the LEDS); and personal dispositions. This last component includes previous psychiatric history, genetic vulnerabilities, and those personality factors thought to influence the way in which stressful events are perceived and responded to. In consequence, the Dohrenwends argue for specifying and separately distinguishing those variables representative of each component that relate to a given stressful incident; they believe that Brown and Harris's method of nonexplicitly combining such variables into one measure "hobbles" the investigation of relationships. Brown and Harris would take issue with certain aspects of this formulation. Although they would not disagree that the various components subsumed under personal dispositions should remain separate, they do not believe that specifying each contextual element associated with events in order to combine them later is a fruitful way forward at this stage of research (see Chapter 1). By contrast, the Dohrenwends feel that such a procedure would limit the overlap in measures (e.g., between events and background factors) consequent upon aggregating all appropriate data to form the context rating. It is clear, therefore, that this central issue needs further attention in order to specify the consequences for theory building of adopting these particular measurement philosophies.

An alternative possibility may stem from considering findings both from laboratory-based stress research and from studies of single severe stressful incidents that have concentrated on identifying individual differences in stress responsiveness. It is already evident that individual differences are a core feature of experimental stress research and that the magnitude of the variations in response to a given stressor can be considerable. Both individual and group differences in stress-adaptive capacities have been demonstrated using noise (e.g., Glass & Singer, 1972; Cohen, Evans, Krantz, & Stokols, 1980), monotony, heat, cold, and shiftwork (e.g., see Hockey, 1983). Another approach has focused upon specific traumatic incidents, again demonstrating the role of individual variation: Lindemann (1944) examined coping strategies following bereavement in the Cocoanut Grove nightclub fire; Chodoff, Friedman, and Hamburg (1964) and Willis (1974) studied coping strategies employed by the parents of children with leukemia; and Henderson and Bostock (1977) assessed coping strategies used by the survivors of a shipwreck. More recently, individual differences in psychological response to the diagnosis of breast cancer were found to be related to survival 5 and 10 years after assessment (Greer, Morris, & Pettingale, 1979; Pettingale, Morris, Greer, & Haybittle, 1985).

The challenge to research inventiveness remains how to allow for individual differences in adaptation to adversity in general-population samples, where the variability of stress experienced (in a contextual sense) is so immense. Recent research has pursued this aim in part through developing scales intended to measure the coping dispositions or behaviors of individuals (e.g., see Pearlin & Schooler, 1978; Coyne, Aldwin, & Lazarus, 1981; Kobasa, Maddi, & Courington, 1981; Pearlin, Menaghan, Lieberman, & Mullan, 1981; Kobasa, Maddi, & Kahn, 1982). A review of the theoretical approaches and empirical studies examining the capacity of individuals to cope with severe events (Silver & Wortman, 1980) concluded that considerable discrepancies exist between them. In particular, and as argued above, empirical data suggest extreme variability in response to stressors, and provide no evidence for a consensual pattern or stage model representing an orderly process of recovery from major crises. It is precisely because of these issues that researchers are now increasingly considering ways of endowing events with context-related weights that include allowances for person-specific dispositions. Dohrenwend and Dohrenwend (1984) have proposed a standard conception of events, but one in which event stress is likely to vary according to the personal dispositions of individuals.

In studies of an Edinburgh hospital population and of general-practice groups, analyses examined the relationship between residual adversity (using the decay model) and psychiatric symptom state (Surtees, Kiff, & Rennie, 1981). The study employed iterative analysis techniques to data obtained from three groups: hospitalized depressed patients, general-practice attenders, and a general-population comparison series. The *maximal* statistical association between adversity and symptom state varied across the study population subgroups according to the duration of the decay periods associated with the most severely threatening event. Considerable variation in decay periods associated with equivalent event magnitudes was demonstrated for different groups. For example, the optimal decay period for depressed female patients was 25-27 weeks; for female general-practice patients it was 42 weeks; and for the (female) community comparison series it was 10-14 weeks. One interpretation of these results is that (as the Dohrenwends suggest) the study groups differed in their (collective) personal dispositions, and coped differently with event stress as a result. There are, of course, a number of alternative possibilities. The events involved could have differed in actual impact, along the lines of the matching idea of Brown and his colleagues (see Chapter 2), and the subjects could have differed in terms of vulnerability factors other than coping style. However, this last possibility is perhaps unlikely, in that the factors would have to be shown to be specific to the different study groups – a perhaps unreasonable expectation (see Surtees *et al.*, 1981, for more details).

The iterative analysis procedure made no attempt to allow for person-specific variation in the change in stress effects with time. An initial strategy to deal with this most difficult problem has now been pursued with the Edinburgh survey data.

Person-Specific Decay Periods

So far, this chapter has been devoted entirely to exploring the relationship between event stress and illness onset; due to constraints of space, the role of other factors in that relationship has not been considered. However, to illustrate a particular and potentially novel approach to the event illness issue that is facilitated by the decay model described here, the role of one other variable is described.

As part of the Edinburgh survey, all respondents were asked questions concerning their behavioral and intrapsychic reactions to actual stressful incidents experienced during the study, where this was possible; if no such incidents were present during that period, the respondents were asked about their reactions in general. A total of 11 different ways in which each woman might have responded to the occurrence of individual stressors was examined. These included seeking professional advice; using prayer or meditation; being angry with oneself or others; ruminating about the situation; taking medication; or attempting to suppress event-related ideation by activity. These questions were asked at the initial study interview, and only those respondents who were free at that time of RDC disorder were included in subsequent analyses. On the basis of responses to these questions, a measure of (maladaptive) coping was derived (see Miller *et al.*, 1985, for further details).

It was assumed that individuals would vary in their capacity to adapt to events of equivalent threat rating on the LEDS. This meant that the decay periods (or event half-lives) of all the events experienced by a given individual were then assumed to reflect, and to be a proxy for, that individual's capacity for resilience to adversity. This additional assumption beyond those already imposed set new analytic problems, which if satisfactorily resolved would enable the investigation of group or individual differences in stress-adaptive capacity.

The demands set for this first empirical investigation, therefore, were to determine whether endowing event threat levels with lifetimes appropriate to an individual's declared capacity to cope with adversity would influence the predictive ability of the modified stress measure. The initial step, of course, was to undertake the analyses *without* imposing the assumption of individual variability in event adaptations, but to establish the additional predictive significance of the coping measure beyond the measures of stress. The initial analyses thus used the mea-

TABLE 6.9. Logistic modeling results of fitting stress measures (binary and continuous) and an index of coping to different measures of case status (Edinburgh data)

			All RDC cases		Major depression only	
Model	Parameters	df [a]	Residual deviance	Change in deviance	Residual deviance	Change in deviance
1	0	305	217.6	–	131.3	–
2	Severe events (yes-no)	304	210.7	6.9	120.7	10.6
3	Severe events + coping	303	195.5	+15.2	114.2	+6.5
4	Adversity (all events)	304	192.1	25.5	109.1	22.2
5	Adversity + coping	303	180.0	+12.1	104.2	+4.9
6	Adversity [b]	304	186.7	30.9	103.2	28.1

[a] Missing value for one case.

[b] Adversity measure influenced by the coping index.

sure of residual adversity as determined previously (using the exponential decay model), and also employed the binary severe event criterion for comparative purposes; both were used in combination with the coping measure and in relation to the two measures of RDC case status previously applied.

The results shown in model 2 (see Table 6.9) indicated the significant relationship between the (context-related) binary measure and onset of RDC psychiatric disorder (all cases, or only the major depressives). Model 3 clearly showed that the coping measure made an additional and highly significant contribution to predicting onset. Repeating these analyses, with the binary criterion replaced by the adversity measure, produced the results shown as models 4 and 5. Once again, coping predicted inception *beyond* the adversity measure. A contrast between models 3 and 5 also revealed that (for the same degrees of freedom) the *joint* effects of adversity and coping produced a greater reduction in scaled deviance than did the combined effects of severe events and coping. The question could now be put: If the stressful half-lives of events were allowed to be influenced at the individual level by the coping measure, would this improve the predictive significance of the adversity measure, consonant with that achieved when their independent effects were assessed?

To try to answer this question, an analysis was undertaken based upon an assumption analogous to that described by Bhattacharya and Holla (1965) in connection with mixtures of exponential distributions. With the assumption of a uniform distribution of the half-life of events,[2] expected values of the uniform order statistics were assigned to the Edinburgh survey respondents according to their ranked position on the coping index. In this way, each individual's coping score (relative to all others in the sample) influenced the half-life of *all* the events she experienced. In practice, all events were considered, with the half-life of the most threatening event scaled being associated with a particular individual's coping score within the range of 6.5 to 19.5 weeks. In con-

---

2. With a half-life expectation of t, then individual half-life parameters are assumed to be *uniformly* distributed between $t - \delta$ and $t + \delta$. With probability density function $1/2\delta$, the expected values of the order statistics of sample size n are given as follows:

$$1.\ t - \delta + [2\delta/(n + 1)]$$
$$2.\ t - \delta + [4\delta/(n + 1)]$$
$$. . . .$$
$$. . . .$$
$$n.\ t - \delta + [2n\delta/(n + 1)]$$

For the specific instance involving the coping measure, t was set equal to 13 weeks and δ to 6.5 weeks. All women in the sample were ranked (ties being taken account of) according to their score on the coping index.

sequence, for an individual with substantial coping resources who had experienced an event of greatest threat, then the procedure would insure that the effect of that event would have decayed completely (according to an exponential change) in about 13 weeks (2 × minimum half-life). In contrast, for an individual also challenged by an event of equal magnitude but with few coping resources, the event would have been over in about 39 weeks.

This procedure was both speculative and empirical, but provided a framework for endowing standard (context-related) event weights with estimates of person-specific stress-adaptive capacities based upon personal attributes. The results of the analysis are shown in Table 6.9 (model 6). Regardless of the case criterion used, residual deviance values for model 6 were *lower* than those for model 4; in essence, the adversity measure modified by coping predicted illness inception better than the measure without this modification. A second point was that the change in deviance achieved with the modified adversity measure (on *one* degree of freedom) equaled that achieved (on *two* degrees of freedom) with the joint effects of adversity and coping in prediction of the onset of major depression, though as can be seen, this was not quite achieved in prediction of the onset of *all* disorders.

Overall, then, the procedure appears to have had the desired effect, in that the predictive capacity of the adversity measure was enhanced by allowing for a person's coping dispositions. This may, of course, have been due in some way to the empirical basis upon which the range of event lifetimes was associated with the coping measure. It is also possible, though – and particularly so in relation to the case criterion covering all RDC disorders assessed – that the full effect of coping might not yet have been achieved.

Discussion

This chapter has investigated the relationship between stressful life events and the onset of diagnosable psychiatric conditions in both hospital and community settings. The work has examined the consequence of imposing, largely by fiat, certain assumptions regarding additivity between events and changes in their stressful effect with time. This work has been pursued to stimulate the development of ideas and perhaps to offer new theoretical insights into etiological processes.

A primary objective in developing the model was to provide a measure of the residual adversity, at a particular time of interest within a given study period, that can be attributed to (selected) classes of events preceding that time. The results based upon the Camberwell studies enabled the relative merits of binary and continuous stress scaling to be determined under conditions when event class was varied, and when the time period for which events had influence was limited, or not. The results indicated the importance of decay as an event property, suggested that the less severe events have a predictive role, and tentatively suggested the presence of a stress ceiling effect.

These results appear, therefore, to underpin the basic assumptions incorporated in the model. But what of evidence for them from other work? Although the direct investigation of these event-specific properties is extremely difficult, several reports are of value. Two studies (Horowitz, Schaefer, & Cooney, 1974; Horowitz, Schaefer, Hiroto, Wilner, & Levin, 1977) provide empirical support, on the basis of the assignment of event weights, for the assumption that the stressful effects of events decrease over time. The belief that time heals is of course widely held by clinicians and is reflected in their advice given at times of clearly event-related crisis (e.g., see Elder, 1984). Such personal experiences provide direct evidence that although the intensity of major event effects fades and memories recede with time, the getting-over period can last not for months but for years. However, it is likely that a distinction should be drawn between the recurrent reappraisal of distant events and the time span for which they are an influence on psychological state. Evidence from several studies (e.g., Paykel, 1978; Brown & Harris, 1978b; Bebbington, Tennant, & Hurry, 1981; Surtees, Miller, et al., 1986) indicates that in the few weeks preceding onset of affective disorder, event rates rapidly increase, in contrast to the situation with controls. Such evidence identifies the immediate post event period as apparently the time of greatest risk; however, the duration over which an elevated (but, by inference, lessening) risk level is present remains essentially unknown. Brown, Harris, and Peto (1973) have suggested in excess of a year for markedly threatening events, whereas others (reviewed by Tennant, 1983) suggest a relatively short period.

Additivity between events continues to be a controversial issue. The evidence so far – based upon analyses in which the temporal interrelationship of events was neglected (Brown & Harris, 1978b, 1986; Finlay-Jones & Brown, 1981) – suggests that minor events, alone or in combination with severe events, contribute little in distinguishing between those with onset of affective disorder and those without onset. Multiple discrete and illness-independent severe events do appear, even when time is neglected, to slightly increase the risk of illness onset. Examination of the relationship between stressors and self-reported depressed mood provided some support for an additive effect involving those stressors rated as least severe (see Miller & Ingham, 1979), but long-term difficulties were included in the analyses. The results shown in Figure 6.2 for the Camberwell community study indicate that it is only when the stressful effect of events is allowed to decay with time that minor events have any important role in combination with severe events in distinguishing between those with and without onset of affective conditions. Such minor events must occur close in time to onset to have an effect.

The LEDS methodology has enabled a quantum leap to be made in stress-illness research through the specification of few but important stressor classes. Overenthusiastic attempts to classify stressors further according to what may be relatively diffuse and inexact attributes may impose limitations on the potential for additional practical and theoretical advances in this research area. Characterizing stressors in ways resembling gene typing will be of potential value only if it can be shown that the rating reliability of the categories involved is satisfactory, and, furthermore, that the relative rarity of the resulting categories does not prejudice analytic possibilities. Analyses on the Edinburgh community study using a typology developed by Miller (e.g., see Miller *et al.*, 1986) have revealed something of the problems associated with the approach. Miller's scheme involves assigning up to six attributes or characteristics to a given event or difficulty. Rating reliability of the chosen categories then has to be demonstrably good, and, in addition, the categories *and* their combinations have to be present in sufficient numbers to facilitate investigation of their relative effects. The Edinburgh data have made it clear that many such categories are extremely rare (e.g., events characterized by particular combinations of attributes were only found after almost 300 woman-years were analyzed), thereby constraining the potential for analysis by such a technique. In spite of the obvious problems associated with this general approach, Finlay-Jones and Brown (1981) have described stressor subtypes distinguishing depressive from anxiety disorders; Tennant, Bebbington, and Hurry (1981) have shown the role of neutralizing events in relation to remission; and Miller and Ingham (1985) have shown the importance of allowing for the interdependence of stressful incidents in predicting symptom variance.

However, other conceptualizations relating stressor challenge to the onset of affective conditions warrant examination but appear relatively intractable in relation to binary stress scaling. The investigation of dose-response, threshold, or cusp-catastrophe surface models will be facilitated by the availability of a continuous measure of adversity. Such a measure is vital for examining the role of factors additional to stress in relation to rapid changes in health state (as in the catastrophe model), and now perhaps amenable to investigation (e.g., see Stewart & Peregoy, 1983). Although the decay model will facilitate investigations along these lines, the assumptions underlying the model demand further research in order to refine them. To achieve this, the ideal development may be to incorporate within the model interviewer-based estimates of the resolution time of each and every stressful event rated, rather than to employ the present rigorous but rather unreal approach. Such a development may provide a bridge between a modeling approach limited by the imposed uniformity of event lifetimes and one allowing the full utilization of actual sequences of incidents. Such a development, of course, will also have to make due allowance for the etiological significance of long-term difficulties, the matching relationships between events and difficulties, the latent effects of experiences in childhood (e.g., parental care and early loss), and the doubtless very different stress-adaptational abilities (decay rate perhaps being seen as a proxy for vulnerability) among individuals. The present work has attempted to include only the most basic elements of such a framework, but has demonstrated that decay and additivity are significant event properties, which when modeled together successfully allow the prediction of inception.

The final analysis in this chapter has perhaps indicated something of the model's greatest potential, worthy of development for the future: the significance of stress decay as one indication of an individual's or group's stress-adaptive capacity or vulnerability. The inherent difficulties in attempting to allow for individual differences in population stress research – an area of increasing interest (e.g., see Rutter, 1985, 1986) – must be overcome if significant new advances are to be made in understanding the psychosocial etiology of psychiatric disorder. This first attempt at linking person-specific coping dispositions to the half-life of events produced encouraging results, but must be viewed with considerable caution in view of the empirical nature of the procedures adopted. The extent, therefore, to which individual differences represented by personality attributes, coping styles, use of support resources, and measures of psychophysiological responsivity may be usefully considered in quantifying the impact of events in population research remains to be investigated. It is just possible that the framework of a viable method now exists. Only time will tell.

Appendix: Exponential (Decay) Model

Let the rate of decay be exponential, and let the stress effect of an event p be k. Then the residual adversity (y) remaining at time t associated with this event is given as follows:

$$y(t) = ke^{\frac{-ct}{k}}$$

where c is a constant.

If c is chosen to give a "standard" half-life (T) from a "standard" initial stress level y_0 (e.g., 1), then

$$\tfrac{1}{2} = e^{cT}$$

$$\therefore \quad c = \frac{\log 2}{T}$$

Hence, the residual adversity due to an event of magnitude k, at time t, is given as follows:

$$y(t) = ke^{\frac{-t\log 2}{Tk}}$$

If, therefore, an individual has experienced events p_0 and p_1 with respective times of t_0 and t_1 and stress magnitudes of k_0 and k_1, then the residual adversity remaining at time t_2 due to their combined effects can be determined as follows. At t_1, the residual effect of k_0 is:

$$k_0 e^{\frac{-t_1\log 2}{Tk_0}}$$

However, at t_1 a new event of magnitude k_1 occurs; therefore, the combined stress is:

$$y_1 = k_0 e^{\frac{-t_1\log 2}{Tk_0}} + k_1$$

Hence the residual adversity at t_2 is:

$$y_2 = y_1 e^{\frac{-(t_2-t_1)\log 2}{Ty_1}}$$

Acknowledgments

The Edinburgh community study described in this chapter was designed and completed by the following staff members of the Medical Research Council (MRC) Unit for Epidemiological Studies in Psychiatry, Edinburgh, Scotland: Jack Ingham, Norman Kreitman, Patrick Miller, Sashi Sashidharan, and myself, together with Christine Dean, who is now at the Department of Psychiatry, Queen Elizabeth Hospital, Birmingham, England. Advice on statistical procedures was provided by John Duffy, Department of Statistics, University of Edinburgh, and the computer programming of the decay model was undertaken by Dilys Rennie, MRC Unit for Epidemiological Studies in Psychiatry.

References

Bebbington, P. E., Sturt, E., Tennant, C., & Hurry, J. (1984). Misfortune and resilience: A community study of women. *Psychological Medicine, 14,* 347-363.

Bebbington, P. E., Tennant, C., & Hurry, J. (1981). Life events and the nature of psychiatric disorder in the community. *Journal of Affective Disorders, 3,* 345-366.

Bhattacharya, S. K., & Holla, M. S. (1965). On a life test distribution with stochastic deviations in the mean. *Annals of the Institute of Statistical Mathematics, 17,* 97-104.

Breslow, N. E., & Day, N. E. (1980). *Statistical methods in cancer research: Vol. 1 The analysis of case-control studies,* Lyon, France: International Agency for Research on Cancer.

Bridges, K. W., & Goldberg, D. P. (1986). The validation of the GHQ-28 and the use of the MMSE in neurological in-patients. *British Journal of Psychiatry, 148,* 548-553.

Brown, G. W. (1974). Meaning, measurement and stress of life events. In B. S. Dohrenwend & B. P. Dohrenwend (Eds.), *Stressful life events: Their nature and effects* (pp. 217-243). New York: Wiley.

Brown, G. W. (1981). Life events, psychiatric disorder and physical illness. *Journal of Psychosomatic Research, 25,* 461-473.

Brown, G. W., & Andrews, B. (1986). Social support and depression. In M. H. Appley & R. Trumbull (Eds.), *Dynamics of stress* (pp. 257-282) New York: Plenum Press.

Brown, G. W., Andrews, B., Bifulco, A., Adler Z., & Bridge, L. (1986). Social support, self-esteem and depression. *Psychological Medicine, 16,* 813-831.

Brown, G. W., Bifulco, A., & Harris, T. O. (1987). Life events, vulnerability and onset of depression: Some refinements. *British Journal of Psychiatry, 150,* 30-42.

Brown, G. W., & Harris, T. O. (1978a). Social origins of depression: A reply. *Psychological Medicine, 8,* 577-588.

Brown, G. W., & Harris, T. O. (1978b). *Social origins of depression: A study of psychiatric disorder in women.* London: Tavistock.

Brown, G. W., & Harris, T. O. (1986). Establishing causal links: The Bedford College studies of depression. In H. Katschnig (Ed.), *Life events and psychiatric disorders: Controversial issues* (pp. 107-187). Cambridge, England: Cambridge University Press.

Brown, G. W., Harris, T. O., & Peto, J. (1973). Life events and psychiatric disorders: Part 2. Nature of causal link. *Psychological Medicine, 3,* 159-176.

Brown, G. W., Sklair, F., Harris, T. O., & Birley, J. L. T. (1973). Life-events and psychiatric disorders: Part 1: Some methodological issues. *Psychological Medicine, 3,* 74-87.

Chodoff, P., Friedman, S. B., & Hamburg, D. A. (1964). Stress defense and coping behavior: Observations in parents of children with malignant disease. *American Journal of Psychiatry, 120,* 743-749.

Cohen, S., Evans, G. W., Krantz, D. S., & Stokols, D. (1980). Physiological motivational and cognitive effects of aircraft noise on children: Moving from the laboratory to the field. *American Psychologist, 35,* 231-243.

Coyne, J. C., Aldwin, C., & Lazarus, R. S. (1981). Depression and coping in stressful episodes. *Journal of Abnormal Psychology, 90,* 439-447.

Dean, C., Surtees, P. G., & Sashidharan, S. P. (1983). Comparison of research diagnostic systems in an Edinburgh community sample. *British Journal of Psychiatry, 142,* 247-256.

Dohrenwend, B. P., Link, B. G., Kern, R., Shrout, P. E., & Markowitz, J. (1985). *Measuring life events: The problem of variability within event categories.* Paper presented at the meeting of the World Psychiatric Association, Section of Epidemiology and Community Psychiatry, Edinburgh.

Dohrenwend, B. S., & Dohrenwend, B. P. (1984). Life stress and illness: Formulation of the issues. In B. S. Dohrenwend & B. P. Dohrenwend (Eds.), *Stressful life events and their contexts*, (pp. 1-27). New Brunswick, NJ: Rutgers University Press.

Elder, A. H. (1984). Death of a spouse. *British Medical Journal, 289*, 665-667.

Endicott, J., & Spitzer, R. L. (1978). A diagnostic interview: The Schedule for Affective Disorders and Schizophrenia. *Archives of General Psychiatry, 35*, 837-844.

Erdreich, L. S., & Lee, E. T. (1981). Use of relative operating characteristic analysis in epidemiology. *American Journal of Epidemiology, 114*, 649-662.

Everitt, B. S., & Smith, A. M. R. (1979). Interactions in contingency tables: A brief discussion of alternative definitions. *Psychological Medicine, 9*, 581-583.

Finlay-Jones, R., & Brown, G. W. (1981). Types of stressful life event and the onset of anxiety and depressive disorders. *Psychological Medicine, 11*, 803-815.

Gaddum, J. H. (1945). Lognormal distributions. *Nature, 156*, 463-466.

Glass, D. C., & Singer, J. E. (1972). *Urban Stress*. New York: Academic Press.

Greer, H. S., Morris, T., & Pettingale, K. W. (1979). Psychological response to breast cancer: Effect on outcome. *Lancet, ii*, 785-787.

Henderson, S., & Bostock, T. (1977). Coping behaviour after shipwreck. *British Journal of Psychiatry, 131*, 15-20.

Hockey, R. (Ed.). (1983). *Stress and fatigue in human performance*. Chichester, England: Wiley.

Horowitz, M. J., Schaefer, C., & Cooney, P. (1974). Life event scaling for recency of experience. In E. Gunderson & R. Rahe (Eds.), *Life stress and illness* (pp. 125-134). Springfield, IL: Charles C Thomas.

Horowitz, M. J., Schaefer, C., Hiroto, D., Wilner, N., & Levin, B. (1977). Life event questionnaires for measuring presumptive stress, *Psychosomatic Medicine, 39*, 413-431.

Ingham, J. G., Kreitman, N. B., Miller, P. McC., Sashidharan, S. P., & Surtees, P. G. (1986). Self-esteem, vulnerability and psychiatric disorder in the community. *British Journal of Psychiatry, 148*, 375-385.

Kobasa, S. C., Maddi, S. R., & Courington, S. (1981). Personality and constitution as mediators in the stress-illness relationship. *Journal of Health and Social Behavior, 22*, 368-378.

Kobasa, S. C., Maddi, S. R., & Kahn, S. (1982). Hardiness and health: A prospective study. *Journal of Personality and Social Psychology, 42*, 168-177.

Levin, M. L. (1953). The occurrence of lung cancer in man. *Acta Unionis Internationalis Contra Cancrum, 9*, 531-541.

Lindemann, E. (1944). Symptomatology and management of acute grief. *American Journal of Psychiatry, 101*, 141-148.

Lilienfeld, A. M., & Lilienfeld, D. E. (1980). *Foundations of epidemiology*. New York: Oxford University Press.

Mari, J. de J. and Williams, P. (1985). A comparison of the validity of two psychiatric screening questionnaires (GHQ-12 and SRQ-20) in Brazil, using relative operating characteristic (ROC) analysis. *Psychological Medicine, 15*, 651-659.

Metz, C. E., Wang, P. L., & Kronman, H. B. (1984). *Rocfit*. Department of Radiology and the Franklin McLean Memorial Research Institute, University of Chicago.

Miettinen, O. S. (1974). Proportion of disease caused or prevented by a given exposure, trait, or intervention. *American Journal of Epidemiology, 99*, 325-332.

Miller, P. McC., Dean, C., Ingham, J. G., Kreitman, N. B., Sashidharan, S. P., & Surtees, P. G. (1986). The epidemiology of life events and long-term difficulties, with some reflections on the concept of independence. *British Journal of Psychiatry, 148*, 686-696.

Miller, P. McC., & Ingham, J. G. (1979). Reflections on the life-events-to-illness link with some preliminary findings. In I. G. Sarason & C. D. Spielberger (Eds.), *Stress and anxiety* (Vol. 6, pp. 313-336). New York: Wiley.

Miller, P. McC., & Ingham, J. G. (1985). Are life events which cause each other additive in their effects? *Social Psychiatry, 20,* 31-41.

Miller, P. McC., Surtees, P. G., Kreitman, N. B., Ingham, J. G., & Sashidharan, S. P. (1985). Maladaptive coping reactions to stress: A study of illness inception. *Journal of Nervous and Mental Disease, 173,* 707-716.

Paykel, E. S. (1978). Contribution of life events to causation of psychiatric illness. *Psychological Medicine, 8,* 245-253.

Pearlin, L. I., Menaghan, E. G., Lieberman, M. A., & Mullan, J. T. (1981). The stress process. *Journal of Health and Social Behavior, 22,* 337-356.

Pearlin, L. I., & Schooler, C. (1978). The structure of coping. *Journal of Health and Social Behavior, 19,* 2-21.

Pettingale, K. W., Morris, T., Greer, S., & Haybittle, J. L. (1985). Mental attitudes to cancer: An additional prognostic factor [Letter to the editor]. *Lancet, i,* 750.

Rutter, M. (1985). Resilience in the face of adversity: Protective factors and resistance to psychiatric disorder. *British Journal of Psychiatry, 147,* 598-611.

Rutter, M. (1986). Meyerian psychobiology, personality development, and the role of life experiences. *American Journal of Psychiatry, 143,* 1077-1087.

Shapiro, M. B. (1979). *Social Origins of Depression* by G. W. Brown and T. Harris: Its methodological philosophy. *Behavior Research and Therapy, 17,* 597-603.

Silver, R. L., & Wortman, C. B. (1980). Coping with undesirable life events. In J. Garber & M. E. P. Seligman (Eds.), *Human helplessness* (pp. 279-340). New York: Academic Press.

Spitzer, R. L., Endicott, J., & Robins, E. (1978). Research Diagnostic Criteria: Rationale and reliability. *Archives of General Psychiatry, 35,* 773-782.

Stewart, I. N., & Peregoy, P. L. (1983). Catastrophe theory modelling in psychology. *Psychological Bulletin, 94,* 336-362.

Surtees, P. G. (1984). Kith, kin and psychiatric health: A Scottish survey. *Social Psychiatry, 19,* 63-67.

Surtees, P. G. (1987). Psychiatric disorder in the community and the General Health Questionnaire. *British Journal of Psychiatry, 150,* 828-835.

Surtees, P. G., Dean, C., Ingham, J. G., Kreitman, N. B., Miller, P. McC., & Sashidharan, S. P. (1983). Psychiatric disorder in women from an Edinburgh community: Associations with demographic factors. *British Journal of Psychiatry, 142,* 238-246.

Surtees, P. G., & Ingham, J. G. (1980). Life stress and depressive outcome: Application of a dissipation model to life events. *Social Psychiatry, 15,* 21-31.

Surtees, P. G., Kiff, J., & Rennie, D. (1981). Adversity and mental health: An empirical investigation of their relationship. *Acta Psychiatrica Scandinavica, 64,* 177-192.

Surtees, P. G., Miller, P. McC., Ingham, J. G., Kreitman, N. B., Rennie, D., & Sashidharan, S. P. (1986). Life events and the onset of affective disorder: A longitudinal general population study. *Journal of Affective Disorders, 10,* 37-50.

Surtees, P. G., & Rennie, D. (1983). Adversity and the onset of psychiatric disorder in women. *Social Psychiatry, 18,* 37-44.

Surtees, P. G., & Sashidharan, S. P. (1986). Psychiatric morbidity in two matched community samples: A comparison of rates and risks in Edinburgh and St. Louis. *Journal of Affective Disorders, 10,* 101-113.

Surtees, P. G., Sashidharan, S. P., & Dean, C. (1986). Affective disorder amongst women in the general population: A longitudinal study. *British Journal of Psychiatry, 148,* 176-186.

Swets, J. A., Pickett, R. M., Whitehead, S. F., Getty, D. J., Schnur, J. A., Swets, J. B., & Freeman, B. A. (1979). Assessment of diagnostic technologies. *Science, 205,* 753-759.

Tennant, C. (1983). Life events and psychological morbidity: The evidence from prospective studies. *Psychological Medicine, 13*, 483-486.

Tennant, C. (1985). Female vulnerability to depression. *Psychological Medicine, 15*, 733-737.

Tennant, C. & Bebbington, P. (1978). The social causation of depression: A critique of the work of Brown and his colleagues. *Psychological Medicine, 8*, 565-575.

Tennant, C., Bebbington, P., & Hurry, J. (1981). The short-term outcome of neurotic disorders in the community: The relation of remission to clinical factors and to 'neutralizing' life events. *British Journal of Psychiatry, 139*, 213-220.

Willis, D. J. (1974). The families of terminally ill children: Symptomatology and management. *Journal of Clinical Child Psychology, 3*, 32-33.

Wing, J. K., Cooper, J. E., & Sartorius, N. (1974). *The measurement and classification of psychiatric symptoms.* Cambridge, England: Cambridge University Press.

PART THREE

LIFE EVENTS AND PHYSICAL ILLNESS

7

Physical Illness: An Introduction

TIRRIL O. HARRIS

The belief that psychosocial factors play a role in the onset of physical illness is as ancient and almost as familiar as the parallel belief about psychiatric conditions. There have been many detailed reviews of the historical genesis of this belief (e.g., Hinkle, 1973, 1977; Lazarus & Folkman, 1984; Lipowski, 1977; Reiser, 1975; and several of the chapters in Goldberger & Breznitz, 1982), and there is no need here for more than a brief outline of how the field has developed.

The Specificity Question

Given the perspective of this volume, perhaps the aspect most deserving of comment is the evolving debate surrounding the specificity issue discussed in Chapter 1. Although the 19th century saw some perceptive clinical reports pinpointing specific stress-illness linkages, these were presented as case histories rather than as part of a developing theory. With the pioneering discussions early in this century and the development of more systematic research, there was a tendency for ideas to polarize in different camps. Those interested in the specific meaning of the psychosocial precipitants in particular disorders followed psychoanalytic precepts, whereas those interested in the physiological aspects pursued more general theories involving homeostasis, and viewed disease in terms of broader groupings or as a whole. In the latter group, Cannon's (1932) theory of the fight-flight reaction, Selye's (1956) general adaptation syndrome, and the ideas of Wolff (1953) are best known; these theorists explored details of a number of biological responses of

Tirril O. Harris. Department of Social Policy and Social Science, Royal Holloway and Bedford New College, University of London, 11 Bedford Square, London WC1B 3RA, England.

the human organism to environmental demands upon it. These responses tended to be presented as occurring in an orchestrated pattern, almost regardless of the nature of these demands. Work on stress reactions stimulated by World War II and the Korean War was still informed by this more general tradition, although its greater thoroughness allows an interested reader to pick out linkages that hint at more specific effects (Grinker & Spiegel, 1945).

The polarization between the major traditions was perhaps inevitable, given the passionate feelings of loyalty both for and against psychoanalysis, which certainly discouraged many concerned with physiological mechanisms from considering the specific psychological differences between various types of stress. Even when the doubtful concept of the "symbolic communication" of the conversion symptom was modified, many still associated the psychosomatic medical tradition with a set of theoretical assumptions involving questionable psychoanalytic propositions at some level. For example, Dunbar (1954) moved from the notion of symptoms communicating a symbolic message to the idea that certain specific personality types were more vulnerable to certain illnesses, and though Alexander (1950) still saw a link between specific diseases and particular unresolved unconscious conflicts, he also left room for a particular constitutional physical vulnerability of tissue or organ that would contribute to determining the somatic nature of the disorder.

Meanwhile, away from the center of debate, a number of studies of particular stress situations proved fertile ground for the development of hypotheses that would ultimately feed back into the specificity debate: for example, Janis's (1958) study of hospital patients facing the stress of surgical operation, and Wolff, Friedman, Hofer, and Mason's (1964) study of parents facing the stress of their children's sickness and ultimate death from leukemia. But although the specific nature of the stress common to all the intensively studied subjects in these reports enhanced the insights of the authors, this did not contribute more generally to specificity theory. The specific nature of the common stress was only the background against which individual variations in coping became the focus of detailed descriptions. And once the importance of coping was recognized, the value of psychoanalytic contributions to theories of disorder was also more easily acknowledged, but this time from the perspective of the theory of defense mechanisms (A. Freud, 1937) rather than of other specific unconscious conflicts. The study of the role of defense mechanisms in both psychological and physical health has continued as a fertile source of ideas and findings (Vaillant, 1977, 1985), but has probably served to deflect attention away from the specificity of the environmental conflict and onto the individual's specific psychic reactive style.

One of the most stimulating and convincing treatments of specific effects can be seen in the experimental work of Graham and colleagues concerning attitude specificity. An early paper (Grace & Graham, 1952) described a number of attitudes that were believed to be associated with certain physiological responses, and in turn with certain diseases. In later work, this group was able to elicit the physiological responses characteristic of these particular disorders by hypnotic induction (Graham, Kabler, & Graham, 1962). Thus each of 20 subjects was given attitude suggestions on two separate occasions – one for hives ("You feel unfairly treated by Dr. X, but there is nothing you can do about it. You are the helpless, innocent victim of unfair, unjust treatment"), and one for hypertension ("You're threatened every instant. You have to watch out"). Five parameters were used to describe five physiological variables. As predicted, there was a relatively greater rise in skin temperature with the hives attitude, and a relatively greater rise in diastolic blood pressure with the hypertension attitude. For the other three measures (systolic blood pressure, pulse, and respiration), no specific predictions had been made, and no significant effect of attitude induction was found. The many controls built into the study design suggest that these results should be taken seriously. Nor can they be interpreted as reflecting differences in general emotionality or "arousal" (along more Selyean lines), such that responses to the hypertension suggestion were "stronger" than those to the hives suggestion, since two earlier studies by the same team were able to contrast the rise in skin temperature produced by the hives suggestion with a significant drop in skin temperature produced by hypnotic induction of the attitude associated with Raynaud disease ("You feel unfairly treated by Dr. X and you want to hit him, choke him, and strangle him") (Graham, Stern, & Winokur, 1958; Stern, Winokur, Graham, & Graham, 1961).

Although this work made an important move in the direction of establishing what may be called the "specificity hypothesis," as Mechanic notes, much of the other evidence in this tradition is fragmentary and illustrative (Mechanic, 1978, p 237). Indeed, attempts to validate these specificities empirically do not appear to have satisfied members of the other camp. In the absence of the findings of recent neurophysiological work, no theory previously advanced could plausibly account for the links proposed between cognitive-affective and neurovegetative-immune patterns. Probably as a result, specificity theory went into decline, and some would say that this disenchantment spread to psychosomatic medicine as a whole during the 1970s. Ironically, this coincided with an increase in concern with the social sources of stress in the environment (McGrath, 1970; Levine & Scotch, 1970). Thus the possibility of developing what Weiner (1982) calls an improved "biopsychosocial" theory had to be further postponed. But unfortunately, as discussed in Chapter 1, the widespread use of checklist measuring instruments such as the Schedule of Recent Experiences gained life events research as a whole the reputation for "focussing on stress as a stimulus that triggers a generalized vulnerability to illness" (Zegans, 1982, p. 143). Therefore yet another polarization seemed to be becoming institutionalized in the specificity debate, with life events outside the specificity camp.

From the vantage point of the 1980s, however, it is now possible to see a way toward Weiner's biopsychosocial approach. In a detailed discussion of the problems of developing multifactorial models of disease onset subtle enough to pick out the complex interactions involved, Depue, Monroe, and Shackman (1979) contrast what they call Alexander's "specificity hypothesis" with Engel's (1968) more generalized view of psychological predisposition to illness (p. 11). They opt for a final perspective somewhere between these two, and conclude by adopting what they call "the qualitative position with respect of psychosocial stimuli in disease models" (p. 15), which places the appraisal process in a central position in the initiation of disease. Their position rests on "the assumption that various emotions are associated with different hormonal patterns"; thus "non-specific theories that postulate general mediators to account for the initiation of many different diseases may no longer be useful" (p. 18). The perspective espoused in this volume is very similar and marries some of the features of recent exciting epidemiological work with earlier aspects of the psychosomatic movement, recent findings in neurophysiology, and, of course, improved measurement of life events and difficulties. As emphasized earlier, traditional psychosomatic research focused more upon personality traits, although these were occasionally then linked with the broad sweep of demographic variables favored by epidemiologists. Even today, a concept of life stress that could form a bridge between the traditional approaches of psychology and epidemiology still takes second place in journals of psychosomatic research; the idea that long-term personality factors predispose a person to particular disorders receives more attention. Where theories have incorporated the notion of somatic illness as a response to stress, there have been competing perspectives: According to one, the physical illness is a substitute for an emotional response that is denied or blocked off, whereas according to others, the intensity of emotional distress itself produces the medical condition.

Zegans (1982) has gone so far as to elaborate seven varieties of these two basic processes. First, the acute bodily response to a stressor may itself cause damage, particularly if an already compromised organ is involved. Second, although the acute response only causes transient insult to a tissue, repeated occurrence may cause permanent tissue damage. (The difference between the first and the second is reminiscent of the difference between life events and long-term difficulties as stressors.) Third, the acute physiological reaction can become chronic if it becomes conditioned to a benign stimulus resembling the stressor and a regular feature of the subject's environment. Fourth, a coping strategy may be used successfully, but the physiological component of the successful coping response is not terminated when the stress is mastered. Fifth, when minor stresses are inappropriately responded to as major assaults, abnormal physiological reactions are possible. Sixth, a physiological response that is appropriate and adequate to cope with a given threat may result in damage to some other aspect of the body through inhibiting a benign but vital body process, or stimulating an irritating one. Finally, coping strategies can misfire when only the behavioral component and not the physiological aspect is inhibited (e.g., fight behavior is inhibited, but not its physiological component). In this instance the physiological aspects of a blocked action can be continuously repeated, since no appropriate cutoff signal is received.

Because in all seven aspects attention is focused upon style of response and defense, rather than upon the stressors themselves and their characteristics, it could be argued that the locus of this controversy is still within the field of personality rather than stress research. In the chapters that follow, we hope to present a case for the proposition that by shifting the direction of vision somewhat more toward the nature of the external stressor rather than the nature of the person, the relevant personality factors may emerge in a clearer perspective. In other words, the earlier failure of psychosomatic research to validate the specificity approach might have been avoided if the nature of the situation preceding onset of each disorder had also been studied, along with those long-term personality factors that might render an individual especially sensitive to that situation. If studies are pursued in this dual manner, the "harder" external material may bring much needed support to "softer" evidence concerning personality, and the presence of one may help to point up the role of the other. For instance, a rather modest and unconvincing correlation between a personality characteristic and a disease may be sharply increased if we consider the presence of a particular personality *and* the presence of a particular, and congruent, stressor. It is also highly likely that the presence of particular types of stressors may help in the search for relevant personality characteristics. Finally, a dual approach will help sort out how far we are dealing with personality dispositions at all, rather than response patterns that have become perpetuated because of "environmental" pressure and facilitation. It is, for example, questionable how far measures of self-esteem reflect a personality characteristic rather than a response to the current social milieu. Of course, it is unlikely that a simple answer will emerge, but the contrasting of "internal" and "external" aspects will allow the issue to be explored rather than prejudged.

Issues in the Study of Life Stress and Physical Disorder

This section of the volume presents examples of studies that have used the Life Events and Difficulties Schedule (LEDS) to examine the role of life events and long-term difficulties in the onset of physical rather than psychiatric conditions. The division of this book into two main parts is not intended to underline the traditional classical dualistic distinction between psyche and soma. It is simply a matter of convenience of presentation; however, studies using the LEDS to investigate the etiology of physical illness do demand some additional considerations. Although most of the points discussed earlier concerning psychiatric disorder apply with equal force to the investigation of somatic disorder, some differences are worth outlining in general before results concerning specific physical disorders are presented.

Intervening Processes

One important difference arises directly from the central role that the meaning of life stress is considered to have in psychiatric disorder. It is intuitively easy to accept that losses are often depressing, or that dangers are often anxiety-provoking, whereas it is difficult to imagine in the same way the types of experience that may be diabetes-inducing or colitis-provoking. In other words, in models developed to explain the etiological role of life events in physical illness, there is more immediate need to take account (even if only implicitly) of intervening processes. Ideally, these processes should be investigated along with the use of the LEDS, and in discussing psychiatric disorder we have already covered many of these cognitive and emotional variables – for instance, as the person's account of the external situation, the person's immediate and distant responses, the support the person receives in the crisis, and the actions taken to change the situation (problem-solving coping). But in the study of physical illnesses there are other such intervening processes. These fall into two broad groupings, which can easily be accommodated within the LEDS interviewing tradition of probing questioning with strict attention to dating: (1) psychiatric symptomatology, which may have physical sequelae in terms of the consequent development of a somatic disorder; and (2) what have been called "coping" responses, including behavioral changes such as in diet, exercise, smoking, and alcohol consumption, which may arise in response to life events and which may then have a physiological impact sufficient to produce an acute illness episode. Other intervening processes that belong more to a laboratory tradition of research include measures of psychophysiological arousal and of fluctuations in neurotransmitters, but here establishment of the time order is bound to be more problematic. Not all the studies described in this section of the volume give details about psychiatric disorder as an intervening variable. But where they do, it is important to distinguish different diagnostic subtypes – for, as will emerge, these can provide crucial links between the meaning of the precipitating life stress and the likely biochemical processes underlying the somatic condition. Thus, to anticipate Chapter 10, distinguishing intervening depression from intervening tension makes it easier to understand why one kind of event (losses) should appear to increase menstrual flow, while another kind of event (challenges) should appear to eliminate it temporarily.

Functional versus Organic Disorder

The issue of diagnostic subgroupings brings us to another important difference in investigations of somatic disorder. There has for many years existed a belief in the distinction between "functional" and "organic" physical complaints: The latter are thought to show clear evidence of physiological changes to tissues and organs, whereas the former are believed to show similar sorts of symptoms upon clinical presentation but to lack such organic pathology upon further investigation. This particular definition of the term "functional" departs somewhat from the 19th-century usage, where it could imply genuine physiological changes too minute to observe or only discernible at postmortem. The contemporary use has a more psychological meaning, as is made clear in a thoughtful outline of the historical development of the term (Trimble, 1982). Trimble pinpoints this terminological transition to the time when Freud's studies of hysterical paralysis (Freud, 1893/1924) moved on from Charcot's perspective of "functional lesion in the grey matter of the cerebral hemisphere on the side opposite the paralysis" (Charcot, 1898, p. 278). Trimble himself is unhappy with current usage, calling it a "meaningless term for undiagnosable symptomatology or a polite eponym for psychiatric disorder" (1982, p. 1770). Although Trimble's dissatisfaction is certainly understandable, the study of this distinction as currently defined is of critical interest to the perspective of this volume, for functional disorders are genuinely expected to be more often precipitated by life stress than are organic conditions. Several of the studies in the following chapters report interesting differences in the expected direction: The same types of provoking agents as those that precede depression (severe events and major difficulties) occur before functional complaints. As will emerge, however, this does not imply that there is no role for life events in "organic" onsets, nor that we must logically adopt one particular position on the meaning of functional disorder in the debate opened up by Trimble.

Nor should these associations with functional disorder allow complacency about current diagnostic categories. First, the category "functional" is only a residual grouping. It is likely that some individuals so diagnosed will ultimately be discovered to have had some undetected organic pathology – if not in the organs specified by the research itself, then perhaps in some other. For example, a girl with a noninflamed appendix may turn out to be suffering from an ovarian cyst (Marsden, 1986). Second, the etiology of many physical complaints is in no less of an exploratory stage than that of most psychiatric disorders, and subgroupings within one overall diagnostic category may well be subject to later revision. For example, it is still not understood exactly how the heavier bleeding of menorrhagia comes about; when this becomes clearer, certain changes to the tissues in the uterus that are now grouped with organic menorrhagia may be considered irrelevant to heavy bleeding, and patients with these particular features may need to be reclassified as functional. Finally, it is always worth considering that within the existing organic group there may be subgroupings that relate differently to different types of life events. One obvious example involves the rapidity of the onset of clear-cut symptoms, and variations on this theme: For instance, patients whose myocardial infarction was preceded by angina can be compared with those without angina (Connolly, 1976). But there are many other possibly useful subcategorizations (e.g., peptic vs. duodenal ulcer).

Illness Behavior and Selection into Treatment

Arising in conjunction with considerations of "functional" complaints is another issue that has so far not been elaborated in this volume, despite its equal relevance for the study of psychiatric disorder: the issue of illness behavior. This is of less importance in population surveys than where samples are recruited among those in treatment, which frequently occurs in studies with a case-control design. Here it is always possible that differences between case and comparison groups have led to treatment seeking rather than to illness itself. Although it is theoretically possible to control for this confounding by using population samples, with rare conditions this can become unreasonably costly and time-consuming, so that case-control studies continue to be a main research focus.

Over the last two decades, Mechanic and his colleagues have opened up this area and provided many insights into the diverse ways illness behavior may confuse interpretation in etiological studies. Mechanic (1962, 1978) defines "illness behavior" as the way people interpret their symptoms and monitor their bodies, how they take remedial action, and how they utilize both formal medical and informal sources of help with health care. Thus it covers both the notion of somatization tendencies and, more recently (Mechanic, 1983), other forms of treatment selection. In the light of the earlier discussion of "functional" disorder, it can be seen that some patients may arrive in departments of physical medicine because of their, and their family doctors', responses to the somatic features of their psychiatric state. Thus one woman who has fainted twice may hurry to her doctor, who refers her on to a neurology department, where thorough testing eventually eliminates a diagnosis of epilepsy; by contrast, another woman may wait for a third blackout before starting to be concerned about herself. Meanwhile, neither of them faints a third time, but the first one has been selected into a case-control study of all new attenders at the department and the second has not. It is possible that the first may have experienced a severe event while the second has not, and that this difference in stressful experience has underlain either the difference in the seriousness with which the women viewed their faintings, or the difference in their willingness to approach a doctor about them (or most probably both these differences). If the hypothesis involves the role of stress in precipitating fainting, it is not enough to establish through careful interviewing that the first woman's severe event did indeed precede her first fainting attack. Unless there is also a random sample of women with an elevated rate of severe events who have fainted without yet attending for treatment, any conclusions from the case-control study about the role of stress in fainting must be subject to caution. The high rate of provoking agents in the case group may be due to their association with sensitive symptom-monitoring and treatment seeking behavior, not to fainting per se. Unfortunately, in many of the studies reported here, it was not possible to extend the research beyond a case-control design, and, as will emerge in Chapter 15, the perspective developed by those working in the area of illness behavior must therefore inform any interpretations or conclusions.

Age

Another factor that deserves special attention in studies of somatic disorder is age. For psychiatric disorder, there is no uniform expectation that risk increases with age; on the contrary, for some disorders such as schizophrenia, risk is decreased (Ciompi, 1985). But risk for a wide range of somatic disorders appears to increase with the more general somatic debility of older age groups. It is therefore not surprising that there is some indication that an etiological role for stress in somatic disorder may be greater in younger age groups – or, in other words, that after a certain point age may replace life stress as the critical factor in promoting onset (Murphy & Brown, 1980). Although age is already routinely controlled for in most studies of stress and psychiatric disorder, this is usually to prevent Type I errors. That is, it is done in order to avoid concluding that a link exists when really one does not, because, say, the higher rate of events in the sick group is spuriously produced by the link of both with another factor. For example, in a study contrasting neurotic with endogenous depression, it might be argued that since patients suffering from the latter type of depression tend to be older than those with the former type, and since older people experience fewer life events than younger people, any differences in life events between the groups might be attributable to age, not to differential diagnostic features. (In fact, this argument ignores the finding that only certain types of events – that is, severe events – are found to precede illness onset in depressives more frequently than they are found among comparison group members, and that severe events do not vary in occurrence by age.) In studies of stress and *somatic* disorder, by contrast, such controls for age may well highlight effects of stress in the younger age groups; such effects might have been attenuated by the inclusion of older patients without life events. In studies of physical illness, in other words, controls for age should guard against Type II errors – that is, rejecting the presence of a link when there is one.

Measurement of Life Events and Difficulties

To turn to the LEDS itself, the aspects that need consideration with a somatic outcome variable are very similar to those that have already emerged in discussing psychiatric disorder. Onset of the physical condition needs to be carefully dated; here, even more than in psychiatric research, there is the danger that the "true" illness process will be overlooked and onset will be dated only in terms of the experiences of pain and dysfunction, which may have arisen some time after key physical changes have begun. It may not be possible to do much about this problem at present except to extend the period of study backward over a longer time. In this way, it may be possible to explore evidence for an increase in life stress some time well before the reported "onset cluster" of subjectively noted symptoms. If the same patterning is found in several studies, this would strengthen the possibility that some internal disease process has been continuing during this extended period, and that these internal changes are related to the earlier life stress. Although this seems to imply that the "true" causal period is likely to be longer in somatic than in psychiatric research, the concept of the internal physical process unnoticed by the subject also allows for the possibility that life events play only a triggering role, pushing above the pain threshold a condition that would have risen above it sooner or later in any case. There is no way of choosing between these two alternatives *a priori*; it is thus always safer to consider both possibilities, and to establish the causal period empirically as the first step in the analysis of the results (see the discussion of triggering as contrasted with formative effects in connection with "brought-forward-time," Brown & Harris, 1978, p. 122).

So far in this book, attention has been focused centrally upon the meaning of any life event or difficulty, and parallels have been pointed out between the specific dimensions of the provoking stressor and the affective quality of the psychiatric disorder (e.g., loss and depression, danger and anxiety, and instrusiveness and schizophrenia). Although there is no reason why similar specificities should not be revealed for stressors before the onset of physical illness (and investigators should always be on the lookout for a new qualitative dimension of life events that can be systematically rated), the original notion promulgated by Selye (1956) of life change that wreaks its effects regardless of meaning, merely through sheer exhaustion of the organism, would appear to have a more plausible place than it does with psychiatric disorder. While the "tiring" quality of events can be considered as a further specific dimension and rated according to the amount of trouble imposed upon the subject, the issues concerning additivity may require different treatment from what they have received so far. It is easier to envisage the addition of a minor difficulty or a nonsevere event as increasing overall exhaustion, in a way in which a collection of minor losses does not seem to produce depression. But none of this amounts to more than saying that the LEDS should be used with previously uninvestigated physical disorders in a way that exploits its full exploratory potential. There is the same wide variety of models to be investigated as there was in the early work on psychiatric conditions; the same range of interplay between event and event and between event and difficulty; and the same opportunity for potentiation by other demographic background experiences.

Not every contribution to this section has exploited all these aspects of the LEDS to the full, but reading through Chapters 8-13 can give a sense of how the instrument can be used to draw powerful and illuminating initial conclusions. One final word: Perhaps one advantage of the LEDS that does not emerge in psychiatric research in quite the way it might is its distinction between contextual and reported dimensions. When one is dealing with psychiatric disorder, the need to defend against the possibility of reporting bias essentially relegates discussion of meaning in cross-sectional research to the effects of the contextual measures. (In longitudinal work much more can be done, as can be seen in the discussion of matching events in Chapter 2.) With physical illness, the self-report dimensions can come more into their own; the impact of reporting style is less likely to introduce bias into the data, and more likely to be an indicator of a genuine etiological effect: Whereas it is vacuous to record that depressed people report having felt depressed by their recent life experiences, it is of more interest if women with one kind of menstrual disorder report that the experiences they have undergone have been depressing, while those with another type of menstrual disorder do not report this, regardless of the actual contextual differences between the experiences of the two groups. This is not, of course, to suggest that respondents will always be able to put into words the precise emotional quality of their response; investigator-based contextual ratings may also be required to supplement the self-report measures if the full etiological contribution of a particular type of stressor to a particular illness is to be revealed. The traditional debate in the psychosomatic research literature, as mentioned earlier, has been between those who believed somatic illness to be enhanced by the denial of affect and those who pinpointed the experience of emotional distress as etiologically crucial. The contrast between contextual and reported ratings allows one to begin to characterize those subjects who are deniers (i.e., for whom reported threat is lower than contextual) and to compare them with those reacting with average or exaggerated responses (i.e., whose reports of threat are the same as or higher than contextual ratings). Perhaps this point does no more than bring us back to where we began, in emphasizing the need to study intervening processes (e.g., reported responses) that take place between stress experience in contextual terms and subsequent disorder, when the outcome is somatic rather than psychiatric. But what has brought us full circle has been an outline of those routine features of the LEDS involving dimensions of meaning that may point up particular perspectives, which themselves then suggest where to look for and identify these crucial intervening variables.

References

Alexander, F. (1950. *Psychosomatic medicine*. New York: Norton.

Brown, G. W., & Harris, T. O. (1978). *Social origins of depression: A study of psychiatric disorder in women*. London: Tavistock.

Cannon, W. B. (1932). *The wisdom of the body* (2nd ed.). New York: Norton.

Charcot, J. M. (1889). *Clinical lectures on diseases of the nervous system*. (Vol. 2). London: New Sydenham Society.

Ciompi, L. (1985). Ageing and schizophrenic psychosis. *Acta Psychiatrica Scandinavica, 71* (Suppl. 319), 93-105.

Connolly, J. (1976). Life events before myocardial infarction. *Jounral of Human Stress, 2*, 3-17.

Depue, R. A., Monroe, S. M., & Shackman, S. L. (1979). The psychobiology of human disease: Implications for conceptualizing the depressive disorders. In R. A. Depue (Ed.), *The psychobiology of the depressive disorders: implications for the effects of stress* (pp. 3-20). London: Tavistock.

Dunbar, H. F. (1954). *Emotions and bodily changes: A survey of literature on psychosomatic interrelationships.* New York: Columbia University Press.

Engel, G. L. (1968). A life setting conductive to illness: The giving-up, given-up complex. *Archives of Internal Medicine, 69,* 293-305.

Freud, A. (1937). *Ego and the mechanisms of defense.* London: Hogarth Press.

Freud, S. (1924). Some points in a comparative study of organic and hysterical paralyses (M. Meyer, Trans.). In *Collected papers of Sigmund Freud* (Vol. 1, pp. 42-58). London: Hogarth Press. (Original work published 1893)

Goldberger, L., & Breznitz, S. (Eds.). (1982). *Handbook of stress: Theoretical and clinical aspects.* New York: Free Press.

Grace, W. J., & Graham, D. T. (1952). Relationship of specific attitudes and emotions to certain bodily diseases. *Psychosomatic Medicine, 14,* 243-251.

Graham, D. T., Kalber, J. D., & Graham, F. K. (1962). Physiological response to the suggestion of attitudes specific for hives and hypertension. *Psychosomatic Medicine, 24,* 257-266.

Graham, D. T., Stern, J. A., & Winokur, G. (1958). Experimental investigation of the specificity of attitude hypothesis in psychosomatic disease. *Psychosomatic Medicine, 20,* 446-457.

Grinker, R. R., & Spiegel, J. P. (1945). *Men under stress.* New York: McGraw-Hill.

Hinkle, L. E., Jr. (1973). The concept of "stress." in the biological and social sciences. *Sciences, Medicine and Man, 1,* 31-48.

Hinkle, L. E., Jr. (1977). The concept of "stress." In Z. J. Lipowski, D. R. Lipsitt, & P. C. Whybrow (Eds.), *Psychosomatic medicine: Current trends and clinical implications.* (pp. 27-49). New York: Oxford University Press.

Lazarus, R. S., & Folkman, S. (1984). *Stress, appraisal, and coping.* New York: Springer.

Janis, I. L. (1958). *Psychological stress: Psychoanalytic and behavioral studies of surgical patients.* New York: Wiley.

Levine, S., & Scotch, N. A. (1970). *Social stress.* Chicago: Aldine.

Lipowski, Z. J. (1977). Psychosomatic medicine in the seventies: An overview. *American Journal of Psychiatry, 134,* 233-244.

Marsden, C. D. (1986). Hysteria – a neurologist's view. *Psychological Medicine, 16,* 277-288.

McGrath, J. E. (1970). *Social and psychological factors in stress.* New York: Holt, Rinehart & Winston.

Mechanic, D. (1962). The concept of illness behaviour. *Journal of Chronic Diseases, 15,* 189-194.

Mechanic, D. (1978). *Medical sociology: A selective view* (2nd ed.). New York: Free Press.

Mechanic, D. (1983). The experience and expression of stress: The study of illness behavior and medical utilization. In D. Mechanic (Ed.), *Handbook of health, health care and the health professions* (pp. 591-607). New York: Free Press.

Murphy, E., & Brown, G. W. (1980). Life events, psychiatric disturbance and physical illness. *British Journal of Psychiatry, 136,* 326-338.

Reiser, M. (1975). Changing theoretical concepts of psychosomatic medicine. In S. Arieti (Ed.), *American handbook of psychiatry* (Vol. 4, pp. 477-500). New York: Basic Books.

Selye, H. (1956). *The stress of life.* New York: McGraw-Hill.

Stern, J. A., Winokur, G., Graham, D. T., & Graham, F. K. (1961). Alterations in physiological measures during experimentally induced attitudes. *Journal of Psychosomatic Research, 5,* 73-82.

Trimble, M. R. (1982). Functional diseases. *British Medical Journal, 285,* 1768-1770.

Vaillant, G. . (1977). *Adaptation to life.* Boston: Little, Brown.

Vaillant, G. E. (1985). An empirically derived hierarchy of adaptive mechanisms and its usefulness as a potential diagnostic axis. *Acta Psychiatrica Scandinavica, 71* (Suppl. 319), 171-180.

Weiner, H. (1982). The prospects for psychosomatic medicine: Selected topics. *Psychosomatic Medicine, 44*, 491-517.

Wolff, C. T., Friedman, S. B., Hofer, M. A., & Mason, J. W. (1964). Relationship between psychological defenses and mean urinary 17-hydroxycorticosteroid excretion rates, Parts I and II. *Psychosomatic Medicine, 26*, 576-609.

Wolff, H. G. (1953). *Stress and disease.* Springfield, IL: Charles C Thomas,

Zegans, L. S. (1982). Stress and the development of somatic disorders. In L. Goldberger & S. Breznitz (Eds.), *Handbook of stress: Theoretical and clinical aspects* (pp. 134-152). New York: Free Press.

8

Appendectomy

FRANCIS CREED

Introduction

Although approximately 80,000 appendectomies are carried out each year in the United Kingdom, Macewen's statement of 1904 remains largely true: "All this removal of diseased appendices does not bring us one step nearer the causation of the disease" (quoted by Barker, 1985, p. 1125). Although attention has been focused on causes of obstruction of the lumen (Horton, 1977; Burkitt, 1971), the etiology of appendicitis is not clear; similarly, the factors that lead to the decision to operate when the appendix turns out to be normal are not known.

Early operation for suspected appendicitis has been partly responsible for the low mortality and morbidity of appendicitis. But the price of this policy has been the removal of a significant number of normal appendices, which can account for up to 40% of appendectomies in young females. Those who have normal appendices removed have recently been more accurately recorded under the diagnosis of "unexplained abdominal pain." Donnan and Lambert (1976) noted that among females aged 15-44 years, the number discharged after the operation with this "diagnosis" was 31 per 10,000 population (compared with 27 per 10,000 for appendicitis).

This chapter examines whether the study of life events can throw any light on the etiology of unexplained abdominal pain that leads to the removal of a normal appendix, as well as on the etiology of appendicitis itself. Since the onset of abdominal pain in each case is sudden and the patient reaches the operating table soon afterwards, these illnesses are especially suited to the life events method of study.

Francis Creed. University Department of Psychiatry, Rawnsley Building, Manchester Royal Infirmary, Oxford Road, Manchester M13 9WL, England.

Etiology of Abdominal Pain in the Absence of Appendicitis

In the case of the normal appendix, there have been numerous suggestions that abdominal pain is a "psychosomatic" complaint. Harding
(1962) speculated from his pathologist's bench that psychological factors
were responsible for the high incidence of removal of normal appendices
among young females – "leaving the smoother life of school to start work,
having a job which is not liked, quarrelling with a boyfriend and other
emotional upsets are commoner at this age than others" (p. 1029). Evidence was provided for this by Ingram, Evans, and Oppenheim (1965),
who found three times more women with social and emotional problems
among those having normal appendices removed than among those with
appendicitis. Barraclough (1967-1968) found evidence that anxiety was
more common among those with normal appendices than among those
with appendicitis. Meyer, Unger, and Slaughter (1964) considered such
abdominal pain to be a hysterical conversion symptom, and found that
the evidence of psychiatric disturbance among those women with normal
appendices was four times that among those with appendicitis. The former group of women also suffered nearly twice as many illnesses during
the subsequent 10 years and underwent more gynecological operations
than those with appendicitis.

Many authors (Meyer *et al.*, 1964; Ingram *et al.*, 1965; O'Rourke &
Milton, 1963; Howie, 1968) have found that those who have normal
appendices removed are more likely to suffer further abdominal pain
over the years following appendectomy than those who have appendicitis. This suggests that in many instances the cause of the pain is unaf-
fected by removal of the appendix. Ingram, *et al.* (1965) suggested that
the pain is caused by contractions of the colon, which is the mechanism
recognized in the irritable bowel syndrome; and it has been demonstrated that distention of the colon can cause pain in the right iliac fossa,
where pain from appendicitis occurs (Swarbrick, Hegarty, Bat, Williams, & Dawson, 1980).

Etiology of Appendicitis

In the case of appendicitis, the etiology of the illness has been studied
at a pathophysiological level. Simultaneous obstruction of the lumen of
the appendix and the introduction of infected material invariably lead
to established appendicitis in controlled experiments (Wangensteen,
Buirge, Dennis, & Ritchie, 1937). There is a pathological evidence that
obstruction of the lumen is important in clinical appendicitis (Horton,
1977; Johnson, 1978), and the condition is said to run in families

(Short, 1946; Howie, 1968; Anderson *et al.*, 1979). It has been described as an illness of civilization because of the rise in prevalence during the course of this century, which suggests that dietary factors are important in the etiology (Burkitt, 1971). But there is no adequate evidence to explain why appendicitis develops when it does in susceptible individuals.

There have been anecdotal reports that the development of appendicitis occurs at times of stress; the case of King Edward VII, who developed appendicitis on the eve of his coronation, is one of these (Paulley, 1955). Goldman (1966) suggested that stress, rather than diet, might be the relevant factor behind the rise in prevalence, but a definite association between stressful life events and the development of appendicitis has not been previously demonstrated.

Using 20 patients with proven appendicitis as a control group for an investigation of irritable bowel syndrome and ulcerative colitis, Fava and Pavan (1976) reported the lowest rate of life events and exit events (according to the method of Paykel) in the appendicitis group. Eylon (1967) found that recent birth events (pregnancy, birth, and weddings) had occurred more commonly among the relatives of patients admitted for appendectomy than in a control group of other patients in a surgical ward.

Ashley (1967) plotted the incidence of proven appendicitis against age and observed a sharp decline after the age of 30 years. The shape of the curve fitted one of the curves derived from a mathematical consideration of possible etiological factors in autoimmune diseases. These calculations indicated, first, that the disease in question is restricted to a carrier population, and, second, that the onset of the disease requires accumulation in a carrier individual of at least two discrete changes that are random in character. Ashley calculated that 12% of the population are at risk of developing appendicitis, and he postulated diet as one factor and infection or vascular factors as the second one. Ashley's model provides a theoretical way in which a life event can be related to the etiology of appendicitis, as it fulfills the criteria of being discrete from diet and occurring randomly in the population.

The present study was designed to examine whether stressful life events were more common in those undergoing appendectomy than in a community comparison group, and whether there was any difference in the pattern or type of life events between the appendicitis and normal-appendix groups. In this way, the role of life events in the etiology of a supposed psychosomatic condition and an organic illness could be compared. In addition, the relationship between life events and psychiatric symptoms was studied, and both events and symptoms were considered to see whether they were associated with continued abdominal pain. The study has been reported briefly in an earlier publication (Creed, 1981).

Subjects and Method

All Caucasian patients aged between 17 and 30 undergoing appendectomy over a 10-month period at three hospitals were considered for interview. Subjects were excluded if, instead of appendicitis, some other cause for their abdominal pain was found at laparotomy. The interview took place on average 4.8 days after the operation, and always when the patient was able to sit comfortably in a side room. The Life Events and Difficulties Schedule (LEDS) was administered, together with the modified Present State Examination (PSE; Wing, Mann, Leff, & Nixon, 1978) and a series of questions relevant to the appendectomy.

As a nonhospitalized comparison group, employees of a local borough council were interviewed. They were matched for age, sex, and social class with the appendectomy group. A number of siblings of the appendectomy patients provided a second nonhospitalized comparison group. At interview, life events were recorded for 1 year – the year before the onset of abdominal pain in the case of the patients, and the year before the interview for the council employees. For the 11 patients who had had long-standing recurrent pain, the first day of the bout of pain that eventually led to the operation was taken as the point of onset.

An additional category of "anticipated events" was employed – those events that were going to occur during the 3 weeks following onset of pain, or interview in the comparison subjects. (Examinations, court appearances, and marriages are examples of anticipated events; the first two carry some predictable short-term threat, though long-term threat is difficult to rate for such events.) All life events were rated in the usual way, but the interviewer was blind to the state of the appendix at the time of interview, and the members of the Bedford College team who carried out the ratings of threat were unaware of whether the subjects belonged to the operation or the community group.

Only after a follow-up study of the patients had been completed 1 year after surgery were the appendix specimens reviewed by a single pathologist, who classified most of them as either "acutely inflamed" or "normal." Those appendix specimens that showed lymphoid hyperplasia or "limited appendicitis" were grouped with the normal specimens for the purpose of this analysis, and the two types together are referred to here as appendices "not acutely inflamed."

At the follow-up interview, the LEDS was repeated to record the events during the year following operation, and the PSE was readministered to determine the patient's mental state at this time. The subjects were questioned about abdominal pain, and reports were classified on a 4-point scale: "none," "trivial," "definite" (pain persistent enough for a clear description to be given, but not disabling), and "disabling" (the patient had attended the doctor and/or been unable to work because of the pain). All statistical analyses used the chi-square test (with Yates's correction where appropriate).

Results

A total of 125 patients were interviewed shortly after appendectomy; of these, 2 refused to complete the interview, and 4 were found to have conditions other than appendicitis that accounted for the abdominal pain. Of the remaining 119 (49 men and 70 women), 63 had "acutely inflamed" appendices, and in 56 the appendix specimens were classified as "not acutely inflamed." The proportion of "acutely inflamed" appendices was similar at the three hospitals. Eleven patients had long-standing recurrent pain, and 10 of these underwent elective surgery. All had appendices that were "not acutely inflamed." The "not acutely inflamed" category included 22 subjects with "mild" appendicitis (lymphoid hyperplasia or "limited appendicitis") and 34 with normal appendices (though 9 of these had elevated white blood cell counts on admission to a hospital). A total of 62 council employees were interviewed as comparison subjects (24 men and 38 women); a further 10 refused interview, and the response rate was therefore 86%.

The two operation groups and the community group were matched for age (mean 21.6 years), marital status, and social class. As noted by Lee (1961), those who fell into the "not acutely inflamed" group were more likely to be female (82%, compared with 38% of the "acutely inflamed" group). During the project, 313 interviews were completed (including those for the follow-up study), and 1,434 life events were recorded. Of these, 42% were rated as having no threat (a rating of 4 on both short-term and long-term threat) and 15% as severe (a long-term threat rating of 1 or 2, focused on the subject). Results are given here in terms of the proportion who experienced an event in a stated period.

TABLE 8.1. Events over 13 weeks prior to operation (patients) or interview (community comparison subjects)

Subject group	Percentage of subjects who experienced:	
	Any life event	An event with threat focused on subject
"Acutely inflamed"	63 (40/63)	54 (34/63) *
"Not acutely inflamed"	88 (49/56)	64 (36/56) *
Community comparison	71 (44/62)	31 (19/62)

Note. n's for the percentages are in parentheses. Adapted from Creed (1981).

* $p < .01$ compared with community group.

Data from Brown and Harris (1978) are presented for comparison: severe events experienced by their depressed patients and by women under 30 years of age in their community sample.

Events during the 13 Weeks before Operation or Interview

When all events were considered, neither group of appendectomy patients differed significantly from the community comparison group (Table 8.1, first column). But considering only those events that were in some way threatening to the subjects (those rated 1, 2, or 3, and subject-focused) altered this pattern. Although there was no difference between the two appendectomy groups, the proportion of subjects who experienced such an event was significantly higher in these groups than in the comparison group (Table 8.1, second column). The commonest examples of such events were breakups of close relationships, examinations, trouble with the police or court appearances, serious arguments at work or at home, and enforced changes of employment. Results were similar for men and women, though the types of events differed: Trouble with the police was more common among men, and splitting up with a boyfriend was more common among women.

These results included anticipated events with those occurring during the 13 weeks prior to onset of pain or interview. If these anticipated events were excluded, the results for threatening subject-focused events were very similar: "acutely inflamed," 51%; "not acutely inflamed," 62%; and community comparison subjects, 31%.

Examination of the results for the 3 weeks prior to onset of pain or interview produced a different picture. When anticipated events were excluded, the "not acutely inflamed" subjects experienced significantly more threatening subject-focused events (36%) than either the "acutely inflamed" group (14%) or the community comparison group (5%) ($p <$ .02). Anticipated events that carried some threat to the subjects were most common in the "acutely inflamed" group, and addition of these events to those for the 3 weeks prior to onset or interview produced a significant difference among the three groups: "acutely inflamed," 22%; "not acutely inflamed," 39%; and community comparison subjects, 5% ($p <$ .01). The threatening anticipated events recorded were forthcoming examinations (6), appearances in court (2), forced job change (1), and enforced migration away from the family (1).

In the 38 weeks after operation, the proportion of subjects in each appendectomy group who experienced at least one such threatening event fell to the level in the community comparison group, suggesting that the raised rate before onset reflects some kind of causal relationship (Figure 8.1, top).

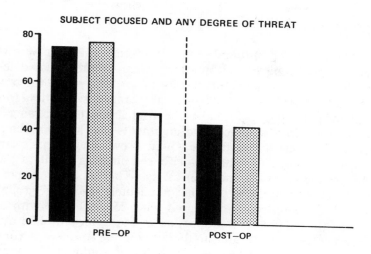

SUBJECT FOCUSED AND ANY DEGREE OF THREAT

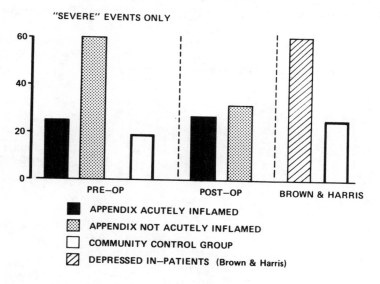

"SEVERE" EVENTS ONLY

■ APPENDIX ACUTELY INFLAMED
▒ APPENDIX NOT ACUTELY INFLAMED
☐ COMMUNITY CONTROL GROUP
▨ DEPRESSED IN-PATIENTS (Brown & Harris)

FIGURE 8.1. Percentage of subjects experiencing an event in the 38 weeks before and after operation for appendectomy subjects, the 38 weeks before interview for the community comparison groups, or the 38 weeks before onset for Brown and Harris's depressed inpatients. Top, subject-focused events with any degree of threat; bottom, severe events only. From "Life Events and Appendicetomy" by F. Creed, 1981, *Lancet, i*, 1381-1385. Copyright 1981 by Lancet Ltd. Reprinted by permission.

Severely Threatening Events

Brown and Harris (1978) found that only those events that were rated as severely threatening in the long term were causally related to the onset of depression. (The commonest events of this type in the present series were serious illness or death in the family, separation from a spouse or long-standing girlfriend or boyfriend, court appearance with the threat of a prison sentence, and arguments that led to a complete disruption of key family relationships.) Of Brown and Harris's sample of depressed patients, 61% had experienced such an event in the 38 weeks before the onset of illness. In the same period before appendectomy in the current study, 59% of the "not acutely inflamed" group had experienced a severe event, compared with 25% of those with acute appendicitis ($p < .001$). The proportion of the latter who had experienced a severe event was similar to that in both the community comparison group in this study and women under age 30 studied in Camberwell by Brown and Harris (1978) (see Figure 8.1, bottom). Separate analyses

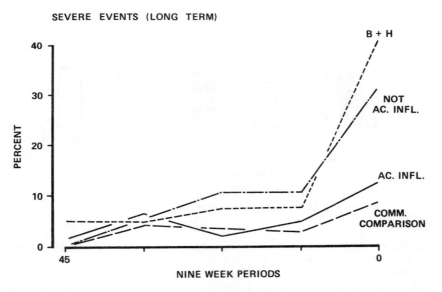

FIGURE 8.2. Percentage of subjects who had experienced a severely threatening event in each of the 9-week periods before surgery for appendectomy subjects ("NOT AC. INFL." and "AC. INFL."), before interview for the present community comparison group ("COMM. COMPARISON"), and before onset for Brown and Harris's depressed inpatients ("B + H"). For those with more than one severe event, the event nearest to surgery/ interview/onset was considered. From "Life Events and Appendicectomy" by F. Creed, 1981, *Lancet, i,* 1381-1385. Copyright 1981 by Lancet Ltd. Reprinted by permission.

by sex revealed a similar pattern, but only with the men did both differences reach statistical significance. In the women, the "not acutely inflamed" group had experienced significantly more severe events than the community comparison group, but the difference between the two appendectomy groups just failed to reach statistical significance (59% vs. 38%), $\chi^2 = 2.84$, $p < .10$.

The 38-week period was used for this comparison because it was the period used by Brown and Harris, but in most instances, as with depression, the severe event preceded the appendectomy by less than 9 weeks (Figure 8.2). The pattern for the 38 weeks after the operation confirmed this close temporal association between severe events and the operation (Figure 8.1, bottom).

Marked chronic difficulties lasting for more than 1 year were recorded among 25% of the "not acutely inflamed" subjects, 21% of those with appendicitis,and 2% of the community comparison subjects ($p < .001$). Difficulties concerning personal relationships were recorded in 30%, 13%, and 8% respectively, of these three groups (for the "not acutely inflamed" group compared to the rest, $p < .01$).

Interpersonal crises were common among the severe events recorded in the "not acutely inflamed" group. Severe life events that were interaction changes or arguments (classified as "miscellaneous") constituted 39% (21/54) of the severe life events recorded for this group, 11% (4/37) of those recorded for the "acutely inflamed" subjects, and 19% (3/16) of those recorded for the community comparison subjects. The difference between the two appendectomy groups was significant ($p < .01$). The number of subjects in each group who had experienced such an event was 19 of 56 (34%) for the "not acutely inflamed" group, 3 of 63 (5%) for the "acutely inflamed" group, and 2 of 62 (3%) for the community comparison group ($p < .001$).

Sibling Comparison Group

If life events play a part in precipitating appendicitis, they should be less common in healthy siblings. The sibling comparison group provided a limited opportunity to test this hypothesis. The accuracy of the LEDS could also be assessed, because first-degree relatives are included in the interview schedule. Thirty-one siblings of the patients were interviewed, and there was complete agreement regarding life events in common for 25 of the sibling-patient pairs (39 events). In the remaining 6 pairs, there was agreement for three events; five events were reported by the subjects only, and only two life events were recorded in the interviews with the siblings that should have been included for the patients but were missed during the original interviews. Neither event was severe.

TABLE 8.2. Proportions of appendectomy patients and their siblings who experienced
life events during the time prior to the onset of the subject's abdominal pain

	Percentage experiencing life events		
	"Acutely inflamed"	"Not acutely inflamed"	Total
Any event threatening to subject (13 weeks before operation)			
Index subjects	50 (8/16)	80 (12/15) *	65 (20/31) *
Siblings	38 (6/16)	27 (4/15)	32 (10/31)
Severe event (38 weeks before operation)			
Index subjects	19 (3/16)	73 (11/15) *	45 (14/31)
Siblings	13 (2/16)	27 (4/15)	19 (6/31)

Note. n's are in parentheses. Adapted from Creed (1981).

* $p < .05$ for index subjects compared with their siblings.

Of the 31 appendectomy subjects whose siblings were interviewed,
65% had experienced an event with some threat to themselves in the 13
weeks before the operation, compared with 32% of their siblings ($p <
.05$). This difference was greater for those in the "not acutely inflamed"
group, and these patients had also experienced significantly more severe
life events than their siblings (Table 8.2).

Relationship to Psychiatric Symptoms

In view of the relationship between severe events and depression, it is
appropriate to ask whether those patients in the "not acutely inflamed"
group were depressed at the onset of their abdominal pain. Those subjects whose score on the PSE for the month prior to onset reached level
4 on the Index of Definition were described as having psychiatric symptoms. Level 4 indicates a total of 10 or more nonspecific symptoms, or
a single key symptom of depression or anxiety without the other related
symptoms (Wing *et al.*, 1978). (This corresponds approximately to the
"borderline" category of Brown and Harris; see Finlay-Jones *et al.*,
1980). Of the total sample (the two patient groups and the comparison
group), 6% (11/181) reached level 5 on the Index of Definition (8 had
depression, 2 had anxiety, and 1 had mixed anxiety/depression). A further 15% (27/181) reached level 4.

Of the "not acutely inflamed" group, 32% (18/56) experienced psychiatric symptoms, compared with 16% (10/62) each of the "acutely
inflamed" group and the community comparison group ($p < .02$). However, although there was an overall relationship between severe life
events and depression similar to that found by Brown and Harris (Table
8.3, bottom line), within the "not acutely inflamed" group, severe

events were common even among the two-thirds who did not have psychiatric symptoms (Table 8.3, second line).

Abdominal Pain during Postoperative Year

Approximately 1 year (average 58 weeks) after the operation, 101 of the 119 appendectomy patients were reinterviewed. Of the original sample, 2 had died (1 in a motorcycle accident and 1 as a result of a congenital cardiac abnormality), 8 refused the second interview, and 8 could not be traced. Of the 101, 41 described "definite" or "disabling" pain in the year after appendectomy; this was usually a pain similar to the one that had led to the operation. Twenty of these 41 patients had both taken time off work and consulted their doctors because of the pain, although only 4 had been referred back to their surgeons.

This continued abdominal pain was most common in the "not acutely inflamed" group; 58% reported it, compared with 24% of those in the "acutely inflamed" group ($p < .001$). If "disabling" pain only was considered, the respective proportions were 25% and 11% ($p < .05$). There was no direct relationship, however, between the experience of severe life events and continued abdominal pain. Of those with continued pain, 44% had experienced a severe life event in the 38 weeks before operation, compared with 38% of those without such pain. The proportions who experienced a severe life event between operation and the follow-up interview were 29% and 33%, respectively.

Psychiatric symptoms, on the other hand, were clearly related to continued abdominal pain. Of the 25 patients with psychiatric symptoms at the time of operation who were followed up, 64% were found to have postoperative pain, compared with 33% of the remainder ($p < .01$). When both pathology of the appendix and psychiatric status at the

TABLE 8.3. Life events and psychiatric symptoms at onset (patients) or interview (comparison group)

Subject group	Percentage who experienced a severe life event in previous 38 weeks	
	Psychiatric symptoms	No psychiatric symptoms
"Acutely inflamed"	40 (4/10)	23 (12/53)
"Not acutely inflamed"	78 (15/18)	53 (20/38)
Community comparison	40 (4/10)	16 (8/52)
Total	58 (25/38)	28 (47/143)

Note. n's are in parentheses. Adapted from Creed (1981).

TABLE 8.4. Abdominal pain and psychiatric status at follow-up

Patient status at time of appendectomy	Percentage with symptoms at follow-up		
	Continued abdominal pain	Psychiatric symptoms	Psychiatric symptoms and abdominal pain
"Acutely inflamed" without psychiatric symptoms	21 (9/42)	5 (2/42)	2 (1/42)
"Acutely inflamed" with psychiatric symptoms	33 (3/9)	44 (4/9)	22 (2/9)
"Not acutely inflamed" without psychiatric symptoms	47 (16/34)	24 (8/34)	15 (5/34)
"Not acutely inflamed" with psychiatric symptoms	81 (13/16)	63 (10/16)	50 (8/16)

Note. n's are in parentheses. Adapted from Creed (1981).

time of operation were considered, the prevalence of continued abdominal pain ranged widely – from 21% for "acutely inflamed" patients without psychiatric symptoms to 81% for "not acutely inflamed" patients with psychiatric symptoms (Table 8.4). The range was 10% to 44% if disabling pain only was considered. There was a close association between depression at follow-up and continued pain.

The presence of psychiatric symptoms at the time of appendectomy was significantly related to a number of factors. For 64% (18/28) of those with psychiatric symptoms, the medical treatment for the suspected appendicitis was initiated by relatives rather than the patients themselves. This compared with 39% (35/91) of those without psychiatric symptoms ($p < .005$). Those with psychiatric symptoms had longer

TABLE 8.5. Length of hospital stay and postoperative complications by appendectomy group and presence of psychiatric symptoms

Psychiatric status at time of appendectomy	"Acutely inflamed"		"Not acutely inflamed"	
	Percentage in hospital for 8 days or more[a]	Percentage with postoperative complications	Percentage in hospital for 8 days or more[a]	Percentage with postoperative complications
Few/no psychiatric symptoms	19 (8/42)	22	36 (12/33)	18
With psychiatric symptoms	11 (1/9)	0	71 (12/17) *	23
Total	18 (9/51)	18	48 (24/50) **	20

[a] n's are in parentheses.

* Comparison of "not acutely inflamed" with and without psychiatric symptoms: corrected $\chi^2 = 3.98$, $p < .05$.

** Comparison of "acutely inflamed" and "not acutely inflamed" groups: corrected $\chi^2 = 9.25$, $p < .01$.

TABLE 8.6. Number of subjects off work for 5 weeks or more following surgery by appendectomy group and psychiatric symptoms

Psychiatric status at time of appendectomy	Percentage off work		
	"Acutely inflamed"	"Not acutely inflamed"	Total
Few/no psychiatric symptoms	26 (11/42)	12 (4/33)	20 (15/75)
With psychiatric symptoms	33 (3/9)	59 (10/17)	50 (13/26) *
Total	27 (14/51)	28 (14/20)	

Note. n's are in parentheses.
*Comparison of those with and without psychiatric symptoms: corrected $\chi^2 = 7.25$, $p < .01$.

hospital stays, and this difference could not be attributed to medical complications (Table 8.5). Those who had psychiatric symptoms at the time of the operation were more likely to report trouble with their scars at the follow-up interview (81% compared to 32%; $p < .001$), and were off work following appendectomy for longer than those without psychiatric symptoms (Table 8.6). These features were most marked in those who had psychiatric symptoms and were in the "not acutely inflamed" group (Tables 8.5 and 8.6). These patients also reported many trivial bodily symptoms both within and outside the gastrointestinal tract and estimated (while still hospitalized) that they would be disabled for longer after the operation (Tables 8.7-8.9). These features show

TABLE 8.7. Reporting of three or more trivial symptoms at time of operation and at follow-up by group and psychiatric symptoms

Psychiatric status at time of appendectomy	Percentage reporting trivial symptoms				
	"Acutely inflamed"		"Not acutely inflamed"		
	At time of operation	At follow-up	At time of operation	At follow-up	Community comparison subjects
Few/no psychiatric symptoms	29 (15/52)	33 (14/42)	50 (17/34) *	41 (13/32)	38 (20/52)
With psychiatric symptoms	62 (5/8)	33 (3/9)	89 (16/18) **	76 (13/17)	70 (7/10)
Total	33 (20/60)		63 (33/52) ***		43 (27/62)

Note. n's are in parentheses.

   * Comparison of "acutely inflamed" and "not acutely inflamed" groups without psychiatric symptoms: $\chi^2 = 4.016$, $p < .05$.

   ** Comparison of "not acutely inflamed" subjects with psychiatric symptoms to those without psychiatric symptoms: corrected $\chi^2 = 6.09$, $p < .02$.

   *** Comparison of total "not acutely inflamed" group with total "acutely inflamed" group: $\chi^2 = 10.14$, $p < .01$. Comparison of total "not acutely inflamed" group with community comparison subjects: $\chi^2 = 4.49$, $p < .05$.

TABLE 8.8. Reported gastrointestinal symptoms at time of operation and at follow-up by appendectomy group and by psychiatric symptoms

| | Percentage reporting gastrointestinal symptoms | | | | |
| | "Acutely inflamed" | | "Not acutely inflamed" | | |
Psychiatric status at time of appendectomy	At time of operation	At follow-up	At time of operation	At follow-up	Total
Few/no psychiatric symptoms	38 (20/52)	38 (16/42)	56 (19/34)	56 (18/32)	45 (39/86)
With psychiatric symptoms	50 (4/8)	22 (2/9)	78 (14/18)	76 (13/17)	69 (18/26)
Total	40 (24/60)	35 (18/51)	63 (35/52) **	63 (31/49)	

Note. n's are in parentheses.

 * Comparison of those with and without psychiatric symptoms: corrected χ^2 = 3.65, n.s.

 ** Comparison of "acutely inflamed" and "not acutely inflamed" groups: corrected χ^2 = 5.23, $p < .05$.

considerable similarity to the illness behaviors reported as common among those with irritable bowel syndrome (Whitehead, Winget, Fedoravicius, Wooley, & Blackwell, 1982).

The "not acutely inflamed" subjects (whether or not they had psychiatric symptoms) were more likely than their counterparts with appendicitis to have a family history of psychiatric illness (48% vs. 21%, $p < .01$); to report conflicts with their parents (29% vs. 13%), $p < .05$); to have suffered previous suspected appendicitis (48% vs. 24%, $p < .01$); and to report dysmenorrhea (63% of female subjects vs. 24%, $p < .05$).

Of those without psychiatric symptoms at the time of appendectomy, 4% of the "acutely inflamed" and 24% of the "not acutely inflamed" subjects had developed depressive symptoms at follow-up ($p < .05$); this finding emphasized that the latter group of subjects were predisposed to develop psychiatric symptoms.

TABLE 8.9. Patients' estimate of length of time to return to full activity after operation (15 days or more)

| | Percentage estimating 15 days or more | |
Psychiatric status at time of appendectomy	"Acutely inflamed"	"Not acutely inflamed"
Few/no psychiatric symptoms	60 (27/45)	61 (22/36)
With psychiatric symptoms	57 (4/7)	86 (12/14) *

Note. n's are in parentheses.

* Comparison of "not acutely inflamed" subjects with psychiatric symptoms with all remaining subjects: χ^2 = 3.39, n.s.

Discussion

Three principal conclusions can be drawn from this study. First, the onset of acute appendicitis, an organic condition with a sudden onset, is *not* associated with the experience of severely threatening life events; it is associated with events carrying short-term threat, including antici- pated events such as examinations and court appearances. Second, the onset of abdominal pain that leads to appendectomy, but without a diagnosis of acute appendicitis, is clearly associated with the experience of severely threatening events, whether or not depressive symptoms are present. Third, continued abdominal pain is most likely in those who either have associated depressive symptoms at the time of operation or develop them soon afterwards.

The measurement of life events in this study showed demonstrable reliability (Creed, 1985). There was little falloff in the reporting of events; the proportion of events that were rated as severely threatening concurs with that in other studies; the differences between groups lay in the rating of threat, rather than the number of events; and these rat- ings were made by the Bedford college raters, who were blind to the subject groups. The role of life events in the two conditions is now con- sidered in more detail.

At present, only those with a family history of appendicitis can be described as vulnerable to developing appendicitis. A positive family history was significantly more common in those with definite appendi- citis, suggesting a constitutional liability for infection to develop at this site in these individuals. According to Ashley's (1967) model, two inde- pendent etiological agents must affect a vulnerable individual together if appendicitis is to develop. A life event carrying short-term threat, which lowers resistance to infection and/or alters colonic contractions, may be one such agent. Exposure to an infective agent may be another. The evidence that exposure to stress lowers residence to infection has been recorded both in animals (Stein, Schiavi, & Camerino, 1976) and in human beings (Bartrop, Lazarus, & Luckhurst, 1977; Schleifer, Kel- ler, Camerino, Thornton, & Stein, 1983). This model is compatible with anticipated events that occur before the onset of appendicitis, as the continued anxiety prior to an important examination or court appear- ance may reasonably be expected to alter the body's normal homeosta- sis. Such life events carry short-term but not necessarily long-term threat, and are focused on the subject.

Vulnerability to having a normal appendix removed is much less easy to define. For those with a family history of appendicitis, it is pos- sible that any right-sided abdominal pain is regarded as potential appen- dicitis, and the subject presents early for surgical treatment. For the "not acutely inflamed" group as a whole in the present study, there was evidence of predisposition to develop psychiatric symptoms, as demonstrated by the family history data and by the fact that a higher proportion of these subjects without psychiatric symptoms at the time of the operation developed such symptoms during the postoperative year, compared to those with inflamed appendices. The "not acutely inflamed" group also tended to report many trivial physical symptoms, to have had more previous histories of suspected appendicitis, and to be disabled longer following the operation. This suggests either that such patients suffer greatly with bodily symptoms or that they have a low threshold for seeking medical treatment.

The role of severe life events in "not acutely inflamed" patients may be twofold. First, a life event may lead to painful contractions of the colon, producing right-sided abdominal pain. The present study has no data to confirm or deny this suggestion, but for those individuals who do not have psychiatric symptoms, this may be the most likely explanation for the direct relationship with stress. Second, the life event and ensuing depressive symptoms may lead to the individual's experiencing greater distress and indicating to others a greater need for medical treatment. There were two findings suggesting this in the present study: Those with psychiatric symptoms were more likely than the remainder to be brought to treatment by close relatives, rather than initiating medical treatment themselves; they were also kept in the hospital longer, and this could not be explained by medical complications.

The difference in the type of life event related to each condition – appendicitis and abdominal pain in the "not acutely inflamed" group – is similar to the difference between events preceding depression and schizophrenia. Brown and Harris (1978) reported that severely threatening events were much less likely to occur before the onset of schizophrenia than the onset of depression, and that schizophrenia could be precipitated by events of relatively minor threat. They have suggested that such a minor threat may cause arousal, which in a predisposed individual may precipitate an onset of florid symptoms. Such a model is close to that envisaged for appendicitis, where the arousal related to an anticipated event (e.g., an important forthcoming examination or a court case) may be similar to that resulting from an actual event (e.g., an accident).

Jacobs, Bar-Nathan, and Iuchtman (1975) also compared the life events experienced by patients admitted with schizophrenia and depression, and found that the depressives had experienced more undesirable events and more events categorized as "exits" (from the social field), which would tend to correspond to the severely threatening events of Brown and Harris used in this study. It was also found that of the 59 events, only 2 occurred significantly more frequently among the depressives: serious arguments with nonresident family members, and serious arguments with fiancé, girlfriend, or boyfriend. In the present study, serious problems in close relationships were responsible for differentiating the "not acutely inflamed" group from the "acutely inflamed" group in terms of both life events and chronic difficulties, and this pattern is similar to that reported by Craig regarding patients with functional abdominal pain (Chapter 9, this volume).

Those who have studied patients with irritable bowel syndrome have found that approximately one-third had normal appendices removed at an earlier stage in the illness (Chaudhary & Truelove, 1962; Keeling & Fielding, 1975). It has been shown that distension of the colon causes pain in many sites – predominantly in the right iliac fossa, the site of pain resulting from appendicitis (Swarbrick et al., 1980). In the present series of appendectomy patients, a quarter of those with episodes of abdominal pain in the year after operation also experienced bowel symptoms.

The present study indicates that continued abdominal pain following appendectomy relates more closely to the development of depression than to the presence of preceeding stress. Although the acute abdominal pain was related to a severe event, the chronic sequelae seemed to result only when the event also led to depressive symptoms. Querido (1959) also found that among patients who had undergone appendectomy, continued abdominal discomfort was not related to preceding stress but occurred in those who were clearly distressed at the time of hospitalization (i.e., suffering from tension and conflict resulting from severe environmental stress). The present study confirms that in some cases removal of a normal or mildly inflamed appendix will not cure abdominal pain. Swarbrick et al. (1980) wrote that "the widespread belief that only the finding of intra-abdominal organic disease is enough to explain a patient's symptoms inhibits the advancement of clinical gastroenterology" (p. 446). The logical step to take with patients who have normal appendices removed is to offer help to those who are seriously distressed by interpersonal crises, to see whether this can relieve the abdominal pain that so often become chronic.

Acknowledgments

This work was carried out while I held a Mental Health Leverhulme Research Fellowship.

References

Anderson, N., Griffiths, H., Murphy, J., Roll, J., Serenyi, A., Swann, I., Cockcroft, A., Myers, J., & St. Leger, A. (1979). Is appendicitis familial? *British Medical Journal, ii,* 697-698.

Ashley, D. J. B. (1967). Observations on the epidemiology of appendicitis. *Gut, 8,* 533-538.

Barker, D. J. P. (1985). Acute appendicitis and dietary fibre: An alternative hypothesis. *British Medical Journal, i,* 1125-1127.

Barraclough, B. M. (1967). Appendicectomy in men. *Journal of Psychosomatic Research, 11,* 203-206.

Barraclough, B. M. (1968). Appendicectomy in women. *Journal of Psychosomatic Research, 12,* 231-234.

Bartrop, R. W., Lazarus, L., & Luckhurst, E. (1977). Depressed lymphocyte function after bereavement. *Lancet, i,* 834-836.

Brown, G. W., & Harris, T. O. (1978). *Social origins of depression: A study of psychiatric disorder in women.* London: Tavistock.

Burkitt, D. P. (1971). The aetiology of appendicitis. *British Journal of Surgery, 58,* 695-699.

Chaudhary, N. A., & Truelove, S. C. (1962). The irritable colon syndrome. *Quarterly Journal of Medicine, 31,* 307-322.

Creed, F. (1981). Life events and appendicectomy. *Lancet, i,* 1381-1385.

Creed, F. H. (1985). *Psychosocial variables and appendicitis.* Unpublished MD thesis, University of Cambridge.

Donnan, S. P. B., & Lambert, P. M. (1976). Appendicitis: Incidence and mortality. In *Population trends* (Vol. 5, p. 26). London: Her Majesty's Stationery Office.

Eylon, Y. (1967). Birth events, appendicitis, and appendicectomy. *British Journal of Medical Psychology, 40,* 317-332.

Fava, G. A., & Pavan, L. (1976). Large bowel disorders: Illness configuration and life events. *Psychotherapy and Psychosomatics, 27,* 93-99.

Finlay-Jones, R., Brown, G. W., Duncan-Jones, P., Harris, T., Murphy, E., & Prudo, R. (1980). Depression and anxiety in the community: Replicating the diagnosis of a case. *Psychological Medicine, 10,* 445-454.

Goldman, M. (1966). Appendicitis: A historical survey. *Hospital Medicine,* 42-46.

Harding, H. E. (1962). A notable source of error in diagnosis of appendicitis. *British Medical Journal, ii,* 1028-1029.

Horton, L. W. L. (1977). Pathogenesis of acute appendicitis. *British Medical Journal, ii,* 1672-1673.

Howie, J. G. R. (1968). The place of appendicectomy in the treatment of young adult patients with possible appendicitis. *Lancet, i,* 1365-1367.

Ingram, P. W., Evans, G., & Oppenheim, A. N. (1965). Right iliac fossa pain in young women. *British Medical Journal, ii,* 149-151.

Jacobs, E. T., Bar-Nathan, J., & Iuchtman, M. (1975). Error-rate factor in the management of appendicitis. *Lancet, ii,* 1032.

Johnson, J. R. (1978). Pathogenesis of acute appendicitis. *British Medical Journal, i,* 305.

Keeling, P. W. N., & Fielding, J. F. (1975). The irritable bowel syndrome: A review of 50 consecutive cases. *Journal of the Irish College of Physicians and Surgeons, 4,* 91-94.

Lee, J. A. H. (1961). "Appendicitis" in young women: An opportunity for collaborative clinical research in the National Health Service. *Lancet, ii,* 815-817.

Meyer, E., Unger, H. T., & Slaughter, R. (1964). Investigation of a psychosocial hypothesis in appendectomies. *Psychosomatic Medicine, 26,* 671-681.

O'Rourke, M., & Milton, G. W. (1963). The results of removing a "normal" appendix. *Australian and New Zealand Journal of Surgery, 33*, 12-15.

Paulley, J. W. (1955). Psychosomatic factors in the aetiology of acute appendicitis. *Archives of the Middlesex Hospital, 5*, 35-41.

Querido, A. (1959). Forecast and follow-up: An investigation into clinical, social and mental factors determining the results of hospital treatment. *British Journal of Preventive and Social Medicine, 13*, 33-49.

Schleifer, S. J., Keller, S. E., Camerino, M., Thornton, J. C., & Stein, M. (1983). Suppression of lymphocyte stimulation following bereavement. *Journal of the American Medical Association, 250*, 374-377.

Short, A. R. (1946). *The causation of the appendicitis.* Bristol, England: John Wright & Sons.

Stein, M., Schiavi, R. C. & Camerino, M. (1976). Influence of brain and behavior on the immune system. *Science, 191*, 435-440.

Swarbrick, E. T., Hegarty, J. E., Bat, L., Williams, C. B., & Dawson, A. M. (1980). Site of pain from the irritable bowel. *Lancet, ii*, 443-446.

Wangensteen, O. H., Buirge, R. E., Dennis, C., & Ritchie, W. P. (1937). Studies in the etiology of acute appendicitis: The significance of the structure and function of the vermiform appendix in the genesis of appendicitis. *Annals of Surgery, 106*, 910-942.

Whitehead, W. E., Winget, C., Fedoravicius, A. S., Wooley, S., & Blackwell, B. (1982). Learned illness behaviour in patients with I.B.S. and peptic ulcer. *Digestive Disease and Sciences, 27*, 202-208.

Wing, J. K., Mann, S. A., Leff, J. P., & Nixon, J. M. (1978). The concept of a "case" in psychiatric population surveys. *Psychological Medicine, 8*, 203-217.

9

Abdominal Pain

TOM K. J. CRAIG

Introduction

The notion that environmental stressors and emotional reaction to these can bring about not only widespread physiological reactions but also pathological changes in bodily organs has a long history. As early as 1884, Stiller pointed to the frequent association between financial losses and the development of peptic ulceration in his patients, and referred to the speculations of earlier observers linking mental anxiety, environmental stressors, and physical disease.

It was commonly believed that such associations must be accounted for by the emotional reaction to stress and consequent physiological arousal, and early efforts at explanation focused largely on factors in the premorbid personality that were believed to determine the nature and strength of emotional responses. Yet, despite many years of effort, convincing evidence has not emerged; for the present, the notion of causal links between particular personality styles or responses to stress and gastrointestinal disease would seem to have been discredited. In recent years, interest has turned from personality and intrapsychic mechanisms toward the external world, not least because of improvements in the measurement of environmental stressors, which have outstripped those in measurement of the less accessible intrapsychic processes (Kimball, 1970). The development of the Life Events and Difficulties Schedule (LEDS) solved many of the problems of low reliability and dubious validity of earlier approaches (Brown, 1974; Birley & Connolly, 1976). At the same time, the development of standardized psychiatric interviews and reliable case definition techniques enabled more rigorous examination of the interplay between environment and emotions than had hitherto been possible.

Tom K. J. Craig. Division of Psychiatry, United Medical and Dental Schools, Guy's Hospital, London SE1 9RT, England; National Unit for Psychiatric Research and Development, Lewisham Hospital, Lewisham High Street, London SE13 6LH, England.

Developed largely for the exploration of the relationship between environmental stressors and psychiatric disorder, the LEDS has now been employed in several studies of physical disorder. Two of these have a direct bearing on the present chapter, providing much of the ground on which the hypotheses explored in the current investigation were based. In the first study, Murphy and Brown (1980) examined a group of 111 women selected from a random sample of the general population because they reported that they had recently developed new physical symptoms of moderate or severe intensity. Every woman was interviewed about her physical and psychiatric state, and about the presence of life events using the LEDS. Thirty of the women were excluded on the basis of having symptoms that could be directly attributable to a psychiatric condition. The remaining 81 "organic" women were compared with a normal population sample matched for life stage and social class. The study demonstrated that severely threatening events, previously shown to be of etiological importance in depression, played a causal role in a wide range of bodily diseases, but only when the onset of somatic symptoms was preceded by the development of a mild affective disorder.

The second of these studies (Creed, 1981, and Chapter 8, this volume) examined patients undergoing appendectomy. It demonstrated that when diagnosis was based on the histological confirmation of inflammation, the same severely threatening events were of etiological importance only in those patients whose appendices turned out to be normal or minimally inflamed on histological examination. Patients with clear evidence of inflammation showed no such relationship, but did have a somewhat elevated rate of less severely threatening events within a 13-week period before appendectomy. Furthermore, affective disorder was more common in patients whose appendices showed no conclusive evidence of inflammation, and it was also associated with the persistence of abdominal pain in the postoperative period. Depression did not appear to play a significant intervening role for organic disorders (i.e., patients with definite inflammation of the appendix) in the manner indicated by the Murphy and Brown investigation.

The present study was conceived with two aims. First, it was intended to follow up the implication in Creed's study that certain nonsevere life events may play an etiological role in organic conditions, and to do so by exploring other dimensions of stressful experience besides that of "threat." Second, it was intended to attempt to reconcile the apparent discrepancy between the Murphy and Brown study and the Creed study regarding the observed role of affective disorder – a discrepancy that apparently cannot be explained on methodological grounds, since both studies used comparable measures of life events and psychiatric symptoms. The most obvious explanation seems to lie in the differing degree of precision employed in making the diagnosis of the physical conditions. Such precision matters, because physical symptoms can arise in the absence of structural organic changes and may represent no more than a somatic component of an affective disorder. Such presentations can be extremely difficult to distinguish clinically from others, in which emotional symptoms arise in response to the experience of bodily discomfort based on organic pathology. For example, how does one distinguish on initial presentation between the tachycardia of acute anxiety and that associated with a "silent" myocardial infarction, or, for that matter, between the types of abdominal pain that led to appendectomy in Creed's study? Although Murphy and Brown (1980) made attempts to rule out somatic complaints that were unequivocally attributable to disturbed affect, it is impossible to be certain that the majority of the remaining patients were suffering from a primary organic disease. As a consequence, their results may reflect little more than the fact that severe events can lead to the development of affective disorders whose somatic components are presented to physicians.

Subjects and Methods

Patients between the ages of 18 and 60 were selected from a consecutive series of attenders at three gastroenterology clinics. Each patient presented at the clinic with an onset of abdominal pain that had occurred within the previous 12 months. The original intention was to study only patients with a first onset, but those suffering a relapse of a prior disorder were included when first onset had been within 3 years of interview and the patient had been free of symptoms in the absence of medication for a year prior to the current episode. All patients were interviewed before the completion of any physical investigative procedures, usually at the first outpatient appointment or within a few days of that.

A comparison group, which had been free of gastrointestinal illness for at least 2 years, was selected from a random sample of persons registered with five general-practice surgeries in the catchment areas of the hospital clinics. This sample allowed for a pairwise match of each patient on the basis of age (within 5 years), sex, marital state, social class, country of birth, and life stage (an index reflecting age and the presence of children in the respondent's household, and known to be related to the frequency of certain life events in the general population).

The Measurement of Life Events and Chronic Difficulties

The method of life events identification and rating, the LEDS, is common to all the studies reported in this volume and was used in unmodified form, with the addition of a number of new dimensions and associated rating scales (see below). As a check on accuracy, dates of events and difficulties were confirmed whenever possible by the examination of official records (registers of births and deaths, travel documents), business letters, personal diaries, and the like. The ratings of the qualitative dimensions involved in the LEDS, and those developed specifically for the investigation, were performed by members of the wider Bedford College research team involved in other life events investigations; raters were unaware of whether subjects were patients or belonged to the comparison series, and were similarly ignorant of the presence or absence of somatic or psychiatric symptoms. This avoided possible bias arising from information relating to the mental or physical state of subjects and their personal reactions to the events or difficulties under review. Two of the qualitative dimensions of life events experience rated in this manner are of relevance to the material to be discussed below.

THREAT

Threat is extensively discussed elsewhere in this volume, and it is sufficient to reiterate that it provides a measure of how distressing or unpleasant the average person would find such an event or difficulty, given a similar biography and current set of circumstances. In keeping with earlier studies of depressive disorder, the present investigation dealt with "severe events" (whose long-term threat was rated as marked or as moderate and focused on the subject alone or jointly with another), "major difficulties" (of similar order of threat and lasting for 2 years or more), and, finally, "provoking agents" (a summary term representing the presence of either severe events or major difficulties alone or in combination).

GOAL FRUSTRATION

A measure of goal frustration was developed specifically for the present study, with the aim of exploring the hypothesis that the frustration of ambition is of causal significance in organic gastrointestinal disease. Like the rating of threat, this was a contextual rating, applied both to events and to chronic ongoing difficulties. The rating was made by members of the wider research team at Bedford College, who, as already noted, had no association with the gastrointestinal study. The requirements of the rating were that there should be evidence that the subject had made consistent and sustained efforts to obtain his or her goal, and that, despite these efforts, the attainment of the goal was irrevocably obstructed by the occurrence of the event or difficulty under consideration. Two examples may serve to illustrate the quality of the experiences that were considered.

1. The subject, a 40-year old commercial artist, sought to return to work once her youngest child started full-time education. She was comfortably well off, and there were no financial or family pressures on her to return to work. She had obtained a diploma in design some 20 years previously, and had worked in a responsible position in a textile company until the birth of her first child. In the course of a year of attempts to find a suitable job, she applied for vacancies in firms in the London area, and also applied toward the end of the year for teaching posts at two local polytechnic institutes. At the last unsuccessful interview, she was told that her diploma was no longer considered adequate qualification for the sort of position she was after, and that with the change in U.K. employment possibilities, there were many younger applicants who were better qualified. Further inquiries confirmed this view, and she realized she would have to settle for a more junior position. This revelation marked the peak of an employment difficulty and was rated as involving a "moderate" degree of goal frustration.

2. The subject, a 30-year old married woman, had a whirlwind romance with an overseas representative of her company. Her lover suggested that she leave her husband and return with him to his own country, later to seek divorce and remarriage. On the planned day of departure, she left a letter for her husband and set off to meet her lover at the airport. He never arrived, and she learned that he had left on an earlier flight without her. This severely threatening life event was rated as involving "marked" goal frustration.

Further illustrative case histories and examples of the rating procedure are reported elsewhere (Craig & Brown, 1984).

Psychiatric Diagnosis

Information on recent psychiatric symptoms was obtained by means of the Present State Examination (PSE; Wing, Cooper, & Sartorius, 1974). In addition to inquiries about current symptoms, a considerable effort was made to date accurately the onset and course of symptoms occurring in the year before interview. Physical onset and psychiatric onset were dated separately, and particular attention was paid to the time relationship between the two. The assessment of psychiatric "caseness" was based on the techniques developed at Bedford College (Brown & Harris, 1978; Finlay-Jones et al., 1980). Briefly, psychiatric disorder was rated by means of consensus team agreement. Those subjects considered by a panel of raters to have experienced a definite psychiatric syndrome of a severity typical of that encountered in outpatient psychiatric clinics were classified as "cases"; those who had symptoms that, while forming recognizable syndromes, were not sufficiently typical, frequent, or intense to be rated as cases were classified as "borderline cases." There were also individuals with psychiatric symptoms that were not sufficient to warrant even a borderline-case rating. The method is known to have good interrater reliability (Brown & Harris, 1978) and to provide a measure of "caseness" broadly comparable to that obtained by other research diagnostic techniques (Dean, Surtees, & Sashidharan, 1983). (For further details, see Finlay-Jones, Chapter 3, this volume.)

In addition, an effort was made to describe the timing of the onset of psychiatric disorder in relation to the onset of somatic symptoms and to the occurrence of stressors. This chapter deals only with those psychiatric disorders that antedated or coincided with physical symptoms. Disorders are referred to here as "onset" when psychiatric symptoms began at some point during the 38 weeks prior to the commencement of somatic symptoms, and as "ongoing" when either (1) the original onset of psychiatric disorder was outside this time period and continued until the onset of physical symptoms, or (2) an event of potential causal impact (i.e., severe event or goal frustration) occurred after the reported onset of psychiatric symptoms. For subjects who reported more than one such event, that closest to physical onset was chosen for the purposes of anchoring psychiatric symptoms.

Finally, all subjects were asked about the experience of emotional disorders earlier in their lives. A positive rating of previous psychiatric disorder was made for those who reported having attended their family doctors for treatment or advice about any of the core symptoms of anxiety and depression recorded by the PSE; for those who reported previous attempts at suicide; and for those who had received psychiatric outpatient or inpatient care.

Physical Diagnosis

Only after all interviews were completed, and after the LEDS and any psychiatric disorder had been rated for both patients and community subjects, were details of the patients' physical diagnoses obtained. These were provided by the patients' consultant physicians on the basis of all available investigative diagnostic tests. Subjects were classed as having an "organic" disorder when there was confirmatory laboratory evidence of disease (e.g., endoscopically visualized active peptic ulceration), and were classed as having a "functional" disorder where no such confirmatory evidence emerged.

Results

A total of 145 patients were approached as meeting the basic inclusion criteria. Of these, 5 refused to participate or failed to complete the interview. A further 5 had other systemic diseases that accounted for their abdominal pain, and these were excluded. Of the remaining 135 patients, 85 were female, and the mean age of the sample was 36 years; 43 were unmarried. Fifty-six patients had a diagnosis of definite organic gastrointestinal disorder, supported by at least one confirmatory diagnostic investigation; the remaining 79 were classified as having a "functional" disorder (Table 9.1). Twenty-eight of the 135 patients had recurrences of an old gastrointestinal disorder (15 organic and 13 functional). Patients with functional disorder were more likely to be female (73% vs. 48%, $p < .01$), single (40% vs. 22%, $p < .02$), and slightly younger (mean ages = 34.6 and 38.3 years, respectively). There were no differences in social class or country of birth. Patients with organic disorder smoked more heavily than either the healthy comparison subjects or the functionally ill, and there were tendencies, which did not reach statistical significance, for the organically ill to have consumed more alcohol and to report more irregularity in their eating habits. Even after the exclusion of patients whose disorder was a recurrence of a previous illness, both groups of patients reported greater frequency of previous gastrointestinal symptoms than their healthy counterparts. The functionally ill also reported significantly more gastrointestinal symptoms in childhood than either the organically ill or the healthy comparison subjects.

TABLE 9.1. Final diagnostic classification of abdominal pain in 140 consecutive clinic attenders

Type of disorder	Final agreed diagnosis	n
Functional disorder	Irritable bowel syndrome	28
	Dyspepsia	14
	Other pain	37
Organic disorder	Esophageal inflammation	6
	Gastritis	6
	Gastric ulcer	5
	Duodenal ulcer	12
	Inflammatory bowel disease	13
	Pancreatitis	2
	Cholecystitis	4
	Other gastrointestinal disorder (appendicitis, diverticulitis, etc.)	8
Systemic organic disease (excluded from study)	Chronic lymphatic leukemia	1
	Hyperparathyroidism	1
	Renal stones	2
	Salpingitis	1

Life Events and Difficulties

When all events were considered, neither group of patients differed from the healthy comparison group. If, however, only those events that were focused on the subject and were at least mildly threatening in the short or long term were considered, differences did emerge. Although there was no significant difference between the two patient groups, both more often reported the experience of at least one such event than did the healthy comparison subjects (see Table 9.2). The commonest examples of such events were enforced changes at work, crises in housing, and breakups of close friendships.

Although the patients experienced a greater number in most categories of life events, those events involving a decrease in the frequency of contact with a close tie as the result of a quarrel were particularly common among subjects with a functional illness: 40% of these patients, compared with only 10% of the organically ill and 17% of the healthy comparison group, reported at least one such event in the 38 weeks prior to onset ($p < .001$). Furthermore, despite the fact that such events were more commonly reported by women in all groups, the excess of this type of event among the functionally ill persisted when the sex of the respondents was taken into account.

SEVERE EVENTS AND PROVOKING AGENTS

Of patients with a functional diagnosis, 57% experienced a severely threatening event focused on the subject prior to onset, compared with 23% of those with an organic diagnosis and 15% of the comparison subjects. This excess of highly unpleasant experiences among the functionally ill remained basically unaltered when the combined category of provoking agents (i.e., severe event or major difficulty) was considered (Table 9.3). Analyses by sex did not affect these findings. The high rate of severe events in the functional group is closely comparable to

TABLE 9.2. Life events in a 38-week period before onset/interview

Subject group	Percentage with any event	Percentage with any event focused on the subject	Percentage with an event with threat focused on the subject
Functional	87 (68/79)	71 (56/79)	63 (50/79) **
Organic	83 (47/56)	61 (34/56)	53 (30/56) *
Healthy comparison	81 (109/135)	62 (84/135)	35 (48/135)

Note. n's for the percentages are in parentheses.

  * $p < .02$ for organic vs. healthy comparison.

 ** $p < .001$ for functional vs. healthy comparison.

TABLE 9.3. Proportion of subjects experiencing at least one event or difficulty of the specified type in a 38-week period before onset/interview

Subject group	Percentage with provoking agent (severe event or major difficulty)	Percentage with goal frustration
Functional	67 (53/79) ***	24 (19/79) *
Organic	23 (14/56)	54 (30/56) **
Healthy comparison	23 (31/135)	9 (12/135)

Note. n's are in parentheses.
  *$p < .01$ for functional vs. healthy comparison.
 **$p < .01$ for organic vs. healthy comparison; $p < .001$ for organic vs. functional.
***$p < .001$ for functional vs. organic and for functional vs. healthy comparison.

that found among those with "not acutely inflamed" appendices studied by Creed (see Chapter 8), as well as to that found in depressed patients in the original Camberwell inquiry (Brown & Harris, 1978); there is good reason to believe that provoking agents played a similarly important etiological role in all three conditions. The majority of the severe events in the functional group involved losses of close ties, and, for the most part, such losses came about as the result of arguments.

GOAL FRUSTRATION

Goal frustration, in complete contrast to threat, was far more common among those with organic disorder (Table 9.3). Both groups of patients experienced more goal frustration that the healthy subjects, but the organic patients had double the rate of the functional patients. Interpretation is complicated by the fact that goal frustration was positively correlated with severity of threat, and the higher rate among the functionally ill might be explained by their higher rate of provoking agents. This indeed was the case: Among patients without a provoking agent, 43% with organic disorders experienced goal frustration, whereas none did so in the functional group. In other words, among those with a functional disorder, there were no events or difficulties characterized by marked goal frustration that were not also provoking agents. For these patients, it is therefore impossible to claim that goal frustration as such played an etiological role. For the organic patients, on the other hand, there is evidence of a powerful causal effect, since this effect was present irrespective of the severity of the provoking agent involved in the goal frustration (Table 9.4). Among this group, the mean time between experiencing the goal frustration and onset of physical symptoms was 4.8 weeks.

In the general-population sample, almost three times as many men as women experienced a goal frustration event or difficulty (16% vs. 5%,

TABLE 9.4. Proportion of subjects experiencing goal frustration by presence of a provoking agent

Subject group	Percentage with no provoking agent	Percentage with provoking agent
Functional	0 (0/26)	36 (19/53)
Organic	43 (18/42)	86 (12/14)
Healthy comparison	3 (3/104)	29 (9/31)

Note. n's are in parentheses.

$p = .05$). One possible explanation is that men are more likely to have greater emotional investment in work or career, and are thereby more often exposed to frustration of their ambitions. For men in the general population, interference with work or career ambitions accounted for 70% of the goal frustration events and difficulties, whereas for women three-quarters concerned failure to achieve a desired outcome in personal relationships. Among *patients*, however, there was no association between sex and goal frustration. Furthermore, work and career frustrations were by far the commonest kind of experience reported by both men and women. The women in this series of patients therefore seemed to be more ambitious, at least in terms of work, than their healthy counterparts. There was no association between goal frustration and age, cultural background, marital status, or social class in this study, and the results remained unaltered if patients suffering a relapse were excluded. Similarly, the effects of goal frustration appeared to be independent of those of tobacco or alcohol consumption.

About a quarter of those subjects with goal frustration had difficulties only, and all except four subjects with goal frustration events had at least one difficulty of at least moderate threat that "matched" the goal frustration event.[1] This observation raises the possibility that it is the presence of chronic stressor, rather than the existence of goal frustration, that is of causal significance. However, difficulties that were neither related to goal frustrations nor linked to a severe event were not associated with onset: 19% (15/79) of the functional patients, 13% (7/56) of the organic patients, and 25% (34/135) of the comparison series had one or more such difficulties on their own.

The fact that virtually all goal frustration was associated with a chronic difficulty (either a difficulty per se or a difficulty that matched

---

1. All four were patients; all had difficulties rated as mildly threatening immediately prior to the event; and in two cases there was anecdotal evidence to suggest that these difficulties had been more severe just outside the study period. All four patients experienced recurrences of an old gastrointestinal disorder.

a goal frustration event) is not surprising. The definition of a goal frustration event specified that a prerequisite was the prior existence of consistent and sustained striving. Such striving could only be detected insofar as it reflected efforts to deal with obstacles in the path to goal attainment, and these obstacles were often sufficient to warrant a difficulty rating. As noted above, for three-quarters of the subjects, such obstacles included at least one crisis rated as a goal frustration event in terms of the LEDS. For the remainder, there were in all instances at least one incident that, while not meeting LEDS criteria for inclusion as a life event, nevertheless represented a crisis within the difficulty and served as a focal point for the goal frustration rating. Two examples may serve to illustrate the principles involved.

1. A 55-year-old married woman and her husband decided to sell their corner shop and retire. They put their shop on the market, and after 2 years eventually attracted a serious buyer. In the intervening time, the husband's health declined, so that the woman was left running the business single-handed. This involved long hours and dealing with aspects of work with which she had not had prior experience. The problems encountered in running the business and her lack of success in finding a buyer were rated as a moderately threatening work difficulty. Goal frustration was rated at the point where the prospective buyer failed to make an offer following a critical building survey report. Although this incident did not meet the formal criteria for rating as an event in the LEDS system, it carried implications for the future: The woman would have to either struggle on as before, or consider dropping the sale price of the business to a point where the couple's retirement plans would have been placed in jeopardy.

2. Some years before the study, another subject's husband had a severe alcohol dependence problem. At the time, he had lost his job and received a number of convictions. Their marriage had come very near to breaking down, but she had thrown herself vigorously into the task of helping with his abstinence and became the motivating force behind his seeking treatment and enrolling in Alcoholics Anonymous (AA). Her policing of his behavior contributed to a moderately severe marital difficulty, with periods of tension and quarreling that persisted throughout the study period. Although her husband still attended AA, he had recently reverted to the fantasy that one day he would be able to return to social drinking.. This change of heart seemed to be linked to an incident concerning the news that an old drinking partner had joined his new work place. This incident provided the focus for the goal frustration rating, but was not considered an event, because there was no evidence that her husband had returned to drink or that he had entirely abandoned the principles of AA.

Such post hoc searching for incidents in those who had experienced a goal frustration difficulty must be viewed with caution. However, the analysis is perhaps sufficient to suggest that the same etiological principle may be involved for events and difficulties involving goal frustration.

The Role of Psychiatric Disorder

As noted in the introduction, the two previous studies using comparable methods to those employed in the present study (Murphy & Brown, 1980; Creed, 1981, and Chapter 8, this volume) reported a higher rate of psychiatric disorder among patients with somatic complaints than could be expected on the basis of rates in the general population, and there was every reason to believe that this would be upheld, even if only for the functionally ill. In order to examine this possibility, subjects with an onset of physical symptoms were categorized by whether the onset of abdominal pain was associated with a psychiatric disturbance of sufficient severity to be classified as a case or a borderline case. Table 9.5 makes clear that both patient groups had a considerable excess of psychiatric symptoms in the 38-week period prior to onset of abdominal pain, compared with a similar period prior to interview in the healthy comparison subjects.

Of particular interest is the suggestion that the functionally ill, compared with those whose gastrointestinal symptoms were based on structural pathology, had relatively more severe psychiatric disorder. Among those patients with psychiatric disorder, the functionally ill exhibited both a higher overall PSE score (mean score of 20.4 for the functionally

TABLE 9.5. Proportion with psychiatric disorder in a 38-week period before onset/interview

Subject group	Percentage classified as psychiatric cases	Percentage classified as psychiatric borderline cases	Percentage classified as psychiatric cases or borderline cases
Functional	34 (28/79) *	20 (16/79) **	56 (44/79) **
Organic	16 (9/56)	32 (18/56) †	48 (27/56) ***
Healthy comparison	8 (11/135)	9 (12/135)	17 (23/135)

Note. n's are in parentheses.

  *p < .01 for functional vs. organic; p < .001 for functional vs. healthy comparison.

 **p < .01 for functional vs. healthy comparison.

***p < .01 for organic vs. healthy comparison.

 †p < .001 for organic vs. healthy comparison.

ill vs. 14.3 for the organic patients, $p < .01$) and a greater likelihood that their disorder would be characterized by specific symptoms of anxiety and depression. In contrast, the emotional disorder in the organic patients typically consisted of reports of nonspecific symptoms of tension, worry, and irritability, together with mild depression of mood. By the end of the study, psychiatric therapeutic intervention had been implemented for six patients, all of whom had functional gastrointestinal disorders.

In order to separate the relative contribution of provoking agents and goal frustration experiences to the two groups of patients and the two orders of severity of psychiatric disorder, a number of linear logistic analyses were performed. For the functionally ill, provoking agents, goal frustration, and psychiatric disorder individually contributed to symptom formation. The contribution of goal frustration was however, largely accounted for by the fact that all were also severely threatening experiences, and the best fit was provided by a model representing a combination of prior provoking agents and psychiatric disorder at case-level severity. For organic patients, provoking agents on their own contributed little to onset. By far the greatest contributions were made by prior goal frustration and psychiatric symptoms at borderline-case-level severity.

This, however, still fell short of a complete explanation. While there was good evidence to suggest that events and psychiatric symptoms together explained more than either alone, it was not possible from the data presented so far to determine to what extent the psychiatric symptoms developed as the consequence of a prior stressor, thereby *intervening* between the stressor in question and onset of somatic symptoms, or to what extent they represented an ongoing psychiatric disorder. The presence of an ongoing psychiatric disorder might itself constitute a risk factor for somatic symptom formation. Table 9.6 presents an analysis addressing this issue. The analysis contrasted the rate of psychiatric disorder among those subjects who reported and did not report a putative etiological agent (i.e., a provoking agent for the functional group or goal frustration for the organic group), according to whether there was a *prior* onset of psychiatric disorder or whether the onset of gastrointestinal disorder occurred in the context of an ongoing emotional disorder.

Both patient groups had a considerable excess of psychiatric symptoms in the 38-week period prior to the onset of their abdominal pain, compared with a similar period prior to interview in the healthy comparison group. Both patient groups also had a high rate of *onset* psychiatric conditions preceding the onset of abdominal pain, and, as would be expected, most of these conditions appeared to be due to the presence of an accompanying etiological agent (see Table 9.6, first column,

TABLE 9.6. Presence of onset and ongoing psychiatric symptoms by presence or absence of a causal agent

Subject group	Percentage with onset of a psychiatric condition			Percentage with an ongoing psychiatric condition			Overall percentage with a psychiatric condition
	Among those with casual agent	Among those with no causal agent	Total	Among those with casual agent	Among those with no causal agent	Total	
Functional	42 (22/53)	12 (3/26)	32 (25/79)	25 (13/53)	23 (6/26)	24 (19/79)	56 (44/79)
Organic	64 (21/33)	9 (2/23)	39 (23/56)	9 (3/33)	4 (1/23)	7 (4/56)	48 (27/56)
Healthy comparison	18 (6/34)	2 (2/101)	6 (8/135)	18 (6/34)	9 (9/101)	11 (15/135)	17 (23/135)

Note. *n*'s are in parentheses.

top two rows).[2] However, though intervening psychiatric symptoms played a similar mediating role for both organic and functional somatic disorders, ongoing psychiatric disorder for the functional group seemed to be important as an etiological agent in its own right. The functional group differed from both the organic group and the healthy comparison group in exhibiting a much higher rate of *ongoing* psychiatric disorder (24%, 7%, and 11%, respectively; see Table 9.6, sixth column).

Finally, the functionally ill patients reported a rate of previous psychiatric episodes (i.e., episodes beyond the time period covered in this investigation, and from which the patients had completely recovered before any subsequent episode current during the time of the study) considerably in excess of the rate for the general population (37% vs. 19%, $p < .01$). However, as Table 9.7 demonstrates, this was entirely due to those subjects who also reported psychiatric symptoms in the time period covered by the interview. The presence of previous psychiatric disorder, in the absence of current symptoms, did not appear to increase the risk of functional illness (Table 9.7). For both the current and previous psychiatric disorder, the predominant diagnosis for both patient groups was that of depression.

Discussion

Life Events/Difficulties and Functional versus Organic Disorder

The association documented here between severely threatening events and difficulties and functional gastrointestinal disorder is perhaps hardly surprising, given the frequency with which stressful experience has been previously linked with functional bowel illness (e.g., Chaudhary & Truelove, 1962). Particularly important are (1) the direct confirmation of Creed's findings concerning abdominal pain that mimics appendicitis, and (2) the fact that both studies are almost exact replications of work with psychiatric patients with depression, where the same quality of severe life experience is of etiological significance (see Chapter 2, this volume).

For organic disease, however, the evidence for stressful experience has been less consistent. Early studies using unstandardized instruments suggested some kind of link with stressful events, but with the introduction of more systematic measures there has been increasing doubt about

2. Even those patients without an etiological agent had a higher rate of onset of psychiatric symptoms occurring before their somatic onset – 10% (5/49) of patients versus 2% (2/101) of the comparison group ($p < .05$). This apparent absence of etiological agents may well have been due to the fact that some were not recorded, either because they did not meet the formal criteria for inclusion or (perhaps less likely) because they were missed by the interview.

TABLE 9.7. Proportion of subjects with a history of previous psychiatric disorder

Subject group	Percentage with previous disorder only	Percentage with previous and current disorder
Functional	10 (8/79)	27 (21/79) *
Organic	13 (7/56)	14 (8/56)
Healthy comparison	12 (16/135)	8 (11/135)

Note. n's are in parentheses.
* $p < .001$ for functional vs. healthy comparison.

the validity of these earlier reports. Piper and his colleagues, utilizing a checklist measure of life events stress, found no relationship among the frequency of life events, their undesirability, and subsequent relapse of gastric or duodenal ulceration (Thomas, Greig, & Piper, 1980; Piper et al., 1981); similarly negative reports exist for ulcerative colitis (Mendeloff, Monk, Siegel, & Lilienfeld, 1970; Feldman, Cantor, Soll, & Bachrach, 1967). These reports together with the study of appendicitis by Creed, suggest that the bulk of evidence is against severe long-term threat's being of significance in organic gastrointestinal disease. If stress does play a role, it is likely to be of a different kind from that involved in affective psychiatric disorder or functional states.

This may be a good part of the reason why many earlier, more impressionistic investigations concluded that there was a link between stress and organic illness. In one of these earlier studies, Davies and Wilson (1937) noted the etiological significance of life events stress among 205 cases of peptic ulcer, and argued that in 84% the symptoms had first begun after an event affecting the subjects' finances, work, or family health. On the basis of personality measures, they argued that ulcer patients were more liable to rebuff and failure because "through their keenness they expose themselves to affronts, failures and disappointments more frequently than their placid neighbours". (p. 1358) There are some similarities between the implications of a personality influence and the finding that the ultimate severity of goal frustration experience appeared to be the result of subjects' own actions in response to earlier warnings of the impending frustration (Craig & Brown, 1984). Indeed, early reports often emphasized attributes of the "ulcer personality," notably apparent ambition and striving nature (Kapp & Rosenbaum, 1947; Kezur, Kapp, & Rosenbaum, 1951). However, this has not been a universal finding of more recent investigations. It may well be that there are many who strive earnestly toward their goals but relatively few who experience the kind of frustration reported in this survey, and that it is only the latter who are at risk of becoming ill.

The Role of Psychiatric Disorder

Up to this point, I have discussed the results only as they pertain to the qualitative experience of particular classes of life events. What of the role of psychiatric disorder? That there is an association between psychiatric and somatic pathology has long been recognized. In a review of psychiatric problems encountered in patients attending general medical outpatient departments, Lipowski (1967) estimated that between 30% and 60% of all inpatients and up to 80% of outpatients suffered from psychiatric illness of sufficient severity to create a problem for the health professions. In the United Kingdom, Culpan and Davies (1960) reviewed 11 studies of psychiatric disorder in medical outpatient settings (all of which used unstandardized clinical assessments of disorder) and showed that about half of newly referred patients to a general hospital were psychiatrically ill.

For gastrointestinal illness, the rates are broadly comparable. Goldberg (1970), using a standardized clinical interview (the Clinical Interview Schedule; Goldberg, Cooper, Eastwood, Kedward, & Shepherd, 1970) found that 34% of individuals attending an outpatient clinic with diseases of the small intestine had concurrent psychiatric disorder. Similarly, using the same measure of psychiatric disorder with 100 consecutive attenders at gastrointestinal clinics, Macdonald and Bouchier (1980) found clear evidence of severe psychiatric pathology in 28 patients and significant psychiatric symptoms in a further 13. These later studies have used more precise operational definition of psychiatric disorder and have produced somewhat lower figures than those reviewed by Lipowski (1967) or Culpan and Davies (1960); nevertheless, it seems reasonable to conclude that at least a third of patients attending general medical and surgical services have diagnosable psychiatric illness, a substantial proportion of which is not detected by the medical staff. Yet such figures as such do little to explain the nature of the association with psychiatric disorder. There are, in fact, at least four possible explanations.

MODEL 1: PHYSICAL PATHOLOGY CAUSING PSYCHIATRIC DISORDER

First, the link can run from pre-existing organic pathology to psychiatric disorder. The existence of a chronic, painful organic condition can bring about depression through patients' reaction to discomfort and their sense of hopelessness and frustration with the limitations the disease places on their ability to cope with everyday life. The present investigation attempted to bypass this most obvious association by focusing on those psychiatric symptoms that were clearly present prior to the onset of pain.

MODEL 2: INDEPENDENT PHYSICAL AND PSYCHIATRIC DISORDERS;
OBSERVED ASSOCIATION DUE TO "CONSULTING" BEHAVIOR

Second, an association between psychiatric disorder and somatic symptoms may arise because depressed individuals may be more likely to *consult* physicians for a perceived somatic disorder, whether or not their symptoms are based on organic change. Such an explanation gains plausibility when one considers the high rate of gastrointestinal symptoms in the general population for which the advice of professionals has not been sought. Thompson and Heaton (1980), for example, found that one-fifth of a sample of apparently healthy subjects had experienced six or more episodes of abdominal pain in the previous year for which they had not consulted their doctors. Furthermore, a persuasive body of evidence has accumulated to suggest that consultation rates among individuals with bodily symptoms are indeed higher in those who are also clinically depressed. Such a possibility must always be borne in mind for hospital-based investigations. It is, however, unlikely to constitute the entire explanation for the results reported. The community-based investigation of Murphy and Brown (1980) was able to demonstrate a similar relationship between psychiatric symptom onset and somatic disorder that clearly antedated any consulting behavior; also, consulting behavior is an unlikely explanation for the association among severe events, depression, and abdominal pain in Creed's study of appendectomy, where the severity of the physical symptoms forced hospital referral in the majority of instances.

MODEL 3: PSYCHIATRIC DISORDER HEIGHTENING SENSITIVITY
TO EXISTING SOMATIC SENSATIONS

Third, psychiatric illness may present with physical symptoms that have no basis in structural pathology. This phenomenon, variously described as "hypochondriasis," "somatoform disorder," or "somatization," has long been recognized clinically, though it is only relatively recently that its close link with affective disorder has come to be fully appreciated. Kenyon (1964), in one of the earlier investigations of hypochondriacal disorders, concluded that the bodily complaints were always secondary manifestations of a primary depressive disorder. Although this sweeping generalization may be debated (such conditions arise at times in the absence of detectable affective disorder), it is clear that somatic complaints, particularly of pain, are a common presenting feature of many depressive disorders.

The simplest explanation for a causal link is that depressed or anxious patients can become abnormally sensitive to existing bodily cues arising from otherwise unnoticed physical processes. Such mechanisms have been invoked to explain the preoccupation with heart rhythm that characterizes some anxious patients, and for this condition, there is some supportive experimental evidence (e.g., Tyrer, Lee, & Alexander, 1980). For functional gastrointestinal disorders, enhanced sensitivity to distension of the bowel with gas has been put forward as one such explanation for their discomfort. Studies of patients with the irritable bowel syndrome (who comprised the largest single diagnostic group among functionally ill patients in the present study) have suggested that as many as two-thirds are excessively sensitive to the sensations produced by distension of the colon; the induction of distension at sigmoidoscopy reproduces symptoms precisely (Swarbrick, Bat, Dawson, Hegarty, & Williams, 1980). These patients also tend to experience pain at an earlier point during progressive distension of the rectosigmoid or sigmoid region of the large bowel (Ritchie, 1973). Distension of the lower esophagus, duodenum, ileum, or colon similarly reproduced unexplained pain in two-thirds of another group of functionally ill patients, in some of whom two widely separate trigger zones were observed (Moriarty & Dawson, 1982). Finally a group of patients with dysphagia, for which no structural pathology could be demonstrated, reported significantly more discomfort as the result of inflating a balloon at different points in the esophagus than either normal subjects or patients with active esophageal inflammation (Edwards, 1982).

Another possibility is that the psychiatric disorder actually causes or increases these bodily symptoms of pain through their impact on intestinal physiology. In other words, some patients may have abnormalities of the motor activity of the bowel, and when stressful experience and/or affective disorder increase bowel motor activity, this abnormality causes the development of pain (Holdstock, Misiewicz, & Waller, 1969). For example, studies of colonic myoelectrical activity have been reported that suggest a characteristic pattern of a persistent excess of slow 3-cycle-per-minute activity in these patients (Snape, Carlson, Matarazzo, & Cohen, 1977; Taylor, Darby, & Hammond, 1978). Furthermore, it is now well established that the normal colon reacts vigorously to a variety of emotional stimuli, and one study at least has shown this reaction to be both more intense in amplitude and of greater duration in patients with established irritable bowel syndrome (Almy, Kern, & Tulin, 1949). Of course, abnormalities of gut motility are not confined to the colon. Many patients with irritable bowel syndrome complain of symptoms that may be attributable to abnormal motility of the esophagus. This may explain a part of the second largest functional group of patients in the present study who presented with dyspeptic symptoms. In a recent investigation (Clouse & Staiano, 1983; Clouse, Staiano, Landau, & Schlascter, 1983), disorders of esophageal motility were observed in half of all patients referred for esophageal manometry. Furthermore, psychiatric disorder as defined by standardized interview was found to be present in 84% of patients with demonstrable abnormalities in smooth muscle contraction, compared with 31% of those whose esophageal motility was judged to be normal.

To sum up, then, both enhanced sensitivity to bodily cues and abnormal gut motility have been proposed to account for the association of psychiatric disorder with functional bowel pain, and of course both can occur together, although there is evidence that abnormal contractility may persist after remission of abdominal pain symptoms (Snape et al., 1977; Taylor et al., 1978).

MODEL 4: PSYCHIATRIC DISORDER PROMOTING RISK OF
PHYSICAL DISEASE

Fourth, psychiatric disorder may provoke or release physical disease. Many of the studies in favor of this hypothesis are based on the association of chronic physical illnesses and equally long-lasting, relatively severe psychiatric disorders. So, for example, there would appear to be an increase in mortality for chronic neuroses (Kerr, Schapira, & Roth, 1969; Sims & Prior, 1978; Tsuang & Woolson, 1978), and there is some evidence of an elevated risk of neoplastic disease among the chronically depressed (Whitlock & Siskind, 1979). Although gastrointestinal illness was observed as a factor in a number of these investigations, none were primarily concerned with these disorders; and given the small number of studies that have specifically sought to demonstrate elevated risk for gastrointestinal disorder among the chronically psychiatrically ill, no firm conclusion can be drawn (West & Hecker, 1952; Hussar, 1968).

But the observation of an association between onset conditions of the two types of illness also has a lengthy tradition. In an exhaustive review of early work, LeShan (1959) commented on the frequency with which it was reported that depressed mood or feelings of helplessness preceded the discovery of neoplastic disease. A well-known theoretical formulation stemming from these early observations is the "giving up-given up" hypothesis of Engel and his coworkers (Engel, 1967; Schmale & Iker, 1966, 1971). Murphy and Brown's (1980) observations in their study of organic disease in a community sample, utilizing measures of event stress and psychiatric disorder identical to those used in the current gastrointestinal investigation, came closest to extending the results of these early investigations. Although, as already noted, there must be some question as to the diagnostic accuracy of this study, the basic finding has been replicated in the current investigation in the organic group. It is particularly noteworthy that both studies demonstrated a relationship between new physical illness and the onset of intervening mild affective symptoms. Chronic psychiatric disorder played no role whatsoever in either the Murphy and Brown study or the present investigation.

How Do Physical Symptoms Arise?

Neither the Murphy and Brown (1980) study nor the present can go much further to explain the mechanism underlying the formation of physical symptoms in these patients, but a number of possibilities can be addressed. First, a mechanism similar to that proposed for the functionally ill in model 3 is possible. That is, an *asymptomatic* organic disease may already have been present before the life crisis and associated emotional symptoms occurred, and such stressors, of sufficient impact to produce a change in mood, may have been sufficient both to affect gut motility in an already diseased organ and to serve to draw attention to bodily cues that were formerly suppressed. For example, early studies of the abdominal pain associated with peptic ulcer disease noted that discomfort was closely correlated with an abnormality in the motility of the ulcerated area of bowel, possibly due to penetration or inflammation of the muscle layer (Ruffin, Baylin, Legerton, & Texter, 1953; Texter, Vantrappen, Lazar, Puletti, & Barboka, 1959).

Another mechanism that can be put forward to explain some upper abdominal pain in both the organically and functionally ill is that of aerophagy (the swallowing of air). This has been shown to be associated with a wide range of gastrointestinal disorders, including peptic ulceration and hiatus hernia (Calloway, Fonagy, & Pounder, 1982); it is also known to occur in anxious patients, where it is productive of both retrosternal and epigastric abdominal pain (Roth & Bockus, 1957). In an investigation of air swallowing during stressful medical procedures, Maddock, Bell, and Tremaine (1949) were able to aspirate three times as much air from the stomachs of anxious patients as they were from those of calm patients.

Although the attraction of providing an explanation that accounts for symptoms in both organic and functional groups cannot be denied, it falls a good way short of a complete formulation. Were this indeed the entire explanation, the organic patients would be expected to display a greater sensitivity to a wide range of stressors, becoming symptomatic in response to lower levels of threat, and to be most sensitive to the immediate impact of stressful events.

Moreover, the association with a particular type of stressful experience (i.e., goal frustration) would not be predicted. The apparently specific nature of the quality of the causal experience suggests the possibility that event stress, in the guise of goal frustration, may be playing a crucial formative role in these disorders.

In terms of likely physiological mediation for goal frustration, it is difficult to envisage any simple pathway. For example, it is now reasonably well established that peptic ulcer disease is brought about through the prolonged exposure of the gastric or intestinal mucosa to gastric acid and pepsin. Such exposure can arise through the excess secretion of acid, decreased emptying of the stomach, or inadequate secretion of mucous and pancreatic bicarbonate. That exposure to acid is the single most important causal factor is supported both by experimental evidence (e.g., Wolf & Wolff, 1943) and by the observation that effective treatments block the effects of acidity, either by neutralization (e.g., Peterson et al., 1977) or by blocking secretion with cimetidine (e.g., Winship, 1978). The precise mechanisms involved probably differ for duodenal and gastric ulceration. In duodenal ulcerations, gastric hypersecretion appears to be an important factor, whereas the pathophysiology of gastric ulceration appears to be related to changes in the quality and quantity of neutralizing mucus (Schrager & Oates, 1978) or bicarbonate (Flemstrom, 1981). Stressful life experiences may contribute to acid hypersecretion, but there is no evidence that they may alter mucus or bicarbonate production. Even the link with acid hypersecretion is debatable. Recent investigations suggest a reduction in secretion (e.g., Badgley, Spiro, & Senay, 1969) or even a biphasic response (Thompson, Richelson, & Malagelada, 1983). Thompson et al. (1983), reviewing earlier reports, suggest that the inconsistencies may have been due to the failure to control for the phase of digestive activity during the experiment, and argue that the true response is biphasic.

Most experimental studies in humans have examined the effects of acute stressors and their immediate impact. Some animal experiments seem to suggest that chronic stressors may be important, and this is borne out by the excess incidence of peptic ulcer disease among individuals in certain occupations characterized by high levels of chronic arousal, such as police officers (Richard & Fell, 1975) and air traffic controllers (Cobb & Rose, 1973). The possible mechanism for this association was explored in a now famous experiment conducted by Brady, Porter, Conrad, and Mason (1958), which examined the effects of a chronic stress (repeated electrical shocks) on the development of gastric ulceration in monkeys. Experimental monkeys were taught to avoid electric shocks by pressing a lever, while others were exposed to shocks over which they had no control. Only the monkeys that had learned to avoid shocks developed gastric lesions.

Unfortunately, later attempts to replicate the findings were unsuccessful. Weiss (1971a, 1971b) in a series of experiments, examined the development of gastric ulcers in rats exposed to electric shock in a similar yoked control design. In contrast to the results of the earlier study, ulcers more often developed in animals that received shocks they were unable to control. Furthermore, if the rats had a warning of impending shock, they were less likely to develop ulcers, as were rats receiving an indication that their efforts had postponed the shock. In contrast, rats that made the greatest number of *excess* responses in an ambiguous situation (where they had no way of predicting whether they would be shocked) were most likely to develop lesions. Weiss (1971b) noted that this latter observation might explain the differences between his and Brady *et al*.'s (1958) observations, as the latter had started to train both members of the yoked pair of monkeys together, selecting as the experimental animal the one that learned the lever-pulling task first. In this way, Brady and his colleagues may have selected the animals emitting the most behavior, and therefore those most similar to Weiss's rats exhibiting excess responses.

Although these experiments, particularly those of Weiss, draw interesting parallels to goal frustration and chronic stressors in human beings, the relevance of animal models of peptic ulcer disease to human disease is questionable. It has proven consistently impossible to produce duodenal ulcers in animals by means of stress. Moreover, the morphological appearance of the lesions produced in these experiments differs from that seen in peptic ulcer disease, being more akin to acute stress ulcers caused by physical trauma (e.g., severe burns) in humans.

Of course, even if goal frustration and chronic stress bring about peptic ulcer disease through alterations in acid secretion, this mechanism cannot explain the association found in the present study with other bowel disease. I have already suggested that one possible link lies with disruption of normal gut motility and heightened sensitivity to bodily cues. This, however, cannot be the entire explanation, as the bulk of current evidence is against any fundamental abnormality of contractility in patients with inflammatory bowel disease (who comprised the largest diagnostic group among the organically ill in the present study). In these conditions, segmental activity (i.e., the frequency and intensity of gut contractions) is not increased, but decreased, and there is no good evidence to suggest increased contractility following stressors (Kern, Almy, Abbot, & Bogdonoff, 1951; Kopel, Kim, & Barbero, 1967). For these disorders, there is strongly suggestive evidence that abnormalities in the immune system contribute to etiology. Kirsner and Shorter (1982), in an extensive review, draw attention to the frequency with which allergic and other immunologically mediated disorders are associated with inflammatory bowel disease, and report studies suggesting that autoimmune processes are implicated in etiology. These authors propose that the disease may begin with some external agent, such as a virus or food additive, that has immunological cross-reactivity with the bowel. This antigen elicits antibody formation, but because its chemical structure is similar to that of some aspect of cells in the gut, the antibodies generated to deal with the invading agent also attack the host. Later, any factor that elicits an immune response, including a stressful event, produces a response that attacks the bowel itself. That stressful experiences can give rise to changes in the immune system is supported by some experimental evidence, though the precise pathways through which this operates remain unknown (e.g., Bartrop, Luckhurst, & Lazarus, 1977; Jemmott & Locke, 1984; Sachar *et al.*, 1973).

In addition, however, an effective theory will need to account for the nature of the emotional arousal that appears to intervene between the occurrence of particular stressors and the onset of physical illness. For the conditions reported here, this emotional response is likely to be different from the profound depression that follows the experience of loss and the anxiety that follows a danger event. Hopelessness, or the "giving up-given up" response to loss, is a more passive response than the striving of those experiencing obstacles to their ambitions. The obvious candidate is anger, and this has been suggested on a number of occasions in the past (e.g., Margolin, 1951). If this is indeed the case, it is unlikely that the standardized psychiatric interview schedules in use today will prove sufficiently sensitive to such subtle patterns in emotional responses.

With improvements in the measurement of life stress and emotional disorders, a number of recent studies, including that reported here, are beginning to provide consistent evidence of the importance of stress and emotional disorder as causal mechanisms for certain gastrointestinal disorders. For the most part, this convergence rests with the group of conditions labeled as "functional" in the present chapter; for these plausible physiological mechanisms can be demonstrated through which changes in the psyche may affect both physiological processes and their subjective perception. For "organic" disorders, where pathological tissue changes can be identified, the evidence of causal relationships remains less widely accepted. Although this skepticism is justified on the grounds of the lack of adequate evidence concerning the physiological processes through which changes in the psyche actually lead to irrevocable changes in organ structure, it is also due in part to a less rational prejudice, itself the persistence of a reaction against the heady days of the 1950s, when virtually all gastrointestinal disorders were regarded as psychophysiological in nature. With improved methods of study and the favorable evidence of recent investigations, however, such prejudice is gradually being overcome, and the pendulum is once more beginning to swing in favor of hypotheses that take account of psychophysiological processes as mediators between psyche and soma.

References

Almy, T. P., Kern, F., Jr., & Tulin, M. (1949). Alterations in colonic function in men under stress. *Gastroenterology, 12,* 425-436.

Badgley, L. E., Spiro, H. M., & Senay, E. C. (1969). Effect of mental arithmetic on gastric secretions. *Psychophysiology, 5,* 633-637.

Bartrop, R. W., Luckhurst, E., & Lazarus, L. (1977). Depressed lymphocyte function after bereavement. *Lancet, i,* 834-836.

Birley, J. L. T., & Connolly, J. (1976). Life events and physical illness. In O. W. Hill (Ed.), *Modern trends in psychosomatic medicine* (pp. 154-165). London: Butterworths.

Brady, J. V., Porter, R. W., Conrad, D. G., & Mason, J. W. (1958). Avoidance behavior and the development of gastro-duodenal ulcers. *Journal of the Experimental Analysis of Behavior, 1,* 69-73.

Brown, G. W. (1974). Meaning, measurement, and stress of life events. In B. S. Dohrenwend & B. P. Dohrenwend (Eds.), *Stressful life events: Their nature and effects* (pp. 217-243). New York: Wiley.

Brown, G. W., & Harris, T. O. (1978). *Social origins of depression: A study of psychiatric disorder in women.* London: Tavistock.

Calloway, S. P., Fonagy, P., & Pounder, R. F. (1982). Frequency in swallowing in duodenal ulceration and hiatus hernia. *British Medical Journal, 285,* 23-24.

Chaudhary, N. A., & Truelove, S. C. (1962). The irritable colon syndrome: A study of the clinical features, predisposing causes and prognosis in 130 cases. *Quarterly Journal of Medicine, 31,* 307-322.

Clouse, R. E., & Staiano, A. (1983). Contraction abnormalities of the oesophageal body in patients referred for manometry: A new approach to manometric classification. *Digestive Disease Science, 28,* 784-791.

Clouse, R. E., Staiano, A., Landau, D. W., & Schlascter, J. L. (1983). Manometric findings during spontaneous chest pain in patients with presumed esophageal "spasms" *Gastroenterology, 85,* 395-402.

Cobb, S., & Rose, R. M. (1973). Hypertension, peptic ulcer and diabetes in air traffic controllers. *Journal of the American Medical Association, 224,* 489-492.

Craig, T. K. J., & Brown, G. W. (1984). Goal frustration and life events in the aetiology of painful gastrointestinal disorder. *Journal of Psychosomatic Research, 28,* 411-421.

Creed, F. (1981). Life events and appendicectomy. *Lancet, i,* 1381-1385.

Culpan, R., & Davies, B. (1960). Psychiatric illness at a medical and a surgical outpatient clinic. *Comprehensive Psychiatry, 1,* 228-235.

Davies, D. T., & Wilson, A. T. (1937). Observations on the life-history of chronic peptic ulcer. *Lancet, i,* 1353-1360.

Dean, C., Surtees, P. G., & Sashidharan, S. P. (1983). Comparison of research diagnostic systems in an Edinburgh community sample. *British Journal of Psychiatry, 142,* 247-256.

Edwards, D. A. W. (1982). "Tender oesophagus" – a new syndrome. *Gut, 23,* 919.

Engel, G. L. (1967). A psychological setting of somatic disease: The giving up-given up complex. *Proceedings of the Royal Society of Medicine, 60,* 553-555.

Feldman, F., Cantor, D., Soll, S., & Bachrach, W. (1967). Psychiatric study of a consecutive series of 34 patients with ulcerative colitis. *British Medical Journal, iii,* 14-17.

Finlay-Jones, R., Brown, G. W., Duncan-Jones, P., Harris, T. O., Murphy, E., & Prudo, R. (1980). Depression and anxiety in the community. *Psychological Medicine, 10,* 445-454.

Flemstrom, G. (1981). Gastric secretion of bicarbonate. In L. R. Johnson (Ed.), *Physiology of the gastrointestinal tract* (pp. 603-616). New York: Raven Press.

Goldberg, D. P., (1970). A psychiatric study of patients with diseases of the small intestine. *Gut, 11,* 459-465.

Goldberg, D. P., Cooper, B., Eastwood, R. R., Kedward, H. B., & Shepherd, M. (1970).

A standardised psychiatric interview for use in community surveys. *British Journal of Preventive and Social Medicine, 24,* 18-23.

Holdstock, D. J., Misiewicz, J. J., & Waller, S. L. (1969). Observations on the mechanism of abdominal pain. *Gut, 10,* 19-31.

Hussar, A. E. (1968). Peptic ulcer in long term institutionalised schizophrenia patients. *Psychosomatic Medicine, 30,* 374-377.

Jemmott, J. B., & Locke, S. E. (1984). Psychosocial factors, immunologic mediation and human susceptibility to infectious diseases: How much do we know? *Psychological Bulletin, 95,* 78-108.

Kapp, F. T., & Rosenbaum, M. (1947). Psychological factors in men with peptic ulcer. *American Journal of Psychiatry, 103,* 700-704.

Kern, F., Almy, T. P., Abbot, F. K., & Bogdonoff, M. (1951). The motility of the distal colon in ulcerative colitis. *Gastroenterology, 19,* 492-508.

Kerr, T. A., Schapira, K., & Roth, M. (1969). The relationship between premature death and affective disorder. *British Journal of Psychiatry, 115,* 1277-1282.

Kenyon, F. E. (1964). Hypochondriasis: A clinical study. *British Journal of Psychiatry, 110,* 478-488.

Kezur, E., Kapp, F. T., & Rosenbaum, M. (1951). Psychological factors in women with peptic ulcer. *American Journal of Psychiatry, 103,* 368-373.

Kimball, C. P. (1970). Conceptual developments in psychsomatic medicine: 1939-1969. *Annals of Internal Medicine, 73,* 307-316.

Kirsner, J. B., & Shorter, R. G. (1982). Recent developments in "non-specific" inflammatory bowel disease. *New England Journal of Medicine, 306,* 775-785, 837-848.

Kopel, F. B., Kim, I. C., & Barbero, G. J. (1967). Comparison of rectosigmoid motility in normal children, children with recurrent abdominal pain, and children with ulcerative colitis. *Pediatrics, 39,* 539-545.

LeShan, L. (1959). Psychological states as factors in the development of malignant disease: A critical review. *Journal of the National Cancer Institute, 22,* 1-18.

Lipowski, Z. J. (1967). Review of consultation and psychosomatic medicine, Part 2. *Psychosomatic Medicine, 29,* 201-224.

Macdonald, A. J., & Bouchier, I. A. D. (1980). Non-organic gastrointestinal illness: A medical and psychiatric study. *British Journal of Psychiatry, 136,* 276-283.

Maddock, W. G., Bell, J. L., & Tremaine, M. J. (1949). Gastro-intestinal gas. *Annals of Surgery, 130,* 512-537.

Margolin, S. G. (1951). The behaviour of the stomach during psychoanalysis: A contribution to a method of verifying psychoanalytic data. *Psychoanalytic Quarterly, 20,* 349-369.

Mendeloff, A. I., Monk, M., Siegel, C. I., & Lilienfeld, A. (1970). Illness experience and life stresses in patients with irritable colon and with ulcerative colitis. *New England Journal of Medicine, 282,* 14-17.

Moriarty, K. J., & Dawson, A. M. (1982). Functional abdominal pain: Further evidence that the whole gut is affected. *British Medical Journal, 284,* 1670-1672.

Murphy, E., & Brown, G. W. (1980). Life events, psychiatric disturbance and physical illness. *British Journal of Psychiatry, 136,* 326-338.

Peterson, W. L., Sturdevant, R. A. L., Frankl, H. D., Richardson, C. T., Isenberg, J. I., Elashoff, J. D., Sones, J. Q., Gross, R. A., McCallum, R. W., & Fordtran, J. S. (1977). Healing of duodenal ulcer with an antacid regimen. *New England Journal of Medicine, 297,* 341-345.

Piper, D. W., McIntosh, J. H., Ariotti, D. E., Calogiuri, J. V., Brown, R. W., & Shy, C. M. (1981). Life events and chronic duodenal ulcer: A case controlled study. *Gut, 22,* 1011-1017.

Richard, W. C., & Fell, R. D. (1975). Health factors in police job stress. In W. H. Kroes & J. L. Hurrell (Eds.), *Job stress and the police officer: Identifying stress reduction techniques* (pp. 73-84). Washington, DC: U.S. Government Printing Office.

Ritchie, J. (1973). Pain from distension of the pelvic colon by inflating a balloon in the irritable colon syndrome. *Gut, 14,* 125-132.

Roth, J. L. A., & Bockus, H. L. (1957). Aerophagia: Its etiology, syndromes and management. *Medical Clinics of North America, 41,* 1673-1696.

Ruffin, J. M., Baylin, G. J., Legerton, C. W., & Texter, E. C., Jr. (1953). Mechanism of pain in peptic ulcer. *Gastroenterology, 23,* 252-264.

Sachar, D. B., Taub, R. N., Brown, S. M., Present, D. H., Korelitz, B. I., & Janowitz, H. D. (1973). Impaired lymphocyte responsiveness in inflammatory bowel disease. *Gastroenterology, 64,* 203-209.

Schmale, A., & Iker, H. (1966). The psychological setting of uterine cervical cancer. *Annals of the New York Academy of Sciences, 125,* 807-813.

Schmale, A., & Iker, H. (1971). Hopelessness as a predictor of cervical cancer. *Social Science and Medicine, 5,* 95-100.

Schrager, J., & Oates, M. D. G. (1978). Human gastrointestinal mucus in disease states. *British Medical Bulletin, 34,* 79-82.

Sims, A., & Prior, R. (1978). The pattern of mortality in severe neurosis. *British Journal of Psychiatry, 133,* 299-305.

Snape, W. J., Carlson, G. M., Matazazzo, S. A., & Cohen, S. (1977). Evidence that abnormal myoelectrical activity produces colonic motor dysfunction in the irritable bowel syndrome. *Gastroenterology, 72,* 383-387.

Stiller, B. (1884). *Die Nervösen Magenkrankheiten.* Stuttgart.

Swarbrick, E. T., Bat, L., Dawson, A. M., Hegerty, J. E., & Williams, C. B. (1980). Site of pain from the irritable bowel. *Lancet, ii,* 443-446.

Taylor, I., Darby, C., & Hammond, P. (1978). Comparison of rectosigmoid myoelectrical activity in the irritable colon syndrome during relapses and remissions. *Gut, 19,* 923-929.

Texter, E. C., Jr., Vantrappen, G. R., Lazar, H. P., Puletti, E. J., & Barborka, C. J. (1959). Further observations on the mechanism of ulcer pain. *Annals of Internal Medicine, 51,* 1275-1294.

Thomas, J., Greig, M., & Piper, D. W. (1980). Chronic gastric ulcer and life events. *Gastroenterology, 78,* 905-911.

Thompson, D. G., Richelson, E., & Malagelada, J. R. (1983). Perturbation of upper gastrointestinal function by cold stress. *Gut, 24,* 277-283.

Thomson, W. G., & Heaton, K. W. (1980). Functional bowel disorders in apparently healthy people. *Gastroenterology, 79,* 283-288.

Tsuang, M. T., & Woolson, R. F. (1978). Excess mortality in schizophrenia and affective disorders. *Archives of General Psychiatry, 35,* 1181-1185.

Tyrer, P., Lee, I., & Alexander, J. (1980). Awareness of cardiac function in anxious, phobic and hypochondriacal patients. *Psychological Medicine, 10,* 171-174.

West, B. M., & Hecker, A. O. (1952). Peptic ulcer: Incidence and diagnosis in psychotic patients. *American Journal of Psychiatry, 109,* 35-37.

Weiss, J. M. (1971a). Effects of coping behavior in different warning signal conditions on stress pathology in rats. *Journal of Comparative and Physiological Psychology, 77,* 1-13.

Weiss, J. M. (1971b). Effects of coping behavior with and without a feedback signal on stress pathology in rats. *Journal of Comparative and Physiological Psychology, 77,* 22-30.

Whitlock, F. A., & Siskind, N. (1979). Depression and cancer. *Psychological Medicine, 9,* 747-752.

Wing, J. K., Cooper, J. E., & Sartorius, N. (1974) *The measurement and classification of psychiatric symptoms.* London: Cambridge University Press.

Winship, D. H. (1978). Cimetidine in the treatment of duodenal ulcer: Review and commentary. *Gastroenterology, 74,* 402-406.

Wolf, S., & Wolff, H. G. (1943). *Human gastric function: An experimental study of a man and his stomach.* New York: Oxford University Press.

10

Disorders of Menstruation

TIRRIL O. HARRIS

Introduction

The common etymological root of the words "hysteria" and "hysterectomy" suggests that the notion of a link between gynecological dysfunction and an intense reaction to stress long predates life events research as we know it today. During this century, gynecological textbooks have given increasing space to psychological factors in the etiology of menstrual disorders. However, in more recent years, certain legal judgments have tilted the focus in the other direction, seeking somatic gynecological causes such as the premenstrual syndrome for disturbed psychological behavior or the hormonal changes of the menopause as an explanation for the melancholia of the middle years. Clearly, debates about the direction of causality – from somatic to psychic or vice versa – can only be vacuous in the absence of trustworthy information about the timing of the factors concerned. Both premenstrual syndrome and the menopause present notorious difficulties in this respect because of the problems of dating clinical changes; as a result, recent research into them is difficult to interpret. The two conditions discussed in this chapter were selected to minimize these problems. Secondary amenorrhea, though sometimes preceded by periods of oligomenorrhea, is usually a marked enough change to be simple to date; and although some menorrhagia sufferers have experienced the problem ever since menarche, most are quite clear that their menstrual pattern underwent noticeable change over a period of only a few months, if not during just one cycle.

Previous research into psychogenic factors possibly affecting these two conditions has fallen into five broad groupings:

Tirril O. Harris. Department of Social Policy and Social Science, Royal Holloway and Bedford New College, University of London, 11 Bedford Square, London WC1B 3RA, England.

1. *Extreme dangers and shocks disturbing menstrual regularity.* Sydenham (1946) reported that of her coinmates in Stanley Camp, Hong Kong, during World War II, only 35% retained regular menstruation, 54% suffered amenorrhea for longer than 3 months, and 5% were irregular with menorrhagia. Bass (1947) reported an incidence of secondary amenorrhea among 800 women internees in the concentration camp of Theresienstadt, ranging from 25% among those who knew they were to stay for a long period to 54% among those who knew they were en route for an unknown destination (i.e., who were in a situation of apparently even greater threat and uncertainty). For the most part, secondary amenorrhea appeared within the first 2 months of incarceration, when anxiety was likely to have been particularly severe. This promptness of onset differentiated such "psychogenic amenorrhea" from that due to malnutrition, which it was claimed eventually caused amenorrhea in 90% of the detained women (Bass, 1947; Stroink, 1947). One study concerning menorrhagia suggests that many with the condition have recently experienced losses of some kind (Blaikley, 1949).

2. *Other life changes that are not necessarily markedly threatening.* These studies have dealt with life changes that are a good deal less unpleasant. They have been facilitated by the presence of certain captive populations – for example, the annual intake into residential colleges, kibbutzim, or the armed forces (Sher, 1946). Drillien (1946) found that at least a quarter of women had missed one or two periods on first entering the army, and Drew and Stifel (1968) found that 10-16% of young women had amenorrhea lasting 2 months or more during their first year of life in a religious order. The absence of comparison groups in these studies reduces confidence in any interpretation, although one study has rated the expected rate of secondary amenorrhea in the general population as between 3% and 7% (Petterson, Fries, & Nillius, 1973). This dearth of community sample information is particularly crucial in interpreting the next group of studies, concerned with biographical background experience.

3. *Background social variables.* Drillien (1946) found that the rate of secondary amenorrhea for army officers was only 1/12th that in other ranks on first entering the army, and suggested that this might be the result of the officers' more frequent earlier experience of separations from home (e.g., in boarding schools). Another study, however, has suggested that those with intellectual occupations are particularly at risk (Fries, Nillius, & Petterson, 1974). Again, less has been reported about menorrhagia, but a history of marital separation or divorce may be relevant (Ballinger, 1977; Greenberg, 1983).

4. *Psychiatric symptomatology.* The role of psychiatric symptomatology is sometimes considered by focusing upon those with outright psychiatric disorder and charting their menstrual pathology (Gregory,

1957; Russell, 1972). More often, those with menstrual disorder are screened for accompanying psychiatric pathology; many studies have reported high levels of psychiatric disorder in women with menorrhagia (Sainsbury, 1960; Greenberg, 1983; Ballinger, 1977; Martin, Roberts, & Clayton, 1980; Gath, Cooper, & Day, 1982; Salter, 1985). Information concerning secondary amenorrhea is less often reported, but Drew and Stifel (1968) suggested that it is probably unrelated to affective symptoms.

5. *Underlying attitudes or personality dispositions.* Finally, there has been some interest in the possible role of attitudes and personality dysfunction. The range of these has varied from rejection of a feminine gender identity, cited as capable of producing secondary amenorrhea (Christie Brown, 1973) or sometimes any gynecological disorder (Rheingold, 1964), to a "strong striving to demonstrate independence by active involvement, a defence against openly feeling anxiety," which is considered likely to predispose women to secondary amenorrhea (Shanan, Brzezinski, Sulman, & Sharon, 1965, p. 464). Extraversion has been identified as a factor predisposing women to spontaneous recovery from secondary amenorrhea (Lodewegens, Bos-Van Rijn, Groenman, & Lappohn, 1977).

The study of menstrual disorders described in this chapter fits squarely into the pattern of inquiry already outlined in earlier chapters: examining onset of somatic disorder, using the Life Events and Difficulties Schedule (LEDS); exploring the role of psychiatric symptomatology as an intervening variable, using the shortened Present State Examination (PSE); contrasting those patients whose somatic symptoms were accompanied by clearly discernible organic pathology with those whose symptoms, lacking such pathology, earned the label "functional disorder"; and exploring the possibility that both life events and psychiatric symptoms play different roles in these two groups of menstrual disorders. The choice of menstrual disorders for study was largely inspired by the success of the LEDS in a general-population sample that was exclusively female – that is, the first Camberwell survey of 1969-1971 (Brown, Ní Bhrolcháin, & Harris, 1975). The choice of a medical condition restricted to women already attending a Camberwell hospital enabled the study to be set up in parallel with the second Camberwell population survey in 1974-1975 (Brown & Harris, 1978).

Subjects and Method

Subject Selection

Subjects consisted of consecutive attenders aged 18-42 at the Kings College/Dulwich hospital group with (1) secondary amenorrhea (not due to pregnancy or during oral contraceptive use), or (2) abnormally heavy uterine bleeding (hereafter referred to as "menorrhagia"). The upper age limit of 42 was selected to try to minimize confounding by biological factors associated with the menopause. Three general-practice surgeries in the same area also agreed to provide appropriate patients as a means of comparing groups from different treatment sources. In the event, few such patients were forthcoming, so the design was simplified and treatment source was ignored. The random community sample provided 224 women in the same age range who had neither disorder; however, because subjects with certain cultural backgrounds (Muslim, Hindu, and Caribbean) had been excluded from this sample, it was also necessary to impose this restriction on the two menstrual disorder groups.

Although it was intended to compare patients with disorders of "organic" origin with others whose disorders could be said to be "functional," information concerning pathological reports was not used to make this categorization until after all psychosocial variables had been collected and rated, and these did not therefore enter into the selection criteria. However, certain decisions were made about the selection of the clinical groups. First, 28 women were excluded because their history of abnormal bleeding before coming to a hospital was more than 5 years in duration. At the time, the study on long-term recall by Neilson and Brown (1984; see also Neilson, Brown, & Marmot, Chapter 12, this volume) had not established that the rate of falloff of recall for severe events was unlikely to threaten research investigating hypotheses concerning the association of such events with onsets so far back in time from interview date. Second, as interviewing proceeded, it became clear that there was a striking age difference between the secondary amenorrhea and the menorrhagia groups: Only 11 of the first 75 menorrhagia patients were under 30 years of age, compared with the majority of those with secondary amenorrhea. Since rates of nonsevere life events are known to vary with age (Brown & Prudo, 1981, p. 591), there was a possibility that a rigid adherence to selecting a consecutive series would lead to difficulty in sorting out which effects were due to age and which were related to diagnosis. A deliberate policy of selecting only younger women was therefore then followed for the last 25 members of the menorrhagia sample. Third, some of the secondary amenorrhea patients had been experiencing irregular intermenstrual intervals of more than 8 weeks. To fix on the most recent gap in menstruation in this group, as if it were a new onset, seemed artificial, and these patients were therefore excluded. The rates of refusal to participate were almost identical in the three groups: 16% for the secondary amenorrhea group, 17% for the menorrhagia group, and 17% for the community comparison group. The final numbers were 65 with secondary amenorrhea, 98 with menorrhagia, and 224 in the comparison group.

Interview

The interview was designed to cover a period of 12 months before onset of disorder, or interview in the comparison group. In the comparison series, it involved only three broad areas: simple demographic items, including a measure of intimate confiding; the PSE (Wing, Cooper, & Sartorius, 1974; see also Finlay-Jones, Chapter 3, this volume); and the LEDS (see Brown, Chapter 1, this volume). Information was also collected about episodes of psychiatric symptomatology prior to the year of onset, and about contacts with psychiatric services and use of psychotropic drugs, although measurement was inevitably less accurate over such a time span than in the main 1-year preonset/preinterview period. Questioning about these episodes was less detailed than in subsequent reports on lifetime experience of affective disorders from this research team (see Harris, Brown, & Bifulco, 1986). However, since the same measures were used in all three groups, it was possible to make comparisons, and any differences that emerged could serve as an approximation of a true estimate of previous disorder. The rating involved one main question ("Have you at any time in your life prior to these 12 months we have been discussing been very depressed at all or seen a doctor for your nerves?"). When there was any hint of prior experience, probes about severity and treatment made it possible to exclude any episode that was clearly very mild. However, the measure was clearly a crude one and of a different order from the strictly defined "caseness" measure applied to the current year. It was likely to include more borderline cases who had seen a general practitioner and fewer true cases who had had no contact with any doctor.

In the two menstrual disorder groups, additional areas were covered. One section dealt with recent gynecological symptoms; this permitted the dating of onset of secondary amenorrhea or menorrhagia as precisely as possible. In dating the latter, particular attention was paid to flooding and clotting, with reports of pain, sweating, dizziness, exhaustion, and so on being given less weight. The probing style of interview resembled that used with the LEDS itself, with frequent cross-checking questions aimed at reducing the reporting biases (both of exaggeration and of underestimation) that are reputed to attend studies of menstrual blood loss (see Harris, 1988, for further details). Another section dealt with previous gynecological health, since this might be considered to increase current vulnerability; it covered areas such as age at menarche, premenstrual tension, dysmenorrhea, contraceptive pill usage, and pregnancies (complications and date of resumption of menstruation). Particular attention was paid here to effects upon libido, appetite, and weight. At the end of the interview, the gynecology patients filled in the Eysenck Personality Inventory (EPI; Eysenck &

Eysenck, 1964), but only a small proportion of the community sample was approached again for this purpose.

Ratings of the tape-recorded interviews followed the criteria already extensively discussed in this volume. The PSE was used as a basis upon which to distinguish cases and borderline cases of depression, anxiety, obsessional neuroses, and other diagnoses according to their "chronicity" before onset of menstrual disorder or interview, along the lines of the Bedford College criteria (Finlay-Jones et al., 1980; Dean, Surtees, & Sashidharan, 1983). The LEDS was used to identify "severe events" (those with marked or moderate long-term contextual threat focused on the subject) and "major difficulties" (rated on the top 3 points of the 6-point contextual severity scale, with a duration of at least 2 years and involving more than physical health problems alone). These were combined in the joint category of "provoking agents," used in the depression research. In addition, qualitative ratings were made of loss, danger, goal frustration, and challenge. Since the last is a new measure, it needs discussion here.

The LEDS Dimension of Challenge

The LEDS dimension of "challenge" has not so far been discussed in this volume. A 4-point scale, dichotomized with points 1 and 2 as definite challenges contrasted with all other events, it involves the notion that a subject, by accepting new responsibility and meeting certain social expectations, can perform in a praiseworthy fashion. Obvious examples are taking on a new job or accepting responsibility for the care of a sick relative. Such events do not necessarily involve any threat as defined by the LEDS, let alone severe threat. Although in some circumstances the failure to meet a challenge successfully may lead to tragic consequences or meet with unpleasant criticism, this is by no means invariable. Like danger, the dimension of challenge looks forward to the future. But what is anticipated is a matter of degree. With a rating of marked challenge there is the assumption that if the subject copes well a severe event as defined by the LEDS will not arise, whereas with a rating of severe danger the occurrence of some future severe event is considered highly likely. Therefore, with challenge, the emphasis is on positive implications; however, a subsequent severe event cannot be ruled out altogether. Likewise, with danger, a severe event is not inevitable, and effective coping on the part of the subject may at times reduce chances of one occurring. However, with danger, unlike challenge, the emphasis is on the negative.

A further difference (though still one of degree) is that, unlike a definite challenge, some dangers involve no real assumption of responsibility by the subject – for example, a relative in the intensive care unit of a hospital is cared for by others. Of course, danger may overlap with challenge when there is a high chance of failing to meet the challenge and when such failure will involve a severe loss experience. Usually, though, any failure to meet a challenge will not be followed by a severe loss, but in a more neutral fashion will merely prevent the attainment of something positive. Thus starting a first job or moving away from the parental home to a place of one's own (to anticipate, both are frequent precursors of secondary amenorrhea) are not typically followed by a severe crisis if not carried out successfully. In the first instance, the person is not usually fired; rather, his or her chances of promotion are reduced. In the second, the person does not usually set the building on fire or develop symptoms of malnutrition, but the place may well be hard to manage, drawing disapproving comments from those who visit.

These two examples are considered definite challenges as defined by the LEDS (in the sense of receiving ratings on the top 2 points of the 4-point scale), as is birth of a first child. Minor challenges (i.e., those rated 3 or 4 on the 4-point scale) include a new job of a kind held before and the birth of a second or subsequent child in comfortable circumstances. Furthermore, the responsibilities arising from an event must last more than 1 week for any degree of challenge to be rated at all. Therefore, the degree of challenge depends not only upon the amount of responsibility the subject assumes as a result of the event, but also upon previous experience in fulfilling such responsibilities. Thus an 18-year-old who must single-handedly nurse her mother bedridden with arthritis is judged to face a greater challenge than a 40-year-old woman in similar circumstances who helped this same mother look after her own sick mother some 20 years earlier. The former is considered a marked challenge, the latter a minor challenge.

From the discussion above, it will be apparent that the LEDS dimension of challenge corresponds closely to Lazarus and Folkman's (1984) use of the term, although their concern with appraisal means that they are describing the self-report rather than the contextual version. They too specify that threat and challenge are not mutually exclusive:

> Challenge appraisals are more likely to occur when the person has a sense of control over the troubled person-environment relationship. Challenge will not occur, however, if what must be done does not call for substantial efforts. The joy of challenge is that one pits oneself against the odds. (Lazarus & Folkman, 1984, p. 36)

Physical Diagnosis: "Functional" versus "Organic" Disorder

Once ratings had been made, information was collected from the hospitals and used to classify patients as suffering from "organic" disorder where there was confirmatory laboratory evidence to account for the menstrual change (e.g., fibroids or polyps in the menorrhagia group, or hyperprolactinemia in the secondary amenorrhea group), or from "functional" disorder in the absence of any such confirmatory evidence.

Results

The Experience of Life Events and Long-Term Difficulties

As in previous studies using the LEDS, the first step was to explore the differing experiences of life events and difficulties in the three groups of women over differing time periods (i.e., before onset, or before interview in the comparison group). Whereas earlier work with various diagnostic groupings had contrasted experiences over a 3-week period with those over a longer time span, the nature of this study suggested a contrast between a 4-week and a longer period, to accord with the standard intermenstrual interval of 4 weeks. There were no differences in the proportion of each group with experience of at least one event of any type when a 1-year period was examined; however, when a 1-month period was taken, the proportion experiencing an event of any type was higher among those with secondary amenorrhea – 66% (43/65), compared with 29% (28/98) in the menorrhagia group and 32% (72/224) in the comparison series ($df = 2$, $p < .01$). This difference did not emerge for severe events in the 1-month period, and nonsevere events were what accounted for the excess experience among the secondary amenorrhea group.

Furthermore, by contrast, when a 12-month rather than a 1-month period was taken, the menorrhagia group experienced more severe events: 56% (55/98) experienced at least one, compared with 28% (18/65) in the secondary amenorrhea group and 29% (66/224) in the comparison series. Further examination revealed that almost all severe events in the menorrhagia group involved losses, and half of them involved husbands or boyfriends; in the community group, not only were there fewer individuals with severe events to start with, but the number of losses and marital events was proportionally lower. Differences in proportions with at least one severe danger event presented a similar pattern, but this was largely due to their association with severe loss experiences in the same individuals. Table 10.1 summarizes these results.

TABLE 10.1. Percentage with a stressful experience of the specified type in the 1 month and 1 year before onset/interview

	1 month			1 year				
Subject group	Severe event	Non-severe event	Any event	Severe event	Severe loss event	Severe danger event	Any provoking agent	Marital/ boyfriend provoking agent
Menorrhagia patients	10 (10/98)	18 (18/98)	29 (28/98)	56 (55/98)	50 (49/98)***	27 (26/98)*	60 (59/98)***	28 (27/98)†
Secondary amenorrhea patients	14 (9/65)	58 (38/65)	66 (43/65)††	28 (18/65)	22 (14/65)	11 (7/65)	31 (20/65)	18 (12/65)**
Comparison group	8 (19/224)	25 (55/224)	32 (72/224)	29 (66/224)	17 (39/224)	15 (34/224)	40 (90/224)	8 (17/224)

Note. n's for the percentages are in parentheses.

    * $p < .02$ for menorrhagia vs. secondary amenorrhea and comparison.

  ** $p < .02$ for secondary vs. comparison.

 *** $p < .01$ for menorrhagia vs. secondary amenorrhea and comparison.

    † $p < .01$ for menorrhagia vs. comparison.

  †† $p < .01$ for secondary amenorrhea vs. menorrhagia and comparison.

Table 10.1 also indirectly provides information about the experience of difficulties in the column headed "Any provoking agent" (i.e., any severe event or major difficulty). Relatively more of the comparison series had a major difficulty without a severe event (this can be seen by comparing the "Severe event" and "Any provoking agent" columns), whereas among the two diagnostic groups, most with a major difficulty also had a severe event. Overall, 32% (31/98) of the menorrhagia group and 9% (6/65) of the secondary amenorrhea group had a major difficulty, compared with 25% (56/224) of the community series (secondary amenorrhea vs. comparison group, $p < .01$).

CONTROLLING FOR DEMOGRAPHIC FACTORS KNOWN TO
INFLUENCE RATES OF LIFE EVENTS

A crucial consideration at this point was to deal with the possible effect of age differences in the three groups. There was, as already noted, some tendency for menorrhagia patients to be older than secondary amenorrhea patients, and even after the adjustment to the sample selection procedure this difference was still large: Only 50% of the menorrhagia and 44% of the comparison group were aged 30 or less, compared with 97% of those with secondary amenorrhea. The latter group, as a corollary, also contained more unmarried women, more in employment, and fewer with children, while the menorrhagia and comparison groups did not differ significantly on any of these items.

Another difference was in social class position. A simple dichotomy was used, in which scale points 1-22 (middle class) were contrasted with points 23-36 (working class) on the Goldthorpe and Hope (1974) grading of occupations; according to this dichotomy, only 18% (12/65) of those with secondary amenorrhea were working-class, compared with 42% (41/98) of the menorrhagia group and 50% (112/224) of the comparison group. (As in earlier studies, the women were classified according to the occupations of their husbands, or, if unmarried and living at home, of their fathers; only if a woman was not living with a male head of household and had been separated from her husband for at least 5 years was her own occupation used as the criterion.) Since it is known that the experience of life events tends to vary particularly with social class and life stage, it was necessary to deal with the possible confounding role of these demographic variables.

There was no suggestion that social class position was in any way confounding the picture of severe events preceding menorrhagia as presented in Table 10.1, nor could the different rates in the menorrhagia and comparison groups be attributed to different distributions between life stages. On the other hand, the relative absence of severe events and major difficulties among secondary amenorrhea patients was almost certainly a function of their higher class position and early life stage.

This, however, did not raise a serious problem of confounding, since it was not proposed that these Camberwell provoking agents were of etiological importance in the onset of secondary amenorrhea. Table 10.1 suggests that if there was any role for life events in secondary amenorrhea, the pathway did not involve severity of contextual threat.

CHALLENGE EVENTS AND SECONDARY AMENORRHEA

If Table 10.1 suggests that menorrhagia may have been responsive to the same kind of provoking agents (particularly losses) known to relate to the development of depression (and to patients with "not acutely inflamed" appendices undergoing appendectomy or with functional gastrointestinal disorder), it also hints that a different process may have been at work with secondary amenorrhea. Nonsevere events seemed to be clustering in the month immediately preceding the date when expected menstruation first failed to occur. A high proportion of those with a nonsevere event (58%, or 25/43) had in fact experienced a definite challenge (e.g., final university examinations, or going abroad to take up a position as an *au pair*). Another 4 women had had an event involving a definite challenge in the 5th to 7th week before onset. One interesting type of challenge, which occurred in as many as 7 of those with secondary amenorrhea, was a reunion with a previous boyfriend (or husband) with whom the relationship had earlier been broken off (sometimes as a severe event in the 12-month period). Here it seems possible that a woman's feelings of responsibility for insuring that the relationship should go as well as possible this time must have been coupled with a need to protect herself against a repetition of any hurt experienced at the time of the earlier breakup. Table 10.2 shows that those with secondary amenorrhea experienced more definite challenges than the comparison group in the 1-month period before onset/interview, and that when the other 48 weeks were taken into account they did not add anything. (Those aged 30 or more were excluded from the comparison group, since it seemed that the experience of challenges declined with age, and the inclusion of older women might therefore prejudice results in favor of the hypothesis by lowering the proportion with a definite challenge in the comparison series.)

TABLE 10.2. Percentage with a major challenge event in the 1 month and 1 year before onset/interview

Subject group	1 month	1 year
Secondary amenorrhea	38 (25/65) *	58 (38/65) *
Comparison group (aged 18–29)[a]	4 (4/113)	32 (36/113)

Note. n's are in parentheses.
[a] Includes depressed cases.
* $p < .001$.

CONTEXTUAL VERSUS SELF-REPORT RATINGS

Consideration of the impact of a life event upon a person's health ideally should involve not only an assessment of its contextual features, but also a more direct assessment of how the person actually appraised it. However, in studies of affective disorder, the use of the LEDS self-report scales is fraught with dangers of bias and circularity: If it is discovered that depressed psychiatric patients report that they have felt depressed in response to their experiences more often than a nondepressed comparison group, it is not clear what can be concluded. These feelings may be "intervening" factors, but they may equally well merely be part of the episode of depressive illness itself. When the dependent variable is a physical illness, however, the reported subjective responses may well make an additional contribution to understanding the origins of the disorder.

It is interesting, therefore, that when this was done the two menstrual disorder groups both differed from the comparison group, but in different ways. Among the menorrhagia patients, 13% of those without a provoking agent (5/39) reported experiencing what had been rated a minor event as severe, while none of the secondary amenorrhea group and only 4% (5/134) of the comparison group did so. On the other hand, those given lower ratings on reported as compared with contextual long-term threat were distributed in the opposite way. Among those with severe events in the year, only 2% (1/55) of menorrhagia patients reported less than moderate feelings of distress, while figures for the comparison and secondary amenorrhea groups were 12% (8/66) and 33% (6/18), respectively ($p < .05$).

There were, in addition, several more secondary amenorrhea patients who, when subjected to probing questions, did not give answers about their subjective distress that justified a lowering of the contextual rating, but whose tendency was to present themselves as well defended against the threat. For example, one young woman with secondary amenorrhea, who had broken off with a boyfriend earlier in the year, said, "Yes, well, I suppose it was pretty awful really, but it made me harder about things. I thought, 'Right, you're not going to hurt me again,' when we got back together." (This was one of those reunions in the 4 weeks before onset.) Another girl of 18 had had to assume chief responsibility when her mother underwent a nervous breakdown, which was associated with insulting her daughter frequently in public. The girl made it quite clear that it was extremely stressful, but at the same time was concerned to emphasize how she had succeeded in protecting herself emotionally: "It changed me a lot, because I resolved there and then never to let myself be hurt by anyone again." This sort of remark was almost unheard of in the menorrhagia group, who described their feelings of pain very fully.

The Experience of Psychiatric Disorder

There were interesting variations among the three groups in their patterns of psychiatric symptomatology: Depression was most common before menorrhagia, tension states were most common before secondary amenorrhea, and anxiety did not appear to differentiate the three groups. The menorrhagia patients had a higher proportion of cases of depression, and the secondary amenorrhea patients a lower rate, than the community series – 27% (26/98), 6% (4/65), and 16% (36/224), respectively (Table 10.3). These figures were probably consequences of the differences already noted in the distribution among the three groups of provoking agents, working-class status, and children living at home.

On the other hand, the rate of cases or borderline cases of nondepressive conditions was not notably higher in the menorrhagia group than in the community comparison group (see Table 10.3, third column). Among those with secondary amenorrhea, however minor clusterings of symptoms involving tension, restlessness, and fatigue *without depression or anxiety* were much more common than in the community series (25% vs. 1%, $p < .05$), although syndromes at a severity comparable to those seen at outpatient psychiatric clinics (i.e., cases) were very rare. In the general population, such tension symptoms tended to be more isolated, whereas among those with secondary amenorrhea there tended to be a clustering of these types of minor symptoms that reached a borderline-case level of severity. Among those depressed before onset of menorrhagia, these tension symptoms were found but

TABLE 10.3. Percentage of each sample with psychiatric disorder of the specified type in the year before onset/interview

Subject group	Case of depression (with or without anxiety/other)	Borderline case of depression (with or without anxiety/other)	Case or borderline case other than depression	Any type of case or borderline case
Menorrhagia patients	27 (26/98) *	20 (20/98) †	12 (12/98)	60 (58/98) ††
Secondary amenorrhea patients	6 (4/65)	6 (4/65)	38 (25/65) †††	51 (33/65) **
Comparison group	16 (36/224) ***	14 (31/224)	7 (15/224)	37 (82/224)

Note. n's are in parentheses.

*$p < .05$ for menorrhagia vs. comparison; $p < .001$ for menorrhagia vs. secondary amenorrhea.
**$p < .05$ for secondary amenorrhea vs. comparison.
***$p < .05$ for comparison vs. secondary amenorrhea.
†$p < .02$ for menorrhagia vs. secondary amenorrhea.
††$p < .001$ for menorrhagia vs. comparison.
†††$p < .001$ for secondary amenorrhea vs. menorrhagia and for secondary amenorrhea vs. comparison.

appeared to form part of the depressive episode; in fact, the only case of a nondepressive disorder was a manic condition (which, of course, has certain affinities with depression).

Overall rates of anxiety, including both cases and borderline cases, and both those with and those without accompanying depression, did not differ significantly among the three groups: 20% (20/98) for menorrhagia patients, 18% (12/65) for secondary amenorrhea patients, and 16% (36/224) for the comparison group. Similarly, when pure anxiety (without depression) was examined, the proportions were again almost identical.

Not only was the proportion of women with *clinical* depression at a caseness level higher among the menorrhagia patients in the year before onset of the menstrual disorder, but among the cases, the proportion attending psychiatric services was also higher: 31% (9/29) of the cases with menorrhagia (including depression and other diagnoses) had been referred to outpatient clinics at some point during their episode before onset of menstrual disorder, and a further 3 had been recommended to attend but either refused or only attended after this onset. The comparable figure in the community series was 8% (3/39), with only one woman failing to attend a psychiatric appointment made for her ($p < .02$). Although there is evidence to suggest that among those rated as cases, referral to outpatient clinics is not necessarily a sign of greater *severity* of depression, referral is often the result of certain symptom features that general practitioners find difficult to handle (Brown, Craig, & Harris, 1985). This difference in the proportion attending psychiatric services therefore suggests that the depressions associated with the onset of menorrhagia had certain qualities that caused doctors to view them as more urgent than those depressions usually found in a community series.

Interestingly enough, these differences did not occur when episodes of psychiatric illness prior to the year of interview or onset of menorrhagia were examined. Of the secondary amenorrhea group, 12% (8/65) had experienced such a previous episode, compared with 29% (28/98) of the menorrhagia and 30% (35/115) of the community series. (The size of the sample was smaller than usual in the comparison series, because this question was not asked in the earlier round of the Camberwell survey in 1969-1971, and 7 responses were "not known.") It was not easy to know how to interpret the difference (which was significant) between those with secondary amenorrhea and the other two groups, in view of their younger age, which would have allowed them much less time to experience a previous episode. What was interesting, however, was the lack of difference in past history between the menorrhagia patients and the comparison group, given the differences between the two groups in the crucial year before menstrual onset/interview. Moreover, the proportion having contact with psychiatric services during these previous episodes was also no different: 29% (8/28) of those in the menorrhagia group saw a psychiatrist during any previous episode, compared with 23% (8/35) in the community series. Nor was there any difference in the numbers who refused psychiatric treatment or who had eccentric or marginal psychiatric contact. For example, one woman in the community series had a psychiatrist friend who helped her with her panic attacks for friendship's sake, and another had drugs mailed to her by her psychiatrist father! Overall, these figures suggest that any differences in caseness between the menorrhagia and the community groups in the crucial year were specifically connected with the circumstances surrounding onset of menorrhagia, and not a sign of a permanently enhanced predisposition to depression among the menorrhagia patients.

Life Events and Psychiatric Disorder

When the experience of life events and difficulties was examined simultaneously with that of psychiatric symptomatology, a twofold pattern emerged that was to some extent expected: Those with depression in the menorrhagia group were also those with the provoking agents, and those with a challenge experience among the secondary amenorrhea group were also those with a nondepressive borderline-case syndrome. In order to explore in more detail whether psychiatric symptoms acted as factors intervening between life stress and menstrual disorder, those whose symptoms *predated* the life events that were being taken as putative causal agents (in other words, those with "ongoing" psychiatric symptomatology) were distinguished from those in whom the onset of psychiatric symptoms *postdated* the life event or start of the major difficulty. This analysis is shown in Table 10.4, and the results suggest that depression may well have mediated the effects of provoking agents, particularly loss, for menorrhagia. Particularly notable among menorrhagia patients was the low number of ongoing depressions, compared with the proportions found not only in this comparison group but also in other random samples of the female general population in similar areas. In the present comparison group, about half the *cases* of depression (19/36) were "chronic" in the sense that the disorder had started at least 12 months before interview; by contrast, among the menorrhagia patients, only less than a third had a disorder that had begun as long as 1 year before onset (and 2 of these were not ongoing at the start of the major difficulties.) When borderline cases were examined along with cases, the ratio of ongoing to onset depression was 10:36 in the menorrhagia group and 29:38 in the comparison group (see the figures for all menorrhagia patients versus the comparison group in the "Depression" columns, Table 10.4). This seemed to imply that something about the experience of menorrhagia was selecting a group with an usually high proportion of onset rather than ongoing depressions; in other words, it pointed to the possibility that the recent onset of depression was involved in the etiology of the menorrhagia. Comparing the figures for menorrhagia patients with and without a provoking agent strengthened this interpretation: The departure from the ratio of ongoing to onset depressions found in the general population (roughly half and half) was even greater among those with a provoking agent (about 1:4) than among those without a provoking agent (1:2). It suggested a causal chain running from provoking agent to onset of menorrhagia and mediated by an intervening depressive condition. The picture with regard to tension mediating the effects of challenge in the secondary amenorrhea group was less clear, but still suggestive.

Other Risk Factors

With a possible role established for life events and psychiatric symptoms in the onset of menorrhagia and secondary amenorrhea, it remained to consider whether any other factors interacted with these to render women more vulnerable to these disorders. Age at menarche tended to be younger among menorrhagia patients than secondary amenorrhea patients: The proportion with menarche before age 14 was 75% (67/89) and 59% (37/63) in the two groups, respectively ($p < .05$; some data missing). Extraversion scores were also higher in the menorrhagia group: 56% (45/80) of menorrhagia and 25% (15/61) of secondary amenorrhea patients scored 14 or more on the EPI (t (138) = 2.55, $p = .012$). Unfortunately, neither of these items had been routinely collected in the comparison group. However, examination of the norms established for the EPI suggested that the secondary amenorrhea group was scoring lower than expected on extraversion (Eysenck & Eysenck, 1964); they might well also have been older than average at menarche, as there is some evidence that four-fifths of girls have menstruated by age 14 (Dewhurst, 1984).

Even in the absence of firm normative material, the differences obtained allow some tentative speculation about what may have been happening. Since vulnerability factors by definition require a provoking agent to be etiologically effective, then among those developing a disorder, the proportion with a vulnerability factor should be higher among those with than among those without a provoking factor (see Chapter 12, where a high Bortner score in the myocardial infarction group was much more frequent among those positive on the workload index).

TABLE 10.4. Percentage of women with specified diagnostic groupings of psychiatric symptomatology in the year before onset of menstrual disorder or interview (case and borderline case disorders combined) by type of life stress

Subject group	Depression (with or without anxiety/other)		Anxiety (without depression)		Other (without depression or anxiety)		Without any symptoms
	Ongoing	Onset	Ongoing	Onset	Ongoing	Onset	
Menorrhagia patients							
With Camberwell provoking agent	12 (7/59)	51 (30/59)	7 (4/59)	2 (1/59)	5 (3/59)	2 (1/59)	22 (13/59)
Without Camberwell provoking agent	8 (3/39)	15 (6/39)	3 (1/39)	5 (2/39)	0 (0/39)	0 (0/39)	69 (27/39)
Secondary amenorrhea patients							
With definite challenge event in the month	12 (3/25)	0 (0/25)	12 (3/25)	0 (0/25)	8 (2/25)	24 (6/25)	44 (11/25)
With definite challenge in the other 11 months	8 (1/13)	0 (0/13)	15 (2/13)	0 (0/13)	8 (1/13)	23 (3/13)	46 (6/13)
With nonchallenge event in the 1 month before onset (but without a definite challenge)	23 (3/13)	0 (0/13)	0 (0/13)	0 (0/13)	8 (1/13)	8 (1/13)	62 (8/13)
With neither of above	7 (1/14)	0 (0/14)	29 (4/14)	0 (0/14)	14 (2/14)	0 (0/14)	50 (7/14)
Comparison group	13 (29/224)	17 (38/224)	6 (13/224)	0 (0/224)	0.4 (1/224)	0.4 (1/224)	63 (142/224)

Note. n's are in parentheses. For those with life stress, "ongoing" and "onset" refer to the periods before and after the life event/start of major difficulty; for those without life stress and for the comparison group, they refer to the periods before and after a date 12 months before interview.

However, this did not occur with these two factors. Neither introversion nor late menarche was associated with definite challenge experiences in the way to be expected of a vulnerability factor. Nor was there any association between either provoking agent or depression and exceptionally high extraversion scores or exceptionally early menarche in the menorrhagia group. Therefore, these factors were probably making an independent contribution to onset and should not be considered as true vulnerability factors.

One of the most frequently cited risk factors for secondary amenorrhea is loss of weight. Because there have been a variety of hypotheses to account for this link, a thorough investigation demands a number of different approaches. Weight loss can be measured in different ways (absolute number of pounds, proportion of weight before loss occurred, amount in relation to the standard for the woman's age and height; see Knuth, Hull, & Jacobs, 1977), and it can occur in different contexts (spontaneously [with or without psychiatric symptoms] vs. self-induced [with or without previous weight gain], the last of these being closest to classical anorexia nervosa). The complexity of the data precludes more than a simple report here (for further details, see Harris, 1988). Self-induced weight loss was more common in the secondary amenorrhea group than in the other two groups, being found in one-third of the sample. However, more than a third of these were dieting as a result of preceding weight gain, which they attributed to the contraceptive pill. Thus, as many as four-fifths of the amenorrhea patients were free of the sort of subclinical anorexia nervosa that has sometimes been called to account for the menstrual syndrome. There was no relationship between weight loss and any of the LEDS measures.

Physical Diagnosis

Unfortunately, because of changes in hospital policy regarding the storage of case notes, and because some subjects had been selected through general practitioners and had not been referred on to hospital treatment, physicians' diagnoses were not available for the complete sample. However, there is no reason to believe that the variables discussed were in any way systematically related to the fact that notes were missing. Coverage was considered adequate for some preliminary analyses of the menorrhagia sample (83%, or 81/98). Of these, 47, or 58%, had had hysterectomies, and therefore excellent information about organic pathology was available for them; it was decided to include the other 34 in the analysis as well, since most had had D & C's and all had had thorough examinations by specialists.

The differentiation between "functional" and "organic" in menorrhagia is possibly more problematic than this same distinction in abdominal disorder or heart disease. In the absence of a clear perspective on the causes of abnormal bleeding (Smith, 1985), there has been some controversy as to what is classifiable as "organic." Given the failure to resolve this debate, it was decided that the most fruitful policy would be to preserve comparability with the only other study in this field that attempted to relate this distinction to psychiatric disorder (Gath et al., 1982). Thus, although recent discussion about the role of polyps as not actually "organic" causes of abnormal bleeding might suggest that these should have been included in the "functional" category (J. R. Newton, personal communication, 1987), they are classified here as "organic." In practice, there were only 5 patients with polyps, and this decision did not affect the results to be reported. It had been anticipated that only about half the menorrhagia group would be "functional," but a surprisingly low number of the 81 whose physical diagnoses were available turned out to be classifiable as "organic," possibly because the upper age limit of 42 was lower than that in other studies. Moreover, preliminary exploration of associations with the independent and intervening variables suggested that it might be worth making further distinctions. For all these reasons, the functional and organic groups were further subdivided according to the physicians' reports. Within the organic group, a distinction was made between those with fibroids or polyps ("organic A") and those with endometriosis or adenomyosis ("organic B"); within the functional group, those with absolutely no physiological abnormalities reported ("functional B") were distinguished from those with something not usually considered relevant to bleeding, such as ovarian cysts or mild cervicitis ("functional A").

Table 10.5 gives results comparing these groups. The differences in rates of provoking agents were not as striking as might have been expected from the work with appendectomy and gastrointestinal patients; only those in the organic A group had a lower rate of provoking agents. However, it was of interest that only one of the five provoking agents in the organic B group involved the kind of marital disruption found more often among those of the functional group. The lack of difference in rates of clinical caseness of depression was also surprising, although the Gath et al. (1982) study, which looked at psychiatric symptomatology among hysterectomy patients, also found no difference between those with organic and functional disorder in terms of PSE Index of Definition and CATEGO. The age differences were not unexpected and accord with ideas arising from the study by Murphy and Brown (1980). There older patients had fewer provoking agents, and also fewer case or borderline-case conditions before onset of various physical illnesses. Murphy and Brown interpreted their findings in terms of the possibility that as age advances, biological factors involved in aging obscure the role of emotional factors. It had therefore been expected that in the present study the functional menstrual conditions would be associated not only with more provoking agents and psychiatric symptomatology, but also with a younger age group. In a similar way, the organic conditions were expected to be associated with lower rates of provoking agents and psychiatric disorder, and with an older age group.

Classifications of secondary amenorrhea usually contrast functional disorders with "discrete" disorders (Hull, et al., 1981; see also Shaw, 1984, p. 282); because the conditions subsumed under the heading "discrete" involve the sorts of pathology specified as "organic" in the dichotomy as discussed in this volume so far, it would have made most sense to follow that distinction here. However, unfortunately, in this particular sample of individuals with secondary amenorrhea, patients nearly all fell into the functional group.[1] Rather than abandon altogether the opportunity to relate the psychosocial variables to some kind of physiological subclassification, two further avenues were pursued. The first, more simple approach is reported here. This followed earlier traditional clinical distinctions among the functional amenorrheas. There seemed some value in exploring these, despite the recent skepticism about their worth; for example, the existence of a separate entity of "postpill amenorrhea" (see below) has become a favorite target (Jacobs, Knuth, Hull, & Franks, 1977; Tolis et al., 1979). The alternative classifications proposed are undoubtedly superior in reflecting endocrinological distinctions that are closer to the likely etiological process and that cut across conventional clinical categories. For example, Hull et al. (1981) distinguish hypothalamic feedback disorders from cycle initiation defects, and Shaw (1984, p. 287) proposes a three-tier hierarchy according to the disturbance of positive or negative estrogen feedback loops. The complications of using routine case notes to impose these classifications would demand a lengthier exposition than is possible in this chapter (for further information, see Harris, 1988).

Results following the first of these avenues, the cruder classificatory

---

1. There were only 4 among the 45 with recorded examples of cystic ovaries (none with Stein-Leventhal syndrome), and only 5 with any degree of hyperprolactinemia, although it has been estimated that among women with amenorrhea the usual proportion with elevated prolactin levels is 15-20% (Franks et al., 1975). (None of these 5 was attributed to a pituitary microadenoma in any case.) It was possible to document initial treatment response to Clomid, Parlodel, and Pergonal, but a number defaulted after only a few months, leaving the sample unsatisfactorily small for any conclusions.

index, are presented in Table 10.6 The four categories distinguished those whose onset of amenorrhea immediately followed cessation of the contraceptive pill (the "postpill" group) from those who had a history of abnormal bleeding preceding the amenorrhea (the "mixed group"), those where additional physiological features led to genuine confusion for some months as to whether the subjects were pregnant rather than amenorrheic (the "pseudocyesis-type" group), and those with no other obvious distinguishing characteristics (the "standard" group). The additional features taken to distinguish the pseudocyesis-type group were abdominal swelling, substantial weight gain, morning sickness, and a militant conviction of pregnancy (often reinforced by medical personnel in the early months of amenorrhea). It could be argued that the first two of these four groups might be expected to have a more somatic, less psychosomatic origin than the third and fourth, and might therefore show lower rates of the specified provoking events.

Table 10.6 shows that the two more organic groups (in the top two rows) had fewer events in the 1 month before onset, and fewer involving

TABLE 10.5. Percentage of women with stressful provoking agent and psychiatric symptomatology by type of menorrhagia

Type of menorrhagia	With provoking agent ***	With marital/ boyfriend provoking agent	With case-level depression	Normal (without even borderline-case psychiatric symptoms)	Aged 32+ ††
Organic A	33 (5/15) †	20 (3/15)	33 (5/15)	40 (6/15)	80 (12/15) †††
Organic B	63 (5/8)	13 (1/8)	0 (0/8) *	75 (6/8)	63 (5/8)
Total organic	43 (10/23)	17 (4/23)	22 (5/23)	52 (12/23)	74 (17/23) §
Functional A	73 (19/26)	35 (9/26)	27 (7/26)	38 (10/26)	50 (13/26)
Functional B	59 (19/32)	30 (9/32)	34 (11/32)	41 (13/32)	22 (7/32) §§
Total functional	66 (38/58) **	31 (18/58)	31 (18/58)	40 (23/58)	34 (20/58)

Note. n's are in parentheses. The composition of each group was as follows: organic A, 12 with myomas, 3 with polyps, total 15; organic B, 5 with adenomyosis, 3 with endometriosis, total 8; functional A, 6 with cervicitis, 3 with cancer of cervix, 3 with ovarian cysts, 3 with inflammation, 2 with cervical polyps, 9 with miscellaneous conditions, total 26; functional B, 32 with genuine absence of organic conditions. In the probability footnotes that follow, the chi-square test was the test of significance.

 *$p < .10$ for organic B vs. all other groups ($df = 1$).
 **$p < .10$ for total functional vs. total organic ($df = 1$).
 ***$p < .05$ for comparison of the four groups ($df = 3$).
 †$p < .025$ for organic A vs. all other groups ($df = 1$).
 ††$p < .01$ for comparison of the four groups ($df = 3$).
 †††$p < .01$ for organic A vs. all other groups ($df = 1$).
 § $p < .01$ for total organic vs. total functional ($df = 1$).
 §§ $p < .01$ for functional B vs. all other groups ($df = 1$).

TABLE 10.6. Percentage of patients with different types of secondary amenorrhea and a comparison group by type of life stress, nondepressive psychiatric symptoms, age at menarche, and age at onset

| Subject group | Any event in 1 month before onset | Challenge event in 1 month before onset | Motherhood situation event in 1 month before onset | Case or borderline case other than depression/ anxiety | Age at menarche | | Aged 20 or less at onset |
					Under 12	14+	
Secondary amenorrhea							
Postpill	44 (8/18)	17 (3/18)	17 (3/18)	22 (7/18)	17 (3/18)	44 (8/18) †	17 (3/18)
Mixed	40 (2/5)	20 (1/5)	20 (1/5)	20 (1/5)	40 (2/5)	20 (1/5)	20 (1/5)
Pseudocyesis type	88 (7/8) ***	38 (3/8)	75 (6/8) ††	25 (2/8)	50 (4/8) *	0 (0/8)	75 (6/8) ***
Standard	76 (26/34) ***	53 (18/34) **	21 (7/34)	26 (9/34)	15 (5/34)	56 (18/32) †	62 (21/34) ***
Random sample comparison (under age 30)	34 (38/113)	4 (4/113)	2 (2/113)	4 (5/113)	20, estimated[a]	20, estimated[a]	13 (15/113)

Note. n's are in parentheses.

[a] From Dewhurst (1984, p. 29).

  * $p < .05$ for pseudocyesis-type vs. the other three types.

 ** $p < .02$ for standard vs. the other three types.

*** $p < .01$ for pseudocyesis-type and standard vs. postpill and mixed.

  † $p < .01$ for postpill and standard vs. mixed and pseudocyesis-type.

 †† $p < .001$ for pseudocyesis-type vs. the other three types.

a definite challenge. The results were to some extent reminiscent of those presented in Table 10.5 in that patterns provided by life stressors were not parallelled by psychiatric symptoms; there was no difference in the proportion with case or borderline-case conditions other than depression or anxiety. On the other hand, age at menarche seemed to be related in a different way: The subjects were likely to be older in the postpill and standard groups, and very much younger in the pseudocyesis-type group.

The contrast between the patterns with regard to 1-month occurrence of events and age at menarche became less puzzling when the nature of the events involved was further examined. Among the pseudocyesis-type group, 6 of the 7 events in the month before onset involved what could broadly be termed "motherhood situations": the subject's marriage or intercourse for the first time, or the marriage or pregnancy of a close peer such as a sister or confidant. Among the standard group, by contrast, only 7 of the 26 events involved such areas (p < .01); the majority involved less "feminine" roles, such as house moves, job changes, examinations, and court cases. It may be of interest that 1 of these 7 in the standard group, with first intercourse as the event, was subsequently given an "abortion" before her diagnosis was returned as secondary amenorrhea, not pregnancy. In other words, she too was presenting a diagnostic picture that confused the medical staff. She was not counted as a pseudocyesis-type patient here because she did not report the additional physical features (e.g., excessive weight gain) that were used here to classify that group. Moreover, the one member of the pseudocyesis-type group who did not experience an event as defined by the LEDS in the 1 month before onset, reported an incident of a very similar nature in the month before her first missed period: A girl in her office who had decided to try to have a baby at the same time that the subject had given up mechanical contraception (some 4 months earlier) announced that she had become pregnant. Since she was neither a confidant nor a household member, this could not qualify as an event according to the LEDS rules, but its similarity to the other events in the pseudocyesis-type group suggests that it might well have played some part in contributing to onset.

It is tempting to speculate that this susceptibility to motherhood situations as opposed to challenges was associated with the lower age at menarche in the pseudocyesis-type group. This possibility is developed further in the "Discussion" section. Among the comparison group, neither motherhood situation events nor challenge events involving the subjects' own careers and residences were as common as among secondary amenorrhea patients, the great majority of events in the community in the month before interview involved interaction changes and illnesses of relatives.

Discussion

The presentation of results for two menstrual disorders simultaneously has involved some complications of exposition, but this disadvantage may have been counteracted by the emergence of a sharper perspective than that which would have arisen from a report focused upon only one of the two conditions. The contrasting patterns, both in the type of life stress preceding each disorder and in the intervening psychiatric symptoms, have served to highlight the role of psychosocial factors in each. It appeared that provoking agents (especially those involving loss) and depression were involved over quite some months in many onsets of menorrhagia; by contrast, secondary amenorrhea appeared to be preceded by challenge experiences within a very recent period, and there also appeared to be some role for intervening tension or fatigue. Furthermore, age at menarche and extraversion scores differed between the two groups. When all these features are considered as a whole, the social class difference between the two groups of patients probably need not be seen as a separate etiological factor, but as a reflection of these contrasting psychogenic pathways. The greater frequency of provoking agents and depression in the working class might well explain why there were more working-class menorrhagia than secondary amenorrhea patients. In fact, the proportion of working-class women was no higher in the menorrhagia than in the community comparison series, so a better way to approach an explanation would be to focus upon features that might explain the greater frequency of middle-class women in the secondary amenorrhea group. Here it could be argued that young women in the middle classes face critical examinations, take up new jobs outside their home towns, and move out of their parents' homes before marriage more often than their working-class counterparts, and that if challenge events play an etiological role in secondary amenorrhea, this class difference is much what might be expected. This would not be incompatible with another, more speculative notion to account for this class difference – namely, that a so far unmeasured predisposition to react to challenges in a way that contributes to secondary amenorrhea may also be associated with a middle-class position.

Shanan et al. (1965) have referred to a "strong striving to demonstrate independence by active involvement" (p. 464) as a candidate for such a predisposition. In a prospective study of the development of transient amenorrhea among American girls entering a kibbutz on first arrival in Israel (a classic event involving definite challenge), they measured both personality and corticosteroid excretion before any onset and found that those who ascribed more activity to characters in projective tests were more likely to become amenorrheic subsequently. They characterized this use of activity as a defense against anxiety, and there can be little doubt that one way of meeting challenges is to involve one-self especially actively in trying to control the situation while simultane-ously suppressing, or even denying, any anxieties arising from it. One is reminded here of some of the self-reports of reaction to threat men-tioned earlier in the secondary amenorrhea group: One girl, for example, threw herself into nursing her mentally deranged mother, while gritting her teeth with determination not to be hurt. And certainly the low rate of onset of psychiatric disorder among the secondary amen-orrhea women would be consistent with the notion of their protecting themselves against such anxieties, with the tension and fatigue states perhaps forming part of such an effort at suppression. In the absence of any measurement of such a cognitive set of dedication, it is not irrele-vant to cite folklore about "stiff upper lips" as part of a middle-class upbringing. But clearly more empirical work needs to be done to explore this line of argument.

Meanwhile, the lower extraversion scores of the secondary amenor-rhea group may also be relevant to this hypothetical predisposition of dedication. Many of the items of the EPI associated with introversion could be seen to involve such a trait (e.g., preferring reading to meeting people, often coming away feeling one could have done better, liking the kind of work one needs to pay close attention to). Although there was no strong evidence here that introversion was interacting with challenge events, the introversion-extraversion dimension deserves more explora-tion. It is noteworthy in this connection that a study in the Netherlands found that extraversion was positively associated with spontaneous recovery from secondary amenorrhea (Lodewegens et al., 1977). This is consistent with the notion that introversion both predisposes individu-als to onset and prolongs the condition.

A further range of evidence for the role of dedication might be found in the recent spate of reports on secondary amenorrhea among athletes (Dale, Gerlach, & Wilhite, 1979; Frisch et al., 1981; Schwartz et al., 1981) and ballet dancers (Frisch, Wyshak, & Vincent, 1980). The high prevalence of this menstrual disorder in these groups is almost always discussed in terms of the somatic effects of prolonged exercise, but such occupations, of course, also particularly involve attributes of challenge and dedication. The tension and competitiveness of such occupations may be as important as body weight, the fat-lean ratio, and energy expenditure in predisposing these individuals to secondary amenorrhea. In this connection it is interesting that a study in Finland (Ronkainen, Pakarinen, Kirkinen, & Kauppila, 1985) found greater dif-ferences between runners and their controls than between joggers and their controls on measures of ovarian hormones and gonadotrophins; the authors interpret this to mean that the strains of competitive train-ing are more crucial than the exercise itself.

One last point should be mentioned: There was no attempt in this study to interview subjects routinely on a self-report scale of challenge. This would have involved questioning about how committed the young women were to successfully meeting the challenges, how much they felt they had geared themselves to the responsibility, and how much this had required them to put aside other thoughts and feelings. It could well be that such a measure could improve on the predictions based on the contextual scale without the attendant problems of reporting bias confronted in studies of psychiatric disorder.

The contrasting picture for menorrhagia of loss and depression preceding onset finds some echo in earlier reports. Greenberg (1983) reported high levels of affective disorder and previous divorce in a sample of women with menorrhagia, and a similar picture has emerged in less specific samples of gynecology patients, many of whom can be assumed (given average proportions among clinic attenders) to have been menorrhagic (e.g., see Ballinger, 1977). Gath et al. (1982), in their study of hysterectomy patients, also found high rates of cases before hysterectomy, using the Index of Definition and CATEGO programs of the PSE. Their figures were somewhat higher than the ones in this study (58% compared with 30%), but this can be explained by the fact that some would have had their psychiatric onset after onset of menorrhagia. (As noted earlier, many women began to feel depressed after several months of abnormal bleeding and before final surgery.) Furthermore, the caseness threshold used by Gath and colleagues was somewhat lower than that of Bedford College. It is worth repeating that, as in the present study, Gath's team found no difference in rates of caseness between the functional group and the organic group. Because of the small numbers in the organic group here, it is difficult to know what to make of the different rates of provoking agents reported in the organic A group, but in the light of Gath et al.'s results it does seem that depression could have been involved in both types of menorrhagia.

Two earlier studies also deserve comment at this point because of the detailed qualitative material they present (although, because systematic measures of life events and psychiatric disorder were not available when these studies were done, a strict comparison with the present results is not feasible). Blaikley's (1949) sensitive discussion of eight cases of menorrhagia and a ninth of postmenopausal bleeding explicitly implicated anxiety (rather than depression), but his report is quite compatible with the disorders' having in practice been mixed cases of anxiety and depression. Certainly there seem to have been provoking agents in all eight cases – six of them "marital" in the sense used in this chapter, and the other two involving major interaction difficulties with relatives in the same household (e.g., one woman was living with a mother-in-law who accused her of stealing from her). Dutton's (1965) report on

155 women with functional uterine bleeding explicitly excluded 920 women whose uterine bleeding could be attributed to organic disease, and he espoused a much broader definition of "organic" than the one used here – one that would have included all the functional A group according to the definitions in Table 10.5. Again, Dutton talked of anxiety rather than depression, and again the sexual aspects of the marital situations were highlighted in his interpretation, although the detailed case histories show that the loss elements were often also marked. Given that his criteria for diagnosing depression were rather unclear (most of his patients apparently rejected the suggestion that they were depressed; Dutton, 1965, p. 399), the low rate of depression in his series should perhaps not be taken as too serious a contradictory finding. Dutton cites Blaikley as a kindred spirit in believing that the ultimate mechanism of uterine bleeding is vasomotor, through vasodilation induced by the activity of the autonomic nervous system.

This brings us face to face with the question of the mechanism by which life stress and psychiatric symptoms may affect menstruation. Studies of the hypothalamic-pituitary axis have for many years suggested a close linkage between pathways involved in the emotions and those mediating hormone release. Numerous publications support the notion that the neurotransmitter dopamine may play a crucial role in inhibiting luteinizing-hormone-releasing hormone (LHRH), which is so crucial in the menstrual cycle (Lachelin, Abu-Fadil, & Yen, 1977; Quigley, Sheehan, Casper, & Yen, 1980). A reduced dopamine turnover has been implicated in the development of depression, particularly in the pervasive loss of motivational incentive associated with the clinical condition (Willner, 1985, Chaps. 8-10). The high rate of motivational incentive implied in the findings involving precipitation of secondary amenorrhea by challenges would be consistent with an increased dopamine turnover, and the low rate of clinical depression further supports this perspective. Moreover, Shanan et al.'s (1965) report of the "strong striving [for] active involvement" in their subjects who did become amenorrheic would tie in with this view. In this connection, it is important to note that previous reports of stress-induced amenorrhea that have mentioned depression as the stress involved may not have paid enough attention to its measurement and its distinction from other neurotic symptoms. Similarly, although bereavements are often mentioned as typical examples of the "stress" involved before amenorrhea, precise numbers are often not forthcoming. Thus Fries et al. (1974) mention bereavements as precursors of amenorrhea, along with change of residence and travel abroad, but do not give relative proportions, let alone discuss whether the bereavements were not also challenge situations. For example, taking on the running of an older married sister's household and family at the age of 19 because the sister has just died may be a challenge demanding dedicated coping activity as well as a bereavement.

The predisposition to such dopaminic interference with LHRH may already be reflected in a girl's age at menarche. In this connection, it is interesting to speculate on the eight patients whose differing clinical presentation (as pseudocyesis-type) was not associated with a later age at menarche. The neuroendocrinological picture in pseudocyesis differs markedly from that in other forms of secondary amenorrhea and has been attributed to a *reduction* in dopamine, possibly as part of a clinical depression, with consequently higher levels of prolactin and luteinizing hormone (Yen, 1986). Certain psychiatrists have also discussed pseudocyesis as a variant of depression in which the depression may be denied (Brown & Barglow, 1971), and certainly the psychosocial context in the few cases reported here had qualitative elements reminiscent of those situations preceding depression. For example, one girl whose best friend announced her pregnancy in the month before onset of the amenorrhea had been engaged to a young man for 2 years, attempting to save enough for a home when they eventually married. Over the preceding 6 months she had become aware that he was no longer contributing to the savings account, but was spending his salary on his motorcycles, and also that the frequency of their dates together had noticeably declined. Another young woman had had three miscarriages during the 3 years she had been married, the first in a premarital pregnancy without which her husband might not have proposed to her. In the months before her amenorrhea, the marriage was deteriorating, and she was one of the few cases of clinical depression in the amenorrhea group. Her menses ceased one month after her younger sister announced she was pregnant.

In these sorts of contexts, where a woman may well have been feeling depressed for some time, the "meaning" of a pregnancy may be interpreted as in some way reparative. Witnessing the "fresh-start" experiences of her peers may suggest to the woman that a pregnancy of her own can offer new hope in her own life. Such a speculation is in line with the psychiatric accounts of Brown and Barglow (1971) and Aldrich (1972), who emphasize that the phantom pregnancy symbolizes a denial of depression: It is as if the woman has in some way changed her hormonal pattern to create a "fresh start" for herself. The suggestion that neuroendocrinological features may underpin this link between these motherhood situation events and amenorrhea gives these speculations somewhat greater plausibility. The psychoanalytic hypothesis that the link would be "explained" by an unconscious desire for pregnancy seems so contrived that doubt is almost automatically thrown on this modest set of associations; setting them into a theoretical context where they cohere with a neuroendocrinological perspective permits a more serious consideration of the data.

Although other neurotransmitters have also been implicated in both the control of LHRH and the experience of clinical depression, none dovetail quite so neatly with the study reported here.[2] One final point is of interest in this discussion of the way in which neuroendocrinological and life event factors may combine to produce amenorrhea: Among those whose amenorrhea followed cessation of oral contraceptives, there was a lower rate of both definite challenge events and other events, suggesting that the inhibition of the menstrual cycle may in some way have related more to the endocrinological effects of the previous pill usage than to experience of events. As mentioned earlier, there has been some disagreement as to the utility of a separate diagnostic category of "postpill amenorrhea," on the grounds that the distribution of causes accounting for it is statistically indistinguishable from that in other amenorrheic women. If life events can be taken as an example of such "causes," then these results suggest that the diagnostic category does have some validity, since Table 10.6 shows them to have been differently related in postpill and standard amenorrhea. It is instructive here to mention that one research team that raised these doubts originally (Jacobs et al., 1977) later revised its opinion: In the light of findings concerning a 13-21% excess of postpill patients who had no weight loss or psychological disturbance to account for their amenorrhea, Hull et al. (1981) concluded, "There has now emerged a small but significant proportion of cases of [postpill amenorrhea] that may be attributable to previous use of oral contraception" (p. 473).

To turn to menorrhagia, it is generally acknowledged that "understanding of the pathology of excessive menstrual blood loss is unfortunately still unclear" (Smith, 1985, p. 294). One point should be made, however: Reports of menstrual blood loss are notoriously unreliable (Hallberg, Hogdahl, Nillson, & Rybo, 1966; Chimbira & Anderson, 1980; Fraser, McCarron, & Markham, 1984), and the retrospective case-control design of the present study had no way of controlling for this source of bias even if facilities for measuring blood loss systematically had been available. The role of provoking agents and depression may be to increase psychic reactivity to menstrual blood loss rather than to increase blood loss itself. Such a model corresponds to the suggestion

---

2. For example, though depletion of noradrenalin has been proposed as crucial in learned helplessness and clinical depression (Gray, 1982; Willner, 1985), it is thought to have a facilitatory, not an inhibitory, role in the control of LHRH. And though endogenous opiates may exert an inhibiting influence upon LHRH similar to that of dopamine (Quigley et al., 1980), their role in depression is much more ambiguous than is that of dopamine. Serotonin and acetylcholine, while also implicated in both depression (Willner, 1985) and control of LHRH (Simonovic, Motta, & Martini, 1974; McCann & Moss, 1975), fit less easily into the theoretical model contrasting depression with motivated response to challenge.

that the role of provoking agents in functional abdominal complaints is to increase sensitivity to pain, rather than to cause any further physiological changes that give rise to "new" pains. The ambiguity of the results on psychosocial factors and functional versus organic menorrhagia might be seen as support for this point of view: It might be argued that other women with fibroids and polyps, but without provoking agents and some degree of depression, would have managed to carry on without attending for medical treatment. Only a general-population study with careful measurement of blood lost, and with careful attention to all sanitary napkins and tampons used, can hope to settle this issue definitively.

Meanwhile, it should be pointed out that many of the conditions studied here involved many other symptoms besides blood loss, and were sufficiently debilitating by any criteria to imply that more than mere reporting bias was at stake in the timing of stressors and depression just before the sudden increase in bleeding. It could well be that advances in gynecology will suggest a different way of grouping the functional and the organic cases, which may show little role for psychosocial factors and reporting bias in the "truly" organic group. Alternatively, it is not impossible that increases in bleeding are physiologically determined in all diagnoses and in a similar way, but a way that does not relate to obvious changes in tissues. Dutton's (1965) faith in autonomic nervous system influences on vasodilation was partly derived from observations that uterine bleeding sometimes follows the administration of cholinergic drugs (p. 403). This may turn out to be more than a mere outdated speculation, and, in conjunction with the results in this chapter, would tie in with some of the new ideas about the role of the cholinergic system in depression (Willner, 1985). Recent research has suggested the involvement of the prostaglandins in menorrhagia, since prostaglandin synthetase inhibitors are successful in reducing bleeding (Smith, 1985), but it is not easy to see how these ideas can be integrated with the psychosocial findings reported here. On the other hand, prostaglandin synthetase inhibitors also have effects on fibrinolysis, and it may be this rather than their impact upon the prostaglandins that gives them their therapeutic power in menorrhagia.

Meanwhile, it would be vainglorious to venture further than this along biochemical pathways at this stage. All that can be hoped is that the contrasting patterns of life stress and psychiatric symptomatology preceding secondary amenorrhea and menorrhagia may provide further clues in the search for these pathways.

Acknowledgments

This study was generously funded by the Mental Health Foundation. I am indebted to Mr. Newton, Mr. Studd, and Mr. Feroze of Kings College Hospital, to Mr. Norman Morris of Charing Cross Hospital, and to Mr. Fairweather of University College Hospital for permission to interview their patients. Mr. Newton also provided helpful guidance on gynecological diagnoses, as did Mr. Haynes of Milton Keynes Hospital; however, they cannot be held accountable for any controversial conclusions in this area, which are entirely my own responsibility.

References

Aldrich, C. K. (1972). A case of recurrent pseudocyesis. *Perspectives in Biological Medicine, 16,* 11-17.

Ballinger, C. B. (1977). Psychiatric morbidity and the menopause: Survey of a gynaecological outpatient clinic. *British Journal of Psychiatry, 131,* 83-89.

Bass, F. (1947). L'amenorrhé au camp de concentration de Terezin. *Gynaecologia, 123,* 211-219.

Blaikley, J. B. (1949). Menorrhagia of emotional origin. *Lancet, ii,* 691-694.

Brown, E., & Barglow, P. (1971). Pseudocyesis: A paradigm for psychophysiological interactions. *Archives of General Psychiatry, 24,* 221-229.

Brown, G. W., Craig, T. K. J., & Harris, T. (1985). Depression: Distress or disease? Some epidemiological considerations. *British Journal of Psychiatry, 147,* 612-622.

Brown, G. W., & Harris, T. (1978). *Social origins of depression: A study of psychiatric disorder in women.* London: Tavistock.

Brown, G. W., Ní Bhrolcháin, M., & Harris, T. (1975). Social class and psychiatric disturbance among women in an urban population. *Sociology, 9,* 225-254.

Brown, G. W., & Prudo, R. (1981). Psychiatric disorder in a rural and an urban population: 1. Aetiology of depression. *Psychological Medicine, 11,* 581-599.

Chimbira, T. H., & Anderson, A. B. M. (1980). Relation between measured menstrual blood loss and patients, subjective assessment of loss, duration of bleeding, number of sanitary towels used, uterine weight and endometrial surface area. *British Journal of Obstetrics and Gynaecology, 87,* 603-609.

Christie Brown, J. (1973). *Feminine gender role-identity and secondary amenorrhea.* Paper presented at the Seventeenth Annual Conference of the Society for Psychosomatic Research, London.

Dale, E., Gerlach, D. H., & Wilhite, A. L. (1979). Menstrual dysfunction in distance runners. *Obstetrics and Gynecology, 54,* 47-53.

Dean, C., Surtees, P. G., & Sashidharan, S. P. (1983). Comparison of research diagnostic systems in an Edinburgh community sample. *British Journal of Psychiatry, 142,* 243-256.

Dewhurst, J. (1984). *Female puberty and its abnormalities.* London: Churchill Livingstone.

Drew, F. L., & Stifel, E. N. (1968). Secondary amenorrhea among women entering a religious life. *Obstetrics and Gynecology, 32,* 47-51.

Drillien, C. M. (1946). Study of normal and abnormal menstrual function in auxiliary territorial service. *Journal of Obstetrics and Gynaecology of the British Empire, 53,* 228-241.

Dutton, W. A. (1965). Psychological fctors in 155 patients with functional uterine bleeding. *Canadian Medical Association Journal, 92,* 398-405.

Eysenck, H. J., & Eysenck, S. B. G. (1964). *Manual of the Eysenck Personality Inventory.* London. University of London Press.

Finlay-Jones, R., Brown, G. W., Duncan-Jones, P., Harris, T., Murphy, E., & Prudo, R. (1980). Depression and anxiety in the community. *Psychological Medicine, 10,* 445-454.

Franks, S., Murray, M. A. F., Jequier, A. M., Steele, S. J., Nabarro, J. D. N., & Jacobs, H. S. (1975). Incidence and significance of hyperprolactinaemia in women with amenorrhoea. *Journal of Clinical Endocrinology, 4,* 597-607.

Fraser, I. S., McCarron, G., & Markham, R. (1984). A preliminary study of factors influencing perception of menstrual blood loss volume. *American Journal of Obstetrics and Gynecology, 149,* 788-793.

Fries, H., Nillius, S. J., & Petterson, F. (1974). Epidemiology of secondary amenorrhea: II. A retrospective evaluation of etiology with special regard to psychogenic factors and weight loss. *American Journal of Obstetrics and Gynecology, 118,* 473-479.

Frisch, R. E., Gotz-Welbergen, A. V., McArthur, J. W., Albright, T., Witschi, J., Bullen, B., Birnholz, J., Reed, R. B., & Herman, H. (1981). Delayed menarche and amenorrhea of college athletes in relation to age of onset of training. *Journal of the American Medical Association, 246,* 1559-1563.

Frisch, R. E., Wyshak, G., & Vincent, L. (1980). Delayed menarche and amenorrhea in ballet dancers. *New England Journal of Medicine, 303,* 17-19.

Gath, D., Cooper, P., & Day, A. (1982). Hysterectomy and psychiatric disorder: Levels of morbidity before and after hysterectomy. *British Journal of Psychiatry, 140,* 335-350.

Goldthorpe, J. H., & Hope, K. (1974). *The social grading of occupations: A new approach and scale.* London: Oxford University Press.

Gray, J. A. (1982). *The neuropsychology of anxiety: An enquiry into the functions of the septo-hippocampal system.* New York: Oxford University Press.

Greenberg, M. (1983). The meaning of menorrhagia: An investigation into the association between the complaint of menorrhagia and depression. *Journal of Psychosomatic Research, 27,* 209-214.

Gregory, B. A. J. C. (1957). The menstrual cycle and its disorders in psychiatric patients: II. *Journal of Psychosomatic Research, 16,* 61-79, 199-224.

Hallberg, L., Hogdahl, A. M., Nillson, L., & Rybo, G. (1966). Menstrual blood loss – a population study. *Acta Obstetrica et Gynaecologica Scandinavica, 45,* 320-351.

Harris, T. O. (1988). *The social and psychological background to menstrual disorders: A study of gynaecological patients with secondary amenorrhea and abnormal uterine bleeding.* Unpublished doctoral dissertation, University of London.

Harris, T. O., Brown, G. W., & Bifulco, A. (1986). Loss of parent in childhood and adult psychiatric disorder: The role of lack of adequate parental care. *Psychological Medicine, 16,* 641-659.

Hull, M. G. R., Bromham, D. R., Savage, P. E., Barlow, T. M., Hughes, A. O., & Jacobs, H. S. (1981). Postpill amenorrhea: A causal study. *Fertility and Sterility, 36,* 472-476.

Jacobs, H. S., Knuth, U. A., Hull, M. G. R., & Franks, S. (1977). Post-pill amenorrhoea – cause or coincidence? *British Medical Journal, ii,* 940-42.

Knuth, U. A., Hull, M. G. R. & Jacobs, H. S. (1977). Amenorrhoea and loss of weight. *British Journal of Obstetrics, 84,* 801-807.

Lachelin, G. C. L., Abu-Fadil, S., & Yen, S. S. C. (1977). Functional delineation of hyperprolactinaemic amenhorroea. *Journal of Clinical Endocrinology and Metabolism, 44,* 1163-1174.

Lazarus, R. S., & Folkman, S. (1984). *Stress, appraisal and coping.* New York: Springer.

Lodewegens, F. J., Bos-Van Rijn, I., Groenman, N. H., & Lappohn, R. E. (1977). The effect of psychic factors on the spontaneous cure of secondary amenorrhoea: A comparison of cases with and without spontaneous cure. *Journal of Psychosomatic Research, 21,* 175-182.

Martin, R. L., Roberts, W. V., & Clayton, P. J. (1980). Psychiatric status after hysterectomy – a one-year prospective follow-up. *Journal of the American Medical Association, 244,* 350-353.

McCann, S. M., & Moss, R. L. (1975). Putative neurotransmitters involved in discharging gonadotrophin-releasing neurohormones and the action of LH-releasing hormone on the CNS. *Life Sciences, 16,* 833-852.

Murphy, E., & Brown, G. W. (1980). Life events, psychiatric disturbance and physical illness. *British Journal of Psychiatry, 136,* 326-338.

Neilson, E. M., & Brown, G. W. (1984). *Psycho-social factors in physical disorders: A preliminary report to the Economic and Social Research Council.* Unpublished manuscript.

Petterson, F., Fries, H., & Nillius, S. H. (1973). Epidemiology of secondary amenorrhea: I. Incidence and prevalence rates. *American Journal of Obstetrics and Gynecology, 117,* 80-86.

Quigley, M. A., Sheehan, K. L., Casper, R. F., & Yen, S. S. C. (1980). Evidence for dopaminergic and opioid activity in patients with hypothalamic hypogonadotrophin amenhorroea. *Journal of Clinical Endocrinology and Metabolism, 50,* 949-954.

Rheingold, J. C. (1964). *The fear of being a woman.* New York: Grune & Stratton.

Ronkainen, H., Pakarinen, A., Kirkinen, P., & Kauppila, A. (1985). Physical exercise-induced changes and season-associated differences in the pituitary-ovarian function of runners and joggers. *Journal of Clinical Endocrinology and Metabolism, 60,* 416-422.

Russell, G. F. M. (1972). Premenstrual tension and psychogenic amenorrhea: Psychophysical interactions. *Journal of Psychosomatic Research, 16,* 279-287.

Sainsbury, P. (1960). Psychosomatic disorders and neurosis in outpatients attending a general hospital. *Journal of Psychosomatic Research, 4,* 261-273.

Salter, J. R. (1985). Gynaecological symptoms and psychological distress in potential hysterectomy patients. *Journal of Psychosomatic Research, 29,* 155-159.

Schwartz, B., Cumming, D. C., Riordan, E., Selye, M., Yen, S. S. C., & Rebar, R. W. (1981). Exercise-associated amenorrhea: A distinct entity? *American Journal of Obstetrics and Gynecology, 141,* 662-670.

Shanan, J., Brzezinski, A., Sulman, F. G., & Sharon, M. (1965). Active coping behaviour, anxiety and cortical steroid excretion in the prediction of transient amenorrhea. *Behavioural Sciences, 10,* 461-465.

Shaw, R. W. (1984). Hypothalamic reproductive failure. In J. Studd (Ed.), *Progress in obstetrics and gynaecology* (Vol. 4, pp. 279-289). London: Longman.

Simonovic, I., Motta, M., & Martini, L. (1974). Acetylcholine and the release of the follicle stimulating hormone-releasing factor. *Endocrinology, 95,* 1373-1379.

Sher, N. (1946). Causes of delayed menstruation and its treatment: An investigation in the Women's Auxiliary Service. *British Medical Journal, i,* 347-349.

Smith, S. K. (1985). Menorrhagia. In J. Studd (Ed.), *Progress in obstetrics and gynaecology* (Vol. 5, pp. 293-308). London: Longman.

Stroink, J. A. (1947). Amenorrhea in wartime. *Gynaecologia, 124,* 160-165.

Sydenham, A. (1946). Amenorrhea at Stanley Camp, Hong Kong, during internment. *British Medical Journal, ii,* 159-160.

Tolis, G., Ruggere, D., Popkin, D. R., Chow, J., Boyd, M., Leon, A., Lalonde, A. B., Asswad, A., Hendelman, M., Scali, V., Koby, R., Arronet, G., Yufe, B., Tweedie, F. J., Fournier, M., & Naftolin, F. (1979). Prolonged amenorrhea and oral contraceptives. *Fertility and Sterility, 32,* 265-268.

Willner, P. (1985). *Depression: A psychobiological synthesis*. New York: Wiley.

Wing, J. K., Cooper, J. E., & Sartorius, N. (1974). *The measurement and classification of psychiatric symptoms: An instruction manual for the Present State Examination and CATEGO programme*. London: Cambridge University Press.

Yen, S. S. C. (1986). Chronic anovulation due to CNS-hypothalamic-pituitary dysfunction. In S. S. C. Yen & R. B. Jaffe (Eds.), *Reproductive endocrinology: Physiology, pathophysiology and clinical management* (pp. 500-545). Philadelphia: W. B. Saunders.

11

Multiple Sclerosis

IGOR GRANT, W. IAN MCDONALD, THOMAS PATTERSON,
AND MICHAEL R. TRIMBLE

The efflorescence, in the past quarter century, of research attempting to link life events to illnesses of various sorts has tended to ignore neurological diseases. The suggestive evidence that has emerged has focused principally on multiple sclerosis (MS), although some has dealt with epilepsy and stroke (Grant, 1985).

This chapter critically reviews the evidence for a link between the social environment and onset and exacerbation of the symptoms of MS. It also describes a recently completed study at the national Hospitals for Nervous Diseases, Queen Square and Maida Vale, London.

Characteristics of MS

MS is a chronic neurological disorder whose cause is unknown. It is the most common neurological disease affecting young adults in temperate climates ("The Progress of Multiple Sclerosis," 1980) and is the leading cause of serious neurological disability among young and middle-aged adults in Western Europe and North America (McKhann, 1982). The disease afflicts women somewhat more frequently than men (60% vs. 40%) and typically has its onset between ages 20 and 40. Early symptoms are often nonspecific and evanescent, and include such complaints as fatigue, clumsiness, visual disturbance, weakness of a limb, and numbness or tingling of parts of the body. Often such symptoms are ascribed, both by the patient and by family members, to fatigue, "stress," or various psychiatric causes. As the disease becomes estab-

Igor Grant and Thomas Patterson. Department of Psychiatry, University of California at San Diego School of Medicine, La Jolla, CA 92093 USA; Veterans Administration Medical Center, San Diego, CA 92161 USA.

W. Ian McDonald and Michael R. Trimble. National Hospitals for Nervous Diseases, Queen Square, London WC1N 3BG, England, and Maida Vale, London, W91TL, England.

lished, more pronounced symptoms, such as weakness or frank paralysis of extremities, loss of sensation, visual loss, abnormal gait, dysarthria, and unusual sensitivity to heat and fatigue, may be evident. Still later symptoms may include dyscontrol of bowel, bladder, and sexual functioning, as well as neuropsychiatric changes (e.g., disturbances in abstracting ability, remembering, and regulation of affect) (Grant, 1986).

The typical course of the disease is intermittent. For example, an initial attack at age 30 may be followed by a complete remission. At the age of 34, there may be an exacerbation leading to only partial clearing of symptoms. Thereafter, repeated attacks may be followed by further remissions with increasing residual disability. After 10 to 15 years, the disease may acquire a progressive downhill course. Approximately 10% of patients will die within 15 years, and the mean survival time has been estimated at 30 years (Confavreux, Aimard, & Devic, 1980). There are several variants to such an intermittent natural history, including an acute, rapidly progressive form; a slow, steadily progressive form; and a benign form characterized by only one or two attacks with permanent remission.

The diagnosis is still made principally on clinical grounds, and requires two attacks and clinical evidence of two separate neurological lesions, although in the presence of certain laboratory findings some variation of these rules is permitted (Poser et al., 1983). Laboratory measures can be useful, including electrophysiological data, such as slowing of the visual evoked response; visualization of plaques of demyelination on neuroradiological examination (magnetic resonance imaging shows particular promise); and certain changes in the protein composition of the cerebrospinal fluid (e.g., oligoclonal bands of immune globulin demonstrated on electrophoresis).

Inspection of the brains of victims shows scattered plaques of demyelination that are widely distributed throughout the white matter, especially in the periventricular zones. The formation of the plaques begins with edema and macrophage infiltration and evolves through several stages; in their final form, the plaques are waxy and relatively avascular. On microscopic examination, the myelin sheath that surrounds the axons seems to be broken down. Electron microscopy has demonstrated pathology in the myelin membrane produced by oligodendrocytes, and immunocytochemical studies suggest that a reduction in myelin basic protein and one of the myelin-associated glycoproteins may precede destructions of the myelin sheath (McFalin & McFarland, 1982a).

The geographic distribution of MS (wherein Caucasoids in northern and temperate climates are affected far more frequently than those living in warm tropical climates), and the presence of certain types of anti-viral antibodies in some patients with MS, have suggested that this disease may have a viral etiology and an autoimmune pathogenesis (McFarlin & McFarland, 1982b). There is evidence that a genetic factor (or factors) influences susceptibility to the disease: Certain groups of MS patients share particular antigens of the HLA type, to a greater degree than expected (Batchelor, Compston, & McDonald, 1978; Compston, 1986).

Treatment is supportive, aimed at maximizing the patient's physical and psychosocial resources despite increasing handicaps. Adrenocorticotropic hormone (ACTH) and steroids can speed remission, but apparently do not alter the ultimate outcome. Immunosuppressive therapy (e.g., azathioprene) is of uncertain benefit, and other approaches to altering the immune system (e.g., injection of myelin basic protein) or reinforcing defenses against viruses (e.g., interferon) have not been shown to be successful.

Observations on the Relationship of Stressful Life Events to Symptoms of MS

Early Descriptions

Virtually from the moment that MS came to be identified as a discrete entity, emotional factors and stressful life events were implicated in its etiology and progression. The earliest pathological descriptions of MS are attributed to Cruveilhier in 1835-1842 and Carswell in 1838. At about the same time what appears to be the first clinical account of multiple sclerosis was written in the autobiography of Augustus D'Esté, who died in 1846. He wrote,

> I attended his [a near relation who seems to have been a father figure] funeral: there being many persons present I struggled violently not to weep. I was, however, unable to prevent myself from so doing. Shortly after the funeral I was obliged to have my letters read to me and their answers written for me, as my eyes were so attacked that when fixed upon minute objects, indistinctness of vision was the consequence. (quoted in Firth, 1948)

Another eloquent autobiographical report was provided in 1919 by B. F. Cummings (under the pseudonym Barbellion of W. N. R.). In his *Journal of a Disappointed Man*, he recorded how powerful emotions and upsetting experiences triggered exacerbations of his symptoms (Barbellion, 1919/1948).

The first complete neurological description of MS, which depicted the disease much in terms that we use today, was provided by Charcot. He, too, commented on the apparent association between stresses in the social environment and onset and exacerbation of the disease. In a lecture on the subject delivered in 1868 at La Salpêtrière, he said;

> But the circumstances most commonly assigned as causes of this disease, by patients, appertain to the moral order – long continued grief or vexation, such, for instance, as may arise from illicit pregnancy, or the disagreeable annoyances and carking cares which a more or less false social position entails. This is often the case as regards certain female teachers. Having said so much with respect to women, the question of male sufferers arises. These are, for the most part, persons who have lost caste, and who, thrown out of the general current, and too impressionable, are ill provided with the means of maintaining what, in Darwin's theory is called the "struggle for life." In short, the etiology is a somewhat trite one such as may be met with again, as it were, at the beginning of all chronic diseases of the central nervous system. (Charcot, 1868/1877, p. 220)

In 1873, the British neurologist Moxon also noted an association between onset of MS and a stressful life event in the following comment on the case of a 28-year-old woman: "Aetiologically it is important to mention another statement the poor creature made when giving a more confidential account to the nurse – viz., that the cause of her disease was having caught her husband in bed with another woman. It was not possible to learn how far this was right; but she was neglected by her friends" (Moxon, 1873, p. 236).

Psychoanalytic Observations

The four decades following the conclusion of World War I witnessed the ascendancy of psychoanalysis as the dominant explanatory theory of human behavior in the United States. Before long, this theoretical framework came to be applied to the problem of MS. As early as 1921, Jelliffe suggested that emotional stress might produce cerebrovascular alterations, which might then favor the development of demyelinating plaques. This theme was picked up by Langworthy and associates in a series of reports based on detailed psychoanalytic study of a small number of cases of MS (Langworthy, Kolb, & Androp, 1941; Langworthy, 1948, 1950). These authors suggested that patients with MS were emotionally immature, caught in entangling neurotic relationships with their mothers. Women caught up in and resentful of such entangling relationships would attempt to strike out for their freedom by marrying against their mothers' will; usually they would select husbands who were passive and in some ways unsuitable by their parents' standards. Onset of illness tended to be associated with a reactivation of the conflict between submission and dominance when husbands became unexpectedly successful, thereby threatening the emotional balance of power in these marriages.

In 1950, the Association for Research in Nervous and Mental Diseases published a set of proceedings that contained several papers on the relationship of stressful life events to onset and exacerbation of multiple sclerosis. Grinker, Ham, and Robbins (1950) performed psychoanalytic interviews with 20 men and 6 women ranging in age from 21 to 54 years. These were apparently patients in various stages of disease, although specifics were not given. The authors suggested that "major changes in a life situation which should have stimulated intense resentment or anger, or which demanded an excessive amount of mental or muscular strain" (p. 458) were often related to precipitations of symptoms, but they did not specify how often this was true or what the events actually were. Furthermore, no patients without MS were studied.

Braceland and Giffin (1950) performed psychiatric interviews with 75 patients aged 18-58 who had MS of varying severity. The authors indicated that they attempted to evaluate the role of "emotional traumas" in disease onset, but "this quest was soon abandoned . . . because it was evident that psychogenic causes could be ascribed not only for multiple sclerosis but for any control series as well" (p. 450). Unfortunately, the authors did not describe their life events inquiry in any detail; nor was it clear from their report whether they actually studied a comparison series in a systematic fashion.

Brickner and Simons (1950) performed a retrospective study of 50 patients with MS looking for notations in their medical records concerning stressful life events related to onset or exacerbation. In 15 of the patient records, there were indications of stressful experiences in relation to symptomatology. In 8 of these the attack occurred during a "prolonged period of tension," and in another 6 the symptom episode developed soon after a life change. There was no comparison group. It was not clear how assiduously neurologists questioned patients about life events or how regularly these were recorded in the chart.

Studies since 1950

The first systematic investigation was reported by Pratt (1951). He interviewed a series of 100 patients with MS aged 15-64. There were 50 men and 50 women, and their modal level of disability was described as "moderate." There was a comparison series of 100 matched for age, sex, and level of disability; most of the controls were patients with other forms of neurological disease. Pratt's interview probed for "emotional antecedents" prior to onset and relapses; 38% of patients with MS and 26% of the comparison series reported emotional stress antedating onset of their disease. This trend in favor of the MS patients was not statistically significant. About one-fourth of each group reported emotional antecedents prior to exacerbations. Although Pratt concluded that there was no difference in the experience of life stress prior to onset of disease in the two groups, he noted that there were specific instances where an emotional stress appeared to have precipitated onset or relapse.

Philippopoulos, Wittkower, and Cousineau (1958) considered various emotional factors in a series of 22 men and 18 women with MS. The patients ranged in age from 20 to 45, and the typical patient's illness had lasted less than 5 years. No event material was collected for the matched comparison series. On the basis of detailed psychiatric interviews, the authors reported that 35 of their 40 MS patients suffered "traumatic experiences" preceding onset of their illness. In most instances these experiences involved "prolonged emotional stress," such as lengthy illness of a family member, new responsibilities or financial burdens, or other threats to a patient's "security system."

As a result of a nationwide survey of MS in Israel, Antonovsky *et al.* (1968) were able to conduct a large case-controlled investigation, one aspect of which dealt with the role of "emotional trauma" in the etiology of MS. The investigators performed structured interviews with 221 patients and 442 sociodemographically matched comparison subjects selected from a stratified population sample. The majority of patients were more than 45 years old at the time of interview, and had suffered from MS for 10 or more years. They inquired about the following prior to onset: life being endangered, serious impairment of health, desperate economic straits, a tragic event to someone close to the respondent, a very difficult interpersonal relationship, a very difficult work situation, geographic moves involving great emotional and physical discomfort, serious frustration, and serious anti Semitism. Only one comparison yielded a significant difference: 19% of MS patients versus 12% of controls reported "very difficult interpersonal relations." The authors concluded that they could not establish a systematic role for pre-existing life experiences in the onset of MS.

In the 1960s, George Engel and his associates published a series of articles in which they discussed the possible relationship between the psychological state of giving up (the so-called "giving up-given up" complex) and onset of various forms of medical illness (Engel, 1968). Mei-Tal, Meyerowitz, and Engel (1970) attempted to test this notion with a series of 32 MS patients who were evaluated in considerable detail using a psychoanalytically oriented interview. Of the 32 patients, 28 experienced onset of symptoms in conjunction with a psychologically stressful situation. It was suggested that the common theme was that they generated the "giving up-given up" complex, evidenced either as pronounced feelings of helplessness or as behavior indicating defensive measures to overcome such feelings. Although this report is rich in illuminating case material, the lack of a comparison series makes it difficult to place the findings in context. Furthermore, a number of the events appeared to be comparatively mild.

In a recent systematic study, Warren and her colleagues (Warren, Greenhill, & Warren, 1982; Warren, Warren, Greenhill, & Paterson, 1982) interviewed a series of 100 consecutive MS patients seen at the Multiple Sclerosis Clinic of the University of Alberta, Canada. The interviews covered a large number of possible biological and environmental antecedents to onset. Embedded in the interview were questions about life circumstances or specific events that might have had a "notable impact on their lives," and that had occurred within 2 years prior to onset of MS. The general categories covered included deaths or illnesses of a close family member or friend, personal illness, changes in the quality of interactions with relatives, changes in marital status, pregnancy and pregnancy-related events, work events, financial adjustments, changes in residence or life style, and miscellaneous or "relatively uncommon" events. Both positive and negative events were included. It was not specified how far back patients had to recollect their life events. Two-thirds developed their initial symptoms between the ages of 20 and 39, but the ages of patients at the time of interview were not given. To judge by the fact that one-third of these patients were not ambulatory, the series probably included a substantial number of rather severely ill persons who had had their illness for many years, and the length of retrospective recall may have been a problem in this study.

Warren and colleagues used group of 100 neurological and rheumatological patients matched for age, sex, race, and general location of early residence as a comparison series. An artificial "age of onset" was specified, based on the age of onset of the MS patient to whom the control was yoked. MS patients reported more events than the comparison group in the 2 years prior to onset (180 vs. 59 total events). The seriousness of the events is uncertain; findings were presented in terms of those reporting "unusual stress" in the 2-year period prior to onset age. According to these self-reports, 79% of MS cases versus 54% of the comparison subjects thought that they were unusually stressed. If only events that received Holmes and Rahe (1967) Social Readjustment Rating Scale weights of 40 or more were considered, then 18% of MS patients and 4% of controls reported at least two events in the 2-year period. The proportion reporting a single such event was not given.

Despite its methodological limitations (e.g., the method of acquiring and recording life event information, and the potentially long anamnestic period), this study provides the first evidence from a reasonably systematic study that MS patients may experience a disproportionate number of life changes prior to onset of their symptomatology.

The National Hospitals-Bedford College Study

The National Hospitals-Bedford College study sought to improve on some of the methodological difficulties of previous research. We attempted to identify MS patients who were at a relatively early stage in the course of their illness; we hoped thereby to obviate some of the more severe problems of long-term forgetting and distortion. In addition, we probed for life events and difficulties anteceding illness using the Life Events and Difficulties Schedule (LEDS).

Subjects

Patients with MS were selected from among inpatients and outpatients at the National Hospitals for Nervous Diseases, Queen Square and Maida Vale. Two methods of selection were used. During a 12-month period, inpatient admissions to the services of several consultant neurologists at the National Hospitals were systematically screened to determine whether they would qualify for the study. To qualify, patients had to carry the diagnosis of probable or definite MS as stipulated in the new diagnostic criteria (Poser *et al.*, 1983). Furthermore, the onset of disease had to be within the past 5 years, and there could be no complicating additional neurological or medical disease. Twenty- six inpatients were selected in this manner. Outpatients were selected through review of the active caseloads of participating consultant neurologists; the same inclusion criteria were used. In this manner, 14 additional patients were identified. After the study was under way, 1 of the inpatients received the diagnosis of cerebellar ectopia, and was therefore excluded. Thus, the total sample size for MS patients was 39. There were 10 men and 29 women, and their average age was 35.6 ± 9.0. The typical patient came from a middle-class socioeconomic background; the average Hope-Goldthorpe rating (Goldthorpe & Hope, 1974) was 14.5 ± 9.4. Of the 39 patients, 82% were married and 71% had children.

Nonpatient community controls were selected from participants in life events studies conducted by Brown, Harris, and associates. There were 10 men and 30 women, whose average age was 35.7 ± 9.7 and whose average Hope-Goldthorpe rating was 15.6 ± 8.9; 70% were married, and 58% had children.

Life Events Method

All subjects were interviewed concerning their experience of life events and difficulties using the semistructured LEDS. For MS patients, the interview began by eliciting a careful history of present illness, which then allowed identification of time of onset of definite symptoms. Questions regarding events and difficulties were then referenced to the year immediately preceding this onset. The average length of time between onset and interview was 2 years, with a range of 3 months to 5 years. Thus, in most instances, patients were reporting on events that had occurred between 18 and 36 months previously. Those in comparison series were asked about events for the year preceding interview.

Once the time frame was defined, the interviewer proceeded to ask questions about the wide variety of events and difficulties covered by the LEDS.

As soon as interviews were complete for several subjects, events and difficulties were discussed among several of the investigators at regular meetings of the Bedford College group, and the core ratings were made for threat, focus, and independence of events and for severity of difficulties. For the purposes of this study, events and difficulties of a "personal health" nature were omitted from analysis in order not to confound predictors with outcomes.

Results

EVENTS

Table 11.1 shows that during the putative "causal period" of 6 months, 62% of MS patients experienced at least one event that carried long-term consequences of a moderately threatening nature. Only 10% of controls reported such events. There were no other significant distributional differences in long-term threat, although somewhat more patients (18%) than controls (10%) reported experiencing very severely threatening events (level 1).

TABLE 11.1. Percentages of subjects reporting events at various levels of long-term threat during the 6 months prior to the interview

Threat level	Comparison	MS patients
	10 (4/40)	18 (7/39) *
2	10 (4/40)	62 (24/39) **
3	40 (16/40)	51 (20/39) ***
4	55 (22/40)	51 (20/39) †

Note. n's for the percentages are in parentheses.

* $\chi^2 = 0.82$, n.s.; ** $\chi^2 = 14.28$, $p < .001$; *** $\chi^2 = 0.44$, n.s.

† $\chi^2 = 0.10$, n.s.

TABLE 11.2. Percentages of subjects reporting events at various levels of short-term
threat during the 6 months before the interview

Threat level	Comparison	MS patients
1	20 (8/40)	31 (12/39) *
2	40 (16/40)	67 (26/39) **
3	22 (9/40)	49 (19/39) ***
4	40 (16/40)	44 (17/39) †

Note. n's for the percentages are in parentheses.
* χ^2 = 0.73, n.s.; ** χ^2 = 2.38, n.s.; *** χ^2 = 3.58, n.s.
† χ^2 = 0.04, n.s.

We also compared the experience of severe threats in the two
groups. "Severe events" were those with a marked long-term threat (level
1) or any moderate long-term threat if focused on the subject. Sixty-two
percent (24/39) of MS patients, as compared to 15% (6/40) of the comparison series, experienced at least one severe threat in the 6-month period (χ^2 = 18.02, $p < .001$). The percent attributable risk (PAR) was 55%
(see Chapter 2, this volume).

These differences in the experience of events with higher levels of
long-term threat were not found for events with various short-term
threat ratings. As shown in Table 11.2, although MS patients tended to
report somewhat more events at all levels of short-term threat, none of
the comparisons was statistically significant.

DIFFICULTIES

Table 11.3 displays the experience of difficulties of various severities by the two groups. More MS patients reported moderate difficulties

TABLE 11.3. Percentages of subjects reporting difficulties at various severity levels

Severity of difficulty	Comparison	MS patients
1	0 (0/40)	8 (3/39) *
2	5 (2/40)	5 (2/39) **
3	18 (7/40)	44 (17/39) ***
4	18 (7/40)	51 (20/39) †
5	35 (14/40)	41 (16/39) ††
6	12 (5/40)	8 (3/39) †††
7	0 (0/40)	3 (1/39) ∫

Note. n's are in parentheses.
* χ^2 = 3.00, n.s.; ** χ^2 = 0.01, n.s.; *** χ^2 = 4.16, $p < .05$.
† χ^2 = 6.13, $p < .02$; †† χ^2 = 0.12, n.s.; ††† χ^2 = 0.50, n.s.
∫ χ^2 = 1.02, n.s.

(levels 3 and 4). When difficulties were dichotomized into severe (levels 1, 2, and 3) and nonsevere (levels 4, 5, and 6), there were again more MS patients reporting severe difficulties: 49% (19/39) of the patients, as opposed to 20% (8/40) of the comparison subjects, reported such difficulties ($\chi^2 = 7.31$, $p < .05$). The PAR was 36% for this analysis.

In terms of type of difficulty, the comparison series as a whole experienced somewhat more housing difficulties, and patients experienced many more difficulties in interactions with their relatives and in their relationships with spouses/steady partners (Table 11.4). As noted earlier, the health difficulty area was removed in order to avoid confounding predictors and outcomes.

EVENTS AND DIFFICULTIES

Brown and Harris (1978) suggested that another way of conceptualizing "severe threats" is to combine events that have serious long-term threat (i.e. level 1 events with subject or other focus, and level 2 events with subject focus) with severe difficulties (levels 1, 2, and 3). Using such an analysis, we found that 77% of the patients with MS (30/39) experienced a severe threat in the 6 months preceding onset, as compared to 35% of the comparison series (14/40) ($\chi^2 = 14.08$, $p < .001$). The PAR was 64%.

EVENTS OVER TIME

Figures 11.1 and 11.2 show the proportions of patients and controls who reported any events or severely threatening events during each of the 12 months preceding onset (or interview date, in the case of con-

TABLE 11.4. Percentages of subjects experiencing difficulties in a number of areas

Area	Comparison	MS patients
Housing	28 (11/40)	8 (3/39) *
Work	18 (7/40)	26 (10/39) **
Money	15 (6/40)	10 (4/39) ***
Leisure/friends	2 (1/40)	0 (0/39) †
Children	18 (7/40)	21 (8/39) ††
Interactions/relations	8 (3/40)	33 (13/39) †††
Social obligation/conflict	5 (2/40)	3 (1/39) ∫
Marital or other intimate relationships	10 (4/40)	49 (19/39) ∫∫
Miscellaneous	8 (3/40)	5 (2/39) ∫∫∫

Note. n's are in parentheses.

* $\chi^2 = 4.58$, $p < .05$; ** $\chi^2 = 0.52$, n.s.; *** $\chi^2 = 0.40$, n.s.
† $\chi^2 = 0.10$, n.s.; †† $\chi^2 = 0.40$, n.s.; ††† $\chi^2 = 6.24$, $p < .02$.
∫ $\chi^2 = 1.00$, n.s.; ∫∫ $\chi^2 = 9.78$, $p < .01$; ∫∫∫ $\chi^2 = 0.20$, n.s.

trols). When all events were considered Figure 11.1, 15-30% of both groups reported an occurrence each month up to 3 months prior to onset (interview). In the last 2 months the curves diverged, with almost twice as many patients as controls reporting some event in the final month.

A similar pattern was seen for events carrying severe long-term threat as defined above (Figure 11.2). The rates of these were on the order of 5-10% per month in both groups until the 6th month. Thereafter, MS patients reported more threatening events. In the last month, the rate of threatening events for patients was quadruple that found in the controls.

Relationship to Past Research and Possible Future Directions

Until the 1980s, although case studies suggested a relationship between stressful life events and onset of MS, the two controlled studies that had been done (Pratt, 1951; Antonovsky et al., 1968) produced negative findings. Warren and associates (Warren, Greenhill, & Warren, 1982; Warren, Warren, et al., 1982) noted that MS patients regarded their lives as particularly stressful in the 2 years prior to onset. At the same time, this group's use of certain notions linked to the Holmes and Rahe (1967) life events instrument, coupled with the likelihood that very long-term anamnestic responses were required, raised questions about the robustness of their findings. The National Hospitals-Bedford College study examined a smaller number of patients and controls. Thus, any conclusions must clearly be tentative. On the other hand, the methods used to derive data on life events and difficulties are considered by many to be "state-of-the-art." Furthermore, the attempt to interview only those patients with relatively recent onset provided somewhat better assurance that memories were not unduly clouded by the passage of time.

The fact that the rate of event reporting by patients and controls was remarkably similar at 6-12 months, and only began diverging in the few months prior to onset, suggests that these findings are probably not artifactual. Furthermore, although there were differences in reports of events of all sorts, patients outstripped controls most dramatically in the area of severe threat. Since the rating of threat was done contextually (i.e., by us), it seems unlikely that inappropriate amplification by patients accounted for the MS-control differences.

Assuming for the moment that these findings at least approximate some underlying "truth," what is their meaning? Do life events and difficulties "cause" MS?

It is obvious that a retrospective case-controlled design of the type reported here cannot assert causality, no matter how intriguing the

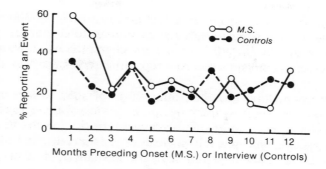

FIGURE 11.1. Report of any event by MS patients ($n = 39$) and controls ($n = 40$).

results. Furthermore, it is clear that at least two factors play an important role in determining vulnerability to MS. The first appears to be a susceptible host. This is suggested by the observation that MS has some tendency to run in families, and that its occurrence is sometimes linked to certain genetic markers.

The second factor appears to be exposure during youth to some environmental agent that is causally linked to MS. It is known, for example, that the risk of MS is highest in temperate and northern climates, and quite low in the tropics. At the same time, when adults from geographic areas of higher prevalence move to areas of lower prevalence, they seem to bring with them the "risk" of their former place of residence. While this appears to hold for adults, it is not true for children who migrate before the age of 15. This suggests that exposure to

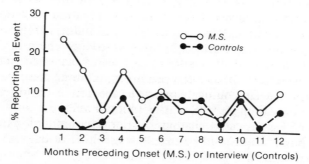

FIGURE 11.2. Report of severely threatening events by MS patients ($n = 39$) and controls ($n = 40$).

some agent in areas of high prevalence occurs during childhood years, and that once such exposure takes place an individual carries a higher likelihood of developing MS to the new geographic site. Whether the environmental agent is a virus or some other transmissible pathogen remains to be established.

We speculate that our data, and those of some of the previous research, are consistent with a "precipitating" role for events and difficulties. Given a biologically vulnerable individual, exposure to severely threatening events and marked difficulties may increase the likelihood that MS will emerge in a person at risk to develop it. It seems possible that onset is "brought forward in time" – a notion discussed extensively by Brown and Harris (1978). This line of reasoning suggests that life events do not determine whether or not MS will develop, but only the timing of onset. If this hypothesis is correct, it is still not clear whether long-term protection from unduly stressful circumstances may forestall the first episode of MS indefinitely.

If we were to accept that life events somehow do "precipitate" onset in some susceptible individuals, what is the mechanism? Here again, there are no answers, but research in psychoimmunology suggests that adversities can alter immune functioning. For example, some bereaved persons show defects in immunity (Bartrop, Lazarus, Luckhurst, Kiloh, & Penny, 1977; Schleifer, Keller, Camerino, Thornton, & Stein, 1983), and this effect has also been noted in some studies of persons who are depressed (Schleifer, Keller, Siris, Davis, & Stein, 1985) and subjected to chronic stresses of other sorts – for example, examinations (Kiecolt-Glaser et al., 1984; Locke et al., 1984). Our group has presented preliminary data that elderly women experiencing severe events and difficulties (determined by a modified LEDS technique) may be immunosuppressed, as evidenced by reduced percentages of T-4 (helper/inducer) lymphocytes and higher percentages of T-8 (suppressor/cytotoxic) lymphocytes (Patterson et al., 1986).

Dysregulation of the immune system is known to accompany MS, although it is not known whether such dysregulation precedes disease onset. It seems possible, however, that clinical onset of MS is preceded by a latent period characterized by some degree of compromise in the neuroimmune system. If this is so, then it seems plausible that severely threatening events, by further compromising immune competence, may act to "permit" the first clinical episode to develop. A test of this notion will require combining some of the modern methods of life events research with sophisticated characterization of immunological competence. One possibility would be to follow a cohort of patients with MS over time, monitoring prospectively their changes in symptoms, life events, and immune functioning.

Acknowledgments

Support for this work was provided by the Medical Research Service of the Veterans Administration and by the Foundations Fund for Research in Psychiatry. We are indebted to Dr. P. C. Gautier-Smith for his enthusiastic support of this study, and particularly his willingness to identify patients who might be suitable as research subjects. Professors John Marshall, J. Newsom-Davis, and P. K. Thomas were also helpful in allowing us access to patients, as were Drs. R. W. Ross Russell, J. A. Morgan-Hughes, P. Rudge, A. N. Gale, R. Clifford Jones, A. J. Lees, P. Bradbury, and E. Byrne. Ms. Marge Zeitsman assisted in scheduling some of our patients. We are grateful to Ms. Laurie Burton and Ms. Megan Cunningham for their help in preparing the manuscript.

References

Antonovsky, A., Leibowitz, U., Medalie, J. M., Smith, H. A., Halpern, L., & Alter, M. (1968). Reappraisal of possible etiologic factors in multiple sclerosis. *American Journal of Public Health, 58,* 836-848.

Barbellion, W. N. R. (pseud. for Cummings, B. F.) (1948). *The journal of a disappointed man.* Harmondsworth, England: Penguin Books, (Original work published 1919)

Bartrop, R. W., Lazarus, L., Luckhurst, E., Kiloh, L. G., & Penny, R. (1977). Depressed lymphocyte function after bereavement. *Lancet, i,* 834-836.

Batchelor, J. R., Compston, A., & McDonald, W. I. (1978). The significance of the association between HLA and multiple sclerosis. *British Medical Bulletin, 34,* 279-284.

Braceland, F. J., & Giffin, M. E. (1950). The mental changes associated with multiple sclerosis (an interim report). *Proceedings of the Association for Research in Nervous and Mental Diseases, 28,* 450-455.

Brickner, R. M., & Simons, D. J. (1950). Emotional stress in relation to attacks of multiple scleroses. *Proceedings of the Association for Research in Nervous and Mental Diseases, 28* 143-149.

Brown, G. W., & Harris, T. O., (1978). *Social origins of depression: A study of psychiatric disorders in women.* London: Tavistock.

Charcot, J. M. (1877). *Lectures on the diseases of the nervous system delivered at La Salpêtrière* (G. Sigerson, Trans.). London: New Sydenham Society. (Original lectures delivered 1868)

Compston, A. (1986). Genetic factors in the aetiology of multiple sclerosis. In W. I. McDonald & D. H. Silberberg (Eds.), *Butterworths international medical reviews – neurology: Vol. 6. Multiple sclerosis* (pp. 56-73). London: Butterworths.

Confavreux, C., Aimard, G., & Devic, M. (1980). Course and prognosis of multiple sclerosis assessed by the computerized data processing of 349 patients. *Brain, 103,* 281-300.

Engel, G. L. (1968). A life setting conducive to illness: The giving up-given up complex. *Annals of Internal Medicine, 69,* 293.

Firth, D. (1948). *The case of Augustus d'Esté.* Cambridge, England: Cambridge University Press.

Goldthorpe, J. H., & Hope, K. (1974). *The social grading of occupations: A new approach and scale.* London: Oxford University Press.

Grant, I. (1985). The social environment and neurological disease. In M. R. Trimble (Ed.), *Advances in psychosomatic medicine* (pp. 26-48). Basel: S. Karger.

Grant, I. (1986). Neuropsychological and psychiatric disturbances in multiple sclerosis. In W. I. McDonald & D. H. Silberberg (Eds.), *Butterworths international medical reviews – neurology: Vol. 6. Multiple sclerosis* (pp. 134-152). London: Butterworths.

Grinker, R. R., Ham, G. C., & Robbins, F. P. (1950). Some psychodynamic factors in multiple sclerosis. *Proceedings of the Association for Research in Nervous and Mental Diseases, 28* 456-460.

Holmes, T. H., & Rahe, R. H. (1967). The Social Readjustment Rating Scale. *Journal of Psychosomatic Research, 11,* 213-218.

Jelliffe, S. E. (1921). Multiple sclerosis and psychonanlysis. *American Journal of Medical Science, 161,* 666-675.

Kiecolt-Glaser, J. K., Garner, W., Speicher, C., Penn, G. M., Holliday, J., & Glaser, R. (1984). Psychosocial modifiers of immunocompetence in medical students. *Psychosomatic Medicine, 46,* 7-14.

Langworthy, O. R. (1948). Relation of personality problems to onset and progress of multiple sclerosis. *Archives of Neurology and Psychiatry, 59,* 13-28.

Langworthy, O. R. (1950). A survey of the maladjustment problems in multiple sclerosis and the possibilities of psychotherapy. *Proceedings of the Association for Research in Nervous and Mental Diseases, 28,* 598-611.

Langworthy, O. R., Kolb, L. C., & Androp, S. (1941). Disturbances of behavior in patients with disseminated sclerosis. *American Journal of Psychiatry, 88,* 243-249.

Locke, S. E., Kraus, L., Lesserman, J., Hurst, M. W., Heisel, S., & Williams, R. M. (1984). Life change, stress psychiatric symptoms, and natural killer cell activity. *Psychosomatic medicine, 46,* 441-453.

McFarlin, D. E., & McFarland, H. F. (1982a). Multiple sclerosis (part 1). *New England Journal of Medicine, 307,* 1138-1187.

McFarlin, D. E., & McFarland, H. F. (1982b). Multiple sclerosis (part 2). *New England Journal of Medicine, 307,* 1246-1251.

McKhann, G. M. (1982). Multiple sclerosis. *Annual Review of Neuroscience, 5,* 219-239.

Mei-Tal, V., Meyerowitz, S., & Engel, G. L. (1970). The role of psychological process in a somatic disorder: Multiple sclerosis. *Psychosomatic Medicine, 32,* 67-86.

Moxon, W. (1873). Case of insular sclerosis of brain and spinal cord. *Lancet, i,* 236.

Patterson, T., Grant, I., McClurg, J., Hollingsworth, J., Yager, J., Young, D., & Nordberg, J. (1986). *The relationship between immune status and stressful life events in an elderly population.* Paper presented at the meeting of the society for Behavioral Medicine, San Francisco.

Philippopoulos, G. S., Wittkower, E. D., & Cousineau, A. (1958). The etiologic significance of emotional factors in onset and exacerbations of multiple sclerosis. *Psychosomatic Medicine, 20,* 458-474.

Poser, C. M., Paty, D. W., Scheinberg, L., McDonald, W. I., Davis, F. A., Ebers, G. C., Johnson, K. P., Sibley, W. A., Silberberg, D. H., & Tourtellotte, W. W. (1983). New diagnostic criteria for multiple sclerosis: Guidelines for research protocols. *Annals of Neurology, 13,* 227-336.

Pratt, R. T. C. (1951). An investigation of the psychiatiric aspects of disseminated sclerosis. *Journal of Neurology, Neurosurgery, and Psychiatry, 14,* 326-336.

The progress of multiple sclerosis. (1980). *British Medical Journal, 281,* 824-825.

Schleifer, S. J., Keller, S. E., Camerino, M., Thornton, J. C., & Stein, M. (1983). Suppression of lymphocyte stimulation following bereavement. *Journal of the American Medical Association, 250,* 374-377.

Schleifer, S. J., Keller, S. E., Siris, S. G., Davis, K. L. & Stein, M. (1985). Depression and immunity. *Archives of General Psychiatry, 42,* 129-133.

Warren, S. A., Greenhill, S., & Warren, K. G. (1982). Emotional stress and the development of multiple sclerosis: Case-control evidence of a relationship. *Journal of Chronic Diseases, 35,* 821- 831.

Warren, S. A., Warren, K. G., Greenhill, S., & Paterson, M. (1982). How multiple sclerosis is related to animal illness, stress, and diabetes. *Canadian Medical Association Journal, 126,* 377-385.

12

Myocardial Infarction

EILEEN NEILSON, GEORGE W. BROWN,
AND MICHAEL MARMOT

Introduction

In a recent review, Haney (1980) estimated that at least 50 studies had included life change variables as they relate to coronary heart disease; as yet, however, no one has managed to integrate this with the even larger literature on stress and heart disease, particularly in terms of the work environment. Syme and Reader edited a significant issue of the *Milbank Memorial Fund Quarterly* in 1967, and the view of heart disease and stress formulated there by Jenkins would still receive wide agreement. Jenkins (1967) states that there are two important categories of socioenvironmental stressors: those that relate through behaviors such as smoking and drinking, and those that create frequent and sustained arousal of the autonomic nervous system, where the interpretative processes of the individual link external events and emotional, neurohumoral, and cardiovascular responses. Given that both these approaches concern potentially long-term processes, it is possible to see room for confusion about life events that occur at particular points in time, and that when studied individually have typically been shown to lead to the development of psychiatric or physical disorder in a matter of weeks or months.

Jenkins emphasizes the importance of frequent and sustained arousal for heart disease, and this makes sense in terms of what is known about the long history of pathological bodily changes stretching over many years that appears to precede a crisis such as myocardial infarction (MI). It suggests that the study of events as such, rather than,

Eileen Neilson and George W. Brown. Department of Social Policy and Social Science, Royal Holloway and Bedford New College, University of London, 11 Bedford Square, London WC1B 3RA, England.

Michael Marmot. Department of Community Medicine, University College Hospital, Gower Street, London WC1E 6BT, England.

say, their long-term untoward consequences, may be relatively unfruitful as a means of obtaining insights into fundamental etiological processes. (This, of course, does not rule out the role of life events as a trigger of MI in someone already physically predisposed.) Moreover, it is possible to conceive of psychosocial processes leading to the kind of sustained arousal that Jenkins has in mind that would not be reflected in a life events instrument. Migrant status, for example, has been implicated in coronary heart disease, but its entire range of consequences may well not be consistently recorded by the Life Events and Difficulties Schedule (LEDS), even though (unlike most instruments) the LEDS covers long-term difficulties as well as events. At present, the LEDS would only reflect such consequences that were clearly unpleasant or associated with exceptional circumstances (e.g., marked social isolation after leaving one's family). Another complication is that many studies have dealt with stressful life events and heart disease only in the sense of precipitating MI in those predisposed by pre-existing atherosclerosis, hypertension, or heart disease. There is now some evidence, though not beyond dispute, that acute stress can trigger MI in such circumstances (Connolly, 1976; Parkes, Benjamin, & Fitzgerald, 1969). However, the major question of whether there are more long-term etiological effects has not been resolved. The present exploratory study was designed to do just this, although we recognized that this would be bound to involve study of a lengthy period of time before any MI.

We therefore first set out to explore the possibility of obtaining accurate information about life events and difficulties over a 10-year period. To our knowledge, we are the first to have tackled this question. However, even if the importance of studying such a lengthy period of time is accepted, it may well be argued that research done so far on the situation in the year or so before MI should have reflected to some degree such a longer-term picture. But from this perspective, it has to be admitted that research so far has not been encouraging. In Sweden, Theorell, Lind, and Floderus (1975) studied 9,097 male construction workers for a 12- to 15-month period, following their completion of a life change instrument very similar to that of Holmes and Rahe (1967). Subsequent diagnoses of coronary disease were made on the basis of death certificates and autopsy reports for those who died, and on the basis of all hospital admissions in the Stockholm area for those who survived. Life change scores did not predict MI. When the men were asked to assess the degree of distress each event had created, there was some discrimination between the MI group and the comparison group (Lundberg, Theorell, & Lind, 1975). This might reflect the fact that such self-reports increased the accuracy of the life events measure used in this study, particularly in the light of the instrument's failure to take account of context (see the comments on the Schedule of Recent Experiences in Chapter 1). However, they could equally have been picking up a factor that has no direct bearing on the etiological role of life events – say, some aspect of personality.

Perhaps more significant is the fact that the only item on the life events list to predict MI was "increased responsibility at work"; 19.4% of those with MI reported this, compared with 9.4% of the rest of the men (Theorell et al., 1975). As the authors point out, excessive overtime work and increased workload have frequently been reported as MI-precipitating factors in retrospective studies (Russek & Zohman, 1958; Russek, 1965; Russek & Russek, 1976; Liljefors & Rahe, 1970; Theorell & Rahe, 1972; Kringlen, 1981). Feelings of overload have also been demonstrated to be correlated with physical changes such as elevated serum lipids (e.g., Friedman, Rosenman, & Carroll, 1958; Rahe & Arthur, 1967). A later analysis of the same data confirmed the importance of the work area (Theorell & Floderus-Myrhed, 1977). A factor analysis of about 60 psychosocial variables produced three indices: unsatisfactory family conditions (e.g., serious conflicts), changes in family structure (e.g., family member leaving home), and workload (e.g., extra job, increased responsibility, too little job responsibility, problems with workmates, unemployed for 30 or more consecutive days). When those who died were excluded, as with the earlier analysis, twice as many of those with MI were high on the final work index (25% vs. 12%), and this again was the only index to relate to outcome. However, the fairly modest difference involved should be noted, as well as the fact that it did not predict death from MI.

A significant study in West Germany by Siegrist, Dittman, Rittner, and Weber (1982) also obtained evidence for an etiological effect, based on a retrospective case-controlled study of 380 male patients with a first MI and a comparison series of 180. Of the MI patients 31% were exposed to three or more "critical negative life events" in the 2 years prior to illness onset, compared with 14% in the comparison group. Although statistically significant, the effect was again at best modest: The population attributable risk (PAR; see Chapter 2) was only 20%. Moreover, it is possible that, since the study period was only 2 years, results were inflated by stressors playing only a triggering role, and longer-term processes were not necessarily involved. The study also covered sources of work overload, social support, and chronic interpersonal difficulties, as well as coronary-prone behavior such as felt need for control. When all these factors were taken into account, the best discrimination was 44% for MI versus 20% for the healthy comparison series, giving a PAR of 30%. This is probably the best result in terms of the impact of psychosocial factors to be published to date, and in this sense the conclusion remains that the etiological effect of psychosocial factors conceived in the broadest sense appears to be modest.

However, evidence that the work environment can be involved in the genesis of MI is impressive. In this same German study, events in the work area appeared to be particularly important (Siegrist *et al.*, 1982, p. 447), and a separate measure of chronic workload was related to onset of MI. (We have already noted other evidence; see also Johnson, 1986.) Siegrist and his colleagues have used the term "active distress" for situations that are threatening or demanding and in which, despite active coping, there is a low probability of a positive outcome (Siegrist *et al.*, 1982; Siegrist, 1985). For men, at least, they argue that the work situation plays a central role in producing active distress and that middle adulthood is a period of particular risk. Most men have achieved a more or less definite status regarding work by their late 30s. Experiences of low job security, layoff, or forced downward mobility can threaten socioeconomic status in a fundamental way and trigger experiences of "active distress." Siegrist and his colleagues believe that the same is true for less dramatic everyday experiences of high workload under control-limiting conditions. They argue that individuals continue to try to resolve such difficulties for two reasons. First, because of circumstances in the job or their own lives taken as a whole, they are unable to escape from the situation or to face it in a positive way; second, their own dispositions, and their appraisal of the situation and of their own coping potential, also play a role. The argument at this point draws upon the literature on "Type A personality," particularly the argument by David Glass (1977) that characteristics such as increased irritability, hostility, and inability to withdraw from imposed demands are used as a coping strategy by individuals who are particularly sensitive about experiencing any sense of loss of control. Results of an ongoing prospective study of cardiovascular risk factors in 416 blue-collar workers have already produced promising material (Matschinger, Siegrist, Siegrist, & Dittman, 1986). One critical set of results suggests that "need for control" exerts a significant influence on systolic blood pressure only under adverse work conditions, such as enforced piecework. Its effect in this instance appears to have been much stronger than that of such well-established risk factors as age, smoking, and obesity.

These recent findings concerning the work environment underline the appropriateness of our decision to place emphasis on ongoing difficulties over a lengthy period of time and to give particular attention to the work situation. Only with such data as a background would it be possible to make a useful assessment of the likely etiological importance of more general life events and difficulties.

The employment section of the LEDS is only one part of an extensive schedule covering a person's relationships and activities as a whole. Although it would certainly have been possible to extend the questioning concerning work, we decided for the sake of comparability with other studies using the LEDS that it was important to keep to the existing LEDS interview schedule. However, we did collect some additional information. There were some obvious gaps in material collected about employment, and some additional probes were included – in particular, the average number of hours worked in each of the study's ten 1-year periods and the length of time taken as vacation during each of them.

Method and Subjects

The Use of the LEDS over a 10-Year Period

Questions and rating procedures for the 10-year version were the same as for the standard LEDS, with some minor amendments. The importance of a narrative approach has been emphasized in Chapter 1. For example, once an event was mentioned, questions about events and difficulties preceding and following it were asked as a matter of course: "And what happened next?" "Did it turn out as you expected?" "Did you think of doing anything else?" Exact dates were not always forthcoming, of course. However, respondents were usually able to report incidents as occurring before or after an incident that had already been dated. We therefore started by asking about events that we had found in pilot work to present the least difficulty in dating (e.g., change of job, change of residence, and a major change in a relationship). Dates for these events then provided anchoring points for questioning about other events and about difficulties.

The LEDS provides questions to elicit further information about events and difficulties once obtained, and an effort was made to use additional probes that had proved useful in pilot interviews. To take some examples, any comment about the self in terms of possible shortcomings (e.g., "I realized I wasn't a brilliant designer") was explored, especially in terms of coping, as this might reflect a difficulty that in turn might relate to the occurrence of an event. Second, a report of an important change in life plan (e.g., change of career) led to questions about dissatisfaction, such as "Was there any particular reason for the change?" Again, the idea was that some kind of difficulty might be revealed. Third, once a problem was mentioned, the person was asked whether anything else like that had happened. Fourth, there were suggested probes for asking about the antecedents of events (e.g., "What led you to make the decision?" "What was it about the situation you didn't like?" "How long had it been going on?").

Study Groups

Four groups of subjects were interviewed. The first two were populations of civil servants selected at random and already part of a much larger ongoing inquiry into heart disease conducted by the London School of Hygiene and Tropical Medicine and the Civil Service Medical Advisory Service.

1. *One-year civil servants*. The first group of 100 civil servants was selected from this much larger random series. We took the opportunity of doing this with a sample of men and women who were attending medical examinations as part of the larger enquiry. Only events and difficulties for the 1 year before interview were asked about.

2. *Ten-year civil servants*. A second series of 49 male civil servants was seen at home in the evenings and questioned about a 10-year period before interview.

3. *Patients*. For the patient sample, two hospitals were used. A total of 75 men were selected who had recently been admitted with a diagnosed MI, but 18 were excluded for reasons such as death or moving out of the area after discharge. A further 14 could not be contacted. Of the remaining 43, 36 were interviewed and 7 refused (16%). Of those seen, 28 had had their first MI in the year before interview, 4 their second, 1 his third, and 1 his sixth.

4. *General-population sample*. A comparison series was obtained by the use of the records kept by general practitioners serving the same area as the patients. A total of 146 men aged 35-60 were selected randomly. Of these, 38 were excluded for reasons such as age and moving from the district, and a further 17 could not be contacted. Of the remaining 91, 67 were interviewed and 24 refused (26%). The comparison group was only selected in terms of age. Matching for other demographic factors was deliberately avoided, since we feared that it might prevent the emergence of crucial explanatory variables. However, a comparison of the two groups showed no significant differences in their composition as far as social class, number of children, current marital status, and race (and, of course, age) were concerned. There were significant differences in terms of educational level and previous divorce, which can be regarded less as evidence of mismatching than as vulnerability factors for MI, since a number of studies have cited upward mobility, status incongruity, and divorce as risk factors for coronary heart disease.

Results of the Methodological Study

Approaches to Validity

The methodological part of the present investigation was intended to establish how far back in time it was possible to date life events and difficulties reasonably accurately. Previous studies of the validity of retrospective reports collected by the LEDS had been restricted to a 12-month period. The quite different matter of the interrater reliability had already been shown to be satisfactory (see Chapter 2). In a further test of reliability, 50 events were rated by two members of the Bedford College team (half of the events had been rated by the original interviewer as carrying "moderate" threat in the long term, and the remainder as carrying "some" threat). When the three sets of ratings were compared, there was disagreement between any two of the three raters about only two events (4%), confirming the previous high levels of interrater reliability.

It is possible to test the validity of life event reports over a 10-year period in three ways. First, validity can be checked via supporting documentation (e.g., death certificates, rent books, letters from the local council, medical records, and hospital outpatient attendance cards). It is only possible to check a minority of events and difficulties in this way, but it is probably important to carry out such checks where possible, since low agreement is bound to reflect a poor instrument; high agreement, however, does not necessarily mean that the instrument is valid for the full range of events and difficulties. When this check has been used, as in the original research on life events and onset of a schizophrenic illness, results have proved highly encouraging (Brown & Birley, 1968).

Second, it is possible to compare the accounts of the subjects and of persons close to them. This is the most obvious approach and was used in the Camberwell research (see Chapter 1). However, it has been pointed out that such reports can be influenced by "family culture" and that there may be collusion in reporting (or not reporting) events (Platt, 1980). Nonetheless, agreement has been so impressive that it is difficult not to give a good deal of weight to such checks. However, two investigators are essential for this method, and we did not have the resources for this in the present study. It seemed in any case too much to ask two members of a family to participate in such an onerous undertaking of covering a 10-year period. Nonetheless, both of the first two approaches were used to a small degree in this study: We took account of any available documentation, and also of any help offered by someone other than the subject who happened to be present at an interview.

We relied on a third method for a systematic test of validity – that of checking "falloff" in terms of the length of time from the date of the reported event or difficulty to the point of interview. The approach assumes that in the general population, events and difficulties reported for the 1 year immediately before interview can be used as a standard for what would be expected to occur in other years, given no falloff in reporting. Earlier research concerning interrespondent agreement indicated that data collected in the year before interview are accurate enough to be used in this way. The validity of reports about earlier years can then be judged by the amount of falloff in the reporting. This approach assumes that for a general-population sample, there is no special reason to experience events or difficulties at one particular point in time more than at any other. This assumption is, of course, not always warranted. It is possible, for example, with a sample of hospital patients that events may tend to cluster in the period immediately before attendance, because this is linked to the experience of a stressor. Because of the possibility, we dealt only with a nonpatient series.

Both the Bedford College team, and more recently one in Edinburgh (Surtees *et al.*, 1986), have used the falloff approach for events covering 1 year (see Chapter 1), and results concerning the falloff of events for the first series of 100 male and female civil servants confirmed the earlier findings. As before, there was *no* falloff over the 12 months in the reporting of severe events. Surprisingly, in the series of civil servants this also held for nonsevere events. (There was a falloff of only 4% in terms of a comparison of the two extreme 20-week periods. This compares with one of about one-third for nonsevere events in the original Camberwell inquiry; see Brown & Harris, 1982.) Of course, the challenge for the present inquiry was to consider the reporting of events and difficulties for the whole decade.

Falloff in 10-Year Period

When the rate of events and difficulties throughout a 10-year period for a second series of civil servants (who were all male) was considered, there was, as would be expected, a falloff in the reporting of events (see Figure 12.1). However, the falloff was only 2.9% per year. Surprisingly, as with the 1-year results, there was no greater falloff for nonsevere events than for severe ones. (Average yearly falloff was calculated by subtracting the rate in year 10, furthest from interview, from that in year 1, nearest to interview; dividing this by the rate in year 1; and dividing this by 9.)

Unfortunately, only after these results were obtained did we realize that these impressive figures might be due to the fact that civil servants are unusually effective in reporting incidents in their lives. This had to be taken seriously, especially as only 61% of the civil servants cooperated, and these individuals might therefore have been particularly motivated to take part in the research. (It should be added, however, that no pressure was put on them to cooperate, as they had been repeatedly contacted to take part in a broader medical inquiry.) It was therefore essential to repeat the exercise with men selected at random from the general population.

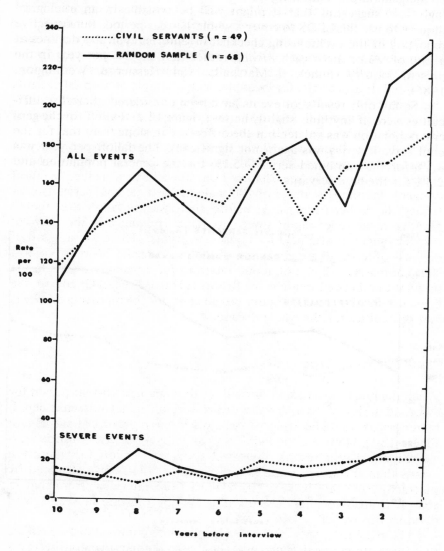

FIGURE 12.1. Rate of events in ten 1-year periods before interview.

For such men, there was a somewhat greater degree of falloff in the reporting of events, but the rate was still only 5.8% per year, compared with 2.9% per year among the civil servants (see Figure 12.1) – a nonsignificant difference. Once again, there was no significant difference between severe and nonsevere events (6.4% and 5.7%, respectively). Falloff per year for the total series was 4.8% for all events. Whether this or the general-population figure of 5.8% was taken, falloff was surprisingly low, suggesting that it might well be possible in an etiological inquiry to use the LEDS to cover a whole 10-year period. Retrospective reporting of life events using checklist inventories typically declines at a rate of 5% or more each *month*, rather that the 5% per year in the present inquiry (Funch & Marshall, 1984; Kessler & Wethington, 1986).

So far, only results for events have been considered. those for difficulties were, if anything, slightly better (Figure 12.2). Falloff for the general population was greater, but the difference in slope from that for the civil servant series was again not significant. The falloff per year was 4.1% for the combined series – 5.1% for the general population and 2.4% for the civil servants.

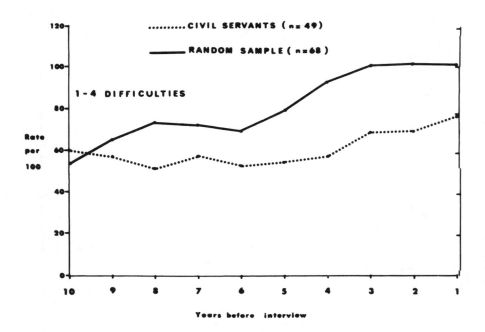

FIGURE 12.2. Rate of difficulties in ten 1-year periods before interview.

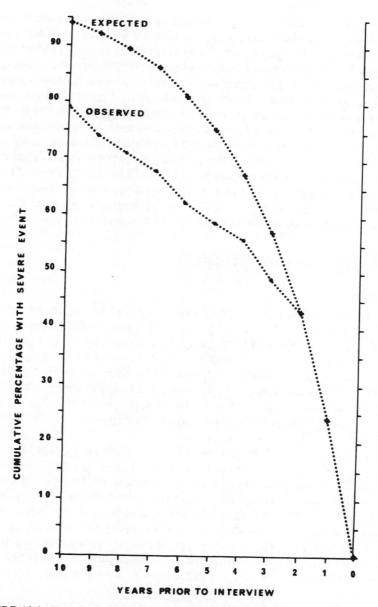

FIGURE 12.3. The observed and expected cumulative percentage of men experiencing one or more severe events in the ten 1-year periods preceding interview.

The falloff results have been considered thus far in terms of *rates* of occurrence. An alternative is to ask whether or not a particular type of event or difficulty has occurred to a person in a given period of time. This, as seen in earlier chapters, has been the usual way of examining the etiological role of provoking agents, and results using this approach were equally impressive. As an illustration, in Figure 12.3, data for severe events in the general-population sample are given in the form of a graph plot of the men experiencing one or more severe events over time. Under the assumption that event exposure would occur randomly, the plot of the *expected* cumulative proportion of individuals experiencing one or more events is exponentially based (see Surtees *et al.*, 1986, p. 41, for details). While by the 3rd year there was a departure from the expected rate of reporting, the difference throughout the final 8 years was never more than about one-quarter of the expected rate.

Results of the Exploratory Etiological Study

Life Events

In the patient inquiry, 32 of the 34 men had had their first MI within the 10-year study period, and 28 within the year before interview. In addition, 5 of the 68 men in the general population had had an MI in the 10 years, for 4 of whom it was a first MI. When the 5 were combined with the 34 patients, there was a total of 39 men with MI. For the 5 with MI in the general population, unlike the hospital series, we had no independent confirmation of the date and nature of the illness from medical records. However, the findings to be reported were in no way changed if these 5 men were excluded.

The size of the MI groups used in the following analyses differed according to the particular issue being tackled. The "purest" group consisted of 28 whose first MI had occurred in the year before interview and for whom there was material on events and difficulties for approximately a 10-year period before MI. It was also possible to consider the 36 men with a first MI occurring at some point in the study period. These included the 28 men with a first MI in the year before interview and 8 men (4 patients and 4 from the general population) who had had their first MI some time in the 9 years before this. (The years for which we had material on events and difficulties before onset for the 8 were 9, 9, 8, 6, 4, 4, 2, and 1, respectively.) Finally, there were 39 men with some form of MI in the 10 years.

Although all events and difficulties revealed by the LEDS were recorded, in the presentation that follows, any that could have been the consequence of the MI or of its antecedents have been ignored – for example, a job change due to high blood pressure prior to the MI, and of course, any job change due to the heart condition itself.

TABLE 12.1. Cumulative percentages with at least one severe event before first MI or interview (for comparison series)

Subject group	Years before first MI/interview					
	6	5	4	3	2	1
First MI[a]	72 (23/32)	69 (22/32)	59 (20/34)	50 (17/34)	43 (15/35)	22 (8/36)
Comparison series	65 (41/63)	62 (39/63)	57 (37/63)	49 (31/63)	43 (27/63)	25 (16/63)

Note. n's for the percentages are in parentheses.
[a]Four with MI excluded because date of first onset not in 6-year period.

We first employed the kind of analysis that has proved so successful with depression (and a number of other physical conditions). Results proved to be largely negative: There was no hint that the experience of a severe event in a 12-month period was related to onset of first MI. Moreover, proportions with at least one severe event during periods ranging from 1 to 6 years before first MI also failed to show a difference (Table 12.1). (Allowance was made for the fact that the full 6-year period was covered for only 32 of the 36 with a first MI in the 10 years.)

However, these results concerned the proportion experiencing at least one severe event. When *number* of events in the 2-year period before first MI was taken into account, a modest association did emerge, although the difference did not reach statistical significance: 28% (10/36) versus 13% (8/63) experienced four or more events with at least "some" long-term threat in the 2 years. The inclusion of other types of events did not increase this difference.[1] The result is similar to one already noted in the large case-controlled study carried out in West Germany (Siegrist *et al.*, 1982), where 31% in the MI group versus 14% in the control series experienced three or more "critical events" in a 2-year period.

Another approach did prove more successful. In the light of the work on gastrointestinal disorder, all severe events were rated in terms of "goal frustration" (see Chapter 9). A clear difference emerged: 31% (11/36) of those with a first MI had a goal frustration event in the 2 years before onset, compared to 6% (4/63) of the comparison series (*p* < .01). Furthermore, the finding concerning four or more events with long-term threat disappeared once goal frustration events were taken into account. Consideration of the dimensions of loss and danger failed to improve on the result (see Chapter 3 for definitions of "loss" and "danger"). In the light of findings to be presented later, it is of interest that 6 of the 11 severe events involving goal frustration in the MI group had to do with work. One subject's business went into liquidation;

1. The best result for severe events was for three or more in the 2 years – 17% (6/35) versus 6% (4/63), a nonsignificant difference.

another lost £7,000 in a business venture; another subject's own taxi was involved in a serious accident for which he did not receive compensation; another was forced to leave a business he had set up and run well; another failed to get a particular job after 3 months searching for work abroad; and tenants asked a final subject to leave his job as porter. The remaining goal frustrations were as follows: One subject's house flooded after he had refurnished it ("my whole home went"); another subject's daughter called off at the last moment her wedding, in which the subject had invested quite substantially (both emotionally and financially); another heard that a girlfriend with whom he had still been trying to repair the relationship had got married; and another was forced to lose contact with one of his two sons after separating from his wife (who kept their house, on which he continued to make payments). It is of interest that goal frustration emerged as important in another study using the LEDS to investigate life events before MI (Connolly, 1976). Although the measure was not developed until after Connolly had published his initial report on events and onset of MI, the written protocols made it possible to rate his data on goal frustration. When this was done, the proportion with a high goal frustration event, even when only a 3-month period was taken, was substantially higher in the MI group – 12% (11/91) versus 1% (1/91) ($p < .01$). In the present series, the comparable figures for 3 months were 14% (5/36) versus 3% (2/63) ($p < .05$).

These results involving life events are clearly of some potential importance. However, in terms of the considerable associations found between life events and other physical conditions, such as gastrointestinal disorders and multiple sclerosis (Chapters 9 and 11), they are perhaps best seen as a hint that some kind of etiological effect arising from psychosocial sources may have been present.

Ongoing Difficulties

Although neither the *major* difficulties predictive of depression nor the goal frustration difficulties involved in gastrointestinal disorder discriminated between MI and comparison groups, findings concerning difficulties were on the whole more encouraging. Figure 12.4 shows the results of an initial exploratory analysis for the *total* MI group (i.e., taking the 10-year period before interview) in terms of the presence of at least one difficulty of moderate severity (levels 1 to 4) in any 1-year period. Difficulties, particularly those relating to health, that had been rated as "illness-related" were excluded (see Chapters 1 and 15 for a discussion of "independence"). For the MI group, the occurrence of at least one difficulty concerning either work, money, or housing was about three times greater than for the comparison series throughout the

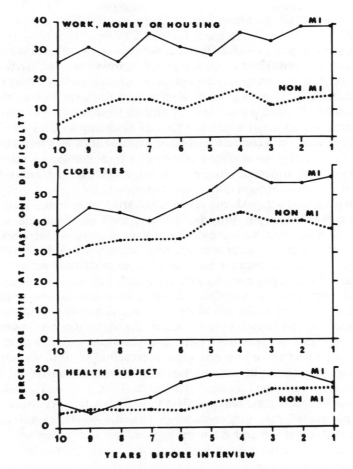

FIGURE 12.4. Proportion of MI subjects (*N*=39) and non-MI subjects (*N*=63) having at least one difficulty in any 1 year.

10-year period. Moreover, the effect appeared to be largely restricted to such difficulties. The proportion in the MI group with at least one difficulty concerning relatives and close friends, including those involving health, exceeded the comparison on average by only one-third during the final 6 years, and the rate of difficulties concerning the subjects' own health was even lower and not significantly different in the MI and comparison series. However, these initial results concerning difficulties ignored the possibility that difficulties occurring after MI could have in some way resulted from the MI. In subsequent analyses, it was essential to take the date of onset into account. (It will be seen that it made no difference to the results.)

Work Events and Difficulties

Since this initial analysis of difficulties suggested, as many other studies have done, that circumstances surrounding work may be particularly critical for MI, events and difficulties involving money and housing were reclassified as "work events" if they were linked with employment – for example, financial problems stemming from a layoff or problems over a lease for an artist who used part of his home as a studio. Three new indices were then created. The basic form of each was settled before any analysis of etiological effects, although a final decision on the exact cutoff point was sometimes made after the actual distribution of scores in the MI and comparison series was examined.

1. *Workload index.* All the men in the study were employed for at least part of the 10-year study period. For the "workload index," two simple measures were first created; both were found to be associated with MI. The more important concerned hours worked. Each year was taken into account separately and counted as positive if an average of more than 51 hours per week had been worked. For the second measure, the person had to have taken only 2 weeks or less vacation in the year (any period of time taken off work was included, whether or not the person actually left home to go on vacation). A person was counted as positive on either of these workload measures if he scored 5 or more in terms of a 10-year period (or the same proportion of time if there were fewer years to consider before onset of MI). Those with a first MI scored higher in terms of hours worked (13/36 vs. 6/63, $p < .001$), and lower in terms of vacation time taken (7/36 vs. 6/63, $p < .02$). As a simplification, a particular year was considered positive on workload if either measure was positive, and an overall workload index was considered positive if a man scored on at least half of the years considered before MI or interview.

2. *Work stress index.* The second index, the "work stress index," followed a similar procedure: A man was rated positive for any particular year if he had either a work difficulty (ratings of 1 to 4), or a work event involving at least "some" long-term threat (ratings of 1 to 3). Years containing a difficulty outnumbered those with an event by a ratio of 62:38. Again, to be positive on the work stress index, a subject had to score on one or the other measure for at least half the years in the period considered.

3. *Nonwork stress index.* Nonwork stress was common, and because of this a somewhat different approach was taken to the third index. Given the failure of the event material to relate in any clear way to onset, only difficulties were taken into account. To be included on the "nonwork stress index," a man had to have experienced the equivalent at least of a "high-moderate" difficulty (rating of 1-3) when scores for

TABLE 12.2. Relationship of three stress indices to onset of first MI

Index	Percentage positive on index		Odds ratio
	First MI	Non-MI	
Nonwork stress	36 (13/36)*	13 (8/63)	3.89
Workload – hours and vacation time (50% criterion)	47 (17/36)**	14 (9/63)	5.36
Work stress – events/difficulties (50% criterion)	31 (11/36)*	10 (6/63)	4.18
Combined work stress (70% criterion)	53 (19/36)**	14 (9/63)	6.70

Note. n's are in parentheses.
* p < .01.
** p < .001.

each year of the period considered were averaged.[2] In practice, everyone included had at least a high-moderate difficulty (1-3) in 7 of the 10 years, or a similar proportion calculated *pro rata*.

Each of the three indices was significantly related to the occurrence of first MI. Because those with MI were only partly derived from a random population series, an odds ratio rather than relative risk was used as a measure of association. For each of the three indices, the odds ratio was approximately 4.0 (first three rows of Table 12.2).

The occupational histories of the MI and comparison series also suggested a difference in work experience. When occupation at time of interview (or last occupation for the 10% who were unemployed), was taken, 44% (17/39) of the total MI series were self-employed (excluding the higher professional grade, covering occupations such as general practitioner and barrister) or belonged to a service occupation, compared with 16% (10/63) of the comparison series (p < .01).[3] When occupational history over the whole 10 years was taken, essentially the same

2. Difficulties were scored as follows: a difficulty rating of 1 = 4, a rating of 2 = 3, a rating of 3 = 2, and a rating of 4 = 1. An average score of 2 was taken as positive. A person with the following pattern of scores would be considered positive: 3, 2, 3, 1, 0, 2, 2, 3, 3, 1 = 20; 20 ÷ 10 = 2.

3. The Hope-Goldthorpe classification of occupations was used (Goldthorpe & Hope, 1974). For the MI and comparison series, the numbers in the relevant service grades were as follows: "large proprietors" (e.g., working owners of large shops), 0 and 0, respectively; "self-employed professionals, lower grade" (e.g., artists), 3 and 2; "small proprietors" (e.g., working owners of small shops), 6 and 4; "self-employed, higher grade" (e.g., shopkeepers), 1 and 2; "service, higher grade" (e.g., cooks, hairdressers), 0 and 1; "service, intermediate grade" (e.g., shop salesmen), 1 and 0; "self-employed, intermediate grade" (e.g., taxi-drivers), 2 and 0; "service, lower grade" (e.g., caretakers, bartenders), 4 and 1.

result emerged. There was a tendency for the self-employed and service occupations to be more often high on the workload index (based on hours worked and vacation time), but this only reached statistical significance when the two series were combined – 45% (11/24) versus 20% (15/75) ($p < .02$). (For the MI and non-MI groups, the results were 9/14 vs. 8/22 and 2/10 vs. 7/53, respectively.)

However, there was a certain amount of overlap between the two work measures, as at times the LEDS rating of difficulties took into account long working hours. A "combined work stress index" was therefore formed, in which a person had to be positive on *either* of the two measures for at least 7 of the 10 yearly periods (or a comparable 70% proportion for those with less than 10 years before first MI). The odds ratio for this new combined index was 6.70 (Table 12.2, row 4).

Overall Stress

Before we proceed, it may be useful at this point to summarize the four stress indices:

1. *Workload index.* Positive in at least 50% of the years in terms of either an average of 51 hours or more per week worked in any year, or 2 weeks or less vacation time in a year.
2. *Work stress index.* Positive in at least 50% of the years in terms of presence of a work difficulty or event.
3. *Combined work stress index.* Positive on one of the first two indices in at least 70% of the years.
4. *Nonwork stress index.* Average of a high-moderate difficulty through total period. (In practice, this resulted in a high-moderate difficulty in at least 70% of years.)

Table 12.3 deals with the combined effect of the last two indices. It shows that when the work and the nonwork stress indices occurred separately, the odds ratios for MI were 4.00 and 1.89, respectively; when they occurred together, the risk approximately doubled (to 7.36) when compared with combined work stress alone. Logistic regression confirmed that both work and nonwork stress were required to predict MI, but clearly the contribution of work stress was the more important.

Finally, it was possible to consider an "overall stress index," taking as positive a person scoring on either the combined work stress index or the nonwork stress index for at least 70% of the years considered. The last row of Table 12.3 shows that 69.4% of those with first MI and 23.8% of the comparison series were positive on one or the other of the component indices of the overall index ($p < .001$), giving an odds ratio

TABLE 12.3. Relationship of various combinations of work and nonwork stress indices to onset of first MI

| | Percentage positive on index | | |
| | | Comparison | Odds |
Index	First MI	series	ratio
None	30.8 (11/36)	76.2 (48/63)	
Combined work stress alone	33.3 (12/36)	11.1 (7/63)	4.00
Nonwork stress alone	16.7 (6/36)	9.5 (6/63)	1.89
Combined work stress and nonwork stress	19.4 (7/36)	3.2 (2/63)	7.36
Total stress index (either combined work stress *or* nonwork stress)	69.4 (25/36) **	23.8 (15/63)	7.27

Note. n's are in parentheses. A logistic regression was performed on the first three indices; its result were as follows:

| | | Reduction | |
Model fitted	Scaled deviance	in deviance	df
Constant	21.85		
(1) Combined work stress	14.58	7.27 *	1
(2) Nonwork stress	5.39	16.46 **	1
(3) 1 + 2	0.42	21.43 **	1

The best-fitting model was 3.
* $p < .01$.
** $p < .001$.

of 7.27 ($p < .001$). Since this was an exploratory study, various other ways of increasing the strength of the prediction were considered. But after reading through the descriptive material and carrying out additional analyses (particularly concerning nonwork events), we were left with the impression that the remaining men with MI were in no way unusual, at least in terms of the various LEDS-based measures of stress.

Given the possibility that the three basic stress measures reflect some etiological effect, there remains the question of length of exposure, bearing in mind that we were particularly concerned to extend measurement back in time for 10 years and explore possible long-term effects. The top half of Table 12.4 shows the proportions scoring on the overall stress index for continuous periods of time before onset of first MI or interview. (In order to avoid possible complications, only the 28 patients with an onset of MI in the year before interview were considered. This gave a period at risk of at least 9 years.) In straightforward statistical terms, leaving aside the question of MI, more people would be expected to qualify as positive when a shorter rather than a longer period was

TABLE 12.4. Percentages positive on overall stress index for various continuous periods from first MI/interview and for particular yearly periods

Time period	Percentage positive		Odds ratio
	From first MI	From interview (comparison series)	
	Length of continuous experience of stress		
10 years	64.3 (18/28) ***	23.8 (15/63)	5.76
8 years	50.0 (14/28) ***	23.8 (15/63)	3.20
6 years	57.1 (16/28) ***	30.2 (19/63)	3.08
4 years	57.1 (16/28) **	31.7 (20/63)	2.87
2 years	57.1 (16/28)	36.5 (23/63)	2.32
1 year	67.9 (19/28)	47.6 (30.63)	2.32
	Year in which stressor occurred		
9th year	71.4 (20/28) ***	38.1 (24/63)	4.06
7th year	64.3 (18/28) *	41.3 (26/63)	2.56
5th year	60.7 (17/28) *	36.5 (23/63)	2.68
3rd year	53.6 (15/28)	39.7 (25/63)	1.75
1st year	64.3 (18/28)	47.6 (30/63)	1.38

Note. n's are in parentheses.
* $p < .05.$
** $p < .02.$
*** $p < .01.$

considered, and this was confirmed. In the comparison series, almost half the men were positive on the index when 1 year was taken, but only a quarter if the 10 years were considered as a whole. However, for those with MI, there was a remarkable stability in the proportion positive, whatever length of time before onset was considered: 67.9% were positive in the year before onset, and as many as 64.3% when the whole 10-year period was considered. This was, of course, just what would be expected if length of exposure was important for onset of MI, and this was reflected in the odds ratios for the various periods. The odds ratio was 2.32 (statistically nonsignificant) for the year of interview and 5.76 for the 10-year period as a whole ($p < .01$). This steady increase in size of association with period at risk, combined with the fact that scores in the MI group for the most part were equally large at any point in the 10-year period, confirmed that length of exposure to stress was of etiological significance. One possible alternative explanation is that there was a falloff in reporting in the non-MI group, but not, for some reason, in the MI group. However, the bottom half of Table 12.4 indicates that for the overall stress index used in this exercise, there was little or no falloff in reporting. The bottom half of Table 12.4 also suggests that if the individual years had been taken as a basis of measurement, the same picture would have emerged as with the more complex index used in the top half of the table, but the result would not have emerged so clearly.

Given that the various stress indices revealed quite powerful effects, it was possible to reconsider the role of goal frustration events. Such events in the 2 years before onset of first MI were related to the stress indices.[4] The association was such that, once the two stress measures were taken into account, goal frustration added nothing to the prediction of MI. But this was an atheoretical formulation. If the goal frustration events were considered in the context of ongoing and related difficulties and events, a case could be made that they might be playing some sort of formative etiological role. In all, 8 of the 11 goal frustration events occurring before MI were associated with ongoing difficulties. In 3 cases, the goal frustration event began a difficulty: For example, a subject's home was badly damaged by burst pipes, and because of lack of insurance, replacement of furnishings and redecoration could only be done gradually. In 2 cases the event ended a difficulty: For instance, the liquidation of a subject's business after a long struggle ended a financial difficulty but represented an enormous failure and confirmed the man's worst fears about the outcome of the difficulty. In 3 other cases, the event was part of an ongoing difficulty. For instance, a subject's daughter called off her wedding at the last minute; while clearly goal-frustrating, this also had an element of confirming a long-term failure in that there had been many years of difficulty with this daughter, including her attendance at a child guidance clinic. Each phase of her childhood had been marked by rebellion and rejection combined with overdependence on her parents. This general picture suggests that a sense of frustration, confirmed and crystallized by an event that was closely linked to a long-term difficulty, may have played a significant role.

Personality Factors and Type A

Much of the stress literature on MI has in fact been dominated by the study of Type A behavior pattern, and we employed two questionnaire measures of such behavior. The first, the 10-item Framingham Type A questionnaire (Haynes, Feinleib, Levine, Scotch, & Kannel, 1978a, 1978b) was quite unrelated to MI. However, a second one composed of 14 bipolar items developed by Bortner (1969) did relate to MI, as an

---

4. Among those with a first MI, 92% (12/13) of those with goal frustration were positive on either work or nonwork stress, compared with 52% (13/23) without goal frustration (p = .06).

earlier study had also shown (Heller, 1979). Each of the 14 items on this measure is composed of two adjectives or phrases with a horizontal line connecting them. One description is considered to describe Type A behavior and the other not (e.g., "never late – casual about appointments"), and the subject marks a vertical line somewhere between the two. The length of the horizontal line used in this study was 50 millimeters, and a subject's score was calculated by measuring the distance of his vertical line in millimeters from the Type B end of the horizontal one. The maximum possible score was therefore 700 (14 × 50). A cutoff score of 425 was used and 34% (12/35, 1 not known) of the MI group and 11% (7/61, 2 not known) of the comparison series scored above the cutoff ($p < .01$). While these results were not particularly impressive, it did seem worthwhile to relate them to work stress using the workload index, as that seemed most relevant to the content of the Bortner questionnaire items. (In fact, associations did not emerge with the two other indices.)

Table 12.5 shows that the Bortner score only related to MI among those positive on the workload index. If the MI and general-population series were combined, the result could be expressed another way. Of the 19 men in the total series with a high Bortner score, 90% (9/10) had MI if they were positive on the workload index and only 30% (3/9) if they did not. Results for those without high Bortner scores were 50% (8/16) and 25% (15/61), respectively. While too much should not be made of this, for methodological reasons, it is still encouraging to see that the patterning of results did not depart from that predicted by a vulnerability model.

Another "psychological" measure used in this inquiry was the Present State Examination (Wing, Cooper, & Sartorius, 1974) with the Bedford College caseness criterion (see Chapter 3). The measure was elaborated so that subjects could be rated not only for the year before interview or MI, but also for details of previous episodes throughout the 10-year period (see Harris, Brown, & Bifulco, 1986). While there was an elevated rate of symptomatology in the MI group before interview, this was mainly at a borderline-case level and largely only *after*

TABLE 12.5. Percentages of high scorers on Bortner Type A scale by rating on workload index

	Percentage with Bortner score of 425 +	
Subject group	Positive on workload index	Not positive on workload index
MI	53 (9/17)	17 (3/18)
Non-MI	11 (1/9)	12 (6/52)

onset of MI (probably in reaction to the long-term threat of such an illness). When the 1 year before onset of MI was compared with the year before interview in the general-population series, the latter, if anything, showed *more*, not less, symptomatology than the patients: 5% (3/63) had case-level depression and 5% (3/63) had borderline-case-level depression in the general-population group, as compared with 3% (1/36) with case-level depression and 6% (2/36) with borderline-case-level depression among the MI group. The same lack of difference was found when the 10-year period was taken as a whole. Overall, the rates were lower than those reported in other chapters in this volume, and this may be attributable to the sex and social class distribution of the groups studied.

Physiological Factors: Smoking and Alcohol Consumption

As in other studies of heart disease, rates of both cigarette smoking and alcohol consumption were higher in the MI group than in the comparison group. Among MI patients, 44% had smoked a minimum of 40 or more cigarettes regularly, compared with 25% of the random sample ($p < .05$); in addition, 46% of patients, but only 25% of the comparison series, had an average weekly consumption of more than 14 units of alcohol ($p < .025$). There was no association between these measures of smoking and drinking and any of the stress indices described earlier, nor was there any connection with a score above 425 on the Bortner scale; thus there was no suggestion that these physiological factors could explain away the LEDS findings. Examination of the data for a potential vulnerability effect proved essentially negative, in contrast to the very similar procedure described in the preceding section and in Table 12.5. Whatever index of stress was used, smoking and alcohol consumption were associated with MI to the same extent in both stressed and unstressed groups. In other words, alcohol, smoking, and stress all appeared to be making independent etiological contributions.

Discussion

The results of the validity study concerning long-term recall were even better than we had hoped. The falloff of some 5% per year after the first year in the reporting of all types of events and difficulties was remarkably low, compared with other instruments, which we have seen typically show this rate of decline per *month*. The results certainly suggest that the kind of long-term retrospective inquiry tackled in the second "Results" section of this chapter is feasible. However, there is one possible shortcoming in the falloff inquiry that should be mentioned (but that, fortunately, would not affect the results of our exploratory etiological inquiry).

Research with women in Camberwell and in the Outer Hebrides has shown a considerable association between rate of events and life stage. Women were divided into three categories: (1) age between 18 and 35 without children at home; (2) any age between 18 and 65 with children at home; and (3) age between 36 and 65 without children at home. In London, there was a drop from 480 events per 100 in the first group to 210 per 100 in the third, with the intermediate group falling in between, but closer to the first group (390 per 100). Comparable differences in rates were obtained in the Outer Hebrides. However, the frequency of severe events was quite unrelated to life stage in either population (see Brown & Prudo, 1981). There is therefore a possibility that since our subjects grew older during the 10-year period, part of the reason for the low rate of falloff was that, for nonsevere events at least, a real falloff in reporting was compensated for by a higher rate of events in the years most distant from interview.

When we looked at our results, there was no relationship between age in the general-population sample and rate of severe events in the *year* before our interview, confirming the results of the two previous inquiries. But there was a hint of a relationship for nonsevere events: The rates were 250 per 100 for those aged 50-54 (40/16) and 170 per 100 for those aged 55-60 (44/26). Although the difference was nonsignificant, it seems safest to conclude until a larger series is available that our results concerning the falloff in reporting of nonsevere events may have been somewhat too favorable. However, both previous work and the present study suggest that such bias should not have influenced the reporting of severe events and, by implication, major difficulties.

The etiological inquiry itself was designed as small-scale, and it is always difficult in this type of research to strike the right balance between placing too much reliance upon the results and being unduly negative about their implications. One major finding is that, in contrast to studies of other disorders (both psychiatric and functional physical conditions), the occurrence of severely threatening events did not predict onset of MI. There were some interesting findings concerning the rate of goal frustration events in the 2 years before MI; leaving these aside, however, the most clear-cut findings emerged when emphasis was shifted to long-term difficulties, particularly concerning work. A combined work stress index, including working long hours, having little vacation time, and other types of stress at work, was particularly highly related to MI: 53% of those with a first MI scored on this index, as opposed to 13% of the comparison series (see Table 12.2). However, a measure of nonwork stress was related to onset as well, and when a total stress index was used, 69.4% in the MI group and 23.8% in the comparison series were positive, giving an odds ratio of 7.27. It is important to note that these results were based on taking as long a period as possible before MI. For most, this was the full 10 years of our inquiry. However, most etiological inquiries have taken far shorter periods. House, Stretcher, Metzner, and Robbins (1986) have recently commented in a study of heart disease on the importance of considering the *stability* of job stress; they point out, "Persons who experience *persistently* elevated stress levels at two or more points in time should be at a significantly increased risk of mortality or serious morbidity, while persons who are high only at a single point but low at other times would have a much lower risk, perhaps not much different from people who experience persistently low levels of stress" (p. 71; emphasis House *et al.*'s). This is an obvious point, but to our knowledge this theme has not been developed in the area of heart disease, although the need for such an approach has been clear for some time (e.g., Fischer *et al.*, 1964).

House *et al.* (1986), in fact, compared stress at two points of time some 10 years apart, and this did enable them to predict mortality rates more effectively. Of course, studying only two points in time is likely to be inadequate, as is a simple self-report measure, but the result does point in the right direction and gives some credence to the key findings in the present inquiry concerning the need to study ongoing stress over an extended period. Table 12.4 illustrates how the differences between the cases and comparison series increased with the length of time that the stress had been experienced: On the overall stress index, the proportions scoring positively after 1 year were 67.9% of cases versus 47.6% in the comparison series, and the percentages rated positively for the 10 years as a whole were 64.3% and 23.8%, respectively. However, although in some ways this inquiry has broken new ground, there is nothing original about the basic finding. The impact of ongoing demands, particularly at work, and of the resulting arousal have been important themes in research on heart disease for several decades. The contribution of this inquiry is to place such work in the context of life events research and to suggest that the impact of such stress may be greater than many have imagined. However, there can be no doubt that coronary heart disease is the outcome of a complex interaction of many variables in which no single variable is likely to predominate (Hinkle, 1967). We are very much aware that we have neglected to take account of factors (e.g., social support) that may ameliorate the processes involved in heavy, ongoing environmental demands (e.g., Marmot & Syme, 1976).

At this point we should perhaps face the possible criticism that the interviewer was not blind to whether a person had suffered MI. This obviously remains a possible source of bias, but it was impossible to meet this criticism with the resources we could employ. We can only reiterate the point made in Chapter 1 that so far there has been no hint that the LEDS is seriously subject to this kind of bias. Where it has been possible to check – for example, in Creed's study of appendectomy patients (see Chapter 8), where the interviewer was blind to diagnoses (functional vs. nonfunctional) and the raters were blind to whether subjects were patients or from the general population – large differences still emerged. Moreover, bias would also have to extend to the finding that a particular set of stressors (particularly concerning work) was important. It also would not explain findings such as those concerning service occupations and self-employment, which presumably were not subject to such bias. However, this possibility cannot be entirely ruled out.

We believe that the result concerning the role of stress over the 10-year period as a whole is perhaps the most significant to emerge from the study, but some others, while more speculative, are perhaps worth pursuing. The link between Type A behavior and various types of stress is an example. The Bortner Type A score of 425 or more only related to MI among those positive on the workload index. When the cases and comparison series were combined, most of those with a high Bortner score had had an MI if they were positive on the workload index, and only about a third had had an MI if they were not. (The proportions with MI among those with low Bortner scores were 50% and 25%, respectively.) These results suggest that, by itself, the Bortner scale may be failing to pick up some crucial component of Type A behavior that is relevant to the development of coronary heart disease. There is a hint in our findings that it is only when the behavior pattern is fully developed and acted out in an extreme form through working long hours, taking little vacation time, and experiencing other types of stressful work and nonwork difficulties that it leads to MI.

Another possible line for future inquiry is that of goal frustration events. In these results there is a strong intuitive link with Type A: The essence of a goal frustration event is confirmation of a failure to control the outcome of a situation – an experience that is likely to provoke anger. Work based on the original, more subtle, interview-based measure of Type A personality (Rosenman & Friedman, 1961, 1974; Friedman & Rosenman, 1959) suggests that those who easily become irascible (Type A_1) are more likely than other Type A subjects to suffer coronary heart disease (Matthews, Glass, Rosenman, & Bortner, 1977). The work is impressive because the measure deliberately tests the subjects' behavior in a provocative situation, instead of merely asking them to check a list of descriptions of their behavior and feelings. Even more recently, this notion of irascibility has been further refined by work on "hot reactors" – subjects whose impatience seems to derive from some basic property of their autonomic nervous system. A measure of "hot reactivity," in fact, showed an impressive improvement in predicting coronary heart disease over other measures of personality, including the Type A_1 measure (Dembrowski, MacDougall, & Shields, 1977; MacDougall, Dembrowski, & Musante, 1979). However, differences between Type B and Type A individuals should not be totally ignored in the light of this new formulation. More of the MI onsets in our series were associated with the work stress indices than with goal frustration events, and a man with a Type A_2 personality is perhaps more likely than a Type B to remain in a difficult work situation over a long period. An example in the present series was the man whose business suffered considerable losses; to make up for them by saving on salaries, he started doing the jobs of those who left. He worked incredibly long hours, he made himself exhausted and ill, and the business collapsed anyway. However, the goal frustration events and their associated difficulties remind us that it is unlikely that a matter can be reduced to personality factors alone. Some of the events have an air of bad luck about them.

The result concerning goal frustration was much the clearest finding to emerge concerning life events as such, and is of particular interest, given its parallels with the role of such events in gastrointestinal disorders with an organic basis (see Chapter 9). However, a higher rate of such events only emerged clearly in the 2 years before onset, and then only in about a third of those with MI; the resulting numbers were too small for us to pursue a more complex analysis. What is interesting, however, is the link between the cognitive-emotional quality of these events and that of those highlighted by the work stress index – a quality of relentless drive and effort, which finds a parallel in the emotional quality of the Type A personality and "hot reactivity." Chesney and Rosenman (1983), in reviewing the biological basis of Type A behavior, point to "the importance of individual *perception* of the challenge inherent in a given situation in determining his or her physiological response to a situation" (p. 30). What is probably involved is a combination of the MI men reacting in a certain way to such events and to some extent creating the events themselves. This exploratory study therefore provides ample evidence that the further investigation of recent life events and MI is likely to be profitable, but that for fundamental insights it is essential for stress over a period of at least 10 years to be studied. Finally, the conclusions of earlier research concerning the particular importance of the work context, at least for men, have been amply confirmed.

Acknowledgments

This research was done with the support of the Economic and Social Research Council. We are very grateful for the help of Dr. E. M. Jepson of the Central Middlesex Hospital and Dr. E. Besterman and Dr. P. Kidner of St. Mary's Hospital, Paddington, concerning the coronary patient series, and for the help of three groups of general practitioners: Drs. J. A. Walker, R. J .S. Milton, R. Lancer, and J. E. F. Anderman; Drs. M. R. Salkind, P. A. C. Julian, G. J. Tobias, and N. C. Hutt; and Drs. G. E. P. Wright, F. Carter, and S. Allan concerning the general-population series.

References

Bortner, R. W. (1969). A short rating scale as a potential measure of pattern behavior. *Journal of Chronic Diseases, 22*, 87-91.

Brown, G. W., & Birley, J. L. T. (1968). Crises and life changes and the onset of schizophrenia. *Journal of Health and Social Behavior, 9*, 203-214.

Brown, G. W., & Harris, T. O. (1982). Fall-off in the reporting of life events. *Social Psychiatry, 17*, 23-28.

Brown, G. W., & Prudo, R. (1981). Psychiatric disorder in a rural and an urban population: 1. Aetiology of depression. *Psychological Medicine, 11*, 581-599.

Chesney, M. A., & Rosenman, R. H. (1983). Specificity in stress models: Examples drawn from Type A behavior. In C. L. Cooper (Ed.), *Stress research* (pp. 21-34). New York: Wiley.

Connolly, J. (1976). Life events before myocardial infarction. *Journal of Human Stress, 3*, 3-17.

Dembrowski, T. M., MacDougall, J. M., & Shields, J. L. (1977). Physiologic reactions to social challenge in persons evidencing the Type A coronary-prone behavior pattern. *Journal of Human Stress, 3*, 2-10.

Fischer, H. K., Dlin, B. M., Winters, W. L., Jr., Hagner, S. B., Russell, G. W., & Weiss, E. (1964). Emotional factors in coronary occlusion: II. Time patterns and factors related to onset. *Psychosomatics, 5*, 280-291.

Friedman, M., & Rosenman, R. H. (1959). Association of specific overt behavior pattern with blood and cardiovascular findings. *Journal of the American Medical Association, 169*, 1280-1296.

Friedman, M., Rosenman, R. H., & Carroll, V. (1958). Changes in the serum cholesterol and blood-clotting time in men subjected to cyclic variation of occupational stress. *Circulation, 17*, 852-861.

Funch, D. P., & Marshall, J. R. (1984). Measuring life events: Factors affecting fall-off in the reporting of life events. *Journal of Health and Social Behavior, 25*, 453-464.

Glass, D. C. (1977). *Behavior pattern, stress, and coronary heart diseases.* Hillsdale, NJ: Erlbaum.

Goldthorpe, J. H., & Hope, K. (1974). *The social grading of occupations. A new approach and scale.* London: Oxford University Press.

Haney, C. A. (1980). Life events as precursors of coronary heart disease. *Social Science and Medicine, 14*, 119-126.

Harris, T. O., Brown, G. W., & Bifulco, A. (1986). Loss of parent in childhood and adult psychiatric disorder: The role of lack of adequate parental care. *Psychological Medicine, 16*, 641-659.

Haynes, S. G., Feinlieb, M., Levine, S., Scotch, N., & Kannel, W. B. (1978a). The relationship of psychosocial factors to coronary heart disease in the Framingham Study: I. Methods and risk factors. *American Journal of Epidemiology, 107*, 362-381.

Haynes, S. G., Feinlieb, M., Levine, S., Scotch, N., & Kannel, W. B. (1978b). The relationship of psychosocial factors to coronary heart disease in the Framingham Study: II. Prevalence of coronary heart disease. *American Journal of Epidemiology, 107,* 384-402.

Heller, R. S. (1979). Type A behavior and coronary heart disease. *British Medical Journal, ii,* 368.

Hinkle, L., Jr. (1967). Some social and biological correlates of coronary heart disease. *Social Science and Medicine, 1,* 129-139.

Holmes, T. H., & Rahe, R. H. (1967). The Social Readjustment Rating Scale. *Journal of Psychosomatic Research, 11,* 213-218.

House, J. S., Stretcher, V., Metzner, H. L., & Robbins, C. A. (1986). Occupational stress and health among men and women in the Tecumseh Community Health Study. *Journal of Health and Social Behavior, 27,* 62-77.

Johnson, J. V. (1986). *The impact of workplace social support, job demands and work control upon cardiovascular disease in Sweden* (Report No. 1). Stockholm: Department of Psychology, University of Stockholm.

Jenkins, C. D. (1967). Appraisal and implications for theoretical development. *Milbank Memorial Fund Quarterly, 65,* 141-152.

Kessler, R. C., & Wethington, E. (1986). *Some strategies for improving recall of life events in a general population survey.* Unpublished manuscript.

Kringlen, E. (1981). Stress and coronary heart disease. In *Twin research: Vol. 3. Epidemiological and clinical studies* (pp. 131-138) New York: Alan R. Liss.

Liljefors, I., & Rahe, R. H. (1970). An identical twin study of psychosocial factors in coronary heart disease in Sweden. *Psychosomatic medicine, 32,* 523-524.

Lundberg, U., Theorell, T., & Lind, E. (1975). Life changes and myocardial infarction: Individual differences in life change scaling. *Journal of Psychosomatic Research, 19,* 27-32.

MacDougall, J. M., Dembrowski, T. M., & Musante, L. (1979). The structured interview and questionnaire methods of assessing coronary prone behavior in male and female college students. *Journal of Behavioral Medicine, 1,* 71-83.

Marmot, M. G., & Syme, S. L. (1976). Acculturation and coronary heart disease in Japanese-Americans. *American Journal of Epidemiology, 104,* 225-247.

Mathschinger, H., Siegrist, J., Siegrist, K., & Dittman, K. H. (1986). Type A as a coping career: Towards a conceptual and methodological re-definition. In T. M. Dembrowski & T. Schmidt (Eds.), *Biological and psychological cardiovascular disease* (pp. 104-126). Heidelberg: Springer.

Matthews, K. A., Glass, D. C., Rosenman, R. H., & Bortner, R. W. (1977). Competitive drive, pattern A and coronary heart disease: A further analysis of some data from the Western Collaborative Study. *Journal of Chronic Diseases, 30,* 489-498.

Parkes, C. M., Benjamin, B., & Fitzgerald, R. G. (1969). Broken heart: A statistical study of increased mortality among widowers. *British Medical Journal, i,* 740-743.

Platt, S. (1980). On establishing the validity of "objective" data: Can we rely on cross-interview agreement? *Psychological Medicine, 10,* 573-581.

Rahe, R. H., & Arthur, R. J. (1967). Stressful underwater demolition team training: Serum urate and cholesterol variability. *Journal of the American Medical Association, 202,* 1052-1061.

Rosenman, R. H., & Friedman, M. (1974). Neurogenic factors in pathogenesis of coronary heart disease. *Medical Clinics of North America, 58,* 268-279.

Russek, H. I. (1965). Stress, tobacco and coronary heart disease in North American professional groups. *Journal of the American Medical Association, 192,* 189-194.

Russek, H. I., & Russek, L. G. (1976). Is emotional stress an etiologic factor in coronary heart disease? *Psychosomatics, 17,* 63-67.

Russek, H. I. & Zohman, B. (1958). Relative significance of hereditary, diet and occupational stress in CHD in young adults. *American Journal of Medical Science, 235*, 266-275.

Siegrist, J. (1985, December). *Social distress and cardiovascular risk: A dynamic approach to social epidemiology.* Paper presented at the seminar on Social Etiology of Disease, Centre National de Recherche Scientifique, Paris.

Siegrist, J., Dittman, K. H., Rittner, K., & Weber, I. (1982). The social context of active distress in patients with early myocardial infarction. *Social Science and Medicine, 16*, 443-454.

Surtees, P. G., Miller, P. M., Ingham, J. G. Kreitmann, N. B., Rennie, D., & Sashidharan, S. P. (1986). Life events and the onset of affective disorder: A longitudinal general population study. *Journal of Affective Disorders, 10*, 37-50.

Syme, S. L., & Reader, L. G. (Eds.). (1967). Social stress and cardiovascular disease [Special issue]. *Milbank Memorial Fund Quarterly, 65*, 9-185.

Theorell, T., & Floderus-Myrhed, B. (1977). Workload and risk of myocardial infarction: A prospective psycholosocial analysis. *International Journal of Epidemiology, 9*, 17-21.

Theorell, T., Lind, E., & Folderus, B. (1975). The relationship of disturbing life changes and emotions to the early development of myocardial infarction and some other serious illnesses. *International Journal of Epidemiology, 4*, 281-293.

Theorell, T., & Rahe, R. H. (1972). Behavior and life satisfaction characteristics of Swedish subjects with myocardial infarction. *Journal of Chronic Disease, 25*, 139-147.

Wing, J. K., Cooper, J. E., & Sartorius, N. (1974). *The measurement and classification of psychiatric symptoms: An instruction manual for the Present State Examination and CATEGO programme.* London: Cambridge University Press.

13

Functional Dysphonia

HARRY ANDREWS AND ALLAN HOUSE

"Functional dysphonia" is usually defined as a difficulty in voice production that cannot be explained by any demonstrable structural lesion of the larynx or by any neurological lesion. It is conventionally separated from disorders of articulation such as dysarthria or stammering, even though those conditions may themselves be psychologically based (Rousey, 1957), but otherwise it covers a wide range of disorders of quality, pitch, volume, or consistency of the voice. Complete disappearance of the voice is called "aphonia" when articulatory movements are attempted and is thereby distinguished from "mutism," which is the disappearance of voice without articulatory movement. The clinical diagnosis is usually made on the basis of an obvious voice disorder coupled with certain more or less characteristic findings on examination of the larynx. Although not essential to the diagnosis, it is common to include observations on associated psychopathology and occasionally to note associated neurological findings.

In this chapter, we describe a study we undertook recently into the life events and difficulties that precede the onset of functional dysphonia. During the course of our interviews, we formed the opinion that there was some aspect of patients' experiences immediately preceding onset that could not readily be described in terms of the available dimensions of stress, such as threat, loss, and goal frustration. Initially we attempted to use the Life Events and Difficulties Schedule (LEDS) dimension of challenge (see Chapter 10) to characterize these experiences, but we did not find this satisfactory and moved on to develop our own measure.

Harry Andrews. Department of Clinical Neurophysiology, The Maudsley Hospital, Denmark Hill, London SE5 8AZ, England.

Allan House. Medical Research Council Project, Department of Neurology, Radcliffe Infirmary, Woodstock Road, Oxford OX2 6HE, England.

Clinical Presentation and Etiology

In peacetime, functional dysphonia is predominantly a disorder of women (Brodnitz, 1969; Aronson, 1973), but when men are placed in stressful circumstances they are by no means immune (Smurthwaite, 1919; Sokolowsky & Junkerman, 1944). Although the average age of a group of functional dysphonics is reported as being the mid-40s, cases have been reported in patients of all ages (Brodnitz, 1971, cited in Aronson, 1973) and even in children (Giacalone, 1981). Brodnitz considered that about half his cases of voice disorder were functional, whereas a British dysphonia clinic reported 30 out of 97 cases to be functional or to have a large functional element when malignant causes were excluded (Simpson, 1971). In another series of consecutive referrals to an ear, nose, and throat (ENT) clinic, 48% of voice disorders received a diagnosis of functional dysphonia (Morrison, Nichol, & Rammage, 1986).

Speculations as to the cause of functional dysphonia come from a variety of sources and are all unsatisfactory. Conversion hysteria (Aronson, Peterson, & Litin, 1966), muscle dysfunction (Aronson, Brown, Litin, & Pearson, 1968a, 1968b; Aminoff, Dedo, & Izdebski, 1978), and psychosomatic disorder (Bloch, 1965; Brodnitz, 1976) have all been proposed. Freud (1905/1953) wrote the case history of "Dora," who suffered from intermittent aphonia and other complaints over a number of years. Her symptoms were presented in terms of infantile sexuality and repression. Other psychoanalytic writers have taken up those themes (Perepel, 1930; Barton, 1960). Psychological stress immediately before onset of dysphonia was often described by earlier writers (Ingals, 1890; Janet, 1920; Smurthwaite, 1919).

There are therefore shortcomings in the current understanding of the condition. First, there is no indication of how important psychosocial factors are in its etiology. Second, the importance of the individual's recent experience when compared with pre-existing psychological factors is unknown. Third, given that recent experience plays some etiological role, it is not known whether there are aspects of it that are specific to the condition or whether the condition is one of a range of abnormal responses to stress of a nonspecific kind. In order to explore the role of psychosocial factors in etiology, we interviewed all women referred to a speech therapy department with a diagnosis of functional dysphonia.

We present our finding in the following order. First, the patient series is described and a preliminary set of LEDS results is given. Second, the elaboration of a new LEDS dimension, "conflict over speaking out" (CSO), is described. Third, findings concerning CSO and the LEDS contextual measures are reported and analyzed.

The Patient Series

Between January 1984 and September 1985, we undertook a study with the Speech Therapy Department at the University Hospital, Nottingham, England, and a consultant ENT surgeon at that hospital. During that time the surgeon saw 257 referrals for the assessment of dysphonia, of whom 121 (47%) were diagnosed as having functional dysphonia. Following examination, all patients were offered speech therapy, and a total of 71 (58%) consecutive adult patients who accepted that offer and attended for their speech therapy assessment were interviewed by us.

Laryngoscopy revealed minor nodular change or edema in 18 and normal cords in 53. There was no instance of complete failure of cord movement on attempted phonation, nor was there any case of complete voice loss (aphonia). During the course of the study, 39 of the patients were re-examined by indirect laryngoscopy, but no instances of missed laryngeal pathology were discovered.

Of the 70 patients, 65 had voices that sounded husky or hoarse at the time of initial speech therapy interview. Of these 65, 10 had in addition episodic whispering speech, and 2 had episodic spasmodic or staccato speech. Only 4 had pure whispering dysphonia, and only 2 had pure spasmodic dysphonia. In addition to these features of speech, 23 also either had pitch that was higher or lower than usual or showed a tendency to unheralded pitch breaks.

During our initial assessment, we obtained information on the onset and course of voice disorder, as well as general information on age, social class, employment status, family and household structure, and social activities. The patients were also interviewed using the Present State Examination; a past psychiatric history was obtained; and they were then interviewed using the LEDS.

Mean age of the subjects was 47.6 years (range 17-81 years) at the time of interview and 43.7 years at the time of the first-ever episode of voice disorder. Because the rarity of functional dysphonia in men suggests that it may be a somewhat different condition, we present only results for the women. Of the original 70 referrals, 60 were women. Four were unable to date the onset of dysphonia with sufficient accuracy; we therefore confined our study to 56 women. If the episode of dysphonia was not the first, onset was dated from the start of the episode leading to referral, provided that at least a year of normal voice had preceded the onset.

The Role of Severe Events and Major Difficulties

An analysis along the lines found to be relevant for depressive conditions suggested the possible presence of a small etiological effect involving the 4-week period before onset. Of the 56 women, 8 experienced an event with severe long-term threat in this period, compared with an average of 2.3 in the six preceding 8-week periods. However, examination of major difficulties did not appear to add to the prediction of dysphonia: 11% (6/56) had a major difficulty (i.e., rated 1-3 on threat, non-health-related, and lasting at least 2 years) at the time of onset, and in all, 21% (12/56) had a severe event or a major difficulty in the 4 weeks before onset. Of the original series of Camberwell women without an onset of depression, 19% (72/382) had such an event or difficulty.

Conflict over Speaking Out

At this point, rather than pursue the analysis any further along traditional lines, we decided to explore the insights we had gained in the interviews themselves, which had suggested that a number of women had experienced unusual situations of a kind not so far described by the LEDS. They appeared to have in common a situation about which many might want to protest or complain, or to intervene verbally in some way; in other words, there was a *challenge* to speak out. But these situations also seemed to be characterized by difficulties that would arise from such forthrightness. That is, there was a *conflict* in the sense that what might be said would probably worsen the situation in which the subject was enmeshed. There was both a challenge to speak out and constraint against doing so, and we therefore called the new dimension "conflict over speaking out" (CSO).

In many situations, people are constrained by a sense of what is acceptable social behavior not to say all that might be said. It is unusual to express openly ambivalent feelings about the physical care of an ailing relative or about the behavior of somebody in authority. The following example illustrates the threshold between one situation given a rating of CSO and another that was not so rated, although it merited consideration. Some of the interpretations were based on the respondent's report of her feelings, but most were in the final analysis contextual, in the sense of a judgment about what it would be reasonable for most people to feel in the situation. The ratings differed from other contextual ratings only in the sense that we did not attempt any rigid distinction between self-report and contextual rating. However, in every instance, self-report was only given weight if it seemed justified in a wider contextual sense.

Case Example: Two Situations Examined for CSO

An unmarried woman in her early 20s presented for the first time with functional dysphonia. She had recently started living with a woman friend; she had left her own flat after a burglary, as she was fearful that it might be broken into again and was sufficiently unsettled to wish not to stay on her own. Soon afterward the friend, Beth, had started to behave in an unusual way – throwing tantrums, having fits of temper, and falling down as if in a faint, to the extent that the patient was apprehensive about leaving her on her own. This upsetting change in behavior was the challenge to speak out or protest. Medical advice had been contradictory. Although it was possible that Beth was simply behaving badly and should be treated accordingly, there was also the possibility that she might be suffering from some form of epilepsy. But on either interpretation, Beth's behavior appeared to be "stress-related," and it would not be unreasonable for the patient to believe that arguments and friction might make this uncertain condition worse. Since such friction might arise if the subject confronted Beth verbally, it would not have been surprising if the subject had experienced a conflict over speaking out in this way.

In addition to contending with this change in Beth's behavior, the patient was also extensively involved in the preparations for the wedding of another friend, Cilla. As the wedding drew nearer, Cilla – a distant friend, in fact – began to make increasingly imperious demands on the patient's time to an extent that most would judge unreasonable, given the tenuousness of their acquaintance. One implication was that if the patient refused to comply, the wedding plans would be placed in jeopardy.

In the case of the first situation, because Beth's behavior was unpleasant and distressing, it constituted a challenge to lessen the unpleasantness of the situation (or at least to prevent its worsening) by saying something. There was also, in contextual terms, constraint upon an appropriate verbal response along the lines of "If you do not stop behaving like this, I'm not prepared to continue this friendship." The basis for a rating of CSO was twofold. First was the contradictory advice about what might be wrong. Because there was uncertainty over which was the appropriate response – confronting bad behavior, or being concerned and sympathetic because the behavior arose from illness – the patient was constrained because it could be unfair to say anything until the medical opinion was less equivocal. Second, she was still dependent on Beth's continuing to allow her to stay, thus avoiding going back to her own flat. Both provided some reason for not speaking out.

In the case of the second difficulty, we felt that there was a challenge – the patient was being imposed upon – but that the conflict over the possibility of her saying to Cilla, for example, "I will only continue to be helpful with your wedding if you moderate the demands you make," was not great enough to rate as CSO. There were three reasons for this. First, the burden upon the patient in terms of preparations for the wedding was insufficient. Second, the negative consequences of such a protest would not be so great in any case: Cilla was neither sick nor argumentative, and a somewhat less well-organized wedding was not so negative an outcome as Beth's health's deteriorating after being hurt by the patient's protest, or the patient's having to go back to live on her own if her protest led to an estrangement. Third, because the degree of friendship was more casual with Cilla than with Beth, the patient was not so obligated to her, and any protest on her part would be unlikely to be thought so unfair.

CSO Ratings of Events and Difficulties

Both events and difficulties could be rated in terms of CSO. The use of this dimension produced much more impressive results. Nineteen women (34%) experienced at least one CSO event in the year before onset – 12 (21%) in the final 4-week period, compared with a maximum of 2 (4%) in any other 4-week period in the year ($p < .05$). Studies have shown that the falloff in reporting of LEDS events in the year before interview is relatively slight (see Chapters 1 and 12), and it was therefore possible to use the occurrence of events outside the 4-week period before onset to establish the expected rate of CSO events in this way.

Twenty-six women (46%) experienced a CSO difficulty at the time of onset. Of these, 8 women had had those difficulties for more than 2 years, and only 1 additional woman had had a CSO difficulty at some time during the year that had resolved before onset. Unfortunately, as was not the case with CSO events, it was not possible to obtain from the patients themselves an expected rate of such CSO difficulties. For this, the LEDS data on a sample of 70 women in the original Camberwell depression study were re-examined for CSO difficulties (CSO events for a sample of 50 were also examined). On a number of occasions, the descriptions of the events and difficulties in the Camberwell women were insufficiently detailed to allow us to make a firm CSO rating. On any occasion where we could only suspect CSO, the difficulty (or event) was rated as positive on CSO. That is, in an attempt to be conservative in regard to the hypothesis we were examining, we attempted wherever possible to find CSO in the experience of the Camberwell women. The results of this comparison are shown in Table 13.1.

Twenty-six (46%) of the dysphonic women and 11 (16%) of the Camberwell women had a CSO difficulty at the time of onset or interview, respectively ($df = 1$, $p < .01$). None of the 3 Camberwell women

TABLE 13.1. CSO events and difficulties experienced by the dysphonic women and by Camberwell women

Subject group	Percentage with CSO event present in past year			Percentage with CSO difficulty present at time of interview/onset	Percentage with CSO event in last 4 weeks or CSO difficulty in year
	Last 4 weeks	Rest of year	Any time during year		
Dysphonic women	21 (12/56)	13 (7/56)	35 (19/56)	46 (26/56)	54 (30/56)
Camberwell women[a]	0 (0/50)	6 (3/50)	6 (3/50)	16 (11/70)	16 (11/70)

Note. *n*'s for the percentages are in parentheses.

[a] The Camberwell women included 50 women who were rated for both events and difficulties, and 20 women who were rated only for difficulties.

with a CSO event had experienced it in the last 4 weeks before interview. When the last 4 weeks were excluded from consideration in both groups, 7 (13%) of the dysphonic women and 3 (6%) of the Camberwell women had at least one CSO event in the rest of the year. This difference was not statistically significant and suggested that the effect of CSO events largely took place in a matter of weeks. The difference between the two groups was increased when they were compared for any experience of CSO event or difficulty in the last 4 weeks. As 8 women had both CSO events and difficulties during this period. 54% (30/56) of the dysphonic series had a CSO event or difficulty in 4 weeks, compared with 16% (11/70) of the comparison series ($p < .001$).

Threat and CSO

These results raised the question of the overlap of CSO with the traditional measures of threat on the LEDS. The overlap in fact was a modest one, suggesting that CSO acted independently of threat in the development of functional dysphonia. For only 6 of the 12 women with a CSO event in the 4-week period before onset was the event severe. However, as might be expected, all but two of the total events rated as CSO in the year had some degree of long-term threat.

The overlap of difficulties was equally modest. Of those with a CSO difficulty, 18% (4/26) had one that was major (i.e., rated 1-3 on severity, non-health-related, and lasting 2 years or more). Of the women with a CSO difficulty, 38% (10/26) had one rated less than 3 (moderate threat). Table 13.2 provides the basic details about the overlap between CSO and threat.

TABLE 13.2. Overlap between CSO and contextual threat/severity

	Percentage with CSO event	Percentage with CSO event or difficulty
Women with at least one event of a given type in the 4 weeks before onset, by highest level of threat		
Severe	75 (6/8)	75 (6/8)
Other moderate	50 (4/8)	63 (5/8)
Mild or no threat	6 (2/32)	59 (19/32)
No event	0 (0/8)	0 (0/8)
Women with at least one difficulty of a given type at onset, by highest level of severity		
Major	33 (2/6)	67 (4/6)
Marked health	25 (2/8)	50 (4/8)
Moderate	43 (6/14)	57 (8/14)
Mild or none	7 (2/28)	50 (14/28)

Note. *n*'s are in parentheses.

Summary

The conclusions that can be drawn from the results can be summarized as follows:

- The experience of events and difficulties prior to the onset of dysphonia is unlike the patterning of experience before the onset of depression (and, for that matter, other conditions discussed in this volume).
- CSO is common before onset of dysphonia, whereas severe events and major difficulties are not.
- The experience of CSO is most common in the 4 weeks before onset.
- CSO is uncommon in the experience of women who do not develop dysphonia.

CSO Reconsidered

At this point in our analysis, it was clearly necessary to reconsider our ratings of CSO and to attempt to formulate principles that would allow us to convey to others what we had done and to carry out tests of interrater reliability.

We had all along sensed that there was often something rather unusual about the way the women had behaved before onset of dysphonia. They seemed, when considered as a group, inclined to stay with situations that others might well have taken steps to leave, or to immerse themselves in problematic situations to an excessive (if not unnecessary) extent. In the light of their accounts of the situations that had developed, they often conveyed an unusual degree of commitment to the other people involved – or, as we came to see it, loyalty. We therefore subsequently did our best in rating CSO to take into account evidence of notable commitment or solicitousness for others. The argument for this was that the degree to which these were present would create conflict over hurting the feelings of others by speaking out (CSO). It was necessary to consider both what the subjects said and how they acted. For example, it would probably be safe to assume that most women would take the needs of a sick relative seriously; however, only in relatively few circumstances would these be seen to be so important that almost everything else would go by the board. It was essential, in making a judgment of "excessive" commitment and solicitousness for others, to do so on the basis of all information. For example, an interviewer might form a quite different impression from the tone in which a narrative account was given and from details of actual behavior than from any judgment the woman herself offered. Such discrepancies between what was said and what was done underlined the need to consider one in the light of the other in rating CSO. However, the course of action taken was given greater weighting than the attitude expressed.

We decided that we had certainly taken such solicitous behavior into account in rating CSO up to this point, but that at the same time there was no reason why it should not be seen in the traditional contextual terms of the LEDS ratings. That is, insofar as women had appeared to exhibit such behavior, it could be seen as likely to contribute to CSO in a particular situation. There were three common scenarios in the CSO events and difficulties we had rated; these had to do with caregiving, family quarrels, and work. The emotions involved were shame and guilt, particularly concerning disloyalty, judged either in terms of what the women told us or in contextual terms (i.e., what it would appear reasonable for a woman to feel). To expand on the idea of CSO, one example of each scenario is given.

Caregiving

A married middle-aged woman paid daily visits to her elderly and frail in-laws who lived nearby. The father-in-law died after a rapid deterioration in his health, and after the funeral, the mother-in-law's condition also worsened. She was unsteady on her feet, seemed not to care for herself, and was confused. She was unwilling to have her daughter-in-law visit her, and because she was profoundly deaf as well as frail, it was impossible to discover whether the worsening was due to grief or increasing frailty or both. No one else in the family visited her and finally the subject moved in with her, in spite of the fact that even the daily visits were unwelcome. The old woman's condition continued to worsen, and the doctor was eventually called when she fell. After the fall, the doctor arranged an admission to an old people's home.

The event rated as having CSO was the subject's moving in to stay with her mother-in-law. Her dedication can be judged by what she gave up. She gave up her comfort – she had to sleep on a camp bed in the front room. She gave up her housework and looking after her husband, who worked full-time – he came to his mother's house after work, was fed there, and either went home afterward or slept on another camp bed in the front room. The old woman had said she did not want her to visit, but her daughter-in-law nonetheless escalated her level of contact. In spite of the old woman's worsening condition, no professional help was called until the fall. The idea that the old woman might be grieving and wanted time on her own to get used to being a widow (a possible interpretation) was not considered. Here was an example of an over-weening commitment to the role of caregiver. The relationship between the two women was strained; the daughter-in-law was not wanted in the house, and they could not talk about what was happening because of the old woman's deafness. In spite of this, the patient made light in the interview of the difficulties she had experienced. What had occurred only emerged after a good deal of questioning.

Our interpretation of the course of events was as follows: After the father-in-law died, it was not clear how well the widow would manage. If she did not manage, then she would have to go into a home (the younger couple's home was not suitable for the mother-in-law to share). If she went into a home straight away because she was not managing, then it could be suspected that not enough was done to help her over the first few weeks of living on her own. It would be shameful to neglect an elderly, frail relative. Rather than just "see how things went" – and thereby take the risk that the mother-in-law would not manage – the subject moved in to live with her. Once the commitment to the mother-in-law had been made, little short of her managing well on her own would have allowed the subject to withdraw.

The central problem for the subject appeared to be whether to leave the old woman to her own devices (which was, after all, what she had asked for). If the subject did that, she might well feel shame if it emerged that the old woman came to harm through lack of support or supervision. The course of action she then embarked on meant that it could never be said that not enough was done. Indeed, the question most easily posed, bearing in mind the setting in which care was offered, was this: Why did the subject do so much? Other relatives could have been asked; the doctor could have been called earlier; the mother-in-law's wishes could have been respected.

On the basis of such considerations, we assumed in contextual terms that the patient would experience thoughts such as "I have looked after both of them; it is someone else's turn," or "I've got other things to do. Why should I give them up to look after someone who does not want me in her house?" The course of action she took prevented her from saying such things, from confronting the mother-in-law with her ingratitude for the very real help she was being offered, and from asking others to step in and help.

Family Quarrels

A middle-aged woman who had recently married for the second time had been trying to persuade her 18-year-old daughter from her first marriage move in with her. The daughter was staying in a house in which she had been squatting for the previous year or so, with friends of whom the subject disapproved because of police trouble and the suspicion of illicit drug abuse. The girl's father had been given custody when the couple had divorced several years ago; the daughter, who had done well at school but had left at age 16 rather than pursue her studies, had left her father's home in the north of the country to come to stay in the same town as her mother, but not to live with her. The mother and daughter saw each other frequently – the daughter would be given money, the mother would do the laundry. Finally, the daughter agreed to come to stay with her mother and stepfather. From the beginning, the three did not get on. The daughter would not help with any aspect of running the house, and she and her stepfather clashed; she enrolled for a course in the local college, then gave it up after a week; she did not change her behavior and continued to have contact with her "bad" (according to her mother) friends.

The event rated as high on CSO was the daughter's coming to live with her mother, the subject. Now it was obviously very important for the subject that her daughter should come to stay; she had been trying to persuade her since her daughter had arrived in town. One could speculate about the reasons why it was so important, from what was known about the breakup of her first marriage and the little contact she had had with the daughter till now, but those reasons were not part of the essential criteria for the rating of CSO. All that was required was that the woman persisted over a lengthy period of time to try to persuade her daughter to come to live with her and her second husband. (The second husband knew very little about this girl, having met her on only a couple of occasions beforehand.) At the same time, the subject had just started her second marriage. Introducing the daughter to the husband involved adjustments being made all around – the stepfather to the daughter, and vice versa; the mother to the daughter, and vice versa; and the mother now living with the daughter from the first marriage, and the second husband. The daughter's behavior over the past year and the fact that the second marriage was only several months old meant that all members of the threesome would find this new living arrangement less than easy. From the way the woman had been behaving, it was obvious that she was committed to re-establishing her relationship with her daughter, to preventing her from being with "bad company," and to persuading her to resume her education.

When the subject was describing the situation, she acknowledged that it was "difficult" having the three living together and that her daughter "did not go out of her way" to make things easy. What concerned her most were her daughter's friends and her suspicions about them; only on close questioning did it emerge that the grounds for her suspicions were flimsy and that her daughter had not been in trouble with the police since she had been staying with her. She was also much exercised by her daughter's lack of interest in the course at the college, which (it also emerged) the subject had arranged for her.

This was essentially a situation of divided loyalties, in which attempting to attend to one risked compromising the other. Our interpretation of the course of action was that the subject behaved as if her loyalties were not divided; she was surprised that the tension at home between all three became difficult to resolve. The subject never attempted to impose conditions on her daughter's behavior, because she thought, she said, that "she [her daughter] would just go back to them [her friends]." The possibility that her daughter and her second husband might not get on, it transpired on questioning, had not occurred to her until the daughter had arrived. The conflict between her commitment to the second marriage and her commitment to her daughter was not therefore acknowledged until the situation had developed to the point where, if she sided with her daughter, her husband would have reason to doubt her investment in the marriage; and if she sided with her husband, the daughter would have reason to doubt the sincerity of the offer of re-establishing the relationship. The subject had engineered a situation in which she could not win. The most obvious way of avoiding expressing the conflicting loyalties in the situation was to temporize, mediate in the quarrels between them, and hope that neither one would insist on the subject's choosing between the two.

Given past events, one might well expect the mother to feel some guilt and shame over the daughter's behavior and its possible origins in the breakup of her parents' (the subject's) marriage. In this context, getting her daughter to stay with her meant that such emotions would be assuaged. However, the course of action produced a set of conflicts over loyalties, and it was those conflicts that were rated as a CSO event when the daughter came to stay.

Work

A middle-aged married woman, a full-time supervisor of a team of hosiers and overlockers in a garment manufacturing business, suspected that her immediate manager was embezzling company funds because the paperwork did not tally with what she knew had been produced. She discussed this with the other supervisors, who supported her in her suspicions but could not give any directly incriminating evidence. Because the subject was the oldest of the supervisors and the longest-standing employee, they insisted that she be the person to make the complaint. (The manager was, in addition to being suspected of embezzlement, also unpopular.)

The subject was a well-considered employee of the firm, both because she had stayed for such a long time (frequent moves are normal in the garment trade) and because she knew one of the directors. Her employment record showed the extent of her loyalty to the firm, and the dilemma she found herself in arose out of that loyalty. If she had been less committed to her job, then, on the assumption that if her manager was found out she might well be implicated in the fraud, she could easily have left. This would probably not have been greatly remarked upon because of the speed of turnover of labor. Also, if she had been less committed to the company, then why should she worry about what her manager was doing? It did not affect her or the wages of the women she supervised. For both personal and financial reasons, she needed to remain in full-time employment, and therefore needed to protect her job. If her suspicions were unfounded, then she could be sure of how her manager would treat her when he heard of her accusation. In addition, she might well be expected to feel conflict over whether voicing her suspicions was a "betrayal" of her manager.

The event being rated here was the subject's being asked by her colleagues to go and speak to the director. She described in the interview conflict over whether she should voice her suspicions, and her dislike of the encouragement from the other supervisors, about whose motives for complaint she was uncertain.

General Considerations

Common to all three of these scenarios was a triad of considerations. First was the evidence from antecedent behavior of the woman's high commitment to some relevant aspect of the situation. Second was the relationship between some course of action taken and the description offered of it. This was the most problematic consideration, as it emerged from each scenario that there was a complex relationship between what was done and what was said. Perhaps the most straightforward expression of our view was that the subjects acted in a certain way so that they could *avoid* saying certain things about what they were doing. Our way of proceeding was this: First, we took close account of what the subject said about her actions in the situation. Then we considered various other courses of action that were open to the subject, and that might well have been chosen by the average woman in that situation. Finally, we asked why *that* course of action was chosen, and why it was described in *that* way. This led to the third consideration, the interpretation of the situation by the women.

As we had sensed that what was important was the discrepancy between the description of the course of action and the feelings that gave rise to and accompanied that course of action, we were disposed to couch our interpretation of the discrepancy in terms of disavowal or denial of unpleasant emotions. In our judgment, these emotions were underreported by the women because the courses of action they engaged in required them to underreport them. Whether such emotions play as important a part as we believe they do is unclear, and there are formidable methodological problems to be addressed before that uncertainty can be resolved.

Reliability of Rating CSO

Some indirect evidence that we were proceeding along roughly the right lines with CSO came from the reliability study we undertook. Three independent trained raters examined the description of 65 events and difficulties in 10 women randomly selected from the dysphonia series. In addition to the brief description of the events and difficulties, a brief narrative of the year in which the events and difficulties occurred was provided, with all reference to dysphonia omitted. The kappa coefficients of interrater agreement for the pairs of raters were .75, .71, and .69.

This suggests that even though it is rather cumbersome to spell out the formulation of CSO, situations in which CSO is likely can be identified reasonably reliably. The probable explanation for the satisfactory interrater reliability is that much of the evidence for CSO comes from a woman's behavior in the developing situation. This further suggests that, at the outset of the study, when we noted that there was something unusual about the way the woman was behaving, we were not reading something into the events and difficulties that was not there. We may have been mistaken in our interpretive account of what we thought was there; our choice of description (CSO) rested on readily available common-sense and psychoanalytical notions. Nonetheless, irrespective of our interpretation, this degree of interrater agreement does suggest that there was *something* unusual about the women's situations before onset.

Discussion

The major methodological consideration of this study must be the complex rating of CSO for events and difficulties. The rating was developed during the study itself, and the reliability exercise, although reassuring, cannot be treated in any sense as definitive. Given that more detailed material was collected on the dysphonia series that on the Camberwell comparison group, it is impossible to rule out bias either on our part in rating the Camberwell series or on the part of the independent raters dealing with the dysphonia events and difficulties. The encouraging level of interrater reliability, however, does suggest that it may be possible to achieve agreement about the complex rating. It also suggests that it may be possible to carry out the rating very largely in contextual terms, in the sense of concentrating on the behavior of the patient, albeit recognizing that she may play a dominant part in creating the context of a CSO event or difficulty.

But given that a *prima facie* case has been made for an etiological effect, there are certain more traditional methodological issues. There are certain problems about the representativeness of our sample of patients. Although it was typical of those reported from other speech therapy departments in terms of the nature of the voice disorder, the age range of the patients, and the preponderance of women, it nonetheless represented a selected sample – namely, those who were prepared to accept the offer of attendance at speech therapy. For the purposes of an initial study, the advantages of studying a speech therapy group outweighed the disadvantages: These patients were more likely to be severe or persistent cases, and the results could therefore be applied to a clinically important group; and the diagnosis of functional dysphonia could be confirmed by a speech therapist with access to ENT reassessment as a way of checking on the reliability of the original diagnosis. Since in this discussion we are more interested in the derivation of a specified hypothesis that applies to at least some dysphonic women, we do not discuss these problems of selection bias further.

The other problem – that of whether antecedent stressors may explain referral into treatment, rather than onset of functional dysphonia – cannot be refuted in this study, but seems to us implausible. First, individuals with functional dysphonia probably refer themselves early for medical advice because it is such a noticeable symptom. Second, general practitioners refer such individuals early for an ENT diagnosis, because a change in voice quality is a common early symptom of laryngeal cancer. It is unlikely, therefore, that self-selection or medical "filtering" would lead to serious bias in sampling a hospital population.

Clinical Observations on Functional Dysphonia

How do our results supplement previous observations about the nature and causes of functional dysphonia?

With respect to the immediate antecedents of dysphonia, most authors have emphasized the nonspecific nature of stress preceding voice disorder. Stress may be overwhelming (battle experience) or crisis-laden (family conflict), but it has not been seen as having inherent qualitative properties that can explain subsequent dysphonia. The findings of our study support the importance of (measurable) stress, and show that there is an element unifying the various types of stresses that are more common in women with dysphonia than in those without, especially in the period immediately before onset.

One phenomenon that has usually been taken to be an indication of the importance of such individual vulnerability is the clear preponderance of women in clinical populations of functional dysphonics. Our finding that difficulties involving the health of others are important stressors may account for much of this sex difference, since it is women who (both in expectation and in reality) bear much of the burden of caring for others. During our clinical interviews, we gained an impression of other aspects of the subjects' vulnerability. What seemed more typical of the courses of action chosen by these women was that they involved a commitment to "soldier on" and not to discuss difficulties, hoping for an improvement while at the same time being unwilling or unable to act in such a way as to bring this about. In other words, we suspect an aspect of vulnerability that is related to personal style in coping with relationships and other problems. Certainly this style cannot be described in standard diagnostic terms; histrionicity is uncommon, as it is in other somatization disorders (Marsden, 1986).

The manifestation of this personal style that most struck us was that these women had become unusually and intractably involved in their immediate social network, unable to disengage themselves from it when it was unsatisfactory and yet equally unable to modify it. A particularly fertile area for further research into this condition would be to explore the nature and origin of this social aspect of vulnerability. In particular, it would be interesting to test hypotheses about specific early experiences that may lead to such a devoted style of personal relationships. Equally, it might be argued that the style arises from a certain type of social situation where the contingencies are largely beyond the subject's control, so that vulnerability is almost entirely socially determined.

One aspect of the etiology of functional dysphonia, which we did study and plan to report elsewhere, is the part played by recognizable psychophysiological states as mediators between the experience of stress and the emergence of the clinical voice disorder. Functional dysphonia is a condition that, almost by definition, involves a disturbance of laryngeal muscular activity, whether it is reduced, increased, uncoordinated, or otherwise inappropriate. In this context, it is interesting that we found muscle tension to be present so often in association with dysphonia, even when there was no formally diagnosable psychiatric disorder. The relationship between muscular dysfunction and stressors preceding the onset of functional dysphonia has been discussed in the literature in two ways. First (and most commonly), muscle dysfunction has been implicated as a feature of the individual's vulnerability; thus it has been suggested that one vulnerability is a long-standing poor technique of voice production or habitual voice abuse (Guthrie, 1939; Jackson, 1940). Against such a background, any stress that increases muscle tension may produce a critical change in laryngeal function. For example, the greater tendency of women to clavicular breathing may explain some of their predisposition (Greene, 1984).

A more specific formulation has postulated a relationship between the underlying psychodynamics of dysphonia and the nature of the resultant muscle dysfunction, and therefore the type of subsequent voice disorder. The whispering dysphonic/aphonic has been seen as more passive and masochistic, and thus as responding to threat with an "appealing" symptom (muscle hypofunction), whereas muscle tension dysphonia arises out of the struggle not to express aggressive feelings (so-called "hyperkinetic" or "hyperfunctional" dysphonia) (Wyatt, 1941; Barton 1960). This is an interesting suggestion, which raises the possibility that different voice pathology may be triggered by different life experiences, depending on the specific content of the challenge presented by the external situation and of the response expected if speaking out should occur. Unfortunately, our sample did not contain a sufficient number with whispering or spasmodic dysphonia to allow us to pursue such a hypothesis; also, the size of our sample was too small to allow subdivision of the CSO events into those likely to produce anger and those likely to produce submissive or passive requests for help.

References

Aminoff, M. J., Dedo, H. H., & Izdebski, K. (1978). Clinical aspects of spasmodic dysphonia. *Journal of Neurology, Neurosurgery and Psychiatry, 41*, 361-365.

Aronson, A. E. (1973). *Psychogenic voice disorders: An interdisciplinary approach to detection, diagnosis and therapy* (Audio Seminars in Speech Pathology). Philadelphia: W. B. Saunders.

Aronson, A. E., Brown, J. R., Litin, E. M., & Pearson, J. S. (1968a). Spastic dysphonia: 1. Voice, neurologic and psychiatric aspects. *Journal of Speech and Hearing Disorders, 33*, 203-218.

Aronson, A. E., Brown, J. R., Litin, E. M., & Pearson, J. S. (1968b). Spastic dysphonia: II. Comparison with essential (voice) tremor and other neurologic and psychogenic dysphonias. *Journal of Speech and Hearing Disorders, 33*, 219-231.

Aronson, A. E., Peterson, H. W., & Litin, E. M. (1966). Psychiatric symptomatology in functional dysphonia and aphonia. *Journal of Speech and hearing Disorders, 31*, 115-127.

Barton, R. T. (1960). The whispering syndrome of hysterical dysphonia. *Annals of Otology, Rhinology and Laryngology, 69*, 156-164.

Bloch, P. (1965). Neuropsychiatric aspects of spastic dysphonia. *Folia Phoniatica, 17*, 301-364.

Brodnitz, F. S. (1969). Functional aphonia. *Annals of Otolaryngology* (St. Louis), *78*, 1244-1253.

Brodnitz, F. S. (1976). Spastic dysphonia. *Annals of Otology, Rhinology and Laryngology, 85*, 210-214.

Freud, S. (1953). Fragment of an analysis of a case of hysteria. In J. Strachey (Ed. and Trans.), *The standard edition of the complete psychological works of Sigmund Freud* (Vol.7, pp. 1-122). London: Hogarth Press. (Original work published 1905)

Giacalone, A. V. (1981). Hysterical dysphonia. Hypnotic treatment of a ten year old female. *American Journal of Clinical Hypnosis, 23*, 289-293.

Greene, M. C. (1984). Functional dysphonia and the hyperventilation syndrome. *British Journal of Disorders of Communication, 19*, 263-272.

Guthrie, D. (1939). Discussion of functional disorders of the voice. *Proceedings of the Royal Society of Medicine, 32*, 447-449.

Ingals, E. F. (1890). Hysterical aphonia. *Journal of the American Medical Association, 15*, 92-95.

Jackson, C. (1940). Myasthenia laryngis: Observations on the larynx as an air column instrument. *Archives of Otolaryngology, 32*, 434-463.

Janet, P. (1920). The troubles of speech. In P. Janet, *The major symptoms of hysteria* (pp. 208-226). New York: Macmillan.

Marsden, C. D. (1986). Hysteria: A neurologist's view. *Psychological Medicine, 16*, 277-288.

Morrison, M. D., Nichol, H., & Rammage, L. A. (1986). Diagnostic criteria in functional dysphonia. *Laryngoscope, 94*, 1-8.

Perepel, E. (1930). On the physiology of hysterical aphonia and mutism. *International Journal of Psychoanalysis, 11*, 185-192.

Rousey, C. L. (1957). The psychopathology of articulation and voice disorders. In L. E. Travis (Ed.), *Handbook of speech pathology* (pp. 819-835). New York: Appleton.

Simpson, I. C. (1971). Dysphonia: The organisation and working of a dysphonia clinic. *British Journal of Disorders of Communication, 6*, 70-85.

Smurthwaite, H. (1919). War neuroses of the larynx and speech mechanism. *Journal of Laryngology, Rhinology and Otology*, 13-20.

Sokolowsky, R. R., & Junkermann, E. B. (1944). War aphonia. *Journal of Speech Disorders, 9*, 193-208.

Wyatt, G. L. (1941). Voice disorders and personality conflicts. *Mental Hygiene, 25*, 237-250.

PART FOUR

EPILOGUE

14

Interlude: The Origins of Life Events and Difficulties

GEORGE W. BROWN AND TIRRIL O. HARRIS

Before we turn to the task of integrating the findings presented in this volume, it is appropriate to pause and ask what gives rise to the life events and difficulties themselves. For if this can be established, a broader perspective on overall etiological processes may be possible.

There is an understandable tendency for psychiatry and medicine to seek explanations inside the individual; this holds even when etiological agents external to the individual are clearly involved. At the other extreme, sociology tends to seek explanations in terms of broad societal processes. Both tend to ignore the practical facts of everyday life and the more or less immediate impact of these on the individual. Although the relevance of the views of both medicine and sociology is so patent that it need not be argued, it is difficult to conceive of any rapprochement between the two without more than a passing concern with an individual's "life structure." This is a term used by Daniel Levinson in his book *The Seasons of a Man's Life* (1978) to tackle the way the internal and external meet in an individual and to reflect the fact that, despite great complexity at any point in time, there is some structure – some regularity. It refers to the current psychosocial totality of the individual and "encompasses not only behavior, but also unexpressed longings, moods, regrets and attitudes about one's life as well as all referents to these activities and feelings" (Sloan, 1987, p. 29). Although we and our colleagues have spent many years attempting in somewhat obsessive detail to try to break down this very structure into component parts, we find it useful to have a concept that recalls its presence. It is too easy to forget the close link and interplay between and among its many disparate manifestations.

George W. Brown and Tirril O. Harris. Department of Social Policy and Social Science, Royal Holloway and Bedford New College, University of London, 11 Bedford Square, London WC1B 3RA, England.

A Two-Strand Perspective

The perspective we have adopted is best captured in Figure 14.1, in which factors impinging on the individual from the external environment in the upper strand (1) are contrasted with factors that are internal and psychological in the lower strand (2). In the first strand, we envisage a wide range of factors that impinge on the individual from outside and that are of potential etiological relevance, such as quality of housing, income, exposure to infective agents, job losses, and unemployment (one's own or one's spouse's). We would also include demographic factors such as father's occupation, which do not strictly directly impinge on the individual but serve as a rough indicator of a range of environmental factors that do. (We deal with this link between life structure and sociocultural factors later.) The second strand, also an integral part of life structure, would include cognitive sets such as low self-esteem, helplessness, aggression, and dependency. It would thus embrace factors traditionally described as personality features, such as long-term traits, but would also include shorter-term emotional states or moods that might combine with them. Thus a long-term sense of low self-worth might combine with a short-term reaction of self-disparagement to produce a very low level of current self-esteem, one of the most frequently cited factors in strand 2.

The mutual interdependence of these inner and outer worlds persists throughout a person's life span, and is just what is captured by the concept of "life structure," represented here by the arrows proceeding in a continuous causal zigzag. Thus adversity in childhood and adolescence (strand 1) may foster a lack of confidence (strand 2), which contributes to taking menial jobs (strand 1), which may further lower the sense of self-worth (strand 2). This particular version of the diagram

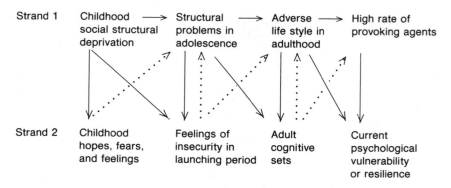

FIGURE 14.1. Speculative causal model of psychosocial experience.

portrays the upper causal strand in rather negative terms, but clearly an alternative might read:

Childhood ———▸ Comfortable ———▸ Low rate of
privilege   life style in   provoking agents
                 adulthood

In Levinson's (1978) terms, strand 2 would count as "self" and strand 1 as "world."

This schema provides a useful backdrop against which to discuss the epidemiology of the life events and difficulties that have been the focus of this volume. Experience with the Life Events and Difficulties Schedule (LEDS) in various surveys has given us some idea of their origins, and we discuss them under the broad headings of the two etiological strands. We are, however, particularly aware of the way in which the processes reflected under one of these headings tend to be related to those under the other. Thus, mindful of the complexity of life structure, we do not wish to suggest in presenting findings under one heading that the other plays no role.

Strand 1

Social Class

Perhaps the most obvious sociodemographic correlate of stressful experiences is social class position. This was forcibly borne in on us during our first general-population study in Camberwell in the early 1970s, in which rates of provoking agents were almost 50% higher among working-class women: Whereas 39% (85/218) of middle-class women had experienced such a severe event or major difficulty, 57% (137/240) of working-class women had done so over the preceding 12 months ($p <$ .001; Brown & Harris, 1978, p. 163). The measure of social class used was the 36-point grading of social occupations developed by Goldthorpe and Hope (1974) divided between points 22 and 23 into "middle-class" and "working-class." Particular weight was placed on the occupation of a husband or cohabitee. But we have re-examined the data using more than a simple dichotomy of class position and a variety of other indices, including a woman's own current or last occupation, her past occupation, and, her educational level (Brown & Harris, 1982). Results were either closely similar to the original findings or somewhat less effective in predicting depression. It would appear, at least for the issues we have tackled, that various approaches to the definition of social class in terms of demographic material give much the same set of results. With all schemes, we found a similar tendency for severe events and major difficulties to increase in frequency as one moves down the social scale. By contrast, nonsevere events did not vary in frequency by social class (Brown & Harris, 1978, 1982).

Life Stage: The Presence of Children at Home

We grouped women according to three main life stages: (1) younger (between 18 and 35 with no children at home); (2) older (between 35 and 65 with no children at home); and (3) women with at least one child at home. In addition, at times we differentiated within the last category in terms of the age of the youngest child. Examination of the Camberwell material suggested that the social class difference in experience of severe events only held among women with children at home. But it was only when types of severe events were considered in addition that the full picture emerged. Almost half the severe events occurring to younger women in both social classes before they had children were of a sociosexual nature (i.e., concerning boyfriends, confidants, or sexual crises such as becoming pregnant while single), whereas among the remaining women the rate of such events declined steadily with each life stage. By contrast, events concerning illness and death greatly increased with life stage.

However, it was really only in the occurrence of what we term "household" events that social class differences in rate of severe events among women with children were found. Such events concern finance and housing, husbands or children (excluding anything involving their health). For health, sociosexual, and other miscellaneous severe events such as tangles with the law (not involving husbands or children), there was no class difference. Marked long-term difficulties presented a very similar picture, with household difficulties accounting for the class difference rather than sociosexual or miscellaneous difficulties, and again only among women with at least one child living at home. However, unlike events, health difficulties also varied with social class and life stage. Clearly, a similar survey today might well show certain differences in detail – housing difficulties might be fewer, and job losses might be more common. But the critical role of household events in differentiating working-class and middle-class women would almost certainly be upheld.

Two other general-population surveys using the LEDS have reported similar associations among provoking agents, social class, and presence of children at home (Bebbington, Sturt, Tennant, & Hurry, 1984, p. 356; Miller et al., 1986). Types of events were not explored in exactly the same way as had been done in Camberwell, but Miller and his colleagues (1986) did show that when all events were taken it was among "independent" events in the areas of work and health that the working-class excess lay. Unsurprisingly, in both these surveys the distribution of depression paralleled the distributions of provoking agents, with particularly high rates among working-class women with children at home, just as had been the case in the original Camberwell study.

Urban-Rural Differences: Industrialized versus Traditional Society

The general-population surveys carried out on the Outer Hebridean islands of North Uist and Lewis led us to elaborate this perspective on the relationship between low social class and provoking agents. Not only were the Camberwell findings not repeated, but there was no association between Hope-Goldthorpe ratings of social status and psychiatric disorder. On the other hand, an index of integration into traditional society turned out to play a parallel role to the one played by social class in the London area. This index represented, on the one hand, an estimate of a woman's household's integration into the economy of the traditional society. Households were classified in terms of the occupation of a core person – usually a husband or father of the subject, although on occasion it was the woman herself. Households engaged in full-time fishing or crofting (farming) were contrasted with those engaged in part-time fishing/crofting and with those in which the core person was solely employed in an occupation more typical of the modern industrial economy (e.g., road mender, publican, administrator, or worker in the local seaweed-processing factory). On the other hand, the index took account of a woman's integration into the church. Rates of provoking agents varied with degrees of both crofting and church attendance, as did rates of depressive disorder: The more integrated groups of women showed lower rates of both. Once again, the differences were particularly noteworthy for women with children at home, and especially involved household events and difficulties (Brown & Prudo, 1981).

The combination of the crofting and churchgoing measures into an index of integration into the traditional society led us to focus more clearly upon industrialization as an independent variable, and to look at the distribution of life events not only within each population but also between the different geographical areas of each survey. With a spectrum ranging from Camberwell at one extreme to full-time crofting or fishing at the other extreme, interesting patterns emerged in the distribution of all types of life events, not only the severe ones. In developing a new classification, we followed notions of "disintegration" suggested by the Leightons and their colleagues (Leighton, Harding, Macklin, MacMillan, & Leighton, 1963) in their classic exploration of psychiatric disorder in Stirling County, Nova Scotia, Canada, but we also elaborated on the Durkheimian notion of "regulation" as one of the features of traditional society (Durkheim, 1897/1952). We distinguished "regular" events (standard transitions that would occur in all communities, such as pregnancy, birth, illnesses, schooling, and retirement) from "irregular" events (less standard transitions, such as changes in residence, job, and interactions involving core relationships, which one might expect to occur less often with more stable and traditional ways of life). These were distinguished from yet a third category of events – "disruptive" ones, which brought not merely change but in many instances some kind of threat (if only in the short term) to the individual life structure (e.g., burglaries, assaults, contacts with police or the courts, divorces, relatives' suicide attempts, serious quarrels, or shocking revelations). Disruptive events were not only more frequent among the Hebridean women, who were least integrated according to the index, but were more frequent in London as a whole than among even the least integrated Hebridean women (Prudo, Harris, & Brown, 1984).

Focusing on such disruptiveness helped us to consolidate a perspective we had been developing about the different backgrounds of anxiety and depressive symptoms in the two populations. The patterning of types of events paralleled a patterning of contact with kin that was related to the morphology of affective disorder: Those with high contact with family of origin were in the most integrated section of Hebridean society and had the fewest disruptive events, whereas those in the least integrated group and with the most disruptive events had least contact with family of origin. This parallel seemed to underline the notion that in close-knit societies, there may be more anxiety than depression (as we had found in the Outer Hebrides, especially in the most integrated group), whereas in city areas, where disruptive events abound, depression may occur more often without anxiety.

Further Cultural Differences: A Spanish Study

The opportunity to pursue these urban-rural patterings using the LEDS in other populations was afforded us recently in northern Spain. The study randomly selected about 200 women from each of three areas: the city of Bilbao; a Spanish-speaking village about 75 miles away from Bilbao; and a Basque-speaking rural area. Results in the rural areas were encouragingly similar to the Hebridean pattern, although perhaps more extreme: The incidence of new cases of clinical depression in the rural Basque-speaking area was almost nonexistent, and the rate of provoking agents was very low (Gaminde & Uria, 1987). The few provoking agents almost exclusively involved illness or death (including not only close relatives and friends, but also livestock). The steep valleys of the

Basque region seemed to have led to an even more extreme closeness with kin in the extended family and an absence of disruptive life events, despite the existence of a militant Basque nationalist movement. It seemed that this political involvement was having little or no effect upon rural life in terms of life events.

Although rates of depression and provoking agents in the Spanish-speaking village were higher than in the Basque-speaking area, they were lower than in the city of Bilbao. But in turn, the Bilbao rates were lower than in the inner-city areas of London we have studied. There was also a difference between Bilbao and Camberwell in rates of certain classes of disruptive events such as marital separations and suicide attempts of relatives; it is tempting to relate this as much to the Roman Catholic culture of the Spanish city as to its later industrialization when compared with London. Certainly in terms of a simple index of church attendance, a higher proportion of the Bilbao sample that of the Camberwell sample were regular churchgoers.

Life Events/Difficulties and Occupational Roles (Including Gender)

So far, our discussion of the link of life events with occupational factors has focused upon the association of social status, defined usually by a husband's or cohabitee's occupation, with the experience of severe events. But as earlier chapters of this book have shown, other dimensions besides severity of threat appear to be important in the etiology of certain psychiatric and physical disorders. Moreover, occupational roles can be an index not just of social status but of other qualitative features, such as the need for quick decision making and the other time pressures that can be faced by business executives and journalists, or the demands for patience and restraint that are imposed on those in the caring professions (e.g., nurses, or housewives looking after young children and elderly invalid relatives).

Although not specifically documented by the LEDS, there is a *prima facie* case for an association between certain occupational categories (e.g., drivers of underground or subway trains) and events rated high on trauma according to the LEDS. Since trauma events do not figure elsewhere in this volume, it is worth briefly spelling out the logic behind their characterization. They embody a very marked short-term threat that may in fact have no long-term threat as defined by the LEDS, but that can, by the very intensity of its immediate impact, upset the subject's basic assumptions about the world. In our experience, they occur extremely rarely in the general population as a whole. Events that involve witnessing gross physical injury, even if only to a stranger, can have such a quality. Thus the frequency of suicide attempts made by individuals throwing themselves on to subway tracks raises the rate of trauma events among such train drivers, and it has been suggested that this occupational group may be subject to a higher than ordinary rate of anxiety disorder as a result (Tata, 1987). In one of our surveys, an overland train driver also experienced a number of trauma events consequent upon the introduction of unmarked level crossings: He narrowly missed colliding with cars on no less than three occasions in the first year of the new system. He was suffering from panic disorder when interviewed some months later. This was much in line with the hypotheses we had developed before elaborating the dimension of trauma – namely, that it would act like severe danger to produce caseness of anxiety. Horowitz (1979) has given another name to his complex of stress reactions, "posttraumatic stress disorder." He has cited many examples of what we would rate as "trauma" events occurring before the onset of this disorder, one classic instance being the suicide of a complete stranger whose body fell from a skyscraper onto the pavement in front of a subject. This is not the place to discuss the possible overlap of posttraumatic stress disorder and onset caseness of pure anxiety, although it is worth documenting that it was as a result of discussing several of the cases in Finlay-Jones's group of onset pure anxiety cases that we originally elaborated the dimension of trauma (see Chapter 3, this volume).

One study that has provided systematic evidence on quality of events and occupational roles, albeit indirect and broadly defined, is Craig's work on gastrointestinal patients (Chapter 9). In the general-population comparison group, goal frustration events were much more common among men than among women; this finding was not unexpected, in the light of ideas about personal goals relating to careers and work, and of sociological accounts of how gender roles affect career commitments and aspirations (Craig & Brown, 1984). Among the gastrointestinal patients, by contrast, there was no sex difference in rate of goal frustration events – a hint that this particular patient group had a higher-than-expected proportion of ambitious, tenacious women, inherently likely to persist in striving until they were met with a goal frustration experience. Again we are faced with the spiral of contributory processes: Was it the long-term ambitious disposition or was it the nature of the occupational career that was ultimately the most important factor in bringing these women face to face with a goal frustration event? For the moment, we cannot give a definite answer. But what we can say is that both elements were probably involved, and that early gender training could well have spared many women in the comparison group from having to face such experiences by weaning them from competitive career orientations and schooling them in the nurturant housewife role.

The mirror image of Craig's result is, of course, the hypothesis suggested by Andrews and House in Chapter 13: that women, in their roles as family mediators and nurses, lay themselves more open to situations involving conflict over speaking out.

From Strand 1 to Strand 2

Previous Experience in Childhood and Adolescence: Lack of Adequate Care in Childhood, and Premarital Pregnancy

In the course of an exploratory study in the greater London district of Walthamstow in 1978, where we sought to chart the chain of circumstances through which childhood loss of mother was correlated with an elevated risk of depression in adulthood, we became aware that certain events early in life resulted somehow in a raised risk of provoking agents in the current environment (Harris, Brown, & Bifulco, 1986, 1987). More important than the early loss of the mother itself in setting a person on such a life course trajectory was the quality of replacement parental care after the loss. If this was judged inadequate (in terms of an index of parental indifference and lax control), risk of current depression was approximately doubled. Further exploration suggested that this link might be mediated by experience of provoking agents, since lack of care was associated with presence of a severe event or major difficulty before onset or interview (Brown, 1989).

Another factor that turned out to play a critical mediating role between childhood lack of care and current depression was the experience of a premarital pregnancy, and again this was found to be associated with experience of a provoking agent in the year before onset/interview (Brown, 1989). A pregnancy of this kind involved any conception before legal marriage, irrespective of whether marriage or a live birth followed. What seemed to be crucial about these premarital pregnancies was that they often trapped women in relationships that they might well not otherwise have chosen and that subsequently became sources of severe events and major difficulties (e.g., housing and financial problems consequent upon a couple's starting a family too young to have built up adequate savings, or marital difficulties with undependable partners). These women also emerged as less upwardly mobile in terms of social class than their peers without such premarital pregnancies.

In interpreting this complex of experiences leading to depression, we outlined a "conveyor belt" of adversities upon which some women were moved inexorably from one crisis to another, starting with lack of care in childhood (often associated with loss of mother) and passing via premarital pregnancy to current working-class status, lack of social support, and high rates of provoking agents. We were, however, fully aware that to attribute this chain of circumstances solely to environmental factors might prove short-sighted. Although it was often hard to see from the women's accounts of their lives how they could have left this conveyor belt once their childhood had located them on it, a more personal element could almost certainly have played a role. According to this perspective, some long-standing feature of their personality – perhaps some form of helplessness or the low self-esteem that often accompanies it – might have contributed to their continuous experience of adversity; thus, perhaps, helpless women more often fail to take steps to extract themselves from poor housing and bad marriages. But we do not here draw any clear-cut boundary between long-term personality traits and shorter-term cognitive-emotional states. At present, they are probably best seen in terms of the general idea of life structure. However, at any point in time, there can be no doubt that personality attributes such as helplessness and low self-esteem can have important consequences in terms of how the external environment is interpreted and dealt with, and the consequences of this can powerfully determine the person's future. We do not despair of attempts to unravel causes from effects within this complex interplay of factors making up a person's life structure; the Islington prospective study allowed us some opportunity to try to sort out the relative contributions of external and internal factors. But first, before exploring this material, it is necessary to state that the positive associations found in Walthamstow between past experiences (here, childhood lack of care and premarital pregnancy) and current experience of severe events and major difficulties were replicated in the Islington sample (Bifulco, Brown, & Harris, 1987).

Negative Elements in Core Relationships
and Low Self-Esteem

So far, the factors we have considered in the present have been relatively crude in terms of what we know of the complexities of a person's life structure. But one of the problems in any attempt to disentangle the contributions of these inner and outer worlds to particular experiences is to tease out their time order and inevitable interplay. Thus, has a woman been made anxious by her husband's volatile temper, or was she more nervous than average before marriage (and possibly contributed to her own state of anxiety by exasperating him further with her indecisiveness)? Prospective studies promise one way forward. As already noted, the Islington longitudinal inquiry afforded a means of assessing a woman's circumstances, attitudes, and behavior that does some justice to the complexity of a person's life structure. The instrument can be seen as covering strand 1 and strand 2 factors at the time of the first contact with a woman, and the strands can therefore be compared in terms of their ability to predict provoking agents in the follow-up period. The instrument, the Self-Evaluation and Social Support Schedule (SESS), deals not only with external manifestations, but with how activities are internally represented (O'Connor & Brown, 1984.) Thus it provides ratings of the identity-enhancing and identity-destructive character of a marriage (i.e., its external, interpersonal nature, based on a woman's detailed reports and perceptions of the husband's behavior) and also the reported impact of these (i.e., how the woman *feels* her marriage has influenced her as a person for better or worse). The SESS deals with security in the marriage, a woman's commitment to the idea of being married, her feelings of competence as a wife, helplessness in relation to her husband, affective concern of the couple, quality of interaction, hostility, dependence, insecurity of attachment, confiding, and primary quality of the marital relationship in terms of a sense of belonging and loyalty. But the SESS also deals with aspects of self that are more internal and less readily related to particular arenas and patterns of activity, such as overall feelings of self-worth, and feelings of satisfaction and dissatisfaction with life. In terms of these strand 2 factors, we had found earlier that low self-esteem was particularly important in predicting later depression once a provoking agent had occurred (Brown, Andrew, Harris, Adler, & Bridge, 1986).

In order to obtain an index of the quality of the interpersonal, external component of life structure, we carried out the following exercise. The 70 scales of the SESS dealing with the "objective" aspects of a woman's life structure were considered. Because we wished them to be of maximal relevance for her internal representations, we used multiple-regression techniques to select the scales that best predicted low self-esteem. The scales deal with all areas of a woman's life – motherhood, marriage, housework, employment, and activities and relationships outside the home, as well as certain measures of financial and other resources. The exercise excluded women with caseness of depression at the time of first interview and was carried out separately for married woman and single mothers, as it was obvious that their ways of life could differ considerably. There was, as would be expected, a good deal of overlap between the scales in predicting low self-esteem, and it should be borne in mind that very much the same results were obtained when a number of measures were exchanged. For example, both overload from work outside the home and financial and social resources potentially available in a crisis were modestly related to low self-esteem for married women (but not for single mothers); however their contribution disappeared once measures dealing with the marital relationship itself were taken into account. These items were related to low self-esteem for married women: negative interaction with children; negative interaction with husband; lack of primary quality of relationship with husband; and security-diminishing characteristics of housework (probably reflecting shortcomings in the practical and financial help a woman received from her husband). And these items were related to low self-esteem for single mothers: negative interaction with children; strife within the home; and lack of a "true" very close relationship (someone named as "very close" with whom there was confiding and frequent contact). (See O'Connor & Brown, 1984.)

These items were used to form a simple dichotomous index, "negative elements in core relationships." Added as positive on the index were 15 women who had a marked non-health-related difficulty that had lasted at least 6 months and involved someone in the home, almost always a husband or child. (Logistic regression showed that such difficulties made an independent contribution to onset once the index had been controlled.) Of course, the measure was highly related to low self-esteem, as the whole exercise of data reduction had been designed to derive an index of life structure involving interpersonal relationships that best predicted a woman's internal sense of self-esteem. Table 14.1 shows that the negative index was related to the later occurrence of a provoking agent, but that this was entirely explained by a greater rate of severe events matching ongoing marked difficulties (D-events) or severe events matching reports of role conflict (R-events). It was quite unrelated to severe events matching domains of reported marked commitment (C-events) without D- or R-events or to nonmatching provoking agents.

Low self-esteem (or negative evaluation of self) was also related to the subsequent occurrence of a provoking agent, and Table 14.1 shows that again this was entirely explained by a raised rate of matching D- or R-events. When negative elements in core relationships and low self-esteem were considered together, the same result emerged: 35% of those with both negative elements in core relationships *and* low self-esteem had a D- or R-event, compared with 15% with one or the other, and only 4% of those with neither. The link of these prior indices with D- or R-events is hardly unexpected, but the failure to relate to other provoking agents is perhaps surprising.

Prior Psychiatric Symptomatology

SYMPTOMATOLOGY AS A PREDICTOR OF PROVOKING AGENTS

Critics of the theory that psychosocial factors have an important role to play in the onset of affective disorder frequently cite prior depressive symptoms as more important than any other predictors of later disorder (see Akiskal, 1985). However, they do not usually specify what the intervening links in this chain might be, and it is therefore of interest to investigate whether such symptomatology can itself relate to the source of provoking agents that may later bring about onset of case depression. In Islington, what we called "chronic subclinical symptomatology" at the time of first contact with the women was found to be an important variable in predicting onset of depression during follow-up, and this therefore needed to be considered as a possible predictor of provoking agents (see Brown, Bifulco, Harris, & Bridge, 1986, for details). These subclinical conditions were almost all borderline cases of anxiety or depression, but included a few nondepressive case conditions. There could be little doubt that both low self- esteem and chronic subclinical symptoms frequently reflected the quality of a woman's relationships: 31% (47/151) with negative elements in core relationships

TABLE 14.1. The association of negative elements in core relationships, low self-esteem, and chronic subclinical symptoms at first interview with type of provoking agent in the follow-up year for 303 Islington women

	Percentage with D- or R- event	Percentage with C-event and not D- or R-event	Percentage with other provoking agent	Total	
Negative elements in core relationships					
Yes	24 (36/151) **	9 (13/151)	21 (46/151)	63	(95/151) **
No	5 (7/152)	9 (14/152)	21 (32/152)	36	(55/152)
Low self-esteem					
Yes	30 (24/81) **	11 (9/81)	26 (21/81)	67	(54/81) **
No	8 (19/222)	8 (18/222)	27 (59/222)	43	(46/222)
Negative elements in core relationships *and* low self-esteem					
Both	35 (22/63) **	11 (7/63)	25 (16/63)	71	(45/63) **
One	15 (16/106)	8 (8/106)	33 (35/106)	56	(59/106)
None	4 (5/134)	9 (12/134)	22 (30/134)	34	(46/134)
Chronic subclinical symptoms					
Yes	31 (21/65) **	9 (5/65)	26 (17/65)	66	(43/65) *
No	9 (22/238)	9 (22/238)	26 (63/238)	45	(107/238)
Negative elements in core relationships *and* discomfiture					
Both	39 (31/80) **	9 (7/80)	24 (19/80)	71	(57/80) **
One	7 (7/104)	9 (9/104)	38 (39/104)	54	(55/104)
None	4 (5/119)	9 (11/119)	18 (22/119)	32	(38/119)

Note. n's for the percentages are in parentheses.

* $p < .01$.

** $p < .001$.

showed chronic subclinical symptomatology at first interview, as compared with 12% (18/152) without the negative index ($p < .001$). Indeed, this link could also be seen in the role of such chronic subclinical symptoms in the etiological process. They showed no association at all with subsequent depression unless a marked difficulty was also present at the time of the first interview. Furthermore, this raised risk was entirely the result of the occurrence of D-events arising out of such difficulties. There was no evidence that such symptoms raised risk of depression except in the presence of ongoing difficulties, which presumably had often played a role in their perpetuation (and perhaps onset) in the first place (Brown, Bifulco, *et al.*, 1986).

It is thus not surprising that, like low self-esteem and negative elements in core relationships, chronic subclinical symptoms were highly related to a D- or R-event, but quite unrelated to other provoking agents (Table 14.1). It finally remained to consider the role of all three indices. The notable finding was that neither the two internal measures (low self-esteem and subclinical symptoms), when combined in a single index of "discomfiture," nor negative elements in core relationships related to D- or R-events *without the presence of the other.* That is, in order to predict such events, discomfiture required the presence of negative elements in core relationships, and vice versa. Since we build on this index in what follows, a less cumbersome way of referring to the factors is desirable. We therefore refer to the presence of discomfiture *and* negative elements in core relationships as a "conjoint index" (negative). The term "discomfiture" has been used because it conveys something of a reactive quality to the environment, and there can be little doubt that much of the low self-esteem and many of the chronic subclinical symptoms we saw were in response to the women's milieu. The term "discomfiture" also reflects the fact that negative feelings and chronic symptoms might be far from overwhelming and could coexist with a good deal of positive feeling. The term is more appropriate than "demoralization," which we also considered using, as this conveys a greater degree of dysphoria and the definite presence of psychiatric symptoms.

LIFE STRUCTURE AND ONSET OF DEPRESSION

These clear-cut results concerning provoking agents raised the question of the relevance of the conjoint index for the onset of depression itself. Would there be the same tendency for all effects to be concentrated in the copresence of factors? Could this be seen as reflecting something about a woman's life structure when external, interpersonal, internal, and even symptomatic reactions seemed to coalesce to keep her upon the conveyor belt to adversity mentioned earlier? In fact, exactly the same patterning of results occurred as with the prediction

TABLE 14.2. The association of negative elements in core relationships and discomfiture (low self-esteem and chronic subclinical symptoms) at first interview with later depression for women with a provoking agent and for all women followed up in Islington

| | Percentage with onset | |
	Those with provoking agent	All women
Negative elements in core relationships		
Yes	29 (28/95) ***	19 (29/151) ***
No	4 (2/55)	2 (3/152)
Low self-esteem		
Yes	33 (18/54) *	23 (19/81) ***
No	13 (12/96)	6 (13/222)
Negative elements in core relationships *and* low self-esteem		
Both	40 (18/45) **	30 (19/63)
One	17 (10/59)	9 (10/106)
None	4 (2/46)	2 (3/134)
Chronic subclinical symptoms		
Yes	35 (15/43)	23 (15/65) ***
No	14 (15/107)	7 (17/238)
Negative elements in core relationships *and* discomfiture		
Both	44 (25/57) ***	33 (26/80) ***
One	7 (4/55)	4 (4/104)
None	3 (1/38)	2 (2/119)

Note. n's are in parentheses.
* $p < .02$.
** $p < .01$.
*** $p < .001$.

of D- or R-events (see Table 14.2). All indices were highly related to onset, with again the clear-cut result that a high rate of onset occurred *only* among those positive on the conjoint index (i.e., scoring positive on both the interpersonal and one of the internal measures) (Table 14.2, last three rows). This result was remarkable for two reasons. First, only 26% (80/303) of the women fell into this high-risk group; and, second, 81% (26/32) of all onsets occurred among them.

It therefore appeared worthwhile to consider finally what might be occurring in more dynamic terms in this relatively small category of high-risk women. Earlier, we had introduced the notion of a personal life structure by deliberately extracting those interpersonal factors that were most closely linked with low self-esteem. Chronic subclinical symptoms were more difficult to place: They were correlated both with low self-esteem ($\gamma = .61$) and with negative elements in core relationships ($\gamma = .51$). We had also earlier established that the entire elevated rate of depression among those with chronic subclinical symptoms was due to the association of these symptoms with marked difficulties and subsequent D-events, and pointed out that there was no hint in the data that they played an etiological role independently of such psychosocial factors (Brown, Bifulco, *et al.*, 1986). (We did not assume that the indices literally contributed to the production of D- or R-events, though they may have – merely that they formed part of some complex aspect of life structure that did.)

Therefore, there was a tight interrelationship among the various factors in the conjoint index (i.e., negative elements in relationships, low self-esteem, and chronic subclinical symptoms) in the production of depression in the Islington women. This, as already seen, reflected the finding that in some way the background life structure led to a very high rate of D- or R-events. The role of life structure in event production, of course, is unsurprising (and, indeed, can be seen as inherent in the notion of severe events' matching difficulties and role conflict). However, there was a second critical process: Once a D- or R-event occurred, risk of depression was greatly heightened in the presence of the conjoint index – that is, it also acted as a vulnerability factor:

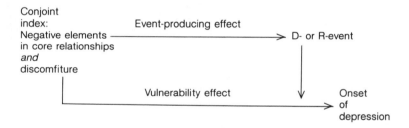

There were 32 onsets of depression in the follow-up period among the 303 women at risk in Islington, and there were 31 women who were positive on the conjoint index and had a subsequent D- or R-event. The risk of depression was very high in this small group of woman – 55% (17/31) – and much of this risk can be seen as a result of vulnerability superimposed on the "event-producing effect." (The vulnerability effect can be judged by the fact that the risk of onset was only 8%, or 1/12, for the rest of the women with a D- or R-event.)

In terms of high risk we have so far discussed 31 women who both were positive on the conjoint index and had a D- or R-event. A second small group of 26 women, who were positive on the conjoint index but did not have a D- or R-event, also proved to be highly at risk. These all had other provoking agents, which, as seen earlier, were unrelated to prior life structure. That is, for this second group, the conjoint index acted simply as a vulnerability factor:

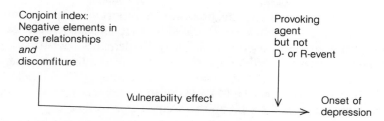

Under these cirumstances, the presence of the conjoint index led to onset in 31% (8/26) of the women. (Only 4 of 81 remaining women with a provoking agent, but without the conjoint index, had an onset.)

For a full etiological model, other factors need to be taken into account, including positive influences such as receiving emotional support in a crisis (Brown, Andrews, et al., 1986). But these results are sufficient to convey that life structure at one point in time was implicated in the development of most of the depression occurring to these women – at least in the context of life in an inner city, where a fifth of the women were single parents. It played a role in the production of D- or R-events and also via a vulnerability effect once a provoking agent had occurred. The upshot was that, in Islington at least, those most at risk of depression in a given year came by and large from a surprisingly small proportion of the total population. Three-quarters of the onsets (25/32) occurred among just over a quarter of the women (26% or 80/303) who at the time of first interview were positive on the conjoint index. However, this picture needs to be seen in dynamic terms. During the year some women, because of life events and lack of support, would have been added to this high-risk category, and others, because of "fresh-start" events or general improvement in their lives, would have been removed.

It is possible that this account has placed too much weight on a psychosocial interpretation of chronic subclinical symptoms in terms of their link with ongoing difficulties (and, we would add, low self-esteem). However, the case that can be made for this in the current material is impressive, and placing rather less emphasis on such a radical interpretation would not in any case change the essence of our conclusions.

The Relative Importance of Early Inadequate Parenting and Current Life Structure

The kind of early experience explored in the Walthamstow project, as might be expected, contributes to this picture. We used an index of early inadequate parenting in terms of either "lack of care" from a key caretaker in childhood, or the presence of reported marked antipathy to such a caretaker. (However, the results were similar if only the lack-of-care measure was used.) Such early inadequate parenting was quite highly related to current life structure as exemplified by the conjoint index: Of those with early inadequate parenting, 47% (34/72) were positive, compared with 19% (44/231) of the remaining women. In terms of the link between the past and subsequent provoking agents, everything was mediated by this current life structure. Early inadequate parenting was entirely unassociated with the occurrence of a D- or R-event, so heavily implicated in onset, unless there was also the relevant event-producing conjoint index (see Table 14.3).

However, there remains the question of the relationship of all this to the broader sociocultural context. How far can the broader findings of epidemiology, the links between demographic groupings and morbidity, be accounted for by the mediation of life events and difficulties of particular types? There are two major problems in documenting this in detail: the multifaceted nature of the links, and the way decisions and choices of the individual mediate the impact of the sociocultural context. It is as though the broader structure provides a setting for the psychologically grounded tendencies of the individual to unravel (we must, of course, bear in mind that these tendencies are partly the result of a prior history of such enactment). Thus the roles provided for us by the wider social context correspond to our past and yet further shape our future identities (for the importance of a role identity, see McCall & Simmons, 1966). Western societies contain well-documented inequali-

TABLE 14.3. Percentage of Islington women with a particular type of stressful experience during follow-up by early inadequate parenting and conjoint index at first interview ($n = 303$)

	First interview		Follow-up period		
Early inadequate parenting	Conjoint index: Negative elements in core relationships *and* discomfiture	D- or R-event	C-event and not D- or R-event	Provoking agent and not D- or R-event or C-event	No provoking agent
Yes	Yes	37 (13/35) *	9 (3/35)	24 (10/35)	26 (9/35) *
No	Yes	40 (18/45)	9 (4/45)	20 (9/45)	31 (14/45)
Yes	No	11 (4/37)	14 (5/37)	27 (10/37)	49 (18/37)
No	No	4 (8/186)	8 (15/186)	27 (51/186)	61 (114/186)

Note. *n*'s are in parentheses.

* $p < .001$ ($df = 3$).

ties in many areas of life, such that some individuals are persistently handicapped in terms of what our consumer-based cultures define as a good life. But as part of this, there is an all-pervasive process of sorting and selection deriving from individual choices and life histories interacting with broader sociocultural factors. For example, in the United Kingdom the quality of public housing differs greatly – both in terms of the accommodation itself and in terms of the surrounding environment – and allocation to this housing is far from random.

It may be argued that such individual selection is perhaps not of great moment for the assessment of structural inequalities. After all, such sorting will not itself change, say, the *overall* rate of unemployment or improve the stock of public housing; it merely settles who will be deprived. It is, however, of significance to the individual and his or her life structure. Moreover, it may be argued that this view underplays the significance for the society as a whole of such a sorting process. For insofar as the experience of adversity in different spheres of life is not random, then this sorting will result in the emergence of multiple problems that would be relatively rare if forms of adversity and deprivation were randomly allocated. Part of our trouble here, of course, is that by taking a random sample of women in Islington we were inevitably forced to deal with a daunting variety of life histories. Thus without larger samples we cannot sort out whether, say, a Turkish background contributes to a different frequency of provoking agents than does a Greek Cypriot background, or to a differential vulnerability when the frequency of such experiences is similar, or to a different cognitive-emotional quality characterizing similar rates of severe events and major difficulties. Moreover, as has been made clear, the individual can play a key role in translating many sociocultural influences into rates of events through strand 2 factors.

Given this level of complexity, an important step will be to spell out individual life histories in even more detail along the lines already touched upon in Figure 14.1. The charting of these life histories retrospectively will prove an important supplement to the increasing number of longitudinal data sets that aim to follow individuals prospectively from childhood. Particularly important is the search for exits from what we have called the "conveyor belt" to adversity. We have noted how past adversity in Islington had little effect on the immediate experience of provoking agents if more recent cirumstances did not have the requisite negative elements. One clue as to what trapped the women on a trajectory to their current negative relationships was provided by their early experience with heterosexual relationships, premarital pregnancy, and early marriage. But without the cultural importance of the role identity of wife and mother for women, perhaps these subjects would never have come near to becoming trapped in this way. And without the cultural emphasis upon the masculine role identity of hard-working provider, perhaps some of the other subjects described in this volume (see Chapter 12) would not have become trapped on a conveyor belt leading to myocardial infarction 10 years later.

References

Akiskal, H. S. (1985). Interaction of biologic and psychologic factors in the origin of depressive disorders. *Acta Psychiatrica Scandinavica, 71*, 131-139.

Bebbington, P., Sturt, E., Tennant, C., & Hurry, J. (1984). Misfortune and resilience: A replication of the work of Brown and Harris. *Psychological Medicine, 14*, 347-363.

Bifulco, A. T., Brown, G. W., & Harris, T. O. (1987). Childhood loss of parent, lack of adequate parental care and adult depression: A replication. *Journal of Affective Disorders, 12*, 115-128.

Brown, G. W. (1989). Causal paths, chains and strands. In M. Rutter (Ed.), *The power of longitudinal data: Studies of risk and protective factors for psychosocial disorders.* Cambridge, England: Cambridge University Press.

Brown, G., Andrews, B., Harris, T. O., Adler, Z., & Bridge, L. (1986). Social support, self esteem and depression. *Psychological Medicine, 16*, 813-833.

Brown, G. W., Bifulco, A. T., Harris, T. O., & Bridge, L. (1986). Life stress, chronic subclinical symptoms and vulnerability to clinical depression. *Journal of Affective Disorders, 11*, 1-19.

Brown, G. W., & Harris, T. O. (1978). *Social origins of depression: A study of psychiatric disorder in women.* London: Tavistock.

Brown, G. W., & Harris, T. O. (1982). Social class and affective disorder. In Ihsan Al-Issa (Ed.), *Culture and psychotherapy* (pp. 125-156). Baltimore: University Park Press.

Brown G. W., & Prudo, R. (1981). Psychiatric disorder in a rural and an urban population: 1. Aetiology of depression, *Psychological Medicine, 11*, 581-599.

Craig, T., & Brown, G. (1984). Goal frustration and life events in the aetiology of painful gastrointestinal disorder. *Journal of Psychosomatic Research, 28*, 411-421.

Durkeim, E. (1952). *Suicide.* London: Routledge & Kegan Paul. (Original work published 1897)

Gaminde, I., & Uria, M. (1987). *Desordenes afectivos y factores sociales en la comunidad autonoma vasca: 3. Comarca de tolosa.* Report to the Basque Government, Bilbao, Spain.

Goldthorpe, J., & Hope, K. (1974). *The social grading of occupations: A new approach and scale.* London: Oxford University Press.

Harris, T. O., Brown, G. W., & Bifulco, A. (1986). Loss of parent in childhood and adult psychiatric disorder: The role of lack of adequate parental care. *Psychological Medicine, 17*, 163-183.

Harris, T. O., Brown, G. W., & Bifulco, A. (1987). Loss of parent in childhood and adult psychiatric disorder: The role of social class position and premarital pregnancy. *Psychological Medicine, 17*, 163-183.

Horowitz, M. J. (1979). Psychological response to serious life events. In V. Hamilton & D. M. Warburton (Eds.), *Human stress and cognition* (pp. 235-263). Chichester, England: Wiley.

Leighton, D. C., Harding, J. S., Macklin, D. B., MacMillan, A. M., & Leighton, A. H. (1963). *The character of danger.* New York: Basic Books.

Levinson, D. (1978). *The seasons of a man's life.* New York: Knopf.

McCall, G., & Simmons, J. (1966). *Identities and interactions.* New York: Free Press.

Miller, P. M., Dean, C., Ingham, J. G. Kreitman, N. B., Sashidharan, S. P., & Surtees, P. G. (1986). The epidemiology of life events and long term difficulties, with some reflections on the concept of independence. *British Journal of Psychiatry, 148,* 686-696.

O'Connor, P., & Brown, G. (1984). Supportive relationships: Fact or fancy? *Journal of Social and Personal Relationships, 1,* 159-175.

Prudo, R., Harris, T. O., & Brown, G. W. (1984). Psychiatric disorder in a rural and an urban population: 3. Social integration and the morphology of affective disorder. *Psychological Medicine, 14,* 327-345.

Sloan, T. S. (1987). *Deciding: Self-deception in life.* New York: Methuen.

Tata, P. (1987). *Post-traumatic stress disorder in train drivers.* Unpublished manuscript.

15

The LEDS Findings in the Context
of Other Research: An Overview

TIRRIL O. HARRIS AND GEORGE W. BROWN

The studies that have been presented in Chapters 2 to 13 using the Life
Events and Difficulties Schedule (LEDS) indicate that life events have
an important, and probably major, etiological role in a variety of psychiatric and physical disorders. However, many research workers may disagree with this conclusion, as on occasions it conflicts with the findings
of a number of studies based on the other approaches to the measurement of life events (and often to the measurement of clinical phenomena as well). Also, at this point we feel the need to face the possible
accusation of parochialism in dealing with work based on only one
instrument. We have spent a good deal of time discussing the strengths
of the LEDS, but it now should be asked whether the results we and our
colleagues have obtained are so different from those of other workers.
And insofar as they are different, can this be explained by differences
between the LEDS and the other life events instruments themselves,
rather than by some correlated source of bias?

Studies of Depression

Two Negative Studies

We start by dealing with depression, because this has been probably the
most widely investigated condition, psychiatric or physical. Two recent
studies are of interest, as they are among the few that have found no
evidence at all for a link between events and development of depression.

Tirril O. Harris and George W. Brown. Department of Social Policy and Social Science,
Royal Holloway and Bedford New College, University of London, 11 Bedford Square,
London WC1B 3RA, England.

The first, a study of middle-aged urban Swedish women (Hällström, 1986), found no suggestion of a link between onset and the presence of severe events or major difficulties defined, as the author claims, by the LEDS. However, in practice, the LEDS was not used; instead, "10 predefined psychosocial stressors" were asked about, and these are far from covering all the types of provoking agents revealed by the LEDS. Many of these involve experiences of a peculiarly private and idiosyncratic nature that can hardly be incorporated in a standard list, such as discovering that one's spouse is a transvestite or meeting for the first time one's adult child who was adopted away at birth. Moreover, quite often it is the women with subsequent onset of depression who experience these less easily classifiable events, while those with the more standard ones (e.g., death of a parent) less often become cases. If Hällström's list is compared with the severe events and major difficulties occurring before onset to the women who became depressed in a recent survey in Islington in north London, *only about half the women would have been included as having a provoking agent*, instead of the 94% we found among these onset cases (see Chapter 2). Furthermore, the list included events that would not usually be counted by the LEDS as severe (e.g., moving house, last child leaving home) and difficulties that often occur at a severity lower than "major" and that therefore would not often be included as provoking agents (e.g., problems with own and husband's work; whether these would be included would depend on the context). The reliance on use of this list is certainly capable of explaining the negative result. The failure to detect the more idiosyncratic stressors would be likely to reduce the number of onsets with a provoking agent, and the inclusion of more minor events and difficulties would be likely to increase those without an onset with such an agent. It would be erroneous to believe that in some way these tendencies would cancel each other out. On the contrary, the false positives and the false negatives would summate to iron out any association buried in the data.

The second study with almost entirely negative results (Breslau & Davis, 1986) is more interesting and less easy to dismiss. A 6-month and a lifetime prevalence of major depression (by *Diagnostic and Statistical Manual of Mental Disorders*, third edition [DSM-III] criteria) was assessed for mothers with children with severe congenital disabilities and for a comparison series of mothers with children free of such disabilities. The two groups of mothers were found not to differ in their experience of depression at the time of interview, as judged by the standard National Institute of Mental Health Diagnostic Interview Schedule. Nor did the women differ in lifetime prevalence, although those in the index group who had at some time been depressed tended to have had more episodes of depression. Despite these fairly clear-cut findings, however, the study probably has not provided the kind of critical test for a social model of depression that the authors claim.

First, there is some ambiguity arising from the time periods covered. Neither "lifetime" nor "6-month" prevalence copes adequately with the central focus of the study on the experience of depression *since* the occurrence of the children's disabilities. Second, major chronic health difficulties experienced by oneself or others constitute the one type of difficulty occurring to women under 65 that has so far failed to relate to an increased risk of depression (see Brown & Harris, 1978, Chapter 8). In the original report of the Camberwell study, it was suggested that in the longer term, coping with such health difficulties may serve to raise a woman's sense of competence and self-worth and thus to protect her from serious depression (Brown & Harris, 1978). But it was also shown that such difficulties *can* lead to depression at their inception and at times of any crisis during the course of the difficulty. In the Breslau and Davis (1986) study, this might have happened when the mothers first learned that the children's disabilities could not be cured. Both findings are compatible with the somewhat anomalous finding by Breslau and Davis that mothers with handicapped children had had more episodes of depression in the past. Also compatible would be the greater prevalence of minor depression among the mothers of the handicapped children. Third, there is an important potential source of bias inherent in the study's design. All the mothers of the handicapped children were in contact with a pediatric specialty clinic; this may have reflected greater morale and sense of competence on the part of attenders, and, because of this, a lower rate of depression than among mothers not in contact with the clinic. Fourth, it is misleading to select one type of difficulty (or crisis for that matter) for study and assume that it is experienced in a broadly comparable way. It is still necessary to consider context – in the present instance, say, the degree of handicap of the children, which may have varied a good deal. And here, as already noted, it is also necessary to face the possibility that the difficulties with the children may have had certain compensating aspects – at least in terms of factors such as feelings of self-worth and self-esteem which appear to play an important role in the etiology of depression (Brown, Andrews, Harris, Adler, & Bridge, 1986).[1]

---

1. One curious aspect of the Breslau and Davis (1986) study may also be worth noting. Those scoring 16 or more on the Center for Epidemiological Studies screening instrument for Depression (CES-D) were far less likely to be rated as having major depression in the chronic stress sample than in the comparison group. This suggests that there might be something unusual about the psychiatric measure, since it would be reasonable to expect a similar ratio of CES-D cases to diagnoses of major depression across stress groups.

Studies Using Checklists

A great many studies of depression have used life events checklists. On other occasions we have spent a good deal of time criticizing them, but in this volume we have avoided becoming too embroiled in these issues. As a recent commentator notes:

> Through the uncritical but widespread use of these lists of "stressful life events," a flood of studies has been created, which have a momentum of their own, which demand that we attend to issues which they have created, and which sidetrack us from the main objective, understanding the life-events disease etiology. Some of the secondary issues raised are: Does the instrument measure stress? How shall we weight the events? How reliable is the recall? Should desirable events be included? etc. The [checklist]-type instrument is, in fact, devastatingly unsuitable for the orderly and detailed study of the etiological role of stressful life experiences in disease and of the possible mechanisms involved. (Kasl, 1983, p. 80)

We have touched on some of these issues in Chapters 1 and 2, and we restrict our comments here to recent longitudinal research. Kasl (1983) is enthusiastic about the likely contribution of longitudinal studies, and there have now been a number dealing with depression. All but three of these (carried out in Islington, Edinburgh, and Los Angeles) have utilized a life events checklist, and unfortunately the longitudinal design has served to add new problems to the already long list of the instrument's shortcomings. The Islington and Edinburgh studies have utilized the LEDS and have obtained positive findings (discussed in Chapter 2). We therefore concentrate on longitudinal studies not using the LEDS.

The basic problem of using a checklist in a longitudinal study is that a questionnaire approach is unable to date event or onset of depression. Because of this, the design itself has to be used to juxtapose events and onset in time, but it is rarely able to do this in a way that meets minimal scientific requirements. In every instance, events assessed at the time of the first contact have been used to predict the occurrence of new symptomatology in the follow-up period; however, in doing this, events occurring in the follow-up period have been entirely ignored. We have seen in Chapter 2 that provoking events usually occur within a few weeks of onset and will therefore be mostly in the follow-up period. The surprising and fatal omission of such events, is, of course, forced upon investigators because of the inability of checklist instruments to date events in relation to changes in symptomatology in the same period. Therefore, although the idea of longitudinal research is methodologically attractive, in practice it has overlooked the fact that events of etiological importance mostly occur within a few weeks of onset, and thus that unless the follow-up period is extremely short, most are bound to be missed.

In recent checklist studies, the lengths of the follow-up periods have varied widely: 9 years (Kaplan, Roberts, Camacho, & Coyne, 1987), 3 years (Warheit, 1979), 1 year (Billing & Moos, 1982; Monroe, 1982), 6 months (Phifer & Murrell, 1986), and 4 months (Andrews, 1981; Henderson, Byrne, & Duncau-Jones, 1981), with only two studies having a follow-up period of 2 months or less (Monroe, 1983; Grant, Hervey, Sweetwood, Yager, & Gerst, 1978; Grant, Yager, Sweetwood, & Olshen, 1982). The study by Grant and his colleagues in California is of particular interest, as it was a 3-year prospective inquiry (albeit by mailed questionnaires) in which life events and psychiatric symptoms were collected every 2 months. The study found little to indicate that life events were causally related to psychiatric symptoms. There are a number of possible reasons for this, including a failure to distinguish new episodes of disorder from fluctuations in an ongoing condition, but the authors emphasize the shortcomings of the life events' instrument itself (Yager, Grant, Hervey, Sweetwood, & Gerst, 1981).

Most of the other longitudinal studies found some evidence for an etiological link. The one carried out in Canberra, Australia, by Henderson *et al.* (1981) found that, in terms of population attributable risk (PAR), 37% of those developing "neurotic depression" in the follow-up period (General Health Questionnaire score higher than 10) had a high life events score at first contact. This compares with a PAR of 86% in the Islington study for the presence of a provoking agent before onset of depression in the follow-up year. It is of interest that if such agents in the follow-up period were to be ignored in the Islington data, a figure as large as 46% would still be obtained on the basis of the presence of at least one marked non-health related difficulty 6 months or more in duration at the time of first interview. This, of course, is just what would be expected, given the importance of severe events matching long-term difficulties (i.e., D-events; see Chapter 2). It suggests that some of the ability of checklist scores at initial contact to predict onset may derive from their reflecting the presence of long-term difficulties, which in turn correlate with a subsequent elevated rate of severe life events. But if this is true, it is necessary to explain the negative results of the California study. Perhaps a 2-month period is not long enough for such a predictive exercise. But, as noted by Kasl (1983), checklist instruments tend to lead to this kind of impasse and speculation, and thus to a call for new research to sort out the inconsistencies and ambiguities. It is therefore a relief to turn to two recent longitudinal studies that have used an alternative, nonchecklist, approach.

Further Longitudinal Studies

Constance Hammen and her colleagues in Los Angeles (Hammen, Mayol, de Mayo, & Marks, 1986) used clinical evaluation of symptomatology and an interview-based assessment of life events. They note that their life events measure was influenced by the LEDS, and that the clinical interview placed particular importance on the distinction between onset of depression, its maintenance, and any relapse. Unfortunately, although this research circumvented many of the shortcomings of prior studies, only 94 students were studied over a 4-month period, all participating in four regular follow-up contacts. Each of these consisted of an interview by telephone covering events that had happened since the last contact and a clinical evaluation covering the same period. Because of the small size of the population, it may have been necessary to lower by more than was desirable the threshold of clinical severity used to define depression. (On the basis of the Islington survey of a high-risk population, only 3 onsets of depression at a caseness level would be expected in 4 months in a population of 94.)

It was possible to use the data prospectively and to deal with new episodes of depression. The events used were "judged to have moderate or severe impact as used by Brown and Harris" (Hammen *et al.*, 1986, p. 117). Of 48 students who were initially low on symptoms, 9 had significant events, but there was no relationship with onset. However, there was an association among those who started off showing some symptoms of depression (Hammen *et al.*, 1986, Table 2). The authors conclude,

> There is a relation between symptoms and events that with appropriate caution can be interpreted as a causal relation. However, the association must be qualified by noting [that] the effect occurs mostly for people who are already symptomatic rather than as onsets in symptom-free persons; that the effect is relatively immediate rather than developing over a longer period; and that although there were no indications that moods cause events to occur, a large proportion of the high-impact events could be construed as at least partly dependent on characteristics or behavior of the person, and often participants who tended to have continuing or recurring depression had such events. (p. 120)

Given the somewhat uncertain clinical basis of the study, these conclusions do not appear to differ from the work already reported in Islington and Edinburgh. Indeed, there appears to be an important convergence about one key issue. We also considered the role of subclinical psychiatric symptomatology (mainly of depression and anxiety) present at the time of our first contact with the women in Islington, and found that this was associated with a higher risk of depression in the follow-up year (Brown, Bifulco, Harris, & Bridge, 1986). However, such subclinical symptoms in Islington were also correlated with low self-esteem, with marked ongoing difficulties, and with the occurrence of severe events in the follow-up year arising out of (i.e., matching) such difficulties. Once these three psychosocial factors were taken into account, there was no evidence of any inherent vulnerability stemming from the subclinical symptoms as such. In other words, we suspect that if Hammen and colleagues had explored the broader context, including the level of support and self-esteem of those without subclinical symptoms, the results would have been fully consistent with those of the Islington and Camberwell surveys.

There has also been a recent prospective study carried out in Brighton, England, of a quite different kind (Bolton & Oatley, 1987). Forty-nine recently unemployed men were selected for study. The men's depression scores were measured by the Beck Depression Inventory (BDI; Beck, Ward, Mendelson, Mock, & Erbaugh, 1961). Interviews took place immediately following job loss (time 1), and again 6-8 months later (time 2). Similar measures were taken for a comparison group of 49 matched men who remained in employment. Of the 20 men who became and remained unemployed, 5 had increases of at least 10 in their BDI scores to reach a level of 18 or more, which is above the level of 16 defined as clinically significant depression (Rush, Beck, Kovacs, & Hollon, 1977). No such changes occurred in the comparison series, and the difference was statistically significant. The study itself was largely concerned with the role of vulnerability and supportive factors, but this basic finding provides clear evidence for an important event-depression link.

For any further critical tests of the link, it is probably necessary to return to some of the early cross-sectional studies. The most important of these is undoubtedly the pioneer work by Paykel and his colleagues (see Paykel, 1974) between 1967 and 1971 at Yale University, which anticipated the first Camberwell inquiry by 1 year. Their life events instrument had at this early stage advanced from a checklist to one using a more flexible mode of interviewing. In a later form, it has been influenced by the LEDS, with the rating of objective negative impact being more or less a contextual one; however, in its initial version it dealt with *general* meaning in terms of undesirability. That is, the event was not considered in context, but a general judgment was made about the degree of unpleasantness of all events of a given type. Depressed *patients* were considered in relation to a series from the general population (Paykel, 1974). In terms of PAR, 33% of patients had an undesirable event of causal importance, compared with 49% of Camberwell patients when the occurrence of a severe event was used as a criterion, and 61% when a severe event or a major difficulty was used. The results are therefore consistent with those reported in Chapter 2, although the size of association was increased by almost half when severe events were used and by 85% when severe events and major difficulties were used. Although such a general measure of meaning is not adequate for dealing, say, with the matching analyses reported in Chapter 2, the approach was without doubt adequate for opening up the area of inquiry and enabled important concepts such as "exit" and "entrance" to be developed.

There have been a number of other cross-sectional investigations. Finlay-Jones (1981), in an interesting paper, has reviewed studies carried out in the 1960s that have been cited as showing no or poor support for the idea of a causal link between life events and depression (e.g., Forrest, Fraser, & Priest, 1965; Hudgens, Morrison, & Barchaa, 1967; Cadoret, Winokur, Dorzab, & Baker, 1972). However, after a detailed scrutiny, he concludes that none provide convincing evidence for refuting a link between life events and depression. He also notes that no study has so far dealt adequately with the role of personality factors and with the possibility that these produce a spurious link. If this should be so, he concludes, they would mainly exert any confounding effect through events brought about by some behavior of the subject.

The "Independence" Dimension

Finlay-Jones's comment about the possible confounding effects of personality raises the issue of "independence" – one of the earliest dimensions used in the LEDS, in an attempt to meet the possibility that an event might be the result of an onset of disorder before symptoms became obvious, rather than a cause. It was argued that by distinguishing events that on logical grounds could not be the result of such an "onset" (because their source was so "independent" of the subject's agency), a test for possible contamination could be made. Events that because of the subject's agency could not be clearly rated as "independent" were relegated to the category "possibly independent." (Compare a house move forced upon a family by the decision of the local council to demolish a whole apartment block with a move decided upon quite voluntarily.)

The presentation of a separate etiological analysis of "independent" events was seen as a preliminary methodological exercise to convince both investigators and readers that an apparent causal link could not simply be the result of bias in measurement. It has been consistently shown that at least half of the severe events occurring before onset of depression are "independent," and in this sense there is a strong case to be made for their etiological role. But once this has been done, it is essential to move on to analyze events that are "possibly independent."

(Those rare "illness-related" events that are likely to be the result of disorder, such as dismissal from a job, are excluded from all analyses of onset, though they may be included in studies of recovery.) It is important to emphasize that the logic behind the concept of "possibly independent" events is not that such events are no longer part of the social stressors in a person's environment; it hardly makes sense that a measure of adversity should ignore a bankruptcy or a marital separation just because the subject has played a part in bringing the event about. However, such a strategy does leave open the question of just what role the subject may play. Our position is that there can be no doubt that the subject plays a key role in bringing about many of the events associated with the onset of depression, but that it is probably no longer useful to see this in terms of the possibility that incipient features of the depressive disorder itself have brought about the raised rate of events. That events on occasion play such a role cannot be ruled out entirely, but it no longer appears at all likely that this is a major reason for the associations that have emerged. Formulating the issue of independence solely in these terms, moreover, fails to face the possible role of personality factors. In order to make a new start in this difficult area, some time ago we refined the original independence scale.

The new scale has 12 points instead of the original 2 (if illness-related events are ignored). To spell out the rationale for each of these points would be tedious here, and details are given in the appendix to this chapter. All except point 1 can be said to tap some quality in the individual that has preceded the event (say, carelessness, a tendency to bring about quarrels, a constitutional weakness leading to both physical and psychiatric illness, etc.). It is therefore possible to argue that significant findings relating to any one of the new scale points, except point 1 (completely independent), may detract from the importance of severe events in bringing about depression and throw the etiological ball firmly back into the court of previous personality; that is, such findings may shift the focus of attention away from the social environment as such. In our first use of the new scale, we showed that the distribution of the ratings for severe events did not differ among the three main classes of depression studied in Camberwell – "neurotic" versus "psychotic" depressed patients, and women with an onset of depression in the general population (Brown & Harris, 1986, pp. 127-128). Results in Islington have proved to be similar, insofar as comparisons can be made. For example, Table 15.1 shows that just over half of those with an onset had had an earlier "independent" severe event.

However, there was one interesting difference in Islington between onset cases and other women. Onset cases had more partners' or subjects' love events, arguments, and breaking off of contact after tension than the other women with severe events – 31% versus 13% ($df = 1$, $p < .05$). These

TABLE 15.1. Independence rating of severe event nearest onset (or nearest interview for nononset women)

Independence	Percentage of onset cases ($n = 29$)		Percentage of other women ($n = 101$)	
A. Independent				
1. Completely independent	34		29	
2. Nearly completely independent	7		11	
3. Negligence by subject impossible to rule out, but not obvious	14	58	11	54
4. Physical illness of subject	3		3	
B. Possibly independent				
5. Subject consents to external events	0		2	
6. Intentional act by subject	0		17	
7. Probably due to carelessness/ negligence	7		10	
8. Arguments and breaking off contact after interpersonal tension	24		11	
9. Breaking off contact without an argument	3		5	
10. Subject's own love events	0		1	
11. Subject's partner's love events	7		1	

are, of course, just the kinds of events that may have an important "personality" component, and we therefore attempted to move beyond the new classification to take into account what we knew of the women and their lives. On the basis of this, we made a judgment in each instance about the likelihood that something unusual about the subject had brought about the severe event. We concluded that this was possible or even likely for 6 of the 13 women with a "possibly independent" event occurring immediately before onset and covered by points 7 to 9. One woman, for example, was bored and dissatisfied with her marriage and began an affair that went badly wrong; another reported being jealous of her husband's affection for their children; another at the time of first interview and in the following year had a major argument with her husband and his family about their children; another found her female lover in bed with a friend who had been her former male lover. We considered only 4 of the events occurring to the women without an onset depression to have similar qualities associated with them.

We are aware that we could be accused of showing naiveté and prejudice in making such judgments. In mitigation, we certainly do not suggest that such incidents necessarily reflect anything untoward or unusual in terms of personality. We merely wished, in the present exercise, to be conservative, and for these 6 women it was clear that some such involvement could not be ruled out. But the other 7 events appeared to be just as unlikely to be related to anything unusual about the women. The one rated "probably due to carelessness/negligence" was clearly very conservatively rated. The woman was a widow with three school-age children who had considerable and understandable money difficulties. The event concerned her being summoned to court for failure to keep up payments on a large fine received by her son some time before. For the remaining 6 of the 13 women with such possibly independent events, the role of unusual personality factors did not appear likely. One, a single mother, had had her first serious relationship with a man since her daughter had been born 6 years earlier. She had seen the relationship as serious and only stopped seeing the man (the severe event) when she found out he was sleeping with someone else. Another woman's husband had been reckless and difficult for years. (Her family had refused to have anything to do with him because of his behavior.) They had separated but had come back together some time before our first contact. In the follow-up year, he began drinking heavily again and later in the year told her he was seeing another woman. These are typical examples.

Therefore, in this exercise, only about one-fifth of the severe events immediately before onset appeared likely to be related to some unusual personality characteristic. But it is in any case important to note that a role for personality does not inevitably mean that a spurious causal effect is involved in the event-depression correlation. It is quite possible – indeed likely – for the occurrence of an event to be brought about by someone's personality and yet for the event still to play a critical intervening role in onset, that is, the picture may be

$$\text{Personality factor} \longrightarrow \text{Event} \longrightarrow \text{Onset}$$

rather than

$$\text{Personality factor} \longrightarrow \text{Event}$$
$$\longrightarrow \text{Onset}$$

Thus, a link between "personality" and events may merely mean that a woman's exceptional behavior has contributed to her experiencing more than the expected number of threatening events. It is a separate issue whether the personality factor independently of the event, or in interaction with it, also raises the risk of depression. Therefore, although this exercise suggested that some severe events occurring before onset could have been a result of a woman's unusual personality, it also suggested that only a small proportion (6/29) of the women developing depression may have been involved.

However, there is a second conceivable source of bias. It is also possible that subclinical symptoms, especially of depression and anxiety (and a few nondepressive conditions at a caseness level), may play a significant role in producing events and thereby in some way may be involved in bringing about spurious findings. We have already touched on this issue in discussing the Los Angeles longitudinal inquiry by Hammen *et al.* (1986). To meet this possibility in the Islington study, all women with clinical and subclinical symptoms at the time of first interview were removed from the analysis of etiological effects; when this was done, an important link still remained between provoking agent and onset – 14% (13/91) versus 1% (1/124) ($p < .001$).

We conclude, therefore, that the case for an important causal role for severe events is a strong one, although the exact role of personality factors in the etiological process has yet to be established. It is impossible to rule out altogether that bias has played some part in our findings, but it seems unlikely to have been a major one. Given that there is an important effect, some consideration needs to be given to alternative theoretical interpretations of the evidence presented in Chapter 2, especially concerning the additivity of events. Here our present perspective runs directly counter to the general position taken by Paul Surtees in Chapter 6.

Additivity and Surtees's Decay Model

Surtees's view of the role of severe events is an interesting alternative perspective to our view that the occurrence of multiple "unrelated" events does not increase the risk of depression. Although there does not always seem to be consistency between the different versions of the decay model in the same data, his work does suggest that there is some improvement in prediction of depression when all events are taken into account. The question is the interpretation to be placed on the often modest differences involved. Because Surtees's approach derives from estimating residual adversity scores based on decay and additivity, the results seem to contradict our conclusion about the overwhelming importance of just one severe event. However, we argue that a straightforward technical issue with no obvious theoretical implications probably explains the differences that have been obtained.

The argument revolves around the way in which the two methods deal with severe events and the fact that the results of the two methods are closely similar for those with an onset, but not for those without. In order to understand the implications of this, it is necessary to recall the basis for a high residual adversity score and to consider how its calculation may influence its correlation with the alternative measure based on the presence or absence of a severe event. Two factors contribute to a high residual adversity score: first, the severity of events at the time they occur; and, second, the proximity in time between the event's occurrence and the point in time for which the score is being calculated. (A third factor, other events occurring between those times, is unimportant for our present argument.) We have seen that severe events tend to accumulate in the few weeks before onset, and so for onset cases of depression, whose adversity score is always calculated at the point of onset, there will have been relatively little time for the score of the severe event to decrease. There will therefore be considerable agreement between the scores based on the adversity index and the simple dichotomy of presence-absence of a severe event occurring in the 6 months before onset. This can be seen for the 37 onset cases in Camberwell, where 92% (24/26) of the women scoring high on the residual adversity index (130+) also had a severe event, and 83% (24/29) of those with a severe event in the 6 months were high on adversity. (The threshold here of 130+ was the same as that used by Surtees in the "B. All events" row of Table 6.2.) But this near-equivalence of the results of the two approaches did not hold for the comparison series of women without an onset. Here the date of interview was the critical point for calculating the residual adversity index, and severe events were distributed evenly over the 6 months before it. Unlike the situation with onset cases, severe events have no reason to accumulate near the last point of the time period studied (onset for cases and interview for noncases). It follows that for a comparison series, a high adversity score will be less tied to the presence of a severe event. In Camberwell, only 70% (48/69) of women with a high score had a severe event, compared with 92% of onset cases ($p < .05$). The alternative (nondecay) approach, by comparison, is still based on the presence or not of a severe event at *any* point in the 6 months.

The upshot of these differences in calculation is that fewer of the nononset women in Camberwell were given a high score by the decay approach than were counted as having a severe event using the Bedford College procedure. This follows directly from the fact that the presence of distant severe events in any sizeable period of time will play a lesser role in calculating the adversity score. And, because of this, it follows that the decay approach will have somewhat more favorable results in terms of indices such as PAR and relative risk. Therefore the modest advantage reported by Surtees for the decay approach, when compared with an index based on the presence or absence of a severe event, is probably largely a function of the fact that the decay approach deals more effectively and less conservatively with the comparison series. We have always recognized that our approach has been conservative in its estimate of etiological effects. This has stemmed from the need at early exploratory stages of research to keep open the possibility of a relatively lengthy causal period. One alternative would be to reduce the size of the causal period; the proportion of nononsets with a severe event would then be reduced by relatively more than the proportion of onsets with a severe event, and an increase in the causal effect of the index of "at least one severe event" would be bound to follow. (As already seen, this follows from the fact that severe events accumulate near the point of any onset, and relatively few will therefore be excluded from the onset group by the omission of the 3-month period furthest from onset.) In fact, when the length of the study period was reduced to 3 months for the Camberwell series the PAR was 71%, which is superior to any so far reported by Surtees for the decay model, and 28 of the 37 onset cases were still selected, the maximum covered by the decay approach. (Relative risk was 8.92, which is comparable to the figure obtained by the decay approach; see Table 6.2.)

We did not reduce the length of the causal period in this way, as it would have meant reducing somewhat the proportion of onset cases with a severe event; this would have had implications for the rest of the analysis, particularly that concerning the role of vulnerability factors. At some point, the length of the period to be taken must be settled empirically. However, since the number of onset cases who only had severe events outside the 5 weeks before onset was relatively low (4 out of 29) in Islington, it will take a larger series culled from a number of studies to obtain a robust estimate of the exact period to be taken. Until this is done, a length of about 6 month seems to be a reasonable reflection of what is known. Meanwhile, it is important to note that in practice the differences in results obtained by the two approaches for the London studies were quite small. (The differences were larger in the Edinburgh study itself, but this was probably due to the surprisingly modest etiological role of severe events in this series. The London studies suggest that the differences are likely to be small when severe events play a major role; see Table 2.1.) We have gone to the trouble of spelling out these somewhat abstruse technical points because of the critical *theoretical* weight Surtees has placed on the modest differences. We interpret these as largely the result of computational differences with no obvious theoretical implications, at least as far as the issue of additivity is concerned.

We do not use this argument to question the potential usefulness of the decay model. Indeed, some such notion has long been part of our conception of the etiological process in depression (see Brown, Harris, & Peto, 1973). However, it does underline the conclusion in Chapter 2 that there is as yet, for depression, surprisingly little evidence of "additivity" across *unlinked* severe events, and little or none for any kind of additivity concerning nonsevere events. Nor, of course, can there be any doubt about the relevance of the notion of decay, in the sense that severe events bring about the onset of depression quite close to their occurrence rather than later. The point at issue is, as already emphasized, the notion of additivity that is at present built into the concept of residual adversity.

Matching and the Notion of Additivity

However, if this position concerning additivity should be correct, a number of issues still require clarification. In particular, what is the nature of the process akin to "additivity" that does occur? We have in mind the fact that, as shown in Chapter 2, in Islington nearly half of the women with severe events occurring very near to the point of onset had had severe events occurring in the prior year to which the events near onset were linked (14/29). One obvious question is this: Why did these women not develop depression in response to the earlier event? Does this not reflect the effect of some accumulation of stress?

In fact, 3 of the 14 women had had an onset in the year before first interview but had then temporarily recovered. One, for example, did so after her husband lost his job as a truck driver when he was arrested for drinking and driving, and she became depressed again in the follow-up year after she learned of his love affair. (All three of these onsets in the prior year involved D-events.) For 7 of the remaining 11 of the 14 women, the final event appeared to be either the culmination of a developing sequence of danger events that ended in a loss, or an event confirming the seriousness of an earlier one that could possibly have been seen as a one-time matter. Examples included the ending of an extramarital affair (after the subject had entered into it 17 weeks earlier); being told that a diseased hip would never get better after several earlier hospital admissions for surgery; a husband's death following the diagnosis of his cancer; a miscarriage after a much-wanted pregnancy in a difficult marriage; and a letter from school about a son's truancy some weeks after the subject had discovered that he had been stealing money from home. Because of the different implications in terms of meaning of danger and loss events, the notion of straightforward additivity would not appear to be applicable in most of these instances. But it might be possible to argue for some (e.g., the woman receiving the letter about her son's truancy) that there would have been no onset if the earlier event had not alerted her to the possibility that the later one was not just an aberration, but might be part of a continuing series in the future.

The events of the remaining 4 of the 14 women may have been better candidates for some kind of additive effect (though, of course, the women themselves may well have seen them in terms of some developing crisis). For one woman, the earlier event involved leaving a difficult husband for a few days "to bring him to his senses," and that led to onset after an incident 30 weeks later where the husband got drunk and created a public disturbance in the place where they both worked. Another woman had had a series of crises over a 6-month period, culminating in a major scene with a friend whom her husband appeared to have involved in some kind of psychotic delusional system. Therefore, in these final four instances, there is some suggestion that additivity may have played a role in the sense that the experience of the prior event provided an essential background for the interpretation of the more recent event, and was thus a necessary condition for the development of depression. But whatever explanation is given, it is important to recall that the events we have been discussing were *linked* to each other and involved one focus. Our own view has already been given – namely, that while additivity was probably often involved in the sense that the onset would not have occurred without the earlier event, the effect is best seen in terms of the woman's final evaluation of a particular set of related circumstances in terms of the hopelessness of her position, in the light of both the past and the present.

Another question involves assumptions about the issue of decay itself. How reasonable is it in any case for Surtees merely to assume that the impact of a stressor declines in some *regular* manner? Although long-term difficulties have not been considered in the decay model, it is certainly relevant that they often appear to remain constant in their ability to produce depression once a "matching" event (i.e., a D-event) has occurred, and also in their ability to perpetuate chronic depression (see Chapter 2). Most marked difficulties are initiated in the first place by a severe event, and the way they subsequently throw up further events would appear to run counter to the notion of decay. For example, in Islington there was no association between the length of a marked difficulty present at first interview and the chances of a subsequent D-event's producing depression – a result that clearly conflicts with the idea that the impact of difficulties declines as a function of time. It can equally be argued that while the difficulties remain "marked" (an empirical question), their *potential* influence does not change. Of the D-events in the follow-up year in Islington 50%, (4/8) led to depression when the difficulties had lasted less than a year, compared with 46% (6/13) when the difficulties had lasted 1-4 years and 43% (6/14) when they had lasted over 4 years.

It may therefore be better to conceive of two forms of decay. Clearly, if depression does not follow fairly quickly on the occurrence of a major loss or disappointment, the development of a disorder at a caseness level becomes much less likely. This has recently been confirmed in a study of unemployed men in south London, where risk of depression was only raised for a limited period soon after the loss of the job (Eales, in press). Some mode of adaptation appears to ward off a full depressive disorder, although symptoms of depression and anxiety at a noncase level may well be present (Brown, Bifulco, *et al.*, 1986). Over and above this fairly immediate dissipation, a second form of decay would be a direct function of the actual *resolution* of the untoward consequences of the event. The need to postulate the presence of this second form is seen in the power of matching D-events to produce depression and the fact that this does not appear to be a function of the length of the difficulty. Such resolution may not only be a matter of clearing up problems in the external world. Where the person's sense of self-worth has been affected, such decay may be a good deal slower than where it has not.

It should also be added that the interpretation of the event in terms of personal responsibility and control is not a simple function of the nature of the event. Research in the area of rape has recently emphasized the importance of women's ability to maintain their sense of personal invulnerability. And in this context, Janoff-Bulman (1979, 1985) has proposed that there are two types of self-blame, one adaptive and the other maladaptive. "Behavioral self-blame" is adaptive and involves blaming one's own behavior, whereas "characterological self-blame" involves blaming one's enduring personality characteristics and is maladaptive: "Thus the rape victim who believes she should not have hitchhiked or should not have walked alone is engaging in behavioral self-blame, whereas the rape victim who believes she is a bad person or a poor judge of character is engaging in characterological self-blame" (Janoff-Bulman, 1985, p. 29). With behavioral self-blame, it is also more easy to conclude that it is possible to do something about avoiding a similar crisis in future. In the earlier of the two reports, Janoff-Bulman (1979) argues for the importance of characterological self-blame in the genesis of depression. Unfortunately, the measure of depression used was not a clinical one, but the relevance of the distinction for the present discussion is obvious. The two types of self-blame identified may be contrasted as forms of "specific" and "generalized" self-blame, and this parallels the distinction between specific and generalized hopelessness in our own model of depression. Finally, it is perhaps also worth bearing in mind that the impact of a crisis is not necessarily restricted to the event itself. Failure to receive support from someone close from whom a person had reason to believe effective support would be forthcoming may constitute an additional loss, although not rated as a life event by the LEDS (Brown, Andrews, *et al.*, 1986).

Additivity and Personal Vulnerability

In *Social Origins of Depression*, we presented evidence that in the presence of a long-term difficulty, a quite trivial event in terms of threat or even an apparently "positive" incident may lead to a major reassessment of one's life; in the same way, when a severe event has occurred some considerable time before onset, a minor one later on may "bring home" the meaning of the original event. Such processes appeared to have brought about an excess of minor events in the 5 weeks before onset in a series of depressed patients (Brown & Harris, 1978, p. 146). Clearly, the result echoes to some extent the finding in the Islington series concerning D-events, and the same kind of mechanism may have been involved. It has not been possible to replicate these findings concerning minor events in the general-population series – both because so few women had an onset of depression with only a major difficulty without a prior severe event, and because the majority of these severe events occurred within 5 weeks of onset.

There is a second related point. In the same Camberwell study, there was evidence that for depressed *patients* the length of time between event and onset tended to be a good deal longer than for women developing depression in the general population (Brown & Harris, 1978, pp. 112-113, 126; see also Surtees & Rennie, 1983). It is therefore possible that the role of minor events will only be clear in a patient series. It also raises the important question of why there should be "delay" in onset in a significant proportion of depressed patients. There was a suggestion in the Camberwell data (though the result just failed to reach statistical significance) that severity of the depression was somewhat greater among those with a "delayed" onset. The matter needs further investigation. However, at present it does not seem too far-fetched to suggest that some kind of defensive process is involved, which, when it fails, brings about a type of depression more likely to be referred for specialist psychiatric treatment. This could be either because the symptoms tend to be somewhat more severe, or because the greater passage of time between event and onset makes the reactive "psychosocial" nature of the conditions less obvious both to the woman and to her general practitioner, who therefore refers her to a hospital. In the light of such issues, the call by Surtees to consider events in a long-term perspective is opportune. In our judgment, however, the field is most likely to develop to the degree that we are able to study decay in empirical terms rather than impose decay functions by fiat. Surtees's exploration of individual characteristics in Chapter 6 is likely to prove a significant step in this direction.

However, while his concept of "person-specific decay" is a move toward empiricism, it does raise further problems. Insofar as it is used to build individual vulnerability into the basic measure of stress at an early stage of the analysis (in the example given, this is coping style), it may promote confusion about what is an understandable reaction to stress and what is a distorted cognition. This is why the approach of the LEDS has aimed to embody an estimate of the "average" reaction, so that distortions or hypersensitivities can be separately estimated; by contrast, the concept of person-specific decay leaves no room for separate estimates, because it builds the subject's coping capacity into the initial measure of adversity. Our criticism is not so much substantive as terminological. It is not substantive, in that person-specific decay is rated prospectively and involves not only emotional reactions but also many behavioral features, and therefore is less subject to all the possible biases of a self-report measure of threat. However, it does appear to depart substantially from the perspective that contextual ratings have been designed to embody – namely, to approach as closely as possible to a "culturally objective" measure of stress.

Thus, while we applaud Surtees's move, we would urge caution about the inclusion of variables involving personal response, and particularly about the terminology he uses. It is misleading to think of the measure as reflecting differences in "adversity" when variation will in part be accounted for by differences in personal response such as in coping style. This does not, however, invalidate the mathematical procedure he has elaborated. As he implies, at some point all analyses have to confront the problem of combining the effects of provoking stressors with the effects of pre-existing (or vulnerability) dispositions, and person-specific decay periods are a promising new way of dealing with this challenge. But it is important to be aware that in the particular example he has chosen, dealing with coping, he has stepped over what others have seen as a critical conceptual boundary between provocation and vulnerability.

The need to keep provoking and vulnerability factors separate has been well argued by Tennant, Bebbington, and Hurry (1981). They maintain that the overlap between the two types of causal factors in our etiological model of depression is too great for a true test of the model: "The contextual rating of an event is based on social data which also serve as 'independent' antecedent variables. . . . This procedure would tend to produce an association between life events [they mean events with severe long-term contextual threat] and other antecedent variables which would not be empirical, and would thus overestimate the causal role of 'life events' in illness" (Tennant et al., 1981, p. 380). They are suggesting that raters will produce an association between provoking agent and onset of depression that is "illicit," because the rules for rating contextual threat specify that certain otherwise minor threat events will be rated as severe because of the presence of a vulnerability factor, and this will tend to confound any conclusions about the relative roles of provoking agents and vulnerability factors in producing depression.

The same point can be made on even stronger grounds for events and marked difficulties. In this case, there is a deliberate attempt by the LEDS to take account of associated difficulties in rating an event. And yet, despite this, we have indicated in Chapter 2 that taking account of a severe event *and* a linked difficulty greatly improves predictive power (in terms of D-events), compared with dealing with severe events alone. In the case of vulnerability factors, the rules concerning rating do not make such a potentially confounding specification. Vulnerability factors are rated as present or absent, irrespective of occurrence of events and difficulties. Moreover, the sort of factors relevant for rating contextual threat rarely coincide exactly with defining characteristics of the vulnerability factors. For example, the presence of *any* young children at home will increase the threat of a financial difficulty; in this sense, the presence of three children under 15 (the vulnerability factor) would not be crucial for deciding the severity of the difficulty, as compared, say, with the presence of two children. Lack of a confiding relationship with husband or boyfriend has the strongest potential for a link with contextual threat and therefore for a confounding effect, but even here it does not appear to be particularly strong. Often the existence of a major marital difficulty forms the background context that characterizes an event as severe (e.g., a pregnancy of the subject) when it would otherwise be of lesser threat. However, much greater "objective" evidence of marital disturbance than mere lack of confiding (say, of violence or of outright neglect) is required for a marital difficulty to be rated as major.

In order to obtain a direct estimate of the possible bias involved in deciding on the presence of a vulnerability factor, we reconsidered the original Camberwell ratings and asked ourselves whether or not, in rating each severe event or major difficulty, knowledge of either lack of intimacy with husband, the presence of three or more children under 15 at home, or lack of employment would be likely to have determined the fact that they were given these particular threat ratings. Or, to put it another way, were the event or difficulty and its immediate context enough for it to have been classified as severely threatening, without knowledge of the presence of one of the vulnerability factors or even a reasonable hunch that it was present? (For example, from being told that a husband and wife did not get on well and had not had sexual intercourse for several years, one might guess that there was no confiding.) The results of the exercise were surprisingly clear-cut (Brown & Harris, 1986). We concluded that only 5 of the 97 women with a provoking agent in the first Camberwell survey had the potential for this kind of contamination, and even this was probably an overestimate, as our judgments were conservative (in the sense of including women for whom there was even only the remotest hint of such a confounding influence).

As a further check, we picked out from the Islington interviews a random selection of events concerning the women's husbands that had involved some long-term threat, and deleted from the description of each event any reference to the quality of the marriage or the husband's past behavior. Events were then rated as severe or not according to the LEDS standards. The results were again clear-cut: All but one (51/52) of the severe events were still rated as severe. Although this particular exercise was highly artificial and the results must therefore be treated with caution, they underline the lack of support for the proposal that provoking agents and vulnerability factors are confounded. It does not therefore appear likely that the kind of bias discussed by Tennant and his colleagues has played a significant role in the vulnerability results that have so far been published.

But the same critics go on to make a further, more contentious point: that the contextual measures of threat are "more accurately described as a measure of general 'social stress' rather than as a 'life event' measure per se" (Tennant et al.,1981, p. 381). This again suggests, like the similar point made by Dohrenwend and his colleagues, that somehow "pure" life events measures are superior (see Chapter 1). Few epidemiologists have the proof or disproof of the vulnerability model as their main purpose; most are in business to predict illness, and thus if a measure of "general social stress" should turn out to have superior predictive power to a sterilized measure of "life events per se," it is to be preferred for that particular task rather than facing all-round rejection on grounds of some "impurity." In fact it is just such "impurity" that, in the light of our earlier discussion in Chapters 1 and 2, we would maintain is the merit of the contextual approach. Indeed, the final reply to criticism is that the contextual ratings almost certainly approximate more closely to the way human beings respond to stressors than do other measures of life events so far produced.

To sum up the issue concerning the distinction between stress and individual vulnerability to stress, although there is general agreement that etiological models should distinguish the two, there is some disagreement over where the boundary should be drawn. On the one hand, Surtees's person-specific decay period seems to include too much of the individual psyche in the measure of stress (i.e., adversity); on the other hand, Tennant and colleagues seem to be excluding too much of the personal biography in their estimate of what is stressful. The contextual approach falls between these two: It defines stress in terms of what reaction would be expected from the *average* person with that particular biography and set of current circumstances, and goes on to deal with vulnerability in terms of further particular characteristics of the individual that will determine whether his or her reaction will depart from that average in the direction of more severe symptomatology. Although this conceptual distinction aids clarity of thought at this stage of research, in the final analysis some way of computing a combination of provocation and vulnerability will be required. In the interim, however, research workers will need to employ a workable boundary between the two concepts that neither overindividualizes nor excessively sterilizes the estimate of stress.

Studies of Nondepressive Conditions

The Specificity Hypothesis and the Term "Event"

We turn now to the nondepressive disorders discussed in other chapters. It becomes apparent that our comments here must be of a different order from those on studies of depression. This is because in other areas measurement of life stress has been even less comparable to the LEDS than in the work on affective disorder, and where there has been some degree of comparability, the relevant studies have already been discussed in the actual chapters. We therefore confine ourselves to a few brief remarks before attempting to integrate the findings into an overall perspective on life events and illness. Throughout, we are particularly concerned with what we call the "specificity hypothesis" – namely, the possibility that specific types of events and difficulties are linked with specific disorders.

Before beginning this review, we should perhaps return to the ambiguity of the term "event." There is very little evidence to suggest that certain events automatically trigger specific emotions. At best, there is some suggestion that various stimuli can trigger in human beings negative emotions generally: "Specific unlearned elicitors of fear, anger or distress separately are hard to find" (Frijda, 1986, p. 257). The immense plasticity of emotion is why we have found it necessary to emphasize context as a crude but reasonably effective device for tapping the relevant concerns, plans, or goals of a person. For, as explained in Chapter 1, these *and* the event are critical for determining meaning and thereby emotion. Such concerns, plans, and goals can be seen as dispositions (i.e., internal representations) that service as standards against which actual situations are tested (Frijda, 1986, p. 336). Therefore, when we refer to "events," we have in mind far more than the event itself: In our contextual ratings, we attempt to deal with relevant dispositions, and this (albeit crudely) must include cultural considerations. We are aware that probably only in the work on matching have we truly approached a reasonably sophisticated treatment of this issue; however, we see our contextual ratings as approximating to what is required, and our theoretical position will not be understood if our use of the term "event" is simply translated as a stimulus with no regard at all to the person and the person's concerns.

Table 15.2 attempts to summarize the key differences between the LEDS and other measures of life stress in a way that clarifies their lack of comparability and that highlights the difficulty of finding much of relevance for the specificity hypothesis in the published literature.[2] The table illustrates the hierarchy of levels on which life stress can be characterized. The level most appropriate to the specificity hypothesis, level 3, is one on which few instruments other than the LEDS have developed dimensions. This level focuses upon the specific qualities of the stressor that are likely to give rise to a specific type of emotional response in the average person experiencing it in those circumstances. The table also provides a summary list of the various LEDS dimensions at that level, which have emerged in the chapters in this volume as of etiological significance for various disorders, and includes examples of a few others not discussed in this volume as further illustration. We have tried to include the best-known instruments in Table 15.2, but there is not room to include all published measures. For example, the Life Events Questionnaire developed by Horowitz et al. (1981) in short (34-item) and long (143-item) forms, and scaled at level 4 on a "presumptive stress" score, has been omitted because the authors focused their subsequent research on only one "inciting" event, which they examined in detail in terms of the response sets it evoked, or its "impact." This later approach corresponds more to the LEDS self-report scale, and the use of the term "impact" could cause some confusion (given that one of the dimensions in the Paykel Inventory is also called "impact," but there it is more of a contextual rating).

Anxiety Disorders

It is interesting that it is with anxiety disorders that there is most scope for comment about other research – possibly because the specificity hypothesis is intuitively as easily acceptable here as with depression; possibly because anxiety disorders constitute, as it were, the other

---

2. Recent changes in some of these instruments may mean that this table will require revision. For example, there are indications that the Psychiatric Epidemiology Research Instrument (PERI) may be changing in the direction of verbal interviews with consensus rating meetings (Dohrenwend, Shrout, Link, Martin, & Skodol, 1986). In other words, it may be moving out of the left-hand set of columns in Table 15.2 (checklists) and into the right-hand set (interviews).

TABLE 15.2. Conceptual levels in the analysis of stress in various life stress measures

Level of description	Checklists					Probing interviews	
	Schedule of Recent Experiences (SRE; Holmes & Rahe, 1967)	Tennant & Andrews (1976) life events inventory	Life Experience Survey (Sarason, Johnson, & Siegel, 1978)	Hassles Uplifts (Kanner, Coyne, Schaefer, & Lazarus, 1981)	Psychiatric Epidemiology Research Interview (PERI; Krasnoff, Askenasy, & Dohrenwend, 1978)	Paykel Inventory (Paykel et al., 1969)	LEDS (Brown & Harris, 1978)
Individuals							
Level 5: Aggregate score of any lower-level scales for a given period	1. Total of individual life change unit (LCU) score	1. Total distress		1. Frequency 2. Cumulative severity 3. Intensity		1. Total of individual LCU score	Additivity not assumed[a]
Events							
Level 4: General stress Valence	1. Readjustment or LCU score	1. Distress scaling 2. Self-caused events	1. Undesirability	1. Severity of each hassle and uplift	1. Amount and desirability of change 2. Effect of respondent's behavior on occurrence of event	1. Positive impact 2. Negative impact 3. LCU score 4. Independence	1. Severity of threat 2. Independence

| Level 3: Cognitive-emotional qualities | 1. Life-threatening | 1. Exit 2. Entrance | 1. Loss 2. Danger 3. Trauma 4. Challenge 5. Goal frustration 6. Conflict over speaking out 7. Intrusiveness 8. Fresh start 9. Exhaustion 10. Motherhood situation 11. Disruptive versus regular 12. Expectedness 13. Stigma 14. Guilt induction 15. Habit change |
| Level 2: Noncognitive-nonemotional qualities | To be developed | | 1. Previous experience 2. Focus 3. Type of relationship 4. Frequency of contact Etc. |

(continued)

TABLE 15.2. *(continued)*

Level of description	Checklists					Probing interviews	
	Schedule of Recent Experiences (SRE; Holmes & Rahe, 1967)	Tennant & Andrews (1976) life events inventory	Life Experience Survey (Sarason, Johnson, & Siegel, 1978)	Hassles Uplifts (Kanner, Coyne, Schaefer, & Lazarus, 1981)	Psychiatric Epidemiology Research Interview (PERI; Krasnoff, Askenasy, & Dohrenwend, 1978)	Paykel Inventory (Paykel et al., 1969)	LEDS (Brown & Harris, 1978)
Level 1B: Basic units	43 listed items	63 listed items	57 listed items	6 types of events may possibly emerge from level 1A below	102 listed items	63 types of events	40 types of events
Minor incidents and life patterns (and sometimes feelings)							
Level 1A: Basic subunit				List of 117 hassles and 135 uplifts			Incident Interview Schedule

[a]Surtees's residual adversity index may be used for this purpose.

"wing" of affective disorder and are thus found frequently enough to be easily studied. However, the fact that they are commonly found together with depression suggests some caution in interpreting findings regarding precipitants unless onsets of anxiety disorders occurring simultaneously with depressive disorders have been distinguished from those without. Thus, although a high rate of bereavements as precipitants has been reported among a series of agoraphobic patients (Sim & Houghton, 1966), this is not necessarily inconsistent with the LEDS findings linking loss (bereavement) with depression and danger with anxiety. It is essential to clarify the original symptom picture of the agoraphobia at the time of its onset.

Research with the LEDS among women in the Outer Hebridean islands has documented that many of the chronic cases of anxiety without depression (usually agoraphobia) had originally been a component part of a depressive bereavement reaction (Prudo, Brown, Harris, & Dowland, 1981). Particularly noteworthy was the tendency for those with nondepressive anxiety conditions preceded by bereavements to have lost a parent, whereas those with a chronic disorder precipitated by the death of a spouse or child tended to have depression without anxiety. Given the protective role played by parents from one's earliest years, their loss might seem intuitively more "dangerous" than loss of a child, and more even than loss of a spouse, who may play a more egalitarian, less protective role than a parent. These results may therefore be interpreted as paralleling Finlay-Jones's findings, in that in the Hebrides those bereavements giving rise to mixed caseness of depression and anxiety had a quality of danger combined with the more obvious element of loss. In our report (Prudo et al., 1981), we described the particular closeness of kinship ties on these islands. On another Gaelic-speaking island off the coast of Northern Ireland, about half of those who married did not live with their spouses as it was considered too disloyal to their kin (Fox, 1978). We sensed some element of this extreme response in the Hebrides, and it is easy to see under such circumstances how a fundamental threat to security could be involved in the death of a close tie. The example also makes the point that a fully effective treatment of "context" in this instance needs to take account of cultural variation in typical concerns.

Miller and Ingham (1985), using the LEDS, independently developed certain qualitative dimensions of events, which they then related to a hierarchy of types of symptomatology (i.e., not only disorders at a caseness level) embracing depression, anxiety, tiredness, and backache. The six dimensions of events elaborated were choice of action, uncertainty of outcome, hopeless situation, personal loss, antisocial act, and threat. This last was a subdivision of contextual threat including all events scored as marked or moderate once those rated as "personal loss" had been excluded. It was therefore relatively close in meaning to "danger" as defined by the LEDS, though not identical (some nonloss events involve hassle rather than danger). Loss emerged as having the greatest association with depression; threat was highly associated with anxiety, as long as it occurred along with at least one of the other dimensions. Also, dimensions such as uncertainty or choice of action without either loss or threat were associated with tiredness. The authors commented on the similarity of their findings to those of the Finlay-Jones study reported in Chapter 3.

Although most other studies of anxiety disorders are not strictly comparable, the brief descriptions of events that are sometimes provided offer some confirmation for the role of danger events. Thus Roberts (1964, p. 192) gives examples of 8 out of 23 precipitant events, all of which would qualify for a rating of severe danger. Another study using the Paykel Inventory and the Research Diagnostic Criteria (RDC) reported suggestive results in terms of the differences between events in the 6 months preceding depression and anxiety disorders (Barrett, 1979). Anxiety sufferers experienced fewer exits, undesirable events, and uncontrollable interpersonal disruptions. It was not, however, possible to read between the lines in the way feasible with Roberts's more detailed accounts, to see whether there was a high rate of severe danger events before anxiety. It is also worth commenting that the threshold for RDC generalized anxiety disorder is likely to be considerably lower than for Bedford College caseness of anxiety, so that a low rate of severe danger events might not in any event constitute a challenge to the specific hypothesis espoused in this volume. Barrett himself comments on the difficulty of pinpointing a definitive onset date among this category of disorders which always tend towards chronicity.

Finally, it is important to comment on Finlay-Jones's finding that parental divorce during childhood can act as a vulnerability factor for onset of anxiety without depression. The literature contains only one study (Faravelli, Webb, Ambonetti, Fonnesu, & Sessarego, 1985) that meets adequate methodological standards, using an established caseness threshold (DSM-III) and a comparison group. However, the series was small and consisted entirely of agoraphobic patients, who, as emphasized earlier, were quite likely to have been suffering from depression along with their anxiety at onset of the episode. The study found higher rates not only of parental divorce, but also of other separations from mother (minimum duration 6 months); the findings are thus more reminiscent of series of depressed subjects (where early loss of mother is important) than of Finlay-Jones's results. This distinction between types of childhood life events and their relationship to differential diagnosis may ultimately prove as illuminating as the distinction between the current dimensions of loss and danger. Although this would be highly speculative, it would seem to be worth commenting on the cognitive-emotional match between the atmospheres of discord that may have preceded the parental divorces – and against which the children may well have had to exercise vigilance – and the current circumstances following danger events, where the individuals are on guard against the occurrence of future crises.

Schizophrenia

As Richard Day points out in Chapter 4, findings concerning life events and schizophrenia, though relatively few, have tended to converge in suggesting that long-term threat or undesirability is not as important as in affective disorder, and that the interval between precipitating event and onset may be shorter than with depression. In terms of the specificity hypothesis, however, even the LEDS findings are no more than suggestive, given that the reanalysis of the data in terms of the dimension of intrusiveness of events has so far always been late in the timetable of each study, and material on intrusiveness has yet to be specially collected. On the other hand, with the detailed information available from the LEDS, such subsequent analyses may provide genuine pointers to what is going on. (Thus the reanalysis of Connolly's [1976] data on myocardial infarction patients, which pointed to the role of goal frustration experiences, was supported by the later study reported in Chapter 12, where material about goal frustration was routinely collected.)

There is certainly a suggestive cognitive-emotional match between the proposed intrusive quality of life events occurring before the acute onset of florid schizophrenic symptoms and the well-established role of high criticism in the home atmosphere in producing relapse, as evidenced by the work on high expressed emotion (EE) (Brown, Birley, & Wing, 1972). Some of this work is particularly impressive, since the explanatory models have been confirmed in a number of important ways by interventions that have succeeded in reducing relapse by training families to minimize their interference and critical comments (Leff & Vaughn, 1985). One final word on schizophrenia and intrusiveness: The study by Steinberg and Durrell (1968), which showed a much higher rate of schizophrenic onset in the early months following first recruitment into the army than during later months, can be interpreted as evidence supporting the role of this dimension of intrusiveness. By definition, entering army life brings with it a definite increase in authoritarian interference.

Physical Illness

We turn now to the reports concerning physical illness. It is necessary to say at the outset that the positive associations reported in these chapters between life events and physical disorders must strike many readers as surprising, in the light of earlier skeptical reviews of the topic (e.g., Andrews & Tennant, 1978). The explanation for this discrepancy, we maintain, derives largely from the manner in which the life events have been measured. A corresponding argument can be raised against the negative evidence linking depressed mood and physical illness (Goldberg, Comstock, & Hornstra, 1979): namely, that by examining illness in general (and thus not distinguishing gastrointestinal from neoplastic from respiratory illnesses), the authors were bound to miss the specific effects of a higher rate of depression in one condition and a lower rate in another. This is discussed again later. Moreover, at this point, it is necessary to warn the reader of an additional complexity. Unlike the research on affective disorders most research into physical disorders has relied on the study of patient series, rather than obtaining "cases" in the general population. This raises the possibility that a psychosocial correlate has only served to bring a person into treatment instead of playing a role in producing the disorder itself. It is sometimes feasible to argue against this possibility on the grounds of the severity of the clinical picture. However, it may well occur, and we include this possibility in some of the etiological models that we formulate.

The chapter in this volume that has most echoes elsewhere in the literature is that on myocardial infarction. Here it is possible to underline the etiological links by emphasizing the way in which dimensions of events and difficulties can have overtones of a quality of personality – as, for example, is the case with overload and frustrations at work and the hard-driving, "hot-reacting" Type A person. If this extension is made for the studies of physical disorders in general, the range of previous findings to be cited can be broadened to include not only work on life events, but also some of the better early psychosomatic studies focusing on personality attributes. Thus, although goal frustration as such was not measured in other early work on patients with gastric/duodenal ulcers, it is interesting that Graham *et al.* (1962) picked out a specific attitude characterizing the typical ulcer patient, which is strongly reminiscent of a goal frustration situation: "felt deprived of what was due to him and wanted to get even (didn't get what he should, what was owed or promised . . .)" (p. 260). Of all the early psychosomatic work, this specificity-of-attitude hypothesis, first proposed in 1952 by Grace and Graham, perhaps offers most by way of corroboration to the specificity of the life stress hypothesis proposed here: Describing attitudes rather than personality traits on the one hand tends to suggest a type of situation that may have provoked that attitude, and on the other hand focuses attention on the time near onset rather than on a longer period. It is therefore disappointing to find that the only other condition discussed both by Graham *et al.* (1962) and by authors in the present volume is multiple sclerosis. The attitude identified by Graham *et al.* – "felt forced to undertake some kind of physical activity, especially hard work, and wanted not to" (1962, p. 260) – is much more specific than the severity of threat/unpleasantness highlighted by Grant, McDonald, Patterson, and Trimble in Chapter 11 of this volume. Graham and colleagues only considered four patients with multiple sclerosis, and it is possible that over a larger sample there would have been a wider range of severe events without this particular feature. But further exploration of Grant *et al.*'s data might also reveal a more specific qualitative aspect to the threat/unpleasantness than emerges in the present analysis, though not necessarily the rather unusual one suggested by Graham and colleagues. In addition, further exploration might also throw light on psychiatric state among the multiple sclerosis patients.

THE ROLE OF PSYCHIATRIC STATUS

In some of the studies of physical disorders reported in this volume, psychiatric status suggested additional evidence for the relevant specific cognitive-affective dimension by indirectly suggesting the typical emotional response to the stressors. Thus the absence of substantial depression or anxiety before myocardial infarction (which, as we shall see, seems to be borne out in the wider literature) was at least consistent with the significance of the types of energetic, hard-driving responses these individuals might have been showing to the work difficulties they were facing (see Chapter 12). Similarly, the relative absence of depression among secondary amenorrhea patients, but the presence of a good deal of minor tension, was consistent with the specific types of challenge situations so often found among these patients (see Chapter 10). Although there is no explicit tradition in the literature on secondary amenorrhea that emphasizes the dimension of dedication in meeting challenge highlighted in Chapter 10 (unlike the frequent references to hard-driving workaholics in the literature on heart disease), reading between the lines in a number of studies does suggest certain parallels. The frequent reports identifying athletes and ballerinas as especially at risk invite the interpretation that their dedication to the competitive challenge of their profession, as much as physiological impact of their exercise, may be of crucial etiological importance. One study in Finland (Ronkainen, Pakarinen, Kirkinen, & Kauppila, 1985) concludes that the strenuous nature of training for competitive running seems to be the crucial factor influencing ovarian hormones and gonadotrophins, rather than the exercise itself. One further comment is in order here: This particular hypothesis has utilized a demographic variable, social occupation (athlete), to highlight a specific cognitive-affective quality (competitive dedication), thus extending the possible range of variables whose clustering may allow a specificity interpretation. It is as if persons who play certain roles are more likely to have certain types of personality dispositions – perhaps because over the years particular types of jobs can mold personality characteristics in the sense that roles can help to mold identities.

In addition, of course, occupations relate to the presence or absence of particular types of life events or difficulties. For example, Caffrey's (1969) comparison of Benedictine monks and Trappist priests fits neatly into the vulnerability model of myocardial infarction suggested here. Although Trappist priests were collectively judged to be as strongly Type A in personality as Benedictine priests, their low rate of myocardial infarction could be attributed to the "lack of role-conflict in their life" (Trappists operate no schools or parishes, as do the Benedictine priests; Caffrey, 1969, p. 102). Another study following a similar framework in relating sociocultural role identities to disease onset was Marmot and Syme's (1976) work on Japanese-Americans, in which those most "acculturated" to Western values, as measured by four indices of upbringing and assimilation, showed a prevalence of coronary heart disease five times greater that that of those least acculturated. Again, the focus was on the link between way of life, type of stressful events, and competitive personality style. Charting these kinds of links between psychological identity and social role makes it easier to see how the broad statistical associations of social epidemiology between demographic factors and disease can be combined with the narrower links usually explored between the psychological and the somatic in a genuinely integrated final perspective. As will emerge later, the concept of a role identity can transform the specificity perspective into what Weiner (1982) calls a genuinely "biopsychosocial" approach rather than merely a psychosomatic one.

Meanwhile, to return to the topic of the psychiatric state before onset of physical illness, the possible role of tension intervening between event and physical illness in the absence of depression or anxiety was also suggested in the study of functional dysphonia (Chapter 13). Here there was a particularly high rate of muscular tension in the laryngeal region, and it is interesting to relate this similarity in the experience of tension in those with secondary amenorrhea and dysphonia to corresponding similarities between the attitudes and stressful situations identified for each condition (see Chapters 10 and 13). On the one hand, the rate of severe loss events was not especially high in either condition, despite a somewhat elevated rate of severe events in general in the dysphonia group in the 4 weeks before onset. One the other hand, the possible predisposing personality traits seemed similar: The dedication proposed as important in secondary amenorrhea patients who responded to a definite challenge has distinct echoes of the loyalty and devotion shown by dysphonia patients who faced conflict over speaking out about irksome, behavior in invalid relatives. As far as further confirmation goes, it is only possible to note that other studies of dysphonia and secondary amenorrhea either have not commented on a high rate of depression or have not used a standardized clinical instrument. The present study of secondary amenorrhea (Chapter 10) probably provides enough evidence to warn us to treat with some caution the speculative remarks about the role of depression that are occasionally made in the clinical literature, especially as few studies distinguish psychiatric state at the time of interview (and thus after onset) from that before onset.

A similar caution is also relevant with regard to psychiatric state and myocardial infarction, where so far as we can see, despite the size of the literature there has as yet been no systematic study of psychiatric symptomatology using a standardized instrument to cover a defined preonset period. Many of the studies have only used simple anxiety and depression scales, or scales on the Minnesota Multiphasic Personality Inventory (MMPI) or Cattell Inventory, which would not be comparable with the Present State Examination (PSE) used in the studies reported in this volume. Kringlen (1981) reports low rates of what he calls "clinical" depression in his study of twins, but gives no indication of how this was assessed. However, the general picture that does emerge from the studies suggests that any depression before myocardial infarction is likely to be very mild and to involve fatigue rather than depressed mood. Thus, lack of energy, feeling blue, and many minor physical complaints were reported more often by those who later developed myocardial infarction than by persons remaining free of heart disease in the Kaiser-Permanente prospective study (Friedman, Ury, Kaltsky, & Siegelaub, 1974). It is fatigue, not depression, that Nixon (1976) cites in his model of the human function curve whereby cardiovascular disease follows upon excessive effort. A similar state of "vital exhaustion and depression" is described by Falger and Appels (1982) as the immediate herald of myocardial infarction, and once again this clearly does not appear to reach the severity threshold even of borderline-case depression, let alone of clinical depression. In their most recent work, Appels, Hoppener, and Mulder (1987) explicitly rename the syndrome "vital exhaustion rather than . . . vital exhaustion and depression as used in preliminary reports," on the grounds that "contrary to expectations almost none of the items referring to depression (guilt feelings; lowered self-esteem) had any predictive power" (p. 10). The literature also gives a general impression that even within the study of coronary heart disease a specificity approach is important, because anxiety (in contrast to depression) and hypochondriasis or hysteria scores relate more clearly to angina pectoris than to myocardial infarction (for a prospective study, see Medalie *et al.*, 1973). One elegant study (Bass & Wade, 1984), using an instrument very similar to the PSE, the Clinical Interview Schedule (Goldberg, Cooper, Eastwood, Kedward, & Shepherd, 1970), compared 46 patients with insignificant coronary obstruction and 53 with significant obstruction as defined by coronary angiography. It did not find a rate of depressive morbidity among the latter group that was any higher than would be expected in a comparable population sample – about 8% in a group where three-quarters of the patients were men.

Bass and Wade's study brings us face to face with the contrast between functional and organic conditions: In their inquiry, patients without significant coronary obstruction had a much higher rate of psychiatric morbidity (mostly anxiety) than those with significant obstruction. This could not be explained by an excess of women or unemployed individuals among those with normal coronary arteries (unemployment and being female are factors likely to increase psychiatric morbidity). This result is strikingly reminiscent of findings reported in Chapters 8 and 9, where those with functional gastrointestinal pain were found to have higher rates of caseness of affective disorder than those with an organic diagnosis. In Creed's and Craig's studies, however, the excess in the functional groups was no less likely to be depression than anxiety, whereas in Bass and Wade's study rates of anxiety neurosis differed more sharply between the two groups of patients. It is tempting once again to relate this difference between rates of anxiety and depression in the different conditions to the specificity hypotheses in another form: namely, that the physical symptoms of anxiety, such as palpitations and especially the hyperventilation syndrome (oppression, tightness across the chest, and profuse sweating), resemble more closely the symptoms of cardiac ischemia than those of gastrointestinal disorder. (This is not to say that other symptoms of cardiac ischemia, such as chest pain, are always easy to distinguish from forms of gastrointestinal disorder, such as esophageal dysfunction.) Bass and Wade (1984) point out that a similarly high incidence of phobic symptoms was reported in previous studies of functional cardiovascular disorder (Wittkower, Rodger, & Macbeth Wilson, 1941; Cohen & White, 1951).

The processes by which depression may contribute to a higher rate of functional gastrointestinal pain have been explored in detail by Craig (Chapter 9); similar processes may obviously also operate to raise sensitivity to pain in other functional conditions. Among other findings reported in this volume and not involving gastrointestinal conditions, only those involving menorrhagia (Chapter 10) are of relevance to this distinction between functional and organic disorders, and here results did not correspond with the hypothesis. Nor did another study of women undergoing hysterectomy find any higher psychiatric morbidity in its functional than in its organic group (Gath, Cooper, & Day, 1982).

However, it is possible that the functional-organic boundary in menor-rhagia may come to be redrawn, and in this connection it is interesting that low rates of depression were found in the endometriosis/ adenomy-osis group of "organic" menorrhagia sufferers in both studies (any psy-chiatric morbidity in that group involved anxiety without depression; D. Gath, personal communication, 1987).

MODELS FOR THE EMERGENCE OF PHYSICAL DISORDERS

What has been emerging, then, has been a series of chains of cir-cumstances, each linking the external situation to the particular disor-der via the specific characteristics and responses of the individual along the following lines:

Social roles and long-term personality dispositions ⟶ Life events/ difficulties ⟶ Emotional psychiatric response ⟶ Physical disorder

And it seems that if the emotional response to life events and difficulties is of the intensity of psychiatric caseness, the disorder itself may be functional and involve less organic pathology (e.g., smaller undetectable lesions or even none at all). For, as noted in Chapter 7, an interest in pursuing the correlates of the functional-organic distinction does not require a commitment to either the modern or the 19th-century per-spective on functional disorders. The last two links in the chain follow two different pathways:

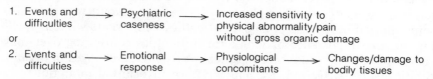

1. Events and difficulties ⟶ Psychiatric caseness ⟶ Increased sensitivity to physical abnormality/pain without gross organic damage

or

2. Events and difficulties ⟶ Emotional response ⟶ Physiological concomitants ⟶ Changes/damage to bodily tissues

Although the first of these models is usually associated with func-tional disorders and the second with organic disorders, there is no rea-son why both, albeit with different relative importance, may not be involved in either organic or functional (in the earlier sense) disorders. In the first model, subjects are coming into treatment because their per-ceptions of physical abnormalities and pain have been heightened by the intensity of their emotional response. They are thus selecting them-selves for diagnosis. This perspective – that psychological distress is an important component of illness behavior – has been well argued by Mechanic (e.g., 1972, 1978), whose studies illuminate the way in which the psychosocial factors influencing perceptions of bodily complaints affect the utilization of medical services. In the second model, it is less the emotional response and its intensity than the physiological concomitants of this response leading to organic changes that play the critical intervening role in bringing the subjects into treatment.

In broad terms, the two models can be seen to reflect a self-selective intervening mechanism for functional disorder and a physiological one for organic disorder (although, as just noted, complex combinations of the models are certainly possible). It should also be pointed out that these models are only crude. The self-selective mechanism proposed by the first model may take a variety of forms. In the simplest instance, the fact that treatment is received may reflect no more than the strength of the person's response; that is, there is no threat to the validity of the proposed causal pathway. However, in certain circumstances, the central causal role of this response may complicate any interpretation of results in terms of specific effects. For example, the physical symptoms of anxiety resemble more closely the symptoms of cardiac ischemia than those of gastrointestinal disorder, and these in turn may lead to differential consultation in terms of medical specialty. In this sense, there may be a misleading sense of specificity where type of psychiatric disorder is concerned, although this would not rule out an important mediating role for affective disorder in general in functional conditions. In a wide-ranging review of these processes, Lloyd (1986) has discussed how increased sensitivity to bodily cues may be supplemented in other instances by "alexithymic" personalities' using somatic symptoms as a form of communication with other people because they find verbal communication problematic. He also reminds us that may somatic symptoms, such as palpitations and headaches, are in fact the ordinary concomitants of psychiatric disorder, but are misinterpreted by the sufferers as signs of a further physical illness. The second model is also somewhat crude, in that it aligns difficulties with events without spelling out the importance of long-term difficulties continuing over may years as the likely cause of the critical physiological changes in organic conditions (as suggested in Chapter 12 for myocardial infarction). By contrast, the first model is much more compatible with a chain of reactions following swiftly after a severe event.

Fortunately, psychiatric symptom schedules registering subthreshold (or borderline-case) morbidity can to some extent act as indicators for the emotional response hypothesized in the second model. Thus Craig's organic group showed a higher rate of borderline-case psychiatric conditions than his comparison group (Chapter 9), just as Murphy and Brown (1980) also reported a possible intervening role for borderline-case symptomatology between provoking agent and physical disorder. In Chapter 11, Grant and colleagues do not report data on psychiatric status, but in concluding they speculate on the possibility that provoking agents may have some effect on the immune system, thus lowering resistance to an infective agent contracted previously. It may well emerge later that the role of borderline-case psychiatric conditions in the onset of such a wide variety of physical disorders consists exactly of this effect upon the immune system in general. Previous discussion of this has often implied that the depressive patterns of symptoms to which this role is attributed may be more than just minor. For example, the frequently cited study by Bartrop, Luckhurst, and Lazarus (1977) deals with the experience of being widowed, after which it is reasonable to expect a high rate of caseness (or at least high borderline caseness) of depression. (In fact, however, this is not clear in the study data.) Another study has confirmed this prospectively, examining suppression of lymphocyte stimulation both before and after the death of wives from breast cancer (Schleifer, Keller, Camerino, Thornton, & Stein, 1983), but again the relationship to depression is not established . However, another retrospective study comparing 49 men with a recent experience of family illness or death with a group of matched controls was able to relate low lymphocyte reactivity to depression as defined by a cutoff score of 17 on the Hopkins Symptom Checklist (Linn, Linn, & Jensen, 1984). Moreover, loneliness (as measured by the UCLA Loneliness Scale) and depression on the 53-item Brief Symptom Inventory were associated with poorer immune function after marital separation (Kiecolt-Glaser et al., 1987).

Certainly the findings of Calloway and Dolan (Chapter 5) among depressed psychiatric patients point to a connection between higher urinary free cortisol and LEDS provoking agents, and this accords well with the body of research on the impact of stress on the pituitary-adrenocortical axis. Furthermore, during the 1970s many studies accumulated suggesting that increases in cortisol were associated with a decreased lymphocyte response to stimulated mitosis and a decreased ability of lymphocytes to destroy foreign cells (e.g., Claman, 1972; for a thorough recent review of the impact of psychosocial factors on immune response, see Jemmott & Locke, 1984, and Stein, Keller, & Schleifer, 1985). But there is no reason why such effects should necessarily involve case rather than borderline-case conditions, nor is it clear that depression must always be involved in these raised rates of psychiatric symptoms. Furthermore, recent work suggests that such a link between affective response and immune function may not always be cortisol-mediated. Among unemployed women, decrease in lymphocyte reactivity was not associated with any significant changes in serum cortisol (Arnetz et al., 1987); and one study with rats suggests that opioid peptides may be the agents that mediate the suppressive effect of stress on natural killer cell cytotoxicity (Schavit, Lewis, Terman, Gale, & Liebeskind, 1984). Clearly, until further evidence is available, this move to incorporate biochemical processes in models involving the LEDS and various illnesses is largely speculative. Meanwhile, the relevant hypothesis to be tested is this:

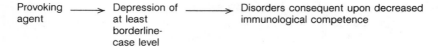

Susceptibility to infectious disease is, of course, only one of several consequences of disturbed immunological functioning; there is clearly room for the development of similar yet differing hypotheses involving other immune-related disorders, such as cancer, autoimmune disorders, and allergies (see Solomon, 1981; Stein, Keller, & Schleifer, 1981). Within the body of studies on susceptibility to infection reviewed by Jemmott and Locke (1984), there is already some hint of specificities, but it is difficult to relate these to the LEDS dimensions on level 3 of Table 15.2. Thus the work linking upper respiratory tract illness and lower secretary immunoglobin A with power-related life change stress in subjects high in inhibited power motivation could be related either to goal frustration or to loss according to the LEDS ratings – or, indeed, to both (McClelland, Floor, Davidson, & Saron, 1980; McClelland, Alexander, & Marks, 1982).

A classic prospective study of infectious mononucleosis in army cadets (Kasl, Evans, & Neiderman, 1979) identified the combination of high motivation toward a military career and poor recent academic performance as highly predictive of the clinical disease; again, however, it is difficult to know whether the poor academic performance would even qualify as a genuine life event according to LEDS rules, let alone a severe one. Totman and Kiff's (1979) study of susceptibility to colds was designed to try to incorporate major features of the LEDS, and deliberately contrasted change and loss aspects of life stress on the Totman Loss Index and the Totman Change Index. In view of the fact that these indices were additive (a number of minor losses could exceed the score of one major loss), it is hard to interpret them in comparable terms with the LEDS. It is thus difficult to know what to make of their finding that the loss index predicted cold symptoms following inoculation with rhinovirus, while the change index predicted virus shedding. However, the Totman and Kiff study does alert one to the possibility that different systems may operate simultaneously through different pathways to promote ill health. The findings suggest, although not explicitly, that life stress may occasionally operate more mechanically than through meaning systems involving emotion or cognition; change per se, without any definite emotional flavor, may exhaust the organism's resources. But further theoretical advances would seem to require these "exhausting" features of particular events to be rated contextually, and not to be left to the generalized scaling procedures concerning social readjustment by which change has hitherto been measured.

TABLE 15.3. Schematic diagram showing various specific linkages for the emergence of particular disorders

Specific dimension of event/difficulty	Specific vulnerability	Psychiatric status	Possible intervening mechanisms			Specific somatic disorder
			Self-selective mechanisms	Speculative physiological response		
Loss	Current and previous low self-esteem	Clinical depression	Not applicable	Not applicable		Not applicable
Loss	?Low self-esteem Early menarche Previous premenstrual tension	Depressive symptomatology	Heightened perception of menstrual blood loss	Unclear; possibly prostaglandins		Menorrhagia
Severe threat Possibly loss	Unclear	Affective symptomatology	Heightened perception of pain, gut contractility, air swallowing	Not applicable		Functional, abdominal pain, including noninflamed appendices
Severe threat Possibly loss	Previous contact with infective agent	Unclear	?Heightened perception of visual blurring, numbness, speech difficulties	Alterations in immune system		Multiple sclerosis
Goal frustration	Striving stubborness	Nonspecific minor syndromes	Unclear	1. Autoimmune process 2. Increased acid secretion		1. Inflammatory bowel disease 2. Peptic ulcer disease

(continued)

TABLE 15.3. *(continued)*

Specific dimension of event/difficulty	Specific vulnerability	Psychiatric status	Possible intervening mechanisms			Specific somatic disorder
			Self-selective mechanisms	Speculative physiological response		
Challenge	Dedication Late menarche	Mild tension syndromes	Possibly punctilious early self-referral	Neurotransmitters (especially dopamine) inhibit luteinizing-hormone-releasing hormone		Secondary amenorrhea (standard)
Motherhood situations	Early menarche	Denial of depression	Unclear	Reduction in dopamine raises levels of luteinizing hormone and prolactin		Pseudocyesis
Conflict over speaking out	Punctiliousness	Laryngeal muscular tension	Unclear	Unclear		Functional dysphonia
Danger	Vigilance against future loss/damage	Anxiety neurosis	Not applicable	Not applicable		Not applicable
Intrusiveness	Sensitivity to criticism/interference	Schizophrenia	Not applicable	Not applicable		Not applicable

SPECIFIC LINKAGES FOR THE EMERGENCE OF
PARTICULAR DISORDERS

In Table 15.3 we summarize the specific linkages suggested by the chapters in this volume, following the model of the chain from background social or psychological factors through life events and difficulties, emotional responses, and the physiological concomitants of these, to the particular illness onset. It will be seen that in some rows the table espouses only one of the two models outlined earlier as intervening between stressor and onset, whereas in other rows it refers to both. Thus in the third row only the first model is portrayed – functional abdominal pain arises from stress only through the self-selective intervening mechanism; in the fifth row, dealing with organic gastrointestinal disorder, only the second model is portrayed, with the self-selective mechanism not considered relevant. In the fourth row both types of mechanism are considered of possible relevance to multiple sclerosis (although this is in no way meant to suggest that the disorder is functional rather than organic), whereas in the eighth row it is unclear whether the functional nature of dysphonia involves a treatment selection mechanism, or whether it merely involves an extension of the psychiatric symptoms of muscular tension. In the second row the table refers to both types of mechanism for menorrhagia, although if knowledge were more advanced this row might have been divided into two – one for functional menorrhagia working through the first self-selective model, and one for organic menorrhagia working through some physiological mechanism involving the prostaglandins or some other factor, perhaps concerning fibrinolysis. But, as is explained in Chapter 10, systematic studies relating organic pathology to menstrual blood loss have not yet established a reliable boundary between functional and organic menorrhagia in clinical diagnostic terms, and a division of the second row of Table 15.3 along those lines would therefore be premature.

Underlying such a series of links is the assumption that different emotions have physiologically distinguishable accompaniments. This issue still remains unsettled, though some of the classic contributions to the debate date from 30 years ago: Ax (1953), Engel (1960), J. Schachter (1957), and S. Schachter (1970) argued for specificity, whereas Levi (1965) argued that catecholamine levels correlate with intensity of either pleasurable or unpleasant emotion, not with its quality. But recent work is encouraging in terms of the validity of the categories of emotion distinguished in ordinary parlance (see Ekman, 1982), and provides support for the impressive earlier conceptualizations of emotion by Tomkins (1962, 1963) and Izard (1971). However, whether or not there is any mileage to be gained from the highly speculative suggestions about physiological mechanisms in the column second from the right in Table 15.3, the causal chains embodied in the rest of the table are still of interest and may suggest further conditions or rows to be explored. Thus an additional chain might run through the personality characteristic of unwillingness to express emotion openly, via loss experiences and the denial of depression, to the onset of breast cancer (Greer, Morris, & Pettingale, 1979; see also LeShan & Worthington, 1956, and Bahnson & Bahnson, 1966).

Clearly, too, in the light of Chapter 14 on the epidemiology of life stress, there ought to be room for another column in which social roles are distinguished from personality dispositions as separate background vulnerability variables. These two types of factors may influence each other in a continuous causal spiral (more ambitious individuals may select jobs whose demands reinforce their hard-driving behavioral style; the woman who has been forced to leave school early may stay in unrewarding employment because she feels she does not have the worthwhile skills to permit any higher ambitions, with yet further ensuing deterioration of her sense of self-worth). These would be typical person-situation interactions of the type that recent work has highlighted (Magnusson, 1985); they have only been omitted from Table 15.3 to avoid undue complexity. Another column ought also to be included to take account of the individual's physiological vulnerability, which is another part of what Roessler and Engel (1974) call "individual response specificity," over and above the "Specific vulnerability" column here.

If the specific links suggested in Table 15.3 are correct, it becomes easier to interpret the negative results obtained in the study of depressed mood and physical illness mentioned earlier (Goldberg et al., 1979). The large proportion of cardiovascular and gastrointestinal patients in that study might well have reported a lower rate of depression than expected, while the positive association found among other patients (e.g., among those with bacterial and viral infections, or with respiratory metabolic or dental disorder) might have been masked. Although we urge caution about the particular physiological mechanisms linking stressor, specific vulnerability, and psychiatric status with somatic disorder, a bolder stance should perhaps be taken on the more general principle that physiological responses to stress will ultimately be found to vary in specific ways, and the notion of one generalized physiological stress response will emerge as untenable. In some sense, the existence of two versions of this latter viewpoint – Cannon's (1926) fight-flight reaction versus Selye's (1950) general adaptation syndrome – already boded its overthrow. This dual perspective is best exemplified in Mason's (1968a, 1968b) classic review of two psychoendocrine systems, the pituitary-adreno-cortical (corresponding to Selye's work) and the sympathetic-adreno-medullary (corresponding to Cannon's). This dichotomy was also elaborated in Henry and Stephens's (1977) distinction between the conservation-withdrawal system of the hippocampal complex and the defense system of the amygdala. Their research was based on animals, but here understandable caution about its relevance for human beings should not develop into rigidities that impede the transfer of knowledge from one species to another. Working with rats and mice, with great sensitivity to their social hierarchies, Henry and Stephens succeeded in developing a model of response to stress that is attractive and easy to apply to human beings.

In sum, then, we are proposing a definite division between varying stressful situations along the lines suggested by Singer (1974) between personal involvement and disengagement. This division would integrate many of the theoretical perspectives hitherto proposed in psychosomatic medicine. According to Table 15.3, and the findings in the earlier chapters, the disorders nearer the top of the table – depression, menorrhagia, functional gastrointestinal disorder, and possibly multiple sclerosis (if we could explore the data in more depth) – would be examples of disorders connected with disengagement. By contrast, the disorders nearer the bottom of the table – secondary amenorrhea, myocardial infarction, and functional dysphonia, and perhaps also organic gastrointestinal disorder, anxiety, and schizophrenia – would be sequelae of involvement/engagement in committed activity of some kind. Of course, disengagement must stem from some form of previous engagement and may take varying periods of time to effect. Klinger (1977) has provided a stimulating overview of this whole area, relating meaning in a person's life to the person's goals and relationships. Although we do not wholly endorse Klinger's integration of the biochemical and the behavioral incentive-disengagement cycle, the perspective outlined here is consistent with his account of the psychosocial phenomenon. This engagement-disengagement dimension is also capable of accommodating another classic concept in the psychosomatic literature, Engel and Schmale's (1967) "giving up-given up" complex. Although careful themselves not to prejudge its nature, these authors end by identifying the "given up" part of the complex with what they call "depression/withdrawal," a clear parallel with disengagement.

If such a dichotomy is espoused, it is tempting to relate it to biochemical knowledge, albeit with caution. The temptation to relate increases in the catecholamines to engagement and decreases to disengagement is reinforced by recent evidence supporting Schildkraut's (1965) early hypothesis concerning their reduction in depression (see also Schildkraut, 1974, and Willner, 1985, for a detailed review), and by work suggesting the role of raised noradrenalin levels in heart disease (see Carruthers, 1969, for an early formulation, and for later relevant evidence see Glass et al., 1980; Contrada et al., 1982; Baroldi, Falizi, & Mariani, 1979). Lundberg and Frankenhauser (1980) extracted two factors: a "distress" factor, with high positive loadings on subjective variables indicative of negative affect and a moderately high positive loading on cortisol excretion; and a factor with high positive loadings on subjective variables indicative of action-proneness and on adrenalin excretion. They cite the parallel work by Ursin, Baade, and Levine (1978), who identified a "cortisol factor" and a "catecholamine factor." From the point of view of the disengagement-involvement dimension proposed here, the parallel is, of course, unmistakable.

Formerly, all catecholamines tended to be discussed in tandem in the context of stress research, but recent reviews have sought to inspire research workers to think in more sophisticated ways about the varieties of biological intervening mechanisms that are posited in so cavalier a fashion (see Steptoe, 1986, 1987, for stimulating discussions along these lines). Furthermore, work on immune function suggests that we should be more sensitive to differences between alpha-adrenergic (norepinephrine-related, and possibly engagement-related) and beta-adrenergic stimulation (possibly less involvement-related, although not necessarily disengaged; see Jemmott & Locke, 1984, p. 97). Frankenhauser's (1983) work with the catecholamines provides the opportunity to consider many such subcategorizations: For example, she has shown that females are less likely to respond to challenging situations by increased catecholamine secretion (see also Frankenhauser, 1975). It is tempting to relate this to the variations in personality style in responding to challenge that are so often commented on in discussions of gender roles, where the aggressiveness of the masculine style and the timidity and obedience of the feminine style are attributed to early socialization (see Oakley, 1972).

Another example of this research team's work with catecholamines is a study of sawmill operators, which reports the association of norepinephrine with irritation and epinephrine with loss of well-being (Frankenhauser & Gardell, 1976). This distinction parallels work with cats, suggesting that a basal amygdaloid defense or fear response involves epinephrine-related activity, whereas the central amygdaloid attack or fight response involves norepinephrine activity (Stock, Schlor, Heidt, & Buss, 1978). This specific distinction between the two catecholamines and the two branches of the fight-flight response echoes the temporarily outmoded Funkenstein hypothesis (1956), based on work with human subjects, that norepinephrine corresponds to "anger out" and epinephrine to "anger in." The distinction also has wider ramifications in terms of social factors, particularly hierachical status, although as yet support for this perspective comes only from animal studies. Lawrence and Haynes (1970) found a greater number of submissive responses from mice receiving epinephrine, and more dominant responses from those receiving norepinephrine. Ely and Henry (1978) also report results suggesting that norepinephrine is specifically involved in the association between social dominance and the sympathetic-adreno-medullary system.

Furthermore, detailed work distinguished the role of dopamine from other catecholamines and suggests that in the very different disorders of schizophrenia and secondary amenorrhea, it may play a more crucial role in onset than the other catecholamines do. But this is just the point at which to pause: There is more than one dopamine system, and there is every indication of complex feedback loops. Knowledge is still far too fluid for us to be able to use neuroendocrinological data as a firm foundation for the specificity hypothesis. Differential dopamine activity has been proposed as relevant for the specific distinction between schizophrenia with positive and with negative symptoms (Mackay & Crow, 1980), but such a specific subcategorization is still highly speculative. What is important is the ability to follow up these speculative specificities systematically within the framework of some kind of model along the lines proposed in Table 15.3, using sensitive and reliable measures of as many links as possible in the chains hypothesized. Thus it would be worth exploring the possibility that intrusive events may be more frequent before onsets of schizophrenia that include the positive symptoms of delusions, hallucinations, and thought disorder (Type I syndrome). Even if the relationship between disturbance of dopaminerigc transmission and Type I (as contrasted with Type II) syndrome is later refuted, systematic study of psychosocial factors involved in the onset and course of the two syndromes may ultimately give rise to yet another neuroendocrinological hypothesis to account for the diagnostic differences.

One final comment is in order: Although pursuit of the perspective involved in Table 15.3 will almost certainly prove productive in scientific terms, there will still be value in pursuing a more general approach in epidemiological studies. As Macintyre (1986) argues, much can be learned by charting the patterning of grosser morbidity indices across different social status and ethnic groups. Not only can this then feed back into the planning of more specific research studies, but it can also more effectively alert those responsible for health policy and planning to what action is required. With the increase in research that crosses interdisciplinary boundaries, and the growth of the biopsychosocial perspective, it becomes ever easier to see both the forest *and* the trees. Nevertheless, just as the art of forestry demands attention to the growth of individual branches and blossoms, we contend that it is mainly through confronting specific etiologies of particular disorders that improvement in our knowledge about the health of members of society will be achieved. Sadly, it does not follow that the social changes entailed by this knowledge will then come about; here the more general approach, which is perhaps better at firing the political imagination, may prove more effective. But meanwhile, given that political, administrative, and professional responsiveness has not proved uniformly indifferent to research findings following the narrower focus, there is room to hope that increasing knowledge about specific etiologies will also prove to be a lever for constructive changes in health policies.

Appendix: New 12-Point Scale of Independence

The first four points deal with "independent" events. Point 1, "Completely independent," describes events whose immediate origin is unconnected with the subject and whose ultimate origin is difficult to attribute to him or her with any plausibility (e.g., a stranger drives into the subject's parked car where he or she is sitting waiting, causing him or her multiple fractures). Point 2 describes events whose immediate origin is unconnected with the subject, but where it is impossible to rule out entirely that some aspect of the subject's behavior might have influenced it (e.g., a friend's deciding to move to a distant part of the country). Point 3, "Negligence by subject impossible to rule out, but not obvious," covers events where influence of the subject's behavior upon the actions of someone else has a certain plausibility, but where there is nothing whatever to suggest that it did occur. Certain accidents to children are included here, though other accidents where the subject's neglect or carelessness is more clearly implicated would fall in a less "independent" category. Point 4 includes all physical illnesses of the subject, this is the least independent of the four "independent" categories and allows for the possibility that somatic complaints may be harbingers of an impending psychiatric breakdown. The rationale for calling this "independent" rather than "possibly independent" derives from an unwillingness to assume the truth of the psychosomatic perspective before it is clearly separately established.

Point 5 is the most independent of the "possibly independent" categories. Called "Subject consents to external events," it deals with events where the subject makes a decision consequent upon some independent incident (e.g., a fall by an elderly mother and a woman's decision to have her come to live with her, where this decision would not have been made without the fall). Point 6 covers intentional actions; it is the classic category of "possibly independent" events, such as a move to a new house or a planned pregnancy. Point 7 describes events that have occurred as a result of the subject's negligence. Thus, since point 3 (see above) is treated conservatively, many events potentially dealt with by point 3 are placed here. The next two points describe events where contact with a key person is disrupted – point 8 after an argument, point 9 without an argument. Point 10 is for events stemming from the subject's romantic susceptibilities that do not really fit points 6 to 9. Point 11 describes events that derive from the romantic susceptibilities of the subject's partner. Although many such events seem to be "independent," our threshold has always been so conservative that anything remotely related to the marital relationship (as opposed to, say, the majority of the partner's health or work events) has been rated only "possibly independent."

References

Andrews, G. (1981). A prospective study of life events and psychological symptoms. *Psychological Medicine, 11*, 795-801.

Andrews, G., & Tennant, C. (1978). Being upset and becoming ill: An appraisal of the relation between life events and physical illness. *Medical Journal of Australia, 1*, 324-327.

Appels, A., Hoppener, P., & Mulder, P. (1987). *A questionnaire to assess premonitory symptoms of myocardial infarction.* Unpublished.

Arnetz, B., Wasserman, J., Petrini, B., Brenner, S.-O., Levi L., Eneroth, E., Salovaara, H., Hjelm, R., Salovaara, L., Theorell, T., & Petterson, I. L. (1987). Immune function in unemployed women. *Psychosomatic Medicine, 49*, 3-12.

Ax, A. F. (1953). The physiological differentiation between fear and anger in humans. *Psychosomatic Medicine, 15*, 443-442.

Bahnson, C. B., & Bahnson, M. B. (1966). Role of the ego defenses: Denial and repression in the etiology of malignant neoplasm. *Annals of the New York Academy of Sciences, 125*, 827-845.

Baroldi, G., Falizi, G., & Mariani, F. (1979). Sudden coronary death: A postmortem study in 208 selected cases compared to 97 "control" subjects. *American Heart Journal, 98*, 20-31.

Barrett, J. E. (1979). The relationship of life events to the onset of neurotic disorders. In J. E. Barrett (Ed.), *Stress and mental disorder* (pp. 87-109). New York: Raven Press.

Bartrop, R. W., Luckhurst, E., & Lazarus, L. (1977). Depressed lymphocyte function after bereavement. *Lancet, i*, 834-836.

Bass, C., & Wade, C. (1984). Chest pain with normal coronary arteries. A comparative study of psychiatric and social morbidity. *Psychological Medicine, 14*, 51-61.

Beck, A. J., Ward, C. H., Mendelson, M., Mock, J., & Erbaugh, J. (1961). An inventory for measuring depression. *Archives of General Psychiatry, 4*, 561-571.

Billings, A. G., & Moos, R. H. (1982). Psychosocial theory and research on depression: An integrative framework and review. *Clinical Psychology Review, 2*, 213-237.

Bolton, W., & Oatley, K. (1987). A longitudinal study of social support and depressiion in unemployed men. *Psychological Medicine, 17*, 453-460.

Breslau, N., & Davis, G. C. (1986). Chronic stress and major depression. *Archives of General Psychiatry, 43*, 309-314.

Brown, G. W., Andrews, B., Harris, T. O., Adler, Z., & Bridge, L. (1986). Social support, self esteem and depression. *Psychological Medicine, 16*, 813-831.

Brown, G. W., Bifulco, A., Harris, T. O., & Bridge, L. (1986). Life stress, chronic psychiatric symptoms and vulnerability to clinical depression. *Journal of Affective Disorders, 11*, 1-19.

Brown, G. W., Birley, J., & Wing, J. K. (1972). Influence of family life on the course of schizophrenic disorders: A replication. *British Journal of Psychiatry, 121*, 241-258.

Brown, G. W., & Harris, T. O. (1978). *Social origins of depression: A study of psychiatric disorder in women.* London: Tavistock.

Brown, G. W., & Harris, T. O. (1986). Establishing causal links: The Bedford College studies of depression. In H. Katschnig (Ed.), *Life events and psychiatric disorders* (pp. 107-187). Cambridge, England: Cambridge University Press.

Brown, G. W., Harris, T. O. & Peto, J. (1973). Life events and psychiatric disorders: 2. Nature of causal link. *Psychological Medicine, 3,* 159-176.

Cadoret, R. S., & Winokur, G., Dorzab, J., & Baker, M. (1972). Disease: Life events and onset of illness. *Archives of General Psychiatry, 26,* 133-136.

Caffrey, B. (1969). Behavior patterns and personality characteristics related to prevalence rates of coronary heart disease in American monks. *Journal of Chronic Diseases, 22,* 93-103.

Cannon, W. B. (1926). The emergency function of the adrenal medulla in pain and the major emotions. *American Journal of Physiology, 33,* 356-372.

Carruthers, M. E. (1969). Aggression and atheroma. *Lancet, ii,* 1170-1171.

Claman, H. N. (1972). Corticosteroids and lymphoid cells. *New England Journal of Medicine, 287,* 388-397.

Cohen, M. E., & White, P. D. (1951). Life situations, emotions, and neurocirculatory asthenia (anxiety neurosis, neurasthenia, effort syndrome). *Psychosomatic Medicine, 13,* 335-357.

Connolly, J. (1976). Life events before myocardial infarction. *Journal of Human Stress, 3,* 3-17.

Contrada, R. J., Glass, D. C., Krakoff, L. R., Krantz, D. S., Kehoe, K., Iseck, W., Collins, C., & Elting, E. (1982). Effects of control over aversive stimulation and Type A behavior on cardiovascular and plasma catecholamine responses. *Psychophysiology, 19,* 408-419.

Dohrenwend, B. P., Shrout, P. E., Link, B. G., Martin, J. L., & Skodol, A. E. (1986). Overview and initial results from a risk-factor study of depression and schizophrenia. In J. E. Barrett & R. M. Rose (Eds.), *Mental disorders in the community* (pp. 184-215). New York: Guilford Press.

Dohrenwend, B. S., Krasnoff, L., Askenasy, A. R., & Dohrenwend, B. P. (1978). Exemplification of a method for sealing life events: The PERI life events scale. *Journal of Health and Social Behavior, 19,* 205-229.

Eales, M. (in press). Affective disorders. *Psychological Medicine.*

Ekman, P. (1982). *Emotions in the human face* (2nd ed.). New York: Cambridge University Press.

Ely, D. L., & Henry, J. P. (1978). Neuroendocrine response patterns in dominant and subordinate mice. *Hormones and Behavior, 10,* 156-169.

Engel, B. T. (1960). Stimulus-response and individual-response specificity. *Archives of General Psychiatry, 2,* 305-313.

Engel, G. L., & Schmale, A. H., Jr. (1967). Psychoanalytic theory of somatic disorder: Conversion, specificity, and the disease onset situation. *Journal of the American Psychoanalytic Association, 15,* 344-365.

Falger, P., & Appels, A. (1982). Psychological risk factors over the life course of myocardial infarction patients. *Advances in Cardiology, 29,* 132-139.

Faravelli, C., Webb, T., Ambonetti, A., Fonnesu, F., & Sessarego, A. (1985). Prevalence of traumatic early life events in 32 agoraphobic patients with panic attacks. *American Journal of Psychiatry, 142,* 1493-1494.

Finlay-Jones, R. (1981). Showing that life events are a cause of depression: A review. *Australian and New Zealand Journal of Psychiatry, 15,* 229-238.

Forrest, A. D., Fraser, R. H., & Priest, R. G. (1965). Environmental factors in depressive illness. *British Journal of Psychiatry, 111,* 243-253.

Fox, R. (1978). *The Tory Islanders: A people of the Celtic fringe.* Cambridge, England: Cambridge University Press.

Frankenhauser, M. (1975). Experimental approaches to the study of catecholamines and emotion. In L. Levi (Ed.), *Emotions: Their parameters and measurement* (pp. 22-35). New York: Raven Press.

Frankenhauser, M. (1983). The sympathetic-adrenal and pituitary-adrenal response to challenge: Comparison between the sexes. In T. M. Dembroski, T. H. Schmidt, & G. Blumchen (Eds.), *Biobehavioral bases of coronary heart disease* (pp. 91-105). New York: S. Karger.

Frankenhauser, M., & Gardell, B. (1976). Underload and overload in working life: Outline of multidisciplinary approach. *Journal of Human Stress, 2*, 35-46.

Friedman, G. D., Ury, H. K., Klatsky, A. L., & Siegelaub, M. S. (1974). A psychological questionnaire predictive of myocardial infarction. *Psychosomatic Medicine, 36*, 327-343.

Frijda, N. G. (1986). *The emotions*. Cambridge, England: Cambridge University Press.

Funkenstein, D. (1956). Norepinephrine-like and epinephrine-like substances in relation to human behaviour. *Journal of Mental Diseases, 124*, 58-68.

Gath, D., Cooper, P., & Day, A. (1982). Hysterectomy and psychiatric disorder: Levels of morbidity before and after hysterectomy. *British Journal of Psychiatry, 140*, 335-350.

Glass, D. C., Krakoff, L. R., Contrada, R., Hilton, W. F., Kehoe, K., Mannucci, E. G., Collins, C., Snow, S., & Elting, E. (1980). Effect of harassment and competition upon cardiovascular and plasma catecholamine responses in Type A and Type B individuals. *Psychophysiology, 17*, 453-463.

Goldberg, D. P., Cooper, B., Eastwood, R. R., Kedward, H. B., & Shepherd, M. (1970). A standardised psychiatric interview for use in community surveys. *British Journal of Preventive and Social Medicine, 24*, 18-23.

Goldberg, E. L., Comstock, G. W., & Hornstra, R. K. (1979). Depressed mood and subsequent physical illness. *American Journal of Psychiatry, 136*, 530-534.

Grace, W. J., & Graham, D. T. (1952). Relationship of specific attitudes and emotions to certain bodily diseases. *Psychosomatic Medicine, 14*, 243-266.

Graham, D. T., Lundy, R. M., Benjamin, L. S., Kabler, J. D., Lewis, W. C., Kunish, N. O., & Graham, F. K. (1962). Specific attitudes in initial interviews with patients having different "psychosomatic" diseases. *Psychosomatic Medicine, 24*, 257-266.

Grant, I., Hervey, L., Sweetwood, H., Yager, J., & Gerst, M. S. (1978). Patterns in the relationship of life events and psychiatric symptoms over time. *Journal of Psychosomatic Research, 22*, 183-191.

Grant, I., Yager, J., Sweetwood, H. L., & Olshen, R. (1982). Life events and symptoms: Fourier analysis of time series from a three-year prospective inquiry. *Archives of General Psychiatry, 39*, 598-605.

Greer, S., Morris, T., & Pettingale, K. W. (1979). Psychological response to breast cancer: Effect on outcome. *Lancet, ii*, 785-787.

Hällström, T. (1986). Social origins of major depression: The role of provoking agents and vulnerability factors. *Acta Psychiatrica Scandinavica, 73,*, 383-389.

Hammen, C., Mayol, A., deMayo, R., & Marks, T. (1986). Initial symptom levels and the life-event-depression relationship. *Journal of Abnormal Psychology, 95*, 114-122.

Henderson, A. S., Byrne, D. G., & Duncan-Jones, P. (1981). *Neurosis and the social environment*. Sydney: Academic Press.

Henry, J. P., & Stephens, P. M. (1977). *Stress, health, and the social environment: A sociobiological approach to medicine*. New York: Springer-Verlag.

Holmes, T. H., & Rahe, R. H. (1967). The Social Readjustment Rating Scale. *Journal of Psychosomatic Research, 11*, 213-218.

Horowitz, M. J., Krupnick, J., Kaltreider, N., Wilner, N., Leong, A., & Marmar, C. (1981). Initial psychological response to parental death. *Archives of General Psychiatry, 38*, 316-323.

Hudgens, R. W., Morrison, H. R., & Barchaa, R. G. (1967). Life events and onset of primary affective disorders. *Archives of General Psychiatry, 16*, 134-145.

Izard, C. E. (1971). *The face of emotion*. New York: Appleton-Century-Crofts.

Janoff-Bulman, R. (1979). Characterological versus behavioral self-blame: Inquiries into depression and rape. *Journal of Personality and Social Psychology, 37*, 1798-1809.

Janoff-Bulman, R. (1985). The aftermath of victimization: Rebuilding shattered assumptions. In C. R. Figley (Ed.), *Trauma and its wake: The study and treatment of posttraumatic stress disorder* (pp. 15-35). New York: Brunner/Mazel.

Jemmott, J. B., III & Locke, S. E. (1984). Psychosocial factors, immunologic mediation, and human susceptibility to infectious diseases: How much do we know? *Psychological Bulletin, 95*, 78-108.

Kanner, A. D., Coyne, J. C., Schaefer, C., & Lazarus, R. S. (1981). Comparison of two modes of stress measurement: Daily hassles and uplifts versus major life events. *Journal of Behavioral Medicine, 4*, 1-39.

Kaplan, G. A., Roberts, R. E., Camacho, T. C., & Coyne, J. C. (1987). Psychological predictors of depression: Prospective evidence from the human population laboratory studies. *American Journal of Epidemiology, 125*, 206-220.

Kasl, S. V. (1983). Pursuing the link between stressful life experiences and disease: A time for reappraisal. In C. L. Cooper (Ed.), *Stress research* (pp. 79-102). New York: Wiley.

Kasl, S. V., Evans, A. S., & Neiderman, J. C. (1979). Psychosocial risk factors in the development of infectious mononucleosis. *Psychosomatic Medicine, 41*, 445-466.

Kiecolt-Glaser, J., Fisher, L., Ogrocki, P., Stout, J., Speicher, C., & Glaser, R. (1987). Marital quality, marital disruption, and immune function. *Psychosomatic Medicine, 49*, 13-31.

Klinger, E. (1977). *Meaning and void: Inner experience and the incentives in people's lives*. Minneapolis: University of Minnesota Press.

Kringlen, E. (1981). Stress and coronary heart disease. In *Twin research: Vol. 3. Epidemiological and clinical studies* (pp. 131-138). New York: Alan R. Liss.

Lawrence, C. W., & Haynes, J. R. (1970). Epinephrine and norepinephrine effects on social dominance behavior. *Psychological Reports, 27*, 195-198.

Leff, J., & Vaughn, C. (1985). *Expressed emotion in families*. New York: Guilford Press.

LeShan, L., & Worthington, R. E. (1956). Loss of cathexes as a common psychodynamic characteristic of cancer patients. *Psychological Reports, 2*, 183-193.

Levi, L. (1965). The urinary output of adrenalin and noradrenalin during pleasant and unpleasant emotional states. *Psychosomatic Medicine, 27*, 80-85.

Linn, M., Linn, B., & Jensen, J. (1984). Stressful events, dysphoric mood, and immune responsiveness. *Psychological Reports, 54*, 219-222.

Lloyd, G. G. (1986). Psychiatric syndromes with a somatic presentation. *Journal of Psychosomatic Research, 30*, 113-120.

Lundberg, U., & Frankenhauser, M. (1980). Pituitary-adrenal and sympathetic-adrenal correlates of distress and effort. *Journal of Psychosomatic Research, 24*, 125-130.

Macintyre, S. (1986). The patterning of health by social position in contemporary Britain: Directions for sociological research. *Social Science and Medicine, 23*, 393-415.

Mackay, A. V. P., & Crow, T. J. (1980). Positive and negative schizophrenic symptoms and the role of dopamine. *British Journal of Psychiatry, 137*, 379-386.

Magnusson, D. (1985). Implications of an interactional paradigm for research on human development. *International Journal of Behavioral Development, 8*, 115-137.

Marmot, M. G., & Syme, L. (1976). Acculturation and coronary heart disease in Japanese-Americans. *American Journal of Epidemiology, 104*, 225-247.

Mason, J. W. (1968a). A review of psychoendocrine research on the plituitary-adrenal cortical system. *Psychosomatic Medicine, 30*, 576-607.

Mason, J. W. (1968b). A review of psychoendocrine research on the sympathetic-adrenal medullary system. *Psychosomatic Medicine, 30*, 631-653.

McClelland, D. C., Alexander, C., & Marks, E. (1982). The need for power, stress, immune function, and illness among male prisoners. *Journal of Abnormal Psychology, 91*, 61-70.

McClelland, D. C., Floor, E., Davidson, R. J., & Saron, C. (1980). Stressed power motivation, sympathetic activation, immune function, and illness. *Journal of Human Stress, 6*, 11-19.

Mechanic, D. (1972). Social psychologic factors affecting the presentation of bodily complaints. *New England Journal of Medicine, 286*, 1132-1139.

Mechanic, D. (1978). Effects of psychological distress on perceptions of physical health and use of medical and psychiatric facilities. *Journal of Human Stress, 4*, 26-32.

Medalie, J. H., Snyder, M, Groen, J. J., Neufeld, H. N., Goldbomt, M. A., & Riss, E. (1973). Angina pectoris among 10,000 men: Five-year incidence and univariate analysis. *American Journal of Medicine, 55*, 583-594.

Miller, P. M., & Ingham, J. G. (1985). Dimensions of experience and symptomatology. *Journal of Psychosomatic Research, 29*, 475-488.

Monroe, S. M. (1982). Assessment of life events. *Archives of General Psychiatry, 39*, 606-610.

Monroe, S. M. (1983). Social support and disorder: Toward an untangling of cause and effect. *American Journal of Community Psychology, 11*, 81-97.

Murphy, E., & Brown, G. W. (1980). Life events, psychiatric disturbance and physical illness. *British Journal of Psychiatry, 136*, 326-338.

Nixon, P. G. F. (1976). Stress and the cardiovascular system. *Practioner, 217*, 765-770, 935-944.

Oakley, A. (1972). *Sex, gender and society.* London: Maurice Temple Smith.

Paykel, E. S. (1974). Recent life events and clinical depression. In E. K. E. Gunderson & R. D. Rahe (Eds.), *Life stress and illness* (pp. 134-163). Springfield, IL: Charles C Thomas.

Paykel, E. S., Myers, J. K., Diendelt, M. N., Klerman, G. L., Lindenthal, J. J., & Pepper, M. P. (1969). Life events and depression: A controlled study. *Archives of General Psychiatry, 25*, 340-347.

Phifer, J. F., & Murrell, S. A. (1986). Etiological factors in the onset of depressive symptoms in older adults. *Journal of Abnormal Psychology, 95*, 282-291.

Prudo, R., Brown, G. W., Harris, T. O., & Dowland, J. (1981). Psychiatric disorder in a rural and an urban population: 2. Sensitivity to loss. *Psychological Medicine, 11*, 601-616.

Roberts, A. (1964). Housebound housewives: A follow-up study of a phobic anxiety state. *British Journal of Psychiatry, 110*, 191-197.

Roessler, R., & Engel, B. T. (1974). The current status of the concepts of physiological response specificity and activation. *International Journal of Psychiatry in Medicine, 5*, 359-365.

Ronkainen, H., Pakarinen, A., Kirkinen, P., & Kauppila, A. (1985). Physical exercise-induced changes and season-associated differences in the pituitary-ovarian function of runners and joggers. *Journal of Clinical Endocrinology and Metabolism, 60*, 416-422.

Rush, A. J., Beck, A. T., Kovacs, M., & Hollon, S. (1977). Comparative efficacy of cognitive therapy and pharmacotherapy in the treatment of depressed outpatients. *Cognitive Therapy and Research, 1*, 17-37.

Sarason, I., Johnson, J. H., & Siegel, J. M. (1978). Assessing the impact of life changes: Development of the Life Experiences Survey. *Journal of Consulting and Clinical Psychology, 46*, 932-946.

Schachter, J. (1957). Pain, fear and anger in hyptertensives and normotensives. *Psychosomatic Medicine, 19*, 17-29.

Schachter, S. (1970). The assumption of identity and peripheralist-centralist controversies in motivation and emotion. In M. Arnold (Ed.), *Feelings and emotions* (pp. 111-122). New York: Academic Press.

Schavit, Y., Lewis, J., Terman, G., Gale, R., & Liebeskind, J. (1984). Opioid peptides mediate the suppressive effect of stress on natural killer cell cytotoxicity. *Science, 223*, 188-190.

Schildkraut, J. J. (1965). The catecholamine hypothesis of affective disorders; A review of supporting evidence. *American Journal of Psychiatry, 122*, 509-522.

Schildkraut, J. J. (1974). Catecholamine metabolism and affective disorders. In E. Usdin & S. Synder (Eds.), *Frontiers in catecholamine research* (pp. 1165-1171). New York: Pergamon Press.

Schleifer, S., Keller, S., Camerino, M., Thornton, J., & Stein, M. (1983). Suppression of lymphocyte stimulation following bereavement. *Journal of the American Medical Association, 250*, 374-377.

Selye, H. (1950). *The physiology and pathology of exposure to stress*. Montreal: Acta.

Sim, M., & Houghton, H. (1966). Phobic anxiety and its treatment. *Journal of Nervous and Mental Diseases, 143*, 484-491.

Singer, M. T. (1974). Presidential address. Engagement-involvement: A central phenomenon in psychophysiological research. *Psychosomatic Medicine, 36*, 1-17.

Solomon, G. F. (1981). Emotional and personality factors in the onset and course of autoimmune disease, particularly rheumatoid arthritis. In R. Ader (Ed.), *Psychoneuroimmunology* (pp. 259-280). New York: Academic Press.

Stein, M., Keller, S., & Schleifer, S. (1981). The hypothalamus and the immune response. In H. Weiner, M. A. Hofer, & A. J. Stunkard (Eds.), *Brain, behavior, and bodily disease*. (pp. 45-61). New York: Raven Press.

Stein, M., Keller, S., & Schleifer, J. (1985). Stress and immunomodulation: The role of depression and neuroendocrine function. *Journal of Immunology, 135*, 827-833.

Steinberg, H. R., & Durrell, J. (1968). A stressful social situation as a precipitant of schizophrenic symptoms: An epidemiological study. *British Journal of Psychiatry, 114*, 1097-1105.

Steptoe, A. (1986). Research programme on breakdown in human adaptation of stress. *Stress Medicine, 2*, 253-257.

Steptoe, A. (1987). The assessment of sympathetic nervous function in human stress research. *Journal of Psychosomatic Research, 31*, 141-152.

Stock, G., Schlor, K. H., Heidt, H., & Buss, J. (1978). Psychomotor behaviour and cardiovascular patterns during stimulation of the amygdala. *Pfluegers Archives, 376*, 177-184.

Surtees, P. G., & Rennie, D. (1983). Adversity and the onset of psychiatric disorder in women. *Social Psychiatry, 18*, 37-44.

Tennant, C., & Andrews, G. (1976). A scale to measure the stress of life events. *Australian and New Zealand Journal of Psychiatry, 10*, 27-32.

Tennant, C., Bebbington, P., & Hurry, J. (1981). The role of life events in depressive illness: Is there a substantial causal relation? *Psychological Medicine, 11*, 379-389.

Tomkins, S. S. (1962). *Affect, imagery, consciousness: Vol. 1. The positive affects*. London: Tavistock.

Tomkins, S. S. (1963). *Affect, imagery, consciousness: Vol. 2. The negative affects*. London: Tavistock.

Totman, R. G., & Kiff, J. (1979). Life stress and susceptibility to colds. In D. J. Oborne, M. M. Gruneberg, & J. R. Eiser (Eds.), *Research in psychology and medicine* (Vol. 1, pp. 141-149). New York: Academic Press.

Ursin, H., Baade, E., & Levine, S. (1978). *Psychobiology of stress*. New York: Academic Press.

Warheit, G. J. (1979). Life events, coping, stress, and depressive symptomatology. *American Journal of Psychiatry, 136*, 502-506.

Weiner, H. (1982). The prospects for psychosomatic medicine: Selected topics. *Psychosomatic Medicine, 44*, 491-517.

Willner, P. (1985). *Depression: A psychobiological synthesis.* New York: Wiley.

Wittkower, E., Rodger, T. F., & Macbeth Wilson, A. T. (1941). Effort syndrome. *Lancet, i*, 531-535.

Yager, J., Grant, I., Hervey, L., Sweetwood, M., & Gerst, M. (1981). Life event reports by psychiatric patients, nonpatients, and their partners. *Archives of General Psychiatry, 38*, 343-347.

16

Summary and Conclusions

GEORGE W. BROWN AND TIRRIL O. HARRIS

This volume has attempted to assemble information about one particular system of measuring life stress, the Life Events and Difficulties Schedule (LEDS). In so doing, we hope not only to inform a wider audience about a method that has not been consistently discussed in reviews of stress research (e.g., Kasl, 1983), but also to provoke discussion of a broad range of issues that are still far from settled. For this reason, considerable attention has been paid to criticisms made of the LEDS, but (we hope) more in the spirit of opening up the debate than in hyperdefensive counterattack. Before these issues are reviewed, however, we summarize the earlier accounts of the use of the LEDS and the resulting findings in the light of the particular perspective the LEDS brings to the study of life events.

Meaning and Emotion

Throughout the presentations in this volume, there has been an assumption that life events play a role in disease largely via meaning. We have seen meaning primarily emerging from plans and purposes inherent in a person's biography and current life structure. For methodological reasons, the contextual approach to measurement that has been for the most part employed avoids using any statement on the respondent's part about meaning. The use of such material in the longitudinal Islington inquiry indicated that the contextual measures are a reasonably accurate estimate, and certainly good enough to get systematic research under way.

It has also been assumed that it is possible to identify specific classes of experiences reflected in life events and difficulties that will correspond in some identifiable way to predispositions to react to these

George W. Brown and Tirril O. Harris. Department of Social Policy and Social Science, Royal Holloway and Bedford New College, University of London, 11 Bedford Square, London WC1B 3RA, England.

experiences with specific disorders. Underlying these assumptions about meaning and specificity of experience has been some notion of the processes by which individuals interact with their environments and by which the cognitive-emotional features of their appraisal produce parallel physiological and neuroendocrinological processes, which finally result in a specific illness. However, life events and difficulties intrude on the complex life structure of the individual and provoke a response from the individual and others in his or her milieu. Only some of this is reflected in the contextual measures of threat. Therefore, although life events have been distinguished from, say, practical and emotional support in dealing with them, any rigid distinction between the two would be misleading, as they are likely to merge as part of a common process in any etiological mechanism that is uncovered. Thus, for example, part of the meaning of a particular crisis is bound to be that support that might reasonably have been expected from a spouse was not forthcoming.

Therefore, although the approach in this volume has involved a distinction between provocation and vulnerability, it has simultaneously emphasized their similarity in cognitive-emotional terms for any specific disorder, in an attempt to respond to the call for "stress research to take into account the dynamic interaction between the situation and the person" (Chesney & Rosenman, 1983, p. 30). So far, the most effective way of conceiving of these specificities has been via categories of emotion and mood. In this way, for example, the two emotions of sadness and anxiety have been distinguished and linked with the two experiences of loss and danger, and these in turn have been linked to the development of clinical depression and of anxiety/phobic disorders, respectively. Moreover, vulnerability in terms of lack of support appears to be vital for depression, but apparently not for the development of anxiety states. For depression the similarity among loss, sadness, and lack of support is obvious; at present, the comparable vulnerability factor for danger and anxiety will remain unclear until interesting leads, such as that of Finlay-Jones on parental divorce in childhood discussed in Chapter 3, are further explored.

However, emotions are unlikely to prove the only means of discerning relevant classes of experience. For example, two events may have very similar emotional impacts, both mildly tiresome but not otherwise worrying or disappointing, but one may produce a great deal of extra work for the subject. Thus if a woman's grown-up daughter's employment takes her out of the common household abroad for 6 weeks, the emotional impact may not be very different according to whether the son-in-law goes with her or not, but the amount of work involved in looking after the grandchildren will vary tremendously – that is, assuming he has an average (or higher) commitment to fatherly behavior. In any case, it is necessary to interpret the notion of "emotion" broadly. Oatley and Bolton (1985), in a discussion of depression, note the sense of dejection and discouragement that can follow a loss and suggest this that should be distinguished from an "emotion" in the usual sense (i.e., involving disturbance of the autonomic nervous system and lasting for discrete time periods). We have not thought it necessary to make this difficult distinction and would class such ongoing states as emotional, albeit ones that are likely to fluctuate in intensity and to have recognizable autonomic accompaniments only on occasions.

Also, despite our emphasis on specific emotions, it may still be useful for some purposes to conceive of relevant emotional experiences in broader terms – not distinguishing, say, positive emotions such as contentment, joy, and warmth from excitement. Randall Collins (1981) has underlined the importance of positive emotions, such as confidence and enthusiasm arising from successful social intercourse, for understanding the structures of the social world. The argument is in a Durkheimian tradition and emphasizes the feelings of solidarity that can arise from everyday conversations; the emphasis is less on the actual content of what is said than on the feeling of belonging that arises from the simple fact of successful participation. The conversational resources employed can be general (arising from class background, employment, or gender) or particular (arising from the history of actual relationships – e.g., bringing up a particular child together, sharing a particular house or a common holiday). Collins conceives of such positive emotions as a form of energy that can be accumulated (slowly) or dissipated (slowly or quickly). Successful experience will lead to a sense of confidence that in turn can lead to further success and provide perhaps additional emotional energy; by contrast, a crisis can lower confidence almost instantly or more slowly. Such energy is undoubtedly one of the correlates of feelings of self-worth and self-esteem, which, with their opposites (feelings of rejection and lack of confidence), provide a key component in our full etiological model of depression. Therefore, in developing an etiological model for conditions such as depression, it may be useful to juxtapose specific emotions such as sadness, failure, and rejection arising from the provoking stressor; more enduring emotional experiences of a general positive or negative kind, arising particularly from ongoing conversations; and the way in which the coming together of the two may lead to some key cognitive-emotional state such as hopelessness. Critical here is probably the way a stressor not only may provoke feelings such as loss and sadness, but at the same time may dramatically undermine positive feelings invested in a particular relationship or role. This may be because the event involves the relationship or role itself, or because the expected support from it does not emerge (Brown, Andrews, Harris, Adler, & Bridge, 1986).

In this view, there are two major sources of relevant emotion. First, there is the emotion arising from everyday activities, much of it of a routine nature; here we would emphasize notions such as feelings of self-worth and self-esteem that are in good part consequences of social performance, and particularly the conversations (or interaction rituals) emphasized by workers in the Durkheimian tradition such as Erving Goffman and Randall Collins. But in this volume on life events we have particularly emphasized a second source, building on the close link between emotion and meaning that in Chapter 1 has been discussed as arising from plans, purposes, and commitments – that is, with intentionality. Oatley (1987), developing this theme, sees emotions typically occurring at the juncture of plans when an estimate of likely outcome is changed, perhaps radically. Emotions "occur as an essential part of the process of management of the conflicts and vicissitudes that arise in human intended action. They function to communicate the occurrence of significant junctures both to ourselves and to others" (Oatley, 1987). Of course, these two sources will tend to be intimately related, in the sense that plans often take for granted that certain key everyday social rituals will continue.

However, the idea of a juncture should probably not be taken too literally. In practice, the accurate establishment of such a point may be difficult because a person's knowledge may not keep in line with changes, actual or anticipated, in the external world. For example, a woman may have been made aware that her husband currently in jail on remand can expect a long sentence for his part in a robbery. In a strict sense, therefore, she knows what is to occur well before the actual sentencing. But this knowledge may not in fact provide a point of juncture, and she may only react to the situation, in the sense of appearing to assimilate its implications, at the time of his sentencing. We do not always know what we know. It may only be when an event has occurred fairly late in a developing sequence that we may truly face a future that could have been fully anticipated. In the instance just given, there had been important changes in the woman's social milieu – her husband was, after all, already in custody.

A related problem is that a person may not be fully aware of the importance of a particular plan until a juncture has been met in the form of a major obstacle. In this context, Bauman (1978, p. 156) quotes Arland Ussher: "The world as world is only revealed to me when things go wrong." The early work in ethnomethodology was particularly geared to illustrate how in everyday life a person typically so takes it for granted that meaningful activity is going on that it is quite unnecessary for him or her to seek explanations or question too deeply the nature of things (Garfinkel, 1967). Much of the time social activity is based on routine, and there is a tendency only in times of crisis for people to offer to themselves (and to an investigator) detailed accounts of what has been going on in motivational terms. In this context, Frijda (1986, p. 335) has argued for the use of the term "concern" since alternatives such as "motive," "plan," or "goal" carry connotations of activity, actual striving, or awareness of a future state to be reached, which are inappropriate for many of the conditions under which emotions can arise. As Frijda points out, the motivational background of emotion is often silent until an emotional event makes it cry out. The term "concern" is also suggested by Klinger (1975). Nonetheless, the term "plan" does convey something of the centrality of the concerns of importance in the genesis of clinical depression.

However, this is not to suggest that plans or concerns are necessarily unconscious. The point is simply that as we go about our daily lives, we take a good deal for granted; we may not consider at all closely plans implicit in routine activity, and thereby face our past and possible future (see Epstein's [1983] discussion of preconscious activity). The notion is akin to the Freudian idea of the preconscious: A rounded knowledge of the person would suggest that certain ideas should be invested with a good deal more feeling and concern than the person actually shows when discussing them. One reason for such inexpressiveness may be the conflict that any fuller recognition would arouse. It may also allow the person to avoid acknowledging lack of success in meeting some core plan. In either circumstance, overt recognition of plans risks creating powerful dysphoric emotions and a push for some action. Most of us are quite happy to live with this kind of half-knowledge; we do our best to live in the present, despite frustrations and disappointments. Herein, as just noted, lies the particular significance of life events: They, with the emotions they arouse, can play havoc with such accommodations. The emotions are likely to be urgent and intrusive and to demand some evaluation of our lives (Costello, 1976). It is therefore not that the thoughts that are aroused are necessarily altogether foreign to us; it is more a matter of their greatly increased salience.

Of course, an event can bring about an entirely new situation. More often, however, we may have come to live with the problem that the event has served to highlight and done our best to create a social milieu that allows the problem to be ignored. In social terms, if something is not spoken about, in some sense it does not exist. In many settings it is possible for participants to know something discreditable about each other and yet act as if it were not so. But this totally changes if one party states openly what has been known by those involved all along. Then it will usually be necessary to act. Malinowski (1937) tells how in the Trobriand Islands a chief had for years been breaking all the rules by giving various privileges to his own son instead of to his mother's brother's son in the way demanded by the matrilineal kinship rules of the culture. Only when the mother's brother's son publicly stated what everybody knew had been going on for years did change occur – and, as so often happens, this was dramatic, involving the suicide of the chief's son. In such an instance, the activity of the human mind parallels that of social circles that collaborate (not always for the same reason) to keep certain facts from becoming salient. But we may, in making these points, be in danger of exaggerating the difficulty of studying plans and junctures. In the Islington longitudinal inquiry, commitment in particular domains such as marriage and motherhood proved to be highly predictive of depression once a matching event occurred. Although ratings of such commitment were not always based on the discussion of clearly formulated plans, they did provide valuable insights into possible etiological mechanisms – and such commitment undoubtedly relates to the kind of intentionality we have been discussing.

For any fully satisfactory knowledge about etiological mechanisms, it will almost certainly be necessary to add the notion of schema or script to that of plans. In essence, this is knowledge relevant to the plan (Oatley, 1987), and it is here we would relate the idea of vulnerability – one that has so far been most fully developed for the etiological model of depression. It might include, for instance, a person's general lack of confidence about his or her ability to form significant new social ties. It has been assumed in the work reviewed that it is the coming together of both junctures in plans and pertinent schemas that is vital. Although we have concentrated on the meaning of junctures brought about by life events, it is clear that changes in meaning can be brought about by the event's being interpreted via a particular schema. But for the present, our major concerns have been the event itself and the meaning arising from the person's biography and immediate context in the sense of concerns, commitments, and plans.

Therefore, we have assumed that there is often a reluctance to face the full implications of our past and our future. There is also a tendency to live in the present, insofar as some of our plans give us satisfaction and enjoyment – states that may come from actual achievement, meeting new challenges that are part of our plans, or experiencing the pleasure of recontacting those close to us after the minor separations of everyday life. But one consequence of such concentration on the present may be to ignore troubles gathering about us: Failure to see the essential incompatibility of our present actions, and failure to recognize how far we have fallen short of some cherished idea, may leave us open to the emotional storm that a life event may bring when these realizations are brought home to us.

Implicit in this account is the conclusion that it is more than the

experience of simple emotions such as sadness and fear that is important for the development of disease. Oatley and Johnson-Laird (1987)
usefully distinguish between "basic" and "complex" emotions. Basic
emotions are universal and are biologically based, and may be experienced by a person without any sense that a particular one has occurred
for a known reason. Complex emotions are derived from such basic
emotions and essentially involve some evaluation of cause; they arise
particularly out of plans and intentions, and the ideas we have of ourself
and those close to us. In this sense, complex emotions are social emotions. Particularly important in their development is a sense of self and
how this may be enhanced or threatened or damaged in various ways.
The story told in Chapter 1 of the woman whose son was attacked illustrates the complex amalgam of ideas and emotions that can occur. Here
the woman probably experienced several of the complex emotions that
Oatley and Johnson-Laird have in mind, but we assume that for some
disorder to ensue, one of these would come to predominate. It is easy
to see in this woman's case that the danger-anxiety component would
predominate, and that in a susceptible person this would provoke the
kind of anxiety/phobic condition described by Finlay-Jones in Chapter
3. (In fact, the woman did develop a severe phobic disorder lasting several months.)

The various contextual ratings of events and difficulties – loss, danger, challenge, intrusiveness, goal frustration, conflict over speaking out
– are attempts, albeit crude, to reflect such complex or social emotions.
But it should also be noted that the work of Finlay-Jones makes clear
that there may be more than one relevant complex emotion arising from
the same event. In his study, the experience of both loss and danger arising from the same event (though sometimes from distinct events) could
lead to the experience of both a depressive and an anxiety disorder. It
is also possible for a person to change the meaning of an event, and
thereby the dominant emotion. One woman having a lengthy affair with
a married man had been led by him to believe that at some point he
would leave his wife and child. A severely threatening event occurred
when he made clear that he would not be able to bring himself to do
this, at which point they separated. A second event involved their coming together again, but now with the implicit understanding that he
would never leave his wife. It would not be surprising if in such circumstances an incipient depressive disorder was turned into another – perhaps a gastrointestinal disorder (from "goal frustration") or an anxiety
disorder (from "danger"). (In fact, our respondent developed a gastric
ulcer.)

So far, we have dwelled on points of juncture and the experience of
marked emotion, and the studies that have been reviewed confirm the

wisdom of this. The onset of nearly all conditions examined usually occurred within a matter of weeks of such a juncture. But the onset of myocardial infarction is a notable exception, and this underlines the importance of also considering ongoing situations. Concentration on the present and the avoidance of the emotional upheaval that can stem from too close a concern with our past and future will be unlikely to allow us to avoid altogether facing ongoing difficulties and frustrations. Indeed, these very demands may be one reason for our reluctance to face the full implications of our situation. Such ongoing experiences may involve various dysphoric moods related, say, to conditions below the LEDS threshold of a difficulty (e.g., a monotonous and unpleasant job), or to more major stressors encompassed by the LEDS (e.g., living with a mentally disturbed spouse). Although it is essential to consider such ongoing experiences in their own right, it is likely that scientific advances will increasingly depend on our ability to bring the study of junctures and ongoing stressors together in some meaningful way, and this has been one of the main underlying aims of the LEDS instrument.

The first chapter of this volume describes the origins and development of the instrument, from a relatively simple count of various categories of incidents to the present complex compilation of "events" with many dimensions or qualities (e.g., loss, danger, intrusiveness, challenge, goal frustration, and fresh start), along with ongoing "difficulties" of varying severities of unpleasantness. The emotions involved are clearly on the whole, in Oatley and Johnson-Laird's (1987) terms, both complex and social.

Chapter 1 explains how the systematic rating of these potential stressors is carried out (usually from a tape recording, after the face-to-face interview), and how the comparability of these ratings is maximized by initial training and supervision of LEDS investigators. It also describes the use of manuals containing rules about which incidents deserve inclusion as "events," of directories containing precedents for the levels of severity of the various dimensions, and of consensus meetings with other raters. The interrater reliability and validity of the various ratings have been found to be higher than those of checklist instruments, and this appears to be related to the style of questioning as well as to the rating procedures. Because respondents are encouraged to talk about experiences in terms of a narrative, interest is usually high, and feelings surrounding the experiences are often relived to some degree in the interview itself. The recall of one incident often leads directly to the recall of others; in this way, reserve about self-disclosure can be reduced. After the respondent has been encouraged to talk at length, thorough probing by the investigator about any anomalies or outstanding points can prompt further recall, and usually manages to resolve any discrepancies in the initial account. This style of interviewing also allows proper attention to be paid to the dating of onset of the outcome variable or disorder, the impossibility of which has been maintained by some researchers (with resulting pessimism about ever finding a convincing relationship between life stress and, say, alcoholism, as outlined in Chapter 1).

Although the LEDS contains a large number of dimensions, the focus of research carried out so far has been on those that aim to predict reactions by reflecting the meaning of the experience for the respondent, rather than on the simpler, more mechanical ratings (e.g., amount of routine change consequent on the event, or number of previous experiences of generally similar events). A table in Chapter 15 (see Table 15.2) conveys the different levels on which dimensions can characterize events, with cognitive-emotional meaning at level 3 and with the simpler dimensions at level 2. The dimension of contextual threat or unpleasantness serves as the basic example of the LEDS method of assessing contextual meaning, although other, rather less general dimensions (e.g., danger or fresh-start events) are also rated contextually and could equally well have been chosen. Deriving from the notion of *verstehen*, or understanding, "contextual threat" may be thought of as the degree of unpleasantness one can expect the average person in that particular set of biographical circumstances to feel. It is contrasted with "reported threat," the degree of unpleasantness the respondent reports actually feeling. Contextual threat may be short-term (lasting less than a week after the event first occurs) or long-term (lasting at least more than 2 weeks, usually several months). The gamut of simpler ratings can often be useful in rating contextual threat, and it is essential that they be considered before a rating of long-term contextual threat is made. However, life is so complex and stress research still so much in its infancy that there are no formulas for linking, say, the following simpler ratings concerning job change with the final contextual rating: changes in working hours, time spent with friends, time spent traveling to work, distance from babysitters, approval of spouse for the new job, consistency with previous career plans, and quality of interaction with new colleagues. Such separate dimensions are inherently difficult, and perhaps impossible, to amalgamate successfully by some method of weighting and summation. There is always the possibility of an unexpected feature that needs to be given particular emphasis: For example, the new supervisor may turn out to be a neighbor of the subject's ex-husband, who has been threatening her for some time and, it may now be feared, may pick up information as to her whereabouts from this supervisor.

The LEDS and Psychiatric Conditions

The LEDS, with its flexible narrative interviewing style, may at first seem less attractive in scientific terms than checklists like the well-known Schedule of Recent Experiences (SRE) of Holmes and Rahe (1967). The account in Chapter 1, however, goes a long way to illustrate how the LEDS ends up with data that are richer not only in terms of depth of understanding of the stressor's impact, but also in terms of broad scientific comparability. In the example just given of the woman with the new job, it can easily take into account the unexpected facts about the supervisor. In Chapter 2, the predictive power of the general dimension of contextual threat or severity is illustrated in regard to clinical depression. Evidence is reviewed from general-population surveys that confirms the role of severe threat. It becomes clear that this rating has a great deal in common with the notion of the undesirability of life events based on a general rather than a contextual judgment, but that it is more discriminating, since "undesirability" also includes events high on short-term but not long-term threat, and also even events with mild long-term threat. The use of the population attributable risk (PAR) statistic is an essential adjunct to relative risk and variance explained in assessing the overall importance of such events. For whereas variance explained focuses largely on those who manage to stay well despite having experienced a severe event, PAR draws attention to how few of those with depression have not had such a provoking agent.

In discussing the process by which severe threat brings about depression, we conclude that the severe events occurring prior to the onset of depression almost always threaten some core aspect of a woman's identity and self-worth. In this sense we are not dealing with the simple emotion of sadness, but something far more complex: The feelings of hopelessness engendered by the experience of loss may become generalized, and low self-esteem, both ongoing and as a result of the event, may play a vital role in this. Although we have concentrated on meaning stemming from the event itself, we also emphasize in Chapter 2 that in the final analysis it will be artificial to proceed in this way without taking account of vulnerability, both in social and in psychological terms, stemming both from the past and from additional current circumstances. In Chapter 14 we have dealt with this in terms of the notion of life structure, although a fully satisfactory treatment must deal with the question of social support, especially in a crisis situation (see Brown *et al.*, 1986). For the present, it needs to be borne in mind that for clinical depression to develop, we assume that there will often be other contributions to the final cognitive-emotional amalgam, particularly from schemas or vulnerability factors; however, we would certainly not rule out that constitutional factors may play a role, either at a cognitive level or in terms of the underlying biochemical processes.

After the initial outline of our earlier findings and the related etiological model of depression, Chapter 2 goes on to present material from our most recent survey, the longitudinal Islington study. First, the chapter details additional refinements to the dimension of severe threat, which indicate that loss and disappointment are particularly implicated in onset. "Loss" here can span a whole range of experiences, from literal departures of persons such as deaths or separations – events that Paykel (1974) has called "exits" – to losses of cherished ideas about oneself, one's roles, or other people's relationships with one. The availability of information collected a year earlier about the activities of Islington subjects involved in such severe events allowed a more sensitive estimate of their personal meaning for the subjects before their current depression, and one that avoided the possibility that current disorder might bias reports of the emotional importance of events.

The Islington data showed that severe events could "match" prior plans or experience to a greater or lesser degree, and in these terms were more or less likely to tip an individual into caseness of depression. First, severe events that matched a marked commitment to a domain in a woman's life such as motherhood were followed by a marked increase in risk of depression; intuitively, this makes a good deal of sense, in that the salience of a loss must vary with the degree to which a person cared for what has been lost. Second, severe events that matched previous areas of role conflict were also more predictive of depression, as, third, were severe events that matched an ongoing marked non-health-related difficulty. The first two findings are clearly consistent with our earlier emphasis on approaching meaning through personal intentions. The important role of events related to an ongoing difficulty can almost certainly be included in these terms as well. But here it is necessary to ask why a person with such a difficulty would not have developed depression before. In his story "Albert Nobbs," George Moore (1922/1976) tells of the experiences of a woman who spends her life disguised as a waiter in a Dublin hotel. A crisis occurs in which she tells her story of deprivation and hardship to someone who discovers her secret: "I thought nobody would ever hear it, and I'd thought I should never cry again. . . . It's all much sadder than I thought it was, and if I'd known how sad it was I shouldn't have been able to live through it" (p. 116). As already argued, it is a common experience that deprivation, hardship, and disappointment can be shifted more or less permanently to some peripheral part of consciousness; one role of life events can be to tell us something central about our lives that we have, in one sense, known all along. The role of matching difficulties and commitments indicates the importance of the loss of something upon which one has heavily staked a part of oneself, and, furthermore, shows that one can lose again something essentially already lost.

These results concerning matching also raise the fundamental theoretical issue of whether or not stressors are additive in some way in their depressogenic effect. On common-sense grounds this is what one would expect, but the question has proved to be highly complex, and results so far do not appear to give much support to such an obvious expectation. The increased risk of depression following a severe event that matches an ongoing difficulty is certainly consistent with the general notion that stresses can have a cumulative depressogenic impact. However, such links by no means conform to the common-sense idea of a series of unrelated crises finally overwhelming a person. For a start, multiple events that are involved in such matching are by definition related to each other, and there are a number of reasons why any additive effect may not be a simple one. For example, often the earlier one may well have been interpretable as a one-time only incident, and the subsequent event may therefore be classed as a disappointment. Such related events are also often part of a developing crisis involving earlier danger events that in themselves are unlikely to provoke depression. Therefore, the situation may be a series of danger events leading to a final loss, rather than a series of losses.

In the light of such considerations, various ways of exploring additivity are pursued in Chapter 2. For example, as just noted, events linked in a chain stemming from one crisis (e.g., hospital admission of husband, diagnosis of his fatal illness, and his death) are not the kind of separate experiences brought about by "unrelated" events (e.g., child in court for stealing, husband's layoff with no other source of income, and emigration of only confidant), and the two kinds of patterning of events have therefore been analyzed separately. In the end, it is concluded that the most parsimonious account remains the view that events and difficulties do not "add" to each other in a routine mechanical fashion, and that just *one* severe loss, including those involved in the kind of "related" chain just discussed, is usually all that is required to produce depressive onset. This conclusion is consistent with the theoretical model that places more emphasis on the thoughts about ourselves arising as a result of a crisis than upon the experience of the crisis itself.

Finally, new evidence bearing upon recovery or improvement from depression is presented and interpreted in a similar way. The experience of fresh-start events, and the reductions in severity of difficulties that precede recovery or improvement, are like mirror images of the processes originally causing the disorder. Again, this supports a theoretical view that gives weight to the generalization of hopelessness, for the experiences preceding recovery often break into the vicious circle of circumstances, mood, and thoughts that have been maintaining this generalization by confronting the subject with a contrary experience embodying new hope of some kind.

In Chapter 3, Robert Finlay-Jones reports his study at the general practice level of women living in the Regent's Park area of London in 1979. He highlights the role of danger experiences in promoting anxiety states, and again reports the contrasting importance of loss in promoting depression. Although in this volume we have not emphasized the issue of vulnerability, this chapter illustrates the kind of analyses that are being carried out. Finlay-Jones is able to show contrasting vulnerability factors for the two conditions: Whereas lack of intimate confiding with partner potentiated the depressogenic effects of severe loss events in his sample, it did not increase risk of an anxiety state after a severe danger event. On the other hand, early separation from father before the age of 11 appeared to act as a vulnerability factor for anxiety conditions, in contrast to the role of early loss of mother for depression; however, he recommends that the evidence be treated cautiously at this stage.

In Chapter 4, Richard Day discusses the role of life events in the onset of schizophrenia. He gives a selective review of the literature, paying most attention to three investigations using the LEDS. The first, 25 years ago in London, was in fact the first study to use the LEDS in its initial version. The other two are recent, and one can almost be viewed as a collection of nine mini-investigations, since the World Health Organization set it up in various centers all over the globe. In each of the studies, it emerged that events at all threat levels seemed to accumulate in the 3 weeks before onset of schizophrenia. Day goes on to discuss causal thinking in epidemiology in general before turning back to the interpretation of these results. He presents further data from an ongoing cohort study on exacerbations of illness in 33 chronic schizophrenics in response to life events, commenting in a way that echoes Chapter 2, in which PAR is recommended as a way of viewing basic data that supplements the tunnel vision of variance explained. In outlining possible explanatory models, he cites work on relapse that has combined investigation of the role of life events with other interacting factors, such as relatives' expressed emotion (EE) in the home and failure to continue prophylactic medication. Future exploration of these models will clearly demand studies of a genuinely multifactorial design. As for the nature of the events themselves, interesting possibilities revealed by recent research concern the role of intrusive events (Harris, 1987). If their importance should be confirmed, it would serve to bring together much more convincingly in theoretical terms the work on the role of EE in the families of schizophrenic patients and relapse (Brown, Birley, & Wing, 1972; Leff & Vaughn, 1985). The idea of a qualitative dimension of intrusiveness can be seen to lie behind both components of the EE index – number of critical comments and degree of emotional overinvolvement. The reason for the patients' particular sensitivity to their experiences probably needs to be sought in a specific set of biochemical and physiological factors characterizing such persons; however, at the same time, the particular cognitive-emotional complex provoked by such events – one of sensitivity to interference or criticism – is probably universal.

In Chapter 5, Paul Colloway and Raymond Dolan relate their findings using the LEDS to endocrine changes in psychiatric patients with depression. Both the hypothalamic-pituitary-adrenal axis and the hypothalamic-pituitary-thyroid axis were investigated. While "nonsuppression" of cortisol levels on the dexamethasone suppression test was associated with endogenous rather than neurotic depression, according to several diagnostic discriminations, it was not related to experience of either severe events or major difficulties before onset. However, experience of either type of provoking agent in the 6 months before onset was associated with higher urinary free cortisol levels. To turn to the hypothalamic-pituitary-thyroid axis, blunted thyroid-stimulating hormone (TSH) responses were related to endogenous (as opposed to nonendogenous) depression according to the Research Diagnostic Criteria (RDC), but not according to the Present State Examination (PSE) or the Newcastle Diagnostic Index. Although blunted TSH responses were not associated with severe events before onset, they were associated with marked difficulties. When the free thyroxine index (FTI) was examined, it emerged that patients with blunted TSH responses and high FTI levels were more likely to have experienced marked difficulties than those with blunted TSH responses and normal FTI levels. Patients with blunted TSH responses and high FTI levels were also more likely to report a history of loss or separation from parents before age 11. On the FTI alone, patients with severe events had higher levels than those without. Therefore, as a general conclusion, various biological measures were related to psychosocial factors both in the present and in the past, while their association with the endogenous-neurotic distinction within the depressed patients was less clear. In discussing their findings in a wider context, Calloway and Dolan convincingly dismiss the old contention that endogenous and neurotic depression differ in terms of precipitation by stress, and challenge the simple dualistic thinking that counterposes biological and psychosocial etiologies. They extend their discussion of the endocrine response to stress to draw out the implications of their own findings on depression for psychosomatic disorders (particularly thyrotoxicosis and Cushing disease), but also for conditions such as neoplastic and infectious diseases that are influenced by the immune system, which is so profoundly affected by cortisol.

In Chapter 6, Paul Surtees returns to the issue of additivity in the etiology of depression and confronts the problem of the time over which events and difficulties act to produce the disorder. By introducing assumptions about the rate at which the threat of events dissipates over time and about the way threats from different events can add together to produce a total amount of residual adversity, he builds a mathematical model that appears to provide a modest improvement on the predictive power of the measure so far employed to understand depression – experience of at least one severe event. He applies the model to the Bedford College Camberwell and Islington data, and also to data collected in Edinburgh. Surtees's approach provides an interesting alternative to the customary LEDS analyses. As we have already noted in Chapter 2, much work remains to be done in investigating additivity. In Chapter 14, however, we discuss ways in which Surtees's model can be improved to pursue this task. In the first place, it completely ignores material on difficulties, which, as we have seen, can be important extra factors regardless of whether they match a severe event. In the second place, the assumption about an initial uniform rate of decay of threat needs supplementing by actual evidence, since sometimes severe events "dissipate" before their appointed time as further positive changes occur and neutralize the threat. Thus, for instance, a woman's unexpected new job can remove the threat of her husband's layoff. We also confront the possibility that the modest improvement provided by the decay approach, compared with taking the presence of just one severe event, is quite unrelated to the question of additivity, and is instead merely the result of a technical feature that reflects the somewhat more conservative method of dealing with the occurrence of severe events in the nononset series in the original nondecay approach. Clearly, the debate must continue, but in the interim we see the perspective that accords importance to just one severe event as the one most likely to deepen our understanding of depression, because it involves a focus on the cognitive sequelae to experience rather than on the mere occurrence of an experience.

The LEDS and Physical Conditions

Part Three of this book is devoted to studies using the LEDS in investigations of physical illness. These require certain additional features of design, which are discussed in Chapter 7. In particular, attention needs to be given to factors intervening between life events and somatic onset: Not only psychiatric disorder, but subclinical emotional distress, may play some role in linking life event and onset of somatic disorder. Fortunately, the threat ratings *reported* by the interviewer can probably be given somewhat more weight than in studies of psychiatric disorder, where the dangers of reporting bias must be seriously considered. Certain responses (e.g., changes in smoking, exercise, and dietary behavior) may also have an important intervening role. Controls for age become even more important than in psychiatric research, because it is more widely accepted that the body's mechanism automatically develops faults with age than that the emotions or the psyche do so, except perhaps in the very last years of life. On the contrary, the conventional wisdom emphasizes a certain psychic improvement with aging – a consolidation and calm above the instabilities of youth. The tendency for physiological problems to appear, as it were, spontaneously with age may mask any somatic effects of stress in the younger groups, if samples are compared without controls for age. Finally, contrasting "functional" with "organic" versions of a condition may also throw a different light on the role of stress in the etiology of a particular physical disorder.

In Chapter 8, Francis Creed reports on his study of 63 appendectomy patients with "acutely inflamed" appendices, about the same number without such inflammation, and a comparison series. The same severe events so crucial for depression (especially those involving interpersonal crises) emerged as more frequent in the group of patients without acute inflammation than among those with inflammation and comparison subjects. Creed used the same 38-week period that was employed in the Camberwell study as a way of preserving comparability, but he notes that in most instances the severe event preceded the appendectomy within 9 weeks. However, those with acute inflammation had an elevated rate of events with at least some (minor) threat in the 3 weeks before the operation, especially when events "anticipated" shortly thereafter were included as a special additional category of event. Marked chronic difficulties of over 1 year's duration were also more frequent in both appendectomy groups than among comparison subjects. A particularly interesting feature of Creed's analysis involved an additional comparison group of siblings. A set of 31 sibling pairs not only provided reassuring information about accuracy of reporting, but confirmed the results on events with severe threat and some threat reported with the other comparison series.

Psychiatric symptoms at a level approximating case or borderline-case disorder were twice as frequent among patients without acute inflammation as among those with appendicitis, the latter having a similar prevalence to the community comparison group. Unfortunately, Creed has not established dates of onset for this psychiatric symptomatology, so it is not feasible to pursue the possibility that it was an intervening mechanism between the events and the abdominal pain. However, he does give evidence about the development of depressive symptoms between first interview and follow-up, which showed a greater rate of onset among those without inflammation; this suggests that differences in experience of psychiatric symptomatology at time of the operation were unlikely to be due only to chronic long-lasting psychiatric conditions. He also presents data that suggest other interesting differences between what were essentially a "functional" group and an "organic" group, such as family history of psychiatric illness, conflicts with parents, and dysmenorrhea; these were more common among those without acute inflammation, while family history of appendicitis was more common among those with acute inflammation.

In discussing his results, Creed contrasts the etiology of definite appendicitis with that of having a normal appendix removed. For definite appendicitis he follows Ashley's (1967) model which proposes that two independent etiological agents must occur together to affect a vulnerable individual. A life event carrying short-term threat, which lowers resistance to infection and/or alters colonic contractions, may be one such agent; exposure to infection may be another, while family history of appendicitis marks a susceptibility to such infection. For individuals who have normal appendices removed, severe life events may lead to painful contractions of the colon, producing right-side abdominal pain. Alternatively, if such events are followed by psychiatric symptoms, they may lead to the subjects' experiencing greater distress and may indicate to others a greater need for medical treatment, as suggested by the fact that those with psychiatric symptoms were more likely than others to be brought into treatment by close relatives rather than initiating treatment themselves. Finally, Creed discusses how continued abdominal pain after appendectomy relates more closely to the development of depression than to the presence of preceding stress.

This first account of the use of the LEDS to study a somatic disorder has in fact set the scene in an important way by highlighting the role of depressogenic provoking agents and of psychiatric symptomatology in the onset of a functional condition. Creed's speculations as to the mechanism by which this may happen invoke increased sensitivity to pain, or perhaps increased pain due to increase in colonic contractions. Although he does not outline it in so many words, his model for the organic disorder opens up a perspective for viewing disorders in which resistance to infection (or, rather, a decrease in this) is the critical feature in onset. This outlook accords more closely with what we have identified as a more general approach to the effects of stress (level 4 in Table 15.2) than it does to the more specific perspectives developed in Chapters 9, 10, and 12 (which correspond more closely to level 3 in the same table). The mere specification of some level of threat, which Creed suggests may be responsible for raising susceptibility to infection, can involve a whole range of different specific qualities of cognition-emotion at the next level below, all of which may contribute to some more generalized lowering of resistance. This theme is taken up again in the discussion of multiple sclerosis in Chapter 11.

In Chapter 9, Tom Craig takes up a similar topic, reporting findings with patients who had abdominal pain suggestive not of appendicitis but of other gastrointestinal disorders. Again, he found that the severe events and major difficulties so important in depression were much more frequent before functional than before organic disorders, and, again, he found a high rate of interpersonal crisis events. However, organic disorders were more frequently preceded by events and difficulties rated high on the new dimension of goal frustration. These frustrations occurred against a background of committed striving for a particular goal, such as winning a court case or saving a company threatened with liquidation. Again, prevalence of psychiatric disorder varied between the groups. The patients with functional disorders showed more psychiatric disturbance at a caseness level of severity and rather more depression than those with organic disorders. Craig's data have allowed him to distinguish between psychiatric symptoms that developed after the critical etiological stressor (i.e., a provoking agent for the functional group and a goal frustration experience for the organic group) and those that were already ongoing before the stressor was experienced. The results suggest that psychiatric state often mediates between provoking agent and functional gastrointestinal conditions. Craig systematically outlines the steps by which this may happen, contrasting the lowering of pain thresholds consequent upon emotional distress with changes in gut motility. In confronting the process by which the specific emotional quality of goal frustration contributes to organic tissue damage, Craig is cautious. He outlines the changes undergone by theories about stress and gastric acid production, and thus refrains from linking this mechanism too closely with the striving and frustration picked out by the LEDS. But he does allow himself some speculation without relating this to biological factors.

In Chapter 10, Tirril Harris reports a study examining two contrasting gynecological conditions with definite onsets, menorrhagia and secondary amenorrhea. Menorrhagia patients showed a raised rate of severe events and major difficulties in the 12 months before somatic onset, and also had higher rates of depression at both case and borderline-case levels than secondary amenorrhea patients or community comparison subjects. Secondary amenorrhea patients, on the other hand, had high rates of more minor events in the month before their menses first disappeared, and also showed more minor tension syndromes without depression than the comparison series. As in Craig's analysis, psychiatric disorder that was ongoing before the crucial type of event has been distinguished from psychiatric disorder that arose between the event and somatic onset; a plausible case emerges that depressive symptoms (either major or minor) mediated between loss experiences and menorrhagia, whereas minor tension syndromes, or no symptoms at all, seemed to mediate between event and amenorrhea later in the menstrual cycle.

Further examination suggested that a large number of the events in the secondary amenorrhea group were definite challenges as defined by the LEDS, involving the subjects in increased responsibilities in a context where they were motivated to do well and where they could succeed if they maintained control of the situation and of any apprehension they might feel. It seemed reasonably likely that the tension syndromes so common in this group could reflect this dedication to rising to the demands of the occasion without complaint, and the number of respondents in this menstrual group with a noncomplaining reporting style gave further support to this perspective. (Reported threat was lower than contextual threat in this group more often than among either comparison subjects or the menorrhagia group.) Another difference between the two menstrual groups, which might well tie in with this postulated disposition of dedication was their degree of extraversion: The amenorrhea patients emerged as more introverted. Physiological predisposition also seemed to play a role, with the amenorrhea group more often experiencing menarche only at age 14 or older. Self-induced weight loss, although playing some role in amenorrhea, could in no way be held to account for the other statistically significant findings.

Comparisons between functional and organic menstrual disorders proved rather disappointing, partly because the numbers of organic patients were so small. Among menorraghia sufferers, a pattern similar to the appendectomy and gastrointestinal results of the preceding two chapters just failed to reach statistical significance; however, when those with endometriosis/adenomyosis were separated off from the other organic patients (with fibroids and polyps), and the boundaries between functional and organic categories correspondingly shifted, there seemed to be some confirmation for the hypothesis. Among amenorrhea sufferers, the functional-organic categorization provided less of interest than did a classification contrasting those with features of pseudocyesis (false pregnancy) and those whose amenorrhea coincided with cessation of oral contraceptives compared with the other patients. This drew attention to a new dimension of events, motherhood situations; these were noticeably more common just before onset in the small pseudocyesis-type group. This unpredicted finding is strikingly reminiscent of some of the more speculative psychoanalytic hypotheses involving a desire for pregnancy (albeit sometimes unconscious) as a background to false pregnancy. In addition, the comparative lack of precipitating challenges among those with "postpill" amenorrhea provides an interesting example of the theory that biochemical and psychosocial factors in etiology can to some extent substitute for each other. Harris allows herself considerable latitude in weaving speculative theories about the mechanisms by which these specific psychosocial qualitative features may translate into neuroendocrinological pathways toward amenorrhea. In focusing upon the possible role of dopamine, however, she does not rule out a role for other biochemical factors. Models proposed for the onset of menorrhagia leave open the possibility that in our present state of knowledge it is premature to try to contrast functional with organic bleeding.

In Chapter 11, Igor Grant, W. Ian McDonald, Thomas Patterson, and Michael Trimble describe their study of multiple sclerosis patients. A careful history of the illnesses insured that only those with an onset definitely datable within the last 5 years were included, and the LEDS interview was applied to the 12 months preceding that onset. Both severe events and marked difficulties in the 6 months before onset or interview were more common among the multiple sclerosis patients than among comparison subjects matched for age, sex, and social class. However, for the period from 6 to 12 months before onset/interview, rates were remarkably similar for the two groups, suggesting that the difference in the more recent period was unlikely to be due to an artifact of reporting bias. In speculating on the mechanism by which these provoking agents can lead to this disorder, the authors cite two possible vulnerability factors, both physiological: a familial tendency to multiple sclerosis linked to certain genetic markers, and early exposure to some environmental agent found in the more temperate climates. They go on to suggest that the provoking agents then act to bring this inherent vulnerability to the point of illness. According to this line of reasoning, life events do not determine whether or not multiple sclerosis will develop, but only the timing of its onset. Grant and colleagues speculate that the increasingly well-known effects of stress upon the immune system may provide the mechanism for releasing these inherent vulnerabilities. Although the authors do not specifically consider the role of short-term threat and of minor long-term threat, it would be intriguing to examine their series in more depth and to relate their findings to Creed's (Chapter 8).

In Chapter 12, Eileen Neilson, George Brown, and Michael Marmot report on a study of patients with myocardial infarction. As a preliminary methodological exercise, it was established that the LEDS could be used retrospectively over a 10-year period, with a satisfactorily low rate of fall off in reporting as distance in time from interview increased; this effect was maintained even after age was controlled for. This of course has reassuring implications, not merely for the study of heart disease, but for all research using the LEDS. When myocardial infarction patients were compared with the comparison group, neither the presence of a severe event nor that of a major difficulty was more frequent among the patients than in the comparison series in any of the ten 1-year periods before onset, although a non-significant trend emerged for patients to have experienced a greater number of severe events over the 10-year period. However, events rated high on goal frustration were five times more common in the 2 years before infarction than in the same period before interview in the comparison subjects. More than half of these events involved the subjects' work, but two-thirds of the patients had not experienced such a goal frustration. However, when the 10-year study period as a whole was considered, the association of psychosocial factors with infarction was substantial; particularly important was the greater experience of work stress among the MI group, although nonwork stress made some contribution.

A combined work stress index was finally used, in which a person (1) had either to have experienced an average weekly workload of more than 51 hours, or to have taken 2 weeks or less of vacation time in a year; or (2) had to have had either a work event or at least some long-term threat (one rated 1-3) or at least a moderate work difficulty (one rated 1-4). In addition, (3) either of these two conditions had to have lasted for 70% of the years in the preonset period. This third requirement concerning duration is of special importance, since in the comparison series almost half were rated as positive on the work stress index if only 1 year was taken, while the proportion was only one-quarter if the whole 10-year period was considered. The proportion who were positive in the infarction group was much the same, whether 1 year or the whole 10-year period was taken; on average, two-thirds were positive. This is perhaps the most critical finding, suggesting as it does the importance of the accumulation of the consequences of stress in the infarction group over a lengthy period of time of at least 10 years. If the 1 year before onset or interview was taken, the difference between MI and comparison series was modest – an odds ratio of 2.32. When the whole 10-year period was considered, this increased to 5.76. Of course, it also suggests that since many studies have examined relatively brief periods of time, the role of psychological factors in etiology may have been underestimated. The result also conforms much more closely to the popular conception of stress accumulating over lengthy periods of time than to the role of a stressor at one point of time, which has so far been emphasized in the studies in this volume.

The Bortner measure of Type A personality not only related to infarction, but was suggestive of an interaction effect with the workload index. (A proper test of this would have required a different overall sampling strategy.) But the authors also comment that this particular measure may need refinement if the reactivity of the vulnerable individual is to be more precisely specified. Here they not only contrast Type A1 personality with Type A personality, but also refer to research suggesting that direct measures of autonomic nervous system arousability may turn out to be better predictors than the behavioral tendencies (e.g., Type A1 personality or irascibility) that act as indicators of this physiological susceptibility. It is interesting to note that psychiatric disorder as normally conceived did not seem to indicate any such form of susceptibility. While several patients showed an elevated rate of depression (particularly at a borderline-case level) after infarction, rates before onset were very similar to those in the comparison series in equivalent periods before interview. Finally, both regular cigarette smoking and higher alcohol consumption were more frequent in the patient group, but there was no suggestion that these had acted to confound the results using the LEDS, nor that they might be interacting with them along the lines of vulnerability factors.

In Chapter 13, Harry Andrews and Allan House discuss their study of women with functional dysphonia. Once again, two problems were confronted. the establishment of a datable onset and the elaboration of a new LEDS dimension. Examination of the experiences of women during the year before onset of their functional dysphonia suggested that although long-term contextual threat might yet again be playing an etiological role, this was not working via the elements of loss and danger usually associated with such threat. What appeared to be involved were situations characterized by a new quality inhibiting outspoken behavior. Compared with some of the other LEDS dimensions such as loss or goal frustration, this one is particularly complicated and less frequently utilized in everyday parlance. The authors therefore emphasize the exploratory nature of their study. They take pains to spell out in detail how on the one hand the environment must provide a challenge to speak out, protest, or complain, and how on the other hand the situation must provide unusual constraints upon such outspoken behavior. Thus a grown-up son who moves away from home to cohabit with his girlfriend only provides a sufficient initial challenge to protest if the mother's previous plans and religious beliefs condemn premarital sex, and the situation only provides sufficient constraints if she is dependent for some important extra benefit upon not losing the son by her open disapproval (e.g., her protests might cause him to withdraw his services in driving her three times a week to visit her old mother in a nursing home some miles away). For the average relatively irreligious mother of the 1980s whose husband is still available to provide daily transport, such an event would involve neither sufficient challenge nor sufficient constraint to qualify for a rating of conflict over speaking out (CSO).

Despite the subtlety of this notion, with adequate training it was possible to reach satisfactory interrater reliability on this dimension. However, some of the interpretations that are made in this chapter are particularly delicate, and it is essential to collect further data for another comparison series with the needs of this rating in mind. Among

those patients without a definite CSO event in the 4 weeks, or CSO difficulty in the 1 year before onset, there was also often some situation that
produced conflict about speaking out but in which the contextual constraints upon doing so were not sufficiently high for a rating of CSO. One
is left speculating as to whether the use of a systematic subjective dimension (reported, or felt, CSO) might not have increased the number of
patients with a relevant qualitative experience, although the authors do
suggest that the conflict situations in which these women found themselves very often derived from their disavowal of the problems being
caused by the situations, or at least their seeming failure to acknowledge
such problems. A reported CSO rating might therefore not add very
many more subjects than those already included using the contextual rating. The use of such self-report measures in future research may be
acceptable, since with a physiological dependent variable the dangers of
a biased conclusion using such measures are less than with a psychological outcome variable. The authors also found a high rate of the PSE
symptom of muscular tension among their sample, and since this tension
was often found in the laryngeal region, they speculate that this may be
an intervening variable between event and dysphonia. This finding is
reminiscent of the report in Chapter 10 that tension states appeared to
mediate between challenge events and secondary amenorrhea.

In their opening remarks, the authors cite Freud's classic case of
Dora as an example of the clinical condition. Ironically, it was only after
the insights emerged from the analysis of this series that it became clear
to us all that Dora too was in a definite CSO situation: On the one hand,
Herr K was pressing his attentions upon her, and on the other, her father
might well have been having an affair with Herr K's wife (Freud,
1905/1925, pp. 36, 145). The fact that when Dora did finally mention
it she was not taken seriously by those around her emphasizes the conflict imposed by society upon a young woman in those times. Although
this is only an exploratory study, the results concerning CSO events and
difficulties present an intriguing model worthy of further pursuit, given
Andrews and House's finding of a high rate of muscular tension. However, until replicated, their results must be viewed with considerable
caution. The insights only arose in the study itself, and it is possible
that the investigators were influenced in the contextual ratings of CSO
by the patients' reports of their responses.

The Origins of Life Events and Difficulties

In Chapter 14, we briefly discuss the social origins of life events and
difficulties as a background to understanding how they can act as the
crucial explanatory factors behind some of the positive associations

uncovered by classical epidemiology, mediating between sociodemographic variables and onset of disorder. Our own general-population studies have revealed that severe events and major difficulties are more common among working-class women at a particular life stage, especially in
inner cities as compared with rural areas; integration into the traditional
society in rural areas seems to override social class and to be linked with
fewer disruptive events. We also outline how certain past experiences
seem to place people on a "conveyor belt" to continuing adversity
throughout life. Particularly important among these past experiences for
women are lack of adequate parental care in childhood and becoming
pregnant before marriage. The conveyor belt leads from these to a series
of negative situations involving their current relationships, which then in
turn throw up severe events and major difficulties. While giving such an
account of this environmental chain of circumstances, we do not ignore
the possibility that more internal psychological factors can play a role in
bringing about events. Thus a woman lacking in confidence may elect to
marry a man who will maltreat her because she has no faith in her ability
to find another husband. With existing knowledge, however, it is impossible to reach an estimate of the relative contributions of the two strands
of causation (external and internal), because the overlap between measures of negative elements in core relationships and personal feelings of
low self-esteem is so great. Nevertheless, it is instructive to note the correspondence among social setting, personal style, and type of life event that
emerges as a result of this overlap.

LEDS Findings in Contrast to Other Research

Chapter 15 aims to provide some kind of overview of the various
findings outlined in the earlier chapters against the background of other
research. Most attention is paid to depression, since it is not only one
of the disorders that has been most widely studied, but also an area in
which many research workers have amended the earlier checklist instruments in an attempt to approximate the rating of severe contextual long-
term threat, and in which there is therefore greatest comparability with
findings emerging with the LEDS. Several recent studies that appear to
have quite different results from those outlined in Chapter 2 are discussed, and explanations are given for the discrepancies in terms of
important differences in the measures, which the authors themselves
seem to have ignored. These differences include not only departures
from crucial LEDS assumptions in rating stressors, but also differences
in approach to the outcome variables, such as their timing and duration,
as well as the cutoff threshold of severity of depression utilized. Particularly important is the critique of the tendency to believe that a longitu-

dinal design as such solves the problems of time order. When all these issues are considered, it is possible to conclude that the weight of evidence does favor a substantial causal link between severe life events and clinical depression.

The Question of Independence

Given this conclusion, it is important to elaborate two issues raised in Chapter 15 in more detail. First is the use of the independence dimension to control for the possibility that the life stress, rather than determining the disorder, is itself the outcome either of an insidious onset of the disorder itself or of a lifelong personality trait predisposing the individual to that disorder. A lengthy discussion concludes that an adequate assessment of the role of stress must eventually include *all* events (both independent and possibly independent) that are not definite results of the disorder, but must also be able to convince the skeptic that the same order of difference between sick and healthy groups is also found when independent events alone are analyzed. It also takes up the theme of Chapter 14 in concluding that events are often a direct result of the life structure of the individual and may also relate to some features of the individual's personality and feelings, both long-term and short-term. (And this undoubtedly holds for some of the other conditions as well – particularly, perhaps, the goal frustration events involved in gastrointestinal disorders and to a lesser extent in myocardial infarction.) However, such links need not be seen in terms of spuriousness, in the sense that personality features (or internal factors) rather than events (or external factors) play the key etiological role. The closeness in time of event and onset suggests that the most plausible interpretation would seem to be that the severe event in these instances is playing a vital intervening role. That is, for the internal factors to influence risk of depression, they must act via a suitable event. However, such internal factors may contribute to depression in other ways. For example, a series of prior crises may have served to drive down a person's sense of self-esteem and sense of control, which then makes an independent contribution to risk once a crisis has occurred. But this would still be within the model concerning provoking agents, vulnerability factors, and sense of generalized hopelessness that we have used to explain the development of clinical depression.

The Question of Additivity

Second, the issue of additivity is addressed in Chapter 15, with particular attention to some of the issues raised by Paul Surtees in Chapter 6.

Although we still maintain that the most fruitful approach is to focus upon the impact of just one severe event, we outline our own approach to additivity in terms of cognitions of hopelessness, which in some sense "add" until they generalize. Next, while accepting in principle the model that stress effects decay with time, we elaborate upon the variations that continuing difficulties together with severe events arising from them (D-events), or a series of interrelated severe events, can bring to that model. Finally, the contribution to postponing (or speeding) this decay that is made by the individual's style of interpreting, or coping with, the event raises broader issues of stress measurement once again. The section of Chapter 15 on depression therefore concludes with a further explication of the value of locating the boundaries between objective/social/external factors and subjective/psychological/internal factors along the lines chosen by the LEDS.

The section of Chapter 15 dealing with the findings concerning disorders other than depression is of necessity more constrained than the section on depression. On the one hand, the field is far broader, and comments are therefore inevitably more sketchy. On the other hand, other research with these disorders has rarely used measures of close enough comparability to the LEDS for comment to be of much substance. This is because few other instruments approach the measurement of stress at the level of such specific cognitive-emotional qualities as loss, danger, or challenge. Most approach it at a more general level of description, such as undesirability or change, and many assume additivity. Thus they give respondents a total score on undesirability, distress scaling, or life change units, which makes comparison with the studies in the present volume highly unsatisfactory. In addition, many earlier studies also adopted a nonspecific approach to *illness*, relating stressful experience to disorder in general rather than to specific disorders such as multiple sclerosis or peptic ulcer. However, one other approach – that by Miller and Ingham (1985), using systematic qualitative dimensions of life events – seems to have reached similar conclusions about the role of danger in the onset of anxiety as contrasted with loss in depression, while agreeing that many constellations of experience show both features simultaneously.

But when the perspective of Chapter 15 is broadened, it becomes possible to see sources of confirmation for some of the hypotheses presented in the earlier chapters. Consideration of specific cognitive-emotional qualities of experience can focus not only on what has happened extraneously to someone (i.e., events and difficulties), but also more broadly on his or her personal style, which may render certain types of events more likely to occur. Thus a striving person may court goal frustrations; a dedicated person may more readily accept new challenges; a polite and compassionate person may take on some responsibilities about which he or she will hesitate to complain; and a person with low self-esteem may become involved in relationships where he or she will be bound to suffer further losses. It also becomes possible to see how these personal styles dovetail with social roles and how the particular types of events that are associated with particular demographic backgrounds give rise to the epidemiological patternings of particular disorders that are now being mapped. Thus the social role of women as nurturant caretakers dovetails both with the higher proportion of females than males among functional dysphonia patients and with the frequency with which the nursing of troublesome invalid relatives gives rise to CSO situations. Thus, also, the higher rates of severe loss experiences and the lower rates of intimacy with one's spouse in working-class samples coalesce to produce a patterning of hopelessness to correspond with the epidemiological findings of more frequent clinical depression with lower social status.

Once the terms of reference of these emotional dimensions are broadened in this way, to include specification of background vulnerability as well as event specification, it becomes possible to explore much of the earlier epidemiological work and the psychosomatic literature on personality for findings germane to the specificities outlined here in connection with precipitating stress. From there, it is possible to move toward speculations about the biological processes that link these cognitive-affective states with disorders in particular physiological systems or organs. A clear example is the contrast between the "overengagement" of the cardiac patient and the "giving up-given up" complex that is central to clinical depression and which seems to precede disorders involving the immune system. The absence of clinical depression before myocardial infarction in the study in this volume underlines this contrast. Singer's (1974) general dimension of engagement/ involvement, which is highlighted by this contrast, can then be plausibly related to the emergent hypotheses that catecholamine activity, both noradrenergic and dopaminergic, is raised in conditions of engagement and reduced in conditions of disengagement. The engagement/ involvement dimension summarizes the familiar contrast between the "fight-flight" system and the "conservation/withdrawal" system. It thus places discussion of the psychosocial meaning of the situation in which the patient has been involved before onset squarely in the context of debate about physiological functioning and the relative roles of the pituitary-adrenocortical and sympathetic-adrenomedullary systems.

But engagement/involvement is still a very broad dimension, and its further refinement may suggest additional specifications of the physiological processes that are postulated as occurring in parallel with the psychosocial experiences. Thus the engagement in a challenge that seems to occur just before many onsets of secondary amenorrhea can be distinguished from the long-term engagement in a potentially frustrating situation that seems to precede myocardial infarction, and from the vigilance imposed by danger events that appears to herald anxiety states. And there is also something that vigilance consequent upon intrusion may have different effects from vigilance against future dangers, at least in those individuals rendered susceptible to schizophrenia by other (perhaps genetic) factors. It is not impossible that further exploration of these varieties of vigilance may lead to regrouping of patients into subcategories that turn out to overlap with subgroupings defined by some of the relevant physiological variables.

One type of specificity that is only briefly referred to in Chapter 15 concerns a person's physiological vulnerability, involving one organ system rather than another in response to, say, a particular disengagement experience. This is usually subsumed under a more general notion of "individual response specificity," which is also assumed to include the long-standing *psychological* response propensities that we spend most time discussing in connection with specificities of vulnerability (see Roessler & Engel, 1974). The role of genetic and constitutional factors clearly requires more attention than we have been able to give it here. Nevertheless, despite the growing awareness that a simple organ system approach is no longer justified in psychosomatic theorizing, and despite the wide-ranging complexities of neuroendocrine functioning, Chapter 15 ends on an optimistic note: Refinement of contextual dimensions of life events and difficulties may be able to play a key role in the advance of psychiatric and psychosomatic knowledge in the coming decades.

Other Issues Involving Use of the LEDS

Inevitably, there are many topics involving the LEDS that cannot be covered in this volume, and many studies using it that have received only passing reference. Examples of the latter include Robinson and Fuller (1985) on diabetes mellitus; Martin, Brown, Goldberg, and Brockington (in press) on puerperal depression; Connolly (1983) on accidents; Reinecker and Zauner (1983), Gorman (1986), and Nadeau (1987) on alcoholism; Flaherty (1987) on impotence; Eales (1985) on the consequences of male unemployment; Ramirez (1986) on breast cancer and its course; Craufurd, Creed, and Jayson (1987) on low back pain; Cooke and Gray (1985) on shoplifting; and Farmer and Creed (in press) on self-poisoning. It should be noted that the studies by and large show substantial correlations between stressors and the onset of each condition, and often important types of specificity emerge. For example, Martin *et al.* (in press) found at best a small association between severe events and onset of major depression in the 3 weeks immediately following birth among a series of women admitted to a psychiatric "mother and baby unit," as compared with puerperal depressions having onsets earlier or later in the peripartum period.

Replication

There are, however, three general issues whose omission would leave this volume incomplete. The first is that of replication and the criteria used to judge its success or failure. A brief recapitulation of the details of the LEDS rating practices is enough to suggest that quite small departures from the routine procedure may introduce sources of variability in the numbers of events recorded, or the severities of their dimensions, such that a study may not be a replication in the true sense of the word. Thus Schmid, Scharfetter, and Binder (1981), believing that they were using the LEDS despite neither having been trained nor using any of the LEDS manuals, reported high rates of falloff (see Brown & Harris, 1982b, for a commentary). Similarly, Hällström (1986) has reported rates of "provoking agents" in a sample of 779 Stockholm women in their middle years, which he does not seem to realize must diverge substantially from rates of "provoking agents" as defined by the LEDS. Since he uses his findings to mount a critique of our model, it is unfortunate that he has failed to achieve a closer degree of replication in the measure he used (for a more detailed description of the differences, see Brown & Harris, 1987). As long as the LEDS system continues relatively unknown, the risk will remain that reports with similar misleading features will continue to appear. In the interim, the best safeguard is for investigators to state that they have been through the training required. Good examples of this practice can be found in Bebbington, Tennant, and Hurry (1981) and Costello (1982), who discuss their training in the "Methods" sections of their reports.

However, the issue of replication does not only concern data collection; it involves following the same procedures concerning analysis. For example, Bebbington *et al.* (1981) have claimed that in spite of using the same LEDS instrument, they obtained quite different results concerning the role of life events in the onset of depression among *patients*. But they changed the original approach in certain critical ways (e.g., taking a shorter period before onset and excluding "possibly independent" events), which would be bound to reduce considerably the size of the etiological effect (Brown & Harris, 1982a). Such practice is highly likely to lead to confusion. We do not argue for slavish repetition; we feel only that innovations should be made with a close regard to past practice so that at every stage of research the new can be related to the old.

Wider Cross-Cultural Applicability

The second issue is that of the use of the LEDS across cultures. The directories of precedents of severity ratings for threat, loss, goal frustration, and so on are largely based on experience in northern Europe. This does not imply that the LEDS can only be used in such cultures; it merely suggests that intercultural variations, being part of the "context" of events, may require different ratings for similar events in different countries. Ultimately, the directories will aim to give examples that embody these principles. Thus a case-controlled study of depressed patients in Nairobi, Kenya, pioneered new ratings for polygamy in Muslim and other cultures (Vadher & Ndetei, 1981). Whereas in Europe such an event would be outside the legal system and would always be rated as severe for the first wife, principles were developed on the basis of consensus ratings in this study whereby on some occasions a husband's taking a second wife was rated as involving little or no long-term threat. Thus, in situations where the new wife was more like a helpmate/companion to the first wife, and the first still had prior access to the husband's ear, the event was not rated as severe. In extending this dimension by consensus, Vadher and Ndetei were in frequent communication with the Bedford College team, just as currently an Australian research team is consulting about threat ratings involving respondents for whom migration to Australia from Hong Kong or Singapore has played a substantial role in their recent life experience.

Such calibration for cultural variation is particularly important for housing and financial difficulties, where local expectations may vary as much as the actual material conditions, thus changing substantially what the average person's reaction might be to such conditions. Research in a rural part of South Portugal documented that somewhat over half the dwellings were without glass windows, running water, a butane cooker, lavatory, plaster ceilings, bath, or tiled floor (Jenkins, 1979, p. 39). LEDS standards developed in London would suggest that these villagers had major housing problems – a judgment almost certainly out of keeping with local feelings. Our own work in a rural area in Scotland did not impose upon us such a reassessment of the severity of housing difficulties, because substantial subsidies had enabled a widespread renovation of crofters' housing in the decade preceding our survey. However, a recent survey in the Basque country, while in no way confronting conditions like those reported by Jenkins in Portugal, marginally adjusted its criteria for judging the severity of housing difficulties (Gaminde & Uria, 1987). So far, the use of the LEDS in Africa and Asia has not involved contextual ratings of dimensions – only the enumeration of events occurring and their classification (see Chapter 4) – but it is envisaged that consultation between the local research teams on the spot and the Bedford College team will prove capable of setting appropriate standards of contextual severity.

One final comment on wider cross-cultural research is perhaps in order: However sensitive the recalibration of stress measurement may be in terms of cross-cultural variations in meaning and context, research may founder without similar sensitivity to cross-cultural variations in the outcome variables. As with so many debates, opinions tend to be polarized. Medical anthropologists often maintain certain diagnoses to be internationally untranslatable, and epidemiologists often fail to see their errors of translation in their enthusiasm to extend the use of standardized instruments throughout the globe (see the volume edited by Kleinman & Good, 1985, and the review of this volume by Klerman, 1987). However, one sensitive study in the People's Republic of China gives grounds for hope in this regard by its subtle comparison of the Chinese diagnosis of neurasthenia and DSM-III major depression, and the use of somatization to mediate between the two (Kleinman, 1986). Although the study did not employ the LEDS, the frequent and detailed descriptions of "major stressors" before onset suggest that these stressors are more similar to LEDS provoking agents than many other categories used by untrained workers claiming to be replicating LEDS surveys (Kleinman, 1986, pp. 87, 105-141). Kleinman cites recent Chinese work in which interest in stress research is beginning to be elaborated, and is optimistic that this may eventually prove a source of insight far beyond the boundaries of China alone.

Wider Applicability across Age Groups

The third issue that must not be omitted also involves the notion of adjusting existing LEDS standards to accommodate the variation in contextual meanings across different groups – this time, across age barriers rather than across different cultures. Working closely with the Bedford College team, Monck and Dobbs have adapted the LEDS or use with teenagers (Monck & Dobbs, 1985) and have produced a special directory for use with that age group (Monck & Dobbs, 1986). Most of the adjustments involved embody the underlying principle that certain incidents make more impact upon adolescents than on adults; thus thresholds for inclusions of incidents as events have been lowered, and thresholds for rating threat have been similarly amended. Thus, whereas an internal vaginal examination by a family doctor would only count as an event for a woman in her 20s if it led to a statement about the probability of her having some serious illness (as defined under LEDS Section 14), any first internal vaginal examination counts as an event for a teenager, no matter how jovial and relaxed the girl or the doctor. Similarly, certain job interviews or driving tests that might not count for adults would be included for adolescents. Plans to develop a LEDS-style interview schedule for even younger children, under secondary school age, are already under way in the Medical Research Council Child Psychiatry Research Unit; these promise to embody some neat additional features, such as the use of "post boxes" to aid children to conceptualize their reports of pleasant and unpleasant reactions to events (Giles, Owen, Nicholls, Rutter, & Sandberg, 1987). Finally, the adaptation of the LEDS for use among the elderly has particularly involved adjustments to the rules involving health-related events and definitions of close ties, and again a special directory for those over 65 is being prepared (Davies & Hulligan, 1985; Wilkinson, Downes, James, Davies, & Davies, 1985).

Criticisms of the LEDS

Economics of Life Events Research

In any volume outlining a particular approach to research, there should be space to review criticisms of its shortcomings; before we conclude this chapter, it is fitting that both practical and methodological criticisms of the LEDS should be discussed. There has been a good deal of misunderstanding about the practical implications of using the LEDS in survey research and a failure to carry out a serious cost-benefit analysis. For example, Kessler and Wethington (1986), in a discussion of the LEDS, note that it has shown considerably better accuracy than has the checklist approach, but go on to state that such "long open-ended interviews" are not feasible for larger-scale population surveys. Their report is of particular interest because they set out to develop an instrument, influenced by the LEDS, that could be used in large-scale surveys; with this in mind, they utilized the latest techniques developed by those in survey research to improve recall. Husbands and wives were interviewed in order to learn about events that one or the other might fail to recall. After screening, 1,332 households were found to be eligible, and interviews with both husbands and wives were obtained in 73% of these. Each interview lasted on average 78 minutes.

Kessler and Wethington emphasize that it has now been well documented that inconsistency in reports in such interviewing is largely due to one respondent's failing to report an event that actually occurred, rather than to one respondent's reporting the occurrence of a fictitious event. They developed a means of testing the accuracy of recall, based on the assumption that the events reported by either spouse did occur. They conclude that reporting reliability in their survey for individual respondents was not satisfactory for any of the severity levels of events (major, moderate, and minor): "Even the most serious events recalled over a 9-month recall period are estimated to be reported with reliability that fails to exceed even a minimally acceptable level" (p.18). However, in a comparable exercise in Camberwell, the same approach based on interviews with depressed patients and close relatives found that 91% of specific severe events occurring to patients over a 12-month period were reported by both patients and relatives. But Kessler and Wethington conclude that reliability was adequate when reports of both husbands *and* wives were considered: For example, they calculated that on the assumption that all the events reported did occur, 72% of the "major events" were reported by either husbands or wives in a 9-month recall period. Nonetheless, this is still well short of the 91% agreement reached by the LEDS, and this improvement over their initial figure was only achieved by using interviews that, unlike the LEDS, required the collaboration of both husbands and wives.

The Kessler and Wethington (1986) report contains a good deal of interesting material, especially about the recall of particular types of events. It also makes some useful suggestions that might improve questioning with the LEDS. For example, the general questions about disappointments, revelations, and anticipation of future negative events might be better asked in the context of the particular domains of the person's life covered earlier in the LEDS (e.g., health or employment), rather than at the end of the interview. It is also clear that Kessler and Wethington can reasonably expect to improve the efficiency of their instrument, in the light of their experience in this first inquiry. However, as it stands, the new instrument falls far short of the LEDS in accuracy. Moreover, it is possible that some of its shortcomings stem from the very fact of the "standardized" approach to interviewing, and that it will not prove possible to remedy these shortcomings by manipulating the wording of questions. We have in mind factors such as the overall tempo of the interview, the emphasis of the LEDS on obtaining a narrative account of events and difficulties, and the stress on following up hints concerning their occurrence no matter where they emerge in the interview as a whole.

Moreover, the economic advantages of Kessler and Wethington's approach are not as obvious as might at first appear. In the original Camberwell population survey, 458 women were seen; the average interview lasted about 2 hours, of which the LEDS took an average of 90 minutes and the shortened PSE 30 minutes. The Kessler and Wethington study carried out 1,954 interviews, each lasting on average 78 minutes, but the proportion of time that was devoted to information other than life events is not specified. Nor is it clear how much extra time was involved in ascertaining events that only concerned the spouse and not the respondent at all (e.g., if a spouse happened to witness a fatal accident to a stranger when the respondent was not present). It is thus not easy to compare the LEDS directly with Kessler and Wethington's strategy in terms of time conservation. However, the contact rate was clearly superior in Camberwell – 83% versus 73% – and this probably had to do with the difficulty of obtaining the collaboration of both husbands and wives. Against this, the rating procedure of the LEDS (using tape recordings) takes longer, and it is necessary to give some backup support with the key contextual scales. But it should be emphasized that the extra time involved in listening to a tape recording in fact saves time during the actual interview, and thus preserves the patience and good will of the respondent. Tape recordings also take pressure off the interviewer, who is freer to keep a check that he or she has covered all the necessary dimensions instead of having to write during the interview. In addition, they allow the interviewer to reassess relationships between events in time, or between event and onset, in a way in which he or she may be too overloaded to do during the interview; thus the possibility of making incorrect assumptions that cannot be revised later is considerably reduced. This "second chance" that the LEDS affords can then be followed up if necessary by telephone or postal inquiry for further clarification. Moreover, tape recording allows use of a flexible semistructured measure of the dependent variable as well, which is even more crucial in dating onset and course of disorder than it is in collecting information about events (see Chapter 15).

To sum up, though Kessler and Wethington's procedure may appear considerably quicker than the LEDS routine of questioning followed by rating tape recordings, it may actually be only a *little* quicker, since two respondents must be contacted, and since the times reported by Kessler and Wethington did not include questioning about dimensions of events. Furthermore, in the final analysis, the costs in terms of time must be weighed against the benefits in terms of the quality of data. A tape recording preserves "meaning" far more directly than notes taken during an interview, because it gives raters access to the exact words, pauses, and tones of voice, and can be available for reliability checks weeks or years later. Moreover, if "cheaper" studies do not lead to convincing cumulative research results, the call for such economies rings somewhat hollow, and the demand for them would appear to relate more to certain attitudes of grant-giving bodies about what is "scientific" than to the need to advance the field as a whole.

Miller and Salter (1984) have suggested that one way to confront the problem of the length of the LEDS interview is to shorten the initial process of identifying incidents that might qualify for inclusion as events by presenting subjects with a checklist and moving on later to collect contextual information orally about those items checked on the list. Provided that there are also enough probing questions to locate any anomalous events not readily classifiable by a checklist, there is no reason in principle why this procedure should not prove acceptable. As yet, however, Miller and colleagues have not reported a systematic direct comparison of the two methods of questioning; until this is done, we can only assert that, when faced with the relative priorities of saving interviewers' time and gathering all the relevant information, we would always opt for the latter.

However, one recent study has gone some way to suggest that an initial checklist can prove cost-effective without much danger of missing severe events, provided that the initial procedure is closely enough tailored to the LEDS (Costello & Devins, 1988). In a sample of women filling in the initial checklist in a family physician's office and interviewed in their homes some time during the ensuing week, almost all whose subsequent LEDS ratings showed they had experienced a severe event had originally filled in the checklist; thus the checklist had a high negative predictive value (.97). Its positive predictive value for severe events, of course, was much less impressive (.27), since without the contextual probes it was difficult to estimate long-term threat. However, because both Costello and Devins and Miller and his colleagues followed their checklist with a probing interview, problems stemming from the low positive predictive value of the checklist would not have threatened their work overall. Costello and Devins attribute the high negative predictive value to the close correspondence of their screening checklist with the domains covered by the LEDS. And there is no doubt that the lack of such a close correspondence could account for the low overlap between checklist and interview reported in other studies (Bebbington, Christopher, Sturt, & Hurry, 1984; Katschnig, 1980; see Chapter 1 for discussion of these). Nevertheless, there is still room for caution. Given that relatively few onset cases are revealed in population surveys, the missing of even some severe events for those with an onset may prove serious, and we would not recommend the use of such screening checklists at present unless it is absolutely necessary or an exploratory study is attempting to open up a new area of inquiry.

The Boundaries of Context

We turn now to more theoretically based criticisms of the LEDS and its approach. It is notable that there has recently been a growing acceptance of the importance of context in the study of stress. Indeed, it is not so much the general notion of a contextual approach that is now criticized, but the location of the specific boundaries that the LEDS defines between event context and the peculiarities of the individual. The critique of Tennant, Bebbington, and Hurry (1981), outlined in Chapter 15, suggests that the LEDS in some sense needs further "purification" so that events may be measured in their own right, uncontaminated by the individual's vulnerability; the critique of Dohrenwend, Link, Kern, Shrout, and Markowiz (1987), outlined in Chapter 1, suggests that events should be characterized by itemizing and combining many detailed features of their context, rather than by allotting them one of the LEDS's more global contextual ratings.

To take the point by Tennant *et al.* (1981) first, as we have already argued, the LEDS's rules for contextual threat are not based upon any of the *specific* vulnerability factors with which severe events have subsequently been combined in analyses testing for interaction. Thus, for example, a woman's confiding in her *husband* does not feature as such in rating threat of any event, although occasionally some event involving an interaction change with a relative or friend leaving town would require consideration of more general aspects of social support, such as whether there were *any* other confidants/relatives left near the subject. Similarly, while a husband's *breadwinning* dependability might form part of the context of, say, news of pregnancy or discovery of dry rot in the house, whether there was *confiding* in him would not be considered. So long as the specific vulnerability factors do not determine threat level, there does not appear to be much danger in using the general features of the person's context to assess the meaning of an event. On the contrary, it is the very ability of the contextual approach to calibrate the weight of a simple event such as a house move with a broader context that permits an estimate of the different risks of disorder following two events that might otherwise be considered identical (house moves).

In regard to the second critique, it is possible that the approach of Dohrenwend and colleagues may, in the longer term, succeed in incorporating these crucial relevant general aspects of context into their detailed specifications for rating particular events. But this will almost certainly involve focusing upon the subject's previous plans and current roles and purposes a good deal more than these researchers do in their present list of "dimensions." The ability to use a systematic measure of ongoing difficulties, such as the LEDS provides, should also aid their task of event specification (e.g., the LEDS D-events). Meanwhile, they themselves acknowledge that in their present instrument, the Psychiatric Epidemiology Research Interview (PERI), intraevent category variability is very large, and they are wise to insert "ultimately" before their statement that "it should be possible to revise life events lists to include under each event category examples of almost all of the important variants of the event" (Dohrenwend *et al.*, 1987, p. 113). As discussed in Chapter 1, until that ultimate point is reached, it is likely that the dimensions they elaborate will fail to pick up those elements of meaning that most reliably predict disorder, since they will be focusing too closely on the event itself and missing relevant features of the wider context. We would reiterate that we doubt whether that issue has a solution in the terms Dohrenwend and colleagues propose.

Kaplan (1964) has discussed the issue in general terms, pointing out that an individual does not choose a friend by summing his or her appraisals of the friend's component traits and habits; the individual reacts to the friend's personality as a whole. Kaplan goes on to suggest that this "configurational" method is probably more widely applicable in the behavioral sciences than the method of "summation," "relying wholly on scalar measures and some (hopefully) appropriate system of weightings" (1964, p. 221). Of course, such a configuration method is the basis of the contextual approach. Perhaps a further reason why there has been reluctance to endorse such an approach is that its ratings of threat have seemed too global to those struggling with the intraevent category variability of their instruments, who are therefore sensitized to just this width of variety. But as Table 15.2 indicates, there are many other contextual dimensions besides threat (e.g., challenge and goal frustration), which can unite events from quite separate categories and which can in this way throw light on the etiology of various disorders. These dimensions occupy an intermediate conceptual level between the simple description of an event category and the global total stress scores (or life change unit scores) of the checklist approach, in which tradition Dohrenwend et al. (1987, p. 114) place the PERI. Therefore, as made amply clear in this volume, espousing a contextual approach does not confine research to a single perspective on stressfulness.

Some research workers, seeking in the interim to bridge the gap between the existing contextual approach and the ultimate goals of the PERI, have advocated the study of single life events (Kessler, Price, & Wortman, 1985). Such studies have proved successful in providing a sufficient number of similar events, with still enough intracategory variability to help systematize new dimensions. Witness, for example, some of the classic early studies by Janis (1958), following patients through the stress of surgery from preoperative to postoperative phases, and by Wolff, Friedman, Hofer, and Mason (1964), following parents through the stress of facing a child's death from leukemia. Studies of other life events that have done fruitful work of this type include research on bereavement, distinguishing, for example, sudden from expected deaths in relationships of a wide range of ongoing qualities (Parkes & Weiss, 1983; Raphael, 1977); studies of pregnancy, distinguishing, for example, premature deliveries from Caesarean sections and normal births (Hobfoll & Lieberman, in press); and research on job loss, distinguishing, for example, those with "a lot" (sic) of other job changes from those with few (Kasl, Gore, & Cobbs, 1975, p. 119). Jacobson (1987) has provided a stimulating discussion of how individuals who have lost their jobs may differ. In an account of a study of 35 unemployed engineers and scientists, he emphasizes the importance of a contextual approach to meaning and shows the same kind of sensitivity to an individual's plans and purposes inherent in the LEDS. Jacobson writes:

> For an engineer, for example, it would be insufficient to infer the meaning of unemployment simply from a statement of the individual's occupational role, including a history of the individual's past or present job responsibilities. Rather, because an engineer may want to pursue either a technological or managerial track, it would be necessary to determine his future preferences, his particular expectations, and his assessment of his career trajectory in order to calculate the likely impact of job loss. (1987, p. 20)

Although in some of his comments Jacobson appears to have underestimated the range of material collected for the present contextual ratings of the LEDS, we would not disagree with the spirit of these comments, nor would we contest the suggestion that the LEDS may fall short in collecting such detail as a matter of course. The material on which such ratings have been based in retrospective research in which the LEDS has been used has almost inevitably been less than ideal, because of the delicate balance between the need for as much information as possible and the possibility of bias if "subjective" material is used in retrospective reporting.

There would thus appear to be two ways of improving the sensitivity of the current contextual ratings. First, as both Kessler *et al.* (1985) and Jacobson (1987) suggest, single life events can be studied. If limited contexts are considered, as in the study of engineers, important insights about context are bound to accumulate; these can certainly then be applied to the rating of *particular* instances. Unfortunately there remains the risk that the interviewer will go too far and thereby justify the criticism that the measures are subject to bias. This can, however, be largely avoided by a longitudinal design. At times it may be possible to capitalize on the future occurrence of one event, such as a plant closure, but even here there may still be difficulties. Reports of plans and commitments at first interview may be influenced by the anticipation of the event; and moreover, the event itself may not provide enough variation in context (e.g., some studies of plant closure have taken place in circumstances where alternative job opportunities have been high). A second approach to a longitudinal design is to question in detail about plans and commitments, covering as far as possible the totality of a person's life – what in Chapter 14 we refer to as "life structure" – and then to wait to see what events occur in the subsequent follow-up period. Events can then be "matched" (as in Islington) with the person's commitments and circumstances, on the basis of knowledge about these that predates the events concerned, since it was obtained at the earlier of the two interviews. On the other hand, in terms of identifying the range of potential contextual variations, it will probably not be possible to collect as much detail as in the study of one event; however, the approach has the advantages of more often dealing with events about which the person can have no advance knowledge, and of enumerating events that vary greatly in type and background context.

Finally, it is necessary to warn those pursuing the first strategy that other severe events beyond the target event may confound the analysis if they are not taken into account. For example, a man who would have survived his job loss without depression because contextually it was less stressful than most may actually have become depressed because his child was killed in a car accident, not because of his job loss.

But even if these criticisms of the contextual approach can be weathered, there is another aspect of the LEDS that is open to criticism. Lazarus and his colleagues have developed an approach to stress measurement that is based on estimating a cumulative score of "hassles" (Kanner, Coyne, Schaefer, & Lazarus, 1981). The type of incident involved is often quite minor (e.g., delays in transport to work on a particular morning, a parking ticket) and would not qualify for inclusion as an event or difficulty in the LEDS. The original rationale for not including such minor incidents in the LEDS was that they would be even more subject to reporting bias than events of more note. However, some incidents not included by the LEDS may well surpass such a threshold of triviality. For example, deaths of pet birds for widows living alone, deaths of in-laws who are not confidants, and uncomplicated births to siblings that are not the first births of that generation are now excluded by the LEDS but may well play some role in various disorders, especially in terms of a new dimension of exhaustion that is now being developed. It is to meet this potential criticism, and to explore the matter further, that the LEDS is now elaborating a companion measure of incidents that can be rated systematically alongside those of life events and difficulties. However, a similar but opposite criticism can be made with even more justification of the study of hassles: namely, that it is essential to take into account the possible role of more serious life events and difficulties before any conclusions about causal processes are drawn. This has not so far been done in a way that allows an estimate of the relative contributions of severe threat or undesirability on the one hand and hassles on the other.

Mention of the elaboration of new dimensions returns us to what has perhaps been the main theme of this book: the importance of specifying, and respecifying, the nature of stress as a step en route to predicting specific disorders. The particular perspective on the nature of stress espoused here has involved classification of events and difficulties by their cognitive-emotional qualities. It has started with the perspective of psychologists like Tomkins, whose analysis of the basic emotions sticks closely to the everyday parlance of perceptive observers of human behavior – distinguishing fear, sadness, anger, disgust, contempt, and the like, and describing more complex combinations and elaborations of these, such as guilt, envy or conflict. When the categorization of stress is kept to this level, it is claimed that insights can emerge that are masked by approaching stress measurement on either a more general level (e.g., total undesirability of all experiences) or a more particular level (e.g., number of previous occasions on which a similar experience had taken place). This approach is unlike the earlier specificity theories, in that it concentrates especially on the actual psychosocial experience before onset rather than on long-standing psychological attitudes, and its tradition of affect analysis owes more to ordinary discourse than to psychoanalysis. Furthermore, its perspective owes much to the microsociological tradition and the ideas of George Herbert Mead (1934) and McCall and Simmons (1966), as has been recently discussed by Oatley and Bolton (1985). For judgments made about the likely emotions to be expected in a certain context take as a critical starting point the understanding of social roles and how they shape our identities, plans, and expectations. It is more than likely that if pursued, this approach will be capable of distinguishing much that was of value in the early specificity hypotheses. There is every reason to believe that further specification of external experiences in this way may throw up hypotheses of parallel specificites in the domain of other contributing variables, such as vulnerability and intervening factors (both psychological and physiological). And it is probable that some of the "attitudes" that were favorite candidates in the earlier specificity theories will now turn out to be internal vulnerability factors that potentiate the specific emotional qualitative impact of the events and difficulties upon the person from outside. Thus, in the sort of situation described in Chapter 13 and encountered so much more frequently before the onset of functional dysphonia than in the comparison group, an unwillingness to express anger may turn out to be crucial in just the way earlier theorists predicted when discussing what they called the "conversion symptom of voice loss." The critical feature, however, may not be the general personality trait but the specific situations in which such persons find themselves, albeit partly created by their own activity. This gives rise to a conflict over speaking out that is magnified by the long-standing unwillingness to say anything hurtful or risky, and this then causes muscular tension, particularly in the laryngeal region. The rather mystical chain of causality in the earlier theories of conversion, which relied heavily on symbolism, is thus not required in order to elaborate the specificity perspective outlined in this volume. A much more direct link is proposed between social role, quality of experience, and physiological responses such as type of neurotransmission. As outlined in Chapter 15, it is not impossible that findings concerning these qualities of stressors may throw up new hypotheses involving the action of different neurotransmitters, which can then feed into biological research.

But whether or not this transition from psychosocial to biological theory occurs, it is clear that the specificity perspective is already proving a fertile source of hypotheses for investigation. For productive research is fully possible without establishing biological mechanisms. The flexibility of the LEDS rating system, along with the detail of material available for analysis (and sometimes reanalysis many years later) from tapes, is ideal for such a progressive elaboration of new qualitative dimensions that match corresponding qualitative predispositions. As we write, we are setting in motion three projects to explore three other new dimensions – of guilt inducing events in obsessive-compulsive neurosis; of relief from the danger of a future loss in manic disorder; and of situations involving dedication and competitive control in anorexia nervosa. At first, only a modest payoff can be expected from such retrospective case-controlled studies, but they may well act as pointers for areas where the greater expenditure demanded by prospective study is going to be worthwhile, especially if the exploratory research has included a wide range of possible vulnerability and intervening variables along with the LEDS. It is very much with this intermediate purpose in mind that this volume has assembled these findings using the LEDS. In the future, measurement of stress may move in a different direction, but in the interim, the perspective of qualitative cognitive-affective contextual dimensions may have served to open up a whole range of hypotheses about psychological and psychosomatic functioning.

References

Ashley, D. J. B. (1967). Observations on the epidemiology of appendicitis. *Gut, 8*, 533-538.

Bauman, Z. (1978. *Hermeneutics and social science*. London: Hutchinson.

Bebbington, P., Christopher, T., Sturt, E., & Hurry, J. (1984). The domain of life events: A comparison of two techniques of description. *Psychological Medicine, 14*, 219-222.

Bebbington, P., Tennant, C., & Hurry, J. (1981). Adversity and the nature of psychiatric disorder in the community. *Journal of Affective Disorders, 3*, 345-366.

Brown, G. W., Andrews, B., Harris, T., Adler, Z., & Bridge, L. (1986). Social support, self-esteem and depression. *Psychological Medicine, 16*, 813-831.

Brown, G. W., Birley, J. T. L., & Wing, J. K. (1972). The influence of family life on the course of schizophrenic disorders: A replication. *British Journal of Psychiatry, 121*, 241-258.

Brown, G. W., & Harris, T. O. (1982a). Disease, distress and depression: A comment. *Journal of Affective Disorders, 4*, 1-8.

Brown, G. W., & Harris, T. O. (1982b). Fall-off in the reporting of life events. *Social Psychiatry, 17*, 23-28.

Brown, G. W., & Harris, T. O. (1987). Stressors and aetiology of depression: A comment on Hällström. *Acta Psychiatrica Scandinavica, 76*, 221-223.

Chesney, M. A., & Rosenman, R. H. (1983). Specificity in stress models: Examples drawn from Type A behavior. In C. L. Cooper (Ed.), *Stress research* (pp. 21-29) New York: Wiley.

Collins, R. (1981). On the microfoundations of macrosociology. *American Journal of Sociology, 86*, 984-1014.

Connolly, J. (1983, September). *Life events before accidental injury*. Paper presented at the World Psychiatric Association International Congress, Vienna.

Cooke, D. J., & Gray, V. (1985). *The role of life events and long-term difficulties in cases of shoplifting*. Unpublished manuscript.

Costello, C. G. (1976). *Anxiety and depression: The adaptive emotions*. London: McGill-Queen's University Press.

Costello, C. G. (1982). Social factors associated with depression: A retrospective community study. *Psychological Medicine, 12*, 329-339.

Costello, C. G., & Devins, G. M. (1988). Two-stage screening for stressful life events and chronic difficulties. *Canadian Journal of Behavioural Science, 20*, 85-92.

Craufurd, D. I., Creed, F., & Javson, M. I. (1987). *Life events and psychological disturbance in patients with low back pain*. Unpublished manuscript.

Davies, A. D. M., & Hulligan, A. (1985). The perception of life stress events by older and younger women. *Perceptual and Motor Skills, 60*, 925-926.

Dohrenwend, B. P., Link, B. G., Kern, R. D. O., Shrout, P. E., & Markowitz, J. (1987). *Measuring life events: The problem of variability within event categories*. In B. Cooper (Ed.), *Psychiatric epidemiology: Progress and prospects* (pp. 103-119). London: Croom Helm.

Eales, M. J. (1985). *Social factors in the occurrence of depression and allied disorders, in unemployed men*. Unpublished doctoral dissertation, University of London.

Epstein, S. (1983). The unconscious, the preconscious, and the self-concept. In J. Suls & A. G. Greenwald (Eds.), *Psychological perspectives on the self* (Vol. 2, pp. 219-247). Hillsdale, NJ: Erlbaum.

Farmer, R., & Creed, F. (in press). Life events and hostility in self poisoning. *British Journal of Psychiatry*.

Flaherty, J. (1987). *Life events and sexual problems*. Unpublished manuscript.

Freud, S. (1925). Fragment of an analysis of a case of hysteria (A. Strachey & J. Strachey, Trans.). In *Collected papers of Sigmund Freud* (Vol. 3, pp. 13-146). London: Hogarth Press. (Original work published 1905)

Frijda, N. H. (1986). *The emotions*. Cambridge, England: Cambridge University Press.

Gaminde, I., & Uria, M. (1987). *Desordens afectivos y factores sociales en la comunidad autonoma vasca: 3. Comarca de tolosa*. Report to the Basque Government, Bilbao, Spain.

Garfinkel, H. (1967). *Studies in ethnomethodology*. Englewood Cliffs, NJ: Prentice-Hall.

Giles, S., Owen, A., Nicholls, J., Rutter, M., & Sandberg, S. (1987). *Children's life events and long-term experiences assessment*. Unpublished manuscript.

Gorman, D. M. (1986). Comment on D. J. Cooke and C. A. Allan's "Stressful life events and alcohol abuse in women." *British Journal of Addiction, 81*, 637-638.

Hällström, T. (1986). Social origins of major depression: The role of provoking agents and vulnerability factors. *Acta Psychiatrica Scandinavica, 73*, 383-389.

Harris, T. O. (1987). Recent developments in the study of life events in relation to psychiatric and physical disorders. In B. Cooper (Ed.), *Psychiatric epidemiology* (pp. 81-102). London: Croom Helm.

Hobfoll, S. E., & Lieberman, Y. (in press). Personality and social resources in immediate and continued stress-resistance among women. *Journal of Personality and Social Psychology.*

Holmes, T. H., & Rahe, R. H. (1967). The Social Readjustment Rating Scale. *Journal of Psychosomatic Research, 11,* 213-218.

Jacobson, D. (1987). Models of stress and meanings of unemployment: Reactions to job loss among technical professionals. *Social Science and Medicine, 1,* 13-21.

Janis, I. L. (1958). *Psychological stress: psychoanalytic and behavioral studies of surgical patients.* New York: Wiley.

Jenkins, R. (1979). *The road to Alto.* Southampton, England: Camelot Press.

Kanner, A. D., Coyne, J. C., Schaefer, C., & Lazarus, R. S. (1981). Comparison of two modes of stress measurement: Daily hassles and uplifts versus major life events. *Journal of Behavioral Medicine, 4,* 1-39.

Kaplan, A. (1964). *The conduct of inquiry: Methodology for behavioral science.* San Francisco: Chandler.

Kasl, S. V. (1983). Pursuing the link between stressful life experiences and disease: A time for reappraisal. In C. L. Cooper (Ed.), *Stress research* (pp. 79-102). New York: Wiley.

Kasl, S. V., Gore, S., & Cobb, S. (1975). The experience of losing a job: Reported changes in health, symptoms and illnes behaviour. *Psychosomatic Medicine, 37,* 106-122.

Katschnig, H. (1980). Measuring life stress: A comparison of two methods. In R. Farmer & S. Hirsch (Eds.), *The suicide syndrome* (pp. 116-123). London: Croom Helm.

Kessler, R. C., Price, R. H., & Wortman, C. B. (1985). Social factors in psychopathology: Stress, social support and coping processes. *Annual Review of Psychology, 36,* 531-572.

Kessler, R. C., & Wethington, E. (1986). *The effect of interview characteristics and depressed mood on the retrospective recall of negative life events.* Unpublished manuscript, Institute for Social Research, University of Michigan.

Kleinman, A. (1986). *Social origins of distress and disease: Depression, neurasthenia and pain in modern China.* New Haven, CT: Yale University Press.

Kleinman, A., & Good, B. (Eds.). (1985). *Culture and depression: Studies in the anthropology and cross-cultural psychiatry of affect and disorder.* Berkeley: University of California Press.

Klerman, G. (1987). [Review of Kleinman, A., & Good, B. (Eds.). *Culture and depression: Studies in the anthropology and cross-cultural psychiatry of affect and disorder*]. *Social Science and Medicine, 9,* 24.

Klinger, E. (1975). The consequences of commitment and disengagement from incentives. *Psychological Review, 82,* 1-25.

Leff, J., & Vaughn, C. (1985). *Expressed emotion in families: Its significance for mental illness.* New York: Guilford Press.

Malinowski, B. (1937). *Sex and repression in savage society.* London: Kegan Paul, Trench, Trubner.

Martin, C. J., Brown, G. W., Goldberg, D. P., & Brockington, I. F. (in press). Psychosocial stress and puerperal depression. *Journal of Affective Disorders.*

McCall, G. J., & Simmons, J. L. (1966). *Identities and interactions.* New York: Free Press.

Mead, G. H. (1934). *Mind, self and society* (C. H. Morris, Ed.). Chicago: University of Chicago Press.

Miller, P., & Ingham, J. G. (1985). Are life events which cause each other additive in their effects? *Social Psychiatry, 20,* 31-41.

Miller, P., & Salter, D. P. (1984). Is there a short-cut? An investigation into the life event interview. *Acta Psychiatrica Scandinavica, 70,* 417-427.

Monck, E., & Dobbs, R. (1985). Measuring life events in an adolescent population: Methodological issues and related findings. *Psychological Medicine, 15,* 841-850.

Monck, E., & Dobbs, R. (1986). *Adolescent life events dictionary of contextual threat ratings.* Unpublished manuscript.

Moore, G. (1976). Albert Nobbs. In J. Michie (Ed.), *The Bodley Head book of longer short stories, 1900-1976* (pp.101-153). London: Bodley Head. (Original work published 1922)

Nadeau, L. (1987). *L'impact des événements critiques tel que mesure par le Life Events and Difficulties Schedule sur la consommation d'alcool et l'admission en traitement des femmes dependantes à l'alcool.* Unpublished doctoral dissertation, University of Quebec, Montreal.

Oatley, K. (1987). *Best laid schemes: A cognitive psychology of emotions.* Unpublished manuscript.

Oatley, K., & Bolton, W. (1985). A social-cognitive theory of depression in reaction to life events. *Psychological Review, 92,* 372-388.

Oatley, K., & Johnson-Laird, P. N. (1987). Towards a cognitive theory of the emotions. *Cognition and Emotions, 1,* 29-50.

Parkes, C. M., & Weiss, R. S. (1983). *Recovery from bereavement.* New York: Basic Books.

Paykel, E. S. (1974). Recent life events and clinical depression. In E. K. Gunderson & R. H. Rahe (Eds.), *Life stress and illness* (pp. 134-163). Springfield, IL: Charles C Thomas.

Ramirez, A. J. (1986). *Life events and breast cancer: Conceptual and methodological issues.* Paper presented at the 16th European Conference on Psychosomatic Research, Athens.

Raphael, B. (1977). Preventive intervention with the recently bereaved. *Archives of General Psychiatry, 34,* 1460-1464.

Reinecker, H., & Zauner, H. (1983). Kritische Lebensreignisse als Risikofaktoren des Alkoholismus [Critical life-events as risk-factors for alcoholism]. *Archiv für Psychiatrie und Nervenkrankheiten, 233,* 333-346.

Robinson, N., & Fuller, J. H. (1985). Role of life events and difficulties in the onset of diabetes mellitus. *Journal of Psychosomatic Research, 29,* 583-591.

Roessler, R., & Engel, B. T. (1974). The current status of the concepts of physiological response specificity and activation. *International Journal of Psychiatry in Medicine, 5,* 359-365.

Schmid, I., Scharfetter, C., & Binder, J. (1981). Lebensereignisse in Abhangigkeit von soziodemographischen variablen. *Social Psychiatry, 16,* 63-68.

Singer, M. T. (1974). Presidential address. Engagement-involvement: A central phenomenon in psychophysiological research. *Psychosomatic Medicine, 36,* 1-17.

Tennant, C., Bebbington, P., & Hurry, J. (1981). The role of life events in depressive illness: Is there a substantial causal relation? *Psychological Medicine, 11,* 379-389.

Vadher, A., & Ndetei, D. M. (1981). Life events and depression in a Kenyan setting. *British Journal of Psychiatry, 139,* 134-137.

Wilkinson, S. J., Downes, J., James, O., Davies, M. G., & Davies, A. D. M. (1985). Life stress and depression in the elderly: experiences from a community study. In A. Butler (Ed.), *Ageing: Recent advances and creative responses* (pp. 250-262). London: Croom Helm.

Wolff, C. T., Friedman, S. B., Hofer, M. A., & Mason, J. W. (1964). Relationship between psychological defenses and mean urinary 17-hydroxycorticosteroid excretion rates, Parts I and II. *Psychosomatic Medicine, 26,* 576-609.

Index

In the absence of a full author index, certain authors can be cross-referenced by consulting the names of their studies.